Introduction to

LOGIC

Introduction to
LOGIC

EIGHTH EDITION

Irving M. Copi

University of Hawaii

Carl Cohen

University of Michigan

Macmillan Publishing Company

NEW YORK

Collier Macmillan Publishers

LONDON

Executive Editor: Helen McInnis
Production Supervisor: Elaine Wetterau
Production Manager: Richard C. Fischer
Text Designer: Nancy Sugihara
Cover Designer: Eileen Burke
Illustrations: ECL Art

This book was set in 10/12 Palatino by Waldman Graphics, Inc., printed by and bound by Halliday Litho. The cover was printed by Halliday Litho.

Macmillan Publishing Company
866 Third Avenue, New York, New York 10022

Collier Macmillan Canada, Inc.

Library of Congress Cataloging in Publication Data

Copi, Irving M.
    Introduction to logic / Irving M. Copi, Carl Cohen. — 8th ed.
        p.   cm.
    ISBN 0-02-325035-6
    1. Logic. I. Cohen, Carl. II. Title.
    BC108.C69   1990
    160—dc20   89-37742
                                                                    CIP

Printing: 2 3 4 5 6 7 8   Year: 0 1 2 3 4 5 6 7 8 9

This book is dedicated to the memory of our mothers and fathers

How the Art of Reasoning is Necessary

When one of his audience said, "Convince me that logic is useful," he said, "Would you have me demonstrate it?"

"Yes."

"Well, then, must I not use a demonstrative argument?"

And, when the other agreed, he said, "How then shall you know if I impose upon you?" And when the man had no answer, he said, "You see how you yourself admit that logic is necessary, if without it you are not even able to learn this much—whether it is necessary or not."

—DISCOURSES OF EPICTETUS

PREFACE

In a republican nation, whose citizens are to be led by reason and persuasion and not by force, the art of reasoning becomes of the first importance.
—THOMAS JEFFERSON

Civilized life depends upon the success of reason in social intercourse, the prevalence of logic over violence in interpersonal conflict.
—JULIANA GERAN PILON

There are obvious benefits to be gained from the study of logic: heightened ability to express ideas clearly and concisely, increased skill in defining one's terms, and enlarged capacity to formulate arguments rigorously and to analyze them critically. But perhaps the greatest benefit is the recognition that reason can be applied in every aspect of human affairs.

Democratic institutions require that citizens think for themselves, discuss problems freely with one another, and decide issues on the basis of deliberation and the weighing of evidence. Through the study of logic we can acquire not only practice in reasoning, but also respect for reason, and thus reinforce and secure the values we prize.

To help achieve these goals, a textbook of logic should contain an ample selection of illustrations and exercises that are of political, scientific, and philosophical interest. These should have been presented by serious writers in honest efforts to solve real problems. Ideally, they should include fallacies as well as paradigms of demonstration. This eighth edition of *Introduction to Logic* contains a substantial number of new examples of these sorts.

An introductory logic course is often the only philosophy course taken by college and university students. It is therefore desirable to include some philosophical issues and arguments in the logic course, if not to interest students in additional philosophy courses, at least to interest them in further thinking and reading in philosophy.

The rate of expansion of human knowledge, especially scientific information, has been accelerating so rapidly in recent years that there is an increasing danger that by the time many students graduate, much of the substantive material learned in their classes may already be out of date. It is only partly in jest that some research laboratories post a sign on their walls reading, "If it works, it's obsolete." There is also an increasing tendency for people to change careers at least once during their lifetimes. So the most valuable thing a student can learn in college is how to think: how to study, to learn, to acquire and process new information. Ideally, every course taken should contribute to this end. In fact, many do not. But it is squarely within the province of logic to focus on this supremely important task. The study of logic can make a permanent and satisfying contribution to the intellectual life of every student. We have tried to make this new edition a more effective instrument for the achievement of this goal.

Some of the changes that have been made are these:

In Part One, thanks to some excellent advice from users of this book, we have moved the material on Deduction and Induction, and on Truth and Validity, from the status of Appendixes back into Chapter One. It is still true that not much use is made of this material until later in the book. But in the overview of Logic presented in Chapter One, these distinctions are essential. In Chapter Three the discussion of Fallacies has been reorganized: related Fallacies are discussed together; some subtleties are explained more fully; and all the chapter's exercises are taken from actual writings. Chapter Four has been reorganized extensively to eliminate the appearance of repetition in classifying definitions in diverse ways.

In Part Two, Chapter Eight has been revised extensively to highlight new ideas and to slow down the rate at which the student is exposed to them. The Logic of Relations, which made its first appearance in the Seventh Edition as Chapter Eleven, has been deleted. It apparently went more deeply into symbolic logic than users of the text for an introductory course in logic were interested in going.

In Part Three, Chapter Fourteen has been modified in various ways, the most obvious one being the enhancement of the treatment of expected value and the replacement of the discussion of gambling at chuck-a-luck by discussions of gambling at roulette and in lotteries. A new Chapter Fifteen, Logic and the Law, has been added, in which the concepts and principles introduced throughout the book are shown to apply to the uses of language and argument in legal settings and to the resolution of legal disputes.

Since the appearance of the previous edition, many readers, both teachers and students, have suggested changes in the book. In many cases these recommendations have been gratefully accepted. Among those whose communications were particularly helpful are Dr. Dennis L. Allison of Austin Community College at Rio Grande Campus in Texas; Professor Kent Baldner, Eastern Illinois University; Mr. Denny Barrett of Youngstown State University in Ohio; Professor Robert W. Beard of Florida State University; Ms. Amelia Bischoff of the University of Michigan's Residential College in Ann Arbor; Professor Frans van der Bogert of Appalachian State University in North Carolina; Professor Charles D. Brown of Auburn University in Alabama; Professor Ludlow Brown of Mercyhurst College, Pennsylvania; Professor D. E. Bushnell of Tulane University, New Orleans; Professor Claro R. Ceniza of De La Salle University in Manila, the Philippines; Professor John W. Copeland of Drew University, New Jersey; Professor William Cox of Macomb Community College, Michigan; Professor Theodore Drange of West Virginia University—Morgantown; Professor Daniel Flage of the University of Texas at Austin; Professor Richard H. Gatchel of Crafton Hills College, Yucaipa, California; Professor Louis R. Geiselman of Hibbing Community College, Minnesota; Professor Eugenio Carpuccio Gonzalez of Caracas, Venezuela;

Professor James A. Gould of the University of South Florida; Professor Joseph G. Grassi of Fairfield University, Connecticut; Professor Thomas R. Grimes of Arkansas State University; Professor Barbara Hannan of the University of Idaho at Moscow; Professor David Hein of Hood College, Frederick, Maryland; Professor Fred Johnson of Colorado State University at Fort Collins; Professor Theodore J. Kondoleon of Villanova University; Professor Charles Lambros of the State University of New York at Buffalo; Professor Larry Laudan of the University of Hawaii at Manoa; Professor Gerald W. Lilje of Washington State University; Professor Eugene Lockwood of Oakton Community College in Illinois; Professor Leemon McHenry of Central Michigan University; Professor Bob Mesle of Graceland College, Lamoni, Iowa; Professor Brendan Minogue of Youngstown State University in Ohio; Professor John Mize of Long Beach City College, California; Professor Harold Morick of the State University of New York at Albany; Professor Nicholas Moutafakis, Cleveland State University; Professor S. O'Connell of Bermuda College, Devonshire, Bermuda; Ms. Cassandra Pinnick of the University of Hawaii at Manoa; Professor R. Puligandla of the University of Toledo; Professor Ronald Roblin of the State University of New York at Buffalo; Professor George Sefler of Purdue University—Calumet, Indiana; Professor Albert Shaw of Glassboro State College, New Jersey; Professor Robert Shoemaker of Hendrix College, Arkansas; Professor Burke Townsend of the University of Montana at Missoula; and Professor John P. Zawadsky of the University of Wisconsin at Stevens Point.

Earlier versions of the new Chapter 15, Logic and the Law, were read by Professors Robert Harris and Jerold Lax of the University of Michigan, and Professor Kenneth Kipnis of the University of Hawaii; their many helpful suggestions for its improvement were much appreciated.

Warm thanks are due to Helen McInnis, Executive Editor of Macmillan's College Division, for her expert editorial advice and unfailing helpfulness in preparing this new edition. We express our gratitude to Elaine W. Wetterau, Senior Production Supervisor, for her needed expertise and generous assistance in seeing this difficult volume through the press.

Most of all we thank our wives for help and encouragement in preparing this new edition.

I. M. C.
C. C.

CONTENTS

Introduction to

LOGIC

PART ONE

Language

1

Introduction

> . . . *this we do affirm—that if truth is to be sought in every division of Philosophy, we must, before all else, possess trustworthy principles and methods for the discernment of truth. Now the Logical branch is that which includes the theory of criteria and of proofs; so it is with this that we ought to make our beginnings.*
>
> —SEXTUS EMPIRICUS

> . . . *bad reasoning as well as good reasoning is possible; and this fact is the foundation of the practical side of logic.*
>
> —CHARLES SANDERS PEIRCE

1.1 *What Is Logic?*

Logic is the study of the methods and principles used to distinguish good (correct) from bad (incorrect) reasoning. This definition must not be taken to imply that only the student of logic can reason well or correctly. To say so would be as mistaken as to say that to run well requires studying the physics and physiology involved in that activity. Some excellent athletes are quite ignorant of the complex processes that go on inside their bodies when they perform. And, needless to say, the somewhat elderly professors who know most about such things would perform very poorly were they to risk their dignity on the athletic field. Even given the same basic muscular and nervous apparatus, the person who has such knowledge might not surpass the "natural athlete."

But given the same native intelligence, a person who has studied logic is more likely to reason correctly than one who has never thought about the general principles involved in that activity. There are several reasons for this. First, the proper study of logic will approach it as an art as well as a science, and the student will do exercises in all parts of the theory being learned. Here, as anywhere else, practice will help to make perfect. Second, a traditional part of the study of logic has been the examination and analysis of fallacies, which are common and often quite "natural" mistakes in reasoning. This part of the subject gives increased insight into the principles of reasoning

3

in general, and an acquaintance with these pitfalls helps to keep us from stumbling into them. Finally, the study of logic will give students techniques and methods for testing the correctness of many different kinds of reasoning, including their own; and when errors are easily detected, they are less likely to be allowed to stand.

The appeal to emotion is sometimes effective. But the appeal to reason is more effective in the long run, and can be tested and appraised by criteria that define correct argument. If these criteria are not known, then they cannot be employed. The study of logic aims to discover and make available those criteria that can be used to test arguments for correctness.

Logic has frequently been defined as the science of the laws of thought. But this definition, although it gives a clue to the nature of logic, is not accurate. In the first place, thinking is studied by psychologists. Logic cannot be "the" science of the laws of thought, because psychology is also a science that deals with laws of thought (among other things). And logic is not a branch of psychology; it is a separate and distinct field of study.

In the second place, if "thought" refers to *any* process that occurs in people's minds, not all thought is an object of study for the logician. All reasoning is thinking, but not all thinking is reasoning. Thus one may "think" of a number between one and ten, as in a parlor game, without doing any "reasoning" about it. There are many mental processes or kinds of thought that are different from reasoning. One may remember something, or imagine it, or regret it, without doing any reasoning about it. Or one may let one's thoughts "drift along" in a daydream or reverie, following what psychologists call free association, in which one image is replaced by another in an order that is not logical. The sequence of thoughts in such free association is often quite significant, and some psychiatric techniques make use of it. The insight into people's characters gained by penetrating the flow of their streams of consciousness is the basis of a very effective literary technique pioneered by James Joyce in his novel *Ulysses*. Conversely, if a person's character is sufficiently well known beforehand, the flow of that person's stream of consciousness can be traced or even anticipated. Sherlock Holmes, we recall, used to break in on his friend Watson's silences, to answer the very question to which Dr. Watson had been "led" in his musings. There seem to be some laws governing reverie, but they are not studied by logicians. The laws that describe the movements of the mind in reverie are psychological, not logical principles. To define "logic" as the science of the laws of thought is to make it include too much.

Logic is sometimes defined as the science of reasoning. This definition is much better, but it also will not do. Reasoning is a special kind of thinking in which problems are solved, in which inference takes place, that is, in which conclusions are drawn from premises. It is still a kind of thinking, however, and therefore still part of the psychologist's subject matter. As psychologists examine the reasoning process, they find it to be extremely complex, highly emotional, consisting of awkward trial-and-error procedures illuminated by sudden—and sometimes apparently irrelevant—flashes of insight. These are all of importance to psychology.

The logician, however, is concerned primarily with the correctness of the completed process of reasoning. The logician asks: Does the problem get solved? Does the conclusion reached follow from the premisses used or assumed? Do the premisses provide good reasons for accepting the conclusion? If the problem gets solved, if the premisses provide adequate grounds for affirming the conclusion, if asserting the premisses to be true warrants asserting the conclusion to be true also, then the reasoning is correct. Otherwise, it is incorrect.

The distinction between correct and incorrect reasoning is the central problem with which logic deals. The logician's methods and techniques have been developed primarily for the purpose of making this distinction clear. All reasoning (regardless of its subject matter) is of interest to the logician—but with this special concern for its correctness as the logical focus.

1.2 *Premisses and Conclusions*

To clarify the explanation of logic offered in the preceding section, it will help to set forth and discuss some of the special terms used by logicians in their work. *Inference* is a process by which one proposition is arrived at and affirmed on the basis of one or more other propositions accepted as the starting point of the process. To determine whether an inference is correct, the logician examines those propositions that are the initial and end points of that process and the relationships between them. *Propositions* are either true or false, and in this they differ from questions, commands, and exclamations. Only propositions can be either asserted or denied: questions may be asked and commands given and exclamations uttered, but none of them can be affirmed or denied, or judged to be either true or false.

It is customary to distinguish between *sentences* and the propositions they may be uttered to assert. Two sentences, which are clearly two because they consist of different words differently arranged, may in the same context have the same meaning and be uttered to assert the same proposition. For example,

> John loves Mary.
> Mary is loved by John.

are two different sentences, for the first contains three words, whereas the second contains five; the first begins with the word "John," whereas the second begins with the word "Mary," and so on. Yet the two sentences have exactly the same meaning. We use the term "proposition" to refer to what such sentences as these are typically uttered to assert.

The difference between sentences and propositions is brought out by remarking that a sentence is always a sentence of a particular language, the language in which it is uttered, whereas propositions are not peculiar to any language. The four sentences

> It is raining.
> Está lloviendo.
> Il pleut.
> Es regnet.

are certainly different, for they are in different languages: English, Spanish, French, and German. Yet they have but a single meaning, and in appropriate contexts may be uttered to assert the proposition of which each of them is a different formulation.

In different contexts exactly the same sentence can be uttered to make very different *statements*. For example, you might utter the sentence

> The present president of the United States is a former congressman.

in 1990 to make a (true) statement about George Bush, but if you had uttered it in 1987 you would have made a (false) statement about Ronald Reagan. In those different temporal contexts, the sentence in question might be uttered to assert different propositions or to make different statements. The terms "proposition" and "statement" are not exact synonyms, but in the context of logical investigation they are used in much the same sense. Some writers on logic prefer "statement" to "proposition," although the latter has been more common in the history of logic. In this book both terms will be used.

Corresponding to every possible inference is an *argument*, and it is with arguments that logic is chiefly concerned. An argument, in the logician's sense, is any group of propositions of which one is claimed to follow from the others, which are regarded as providing support or grounds for the truth of that one. Of course, the word "argument" is often used in other senses, but in logic it has the sense just explained.

An argument, in the logician's sense, is not a mere collection of propositions, but has a structure. In describing this structure, the terms "premiss" and "conclusion" are usually employed. The *conclusion* of an argument is the proposition that is affirmed on the basis of the other propositions of the argument, and these other propositions, which are affirmed (or assumed) as providing support or reasons for accepting the conclusion, are the *premisses* of that argument.

The simplest kind of argument consists of just one premiss and a conclusion that is claimed to follow from it, or to be implied by it. An example in which each is stated in a separate sentence is the following:

> The United States is a net energy importer. Therefore, it is a mathematical certainty that the nation as a whole is better off, not worse off, with lower prices for oil.[1]

---

[1]"Oil Drip," *The New Republic*, April 28, 1986, p. 7.

Here the premiss is stated first and the conclusion second. But the order in which they are stated is not significant from the point of view of logic. An argument in which the conclusion is stated in the first sentence and the premiss in the second is:

> Great cases like hard cases make bad law. For great cases are called great because of some accident of immediate or overwhelming interest which appeals to the feelings and distorts the judgment.[2]

In some arguments the premiss and conclusion are stated in the same sentence. The following is a one-sentence argument whose premiss precedes its conclusion:

> Because sensations are essentially private, we can have no way of knowing how the world appears to other people.[3]

Sometimes the conclusion precedes the premiss in a one-sentence argument, as in the following example:

> Cooling atoms down is equivalent to slowing them down, since temperature is a measure of how fast atoms or molecules are bouncing around (absolute zero means absolute stillness).[4]

When reasons are offered in an effort to persuade us to perform a specified action, we are presented with what is in effect an argument even though the "conclusion" may be expressed as an imperative or command. Consider, for example, the following two passages:

> Wisdom is the principal thing; therefore get wisdom.[5]

and

> Neither a borrower, nor a lender be;
> For loan oft loses both itself and friend.[6]

Here too the command may either precede or follow the reason (or reasons) offered to persuade the hearer (or reader) to do what is commanded. For the sake of uniformity and simplicity, it is useful to regard commands, in these contexts, as no different from propositions in which hearers (or readers) are told that they *should*, or *ought to*, act in the manner specified in the command. Exactly what difference, if any, there is between a command to do something and a statement that it should or ought to be done is a difficult problem that need not be explored here. By ignoring that difference (if there really is one), we are able to regard both kinds of arguments as structured groups of propositions.

---

[2]Mr. Justice Felix Frankfurter, *Dennis v. United States,* 341 U.S. 494 (1951).

[3]Richard L. Gregory, "Sensations," *The Oxford Companion to the Mind* (Oxford: Oxford University Press, 1987), p. 700.

[4]"Slow Atoms," *The Economist,* October 22, 1988, p. 96.

[5]*Proverbs* 4:7.

[6]William Shakespeare, *Hamlet,* I, iii.

Some arguments offer several premises in support of their conclusions. On occasion the premises are enumerated as first, second, third—or as (a), (b), (c), as in the following argument, in which the statement of the conclusion precedes the statements of the premisses:

> To say that statements about consciousness are statements about brain processes is manifestly false. This is shown (a) by the fact that you can describe your sensations and mental imagery without knowing anything about your brain processes or even that such things exist, (b) by the fact that statements about one's consciousness and statements about one's brain processes are verified in entirely different ways, and (c) by the fact that there is nothing self-contradictory about the statement "X has a pain but there is nothing going on in his brain."[7]

In the following argument the conclusion is stated last, preceded by three premisses:

> Since happiness consists in peace of mind, and since durable peace of mind depends on the confidence we have in the future, and since that confidence is based on the science we should have of the nature of God and the soul, it follows that science is necessary for true happiness.[8]

Counting the premisses of an argument is not terribly important at this stage of our study, but it will gain importance as we proceed to analyze and diagram more complicated arguments later. To list the premisses of the preceding argument, we cannot appeal simply to the number of *sentences* in which they are written. That they are all in a single sentence should not be allowed to disguise their multiplicity.

It should be noted that "premiss" and "conclusion" are relative terms: one and the same proposition can be a premiss in one argument and a conclusion in another. Consider, for example, the argument:

> Now human law is framed for the multitude of human beings. The majority of human beings are not perfect in virtue. Therefore human laws do not forbid all vices.[9]

Here the proposition that *human laws do not forbid all vices* is the conclusion, and the two propositions preceding it are premisses. But this argument's conclusion is a premiss in the following (different) argument:

> . . . vicious acts are contrary to acts of virtue. But human law does not prohibit all vices, ... Therefore neither does it prescribe all acts of virtue.[10]

No proposition by itself, in isolation, is either a premiss or a conclusion. It is a premiss only where it occurs as an assumption in an argument. It is a conclusion only where it occurs in an argument in which it is claimed to follow from propositions assumed in that argument. Thus "premiss" and

---

[7]U. T. Place, "Is Consciousness a Brain Process?" *The British Journal of Psychology,* February 1956.

[8]Gottfried Leibniz, *Preface to the General Science.*

[9]Thomas Aquinas, *Summa Theologica,* I–II, Question 96, Article 2.

[10]Ibid., Article 3.

"conclusion" are relative terms, like "employer" and "employee." A person alone is neither employer nor employee, but may be either in different contexts: employer to one's gardener, employee of the firm for which one works.

The preceding arguments either have their premises stated first and their conclusions last or their conclusions stated first, followed by their premises. But the conclusion of an argument need not be stated either at its end or at its beginning. It can be, and often is, sandwiched in between different premisses offered in its support. This arrangement is illustrated in the following:

> Since freedom and well-being are the necessary conditions of action and successful action in general, every agent must regard these conditions as necessary goods for himself, since without them he would not be able to act for any of his purposes, either at all or with general chances of success.[11]

Here the conclusion that *every agent must regard these conditions as necessary goods for himself* is asserted on the basis of the propositions that precede and follow it.

To carry out the logician's task of distinguishing good from bad arguments, one must be able to recognize arguments when they occur and to identify their premises and conclusions. Given that a passage contains an argument, how can we tell what its conclusion is, and what are its premises? We have already seen that an argument can be stated with its conclusion first, or last, or in between its several premises. Hence the conclusion of an argument cannot be identified in terms of its position in the formulation of the argument. How, then, can it be recognized? Sometimes by the presence of special words that attach to the different parts of an argument. Some words or phrases typically serve to introduce the conclusion of an argument.

We call such expressions "conclusion-indicators." The presence of any of them often, though not always, signals that what follows is the conclusion of an argument. Here is a partial list of *conclusion-indicators*:

therefore	for these reasons
hence	it follows that
thus	we may infer
so	I conclude that
accordingly	which shows that
in consequence	which means that
consequently	which entails that
proves that	which implies that
as a result	which allows us to infer
for this reason	which points to the conclusion that

Other words or phrases typically serve to mark the premises of an argument. Such expressions are called "premiss-indicators." The presence of any

---

[11]Alan Gewirth, "Human Rights and Conceptions of the Self," *Philosophia*, Vol. 18, Nos. 2–3, July 1988, p. 136.

one of them often, though not always, signals that what follows is a premiss of an argument. Here is a partial list of *premiss-indicators*:

since	as indicated by
because	the reason is that
for	for the reason that
as	may be inferred from
follows from	may be derived from
as shown by	may be deduced from
inasmuch as	in view of the fact that

Once an argument has been recognized, these words and phrases help us to identify its premisses and conclusion. But not every passage containing an argument need contain these special logical terms. Consider, for example:

> In 20 years' time the only maple leaf left in Canada might be on the national flag. Acid rain is killing the maple trees of central and eastern Canada, as well as in New England.[12]

Although neither conclusion-indicators nor premiss-indicators appear here, this is plainly an argument whose conclusion is stated first, and is followed by a premiss offered in support of it. The same structure appears in the following example:

> A little neglect may breed great mischief. . . . for want of a nail the shoe was lost; for want of a shoe the horse was lost; and for want of a horse the rider was lost.[13]

Although this might be regarded as *stating* a well-known truth, and then *illustrating* it by reference to the missing horseshoe nail and the consequent loss of the rider, it can at least equally well be understood as an argument whose conclusion is stated first and followed by three premisses that are claimed to support it. A somewhat more complicated example of an argument in whose formulation neither conclusion-indicators nor premiss-indicators appear is the following:

> It takes obtuse reasoning to inject any issue of the "free exercise" of religion into the present case. No one is forced to go to the religious classroom and no religious exercise or instruction is brought to the classrooms of the public schools. A student need not take religious instruction. He is left to his own desires as to the manner or time of his religious devotions, if any.[14]

Here the conclusion, which can be paraphrased as "the present case has nothing to do with the 'free exercise' of religion," is stated in the first sentence. The last three sentences offer grounds or reasons in support of that conclusion. How can we know that the first sentence states the conclusion

---

[12]"Maple Syrup," *The Economist*, April 4, 1987, p. 63.
[13]Benjamin Franklin, *Poor Richard's Almanac*, 1758.
[14]Mr. Justice Douglas, for the Supreme Court, *Zorach v. Clauson*, 343 U.S. 306 (1952).

and that the other three express premisses? Context is enormously helpful here, as indeed it usually is. Also helpful are some of the phrasings used in expressing the various different propositions involved. The phrase "it takes obtuse reasoning to inject . . ." suggests that the question of whether "free exercise" of religion is involved in the case is precisely the point of disagreement. It suggests that someone has claimed that there is an issue of religious freedom in the case and that the court rejects that claim and will therefore argue against it. The other propositions are stated in matter-of-fact terms, suggesting that there is no dispute about them, and thus no question of their being acceptable as premisses.

Not everything said in the course of an argument is either a premiss or the conclusion of that argument. A passage that contains an argument may also contain other material, which may sometimes be irrelevant, but often supplies important background information that enables the reader or hearer to understand what the argument is about. For example, consider the argument contained the following passage:

> Untreated glaucoma is a leading cause of painless, progressive blindness. Methods for early detection and effective treatment are available. For this reason blindness from glaucoma is especially tragic.[15]

The third proposition contained in this passage is the conclusion, as is shown by the presence of the conclusion indicator "for this reason." The second proposition is the premiss. The first proposition is not part of the argument at all, strictly speaking. But its presence permits us to understand that the *available methods* referred to in the premiss are methods for early detection and effective treatment *of chronic glaucoma*.

If we wished to give a *complete* analysis of the preceding argument, we might want to rephrase its constituent propositions as follows:

PREMISS: Methods for early detection and effective treatment of chronic glaucoma are available.
CONCLUSION: Blindness from chronic glaucoma is especially tragic.

Another illustration of this point is found in one of Schopenhauer's essays:

> If the criminal law forbids suicide, that is not an argument valid in the Church; and besides, the prohibition is ridiculous; for what penalty can frighten a person who is not afraid of death itself?[16]

Here the material before the first semicolon is neither premiss nor conclusion. But without some such information we should not know what "prohibition" is referred to in the conclusion. Here the conclusion is *the criminal law's prohibition of suicide is ridiculous*. The premiss offered in its support is *no penalty*

---

[15]*Harvard Medical School Health Letter*, April 1979, p. 2.

[16]Arthur Schopenhauer, "On Suicide," in *Complete Essays of Schopenhauer*, Book V, *Studies in Pessimism*, trans. T. Bailey Saunders (New York: Wiley Book Company, 1942), p. 26.

can frighten a person who is not afraid of death itself. This example also shows that propositions can be asserted in the form of "rhetorical questions," which are used to make statements rather than to ask questions, even though they are interrogative in form.

Other examples of arguments containing statements formulated as rhetorical questions are

> . . . if there is no one who desires to be miserable, there is no one, Meno, who desires evil; for what is misery but the desire and possession of evil?[17]

and

> If a man say, I love God, and hateth his brother, he is a liar: for he that loveth not his brother whom he hath seen, how can he love God whom he hath not seen?[18]

In analyzing Schopenhauer's argument, and the earlier one concerning the free exercise of religion, it was helpful to rephrase some of their constituent propositions. The purpose in each case was to minimize our dependence on their contexts for an understanding of the arguments and of the roles played in them by their constituent propositions. This will be a pervasive concern in much of the rest of this book. We often want to focus on a proposition itself: we might want to know whether it is true or false, what it implies, whether it is implied by some other proposition, or whether it is a premiss or the conclusion of a given argument. In such cases it will be useful to have a formulation of the proposition that can be understood as independently of context as may be possible.

Sometimes the propositional nature of a constituent of an argument is disguised by its expression as a noun phrase rather than a declarative sentence. This occurs in the following:

> Ethan Nadelmann, an assistant professor at the Woodrow Wilson School of Public and International Affairs at Princeton University, argues that prohibition [of hard drugs] has been an utter failure. He cites the surge of killings by drug dealers in cities like Washington and New York, the clogging of state and Federal courts and prisons with drug prisoners, the political disruption of Columbia by [drug] traffickers, and drug-related corruption throughout the world.[19]

That this passage is indeed an argument is partly obscured by the grammatical form in which its premises, which are preceded by the conclusion, are expressed. These premises may be helpfully rephrased as declarative sentences, and would then be set forth as follows:

Killings by drug dealers in cities like New York and Washington have surged;

[17]Plato, *Meno,* 78A.
[18]I John 4:20.
[19]*The New York Times,* May 15, 1988, Section 1, p. 12.

state and Federal courts and prisons have become clogged with drug prisoners;
Columbia has been politically disrupted by drug traffickers;
and drug-related corruption has appeared throughout the world.

It is then evident that the proposition which precedes these premisses is the
conclusion of the argument:

> The prohibition [of hard drugs] has been an utter failure.

Although every argument has a conclusion, the formulations of some arguments do not contain explicit statements of their conclusions. How can
such an argument be understood and analyzed? The unstated conclusion of
such an argument is often indicated by the context in which the argument
occurs. Sometimes the stated premisses inescapably suggest what the unstated conclusion must be, as in

> If he's smart, he isn't going to go around shooting one of them, and he's smart.[20]

Here the context is required for us to know what "one of them" might be.
But no context is needed for us to know that the conclusion is

> He isn't going to go around shooting one of them.

Another example of an argument with an unstated conclusion is

> The spectacular beauty of Northern California's Mendocino and Humboldt coasts
> draws huge flocks of tourists each year from across the United States and around
> the world. . . . The region abounds with diverse marine life, including endangered
> whales, seals, walruses and sea birds, and the fisheries of this region are some of
> the most important on the West Coast. The Fish and Wildlife Service has said that
> oil development would have 'potentially devastating impacts' on these resources.[21]

From the four stated premisses of this argument its conclusion—not stated—
may readily be inferred:

> Oil development should not be permitted in the waters off Northern California's
> Mendocino and Humboldt coasts.

Some of you might be "put off" at being told that in analyzing an argument
with an unstated conclusion you must already know what follows logically,
or what might seem to the arguer to follow logically, from the stated premisses. After all, it is logic that you are supposed to be learning from this book!
How can the book presuppose that you already know logic? If you did, why
would you be studying the subject? This objection is not difficult to answer.
Some logical ability is presupposed in the study of any subject, including

---

[20]George V. Higgins, *The Friends of Eddie Coyle* (New York: Ballantine Books, 1981), p. 121.
[21]Lisa Speer and Sara Chasis, "Don't Pull the Plug on Offshore Waters," *The New York Times*,
June 25, 1988, p. 15.

logic itself. The study of logic can be expected to *sharpen* your logical sense, *improve* your ability to analyze arguments, and provide you with effective techniques for appraising arguments as good or bad, or as better or worse. But some logical sense must be there to be sharpened, and some analytical ability must already exist to be improved. As C. I. Lewis, an important twentieth-century logician, wrote

> The study of logic appeals to no criterion not already present in the learner's mind . . . for the very business of learning through reflection or discussion presumes our logical sense as a trustworthy guide.[22]

In summary: an argument is a group of propositions of which one, the conclusion, is claimed to follow from the others, which are premisses. Propositions are typically stated in declarative sentences, but they sometimes appear as commands, rhetorical questions, or noun phrases. An entire argument can be stated in a single sentence, but often several sentences are employed in its formulation. In the presentation of an argument, its conclusion may either precede or follow all the premisses, or it may come between two of them. Or the conclusion may not be stated explicitly, but be made clear by the context or implied by the very statement of the premisses. The presence of special terms functioning as premiss-indicators or conclusion-indicators often helps us to identify and distinguish the premisses and conclusion of an argument. A passage containing an argument may also contain propositions that are neither premisses nor conclusion of that argument, but contain information that helps the reader or hearer to understand what the premisses and conclusion are about. In analyzing an argument, it is often useful to distinguish separate premisses that may be conjoined in a single sentence. And in reporting the result of our analysis of an argument into its premiss (or premisses) and conclusion, it is customary and helpful to formulate each single premiss, and the conclusion, in a separate declarative sentence that can be understood independently of the context.

EXERCISES

Identify the premisses and conclusions in the following passages, each of which contains just one argument.[23]

★ 1. But the price of fossil and nuclear fuel is only a small fraction of their total cost. Society pays the other cost for damaged health and property, oil spills in the oceans, polluted or poisoned rivers, lakes and beaches, acid rain, killed or poisoned fish and oyster beds, and human misery.

—MOSES CAMMER, "Solar Energy Will Prove Itself Cheaper,"
The New York Times, July 12, 1988, p. 28

[22]C. I. Lewis, *Mind and the World-Order* (New York: Charles Scribner's Sons, 1929), p. 3.
[23]Solutions to starred exercises will be found at the back of the book on pages 503–548.

2. It is hard to argue that Western astrology must be true because it has such a long tradition behind it, because Chinese and Indian astrology have equally long traditions. If one is right, the others are wrong.

—MARTIN GARDNER, "Seeing Stars," *The New York Review of Books,*
June 30, 1988, p. 4

3. FairTest charged that another examination, the Scholastic Aptitude Test, which most colleges use as one measure of which high school students they admit, was biased against girls, again pointing out that they as a group scored lower on that test even though they earned better grades than boys.

—LEE A. DANIELS, "Groups Charge Bias in Merit Scholarship Testing,"
The New York Times, June 29, 1988, p. 25

4. Lying is as much a part of normal growth and development as telling the truth. The ability to lie is a human achievement, one of those abilities that tends to set them apart from all other species.

—ARNOLD GOLDBERG, "Lies: Mental Disorder or Normal Growth?"
The New York Times, May 17, 1988, p. 19

★ 5. The light that we see from distant galaxies left them millions of years ago, and in the case of the most distant object that we have seen, the light left some eight thousand million years ago. Thus, when we look at the universe, we are seeing it as it was in the past.

—STEPHEN W. HAWKING, *A Brief History of Time: From the Big Bang
to Black Holes* (Toronto: Bantam Books, 1988), p. 28

6. . . . the advanced technologies applied in supercomputers tend to quickly permeate the entire computer industry. So the nation that leads in supercomputer development tends to have a jump on other countries in producing more powerful—and more lucrative—lower-level computers.

—DWIGHT B. DAVIS, "Supercomputers: A Strategic Imperative?"
High Technology, May 1984, p. 44

7. Forbear to judge, for we are sinners all.

—WILLIAM SHAKESPEARE, *Henry VI, Part III,* iii

8. [M]ales born into poverty are more likely to commit crimes as teenagers and adults than are more privileged males. So a boom in births among poor mothers can be expected to exert upward pressure on the crime rate 15 to 20 years later.

—DAVID E. BLOOM and NEIL G. BENNETT, "Future Shock,"
The New Republic, June 19, 1989, p. 18

9. He that loveth not knoweth not God; for God is love.   —I John 4:8

★ 10. Thomas Moore, the director of domestic studies at the Hoover Institution at Stanford University, argues that poverty statistics overstate the number of poor people because researchers don't add in such noncash benefits as food stamps or Medicaid when calculating family incomes.

—VICTOR F. ZONANA, "Population Puzzle," *The Wall Street Journal,*
June 20, 1984

11. Since there are no mental diseases, there can be no treatments for them.

—DR. THOMAS S. SZASZ, in Carol Levine, ed.,
Taking Sides: Clashing Views on Controversial Bio-Ethical Issues
(Guilford, Conn.: The Dushkin Publishing Group, Inc., 1984), p. 179

12. Although the game is Scottish in its ancestry, golf has become an unde-niably American pastime. An estimated 21.7 million Americans are golfers and, according to the National Golf Foundation, 8 million more will be playing by the year 2000.   —"Leonardo of the Links," *New York Times Magazine,*
November 13, 1988, p. 50

13. Since an individual's lifetime earnings typically follow an up-and-down pattern—low while a young adult, highest just before retirement, and then a leveling or reduction—there always will be a "natural level" of income inequality at any one time, if only because of the age distribution.
—MARK LILLA, "Why the 'Income Distribution' Is So Misleading,"
The Public Interest, No. 77, Fall 1984, p. 63

14. Missiles are easier to defend than cities, for two reasons: first, missile sites are small and tough, whereas cities are large and vulnerable; second, a defense of missile sites is considered effective if it can save half the missiles, whereas a defense of cities has to try to save them all.
—FREEMAN DYSON, "Reflections: Weapons and Hope,"
The New Yorker, February 13, 1984, p. 103

★ 15. But the peculiar evil of silencing the expression of an opinion is, that it is robbing the human race; posterity as well as the existing generation; those who dissent from the opinion, still more than those who hold it. If the opinion is right, they are deprived of the opportunity of exchanging error for truth: if wrong, they lose, what is almost as great a benefit, the clearer perception and livelier impres-sion of truth, produced by its collision with error.
—JOHN STUART MILL, "On Liberty" (1859), in Max Lerner, ed., *Essential Works*
of John Stuart Mill (New York: Bantam Books, Inc., 1961), p. 269

16. It is difficult to gauge the pain felt by animals, because pain is subjective and animals cannot talk.
—"The Ethics of Animal Testing," *The Economist*, April 7, 1984, p. 87

17. Any attempt to base logical principles on something more ultimate, whether it be our system of contingent rules for the use of language or anything else, must be self-defeating. For the attempt consists of deducing conclusions from premises and for deduction to be possible the prior validity of logical laws is a prerequisite.   —DAVID MITCHELL, *An Introduction to Logic*
(London: Hutchinson University Library, 1962), p. 134

18. [Members of a twelve-member faculty committee at the Colorado School of Mines] . . . say that future engineers will be called on increasingly to work on interdisciplinary teams and be faced with greater public scrutiny and government regulation.
Accordingly, says the faculty report, the school should help students develop a "broader view of the social and political implications of [their] actions, better communicative skills, more intellectual mobility, better management capabilities, and a higher commitment to the preservation of the environment."
—ROBERT L. JACOBSON, in *The Chronicle of Higher Education*, July 9, 1979

19. Thinking is a function of man's immortal soul. God has given an immortal soul to every man and woman, but not to any other animal or to machines. Hence no animal or machine can think.
—A. M. TURING, "Computing Machinery and Intelligence,"
Mind, Vol. 59, 1950

★ 20. A gray surface looks red if we have been looking at a blue-green one; plain paper feels smooth if we have been feeling sandpaper or rough if we have been feeling plate glass; and tap water tastes sweet if we have been eating artichokes. Some part of what we call red or smooth or sweet must therefore be in the eyes or fingertips or tongue of the beholder, feeler, or taster.

—B. F. SKINNER, *Beyond Freedom and Dignity*

21. Good sense is of all things in the world the most equally distributed, for everybody thinks himself so abundantly provided with it, that even those most difficult to please in all other matters do not commonly desire more of it than they already possess. —RENÉ DESCARTES, *A Discourse on Method*

22. Courtly love was understood by its contemporaries to be love for its own sake, romantic love, true love, physical love, unassociated with property or family, and consequently focused on another man's wife, since only such an illicit liaison could have no other aim but love alone.

—BARBARA TUCHMAN, *A Distant Mirror, The Calamitous 14th Century*

23. Citizens who so value their "independence" that they will not enroll in a political party are really forfeiting independence, because they abandon a share in decision making at the primary level: the choice of the candidate.

—BRUCE L. FELKNOR, *Dirty Politics*

24. . . . for a producer to convince the institutions which finance movies that his film will be profitable, he has to line up a "bankable" star; and if he has a project for a political movie, the star is unlikely to sign on if he doesn't agree with the film's politics. Which means that the political movies the public is getting from Hollywood today represent, by and large, the political thinking of actors.

—RICHARD GRENIER, "Jane Fonda & Other Political Thinkers,"
Commentary, June 1979

★ 25. In his mid-thirties, Boswell said of himself, "I am sensible that I am deficient in judgement, in good common sense. I ought therefore to be diffident and cautious. . . ."

—IRVIN EHRENPREIS, review of Frank Brady, *James Boswell: The Later Years, 1769–1795*, in *The New York Review of Books*, March 28, 1985, p. 3

26. The investigation of supernatural phenomena lies outside the realm of science. Therefore, science can neither prove nor disprove the existence of God.

—JAMES A. HOPSON, letter to the editors, *The New Republic*,
September 12, 1983, p. 4

27. We cannot for a moment believe that knowledge has reached its final goal, or that the present condition of society is perfect. We must therefore welcome from our teachers such discussions as shall suggest the means and prepare the way by which knowledge may be extended, present evils be removed and others prevented. —The University of Wisconsin Board of Regents, 1894, quoted in Richard Hofstadter and Walter P. Metzger, *The Development of Academic Freedom in the United States*

28. In a primitive society in which each family can raise only enough food for itself, everybody lives on the land. When farm productivity doubles, each farm family can grow enough for two, and half the population is freed to work in industry. When each farm family can grow enough food for three, only a third of the population need stay on farms, and so on. It follows as almost a matter of

simple arithmetic that the percentage of total population on farms must be inversely proportional to the productivity of farm labor.

—DANIEL B. SUITS, *Principles of Economics*

29. The doctrine of deterrence holds that a nuclear aggressor will not act if faced with a threat of retaliation in kind. It rests, therefore, on the willingness to use these weapons in response to attack.

—CHARLES KRAUTHAMMER, "On Nuclear Morality,"
Commentary, Vol. 76, No. 4, October 1983, p. 48

★ 30. It is probably true that the least destructive nuclear weapons are the most dangerous, because they make it easier for a nuclear war to begin.

—FREEMAN DYSON, "Reflections: Weapons and Hope,"
The New Yorker, February 6, 1984, p. 60

1.3 *Diagrams for Single Arguments*

Argumentative passages often contain more than a single argument. But to deal with the problem of analyzing complex argumentative passages (as in Section 1.5) it is useful to establish first a standard method of analyzing *single* arguments. A powerful yet simple method of doing this, and of exhibiting the structure of arguments diagrammatically, was devised some years ago by Professor Monroe Beardsley, and subsequently developed by Professor Stephen N. Thomas and Professor Michael Scriven.[24] With only minor modifications we follow their lead in this matter.

A diagram of something is a *spatial* representation of it, like a blueprint of a building or a machine, a graph showing population or income distribution, or a wiring diagram for electrical equipment. We will adopt the convention of placing the argument's conclusion below its premiss or premisses and will use an arrow as our diagrammatic conclusion-indicator. As a first approximation to our diagrams, we set forth the argument

> Given that every carrier of the disease is a potential spreader of the disease, we *must* protect the uncontaminated from the contaminated.[25]

as

> Every carrier of the disease is a potential spreader of the disease.
> ↓
> We *must* protect the uncontaminated from the contaminated.

[24]Monroe C. Beardsley, *Practical Logic* (Englewood Cliffs, N.J.: Prentice-Hall, Inc., 1950); Stephen N. Thomas, *Practical Reasoning in Natural Language* (Englewood Cliffs, N.J.: Prentice-Hall, Inc., 1973); Michael Scriven, *Reasoning*, (New York: McGraw-Hill Book Company, 1976).

[25]Karel Capek, *The White Plague*, quoted by Susan Sontag in "AIDS and Its Metaphors," *The New York Review of Books*, Vol. 35, No. 16, October 27, 1988, p. 92.

And the argument

> The safest prediction is always for more of the same, because inertia is a powerful force.[26]

whose conclusion is stated first and its one premise second is set forth as

Inertia is a powerful force.

↓

The safest prediction is always for more of the same.

When we encounter arguments with two or more premises, rearranging them becomes more tedious, and our diagrams become too cluttered. It is more convenient to number the constituent propositions in the order of their occurrence in the passage and to let the numbers assigned to them, enclosed in circles, appear in our diagrams instead of the full sentences in which they are stated. When constructed in this way a diagram displays the structure of the argument with maximum clarity. In numbering the premises and conclusions of arguments, it is helpful to put brackets around each one, with its circled number either above it or directly in front of it, as in the following passage:

> ① [The time for a national high-speed passenger railroad system has come.] ② [Airlines cannot keep up, and in their frenzied attempt to do so have subjected passengers to poor service and, what is worse, life-threatening conditions.] ③ [The upkeep costs of the heavily travelled interstate highways, never intended or constructed to take such pounding, are soaring.][27]

Now we can use the circled numbers to represent the propositions that they label and diagram the argument in this way:

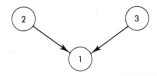

In this argument each of the two premises supports the conclusion *independently*. Each supplies some warrant for accepting the conclusion and would do so even in the absence of the other premise.

A decision must be made at this point about the "arithmetic" of such arguments. Should we count this as a single argument with two premises and one conclusion, or should we say that here we have two different arguments with the same conclusion? Emerging practice is to say that it is *one*

---

[26]Robert J. Samuelson, *Newsweek*, January 11, 1988, p. 41.

[27]Leo D. Marks, "Time to Start on High-Speed National Rail," *The New York Times*, October 15, 1988.

argument with two independent premisses. The principle seems to be that the number of conclusions determines the number of arguments. So by a "single argument" is meant an argument to a single conclusion, regardless of how many premisses are adduced in its support.

Not every premiss in an argument provides the kind of independent support for the conclusion that those in the preceding argument do. Some premisses must work together to support their conclusion. When this happens, the cooperation they display can be exhibited in the argument's diagram. This situation is illustrated by the following argument. Incidentally, it may be useful to circle any premiss-indicators or conclusion-indicators that may be present in the argument being analyzed.

> ① [If an action promotes the best interests of everyone concerned, and violates no one's rights, then that action is morally acceptable.] ② [In at least some cases, active euthanasia promotes the best interests of everyone concerned and violates no one's rights.] (Therefore,) ③ [in at least some cases active euthanasia is morally acceptable.][28]

Here neither of the two premisses supports the conclusion independently. If the principle expressed in the first premiss were true, but there were no case in which active euthanasia promoted everyone's best interests, the conclusion would have been given no support at all. And if there were cases in which active euthanasia promotes everyone's best interests, but the principle expressed in the first premiss were not true, the conclusion—that active euthanasia is morally acceptable in some cases—would remain without support. Thus, each premiss here supports the conclusion through the *mediation* of the other premiss. Both are needed, in contrast to the independent or *immediate* support for its conclusion that each premiss provided in the earlier example, about the need for a high-speed passenger railroad system. That the two premisses do work cooperatively in this argument, rather than independently, is represented in the diagram by connecting their numbers with a brace, as shown, and drawing a single arrow leading from the pair of them to the conclusion.

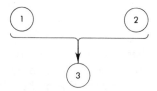

In an argument containing three or more premisses, one (or more) might provide independent support for the conclusion while two (or more) of the other premisses provide support only in combination. This situation is illustrated by the following argument:

---

[28]James Rachels, cited in T. A. Mappes and J. S. Zembaty, eds., *Social Ethics*, 3rd ed. (New York: McGraw-Hill Book Company, 1987), p. 79.

① [Desert mountaintops make good sites for astronomy.] ② [Being high, they sit above a portion of the atmosphere, enabling a star's light to reach a telescope without having to swim through the entire depth of the atmosphere.] ③ [Being dry, the desert is also relatively cloud-free.] ④ [The merest veil of haze or cloud can render a sky useless for many astronomical measures.][29]

Here propositions ②, ③, and ④ provide support for proposition ①, which is the conclusion. But they offer their support in different ways. The single statement ② by itself supports the claim that mountaintop locations are good sites for telescopes. But the two statements ③ and ④ must work together to support the claim that *desert* locations are good sites for telescopes. The diagram showing this difference is

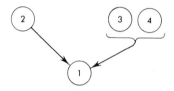

An argument in whose formulation the conclusion is sandwiched in between two premises is the following:

(Since) ① [morals . . . have an influence on the actions and affections] (it follows that) ② [they [morals] cannot be derived from reason;]. . . (because) ③ [reason alone as we have already prov'd, can never have any such influence.][30]

The diagram for Hume's argument is

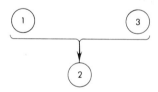

Finally, an argument whose conclusion is not explicitly stated can have that conclusion represented in the argument's diagram by a number in a *broken* circle, as in the following example:

What was striking was that ① [every politician or journalist I talked to, including the young intellectuals who back the PLO, claimed that Egyptian young people would not want to fight again.] . . . ② [Moreover, the widening of the Suez Canal is now going forward and the cities on its banks are being rebuilt.] ③ [A nation planning to make war would not be likely to block its route of attack in this way.][31]

[29]Blanchard Hiatt, *University of Michigan Research News*, Vol. 30, Nos. 8–9, August–September 1979, p. 5.

[30]David Hume, *A Treatise of Human Nature*.

[31]Arthur Hertzberg, "The View from Cairo," *The New York Review of Books*, June 26, 1980, p. 45.

The first thing to notice is that this argument has an unstated conclusion, which we number in the way indicated:

(4) [Egypt will not attack [Israel] across the Suez Canal again.]

Having all its propositions indicated and labeled, we can represent the argument by the following diagram:

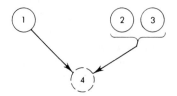

EXERCISES

Diagram the arguments in the following passages, each of which contains a single argument.

★ 1. American farmers produce more food and fiber than they could profitably sell on a free market. In cold economic terms, that means that we have more farmers than we need.   —*The New Republic,* August 11 and 18, 1986, p. 5

2. Even if heroin should prove to be identical to morphine in terms of how it affects patients, it has the advantage of being much easier to inject. . . . The drug is 50 times more soluble than morphine, and when you have a wasted person who has very little muscle mass and very little fat, an injection is extremely painful. Five cc's of morphine is a tablespoon, and there is no place to put it. The equivalent dose of heroin is so small that it can be given to anyone.
—DAVID HOLZMAN, "Heroin for Patients a Painful Issue,"
Insight, October 3, 1988

3. Only in a reasonably tolerant society can civil disobedience flourish. That means we should expect more of it in a more just society, especially as a more just society is more likely to tolerate extreme views.
—BARRY R. GROSS, review of Kent Greenawalt, *Conflicts of Law and Morality,* in
Ethics, Vol. 89, No. 1, October 1988, p. 170

4. I believe that we must use clean, safe nuclear power. . . . [T]he more dependent we become on foreign oil, the less our national security is enhanced.
—VICE PRESIDENT GEORGE BUSH, in the Bush–Dukakis presidential debate,
Los Angeles, October 15, 1988

★ 5. I've opposed the death penalty all of my life. I don't see any evidence that it's a deterrent and I think there are better and more effective ways to deal with violent crime.
—GOVERNOR MICHAEL DUKAKIS, in the Bush–Dukakis presidential debate,
Los Angeles, October 15, 1988

6. By making drugs a criminal matter, we have in fact made the problem worse. If we decriminalize, at least we would only have a massive public-health problem, a massive corruption problem and a massive foreign-policy problem.
—GEORGETTE BENNETT, *Newsweek,* May 30, 1988, p. 37

7. And there must be simple substances, since there are composites; for the composite is only a collection or *aggregatum* of simple substances.
— G. W. LEIBNIZ, *The Monadology*, (1714), #2; in *Leibniz Selections* (New York: Charles Scribner's Sons, 1971), p. 533

8. Heating a piece of material is equivalent to increasing the energy of motion of the constituents of that piece, be they atoms or electrons or other particles. In a hot material, the atoms or electrons perform all kinds of motions, oscillations, straight flights, etc. The greater the temperature, the higher the energy of the motions. Thus, temperature is equivalent to energy.
— VICTOR WEISSKOPF, "The Origin of the Universe," *The New York Review of Books*, Vol. 36, No. 2, February 16, 1989, p. 10

9. Dr. Oliver Wendell Holmes once laid out the dictum that the key to longevity was to have a chronic incurable disease and take good care of it. Even now, 150 years later, this works. If you have chronic arthritis you are likely to take a certain amount of aspirin most days of your life, and this may reduce your chances of dropping dead from coronary thrombosis. When you are chronically ill, you are also, I suppose, less likely to drive an automobile, or climb ladders, or fall down the cellar stairs carrying books needing storage, or smoke too much, or drink a lot.
— LEWIS THOMAS, *The Youngest Science* (New York: The Viking Press, Inc., 1983), p. 149

★ 10. A just society cannot possibly pay everyone the same income, since the aptitudes and efforts of individuals diverge dramatically, and since the common good is far better served, accordingly, by systematic inequalities of reward.
— MICHAEL NOVAK, *Commentary*, Vol. 76, No. 6, December 1983, p. 30

11. To say I believe in spanking children implies that spankings are in some way essential to their proper upbringing. I do not hold that opinion; therefore, I do not believe in spankings.
— JOHN ROSEMOND, "Parent Power," syndicated column, August 30, 1983

12. . . . since reduction of sodium may prevent the development of hypertension in some people and since a high-salt diet is almost certainly not beneficial, reduced salting of food and reduced consumption of salty snack foods is probably a good idea.
— "Science and the Citizen," *Scientific American*, Vol. 249, No. 2, August 1983, p. 60

13. Competent individuals are at liberty to make their own medical treatment decisions; incompetent individuals are not. Thus, competence and liberty are inextricably interwoven.
— GEORGE J. ANNAS and JOAN E. DENSBERGER, "Competence to Refuse Medical Treatment: Autonomy Vs. Paternalism," *Toledo Law Review*, Vol. 15, Winter 1984, p. 561

14. Dost thou love Life? Then do not squander Time; for that's the stuff Life is made of.
— BENJAMIN FRANKLIN, *Poor Richard's Almanac*, 1746

★ 15. **Q.** Dr. Koop, why does the government need to intervene in the treatment of handicapped infants?
A. The Rehabilitation Act of 1973 states that it is illegal in any institution that receives federal aid to discriminate against anyone on the basis of race, creed, color, religion, ethnic origin or handicap. We have good evidence that many children are deprived of their civil rights by being treated in a different way than they would be treated if they were not handicapped.
— Interview with Surgeon General C. Everett Koop, in *U.S. News & World Report*, January 16, 1984, p. 63

16. Furthermore, if you look at the history of the death penalty in this country, you'll find that its application has been arbitrary, capricious and discriminatory.

Q. In what ways?

A. The poor and minorities tend to be overrepresented on death row. Blacks who kill whites are overrepresented in relation to blacks who kill blacks. That tells us something about the way the system works.

People who can afford expensive lawyers can beat the system when it comes to the death penalty as well as other kinds of punishment.

—PATRICK V. MURPHY, interview in *U.S. News & World Report*,
April 20, 1981, p. 50

17. In his analysis of the death penalty in America, David Bruck argues that capital punishment is invalid due to its racially discriminatory impact. I suggest such reasoning proves too much. If, as I suspect is true, juries and judges impose *all* penalties more harshly on blacks than on whites (or more harshly when the victim is white), Mr. Bruck's analysis would lead to the conclusion that all criminal sanctions are invalid.

—C. EDWARD FLETCHER III, letter to the editor, *The New Republic*,
January 23, 1984, p. 4

18. For Mr. Bruck, distribution of the death penalty to a few murderers, capriciously selected, argues for its abolition. But if something is badly distributed, surely the distribution is at fault, not what is being distributed. Or does Mr. Bruck contend that maldistribution is inherent in the death penalty? I can't see why it would be . . . Mr. Bruck argues . . . illogically. . . .

—ERNEST VAN DEN HAAG, letter to the editor,
The New Republic, January 23, 1984, p. 2

19. Prisons are . . . necessary. The existence of prisons and the prospect of incarceration make up a backdrop of deterrence that keeps the crime rate from overflowing. Prisons also serve the melancholy social task of consuming the youth of violent offenders and returning them to the community drained of the vitality necessary for aggression. Finally, prison sentences serve the morally unifying and emotionally releasing purpose of expressing communal reprobation through ceremonies of degradation that bind people together in separating them from the criminal. —GRAHAM HUGHES, "American Terror,"
The New York Review of Books, January 25, 1979

★ 20. Hunting, . . . particularly the hunting of large animals, is so complicated, difficult and hazardous that the cooperation of numerous individuals is needed. It can be inferred, therefore, that Peking man was more likely to have been living in a group than in solitude when he began to hunt deer.

—WU RUKANG and LIN SHENGLONG, "Peking Man,"
Scientific American, Vol. 248, No. 6, June 1983, p. 94

21. There are more people learning English as a second language than speak it as their first. It is therefore discourteous to address a foreigner in his own language, since it deprives him of the opportunity to improve his English.

—From a letter from the Earl of St. Germans to *The Independent*,
quoted by David Broder of the Washington Post Service, July 2, 1989

22. Mr. Kondracke asks, "What justification can there be for taxing interest at a lower rate than other forms of income?" How about these:

Tax-free interest encourages saving, which lowers interest rates, which lowers the deficit, which lowers Federal borrowing, which lowers interest rates, etc.

Tax-free interest can be targeted to provide low-interest mortgages, which are the backbone of the American Dream.

Tax-free interest encourages thrift, which will provide security to us all in our old age. —LAWRENCE J. KRAMER, letter to the editor,
The Wall Street Journal, September 11, 1984, p. 27

23. Proponents of the bill . . . argue that legalizing heroin for medicinal purposes would not contribute to the nation's drug abuse problem because the amounts involved—about 400 pounds a year—would be small, and because the heroin would be manufactured, stored and administered under strict security.
—JEAN COBB, "Heroin in Hospitals," *Common Cause*,
Vol. 10, No. 6, November–December 1984, p. 35

24. Every time an obscenity case is to be argued here, my office is flooded with letters and postal cards urging me to protect the community or the Nation by striking down the publication. The messages are often identical even down to commas and semicolons. The inference is irresistible that they were all copied from a school or church blackboard. Dozens of postal cards often are mailed from the same precinct. —MR. JUSTICE DOUGLAS, concurring opinion,
Memoirs v. *Massachusetts*, 383 U.S. 413

★ 25. In 1972 Justice Thurgood Marshall wrote that "punishment for the sake of retribution is not permissible under the Eighth Amendment." That is absurd. The element of retribution—vengeance, if you will—does not make punishment cruel and unusual, it makes punishment intelligible. It distinguishes punishment from therapy. Rehabilitation may be an ancillary result of punishment, but we punish to serve justice, by giving people what they deserve.
—GEORGE F. WILL, "The Value of Punishment,"
Newsweek, May 24, 1982, p. 92

1.4 *Recognizing Arguments*

Thus far the reader's attention has been directed to passages already identified and labeled as expressing arguments. There the problems were, first, to distinguish their premisses and conclusions and, second, to diagram the arguments to exhibit their structures more clearly. In this section we consider the prior problem of deciding whether an argument is present in a given passage.

The presence or absence of premiss-indicators or conclusion-indicators is helpful, though not always decisive, as was noted in Section 1.2. Extremely important is the context in which the passage (spoken or written) occurs. In a formal debate, in a law court, or in a legislative chamber, one naturally *expects* to encounter arguments. And the announced or scheduled agenda in such contexts helps us to understand *what* is being asserted in alleged support of *what* conclusion.

A proposition by itself is *not* an argument. A proposition is said to be "true" or "false," whereas we use different terms to describe analogous characteristics of arguments, such as "correct" or "incorrect," "valid" or "invalid," "sound'" or "unsound," "demonstrative," "plausible," or "fallacious."

An argument is a group of propositions of which one, the conclusion, is claimed to be true on the basis of other propositions, the premises, that are asserted as providing grounds or reasons for accepting the conclusion. But not every passage containing several propositions is an argument. Consider the following account of the last days of Hitler's Third Reich, in April 1945:

> The Americans and Russians were driving swiftly to a junction on the Elbe. The British were at the gates of Hamburg and Bremen and threatening to cut off Germany from occupied Denmark. In Italy Bologna had fallen and Alexander's Allied forces were plunging into the valley of the Po. The Russians, having captured Vienna on April 13, were heading up the Danube. . . ."[32]

Here every proposition contained in the paragraph is asserted, but no claim is made either explicitly or implicitly that any of them provides grounds or evidence for any other. So no argument is present.

It is useful to remark at this point that not only arguments, but also some compound propositions contain two (or more) other propositions of which both (or all) are asserted. For example, the last sentence of the passage just quoted is a conjunction of two propositions: *the Russians had captured Vienna on April 13,* and *they were heading up the Danube*—here conjoined only by commas. Other conjunctions are expressed more straightforwardly, for example, "Roses are red and violets are blue" or "Jack and Jill went up the hill." Still others are more complex, as when they have more than two components, or when their components are themselves compound. It is obvious that asserting the conjunction of two propositions is strictly equivalent to asserting each of the component propositions themselves.

But that is not true of other kinds of compound propositions. In alternative propositions, such as

> Circuit Courts are useful, or they are not useful.[33]

and

> Either wealth is an evil or wealth is a good. . . .[34]

neither of their components is asserted, only the compound "either–or" alternative or disjunctive propositions are asserted. And in hypothetical or conditional propositions such as

> If we were sure that the earth is as much lighted by the sun as one of these clouds, no question would remain about its being no less brilliant than the moon.[35]

[32]William L. Shirer, *The Rise and Fall of the Third Reich* (New York: Simon and Schuster, 1960), p. 1437.

[33]Abraham Lincoln, annual message to Congress, December 3, 1861.

[34]Sextus Empiricus, *Against the Logicians.*

[35]Galileo Galilei, "The First Day," in *Dialogue Concerning the Two Chief World Systems,* 1632 (Berkeley: University of California Press, 1962), p. 89.

and

> If the President defied the order, he would be impeached.[36]

neither of their component propositions is asserted; only the compound "if–then" hypothetical propositions are asserted. So in diagramming an argument, one must diagram each alternative proposition and each hypothetical proposition as a single (compound) proposition, because each constituent proposition of an argument is asserted in that argument: either as one of the premisses or as the conclusion.

Because neither alternative nor hypothetical propositions involve the assertion of their component propositions, they are not—by themselves—arguments. In this respect a hypothetical proposition is very different from an argument that might resemble it very closely. Consider the hypothetical proposition

> If no honest work can demean the dignity of a human being, any task can be performed with pride.

Neither its first component proposition *No honest work can demean the dignity of a human being* is asserted, nor is its other component proposition *any task can be performed with pride.* What is asserted is only that the former implies the latter, but both could be false for all the statement in question says. No premiss is asserted, no inference is made, no conclusion is claimed to be true: there is no argument here. But consider the following:

> Any task can be performed with pride, because no honest work can demean the dignity of a human being.[37]

Here we *do* have an argument, as is suggested by the presence of the premiss-indicator "because." The proposition *no honest work can demean the dignity of a human being* is asserted as premiss, and the proposition *any task can be performed with pride* is claimed to follow from that premiss and is asserted to be true. A hypothetical proposition may look like an argument, but it is not—by itself—an argument, and the two should not be confused.

Context, however, is extremely important here. And included in context is what can be called "common knowledge." For example, it is common knowledge that society has not yet finally settled matters of justice and retribution. In the light of this common knowledge, an argument is expressed in the following hypothetical proposition:

> If matters of justice and retribution were simple, society would have settled them as easily as it has settled on the advantages of paved roads.[38]

---

[36]Victoria Schuck, "Watergate," *The Key Reporter*, Vol. 41, No. 2, Winter 1975–1976.

[37]Judith Martin, "The Pursuit of Politeness," *The New Republic*, August 6, 1984, p. 34.

[38]Diane Johnson, review of Susan Jacoby, *Wild Justice: The Evolution of Revenge*, in *The New York Review of Books*, Vol. 31, No. 2, February 16, 1984, p. 40.

For in the given hypothetical proposition, the component that is implied, *society would have settled them as easily as it has settled on the advantages of paved roads,* is false, And in the light of this contextual information we immediately infer that the "if" component of that hypothetical proposition must be false also—and that is the unstated conclusion of the argument expressed by the hypothetical proposition in question:

Matters of justice and retribution are *not* simple.

To diagram the argument expressed in that hypothetical proposition cited just above, we could represent that proposition itself as ①, the common knowledge *denial* of its component that is implied in it as ② , and the unstated conclusion that is the *denial* of its "if" component as ③ . So the diagram for the preceding argument is

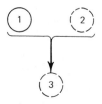

Similarly, we often express our judgment on some matter by formulating an argument in the form of a hypothetical proposition of which the second component is not merely false but absurd, thus underscoring our judgment, which is the emphatic denial of the "if" component. Looking at some ultramodern work of art, for example, the viewer may respond by saying: "If that's an artistic masterpiece, I'm a monkey's uncle!" Clearly, this would be intended as an argument whose conclusion is the *denial* that the work in question is an artistic masterpiece. This argument is likewise diagrammed as

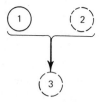

We have already remarked that although every argument contains several propositions, not every passage in which several propositions are asserted need contain an argument. For an argument to be present, one of those asserted propositions must be claimed to follow from other propositions asserted to be true, which are *presented* as grounds for, or reasons for believing, the conclusion. This claim may be either explicit or implicit. It may be made explicit by the use of premiss-indicators or conclusion-indicators or by the occurrence of such words as "must," "should," "ought," or "necessarily" in the conclusion. But the presence of these argument-indicators is not always decisive. Some argument-indicators have other functions as well. For example, if we compare

Since Kleo graduated from medical school her income is probably very high.

with

Since Kleo graduated from medical school there have been many changes in medical techniques.

we see that although the first is an argument in which the word "since" indicates the premiss, the second is not an argument at all. In the second, the word "since" has temporal rather than logical significance: what is asserted is that many changes in medical techniques developed *after* Kleo graduated from medical school, without the slightest suggestion that there is any evidential connection between her graduation and those changes. These two different meanings of the term combine to give deeper texture to a line from the song "Stormy Weather":

Since you went away, it's been raining all the time.

Such words as "because" and "for" also have other than strictly logical uses. Compare the following two passages:

(1) Encryption and decryption keys must be protected more securely than any other secret message, because these are the keys that allow either the intended recipient of a cipher message or a spy to decipher it.[39]
(2) We have decided to write this article together because of our deep belief that the security of free peoples and the growth of freedom both demand a restoration of bipartisan consensus in American foreign policy.[40]

The first passage is plainly an argument. Its conclusion is that encryption and decryption keys must be protected more securely than any other secret message; its premiss (that these are the keys that allow either the intended recipient of a cipher message or a spy to decipher it) is marked by the word "because." But in the second passage there is no argument at all. That the authors chose to write their article together is not a conclusion; it is not inferred; it is a fact that they are here explaining. The word "because" does not mark a premiss in this passage; what follows it is not evidence, or grounds, or reasons for believing what we already know to be true from looking at the first page of the article. "Because" is here an indication of an *explanation* of the decision by these two authors—one a prominent Republican, the other a prominent Democrat—to write about American foreign policy jointly. Both of these passages assert two propositions, and in both cases the

[39]"Most Ferocious Math Problem Is Tamed," *The New York Times,* October 12, 1988, p. 11.
[40]Henry Kissinger and Cyrus Vance, "An Agenda for 1989," *Newsweek,* June 6, 1988, p. 31.

two propositions are linked by the word "because"—but in one case we are presented with an argument, and in the other case we are not.

The difference between these arguments and nonarguments is primarily one of purpose or interest. Either can be formulated in the pattern

$$Q \text{ because } P.$$

If we are interested in establishing the *truth of Q* and *P* is offered as evidence for it, then "*Q because P*" formulates an argument. However, if we regard the truth of *Q* as being unproblematic, as being at least as well established as the truth of *P*, but are interested in explaining *why Q is the case*, then "*Q because P*" is not an argument but an explanation. The two examples discussed are fairly easy to distinguish, the first being an argument and the second an explanation. But not all examples are so easily classified. In each case, the context may help to make clear the intention of the writer or speaker. Normally, if the purpose is to establish the truth of a proposition, it is an argument that is formulated. If the purpose is to explain or account for something, then it is an explanation that is formulated. Explanations will be discussed in greater detail in Chapter 13. Meanwhile, it is important to be able to distinguish *what* is being explained from what the explanation *is*. In the second example above, quoted from Henry Kissinger and Cyrus Vance, *what* is being explained is their decision to collaborate on an article although they are members of different political parties. And the explanation *is* that they believe that bipartisan consensus is needed in foreign policy.

Recognition and analysis of arguments go hand in hand. Unless it is at least suspected that an argument is present, there is no motivation to apply the method of analysis and to construct a diagram. And often recognition is effected by trying the method of argument analysis and finding that it *does apply* to the passage in question.

EXERCISES

Only some of the following passages contain arguments. Find those with arguments and diagram the arguments they contain. In the case of explanations, indicate what is being explained and what the explanation is.

★ 1. Now every developed capitalist nation simultaneously plays the role of colony and metropolis with respect to other such nations. . . . Thus, war today between two developed nations would not be a war *for* markets but, instead, a war *against* their markets.   —YURI ORLOV, "Before and After Glasnost," *Commentary*, October 1988, p. 24

2. Because their best physicists were not zealous for weapons, because they made uncorrected mistakes, because Hitler was Hitler, and because men like Speer always had more urgent production priorities, the Germans never really tried to make an atomic bomb.

—"Hitler and the Bomb," *New York Times Magazine*, November 13, 1988, p. 64

3. According to *AV Magazine*, Argentina's Minister of Education and Justice, Dr. Julio Raul Rajneri, has announced a ministry resolution to outlaw dissection of animals for teaching purposes. ". . . Taking into account that biology is the science of life, and that it is not coherent to base the teaching of such a science on the death of other beings . . . the ministry resolves to ban vivisection and dissection of animals in all teaching establishments. . . ."
—*National Association for Biomedical Research Update*, July 8, 1988

4. The steep climbing angle jet transports require for noise alleviation would cause passengers in rearward-facing seats to hang from their seat belts, instead of having the comfort that a back rest provides forward-facing seats in steep climbs. Because of this discomfort and the possible preference of passengers to look forward, coupled with the safety questions, the views of passengers should be established before rearward-facing seats are adopted.
—JEROME LEDERER, "Facing Rear Adds Little Air Safety,"
The New York Times, March 6, 1989, p. 24

★ 5. Detection of a celestial gamma ray source with 20,000 times more energy output than the sun has scientists perplexed because the characteristics of its radiation do not conform to conventional theories of physics. The radiation appears to be either a new twist on a common occurrence or a new occurrence altogether.
—*Insight*, November 14, 1988, p. 58

6. Federal law prohibits buying fetal tissue from women who abort and from abortion clinics, thus minimizing the likelihood that a dehumanizing market in fetal tissue will develop.
—JOHN A. ROBERTSON, *The New York Times*, December 10, 1988

7. The right wing disliked Orwell because he was a socialist, and the left wing disliked him because he told the truth.
—FREEMAN DYSON, "Reflections: Weapons and Hope,"
The New Yorker, February 20, 1984, p. 64

8. Capitalism succeeds because it is an economic theory designed for sinners, of whom there are many, just as socialism fails because it is a theory designed for saints, of whom there are few.
—SAMUEL MCCRACKEN, review of Michael Novak, *The Spirit of Democratic Capitalism*, in *Commentary*, Vol. 74, No. 1, July 1982, p. 76

9. High interest rates are not to blame for keeping Europe behind the Americans and the Japanese. The reasons are excessive welfare spending, rigid labor markets, obsolete plants, slow adjustment to innovation and lack of long-term confidence—"Eurosclerosis," one West German economist calls it.
—ALFRED ZANKER, "Silver Linings for Europe in High U.S. Interest Rates,"
U.S. News & World Report, July 30, 1984, p. 51

★ 10. . . . a decaying satellite can look like an incoming warhead to a sensor. That is the reason we have a man in the loop.
—GENERAL JAMES HARTINGER, Chief, Air Force Space Command,
"Nuclear War by Accident—Is It Impossible?" interview in
U.S. News & World Report, December 19, 1983, p. 27

11. . . . the number of strategic warheads on each side far exceeds the number of significant nonmilitary targets, so the majority of the weapons must be aimed at military targets if they are aimed at anything at all.
—FREEMAN DYSON, "Reflections: Weapons and Hope,"
The New Yorker, February 6, 1984, p. 72

12. In Iowa, for instance, the striped skunk is one of the most commonly run-over mammals, because of a skunk's natural defensive tactic. It stands its ground and ejects its notorious odor. Unfortunately for skunks, such a stand can be its last, as it does nothing to repel an oncoming pickup.
　　　　　　—CHARLIE CREEKMORE, "Flattened Fauna," *Science 84*, June 1984, p. 78

13. The extraordinary ability of satellites to see, to listen and to communicate would, however, greatly amplify the effectiveness of military forces in war-time. For that reason satellites would become particularly tempting targets as soon as hostilities seemed imminent.
　　　　　　—RICHARD L. GARWIN, KURT GOTTFRIED, and DONALD L. HAFNER,
　　　　　　　　"Antisatellite Weapons," *Scientific American*, June 1984, p. 45

14. New workers need capital, even if it is only a plough, so countries with a growing workforce have to invest more—or spread their investment more thinly.
　　　　　　—"Demography Comes of Age," *The Economist*, July 14, 1984, p. 76

★ 15. Treason doth never prosper: what's the reason?
　　　　For if it prosper, none dare call it treason.
　　　　　　—SIR JOHN HARINGTON, *Epigrams*, Book iv, No. 5

16. Because the U.S.S.R. has important facilities in the Arctic region, where it is difficult to have a clear line of sight to a geosynchronous satellite above the Equator, the Russians have introduced highly elliptical orbits for many of their Molniya-class communications and early-warning satellites.
　　　　　　—RICHARD L. GARWIN, KURT GOTTFRIED, and DONALD L. HAFNER,
　　　　　　　　"Antisatellite Weapons," *Scientific American*, June 1984, p. 46

17. High among the reasons for the woeful infant death rate in the Third World are undernourished mothers: They give birth to underweight babies and then haven't the strength—or the milk—to care for them. Food production has been falling steadily in the Third World for a decade now, so there are more under-nourished mothers than ever.　　　　—JUNE KRUNHOLZ, "Third-World Success,"
　　　　　　　　The Wall Street Journal, May 24, 1983

18. . . . there has never been a default on any item of the federal government's obligation; that is why the credit rating of the government is the standard against which all others are measured.
　　　　　　—ROBERT HEILBRONER, "Reflections (The Deficit),"
　　　　　　　　The New Yorker, July 30, 1984, p. 50

19. . . . a mammogram . . . has shown a slight shadow on the X-ray. If this were anything to worry about, there ought to be a palpable mass where the X-ray suggests one. And there isn't. Don't worry. . . .
　　　　　　—DR. RUSSELL STEARNE, quoted in Mark Kramer, "Benign Violence,"
　　　　　　　　The Atlantic Monthly, Vol. 251, No. 5, May 1983, p. 48

★ 20. According to BLS [the Bureau of Labor Statistics], a couple with two children needs 67 percent more income than a childless couple. This implies that adults spend about two thirds as much on their children as on themselves.
　　　　　　—CHRISTOPHER JENCKS, "The Hidden Prosperity of the 1970s,"
　　　　　　　　The Public Interest, No. 77, Fall 1984, p. 57

21. . . . we often learn about causes from cures: if ingesting a chemical cures a disease, we may learn that the disease was caused by a lack of that chemical.
　　　　　　—ERNEST VAN DEN HAAG, "Thinking About Crime Again,"
　　　　　　　　Commentary, Vol. 76, No. 6, December 1983, p. 73

22. Well over half of all public lands in Alaska and the Western states (where the odds are best for finding rich ore deposits) are closed or severely restricted to exploration and development—some because the mineral potential is not obvious, others because obvious potential is viewed as a "threat" to other possible land uses, and still others because prohibiting mineral activities is easier than developing a land-management scheme that will protect ecological values and permit mineral uses.

—PAUL K. DRIESSEN and WILBERT DARE, "Readers Report,"
Business Week, January 14, 1985, p. 5

23. . . . [C]lients should try to go through the entire first interview without even mentioning money. If you ask for a salary that is too high, the employer concludes that he can't afford you. If you ask for one that is too low, you're essentially saying, "I'm not competent enough to handle the job that you're offering."

—JAMES CHALLENGER, "What to Do—and Not to Do—When Job Hunting,"
U.S. News & World Report, August 6, 1984, pp. 63–66

24. Saying that, as a society, "We value self-sufficiency (and) we are offended by poverty," Moynihan [Senator Daniel Patrick Moynihan, D–N.Y.] contends that "It follows that we should not tax individuals, much less families, to the point where they are officially poor and potentially dependent."

—Washington Post Service, *The Honolulu Advertiser*, April 8, 1985, p. A-4

★ 25. The Tudor government in England was quite willing to reintroduce slavery into England and passed an act of Parliament making the enforcement of slavery legal, but it failed because there was an inexhaustible well of paupers to draw upon, cheaper by far than slaves, and much easier to control.

—J. H. PLUMB, review of *Slavery and Human Progress*,
in *The New York Review of Books*, January 17, 1985, p. 32

1.5 *Passages Containing Several Arguments*

We turn now to the problem of diagramming passages containing more than a single argument. In English (and any other natural language) it is possible to weave the strands of argument among one another in various ways, some of them quite complicated. As logicians our task here is to exhibit the complexities clearly, using diagrams to help us understand the logic of the passage.

In a complex passage it often happens that the conclusion of one argument serves as the premiss for another. More than two arguments may be present, and they may be so articulated that an extended line of reasoning cascades through several arguments to reach a final conclusion. In such argumentative passages there is a flow, a general direction, along which the speaker or writer intends the hearer or reader to follow.

To understand such complex reasoning, one must try to see how the single arguments in the passage are so arranged as to lead one rationally to accept the final conclusion. Each component argument may play a leading or a bridging role; the passage as a whole can best be understood by analyzing each of its component parts, using the methods of diagramming developed in earlier sections, and then noting the articulation of the parts in the larger whole. To appraise any chain of arguments as good or bad, cogent or faulty, one must have a thorough grasp of the entire structure.

In oral presentation this is more difficult to accomplish than it is for a written passage. But acquiring facility at analyzing written argumentative passages will help one to develop the habits and insights required to cope with spoken arguments.

Practicing these logical skills will help one to read more carefully and thus with greater comprehension. These skills enable their possessor to see with maximum clarity what conclusion is being urged, on the basis of what evidence, and to understand how the speaker or writer claims that the conclusion is derived from the premises. These analytical skills also help us to organize our own arguments more effectively—marshalling the evidence for our conclusions in the clearest possible fashion, and formulating the premisses we offer in support of our conclusions with greatest force and precision.

The number of arguments in a passage is determined (as we noted earlier) by the number of conclusions it contains. So a passage in which two distinct conclusions are inferred from the same premiss or group of premisses will count as containing two arguments. A remarkably clear example is the following passage:

> You can read about a country's history and culture, you can pore over travel brochures . . . but you can't get a true feeling for the people and the culture without witnessing both first hand. That's why there is no substitute for sending your children abroad to study, and why hosting a foreign student yourself can be a valuable experience for your family.[41]

Here the premiss is ① [you can't get a true feeling for the people and the culture without witnessing both first hand], the first conclusion is ② [there is no substitute for sending your children abroad to study], and the second conclusion is ③ [hosting a foreign student yourself can be a valuable experience for your family]. This passage contains two arguments, as is displayed by the diagram

An example of a two-argument passage in which each conclusion is inferred from the same *pair* of premisses is

> To hasten the social revolution in England is the most important object of the International Workingmen's Association. The sole means of hastening it is to make Ireland independent.
> Hence the task of the "International" is everywhere to put the conflict between

[41]Carol Steinberg, "Family," *Venture*, April 1983, p. 68.

England and Ireland in the foreground, and everywhere to side openly with Ireland.[42]

The premises here are ① [to hasten the social revolution in England is the most important object of the International Workingmen's Association] and ② [The sole means of hastening it is to make Ireland independent], and the conclusions are ③ [the task of the "International" is everywhere to put the conflict between England and Ireland in the foreground] and ④ [everywhere [the task of the "International" is] to side openly with Ireland]. The diagram for this argumentative passage is

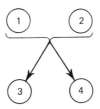

Some passages may contain two or more arguments that do not overlap either in their premises or conclusions but have been placed next to each other because of their common subject matter. They may come in simple succession, as in

> She is a woman, therefore may be won;
> She is Lavinia, therefore must be lov'd.[43]

Here the component propositions are ① [she is a woman] ② [she may be won], ③ [she is Lavinia], and ④ [she must be lov'd]. The diagram for this argumentative passage is

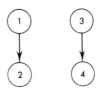

Or two arguments in a single passage may have their premises and conclusions intertwined, although still independent of each other. In the following passage from John Locke's influential *Second Treatise of Government*, the two conclusions are stated first, followed by the premises offered in their support:

> It is not necessary—no, nor so much as convenient—that the legislative should be always in being; but absolutely necessary that the executive power should, because there is not always need of new laws to be made, but always need of execution of the laws that are made.

[42]Karl Marx, Letter 141, 9 April 1870, *Karl Marx and Friedrich Engels Correspondence 1846–1895* (New York: International Publishers, 1936), p. 290.
[43]William Shakespeare, *Titus Andronicus*, II, i.

Here the component propositions are ① [it is not necessary or convenient that the legislative [branch of government] should be always in being]; ② [it is absolutely necessary that the executive power should be always in being]; ③ [there is not always need of new laws to be made]; and ④ [there is always need of execution of the laws that are made]. The diagram for this argumentative passage is

which shows that the second argument's conclusion comes between the premiss and conclusion of the first argument and that the first argument's premiss comes between the premiss and conclusion of the second argument, as well as showing that both conclusions are stated before their premisses.

A more interesting arrangement of two or more arguments in the same passage occurs when the conclusion of one argument is also a premiss of another. A simple example is the following:

① [The majority of our college students enroll in higher learning for vocational reasons.] ② [Such students, (therefore,) view their stay at college as a series of hurdles culminating in a credential and a post-graduate job.] (Consequently,) ③ [the values harbored by the majority of students coincide rather precisely with the values of the business establishment in general and the college administrators.][44]

The diagram for this passage is

which shows that there is an intermediate conclusion or subconclusion ② that is inferred from the given premiss ① and is itself a premiss from which the final conclusion ③ is inferred.

Another passage of the same complexity but with its constituents differently arranged is

[44]David Slive, letter to the editor, *Academe*, February 1980, p. 59.

① [The death penalty is further warranted] (because) ② [it is the only practical way to make certain that a murderer will not repeat his crime.] ③ [Under today's permissive, revolving-door justice, it is almost an everyday occurrence to read where a convicted murderer, after serving a relatively short sentence, has killed again.][45]

Its diagram is

A passage containing a slightly longer "chain" argument is

At first sight it seems plausible to say that (since) ① [reasons can be given for pieces of behaviour we usually call "irrational,"] ② [even this behaviour is, after all, rational, but at the unconscious level.] (It is a short step to the conclusion that) ③ [Freud has shown irrational behaviour to be "really" rational] and that ④ [we are, (therefore,) more rational than we usually suppose.][46]

Its diagram is

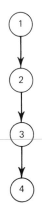

In some argumentative passages the final conclusion is not inferred from the subconclusion alone, but from it together with one or more premisses

[45]Frank G. Carrington, *Neither Cruel Nor Unusual.*

[46]Peter Alexander, "Rational Behaviour and Psychoanalytic Explanation," in Richard Wollheim, ed., *Freud: A Collection of Critical Essays* (Garden City, N.Y.: Anchor Books, 1974), pp. 306–307.

that are adduced in additional support for the final conclusion. We have this situation in the following:

> . . . ① [wealth is not sought except for the sake of something else,] (because) ② [of itself it brings us no good, but only when we use it, whether for the support of the body or for some similar purpose.] ③ [Now the highest good is sought for its own, and not for another's sake.] (Therefore) ④ [wealth is not man's highest good.][47]

as the following diagram shows.

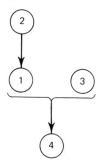

In somewhat more complicated argumentative passages, the final conclusion is inferred from two or more premises, all of which were themselves the conclusions of earlier arguments in the passage. That is the case in the following argument:

> ① [Unlike land-based intercontinental ballistic missiles (ICBM's) such as the Minuteman and its proposed replacement, the MX, [sea-launched ballistic missiles] SLBM's on submerged submarines are difficult to locate accurately;] (hence) ② [they are essentially invulnerable to a preemptive "counterforce" attack and seem certain to remain so for the foreseeable future.] Moreover, ③ [U.S. ballistic-missile submarines, by virtue of their range and mobility, are capable of launching a prompt retaliatory strike on the U.S.S.R. from many directions.] (thereby) ④ [complicating any attempt to thwart a counterattack by means of an anti-ballistic-missile (ABM) system.]. (In short,) ⑤ [SLBM's come close to being an ideal deterrent force against a nuclear attack.][48]

whose diagram

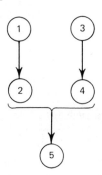

[47]Thomas Aquinas, *Summa Contra Gentiles*, in Anton C. Pegis, ed., *Basic Writings of St. Thomas Aquinas* (New York: Random House, 1945).

[48]"Science and the Citizen," *Scientific American*, Vol. 248, No. 5, May 1983, p. 88.

shows that ⑤ is inferred from ② and ④, each of which was itself inferred earlier in the passage.

Diagramming another complex argumentative passage reminds us how to treat noun phrases that—in the context—have propositional roles in the argument.

① [Looking ahead, the Labor Department sees manufacturing's share of nonfarm jobs, which stood at close to 24 percent in 1969, dropping to about 19 percent by 1990.]
The reasons for the fall are threefold: (Because of) ② [high interest rates] and ③ [low birth rates,] ④ [the American appetite for autos, refrigerators and other big-ticket items is waning.] ⑤ [More of what is bought here is being produced abroad.] And ⑥ [American industry is becoming increasingly automated.][49]

The diagram is

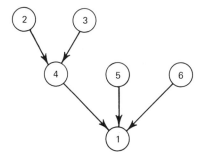

Here bracketing and numbering the noun phrases ② and ③ indicates that they are understood to express propositions, which (after deleting the word "of") might be rephrased as "interest rates are high" and "birth rates are low."

Sometimes we *assume* a proposition in order to explore its consequences, to see what else would be the case if the proposition in question were true. That amounts to "asserting the proposition for the sake of the argument," and it occurs in the following argumentative passage. For stylistic reasons, to avoid the monotony of saying the same thing in the same way, authors may say the same thing in different ways; that is, they may formulate a single proposition in various different sentences. This also happens in the following passage—as is shown by our assigning the same number to different formulations of the same proposition:

When ① [the state levies a sales tax,] ② [the cost of the taxed commodity rises.] (Because) ② [the cost of the commodity is higher,] ③ [less of it is sold—gasoline or liquor or cigarette sales, for example, always suffer when taxes are placed on them.] (It follows that) ④ [the sales tax must affect individuals other than just the buyers.] ⑤ [The seller of the commodity must bear some of the tax] (because) ③ [his sales have declined] and presumably ⑥ [so has his income.] ⑦ [The

---

[49]"Jobs—A Million That Will Never Come Back," *U.S. News & World Report*, September 13, 1982, p. 53.

workers or other suppliers of services who produce the commodity will also be penalized,] (because) ③ [less of the taxed commodity will be bought] (and therefore) ⑧ [fewer people will be employed making it.] In other words, ⑨ [the incidence, or burden, of a tax is often much more complex than appears on the surface.][50]

The following diagram presents the logic, if not the rhetoric, of the passage in question.

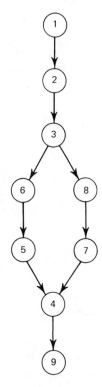

EXERCISES

Analyze and diagram the arguments in the following passages, each of which contains more than one argument.

★ 1. General Mercier, leaving for Rennes to appear as a witness, issued his Order of the Day: "Dreyfus will be condemned once more. For in this affair someone is certainly guilty and the guilty one is either him or me. As it is certainly not me, it is Dreyfus." —BARBARA W. TUCHMAN, *The Proud Tower*
(New York: The Macmillan Company, 1966), p. 257

2. The Creative is heaven, therefore it is called the father. The Receptive is the earth, therefore it is called the mother. —*The I Ching* or *Book of Changes*
(Princeton, N.J.: Princeton University Press, 1967), p. 274

[50]Robert Heilbroner and Lester Thurow, *Five Economic Challenges* (Englewood Cliffs, N.J.: Prentice-Hall, Inc., 1981), pp. 60–61.

3. Soviet policy is not driven by internal necessity, so it can change. But because it is driven by power, interest and conviction, it will not change easily.
—STEPHEN SESTANOVICH, "What Gorbachev Wants,"
The New Republic, May 25, 1987, p. 23

4. A non-nuclear world can never be restored. Any moderately industrialized country can make nuclear weapons, and any rich country can buy them. Thus the West will always need some nuclear weapons against the chance that a strong hostile power or a state under the control of an irrational leader will obtain them.
—EUGENE V. ROSTOW, "Why the Soviets Want an
Arms-Control Agreement, and Why They Want It Now,"
Commentary, Vol. 83, No. 2, February 1987, p. 25

★ 5. I have a heart, and therefore I love; but I am your daughter, and therefore I am proud.
—WILLIAM S. GILBERT and ARTHUR S. SULLIVAN, *H.M.S. Pinafore*, Act I

6. It is impossible to be specific about the future of any branch of science since there is no way of forecasting unexpected and surprising discoveries. (If there were, they wouldn't be unexpected and surprising, and they could be made without delay.)
—ISAAC ASIMOV, "The Med-Surg Miracle Tour,"
Creative Living, Summer 1988, p. 2

7. Higher interest rates are badly suited to cooling an economy in which the trade balance is a worry, because they strengthen the currency, and hence make exports dearer and imports cheaper.
—"Business," *The Economist*, September 2, 1988, p. 53

8. [D]rug use is wrong because it is immoral, and it is immoral because it enslaves the mind and destroys the soul.
—JAMES Q. WILSON, quoted by George Will in "How Reagan
Changed America," *Newsweek*, January 9, 1989, p. 15

9. As force is always on the side of the governed, the governors have nothing to support them but opinion. It is therefore on opinion only that government is founded.
—DAVID HUME, cited in Keith Thomas, "Just Say Yes,"
The New York Review of Books, Vol. 35, No. 18, November 24, 1988, p. 43

★ 10. . . . almost every advertisement you see is obviously designed, in some way or another, to fool the customer: the print that they don't want you to read is small; the statements are written in an obscure way. It is obvious to anybody that the product is not being presented in a scientific and balanced way. Therefore, in the selling business, there's a lack of integrity.
—RICHARD P. FEYNMAN, *"What Do You Care What Other People Think?"*
(New York: W. W. Norton & Company, Inc., 1988), p. 218

11. When drug dealers kill in the course of their business, they often kill other drug dealers. . . . If the bill [allowing the death penalty for drug dealers who kill in the course of their business] works as it is supposed to, drug dealers will be deterred from killing other drug dealers. With less of a threat of death from other dealers, we can expect more people to engage in drug dealing and the peddling of drugs to rise.
—RICHARD LEMPERT, "Death for Drug Killings Means Politics as Usual,"
The New York Times, June 25, 1988, p. 14

12. [H]ypochondriacs are using physical symptoms as a nonverbal way of telling other people that something has gone wrong in their lives. To tell someone

about your aches and pains is really to ask them to help. So the hypochondriac is asking others for special consideration—for attention, sympathy and support. This interpretation suggests that if you put a hypochondriac on a desert island, his symptoms would disappear.

—"The Problem of Overweight," *Harvard Medical School Health Letter,* Vol. 11, No. 11, September 1986, p. 7

13. Energy in its various forms, from heat to gasoline, plays a larger part in the budgets of poor families than well-to-do families. This is because energy is largely used for essentials. For families in the lowest ten percent of households, energy accounts for a full third of household expenditures; whereas for households in the top ten percent, it absorbs only five percent of household expenses. Therefore, a jump in energy costs will penalize the poor much more severely than the rich.

—ROBERT HEILBRONER and LESTER THUROW, *Five Economic Challenges* (Englewood Cliffs, N.J.: Prentice-Hall, Inc., 1981), p. 123

14. . . . the necessity of financing the very large prospective deficits that will remain even at high levels of output will cause a competition between government and business for access to available funds—a competition that the federal government is certain to win. The government is certain to win because the Treasury will price its new bond issues, or adjust their interest rates, to whatever levels are needed to tempt households, banks, and businesses to buy its bonds. The consequences are twofold: First, the absorption of funds by the federal government will leave that much less available for other uses, whether private or state and local. Second, the struggle among borrowers for the nation's savings will raise interest rates.   —ROBERT HEILBRONER, "Reflections (The Deficit),"

The New Yorker, July 30, 1984, p. 54

★ 15. The lower strata of the middle class—the small tradespeople, shopkeepers, and retired tradesmen generally, the handicraftsmen and peasants—all these sink gradually into the proletariat, partly because their diminutive capital does not suffice for the scale on which modern industry is carried on, and is swamped in the competition with the large capitalists, partly because their specialized skill is rendered worthless by new methods of production. Thus the proletariat is recruited from all classes of the population.

—KARL MARX and FRIEDRICH ENGELS, *The Communist Manifesto,* 1848 (New York: International Publishers, 1971), p. 9

16. Hunting was a valuable adaptation to the environment since meat could supply more calories and protein than a vegetarian diet. Peking man was evidently able to compete successfully with large carnivores as a hunter. An abundance of fossil bones of mammals of various sizes found in the cave indicates that Peking man not only hunted small game but also was capable of killing large animals.

—WU RUKANG and LIN SHENGLONG, "Peking Man," *Scientific American,* Vol. 248, No. 6, June 1983, p. 93

17. Because nursing homes charge private patients much more than Medicaid pays, private patients are usually preferred over Medicaid patients. As a result, Medicaid patients often have difficulty gaining access to nursing homes. Simi-

larly, since severely disabled patients require more expensive care than the average patient does, fewer nursing homes will accept them.

—ALICE M. RIVLIN and JOSHUA M. WEINER, The Brookings Institution,
"Study Urges Federal Insurance for Long-Term Health Care of the Elderly,"
The New York Times, May 18, 1988, p. 24

18. [C]ontemporary standards of decency confirm our judgment that such a young person [15 years old] is not capable of acting with the culpability that can justify the ultimate [death] penalty. Inexperience, less education, and less intelligence make the teen-ager less able to evaluate the consequences of his or her conduct while at the same time he or she is more apt to be motivated by mere emotion or peer pressure than is an adult.

Juvenile executions could not be expected to deter people under 16 from committing murder because the likelihood that the teen-age offender has made the kind of cost-benefit analysis that attaches any weight to the possibility of execution is so remote as to be virtually nonexistent.

—JUSTICE JOHN PAUL STEVENS, *Thompson* v. *Oklahoma,* June 29, 1988

19. McGeorge Bundy, advisor on major elements of U.S. foreign policy over the past twenty years, remarks that in one sense our deterrent policies have obviously worked: there has been no nuclear war. In the same sense, he reminds us, the deterrent policies of Finland, Austria, Canada and Mexico have worked as well. . . . And these nations can equally well claim on behalf of their policies that "there has been no war against them, and no coercion that has prevented their citizens from living lives decisively better than those of the generation before them." Clearly, Bundy says, "the judgment that deterrence has worked is not a judgment that any particular form of deterrence was the best available—or even that it was necessary. . . . It is only an assumption, and one not open to proof, that the nuclear weapon [is] indispensable to [deterrence].

—*Report from the Center for Philosophy and Public Policy,*
University of Maryland, Vol. 3, No. 3, Summer 1983, p. 3

★ 20. A disease entity is defined by signs and symptoms generated by objective—that is, organic—determinants. Thus . . . illness is organic. Since mental disturbances are not organic, mental illness is not illness.

—Attributed to Dr. Thomas Szasz in Carol Levine, ed.,
Taking Sides: Clashing Views on Controversial Bio-Ethical Issues
(Guilford, Conn.: The Dushkin Publishing Group, Inc., 1984), p. 181

21. While savings may be hoarded rather than channeled into productive investments, the demand generated by increased consumption necessarily induces increased investment, and hence promotes the greatest possible utilization of a society's resources. Hence, rather than encouraging individual thrift, the appropriate economic role for government is to generate consumption through such devices as public works programs, which put more money in the hands of the poorer classes (whose lack of surplus wealth gives them a greater "propensity to consume" than the wealthy).

—ROBERTA SCHAEFER and DAVID SCHAEFER, "The Political Philosophy of
J. M. Keynes," *The Public Interest,* No. 71, Spring 1983, p. 53

22. Shielding against radiation is not the only prerequisite for an adequate shelter. Once the attack has occurred, people must remain inside the shelters

until the outside fallout decays to a safe level, a period that may exceed one month if the intensity of fallout has been great. Therefore, the shelter must have adequate ventilation and sanitation facilities, and it must be stocked with sufficient food, water, and other supplies.

—ARTHUR J. VANDER, "The Delusion of Civil Defense,"
LSA, The University of Michigan, Ann Arbor, Spring 1983, p. 10

23. . . . nuclear warheads are not weapons, as one normally understands the term. No nation can use them to achieve a political end, since if its bluff were called, it would be left with the option of capitulating or committing national suicide. Nuclear warheads are unusable to halt a conventional attack since their use would almost certainly lead to an all-out nuclear exchange and the destruction of all that we were trying to protect. Nuclear weapons are useful only in a cancelling-out process—to deter the other side from using them.

—GEORGE W. BALL, "Sovietizing US Policy," *The New York Review of Books*,
Vol. 31, No. 1, February 2, 1984, p. 34

24. The free-market remedy for inflation is mass unemployment. This remedy imposes severe economic, social and political costs. It is also cruelly inequitable, since it places the burden of the struggle against inflation on those least able to bear it. It is also unavailing, since mass unemployment will inevitably create a demand for reflation, and with reflation prices and interest rates will shoot up again.   —ARTHUR SCHLESINGER, JR., "Should Conservatives Embrace Big Government?" *The Wall Street Journal*, February 3, 1983

★ 25. Why should selective cutting be implemented? The Amazonian forest contains 20 to 60 trees an acre, but only one or two can be used for industrial purposes. Only these trees can be felled economically because exploration requires heavy, expensive, high-oil-consumption equipment. This machinery can be amortized only by cutting large, high-yield trees. The main advantage of selective cutting is that the younger trees get more access to light and water, accelerating the natural growth cycle of the forest.

—ALLEN FALK, "Amazon Tree Cutting Better Than Burning,"
The New York Times, November 14, 1988, p. 22

26. There is no possibility, it would seem, of controverting the committed Marxist. His Marxism makes him invulnerable to argument since, among other things, it enables him to assume that those who disagree with him do so because they are, as the editors write, spokesmen for "narrow political interests and biases." —STEPHEN MILLER, review of Bertell Ollman and Edward Vernoff, eds.,
The Left Academy: Marxist Scholarship on American Campuses,
in *The Public Interest*, No. 71, Spring 1983, p. 140

27. In physics, we deal with what have been characterized as "limiting cases"—situations that can be so highly idealized and simplified that they can be subjected to predictive law. We can talk about "the" electron, because each electron is like every other electron. But since no two living things are exactly alike, biological laws are statistical, and since biological systems are so complex the laws are usually nonpredictive. This makes biology a science with goals, methods, and a philosophy very different from those of physics.

—JEREMY BERNSTEIN, "The Evolution of Evolution,"
The New Yorker, January 23, 1984, p. 98

28. In inflationary times it is obviously advantageous to borrow money at normal interest rates because dollars will be cheaper and more plentiful when it comes time to repay the loan. Therefore businesses seek to borrow funds—but banks are loath to lend, for exactly the same reasons.

Two results follow. First, interest rates go ever higher to compensate banks for the falling value of the dollars they will receive. . . .

Second, banks refuse to lend for more than short periods of time. The result is that business has to take on short term loans at high interest rates.

—ROBERT HEILBRONER and LESTER THUROW, *Five Economic Challenges* (Englewood Cliffs, N.J.: Prentice-Hall, Inc., 1981), p. 28

29. The language being considered on the labels [of cigarette packages] would require warning of the increased danger of heart disease, lung cancer and emphysema; of hazards to pregnant women of miscarriage and birth deformities, and of the risk of addiction.

The tobacco industry, in a real triumph of doubletalk, is still arguing against strict labeling on the grounds that (a) you don't need it because everyone knows the dangers connected with smoking and (b) you should not have tougher labels because there is no established causal link between smoking and disease, only some statistical "questions."

If you believe either of these arguments you probably also believe in the Easter Bunny, but since some 32 percent of the public still smokes, there obviously are a lot of people who don't or won't recognize the dangers or who do believe in the Easter Bunny.   —JUDY MANN, " 'Sure' Way to Cut Number of Smokers," *Washington Post Service*, April 2, 1982

★ 30. ". . . You appeared to be surprised when I told you, on our first meeting, that you had come from Afghanistan."

"You were told, no doubt."

"Nothing of the sort. I *knew* you came from Afghanistan. From long habit the train of thoughts ran so swiftly through my mind that I arrived at the conclusion without being conscious of intermediate steps. There were such steps, however. The train of reasoning ran, 'Here is a gentleman of medical type, but with the air of a military man. Clearly an army doctor, then. He has just come from the tropics, for his face is dark, and that is not the natural tint of his skin, for his wrists are fair. He has undergone hardship and sickness, as his haggard face says clearly. His left arm has been injured. He holds it in a stiff and unnatural manner. Where in the tropics could an English army doctor have seen much hardship and got his arm wounded? Clearly in Afghanistan.' The whole train of thought did not occupy a second. I then remarked that you came from Afghanistan, and you were astonished."

It is simple enough as you explain it," I said, smiling.

—A. CONAN DOYLE, *A Study in Scarlet*, Chapter 2

1.6 *Deduction and Induction*

Arguments are traditionally divided into two different types, *deductive* and *inductive*. Every argument involves the claim (noted earlier) that its premises provide some grounds for the truth of its conclusion; but only a deductive argument involves the claim that its premisses provide *conclusive* grounds for its conclusion. When the reasoning in a deductive argument is correct, we call that argument *valid*; when the reasoning of a deductive argument is incorrect, we call that argument *invalid.*

We may therefore define *validity* as follows: A deductive argument is valid when its premisses, if true, do provide conclusive grounds for the truth of its conclusion. In a deductive argument (but not in an inductive argument) premisses and conclusion are so related that it is absolutely impossible for the premisses to be true unless the conclusion is true also.

In every deductive argument, either the premisses succeed in providing conclusive grounds for the truth of the conclusion, or they do not succeed. Therefore, every deductive argument is either valid or invalid. This is a point of some importance: if a deductive argument is not valid, it must be invalid; if it is not invalid, it must be valid. But note that the terms "valid" and "invalid" do not apply to inductive arguments; for inductive arguments other terms of appraisal will be required.

In the realm of deductive logic the central task is to clarify the relation between premisses and conclusion in valid arguments, and thus to allow us to discriminate valid from invalid arguments. The theory of deduction, including both traditional logic and symbolic logic, is the substance of Part Two of this book.

An inductive argument makes a very different claim—not that its premisses give conclusive grounds for the truth of its conclusion, but only that its premisses provide *some* support for that conclusion. Inductive arguments, therefore, cannot be "valid" or "invalid" in the sense in which these terms are applied to deductive arguments. Of course, inductive arguments may be evaluated as better or worse, according to the degree of support given to their conclusions by their premisses. Thus, the greater the likelihood, or probability, which its premisses confer upon its conclusion, the greater the merit of an inductive argument. But that likelihood, even when the premisses are all true, must fall short of certainty. The theory of induction, and the methods of calculating probabilities, are presented in Part Three of this book.

The distinction between deductive and inductive arguments is sometimes drawn in a different way—centering upon the relative generality of their premisses and conclusions. Deductive inferences, it is sometimes said, move from the general to the particular, while inductive inferences move from the particular to the general.[51] This way of distinguishing them proves unsatisfactory upon analysis.

In that tradition, the classical example of a deductive argument

> All humans are mortal.
> Socrates is human.
> Therefore Socrates is mortal.

[51]William Whewell, in *The Philosophy of the Inductive Sciences*, long ago put it thus: ". . . in Deduction we infer particular from general truths; while in Induction we infer general from particular. . . ."

does indeed have a particular conclusion,[52] inferred validly from two premisses of which the first is a general or universal proposition. It is also true that a very common form of inductive argument is one in which a general or universal conclusion is inferred from a group of premisses all of which are particular, as in this example:

> Socrates is human and mortal.
> Xanthippe is human and mortal.
> Sappho is human and mortal.
> Therefore probably all humans are mortal.

But this method of distinguishing between deduction and induction does not always work. The difficulty lies in the fact that a valid deductive argument may have universal propositions for its conclusion as well as for its premisses, as in

> All animals are mortal.
> All humans are animals.
> Therefore all humans are mortal.

And a valid deductive argument may have particular propositions for its premises as well as for its conclusion, as in

> If Socrates is human then Socrates is mortal.
> Socrates is human.
> Therefore Socrates is mortal.

Moreover, an inductive argument need not rely only upon particular premisses, but may have universal (i.e., general) propositions for its premises as well for its conclusions, as in

> All cows are mammals and have lungs.
> All whales are mammals and have lungs.
> All humans are mammals and have lungs.
> Therefore probably all mammals have lungs.

And further, an inductive argument may have a particular proposition as

---

[52]The term "particular" is used by Whewell, and other logicians in his tradition, to refer to propositions about a single thing (e.g., Socrates) as well as to propositions about some but not necessarily all members of a given class (e.g., some humans). More recent logical practice uses the phrase "particular propositions" to refer only to the latter group. At this point we are examining Whewell's view, and therefore follow his usage.

Later in this book, singular propositions are discussed in detail in Section 7.2 of Chapter 7 and in Section 10.1 of Chapter 10; particular propositions (in the current sense) are discussed in Section 5.1 of Chapter 5 and in Section 10.3 of Chapter 10.

its conclusion, as in

> Hitler was a dictator and was ruthless.
> Stalin was a dictator and was ruthless.
> Castro is a dictator.
> Therefore Castro is probably ruthless.

These counterexamples show that it is not satisfactory to characterize deductive arguments as those in which particular conclusions are inferred from general premisses; nor is it satisfactory to characterize inductive arguments as those in which general conclusions are inferred from particular premisses.

The fundamental difference between these two kinds of argument lies in the claims that are made about the relations between premisses and conclusion. Deductive arguments are those in which a very strict or close relationship is claimed to hold between their premisses and conclusions. If a deductive argument is valid then, given the truth of its premisses, its conclusion *must* be true no matter what else may be the case.

For example: If it is true that all humans are mortal, and if it is true that Socrates is a human, then it must be true that Socrates is mortal no matter what else may be true in the world and no matter what other premisses are added or other information discovered. If we find that Socrates is ugly, or that angels are immortal, or that cows give milk, it affects the validity of the argument not one bit; the conclusion that Socrates is mortal follows from any enlarged set of premisses with deductive certainty, just as it did from the two premisses originally given. If an argument is valid, nothing additional in the world can make it *more* valid; if a conclusion is validly inferred from some set of premisses there is nothing that can be added to the set that would make that conclusion follow more validly or more strictly or more logically.

But the relation between premisses and conclusion claimed for an inductive argument, even the best of that kind, is much less strict, and very different in kind. Consider the following inductive argument:

> Most corporation lawyers are Conservatives.
> Barbara Shane is a corporation lawyer.
> Therefore Barbara Shane is probably a Conservative.

This is a pretty good inductive argument; its first premiss is true, and if its second premiss is true also, its conclusion is more likely true than false. But in this case, by adding new premisses to the original pair the resulting argument may be substantially weakened, or (depending on the premisses added) strengthened. Suppose we add the premiss that

Barbara Shane is an officer of the American Civil Liberties Union (ACLU).

and also add the (true) premiss that

Most officers of the ACLU are not Conservatives.

Now the conclusion [that Barbara Shane is a Conservative] no longer seems very probable; the original inductive argument has been greatly weakened by the presence of this additional information about Barbara Shane. Indeed, if the final premiss were transformed into the universal proposition

No officers of the ACLU are Conservatives.

the opposite of the original conclusion would now follow deductively, that is, validly, from the set of premisses affirmed.

On the other hand, if we enlarge the original set of premisses by adding the following additional premisses instead:

Barbara Shane served in the cabinet of President Ronald Reagan.

and

Barbara Shane has long been an officer of the National Rifle Association.

then the original conclusion follows with a greater likelihood from this enlarged set of premisses than it did from the original set.

The strength of the *claim* about *the relation between the premisses and the conclusion* of the argument is the nub of the difference between deductive and inductive arguments. We characterize the two types of arguments as follows: A *deductive* argument is one whose conclusion is claimed to follow from its premisses with absolute necessity, this necessity not being a matter of degree and not depending in any way upon whatever else may be the case; in sharp contrast, an *inductive* argument is one whose conclusion is claimed to follow from its premisses only with probability, this probability being a matter of degree and dependent upon what else may be the case.

Although probability is the essence of the relation between premisses and conclusion in inductive arguments, such arguments do not always acknowledge explicitly that their conclusions are inferred only with some degree of probability. On the other hand, the mere presence of the word "probability" within an argument is no sure indication that the argument is inductive, because there are some strictly deductive arguments *about* probabilities themselves. Arguments of this kind, in which the probability of a certain combination of events is deduced from the probabilities of other events, are discussed in Chapter 14.

1.7 *Truth and Validity*

Truth and falsehood may be predicated of propositions, but never of arguments. And the attributes of validity and invalidity can belong only to deductive arguments, never to propositions. There is a connection between the validity or invalidity of an argument and the truth or falsehood of its premisses and conclusion, but the connection is by no means a simple one. Indeed, it is so complex that the whole of Part Two of this book is devoted to the problem of determining the validity or invalidity of deductive arguments. So only a brief preliminary discussion of validity will be presented in this section.

It is important to realize that an argument may be valid while one or more of its premisses is untrue. This point was made forcefully by Abraham Lincoln, in one of his debates with Judge Stephen Douglas, in 1858. Lincoln was attacking the Dred Scott decision, which obliged the return of slaves, who had escaped into northern states, to their owners in the south.

> [W]hat follows as a short and even syllogistic argument from it [i.e., from the Dred Scott decision]? I think it follows, and submit to the consideration of men capable of arguing, whether as I state it in syllogistic form the argument has any fault in it:
>
> Nothing in the Constitution or laws of any State can destroy a right distinctly and expressly affirmed in the Constitution of the United States.
>
> The right of property in a slave is distinctly and expressly affirmed in the Constitution of the United States.
>
> Therefore, nothing in the Constitution or laws of any State can destroy the right of property in a slave.
>
> I believe that no fault can be pointed out in that argument; assuming the truth of the premises, the conclusion, so far as I have capacity at all to understand it, follows inevitably. There is a fault in it as I think, but the fault is not in the reasoning; but the falsehood in fact is a fault of the premises. I believe that the right of property in a slave *is not* distinctly and expressly affirmed in the Constitution, and Judge Douglas thinks it *is*. I believe that the Supreme Court and the advocates of that decision [the Dred Scott decision] may search in vain for the place in the Constitution where the right of property in a slave is distinctly and expressly affirmed. I say, therefore, that I think one of the premises is not true in fact.[53]

Arguments may exhibit differing combinations of true and false premises and conclusions. Here follow seven different examples; their contents are trivial and contrived, but that will put the special features of each example in sharp relief. Using these examples we may formulate important principles concerning the relations of truth and validity.

Some valid arguments contain only true propositions, as, for example:

I.
    All whales are mammals.
    All mammals have lungs.
    Therefore all whales have lungs.

---

[53]Abraham Lincoln, in Roy R. Basler, ed., *The Collected Works of Abraham Lincoln* (New Brunswick, N.J.: Rutgers University Press, 1953), Vol. III, p. 231.

But an argument may also consist entirely of false propositions and nevertheless be valid, as, for example:

II.
> All spiders have ten legs.
> All ten-legged creatures have wings.
> Therefore all spiders have wings.

This argument is valid because if its premises were true its conclusion would have to be true also—even though in fact they are all false.

Moreover, an argument may have premises that are all true, and have a true conclusion, and nevertheless be invalid, as in the following example:

III.
> If I owned all the gold in Fort Knox then I would be wealthy.
> I do not own all the gold in Fort Knox.
> Therefore I am not wealthy.

The premisses could be true and the conclusion false—as is clear when one considers that if I were to inherit ten million dollars, the premisses would remain true, although the conclusion would become false. Of course the argument would remain invalid.

This point is further illustrated by the following argument, which has precisely the same form as Example III:

IV.
> If Rockefeller owned all the gold in Fort Knox, then Rockefeller would be wealthy.
> Rockefeller does not own all the gold in Fort Knox.
> Therefore Rockefeller is not wealthy.

The premisses of this argument are true, and its conclusion is false. Such an argument cannot be valid, because it is impossible for the premisses of a valid argument to be true while its conclusion is false.

Arguments with false premisses and true conclusions may be valid or invalid. Here is an example of a valid argument with false premisses and a true conclusion:

V.
> All fishes are mammals.
> All whales are fishes.
> Therefore all whales are mammals.

And here is an example of an invalid argument with false premisses and a true conclusion:

VI.
> All mammals have wings.
> All whales have wings.
> Therefore all whales are mammals.

Finally, there are invalid arguments whose premisses and conclusions are all false, as, for example:

VII.
    All mammals have wings.
    All whales have wings.
    Therefore all mammals are whales.

Effective methods for establishing the validity or invalidity of deductive arguments will be presented and explained in Part Two of this book—but it is clear from these seven examples that there are valid arguments with false conclusions (Example II), as well as invalid arguments with true conclusions (Examples III and VI). Hence it is clear that the truth or falsity of an argument's conclusion does not by itself determine the validity or invalidity of that argument. And the fact that an argument is valid does not guarantee the truth of its conclusion. (Example II)

By laying out these seven examples of deductive arguments on the two following charts, we may better appreciate their variety. The first chart, of *invalid* arguments, shows that there are invalid arguments with every combination of true and false premisses and conclusions:

| | *Invalid Arguments* | |
	True conclusion	*False conclusion*
True premisses	Example III	Example IV
False premisses	Example VI	Example VII

The second chart, of *valid* arguments, shows that valid arguments have only three of those combinations of true and false premisses and conclusions:

| | *Valid Arguments* | |
	True conclusion	*False conclusion*
True premisses	Example I	
False premisses	Example V	Example II

The blank position on the second chart exhibits graphically a point of the most fundamental importance: *if an argument is valid and its conclusion is false, not all its premisses can be true.* And also: *if an argument is valid and its premisses are true, we may be certain that its conclusion must be true also.* Some perfectly valid arguments do have false conclusions—but any such argument must have at least one false premiss.

When an argument is valid, *and* all of its premisses are true, we call it *"sound."* The conclusion of a sound argument obviously must be true. If a deductive argument is not sound—which means either that it is not valid or that not all of its premisses are true—it fails to establish the truth of its conclusion.

To test the truth or falsehood of premisses is the task of science in general, since premisses may deal with any subject matter at all. The logician is not so much interested in the truth or falsehood of propositions as in the logical relations between them, where by the "logical" relations between propositions we mean those which determine the correctness or incorrectness of arguments in which they may occur. Determining the correctness or incorrectness of arguments falls squarely within the province of logic. The logician is interested in the correctness even of arguments whose premisses might be false.

A question might be raised about the value of this last point. It might be suggested that we ought to confine ourselves to arguments that have true premisses, ignoring all others. But as a matter of fact we are interested in, and must often depend upon, the correctness of arguments whose premisses are not known to be true. Examples of such situations suggest themselves readily. A scientist who is interested in verifying scientific theories by deducing testable consequences from them does not know beforehand which theories are true. Were that known, there would be no need for (further) verification. In our everyday affairs, we must often choose between alternative courses of action. Where these courses are genuine alternatives that cannot all be adopted, we may try to reason about which should be chosen. Such reasoning generally involves figuring out the consequences of each of the different actions among which we must choose. One might argue, suppose I choose the first alternative, then such and such will be the case. On the other hand, assuming that I choose the second alternative, then something else will follow. In general, we are inclined to choose among alternative courses of action on the basis of which set of consequences we prefer to have realized. In each case, we are interested in reasoning correctly, lest we deceive ourselves. Were we interested only in arguments that have true premisses, we should not know which line of argument to consider until we knew which of the alternative premisses was true. And if we knew which premiss was true, we should not be interested in the arguments at all, because our purpose in considering the arguments was to help us decide which alternative premiss to *make* true. To confine our attention to arguments with true premisses alone would be self-defeating and stultifying.

So far we have been speaking only about propositions and the arguments that contain them as premisses and conclusion. As has been explained, these are not linguistic entities such as sentences, but what sentences may be uttered to assert. Whether the actual process of thinking or reasoning requires language or not is an open question. It may be that thinking requires the use of symbols of some sort, words or images or what not. We all feel a certain sympathy with the youngster who was told to think before speaking, and replied, "But how can I know what I think until I hear what I say?" Perhaps all thinking does require words or some other kind of symbols, but that is not a question that concerns us here. It is obvious that the communication of any proposition or any argument requires symbols and involves language. In the rest of this book, we are concerned with *stated* arguments, whose propositions are formulated in language.

The use of language, however, complicates our problem. Certain accidental or misleading features of their formulations in language may make more difficult the task of investigating the logical relations among propositions. It is part of the task of the logician, therefore, to examine language itself, primarily from the point of view of discovering and describing those aspects of it which tend to obscure the difference between correct and incorrect argument. It is for this reason that Part One of this book is devoted to language.

1.8 *Problem Solving*

A great deal of what we do is a matter of habit. As we go to work or school, we usually move along a well-established route, with surroundings so familiar that we scarcely notice them. But if our normal progress is interrupted by some obstacle, an excavation or a barricade, *that* captures our attention. Our progress becomes problematic. We must think about what to do next. We recognize that we have a problem. We must consider what to do about it.

It has been argued very plausibly that every problem, however abstract, arises from some kind of conflict between a belief and a situation to which the belief seems inappropriate. From this collision between situations and beliefs that do not "fit" them there arises the discomfort of doubt. And it is doubt that stimulates inquiry. As Charles Sanders Peirce wrote: "The irritation of doubt causes a struggle to attain a state of belief. I shall term this struggle *Inquiry*. . . ."[54]

In Section 1.1 we remarked that the skills included in "logical ability" are useful in solving problems. The most fruitful and dependable kind of Inquiry is the application of reason to solving problems. This involves all aspects of what Peirce called Inquiry: examining and reexamining the problematic situation from every point of view that occurs to us, marshalling all relevant information that is available, and seeking as persistently as we can for some new insight into the situation or some new combination of possible beliefs that will enable us to dispel the discomfort or irritation of doubt.

As William James put it,

> The individual has a stock of old opinions already, but he meets a new experience that puts them to a strain. Somebody contradicts them; or in a reflective moment he discovers that they contradict each other; or he hears of facts with which they are incompatible; or desires arise in him which they cease to satisfy. The result is

---

[54]Charles Sanders Peirce, "The Fixation of Belief" (1877), reprinted in Irving M. Copi and James A. Gould, eds., *Readings on Logic*, 2nd ed. (New York: Macmillan Publishing Company, 1972), p. 62.

an inward trouble to which his mind till then had been a stranger, and from which he seeks to escape by modifying his previous mass of opinions. He saves as much of it as he can, for in this matter of belief we are all extreme conservatives. So he tries to change first this opinion, and then that (for they resist change very variously), until at last some new idea comes up which he can graft upon the ancient stock with a minimum of disturbance of the latter, some idea that mediates between the stock and the new experience and runs them into one another most felicitously and expediently.[55]

John Dewey's formulation of this important conception is the following:

. . . thinking takes its departure from specific conflicts in experience that occasion perplexity and trouble. Men do not, in their natural estate, think when they have no troubles to cope with, no difficulties to overcome. A life of ease, of success without effort, would be a thoughtless life, and so also would a life of ready omnipotence.[56]

The serious problems of human life, broadly speaking, have to do with the avoidance of suffering and the achievement of happiness. To achieve these goals we try to learn about causes and effects. Traditional medical investigators sought to discover the causes of specific diseases, in order that patients might be cured and that diseases might be wiped out by eliminating their causes. With more recent emphasis on "wellness," that is, on health maintenance and promotion, inquirers seek to identify those aspects of diet, hygiene, and exercise that produce physical and mental strength and vigor. Today's science and technology have enormously advanced our understanding and control of the world around us. The scientific laws discovered, the scientific hypotheses and theories devised, the machinery and instruments invented, all represent so many problems solved, so much effective thinking and productive reasoning. These topics are treated at length in Chapters 12 and 13.

Up to now in this chapter we have focused our attention on identifying and analyzing other people's arguments. When you solve a problem you must draw your own inferences, you must construct your own arguments. Some of the premises used describe the problematic situation you confront. Other premises contain information that you believe to be relevant to the problem's solution. If the problem is at all difficult, you may find in the course of your thinking that the situation has been misdescribed. Or you may find that the information at hand is not sufficient for solving the problem. Here, as anywhere else, practice makes perfect.

A useful kind of exercise to help strengthen one's problem-solving abilities is the logical puzzle, or "brain-teaser." In this kind of exercise the problematic situation is presented as a mass of more or less unrelated data or propositions given as true in the statement of the puzzle. And a specific question or group of questions are posed, the answers to which will constitute the solution to

---

[55]William James, *Pragmatism* (New York: Longmans, Green and Co., 1907), pp. 59–60.
[56]John Dewey, *Reconstruction in Philosophy* (Boston: Beacon Press, 1957), pp. 138–139.

the problem. There is a good deal of plausibility to some of these puzzles. From such information or data, a detective or police inspector might have the challenging task of reconstructing the anatomy of a crime in sufficient detail to permit the apprehension and arrest of the felon responsible for it. Or a newspaper reporter might be required to analyze and rearrange such data to produce an intelligible and thus printable journalistic story. Or a scientist might accept the task of explaining the apparently unrelated data by appealing to scientific laws and theories from which just those data might have been predicted to emerge in the circumstances that gave rise to them.

From the data given in puzzles of this sort, a few inferences can perhaps be drawn immediately—and, in some particularly elementary puzzles, that might be sufficient to establish the answer to the question posed. For example, consider the following illustration:

> In a certain flight crew the positions of pilot, copilot, and flight engineer are held by Allen, Brown, and Carr, though not necessarily in that order.
> The copilot, who was an only child, earns the least.
> Carr, who married Brown's sister, earns more than the pilot. What position does each person hold?

We can immediately draw several inferences that tell us Carr's position. Since Carr earns more than the pilot, Carr is not the pilot. And since Carr earns more than the pilot, and the copilot earns the least, it follows that Carr is not the copilot either. Hence Carr must be the flight engineer.

Next we can infer that since Brown has a sister, Brown was not an only child and therefore Brown is not the copilot. And we can infer that Brown is not the flight engineer from our identification of Carr as the flight engineer. Hence Brown must be the pilot. And by elimination Allen must be the copilot.

There is no fixed pattern of inference and argument that will lead to the solution of every puzzle of this sort, just as there is no fixed pattern that will lead to the resolution of every problem. But where the puzzle is, like the flight crew puzzle, to match persons with positions, and where the puzzle is even a little more complicated than the one just considered, it is sometimes useful to construct a diagram or matrix. Consider the following puzzle:

> Alonzo, Kurt, Rudolf, and Willard are four creative artists of great talent. One is a dancer, one is a painter, one is a singer, and one is a writer, though not necessarily in that order.
> (1) Alonzo and Rudolf were in the audience the night the singer made his debut on the concert stage.
> (2) Both Kurt and the writer have had their portraits painted from life by the painter.
> (3) The writer, whose biography of Willard was a best-seller, is planning to write a biography of Alonzo.
> (4) Alonzo has never heard of Rudolf.
> What is each man's artistic field?

To keep track in one's mind of this many facts and the several conclusions that might be inferred from them would be confusing and difficult. Even writing them down in the form of notes might simply produce more clutter. A good method of keeping track of this information and the intermediate inferences or subconclusions drawn, in a way that will be useful and suggestive of further inferences, is to draw an array or diagram in which there is room to represent every possibility. In the present case we would construct a four-row by four-column rectangular array as follows.

	Dancer	*Painter*	*Singer*	*Writer*
Alonzo				
Kurt				
Rudolf				
Willard				

Now if we are led to the conclusion that the individual whose name is at the left cannot be the artist whose field heads one of the columns, we can write an "N" (for "No") in the cell or box to the right of that individual's name and in the column headed by the field in question. For example, if we decide that Rudolf is not the singer, we write an "N" in the third box from the top in the third column. Or if we decide that Rudolf is the dancer, we write a "Y" (for "Yes") in the box in the row headed by his name and in the column headed by the category *dancer*.

In the present puzzle we can infer from (1) that neither Alonzo nor Rudolf is the singer, so we write "N" opposite their names in the third column. From (2) we know that Kurt is neither the painter nor the writer, so we write "N" opposite his name in the second and fourth columns. From (3) we see that the writer is neither Alonzo nor Willard, so we enter "N" opposite their names in the fourth column. Our matrix now looks like this:

	Dancer	*Painter*	*Singer*	*Writer*
Alonzo			N	N
Kurt		N		N
Rudolf			N	
Willard				N

By elimination it is now clear that Rudolf is the writer, so we insert a "Y" in the box opposite his name in the column headed *writer* and place an "N" in the remaining boxes in his row. Next we notice that according to (2) Rudolf has had his portrait painted from life by the painter, while according to (4)

Alonzo does not know Rudolf, from which it follows that Alonzo is not the painter and we enter an "N" in the box under *painter* in the row to the right of Alonzo's name. By elimination, again, we know that Alonzo is the dancer and we write a "Y" in the box next to his name. But then neither Kurt nor Willard can be the dancer, so we write "N" next to each of their names in the first column. This leaves *singer* as the only category possible for Kurt, and in the remaining empty box in his row we duly write a "Y." We then write an "N" under *singer* in the row opposite Willard's name, and (again by elimination) we conclude that Willard must be the painter and write a "Y" in the last empty box in the matrix, which now looks like this:

	Dancer	Painter	Singer	Writer
Alonzo	Y	N	N	N
Kurt	N	N	Y	N
Rudolf	N	N	N	Y
Willard	N	Y	N	N

And from these entries we can read off that Alonzo is the dancer, Kurt is the singer, Rudolf is the writer, and Willard is the painter.

Some problems in reasoning must be approached in a different way. The relations between concepts (like "father and son"), or the meanings of the terms used (like "twin"), may have to be relied upon to formulate the premisses in a chain of arguments leading to the conclusion that is the solution. The following problem is a good example. Before turning to its solution, which appears below, readers may wish to accept the challenge in reasoning that it presents.

THE PROBLEM: Mr. Short, his sister, his son, and his daughter are fond of golf and often play together. The following statements are true of their foursome:

(1) The best player's twin and the worst player are of opposite sex.
(2) The best player and the worst player are the same age.
Which one of the foursome is the best player?

THE SOLUTION: We construct a series of arguments leading to the answer, using the relative ages of the several players in our first premisses. The best player and the best player's twin are the same age, by the very meaning of the word "twin." By statement (2) the best player and the worst player are the same age. By statement (1) the best player's twin and the worst player are of opposite sex and are therefore two different people. So three of the four golfers are the same age. Obviously, Mr. Short must be older than both his son and his daughter, so the three golfers who are the same age are Mr. Short's sister, son, and daughter. It follows that the twins mentioned in statement (1) are Mr. Short's son and daughter. One of these twins must be the best player.

If the best player were Mr. Short's son, then by statement (1) his twin, who is Mr. Short's daughter, would be of the opposite sex from the worst player. That would imply that Mr. Short (as the only remaining male) is the worst player. But Mr. Short cannot be the worst player, because we know from statement (2) that the best player and the worst player are the same age, and a man cannot be the same age as his own son. Therefore the best player cannot be Mr. Short's son. Therefore the best player must be Mr. Short's daughter.

It must be remarked that real problems in the real world are not as neat and tidy as these logical puzzles. In the first place, many real problems are not accurately described in the first instance, and their misdescription could be sufficiently misleading to prevent *any* solution from being correct. To solve them might absolutely require that some part or parts of the initial description be rejected or replaced. But that would be totally inappropriate in seeking to solve a logical puzzle. In the second place, to solve *some* real problems might require us to make important scientific discoveries, to invent and use previously unimagined instruments or equipment, or to search as yet unexplored territories, whereas the information contained in the statement of a logical puzzle must be sufficient for it to be solved—needing no supplementation beyond such items of common knowledge as that twins are of the same age or that a father must be older than his children. And, finally, real problems do not come with an explicitly formulated question whose answer would certify that the problem has been solved. Many real problems are identified as such, initially at least, only by the obscure feeling that something is wrong rather than by an explicit question whose answer cannot immediately be supplied. Despite these differences, however, contrived exercises in reasoning are useful in studying logic.

EXERCISES IN REASONING

The following problems require reasoning for their solution. To prove that an answer is correct requires an argument (often containing subsidiary arguments) whose premises are contained in the statement of the problem—and whose final conclusion is the answer to it. If the answer is correct, a valid argument proving it can be constructed. In working at these problems, readers are urged to concern themselves not merely with discovering the answers, but also with formulating arguments to prove those answers correct.

★ 1. In a certain mythical community, politicians never tell the truth, and non-politicians always tell the truth. A stranger meets three natives and asks the first of them, "Are you a politician?" The first native answers the question. The second native then reports that the first native denied being a politician. The third native says that the first native *is* a politician.

How many of these three natives are politicians?

2. Of three prisoners in a certain jail, one had normal vision, the second had only one eye, and the third was totally blind. The jailor told the prisoners that from three white hats and two red hats he would select three and put them on the prisoners' heads. None could see what color hat he wore. The jailor offered freedom to the prisoner with normal vision if he could tell what color hat he wore. To prevent a lucky guess, the jailor threatened execution for any incorrect answer. The first prisoner could not tell what hat he wore. Next the jailor made the same offer to the one-eyed prisoner. The second prisoner could not tell what hat he wore either. The jailor did not bother making the offer to the blind prisoner, but he agreed to extend the same terms to him when he made the request. The blind prisoner said

> I do not need to have my sight;
> From what my friends with eyes have said,
> I clearly see my hat is ———!

How did he know?

3. On a certain train, the crew consists of the brakeman, the fireman, and the engineer. Their names listed alphabetically are Jones, Robinson, and Smith. On the train are also three passengers with corresponding names, Mr. Jones, Mr. Robinson, and Mr. Smith. The following facts are known:
   a. Mr. Robinson lives in Detroit.
   b. The brakeman lives halfway between Detroit and Chicago.
   c. Mr. Jones earns exactly $20,000 a year.
   d. Smith once beat the fireman at billiards.
   e. The brakeman's next-door neighbor, one of the three passengers mentioned, earns exactly three times as much as the brakeman.
   f. The passenger living in Chicago has the same name as the brakeman.
What was the engineer's name?

4. The employees of a small loan company are Mr. Black, Mr. White, Mrs. Coffee, Miss Ambrose, Mr. Kelly, and Miss Earnshaw. The positions they occupy are manager, assistant manager, cashier, stenographer, teller, and clerk, though not necessarily in that order. The assistant manager is the manager's grandson, the cashier is the stenographer's son-in-law, Mr. Black is a bachelor, Mr. White is twenty-two years old, Miss Ambrose is the teller's step-sister and Mr. Kelly is the manager's neighbor.
   Who holds each position?

★ 5. Benno Torelli, genial host at Hamtramck's most exclusive nightclub, was shot and killed by a racketeer gang because he fell behind in his protection payments. After considerable effort on the part of the police, five suspects were brought before the district attorney, who asked them what they had to say for themselves. Each of them made three statements, two true and one false. Their statements were

LEFTY: I did not kill Torelli. I never owned a revolver in all my life. Spike did it.

RED: I did not kill Torelli. I never owned a revolver. The others are all passing the buck.

DOPEY: I am innocent. I never saw Butch before. Spike is guilty.

SPIKE: I am innocent. Butch is the guilty one. Lefty did not tell the truth when he said I did it.

BUTCH: I did not kill Torelli. Red is the guilty one. Dopey and I are old pals.

Whodunnit?

6. Five men who were buddies in the last war are having a reunion. They are White, Brown, Peters, Harper, and Nash, who by occupation are printer, writer, barber, neurologist, and heating contractor. By coincidence, they live in the cities of White Plains, Brownsville, Petersburg, Harper's Ferry, and Nashville, but no man lives in the city having a name similar to his, nor does the name of his occupation have the same initial as his name or the name of the city in which he lives.

The barber doesn't live in Petersburg, and Brown is neither a heating contractor nor a printer—nor does he live in Petersburg or Harper's Ferry. Mr. Harper lives in Nashville and is neither barber nor writer. White is not a resident of Brownsville, nor is Nash, who is not a barber, nor a heating contractor.

With only the information given above, determine the name of the city in which Nash resides.

7. Daniel Kilraine was killed on a lonely road, two miles from Pontiac, Michigan, at 3:30 A.M., March 17 of last year. Otto, Curly, Slim, Mickey, and the Kid were arrested a week later in Detroit and questioned. Each of the five made four statements, three of which were true and one of which was false. One of these persons killed Kilraine.

Their statements were

OTTO: I was in Chicago when Kilraine was murdered. I never killed anyone. The Kid is the guilty one. Mickey and I are pals.

CURLY: I did not kill Kilraine. I never owned a revolver in my life. The Kid knows me. I was in Detroit the night of March 17.

SLIM: Curly lied when he said he never owned a revolver. The murder was committed on St. Patrick's Day. Otto was in Chicago at this time. One of us is guilty.

MICKEY: I did not kill Kilraine. The Kid has never been in Pontiac. I never saw Otto before. Curly was in Detroit with me on the night of March 17th.

THE KID: I did not kill Kilraine. I have never been in Pontiac. I never saw Curly before. Otto erred when he said I am guilty.

Whodunnit?

8. A woman recently hosted a political meeting to which she invited five guests. The names of the six people who sat down at the circular table were Abrams, Banjo, Clive, Dumont, Ekwall, and Fish. One of them was deaf, one was very talkative, one was terribly fat, one simply hated Dumont, one had a vitamin deficiency, and one was the hostess. The person who hated Dumont sat directly opposite Banjo. The deaf one sat opposite Clive, who sat between the one who had a vitamin deficiency and the one who hated Dumont. The fat one sat opposite Abrams, next to the deaf person and to the left of the one who hated Dumont. The person who had a vitamin deficiency sat between Clive and the

one who sat opposite the person who hated Dumont. Fish, who was a good friend of everyone, sat next to the fat person and opposite the hostess.

Identify each of these people, matching name and description.

9. Three people went into a hotel and rented a room for $30, each paying $10 for his share. Later, the clerk discovered that the price of the room was only $25. He handed the bellman five $1 bills and asked him to return them to the three people. The bellman, not knowing how to divide $5 among three people, instead gave each person $1, and the rest to charity.

The three people originally paid ten dollars each, but each received $1 back, so they have now paid a total of $27 for the room. Add to that the $2 that the bellman gave away, and you have a total expenditure of $29 instead of $30. What happened to the other dollar?

★ 10. A jeweler has ten diamonds, nine of them exactly the same weight, the tenth slightly different. They are all mixed together, and his problem is to select the one that is different and to tell whether it is lighter or heavier than the others. How can he do this by making only three uses of his balance scale?

11. Nine men—Brown, White, Adams, Miller, Green, Hunter, Knight, Jones, and Smith—play the nine positions on a baseball team. (The battery consists of the pitcher and the catcher; the infield consists of the first, second, and third basemen and the shortstop; and the outfield consists of the right, left, and center fielders.) Determine, from the following data, the position played by each man.

    a. Smith and Brown each won $10 playing poker with the pitcher.
    b. Hunter is taller than Knight and shorter than White, but each of these weighs more than the first baseman.
    c. The third baseman lives across the corridor from Jones in the same apartment building.
    d. Miller and the outfielders play bridge in their spare time.
    e. White, Miller, Brown, the right fielder, and the center fielder are bachelors; the rest were married.
    f. Of Adams and Knight, one plays outfielder position.
    g. The right fielder is shorter than the center fielder.
    h. The third baseman is the brother of the pitcher's wife.
    i. Green is taller than the infielders and the battery, except for Jones, Smith, and Adams.
    j. The third baseman, the shortstop, and Hunter made $150 each speculating in gold.
    k. The second baseman is engaged to Miller's sister.
    l. The second baseman beat Jones, Brown, Hunter, and the catcher at cards.
    m. Adams lives in the same house as his own sister, but dislikes the catcher.
    n. Adams, Brown and the shortstop lost $200 each speculating in copper.
    o. The catcher and his wife have three daughters, and the third baseman and his wife have two sons, but Green is being sued for divorce.

12. In a certain bank there were eleven distinct positions, namely, in decreasing rank, President, First Vice-President, Second Vice-President, Third Vice-President, Cashier, Teller, Assistant Teller, Bookkeeper, First Stenographer, Second Stenographer, and Janitor. These eleven positions are occupied by the following,

here listed alphabetically: Mr. Adams, Mrs. Brown, Mr. Camp, Miss Dale, Mr. Evans, Mrs. Ford, Mr. Grant, Miss Hill, Mr. Jones, Mrs. Kane, and Mr. Long. Concerning them, only the following facts are known:

   a. The Third Vice-President is the pampered grandson of the President but is disliked by both Mrs. Brown and the Assistant Teller.
   b. The Assistant Teller and the Second Stenographer shared equally in their father's estate.
   c. The Second Vice-President and the Assistant Teller wear the same style of hats.
   d. Mr. Grant told Miss Hill to send him a stenographer at once.
   e. The President's nearest neighbors are Mrs. Kane, Mr. Grant, and Mr. Long.
   f. The First Vice-President and the Cashier live at the exclusive Bachelor's Club.
   g. The Janitor, a miser, has occupied the same garret room since boyhood.
   h. Mr. Adams and the Second Stenographer are leaders in the social life of the younger unmarried set.
   i. The Second Vice-President and the Bookkeeper were once engaged to be married to each other.
   j. The fashionable Teller is the son-in-law of the First Stenographer.
   k. Mr. Jones regularly gives Mr. Evans his discarded clothing to wear, without the elderly Bookkeeper knowing about the gift.

Show how to match correctly the eleven names against the eleven positions occupied.

13. Alice, Betty, Carol, and Dorothy were a lifeguard, a lawyer, a pilot, or a professor. Each wore a white, yellow, pink, or blue dress. The lifeguard beat Betty at tennis, and Carol and the pilot often played bridge with the women in pink and blue dresses. Alice and the professor envied the woman in the blue dress, but this was not the lawyer, as she always wore a white dress.

What was each woman's occupation and dress color?

14. In the same mythical community described in Exercise 1, a stranger meets three other natives and asks them: "How many of you are politicians?" The first native replied, "We are all politicians." The second native said, "No, just two of us are politicians." The third native then said, "That isn't true either."

Was the third native a politician?

CHALLENGE TO THE READER
   Here is a final problem in reasoning whose solution will require the construction of a set of sustained arguments. It isn't easy—but solving it is well within your power, and will give you great pleasure.

15. You are presented with a set of twelve metal balls, apparently identical in every respect: size, color, and so on. In fact, eleven of them are identical, but one of them is "odd"—it differs from all the rest in weight only; it is either heavier, or lighter, than all the others. You are given a balance scale, on which the balls can be weighed against one another. If the same number of balls are put on each side of the balance, and the "odd" ball is on one side, that side will go down if the odd ball is heavier, or up if the odd ball is lighter; the two sides

will balance if the odd ball is not among those weighed and the same number of balls are placed on each side. You are allowed three weighings only; any removal or addition of a ball constitutes a separate weighing.

Your challenge is this: devise a set of three weighings that will enable you to identify the odd ball wherever it may lie in a random mixing of the twelve balls, *and* that will enable you to determine whether the odd ball is heavier or lighter than the rest.

2

The Uses of Language

It is indeed not the least of the logician's tasks to indicate the pitfalls laid by language in the way of the thinker.

—Gottlob Frege

. . . the woof and warp of all thought and all research is symbols, and the life of thought and science is the life inherent in symbols; so it is wrong to say that a good language is important to good thought, merely; for it is the essence of it.

—Charles Sanders Peirce

Careful and correct use of language is a powerful aid to straight thinking, for putting into words precisely what we mean necessitates getting our own minds quite clear on what we mean.

—William Ian Beardmore Beveridge

2.1 *Three Basic Functions of Language*

Language is so subtle and complicated an instrument that we often lose sight of the multiplicity of its uses. But there is real danger in our tendency to oversimplify.

Those who take too narrow a view of the legitimate uses of language find words constantly being "wasted"—at social functions, for example. Thus the complaint: "So-and-so always asks me how I am. What a hypocrite! He doesn't care in the least how I am!" Remarks like these reveal a failure to understand the complex purposes for which language is used. That is shown also in the deplorable conduct of those bores, who, when asked how they are, actually proceed to describe the state of their health. But people do not usually talk at parties to instruct each other. And ordinarily "How are you?" is a friendly greeting, not a request for a medical report.

The philosopher George Berkeley remarked long ago in his *Treatise Concerning the Principles of Human Knowledge* that

> . . . the communicating of ideas . . . is not the chief and only end of language, as is commonly supposed. There are other ends, as the raising of some passion,

the exciting to or deterring from an action, the putting the mind in some particular disposition; to which the former is in many cases barely subservient, and sometimes entirely omitted, when these can be obtained without it, as I think does not infrequently happen in the familiar use of language.

More recent philosophers have elaborated in great detail the variety of uses to which language can be put. In his *Philosophical Investigations* Ludwig Wittgenstein insisted rightly that there are "countless different kinds of use of what we call 'symbols,' 'words,' 'sentences.'" Among the examples suggested by Wittgenstein are giving orders, describing the appearance of an object or giving its measurements, reporting an event, speculating about an event, forming and testing a hypothesis, presenting the results of an experiment in tables and diagrams, making up a story, play-acting, singing catches, guessing riddles, making a joke and telling it, solving a problem in practical arithmetic, translating from one language into another, asking, thinking, cursing, greeting, and praying.

Some order can be imposed on the staggering variety of language uses by dividing them into three very general categories: the *informative*, the *expressive*, and the *directive*. This threefold division is admittedly a simplification, perhaps an oversimplification, but it has been found very useful by many writers on logic and language.

The first of these uses of language is to communicate information. Ordinarily, this is accomplished by formulating and affirming (or denying) propositions. Language used to affirm or deny propositions, or to present arguments, is said to be serving the *informative* function. Here we use the word "information" to include misinformation: false as well as true propositions, incorrect as well as correct arguments. Informative discourse is used to describe the world, and to reason about it. Whether the alleged facts are important or unimportant, general or particular, does not matter; in any case the language used to describe or report them is being used informatively.

Just as science provides us with the clearest examples of informative discourse, so lyric poetry furnishes us the best examples of language serving an *expressive* function. The following lines of Burns

> O my Luve's like a red, red rose
> That's newly sprung in June:
> O my Luve's like the melodie
> That's sweetly play'd in tune!

are definitely not intended to inform us of any facts or theories concerning the world. Here the poet's concern is not with knowledge but with feelings and attitudes. The passage was not written to report any information, but to express certain emotions that the poet felt very keenly and to evoke similar feelings in the reader. Language serves the expressive function whenever it is used to vent or to arouse feelings or emotions.

Here we are using the term "express" in a somewhat narrower way than usual. It is perfectly natural to speak of expressing a feeling, an emotion, or an attitude. But one ordinarily speaks also of expressing an opinion, a belief, or a conviction. To avoid confusing the informative and expressive functions of language, we shall speak instead of *stating* or *declaring* an opinion, or a belief, and reserve the term "express" in this chapter for revealing or communicating feelings, emotions, and attitudes.

Not all expressive language is poetry. We express sorrow by saying "That's too bad" or "Oh my" and enthusiasm by shouting "Wow!" or "Dynamite!" The lover expresses delicate passion by murmuring "Darling!" or private words of endearment. The poet expresses complex and concentrated emotions in a sonnet or some other verse form. A worshipper's feeling of awe and wonder at the vastness and mystery of the universe may be expressed by reciting the Lord's Prayer or the twenty-third Psalm of David. All these uses of language are not intended to communicate information but to express emotions, feelings, or attitudes. Expressive discourse *as expressive* is neither true nor false. To apply only the criteria of truth or falsehood, correctness or incorrectness, to expressive discourse like a lyric poem is to miss its point and to lose much of its value. One whose enjoyment of Keats's sonnet "On first looking into Chapman's Homer" is diminished by knowing that it was Balboa rather than Cortez who discovered the Pacific Ocean is a "poor reader" of poetry. The purpose of the poem is not to teach history. Of course some poems do have an informative content that may be an important ingredient in their total effect. Some poetry may well be "criticism of life," in the words of a great poet. But such poems are more than *merely* expressive, as we are using the term here. Such poetry may be said to have a "mixed usage" or to serve a multiple function. This notion will be discussed further in the following section.

Expression may be analyzed into two components. When one curses while alone, or writes poems that are shown to no one, or prays in solitude, the language used functions to express the feelings of the speaker or writer, but it is not intended to evoke a similar attitude in anyone else. On the other hand, when an orator seeks to move others to share his or her enthusiasm, when a lover uses poetic language in courtship, when the crowd cheers its athletic team, the language used not only expresses the feelings of its speakers but is intended to evoke similar feelings in the hearers. Expressive discourse, then, is used either to *express* the speaker's feelings or to attempt to *evoke* certain feelings on the part of the auditor. Of course it may do both.

Language serves the *directive* function when it is intended to cause (or prevent) overt action. The clearest examples are commands and requests. When a parent tells a child to wash up for dinner, the intention is not to communicate any information or to express or evoke any particular emotion. The language is intended to get results, to cause action of the indicated kind. When a theater-goer says to the ticket-seller, "Two, please," the language is again being used directively, to produce *action*. Between commands and requests the differences are rather subtle—for almost any command can be converted into a request with suitable changes in the tone of voice, or merely by adding the word "please." A question also may be classified as directive discourse when, as ordinarily, it is posed to request an answer.

In its nakedly imperative form, directive discourse is neither true nor false. A command such as "Close the window" cannot be either true or false in any literal sense. We may indeed disagree about whether a command has been obeyed or disobeyed, but we never disagree about whether a command is true or false, because those terms simply do not apply to it. However, commands and requests have other attributes—reasonableness or propriety, unreasonableness or impropriety—that are somewhat analogous to the truth or falsehood of informative discourse. We saw, in Section 1.2, that reasons can be given for an action to be performed; and when the statement of those reasons accompanies the command, the whole can be regarded as an argument. For example:

> Drive defensively. Remember that the cemetery is full of law abiding citizens who had the right of way.[1]

In treating discourse of this kind as an argument, we regard the command that it contains as a proposition in which the recipients of the command are told that they should, or ought to, perform the action commanded. Exploring these issues, some writers have been led to develop a "logic of imperatives," but to discuss it is beyond the scope of this book.[2]

2.2 *Discourse Serving Multiple Functions*

The examples of informative, expressive, and directive discourse in the preceding section were chemically pure specimens, so to speak. This threefold division of the kinds of communication is illuminating and valuable, but it cannot be applied mechanically, because almost any ordinary communication will probably exemplify, to a greater or lesser extent, all three uses of language. Thus a poem, which might be primarily expressive discourse, may have a moral, and thus, in effect, may direct the reader (or hearer) to lead a different kind of life. Wordsworth wrote:

> The world is too much with us: late and soon,
> Getting and spending, we lay waste our powers:
> Little we see in Nature that is ours. . . .

And of course a poem may contain a certain amount of information as well.

On the other hand, although a sermon may be predominantly directive, seeking to cause certain appropriate action by members of the congregation (whether to abandon their evil ways, or to contribute money to the church, or what not) it may express and evoke sentiments, thus serving the expressive function, and may also include some information, such as the glad tidings of the Gospels. And a scientific treatise, essentially informative, may express something of the writer's own enthusiasm, and may also, at least

---

[1]Ann Landers, "You Could Be Dead Right!" syndicated column, August 26, 1988.

[2]For an introduction to this topic, the interested reader can consult Nicholas Rescher, *The Logic of Commands* (London: Routledge & Kegan Paul Ltd., 1966).

implicitly, bid the reader to verify independently the author's conclusion. Most ordinary uses of language are mixed.

When language serves mixed or multiple functions the speaker surely need not be using it that way out of confusion. Rather, effective communication demands certain combinations of functions. Outside of the context of clear and formal relationships—parent to child, employer to employee—one cannot simply issue an order and expect to have it obeyed; bald commands arouse resentment or antagonism, and are often self-defeating. Consequently, a certain indirection must often be used. Normally, to cause the action we seek we do not flatly issue an imperative; a more subtle method of producing the desired result is usually necessary.

Actions often have very complex causes. Motivation is more properly the study of the psychologist than the logician, but it is common knowledge that actions usually involve both what the actor *wants,* and what the actor *believes.* People who are hungry, and desire food, will not put what is before them into their mouths unless they believe that it is food; if they have no doubt that it is food they may not touch it unless they have some desire to eat.

Now wants and desires are special kinds of what we have been calling attitudes or feelings; and beliefs are commonly influenced by information received. Consequently, we sometimes succeed in causing others to act by evoking in them appropriate attitudes, and sometimes by giving them information that affects their relevant beliefs.

Suppose that your aim is to get your listeners to contribute to a particular charitable organization. Assuming your listeners to be benevolent in attitude, you may stimulate them to action by informing them of the good works done by that charitable organization, of the fine results their contribution will support. Your language is directive, its purpose being to cause action. But a naked command is not likely to accomplish, in such a case, what solid information may. Suppose, on the other hand, that your listeners are already fully persuaded that the charitable organization in question does accomplish benevolent results. A simple request for their money is again likely to fail— but you may succeed in causing them to contribute to that charitable organization by somehow arousing or sufficiently enhancing their benevolent feelings or emotions. In this case you achieve your end by using expressive discourse; you make a "moving appeal." Thus again your language naturally has mixed uses, functioning both expressively and directively.

Suppose, finally, that you are seeking a donation from people who have neither a benevolent attitude nor a belief that the charitable organization in question serves a benevolent purpose. Then you must use language both expressive and informative—and the language used, aiming at action, will serve all three functions at once, not accidentally but deliberately and essentially, as necessary to successful communication.

Another interesting and important mixed use of language has often been called *ceremonial.* In this category are included many different kinds of phrases, ranging from trivial words of greeting to the portentous language of state documents, and the verbal rituals performed on holy days in houses of worship. Ceremonial discourse can always be regarded as a mixture of expressive and directive discourse, rather than as a separate kind that is unique. For example, ceremonial greetings at social gatherings express and evoke goodwill and sociability. For some speakers they may be intended also to serve the directive purpose of causing their hearers to act in certain ways— to patronize the speaker's business, to offer employment, or to extend an invitation to dinner. At the other extreme, the impressive language of the marriage ceremony is intended both to emphasize the solemnity of the occasion (its expressive function) and to cause the bride and groom to perform in their new roles with heightened appreciation of the seriousness of their marriage vows (its directive function).

Ceremonial language is often not recognized for what it is. Thus John Kenneth Galbraith, in *The Affluent Society*, wrote

> In some measure the articulation of the conventional wisdom is a religious rite. It is an act of affirmation like reading aloud from the Scriptures or going to church. The business executive listening to a luncheon address on the virtues of free enterprise and the evils of Washington is already persuaded, and so are his fellow listeners, and all are secure in their convictions. Indeed, although a display of rapt attention is required, the executive may not feel it necessary to listen. But he does placate the gods by participating in the ritual. Having been present, maintained attention, and having applauded, he can depart feeling that the economic system is a little more secure. Scholars gather in scholarly assemblages to hear in elegant statement what all have heard before. Yet it is not a negligible rite, for its purpose is not to convey knowledge but to beatify learning and the learned.

There is still another use of language, somewhat akin to the ceremonial, that fits less well into our threefold division of language functions. When you are asked by a friend to meet him at a certain time and place, and you reply: "I will, I promise," your words do more than report your attitude or predict your conduct; they have the function of making the promise itself. Similarly, at the end of the marriage ceremony, when the minister or magistrate says, "I now pronounce you husband and wife," though the words may seem merely to report what the speaker is doing, their utterance, in this setting, actually constitutes the doing of it. These are instances of the *performative* use of language. A performative utterance is one which, when uttered in appropriate circumstances, actually performs the act it appears to report or describe. There appear to be a class of what are called "performative verbs"—verbs that denote an action that is typically accomplished, in appropriate circumstances, by using that verb in the first person. Other examples are these: I congratulate you . . . ; I apologize for my . . . ; I suggest that . . . ; I christen this ship . . . ; I accept your offer . . . ; and so on. The workings of performative verbs do not appear to be amalgams of the three major functions previously distinguished, but are tied in special ways to the circumstances in which they are uttered.[3]

---

[3]The notions of performative utterance and performative verb were first developed by the late Professor John Austin of Oxford University; see his *How to Do Things with Words* (London: Oxford University Press, 1962).

2.3 *The Forms of Discourse*

A sentence is often defined as the unit of language that expresses a complete thought. In textbooks of grammar sentences are commonly divided into four categories, called declarative, interrogative, imperative, and exclamatory. But these four grammatical categories do not coincide with those of assertions, questions, commands, and exclamations. We may be tempted to identify form with function—to think that declarative sentences and informative discourse coincide, and that exclamatory sentences are suitable only for expressive discourse. Or we may think that directive discourse consists exclusively of sentences in the imperative or (regarding questions as always being requests for answers) the interrogative mood. Were such neat identifications possible the problem of communication would be immensely simplified—for then we should be able to tell the intended function of a passage simply by its form, which is open to direct inspection. But those who identify form with function are not sensitive readers, for that identification often leads them to misunderstand what is said, and they "miss the point" of much that is to be communicated.

It is a mistake to believe that everything in the form of a declarative sentence is informative discourse, to be valued if true and rejected if false. "I had a very nice time at your party" is a declarative sentence, but its function need not be informative at all, but rather ceremonial or expressive, expressing a feeling of friendliness and appreciation. Many poems and prayers are in the form of declarative sentences, despite the fact that their functions are not informative. To consider them as simply informative and to evaluate them as simply true or false would be to shut oneself off from many valuable aesthetic and religious experiences. Again, many requests and commands are stated indirectly—perhaps more gently—by means of declarative sentences. The declarative sentence "I would like some coffee" should not be taken by a waiter to be a mere report of the psychological fact it apparently asserts about the customer, but as an order or request for action. Were we invariably to judge the truth or falsehood of declarative sentences such as "I'd appreciate some help with this" or "I hope you'll be able to meet me after class at the library," and do no more than register them as information received, we should soon be without friends. These examples should suffice to show that the declarative form is no certain indication of the informative function. Declarative sentences lend themselves to the formulation of every kind of discourse.

It is the same with other forms of sentences. The interrogative sentence "Do you realize that we're almost late?" is not necessarily a request for information but may be a request to hurry. The interrogative sentence "Isn't it true that Russia and Germany signed a pact in 1939 that led to the Second World War?" may not be a question at all but either an oblique way of communicating information or an attempt to express and evoke a feeling of hostility toward Russia, functioning informatively in the first instance and expressively in the second. Even a grammatical imperative, as in official documents beginning "Know all men by these presents that . . . ," may not be a command but rather informative discourse in what it asserts and expressive discourse in its use of language to evoke the appropriate feelings of solemnity and respect. In spite of its close affinity to the expressive, an exclamatory sentence may serve a quite different function. The exclamation "Good Lord it's late!" may in context be a request to hurry. And the exclamation "What a beautiful view!" uttered by a realtor to a potential customer may be intended to function more directively than expressively.

Much discourse is intended to serve two or possibly all three functions of language at once. In such cases each aspect or function of a given passage is subject to its own proper criteria. A passage having an informative function may have that aspect evaluated as true or false. The same passage serving a directive function may have that aspect evaluated as proper or improper, right or wrong. And if there is also an expressive function served by the passage, that component of it may be evaluated as sincere or insincere, as valuable or otherwise. To evaluate a given passage properly requires knowledge of the function or functions it is intended to serve.

Truth and falsehood, and the related notions of correctness and incorrectness of argument, are more important in the study of logic than are the others mentioned. Hence, as students of logic, we must be able to differentiate discourse that functions informatively from that which does not. And we must be able further to disentangle the informative function a given passage serves from whatever other functions it may also be serving. To do this "disentangling," we must know what different functions language can serve and be able to tell them apart. The grammatical structure of a passage often indicates its function, but there is no *necessary* connection between function and grammatical form. Nor is there any strict relation between function and content—in the sense of what might seem to be asserted by a passage. This is very clearly shown by an example of Bloomfield's in his chapter on "Meaning":

> A petulant child, at bedtime, says *I'm hungry,* and his mother, who is up to his tricks, answers by packing him off to bed. This is an example of displaced speech."[4]

The child's speech here is directive—even though it does not succeed in procuring the wanted diversion. By the function of a passage we generally mean the intended function. But that, unfortunately, is not always easy to determine.

When a passage is quoted in isolation, it is often a difficult question what language function the passage is primarily intended to serve. The reason for this difficulty is that context is extremely important in determining the answer to such a question. What is imperative or flatly informative, by itself, may in its actual context function expressively, as part of a larger whole whose poetic effect is derived from all its parts in their arrangement. For example, in isolation,

---

[4]See Leonard Bloomfield, *Language* (New York: Henry Holt and Company, Inc., 1933).

> Come to the window.

is an imperative serving the directive function, and

> The sea is calm tonight.

is a declarative sentence serving an informative function. But both are from Matthew Arnold's poem "Dover Beach," and in that context chiefly serve the poem's expressive function.

It is important also to distinguish between the proposition that a sentence formulates and some fact about the speaker for which the utterance of that sentence is evidence. When a person remarks, "It is raining," the proposition asserted is about the weather, not about the speaker. Yet making the assertion is evidence that the speaker believes it to be raining, which is a fact about the speaker. It also may happen that people make statements that are ostensibly about their beliefs, not for the sake of giving information about themselves, but simply a way of saying something else. To say "I believe that gold should not be used as a standard for currency" is ordinarily not to be construed as a psychological or autobiographical report about the beliefs of the speaker, but is simply a way of asserting or recommending that gold should not be so used. Similarly, when a speaker utters a command, it is reasonable to infer that the speaker wants something done; indeed, under some circumstances merely to assert that one has a specific desire is, in effect, to give a command or make a request. An exclamation of joy gives evidence that the speaker is joyful, even though the speaker makes no assertion in the process. But to affirm, as a psychological report, that the speaker is joyful is to assert a proposition, something quite different from exclaiming joyously.

In Section 1.4 the problem of recognizing arguments was discussed. The difference between an argument and an explanation was noted, and it was remarked that their difference depended on the intentions of the speaker or writer. We can now look a little more deeply into the matter. Consider the following letter to the editor, published in *The Honolulu Advertiser* (March 6, 1984, p. A-9):

> I oppose the idea of holding prayer in our public schools. First of all, parents have ample opportunity to hold prayer in their homes, if this is what they wish to do. Also, they are free to send their children to a religious school of their choice.
>
> It is doubtful that a prayer could be composed that would be acceptable to all the various religious groups in our community, and in any case, it is not a proper function of the state to devise prayers that its citizens are obligated to use.
>
> It would be equally inappropriate if the Sunday schools were to attempt to teach the "three R's." The public schools and the religious schools were each designed with a specific purpose in mind and each should confine itself to its own area of expertise.
>
> Our Constitution has wisely declared that there should be no connection between church and state. For the sake of everyone's freedom, let's keep it that way.

It begins with the statement "I oppose the idea of holding prayer in our public schools." But this is not a simple autobiographical report of what the writer supports or opposes, as would be appropriate if she were being interviewed as a public figure whose likes and dislikes might be a matter of popular interest or as a subject whose psychological profile was being constructed by a social scientist. If it were, the rest of the letter could be taken as *explaining* the writer's opposition to school prayer. Instead, the beginning statement is the writer's way of saying that *it is a bad idea to hold prayer in our public schools* or that *we all should oppose it.* One can tell that by the several judgmental remarks in what follows the first sentence, such as "it is not a proper function of the state to . . . ," "It would be equally inappropriate . . . ," "each [of the public schools and the religious schools] should confine itself to its own area of expertise," and the final exhortation "let's keep it that way." The letter is *not* an explanation of the writer's opposition to school prayer. It is an argument intended to persuade her readers that school prayer is a bad thing. Her intention is not to explain her own feelings but to persuade others to share them.

This is not to accuse the writer of any kind of deception or subterfuge. Her language is entirely appropriate. The first sentence of her letter is a perfectly legitimate method of announcing the conclusion of the extended argument that her letter contains.

In subsequent chapters we shall develop certain logical techniques that can be applied quite mechanically to test the validity of an argument. But there is no mechanical technique for recognizing the *presence* of an argument. *There is no mechanical method of distinguishing language that is informative and argumentative from language that serves other functions instead.* This requires careful thought, and demands an awareness of and sensitivity to the flexibility of language and the multiplicity of its uses.

EXERCISES

I. What language functions are *most probably intended* to be served by each of the following passages?

★ 1. The atrocious crime of being a young man, which the honorable gentleman has with such spirit and decency charged upon me. I shall neither attempt to palliate nor deny; but content myself with wishing that I may be one of those whose follies may cease with their youth, and not of that number who are ignorant in spite of experience.

—WILLIAM PITT, speech in the House of Commons

2. Judges do not know how to rehabilitate criminals—because no one knows.
—ANDREW VON HIRSCH, *Doing Justice—The Choice of Punishment*

3. When tillage begins, other arts follow. The farmers therefore are the founders of human civilization.   —DANIEL WEBSTER, "On Agriculture"

4. The only thing necessary for the triumph of evil is for good men to do nothing.   —EDMUND BURKE, letter to William Smith

★ 5. They have no lawyers among them, for they consider them as a sort of people whose profession it is to disguise matters. —SIR THOMAS MOORE, *Utopia*

6. Pleasure is an actual and legitimate aim, but if anyone says that it is the only thing men are interested in, he invites the old and legitimate reply that much of the pleasure they actually get would have been impossible unless they had desired something else. If men have found pleasure in fox-hunting, it is only because for the time they could forget about hunting pleasure, and hunt foxes.
—BRAND BLANSHARD, *The Nature of Thought*

7. The bad workmen who form the majority of the operatives in many branches of industry are decidedly of the opinion that bad workmen ought to receive the same wages as good. —JOHN STUART MILL, *On Liberty*

8. War is the greatest plague that can afflict humanity; it destroys religion, it destroys states, it destroys families. Any scourge is preferable to it.
—MARTIN LUTHER, *Table Talk*

9. Human history becomes more and more a race between education and catastrophe. —H. G. WELLS, *The Outline of History*

★ 10. The man who insists upon seeing with perfect clearness before he decides, never decides. —HENRI-FREDERIC AMIEL, *Amiel's Journal*

11. Among other evils which being unarmed brings you, it causes you to be despised. —NICCOLO MACHIAVELLI, *The Prince*

12. Eternal peace is a dream, and not even a beautiful one. War is a part of God's world order. In it are developed the noblest virtues of man: courage and abnegation, dutifulness and self-sacrifice. Without war the world would sink into materialism. —HELMUTH VON MOLTKE

13. Language! the blood of the soul, sir, into which our thoughts run, and out of which they grow.
—OLIVER WENDELL HOLMES, *The Professor at the Breakfast Table*

14. I believe that war is at present productive of good more than of evil.
—JOHN RUSKIN

★ 15. A little philosophy inclineth man's mind to atheism; but depth in philosophy bringeth man's mind about to religion. —FRANCIS BACON, *Essays*

16. You'll never have a quiet world until you knock the patriotism out of the human race. —GEORGE BERNARD SHAW, *O'Flaherty, V.C.*

17. If [he] does really think that there is no distinction between virtue and vice, why, sir, when he leaves our houses let us count our spoons.
—SAMUEL JOHNSON

18. Man scans with scrupulous care the character and pedigree of his horses, cattle, and dogs before he matches them; but when he comes to his own marriage he rarely, or never, takes any such care.
—CHARLES DARWIN, *The Descent of Man*

19. The story of the whale swallowing Jonah, though a whale is large enough to do it, borders greatly on the marvelous; but it would have approached nearer to the idea of miracle if Jonah had swallowed the whale.
—THOMAS PAINE, *The Age of Reason*

★ 20. War has the deep meaning that by it the ethical health of the nations is preserved and their finite aims uprooted. And as the winds which sweep over the ocean prevent the decay that would result from its perpetual calm, so war protects the people from the corruption which an everlasting peace would bring upon it. —GEORG HEGEL, *The Philosophy of Law*

21. That all particular appetites and passions are toward *external things themselves*, distinct from the *pleasure arising from them*, is manifested from hence—that there could not be this pleasure were it not for that prior suitableness between the object and the passion; there could be no enjoyment or delight from one thing more than another, from eating food more than from swallowing a stone, if there were not an affection or appetite to one thing more than another.
—JOSEPH BUTLER, sermon, "Upon the Love of Our Neighbor"

22. "An unhappy alternative is before you, Elizabeth. From this day you must be a stranger to one of your parents. Your mother will never see you again if you do *not* marry Mr. Collins, and I will never see you again if you do."
—JANE AUSTEN, *Pride and Prejudice*

23. "Of this man Pickwick I will say little; the subject presents but few attractions; and I, gentlemen, am not the man, nor are you, gentlemen, the men, to delight in the contemplation of revolting heartlessness, and of systematic villainy." —CHARLES DICKENS, *Pickwick Papers*

24. You praise the men who feasted the citizens and satisfied their desires, and people say that they have made the city great, not seeing that the swollen and ulcerated conditions of the State is to be attributed to these elder statesmen; for they have filled the city full of harbors and docks and walls and revenues and all that, and have left no room for justice and temperance.   —PLATO, *Gorgias*

25. A civil war is like the heat of a fever; but a foreign war is like the heat of exercise, and serveth to keep the body in health.   —FRANCIS BACON, *Essays*

II. For the following passages, indicate what propositions they may be intended to assert, if any, what overt actions they may be intended to cause, if any, and what they may be regarded as providing evidence for about the speaker, if anything.

★ 1. I will not accept if nominated and will not serve if elected.
—WILLIAM TECUMSEH SHERMAN, message to the Republican National Convention, 1884

2. The government in its wisdom considers ice a "food product." This means that Antarctica is one of the world's foremost food producers.
—GEORGE P. WILL, "Government, Economy Linked"

3. Criticism is properly the rod of divination: a hazel switch for the discovery of buried treasure, not a birch twig for the castigation of offenders.
—ARTHUR SYMONS, *An Introduction to the Study of Browning*

4. Without music, earth is like a barren, incomplete house with the dwellers missing. Therefore the earliest Greek history and Biblical history, nay the history of every nation, begins with music.
—LUDWIG TIECK, quoted in Paul Henry Lang, *Music in Western Civilization*

★ 5. Research is fundamentally a state of mind involving continual reexamination of doctrines and axioms upon which current thought and action are based. It is, therefore, critical of existing practices.

—THEOBALD SMITH, *American Journal of Medical Science,* Vol. 178, 1929

6. I have tried sedulously not to laugh at the acts of man, nor to lament them, nor to detest them, but to understand them.

—BARUCH SPINOZA, *Tractatus Theologico-politicus*

7. Of what use is political liberty to those who have no bread? It is of value only to ambitious theorists and politicians. —JEAN PAUL MARAT

8. While there is a lower class I am in it, while there is a criminal element I am of it, and while there is a soul in prison I am not free. —EUGENE DEBS

9. If there were a nation of gods they would be governed democratically, but so perfect a government is not suitable to men.

—JEAN JACQUES ROUSSEAU, *The Social Contract*

★ 10. There are three classes of citizens. The first are the rich, who are indolent and yet always crave more. The second are the poor, who have nothing, are full of envy, hate the rich, and are easily led by demagogues. Between the two extremes lie those who make the state secure and uphold the laws.

—EURIPIDES, *The Suppliant Women*

11. I am convinced that turbulence as well as every other evil temper of this evil age belong not to the lower but to the middle classes—those middle classes of whom in our folly we are so wont to boast.

—LORD ROBERT CECIL, *Diary in Australia*

12. God will see to it that war shall always recur, as a drastic medicine for ailing humanity. —HEINRICH VON TREITSCHKE, *Politik*

13. I would rather that the people should wonder why I wasn't President than why I am. —SALMON P. CHASE

14. He [Benjamin Disraeli] is a self-made man, and worships his creator.

—JOHN BRIGHT

★ 15. We hear about constitutional rights, free speech and the free press. Every time I hear these words I say to myself, "That man is a Red, that man is a Communist." You never heard a real American talk in that manner.

—FRANK HAGUE, speech before the Jersey City Chamber of Commerce, January 12, 1938

16. Even a fool, when he holdeth his peace, is counted wise; And he that shutteth his lips is esteemed as a man of understanding. —Proverbs 17:28

17. A word fitly spoken is like apples of gold in settings of silver.

—Proverbs 25:11

18. I have sworn upon the altar of God eternal hostility against every form of tyranny over the mind of man. —THOMAS JEFFERSON

19. A free man thinks of nothing less than of death, and his wisdom is not a meditation upon death but upon life. —BARUCH SPINOZA, *Ethics*

★ 20. I have seen, and heard, much of Cockney impudence before now; but never expected to hear a coxcomb ask two hundred guineas for flinging a pot of paint in the public's face.

—JOHN RUSKIN, on Whistler's painting "Nocturne in Black and Gold"

21. When people who are tolerably fortunate in their outward lot do not find in life sufficient enjoyment to make it valuable to them, the cause generally is, caring for nobody but themselves. —JOHN STUART MILL, *Utilitarianism*

22. A young man is not a proper hearer of lectures on political science; for he is inexperienced in the actions that occur in life, but its discussions start from these and are about these; and, further, since he tends to follow his passions, his study will be vain and unprofitable, because the end aimed at is not knowledge but action. —ARISTOTLE, *Nichomachean Ethics*

23. Men are never so likely to settle a question rightly as when they discuss it freely. —THOMAS BABINGTON, Lord Macaulay

24. Mankind has grown strong in eternal struggles and it will only perish through eternal peace. —ADOLPH HITLER, *Mein Kampf*

25. But of the many falsehoods told by them, there was one which quite amazed me;—I mean when they said that you should be upon your guard and not allow yourselves to be deceived by the force of my eloquence. To say this, when they were certain to be detected as soon as I opened my lips and proved myself to be anything but a great speaker, did indeed appear to me most shameless—unless by the force of eloquence they mean the force of truth; for if such is their meaning, I admit that I am eloquent. But in how different a way from theirs! —PLATO, *Apology*

2.4 *Emotive Words*

We now turn from our discussion of sentences and more extended passages to examine the *words* with which they are built. A single sentence, as we have seen in Section 2.2, can serve an informative as well as an expressive function simultaneously. To do the former the sentence must formulate a proposition, and to do that its words must have literal or cognitive meaning, referring to objects or events, and to their attributes or relations. When the sentence expresses an attitude or feeling, however, some of its words may also have emotional suggestiveness or impact. A word or phrase can have both a *literal* meaning and an *emotional* impact. The latter is commonly called the word's "emotive meaning."

The literal meanings and the emotive meanings of a word are largely independent of one another. For example, the words "bureaucrat," "government official," and "public servant" have almost identical literal meanings— but their emotive meanings are very different. "Bureaucrat" tends to express resentment and disapproval, while the honorific "public servant" tends to express respect and approval. "Government official" is more nearly neutral than either of the others.

As John Kenneth Galbraith put it in *The Affluent Society,*

> The notion of a vested interest has an engaging flexibility in our social usage. In ordinary intercourse it is an improper advantage enjoyed by a political minority to which the speaker does not himself belong. When the speaker himself enjoys it, it ceases to be a vested interest and becomes a hard-won reward. When a vested interest is enjoyed not by a minority but by a majority, it is a human right.

It is important to realize that one and the same thing can be referred to by words that have very different emotive impacts. It might be thought that the emotive impact of a word is always connected with some quality of its referent. As Shakespeare wrote,

> What's in a name? That which we call a rose
> By any other name would smell as sweet.

It may be that the actual fragrance of roses would remain the same through any change of name we might assign them. But our attitude toward them would very likely change if we began to refer to roses as, say, "skunkweeds." An illustration of this kind of connection between attitude and terminology was reported by Professor Harold J. Lasky in a letter to Bertrand Russell:

> I find that when one presents the student-mind with syndicalism or socialism namelessly they take it as reasonable and obvious; attach the name and they whisper to the parents that nameless abominations are being perpetrated.

Changes in the other direction are familiar; sellers of canned horse mackerel move much more of their merchandise now that they call it "tunafish." As a popular syndicated columnist has written,

> Americans have a genius for inventing new phrases to replace old ones with which we are no longer comfortable. Undertakers became morticians. Janitors became maintenance men. Old people became senior citizens. Lie detector experts are in the process of becoming truth verifiers. The reality doesn't change; only our way of describing it.[5]

Choosing the name that suggests the desired flavor is an old practice, especially in wartime propaganda. A crushing defeat of one's own army is likely to be called, for popular consumption, a "temporary setback"; a massive retreat may be recounted as an "orderly consolidation of forces." During World War II the British novelist and diplomat Harold Nicolson made the following entry in his diary:

> I notice that when we get on both sides of an enemy, that enemy is described as "surrounded," but when the enemy get on both sides of us, we are told that we have driven a "wedge" between his two armies.[6]

The flight from less comfortable to more comfortable terms can have only the most temporary success. When "undertaker" is replaced by "mortician" the latter begins to lose its attraction and eventually must be replaced by "funeral director," and so on. As Germaine Greer wrote in *The Female Eunuch*:

> It is the fate of euphemisms to lose their function rapidly by association with the actuality of what they designate, so that they must be regularly replaced with euphemisms for themselves.

---

[5]Ernest Conine, *Los Angeles Times Service*, April 6, 1975.
[6]Harold Nicolson, *The War Years*, in Nigel Nicolson, ed., *Diaries and Letters* (New York: Atheneum Publishers, 1967), Vol. II.

The story is told that President Harry Truman's wife, Bess, was asked by her friends to try to stop him from saying "manure," to which she replied that it had taken her forty years to get him to *start* saying "manure."

Language does have a life of its own, independent of the facts it is used to describe. Certain physiological activities pertaining to reproduction and elimination can be unemotionally described using a medical vocabulary, without offending the most squeamish taste; the description of the same activities using the four-letter synonyms of these terms may shock all but the most hardened listeners. Using our terminology, we may say that the two sets of words have the same literal or descriptive meanings, but are moderately or sharply opposed in their emotive meanings.

Sometimes the emotive meaning of a word or phrase may arise, in the mind of a given person, not from the thing it literally referred to, but from the context in which it was first learned or encountered. One writer has reported

> . . . the illuminating story of a little girl who, having recently learned to read, was spelling out a political article in the newspaper. "Father," she asked, "what is Tammany Hall?" And her father replied in the voice usually reserved for the taboos of social communication, "You'll understand that when you grow up, my dear." Acceding to this adult whim of evasion, she desisted from her inquiries; but something in Daddy's tone had convinced her that Tammany Hall must be connected with illicit *amour,* and for many years she could not hear this political institution mentioned without experiencing a secret non-political thrill.[7]

For many of us there are certain words or phrases that, because of some special association in our lives, carry a private emotional suggestiveness we may be reluctant to admit.

The contrast between literal and emotive meanings, and the manipulative uses of their differences, led the philosopher Bertrand Russell to devise an amusing and instructive word game. He "conjugated" an "irregular verb" thus:

> I am firm; you are obstinate; he is a pigheaded fool.

The London *New Statesman and Nation* subsequently ran a contest soliciting such irregular conjugations and picked among the winners the following:

> I am righteously indignant; you are annoyed;
> he is making a fuss about nothing.

> I have reconsidered it; you have changed your mind;
> he has gone back on his word.

In his lively book entitled *How to Think Straight,* Robert Thouless made an experiment designed to show the importance of emotively colored words in poetry. There he examined two lines from Keats's "The Eve of St. Agnes":

[7]Margaret Schlauch, *The Gift of Tongues* (New York: Viking Press, Inc., 1942).

> Full on this casement shone the wintry moon,
> And threw warm gules on Madeline's fair breast.

He proposed to show that their beauty arises primarily from the proper choice of emotionally colored words by showing how that beauty is lost completely if those words are replaced by neutral ones. Selecting the words "casement," "gules," "Madeline," "fair," and "breast," Mr. Thouless wrote

> *Casement* means simply a kind of window with emotional and romantic associations. *Gules* is the heraldic name for red, with the suggestion of romance which accompanies all heraldry. *Madeline* is simply a girl's name, but one calling out favorable emotions absent from a relatively plain and straightforward name. *Fair* simply means, in objective fact, that her skin was white or uncolored—a necessary condition for the colors of the window to show—but also fair implies warm emotional preference for an uncolored skin rather than one which is yellow, purple, black, or any of the other colors which skin might be. *Breast* also has similar emotional meanings, and the aim of scientific description might have been equally well attained if it had been replaced by such a neutral word as *chest*.

> Let us now try the experiment of keeping these two lines in a metrical form, but replacing all the emotionally-colored words by neutral ones, while making as few other changes as possible. We may write:

>> "Full on this window shone the wintry moon,
>> Making red marks on Jane's uncolored chest."

> No one will doubt that all of its poetic value has been knocked out of the passage by these changes. Yet the lines still mean the same in external fact; they still have the same objective meaning. It is only the emotional meaning which has been destroyed.[8]

To the extent that humorous impact is to be included in emotive meaning, the revised lines of "poetry" have considerable emotive meaning, though very different from that possessed by the original verses.

EXERCISES

1. Give five original "conjugations of irregular verbs" in which literally the same activity is given a laudatory description in the first person, a fairly neutral one in the second person, and a derogatory one in the third person.

2. Select two brief passages of poetry and perform Thouless's "experiment" on them.

2.5 *Kinds of Agreement and Disagreement*

The "irregular verb" conjugations mentioned in the preceding section make one thing abundantly clear. The same state of affairs can be described in different words that express widely divergent attitudes toward it. And to the

[8]Robert H. Thouless, *How to Think Straight* (New York: Simon and Schuster, Inc., 1939).

extent that anything can be described by means of alternative phrases—one of which expresses an attitude of approval, another an attitude of disapproval, still another a more or less neutral attitude—there are different kinds of agreement and disagreement that can be communicated about any situation or activity.

Two people may disagree as to whether or not something has happened, and when they do, they may be said to have *disagreement in belief.* On the other hand, they may agree that an event has actually occurred, thus agreeing in belief, and yet they may have strongly divergent or even opposite attitudes toward it. One who approves of it will describe it in language that expresses approval; the other may choose terms that express disapproval. There is disagreement here, but it is not disagreement in belief as to what has occurred. The disagreement manifested is rather a difference in feeling about the matter, a *disagreement in attitude.*[9]

With respect to any matter, two persons may agree in belief and disagree in attitude, or they may agree in both belief and attitude. It is also possible for people to agree in attitude despite disagreeing in belief. One may believe that so-and-so has reconsidered a question and changed his position, and so praise him for "listening to the voice of reason," while the other may believe that he has *not* changed his mind and praise him for "refusing to be swayed by blandishment." This third kind of situation often occurs in politics; people may support the same candidate for different and even incompatible reasons. There is a fourth possibility also, in which the disagreement is complete. One speaker, believing that so-and-so has changed his mind, may strongly approve of him for having wisely reconsidered the matter, while the second speaker, believing that he has *not* changed his mind, may just as vigorously disapprove of him for being too pigheaded to admit his mistake. Here there is disagreement in belief and also disagreement in attitude.

So when the resolution of disagreement is our goal we must attend not only to the facts in a given case, but to the varying attitudes of the disputants toward those facts. For different kinds of disagreement, different methods to achieve resolution are called for. So if we are unclear as to what kinds of disagreement exist, we shall be unclear as to what methods should be used. Disagreement in *belief* can best be resolved by ascertaining the *facts.* To decide them, if it is sufficiently important, witnesses could be questioned, documents consulted, records examined, and so on. When the facts are established and the issue decided, the disagreement is likely to be resolved. The methods of scientific inquiry are available here, and it will suffice to direct them squarely at the question of fact about which there is disagreement in belief.

---

[9]We are indebted to our late colleague and friend, Professor Charles L. Stevenson, for the terms agreement and disagreement "in belief" and agreement and disagreement "in attitude," and to him also for the notion of "persuasive definition," which will be discussed in Chapter 4. See his *Ethics and Language* (New Haven, Conn.: Yale University Press, 1944).

On the other hand, if there is disagreement in *attitude* rather than disagreement in belief, the techniques appropriate for settling it are rather different, being more varied and less direct. To call witnesses, consult documents, or the like, to the end of establishing that the event did (or did not) take place would be fruitless in resolving such a dispute, because the facts of the case are not at issue; the disagreement is not over what the facts *are* but over how they are to be valued. Efforts to resolve this disagreement in attitude may involve reference to many factual questions, but not the one about which there is attitudinal conflict. Instead, it may be fruitful to consider the consequences of that event and what happy (or unhappy) consequences would have been entailed had it not occurred. Questions of motive and of intention are of great importance here. These are all factual questions, to be sure, but none of them is identical with what would be the issue if the disagreement were in belief rather than in attitude. Still other methods are available that may resolve a disagreement in attitude. Persuasion may be attempted, with its extensive use of expressive language. Rhetoric may be of paramount utility in unifying the will of a group, in achieving unanimity of attitude—but of course it is wholly worthless in resolving a question of fact.

A word of warning: Such words as "good" and "bad," "right" and "wrong," in their strictly ethical uses tend to have very strong emotive impacts. When we characterize an action as *right*, or a situation as *good*, we express an attitude of approval toward it, whereas when we characterize it as *wrong* or *bad* we are expressing disapproval. That cannot be denied. Some writers on ethics deny, however, that these terms have any literal or cognitive meaning; only emotive meaning is allowed them. Other writers on ethics vigorously insist that such terms do have cognitive meaning, and do refer to objective characteristics of what is being discussed. In this quarrel the student of logic need not take sides. We must insist, however, that not every attitude of approval or disapproval implies a moral judgment. Besides moral values there are aesthetic values, and beyond these two types there are surely personal values reflecting individual preferences or tastes. A negative attitude toward a thing—some food or item of dress—need not involve either ethical or aesthetic judgment, yet it may be given strong verbal expression.

Where disagreement is in attitude rather than in belief, the most vigorous—and, of course, genuine—disagreement may be expressed in statements all of which are literally true. An illuminating example of this sort is reported by Lincoln Steffens in his *Autobiography*. Shortly after the turn of the century, Steffens, in his capacity as a "muckraker," went to Milwaukee to prepare an exposé of "that demagogue," Robert La Follette, then governor of Wisconsin. Steffens called first on a banker, who said that La Follette was "a crooked hypocrite who stirred up the people with socialist-anarchist ideas and hurt business." Steffens asked the banker for evidence, and described what ensued as follows:

> . . . the banker set out to demonstrate . . . hypocrisy, socialism-anarchism, etc., and he was going fast and hot till I realized that my witness had more feeling than

facts; or if he had facts, he could not handle them. He would start with some act of La Follette and blow up in a rage. He certainly hated the man, but I could not write rage.[10]

Steffens's conversation with the banker was interrupted by the arrival of an attorney, who was prepared to present the "evidence" against La Follette. Steffens's account proceeds:

> When I told him how far we had got, the banker and I, and how I wanted first the proofs of the dishonesty alleged, he said: "Oh, no, no. You are getting off wrong. La Follette isn't dishonest. On the contrary, the man is dangerous precisely because he is so sincere. He's a fanatic."

We may remark that the third possibility mentioned previously is perfectly exemplified in the present example. There was disagreement in belief between the banker and the lawyer on the question of La Follette's honesty. But this factual question was completely overshadowed by that of attitude. Here there was vigorous agreement. Both disapproved of La Follette and his actions: curiously enough, the banker because the governor was "a crooked hypocrite," the lawyer because the governor was "so sincere." Then the lawyer got down to cases. His motive here was to achieve agreement with Steffens. The report continues:

> The attorney, with the banker sitting by frowning, impatient, presented in good order the charges against La Follette, the measures he had furthered, the legislation passed and proposed, his political methods. Horrified himself at the items on his list and alarmed over the policy and the power of this demagogue, he delivered the indictment with emotion, force, eloquence. The only hitch was that Bob La Follette's measures seemed fair to me, his methods democratic, his purposes right but moderate, and his fighting strength and spirit hopeful and heroic.

What happened here was that the lawyer's statement of the facts, which presumably Steffens agreed with the lawyer in believing, was not sufficient to produce the kind of agreement in attitude that the lawyer desired. Steffens's attitude toward those facts was altogether different from the lawyer's. Adducing more evidence that the facts were as described—literally—would not have brought the two men a hair's breadth nearer to agreement—in attitude. The lawyer's "emotion, force, eloquence" were relevant, but not sufficient. What the lawyer regarded as newfangled innovations and radical departures from established order, Steffens tended to regard as progressive improvements and the elimination of antiquated prejudice. Both would agree on the fact that change was involved. But their evaluations were different. The reverse was the case with the lawyer and the banker. Their evaluations were the same, even though they disagreed on the factual question of whether La Follette was hypocritical or sincere.

[10]Lincoln Steffens, *The Autobiography of Lincoln Steffens* (New York: Harcourt Brace Jovanovich, Inc., 1931).

The lesson we may draw from these considerations is simple but important. When two parties appear to disagree and formulate their divergent views in statements that are logically consistent with each other, both being perhaps literally true, it would be a mistake to say that the parties do not "really" disagree or that their disagreement is "merely verbal." They are not merely "saying the same thing in different words." They may, of course, be using their words to affirm what is literally the same fact, but they may also be using their words to express conflicting attitudes toward that fact. In such cases, their disagreement, although not "literal," is nevertheless *genuine*. It is not "merely verbal," because words function expressively as well as informatively. And if we are interested in resolving disagreements, we must be clear about their nature, since the techniques appropriate to the resolution of one kind of disagreement may be hopelessly beside the point for another.

Knowledge of the different uses of languages is an aid in understanding what kinds of disagreements may be involved and is thus an aid in resolving them. Drawing the indicated distinctions does not by itself solve the problem or resolve the disagreement, of course. But it clarifies the discussion and reveals the kind and locus of the disagreement. And if it is true that questions are more easily answered when they are better understood, then the study of the different uses of language is of considerable value.

EXERCISES

Identify the kinds of agreement or disagreement exhibited by the following pairs.

★ 1. a. Answer a fool according to his folly, lest he be wise in his own conceit.
—Proverbs 26:5
   b. Answer not a fool according to his folly, lest thou also be like unto him.
—Proverbs 26:4

2. a. For when the One Great Scorer comes
   To write against your name,
   He marks—not that you won or lost—
   But how you played the game.   —GRANTLAND RICE
   b. Winning isn't everything. It's the only thing.   —VINCE LOMBARDI

3. a. Opportunity knocks but once.
   b. It's never too late to mend.

4. a. A stitch in time saves nine.
   b. Better late than never.

5. a. Absence makes the heart grow fonder.
   b. Out of sight, out of mind.

6. a. The race is not to the swift, nor the battle to the strong.
—Ecclesiastes 9:11
   b. But that's the way to bet.   —JIMMY THE GREEK

7. a. For that some should rule and others be ruled is a thing not only necessary, but expedient; from the hour of their birth, some are marked out for

subjection, others for rule. . . . It is clear, then, that some men are by nature free, and others slaves, and that for these latter slavery is both expedient and right.

—ARISTOTLE, *Politics*

b. If there are some who are slaves by nature, the reason is that men were made slaves against nature. Force made the first slaves, and slavery, by degrading and corrupting its victims, perpetuated their bondage.

—JEAN JACQUES ROUSSEAU, *The Social Contract*

8. a. War alone brings up to its highest tension all human energy and puts the stamp of nobility upon the peoples who have the courage to face it.

—BENITO MUSSOLINI, *Encyclopedia Italiana*

b. War crushes with bloody heel all justice, all happiness, all that is God-like in man. In our age there can be no peace that is not honorable; there can be no war that is not dishonorable.   —CHARLES SUMNER

9. a. Next in importance to freedom and justice is popular education, without which neither freedom nor justice can be permanently maintained.

—JAMES A. GARFIELD

b. Education is fatal to anyone with a spark of artistic feeling. Education should be confined to clerks, and even them it drives to drink. Will the world learn that we never learn anything that we did not know before?

—GEORGE MOORE, *Confessions of a Young Man*

★ 10. a. Belief in the existence of god is as groundless as it is useless. The world will never be happy until atheism is universal.

—J. O. LA METTRIE, *L'Homme Machine*

b. Nearly all atheists on record have been men of extremely debauched and vile conduct.   —J. P. SMITH, *Instructions on Christian Theology*

11. a. I know of no pursuit in which more real and important services can be rendered to any country than by improving its agriculture, its breed of useful animals, and other branches of a husbandman's cares.

—GEORGE WASHINGTON, letter to John Sinclair

b. With the introduction of agriculture mankind entered upon a long period of meanness, misery, and madness, from which they are only now being freed by the beneficent operations of the machine.

—BERTRAND RUSSELL, *The Conquest for Happiness*

12. a. Whenever there is, in any country, uncultivated land and unemployed poor, it is clear that the laws of property have been so far extended as to violate natural right.   —THOMAS JEFFERSON

b. Every man has by nature the right to possess property of his own. This is one of the chief points of distinction between man and the lower animals.

—POPE LEO XIII, *Rerum novarum*

13. a. The right of revolution is an inherent one. When people are oppressed by their government, it is a natural right they enjoy to relieve themselves of the oppression, if they are strong enough, either by withdrawal from it, or by over-throwing it and substituting a government more acceptable.

—ULYSSES S. GRANT, *Personal Memoirs, I*

b. Inciting to revolution is treason, not only against man, but against God.

—POPE LEO XIII, *Immortalie Dei*

14. a. Language is the armory of the human mind; and at once contains the trophies of its past, and the weapons of its future conquests.

—SAMUEL TAYLOR COLERIDGE

b. Language—human language—after all, is little better than the croak and cackle of fowls, and other utterances of brute nature—sometimes not so adequate.
—NATHANIEL HAWTHORNE, *American Notebook*

★ 15. a. How does it become a man to behave towards the American government today? I answer, that he cannot without disgrace be associated with it.
—HENRY DAVID THOREAU, *An Essay on Civil Disobedience*

b. With all the imperfections of our present government, it is without comparison the best existing, or that ever did exist. —THOMAS JEFFERSON

16. a. Farming is a senseless pursuit, a mere laboring in a circle. You sow that you may reap, and then you reap that you may sow. Nothing ever comes of it.
—JOANNES STOBAEUS, *Florilegium*

b. No occupation is so delightful to me as the culture of the earth.
—THOMAS JEFFERSON

17. a. Our country: in her intercourse with foreign nations may she always be in the right; but our country, right or wrong!
—STEPHEN DECATUR, toast at a dinner in Norfolk, Virginia, April 1816

b. Our country, right or wrong. When right, to be kept right; when wrong, to be put right.[11] —CARL SCHURZ, speech in the Senate, January 1872

18. a. A bad peace is even worse than war. —TACITUS, *Annals*

b. The most disadvantageous peace is better than the most just war.
—DESIDERIUS ERASMUS, *Adagia*

19. a. It makes but little difference whether you are committed to a farm or a county jail. —HENRY DAVID THOREAU, *Walden*

b. I know few things more pleasing to the eye, or more capable of affording scope and gratification to a taste for the beautiful, than a well-situated, well-cultivated farm. —EDWARD EVERETT

★ 20. a. Thought, like all potent weapons, is exceedingly dangerous if mishandled. Clear thinking is therefore desirable not only in order to develop the full potentialities of the mind, but also to avoid disaster.
—GILES ST. AUBYN, *The Art of Argument*

b. Reason is the greatest enemy that faith has: it never comes to the aid of spiritual things, but—more frequently than not—struggles against the divine Word, treating with contempt all that emanates from God.
—MARTIN LUTHER, *Table Talk*

2.6 *Emotively Neutral Language*

The expressive use of language is just as legitimate as the informative. There is nothing wrong with emotive language, and there is nothing wrong with language that is nonemotive, or neutral. Similarly, we can say that there is nothing wrong with pillows and nothing wrong with hammers. True enough; but we will not succeed in trying to drive nails with pillows, nor will we be comfortable resting our heads on hammers. We may preserve the literal meaning of a poet's romantic lines when we replace his emotive language

---

[11]On this kind of disagreement G. K. Chesterton commented in *The Defendant* that "'My country, right or wrong' is like saying 'My mother, drunk or sober.'"

with matter-of-fact speech, but we will lose a very great deal in doing so. In some kinds of poetry emotively colored language is properly preferred to neutral language. In other spheres, language that is neutral is preferable to that which is emotively colored.

Which spheres are those? Neutral language is to be prized when factual truth is our objective. When we are trying to learn what really is the case, or trying to follow an argument, distractions will be frustrating—and emotion is a powerful distraction. The passions tend to cloud the reason; this truth is reflected in the usage of "dispassionate" and "objective" as near synonyms. Therefore, when we are trying to reason about the facts in a cool and objective fashion, referring to them in strongly emotive language is a hindrance rather than a help.

Here are some examples. In economics it is a serious question whether a given degree of government control will have a positive or negative effect upon productivity or efficiency. Making that determination regarding some specific policy will be more difficult if the phenomena in question are referred to with emotively colored expressions like "bureaucratic interference" or "irresponsible license." In philosophy, too, emotive meaning can get in the way. William James, in his essay "The Dilemma of Determinism," defended his "wish to get rid of the word 'freedom'" on the grounds that "its eulogistic associations have . . . overshadowed all the rest of its meaning." He rightly preferred to discuss the issue using the words "determinism" and "indeterminism" because, he said, "their cold and mathematical sound has no sentimental associations that can bribe our partiality either way in advance." We should do well to follow James's example.

Indeed, the almost automatic response to some terms heavy with emotive meaning may seriously interfere with an objective appraisal of the facts we are concerned about. In the work of professional opinion polling it has long been recognized that interviewers must be very careful not to prejudice the responses they receive by using emotive phrasing in the questions they ask. Careful studies of this emotive factor in polling have been done; in one such study, the favorable reaction to "explaining our point of view" while reporting the news was cut almost in half when that expression was replaced by "including some propaganda." One negatively charged word—propaganda—changed the polling result dramatically.[12]

Of course, one may wonder whether the change of such a key term in a question does not essentially alter the question itself. But the logical point remains: If our aim is to communicate information, and if we wish to avoid being misunderstood, we should use language with the least possible emotive impact. In science, for example, where an earlier tradition used such terms as "noble" and "base" to characterize metals like gold and iron, we have learned that progress is supported by the cultivation of a set of emotively neutral terms, and this has been done systematically in the physical sciences.

[12]Stuart Chase, *The Proper Study of Mankind* (New York: Harper & Row, Publishers, Inc., 1948).

It follows that whenever we encounter highly emotive language as we are investigating the literal truth or falsity of a view, or its logical implications, our task will be facilitated if we translate those passages into formulations as nearly neutral as possible. Suppose that we are interested in the conflict between freedom and other values, as it appears in the clash between civil libertarians and feminists over the legal permissibility of certain kinds of sexually explicit literature and films. Here is one account of what its author calls the "squabble over pornography."

> We are presented with the amusing spectacle of pornography, clad in armor borrowed from the heroic struggles for freedom of speech, and using Miltonic rhetoric, doing battle with feminism, newly draped in the robes of community morality, using arguments associated with conservatives who defend traditional sex roles. . . . In the background stand the liberals, wringing their hands in confusion because they wish to favor both sides and cannot.[13]

Now, can this passage be translated into more nearly neutral language that gives a fair account of the theoretical conflict under discussion? No more information is presented by the author in the passage cited than in the following:

> The right to publish sexually explicit books and films has been supported by those using the traditional arguments in defense of free speech, while it has been attacked by feminists who have, for this purpose, adopted a more conservative position associated with traditional morality. Many liberals are troubled by their inability to decide which side in this conflict they will join.

The conflict in question, which has indeed caused bitter disagreement among old political allies, is both interesting and complicated. No intellectual gain is made by sprinkling the account of it with emotional and sarcastic phrases like "Miltonic rhetoric," "feminism, newly draped in the robes of community morality," and "liberals, wringing their hands in confusion." Students of logic, and citizens seeking to build a good community, will want to understand the issues at stake in this controversy, the arguments and evidence on both sides. Serious thinkers will approach the continuing debate over such issues thoughtfully and with care, seeking—as David Hume advised in all such matters—to follow the argument where it leads, rather than to belittle the participants by caricaturing their roles in what is called "an amusing spectacle."

Playing upon emotion, rather than appealing to reason, is a common device of those who profit from the distortion of the truth. The most flagrant displays of such efforts to manipulate are in the world of advertising, where the overriding aims are always to persuade, to sell, and often to exploit. We must be constantly on our guard against these uses of emotionally charged language, and against their uses in political campaigns where almost every rhe-

---

[13] Allan Bloom, "Liberty, Equality, Sexuality," *Commentary*, April 1987, p. 24.

torical trick is played and replayed. Our best defenses are thoughtful sensitivity to language and its different uses, and skill in recognizing the assorted efforts of unscrupulous persons to make the worse appear the better cause.

EXERCISE

Select a brief passage of highly emotive writing from some current periodical and translate it in such a way as to retain its informative significance, while reducing its expressive significance to a minimum.

3

Fallaces

. . . arguments, like men, are often pretenders.

—PLATO

It would be a very good thing if every trick could receive some short and obviously appropriate name, so that when a man used this or that particular trick, he could at once be reproved for it.

—ARTHUR SCHOPENHAUER

That logical error is, in the last analysis some sort of inadvertence, is an indispensable assumption of the study [of logic].

—C. I. LEWIS

3.1 *What Is a Fallacy?*

A fallacy is an error in reasoning. As logicians use the word it designates not any mistaken idea or false belief, but *typical* errors, mistakes that arise commonly in ordinary discourse, and that render unsound the arguments in which they appear.

An argument, whatever its subject or sphere, is generally constructed to prove that its conclusion is true. But any argument can fail to fulfill this purpose in either of two ways. One way it can fail is by assuming a false proposition as one of its premises. We saw, in Chapter 1, that every argument involves the claim that the truth of its conclusion follows from, or is implied by, the truth of its premises. So if its premises are not true, the argument fails to establish the truth of its conclusion, even if the reasoning based on those premises is valid. To test the truth or falsehood of premises, however, is not the special responsibility of the logician; it is rather the task of inquiry in general, since premises may deal with any subject matter whatever.

The other way that an argument can fail to establish the truth of its conclusion is for its premises not to imply its conclusion. Here we do have the special province of the logician, whose chief concern is the logical relations between premisses and conclusion. An argument whose premisses do not imply its conclusion is one whose conclusion *could* be false *even if* all its premisses were true. In cases of this kind the reasoning is bad, and the argument is said to be *fallacious,* or to be a *fallacy.*

There are many ways in which reasoning can go astray, many *kinds* of mistakes that may be made in argument. Each fallacy, as we shall use the term, is a type of incorrect argument. Since each fallacy is a type, we can say of two or more different arguments that they contain or commit the same fallacy. That is, they exhibit the same kind of mistake in the reasoning process.

It is customary in the study of logic to reserve the term "fallacy" for arguments which, although incorrect, are psychologically persuasive. Some arguments are so obviously incorrect as to deceive and persuade no one. But fallacies are dangerous because most of us are, at one time or another, fooled by some of them. We therefore define a fallacy as: a type of argument that may seem to be correct, but that proves, upon examination, not to be so. It is profitable to study these mistaken arguments, because the traps they set can best be avoided when they are well understood. To be forewarned is to be forearmed.

How many different kinds of mistakes in arguments—different fallacies— must be distinguished? Aristotle, the first systematic logician, identified 13 types;[1] very recently a listing of more than 113 has been developed![2] There is no precisely determinable number of fallacies, since much depends, in counting them, upon the system of classification used. We distinguish 17 fallacies here—the most common and most deceptive categories of mistakes in reasoning—divided into two large groups, called *fallacies of relevance* and *fallacies of ambiguity.* Mastering these will enable the student to detect the most troublesome errors in reasoning, and will promote that sensitivity needed to detect errors of related kinds as well.

---

[1]Aristotle, *Sophistical Refutations,* in W. D. Ross, ed., *The Works of Aristotle* (New York: Oxford University Press, Inc. 1928), Vol. I.

[2]To the best of our knowledge the most comprehensive—or at least voluminous—list of fallacies is given by David Hackett Fischer in his book *Historian's Fallacies* (New York: Harper & Row, Publishers, Inc., 1970). The index for Fischer's book contains entries for 112 different fallacies, but in the body of his book he discusses and names more than are listed in his index. Fifty-one fallacies are "named, explained, and illustrated" by W. Ward Fearnside and William B. Holther in their book *Fallacy: The Counterfeit of Argument* (Englewood Cliffs, N.J.: Prentice-Hall, Inc., 1959). A historical, critical, and theoretical treatment of the topic is given by C. L. Hamblin in his book *Fallacies* (London: Methuen & Company, Ltd., 1970). Another excellent treatment of this topic is that of John Woods and Douglas Walton in their book *Argument: The Logic of the Fallacies* (Scarborough, Ontario: McGraw-Hill Ryerson Ltd., 1982). An insightful criticism of the more usual methods of classifying fallacies is found in Howard Kahane, "The Nature and Classification of Fallacies," in J. Anthony Blair and Ralph J. Johnson, eds., *Informal Logic* (Inverness, Calif.: Edgepress, 1980). All these books can be warmly recommended to readers who wish to go more deeply into the subject of fallacies.

3.2 *Fallacies of Relevance*

When an argument relies upon premises that are not relevant to its conclusion, and that therefore cannot possibly establish its truth, the fallacy committed is one of relevance. *"Irrelevance"* may perhaps better describe the problem: but the premises are often *psychologically* relevant to the conclusion, and that explains their seeming correctness and persuasiveness. How psychological relevance can be confused with logical relevance is explained in part by the different uses of language distinguished in Chapter 2; the mechanics of these confusions will become clearer in the analyses, below, of the 12 different fallacies in this group.

Latin names have traditionally been given to many fallacies; some of these—like "ad hominem"—have become part of the English language. We will use here both the Latin and the English names.

1. The Argument from Ignorance—Argument *ad Ignorantiam*

This is the mistake that is committed whenever it is argued that a proposition is true simply on the basis that it has not been proved false, or that it is false because it has not been proved true. We realize, upon reflection, that many false propositions have not yet been proved false, and many true propositions have not yet been proved true—and thus our ignorance of how to prove or disprove a proposition does not establish either truth or falsehood. This fallacious appeal to ignorance appears most commonly in misunderstandings of developing science—where propositions whose truth cannot yet be established are mistakenly held false for that reason, and also in the world of pseudo-science, where propositions about psychic phenomena and the like are fallaciously held true because their falsehood has not been conclusively established.

Famous in the history of science is the argument *ad ignorantiam* given in criticism of Galileo, when he showed leading astronomers of his time the mountains and valleys on the moon that could be seen through his telescope. Some scholars of that age, absolutely convinced that the moon was a perfect sphere, as theology and Aristotelian science had long taught, argued against Galileo that although we see what appear to be mountains and valleys, the moon is in fact a perfect sphere, because all its apparent irregularities are filled in by an invisible crystalline substance. And this hypothesis, which saves the perfection of the heavenly bodies, Galileo could not prove false! Legend has it that Galileo, to expose the argument *ad ignorantiam*, offered another of the same kind as a caricature. Unable to prove the nonexistence of the transparent crystal supposedly filling the valleys, he put foward the equally probable hypothesis that there were, rearing up from the invisible crystalline envelope on the moon, even greater mountain peaks—but made of crystal and thus invisible! And this, he pointed out, his critics could not prove false.

Those who strongly oppose some great change are often tempted to argue against the change on the ground that it has not yet been proved workable or safe. Such proof is often impossible to provide in advance, and the appeal of the objection is commonly to ignorance mixed with fear. Such an appeal will often take the form of rhetorical questions which suggest, but do not flatly assert, that the proposed changes are full of unknown peril. When, for example, the technology for cutting and recombining DNA (what has been called "genetic engineering") was first being considered in the 1970s, some who sought to forbid such research appealed to our ignorance of its long-term consequences. One critic, formulating his appeal *ad ignorantiam* in highly emotive language, wrote in a letter to *Science*:

> If Dr. Frankenstein must go on producing his biological monsters . . . [h]ow can we be sure what would happen once the little beasts escaped from the laboratory?[3]

In some circumstances, of course, the fact that certain evidence or results have not been got, after they have been actively sought in ways calculated to reveal them, may have substantial argumentative force. New drugs being tested for safety, for example, are commonly given to mice or other rodents for prolonged periods; the absence of any toxic effect upon the rodents is taken to be evidence (although not conclusive evidence) that the drug is probably not toxic to humans. Consumer protection often relies upon evidence of this kind. In circumstances like these we rely not on ignorance but upon our knowledge, or conviction, that if the result we are concerned about were likely to arise, it would have arisen in some of the test cases. This use of the inability to prove something true supposes that investigators are highly skilled, and that they very probably would have uncovered the evidence sought had it been possible to do so. Tragic mistakes are sometimes made in this sphere even so; but if the standard is set too high—if what is required is a conclusive proof of harmlessness that cannot ever be given—consumers will be denied what may prove to be valuable, even lifesaving, medical treatments.

Similarly, when a security investigation yields no evidence of improper conduct by the person investigated, it would be wrong to conclude that the investigation has left us ignorant. A thorough investigation will properly result in his being "cleared." *Not* to draw a conclusion, in some cases, is as much a breach of correct reasoning as it would be to draw a mistaken conclusion.

There is one special context in which the appeal to ignorance is common and appropriate, namely, in a criminal court, where an accused person is presumed innocent until proved guilty. We adopt this principle because we recognize that the error of convicting the innocent is far more terrible than that of acquitting the guilty—and thus the defense in a criminal case may legitimately claim that if the prosecution has not proved guilt beyond a reasonable doubt, the only verdict possible is not guilty. A recent opinion of the

---

[3]Erwin Chargaff, *Science*, Vol. 192, 1976, p. 938.

United States Supreme Court strongly reaffirmed this standard of proof in these words:

> The reasonable-doubt standard . . . is a prime instrument for reducing the risk of convictions resting on factual error. The standard provides concrete substance for the presumption of innocence—that bedrock axiomatic and elementary principle whose enforcement lies at the foundation of the administration of our criminal law.[4]

But *this* appeal to ignorance succeeds only where innocence must be assumed in the absence of proof to the contrary; in other contexts such an appeal is indeed an argument *ad ignorantiam.*

2. The Appeal to Inappropriate Authority—Argument *ad Verecundiam*

In attempting to make up one's mind on a difficult or complicated question, it is entirely reasonable to be guided by the judgment of an acknowledged expert who has studied the matter thoroughly. When we argue that a given conclusion is correct on the ground that an expert authority has come to that judgment we commit no fallacy. Indeed, such recourse to authority is necessary for most of us on very many matters. Of course, an expert's judgment is not conclusive proof; experts disagree, and even in agreement they may err; but expert opinion is surely one reasonable way to support a conclusion.

The fallacy *ad verecundiam* arises when the appeal is made to parties having no legitimate claim to authority in the matter at hand. Thus, in an argument about morality, an appeal to the opinions of Darwin, a towering authority in biology, would be fallacious, as would be the appeal to the opinions of a great artist, like Picasso, to settle an economic dispute. But care must be taken in determining whose authority is reasonably to be relied upon, and whose rejected. While Picasso was not an economist, his judgment might plausibly be given some weight in a dispute pertaining to the economic value of an artistic masterpiece; and if the role of biology in moral questions were in dispute, Darwin might indeed be an appropriate authority.

The most blatant examples of misplaced appeals to authority appear in advertising "testimonials." We are urged to drive an automobile of a given make because a famous golfer or tennis player affirms its superiority; we are urged to drink a beverage of a certain brand because some movie star or football coach expresses enthusiasm about it. Wherever the truth of some proposition is asserted on the basis of the authority of one who has no special competence in that sphere, the appeal to misplaced authority is the fallacy committed.

This appears to be a simpleminded mistake that is easy to avoid, but there are circumstances in which the fallacious appeal is very tempting, and therefore intellectually dangerous. Here are two examples: In the sphere of international relations, in which weapons and war unhappily play a major role,

---

[4]Mr. Justice Brennan, writing for the Court, *In re Winship*, 397 U.S. 358 (1970).

one opinion or another is commonly supported by appealing to those whose special competence lies in the technical design or construction of weapons. Physicists like Robert Oppenheimer or Edward Teller, for example, may indeed have the knowledge to give authoritative judgments regarding how certain weapons can (or cannot) function; but their knowledge in this sphere does not give them special wisdom in determining political goals to be pursued. An appeal to the strong judgment of a distinguished physicist on the wisdom of ratifying some international treaty would be an argument *ad verecundiam*. Similarly, we admire the depth and insight of great fiction—say in the novels of Alexander Solzhenitsyn or Saul Bellow—but resorting to their judgment in determining the real culprit in some political dispute would be an appeal *ad verecundiam*.

It is sometimes difficult to know whether a given "expert," alleged to be an authority in a particular sphere, is properly to be relied upon. That judgment itself may require careful thought, and we may later regret that we chose to rely upon an expert who turns out to have been mistaken. If that expert's good reputation was deserved, however, such a choice is no fallacy. The error becomes one of reasoning—the fallacy *ad verecundiam*—when the appeal is plainly inappropriate, the authority relied upon not legitimate.

3. Complex Question

Of all the fallacies in everyday reasoning, one of the most common is this: asking a question in such a way as to presuppose the truth of some conclusion buried in that question. The question itself is likely to be rhetorical, no answer genuinely sought. But putting the question seriously, and taking it seriously, often achieve the questioner's purpose, fallaciously.

Thus an executive of a utility company may ask: "Why is the private development of resources so much more efficient than any public control?" Or a homeowner may ask about a proposed increase in the property tax: "How can you expect the majority of the voters, who rent but don't own property and don't have to pay the tax, to care if the tax burden of others is made even more unfair?" Such questions, frequently appearing on the editorial pages of newspapers, and heard on television talk shows, have as their object the acceptance of the truth of certain propositions—that private development is more efficient than public control; or that the burden of a proposed tax on the property owner is unfair, and that those who rent rather than own their homes are not affected by increasing the tax on property—without having to assert or defend those alleged truths forthrightly. Complex Question is perhaps the most widely practiced of the devious devices used in what is known as "yellow journalism." Its presence may be suspected whenever the question is accompanied by the aggressive demand that it be answered "yes or no."

The danger that complex questions present, especially when they are put before a legislative (or other decision-making) body, has resulted in giving privileged position, in parliamentary procedure, to the motion to *divide the question*. Thus, for example, a motion that the body "postpone a given matter for one year," may wisely be divided into the decision to postpone it, and *if* that is done, then to determine the length of the postponement. Some members may warmly support the postponement itself, yet find the one-year period intolerably long; if the opportunity to divide the question were not given priority, the body might be maneuvered into taking action upon a motion which, because of its complexity, cannot be decided intelligently. Often a presiding officer, having the duty to promote a fully rational debate, will solicit the motion to divide the question before beginning the substantive debate.

Fallacious complexity can appear in discourse of different forms. In its most explicit form it occurs in a dialogue in which one party poses a question that is complex, a second party answers it, and the first party then draws a fallacious inference for which that answer was the ground. For example:

LAWYER: The figures seem to indicate that your sales increased as a result of these misleading advertisements. Is that correct?
WITNESS: They did not!
LAWYER: But you do admit, then, that your advertising was misleading. How long have you been engaging in practices like these?

More commonly, however, the fallacy takes a less explicit and trickier form, in which a single speaker, or writer, deliberately poses the complex question, answers it himself, and then goes on to draw the fallacious inference. Or, still less explicitly, the complex question may be posed and the fallacious inference drawn without the answer to the question having been stated at all, but merely suggested or presupposed.

4. Argument *ad Hominem*

The phrase "ad hominem" translates into "against the man." It names a fallacious attack, in which the thrust is directed not at the conclusion one wishes to deny, but at the person who asserts or defends it. This fallacy has two major forms, because there are two different ways in which the attack can be directed.

A. The Argument *ad Hominem, Abusive*
It is very common in rough-and-tumble argument to disparage the character of the opponents, to deny their intelligence or reasonableness, to question their integrity, and so on. But the personal character of an individual is logically irrelevant to the truth or falsehood of what that person says, or the correctness or incorrectness of that person's argument. To contend that proposals are bad or assertions false because they are proposed or asserted by "radicals" (of the left or right) is a typical example of the fallacy *ad hominem, abusive*.

Abusive premisses are irrelevant—but they may sometimes persuade by the psychological process of transference. Where an attitude of disapproval toward a person can be evoked, the field of emotional disapproval may be so extended as to include disagreement with the assertions that person makes.

There are many variations in the patterns of *ad hominem* abuse, of course. Sometimes the opponent is abused for being of a certain persuasion—an atheist or a communist. Sometimes a conclusion is condemned simply because it is one shared by persons who are believed to be vicious or of bad character. Many contend that Socrates, at his famous trial in Athens, was found guilty of impiety partly because of his close association with persons widely known to have been disloyal to the state, and rapacious in conduct. "Guilt by association" was repeatedly suggested in the United States during the 1950s, by the Committee on Un-American Activities of the House of Representatives, when misconduct was alleged in part because of the support given by those accused to political causes (e.g., civil liberties, and racial equality) supported also by the Communist Party. Because argument *ad hominem, abusive* commonly takes the form of attacking the source or the genesis of the opposing position—which is not relevant to its truth, of course—it is sometimes called "the Genetic Fallacy."

There is one context in which an argument that appears to be *ad hominem* is not fallacious. In a court of law, or other formal proceedings, when sworn testimony is given and it is believed by opponents to be perjury, deliberate falsehood, the unreliability of the person giving that testimony may appropriately be exhibited. Efforts may be made to "impeach the witness," to call his truthfulness into question. The argument is not fallacious if the credibility of the witness, and his sworn testimony, is thus undermined; but if one goes on to infer that the attack establishes the *falsehood* of that to which the witness testified, instead of concluding merely that the discredited testimony does not establish its truth, then the reasoning would be fallacious. To impeach a witness it will not suffice merely to assert that he is a liar; it must be shown from the pattern of that witness's past conduct, or from the inconsistency of the sworn testimony that witness has given.

A legendary example of the abusive variety of *ad hominem* also arose in a courtroom, in Britain. There the practice of law has long been divided between solicitors, who prepare cases for trial, and barristers, who argue or "plead" cases in court. Ordinarily, their cooperation is admirable, but sometimes it leaves much to be desired. On one such latter occasion, the barrister ignored the case completely until the day it was to be presented at court, depending upon the solicitor to investigate the defendant's case and prepare the brief. Arriving at court just a moment before the trial was to begin, he was handed his brief by the solicitor. Surprised at its thinness, he glanced inside to find written: "No case; abuse the plaintiff's attorney!"

B. The Argument *Ad Hominem, Circumstantial*
In this variety of the *ad hominem* fallacy, it is the irrelevant connection between

the beliefs held and the circumstances of those holding it that gives rise to the mistake. An opponent ought to accept (or reject) some conclusion, it is argued fallaciously, merely because of that person's employment, or nationality, or other circumstances. Thus it may be unfairly suggested that a clergyman must accept a given proposition because its denial would be incompatible with the Scriptures. A political candidate, it may be claimed, must support a given policy, since it is a policy explicitly defended in the platform of his party. Such argument is irrelevant to the *truth* of the proposition in question—it simply urges the *acceptance* of it by some individual because of his or her situation and convictions. Sport hunters, accused of barbarism for sacrificing unoffending animals merely for amusement, sometimes reply to their critics: "Why do *you* feed on the flesh of harmless cattle?" But this reply is plainly *ad hominem*, at the person; the reply does not even begin to prove that it is right to sacrifice animal life for human amusement, but merely that the critics cannot consistently decry that conduct because of their own circumstances—in this case their not being vegetarians. The term *tu quoque*, meaning "you're another" is sometimes used to name this circumstantial variety of the *ad hominem*.

The circumstances of the opponent are not the issue in serious argument; therefore, such premises are not to the point. Calling attention to those circumstances may be psychologically effective in winning assent to one's conclusion from one's opponent; but however persuasive it may prove, argument of this kind is essentially fallacious.

A classic example of a circumstantial *ad hominem* argument appears in Plato's dialogue, *Crito*, in which the mythical Laws of Athens—the state personified—speak to Socrates, seeking to prove to him that he would be wrong to flee from the sentence of death that had been imposed upon him by the Athenian court:

> Of all Athenians you have been the most constant resident in the city, which, as you never leave, you may be supposed to love. . . . Nor had you any curiosity to know other states or their laws; your affections did not go beyond us and our state; we were your special favorites and you acquiesced in our government of you. . . . Moreover you might, in the course of the trial, if you had liked, have fixed the penalty at banishment; the state which refuses to let you go now would have let you go then. But you pretended that you preferred death to exile, and that you were not unwilling to die. And now you have forgotten these fine sentiments. . . . [5]

The circumstances of one's opponents are also sometimes used, fallaciously, as the reasons for rejecting a conclusion they support—as when it is argued, without relevance to the truth of the conclusion, that their judgment is dictated by their special situation, rather than by reasoning or evidence. An argument whose conclusion is favorable to some minority deserves dis-

---

[5]Plato, *Crito*, No. 52; Jowett Translation (New York: The Macmillan Company, 1892), Vol. I, p. 436.

cussion on its merits; it is fallacious to attack it simply on the ground that it is presented by a member of that minority and therefore self-serving. Manufacturers, as another example, may be expected to favor a protective tariff—but when their arguments in favor of a tariff are rejected merely on the grounds that they are manufacturers and therefore may be expected to hold that view, the critic is committing a fallacy *ad hominem*, circumstantial.

The connection between the abusive and the circumstantial varieties of argument *ad hominem* is not difficult to see; the latter may be regarded as a special case of the former. The first use of the circumstantial *ad hominem* charges one's adversaries with *inconsistency*—among their several beliefs, or between what they preach and what they practice—which is a kind of reproach or abuse. The second use of the circumstantial *ad hominem* charges one's adversaries with being so *prejudiced* that their alleged reasons are mere rationalizations or conclusions dictated in reality by self-interest. And that is certainly to abuse them. This particular kind of *ad hominem* is sometimes called "poisoning the well," for obvious reasons.

5 and 6. Accident and Converse Accident

These two fallacies arise as a result of the careless, or deliberately deceptive use of generalizations. In political and moral argument, and in most affairs of importance in community life, we rely upon statements of how things generally are, how people generally behave, and the like. But, even when general claims are entirely plausible, we must be careful not to apply them to particular cases too rigidly. Circumstances alter cases; a generalization that is true by and large may not apply in a given case, for good reasons having to do with the special (or "accidental") circumstances of that case. When we apply a generalization to individual cases that it does not properly govern, we commit the *fallacy of Accident*. When we do the reverse, and carelessly or by design, apply a principle that is true of a particular case to the great run of cases, we commit the *fallacy of Converse Accident*.

Experience teaches us that many generalizations, although widely applicable and useful, have exceptions for which we must be on guard. In the law, principles that are sound in general sometimes have very specifically identified exceptions. For example, the rule that hearsay testimony may not be accepted as evidence in court, is not applicable when the party whose oral communications are reported is dead, or when the party reporting the hearsay does so in conflict with his own best interest. Almost every good rule has appropriate exceptions; we argue fallaciously when we reason on the supposition that some rule applies with universal force.

Socrates, in a dialogue with the young Euthydemus who plans to become a statesman, draws from Euthydemus a commitment to many of the conventionally accepted moral truths—that it is wrong to deceive, unjust to steal, and so on. Then Socrates (as recounted by Xenophon in his report of the dialogue) presents a series of hypothetical cases in which Euthydemus reluctantly agrees that it would appear right to deceive (to rescue our country-men), and just to steal (to save a friend's life), and so on. For all those who may try to decide specific and complicated issues by appealing mechanically to general rules, the fallacy of Accident is a genuine and serious threat. The logician H. W. B. Joseph observed that "there is no fallacy more insidious than that of treating a statement which in many connections is not misleading as if it were true always and without qualification."[6]

Accident is the fallacy we commit when we move carelessly or too quickly *from* a generalization; Converse Accident is the fallacy we commit when we move carelessly or too quickly *to* a generalization. We are all familiar with those who draw conclusions about all persons in a given category because of what may be true about one or a few persons in that category; we know, and need to remember, that although a certain drug may be innocuous in some circumstance it is not therefore innocuous in all circumstances. Considering the effect of alcohol only on those who indulge in it to excess, one may conclude that all liquor is harmful and urge that its sale and use should be forbidden by law. Converse Accident is a kind of fallacious reasoning whose error is plain to everyone when exposed; yet it is a convenient deception, upon which many persons are tempted to rely when they argue inattentively or with great passion.

7. False Cause

The nature of the connection between cause and effect—and how we can determine whether such a connection is present or absent—are central problems of inductive logic and scientific method. These problems are discussed in detail in Part Three of this book. It is easy to see, however, that any reasoning which relies upon treating as the cause of a thing what is not really its cause must be seriously mistaken; in Latin this mistake has been called the fallacy of *non causa pro causa*; we call it more simply *false cause*.

One variety of false cause is most common, and often very misleading—the error of concluding that an event is *caused* by another simply because it *follows* that other. We know, of course, that mere temporal succession does not establish a causal connection; but we can be tricked. If very peculiar weather conditions are experienced just after the underground testing of a nuclear device, some will argue, fallaciously, that the tests were the cause of those conditions. If an aggressive move in foreign policy is followed by an international event for which we had been hoping, some may mistakenly conclude that the aggressive policy was the cause of that event. In primitive beliefs the error is sometimes blatant; we will all reject as absurd the claim that beating drums is the cause of the sun's reappearance after an eclipse, despite the evidence offered that every time drums have been beaten during

[6]H. W. B. Joseph, *An Introduction to Logic* (New York: Oxford University Press, 1906).

an eclipse the sun has reappeared! This variety of false cause is widely called the fallacy of *post hoc ergo propter hoc* (after the thing, therefore because of the thing)—and while the mistake is easy to detect in many circumstances, there are times when even the best of scientists, or statesmen, may be misled.

8. Begging the Question—*Petitio Principii*

To beg the question is to assume the truth of what one seeks to prove, in the effort to prove it. That would seem to be a silly mistake, evident to all—but how silly or obvious the mistake is depends largely on the way in which the premises of the argument are formulated. Their wording often obscures the fact that buried within one of the premises assumed lies the conclusion itself. This fallacy is illustrated by the following argument, reported by the logician Richard Whately: "To allow every man unbounded freedom of speech must always be, on the whole, advantageous to the state; for it is highly conducive to the interests of the community that each individual should enjoy a liberty, perfectly unlimited, of expressing his sentiments."[7]

Sometimes we fall into this mistake when, in the effort to establish our conclusion, we cast about in search of premises that will do the trick. Of course the conclusion itself, disguised in other language, certainly will do the trick! Among all the fallacies of relevance, therefore, it will be seen that this is the one case in which the error does not lie in the fact that the premises are not relevant or that they cannot establish the conclusion. They are not *ir*relevant, they *do* prove the conclusion—but they do so trivially. A *petitio principii* is always valid—but always worthless, too.

Those who fall into this error often do not realize that they have assumed what they set out to prove. The fact of that assumption can be obscured by confusing and therefore unrecognized synonyms, or by a chain of intervening argument. Every *petitio* is a *circular argument*, but the circle that has been constructed may—if it is large or fuzzy—go quite undetected.

Powerful minds are sometimes snared by this fallacy—as may be illustrated by a highly controversial issue in the history of philosophy. Logicians have long sought to establish the reliability of inductive procedures by establishing the truth of what is called "the principle of induction." This is the principle that the laws of nature will operate tomorrow as they operate today, that in basic ways nature is essentially uniform, and that therefore we may rely upon past experience to guide our conduct in the future. "That the future will be essentially like the past" is the claim at issue—but this claim, never doubted in ordinary life, turns out to be very difficult to prove. Yet some thinkers have claimed that they could prove it by showing that, when we have in the past relied upon the inductive principle, we have always found that this method has helped us to achieve our objectives. They ask: why conclude that the future will be like the past? Because it always has been like the past.

But, as David Hume pointed out, this common argument is a *petitio*, it begs

[7]Richard Whately, *Elements of Logic* (London, 1826).

the question. For the point at issue is whether nature *will continue* to behave regularly; that it *has* done so in the past cannot serve as proof that it *will* do so in the future—unless one assumes the very principle that is here in question: that the future will be like the past! And so Hume, granting that in the past the future has been like the past, asks the telling question with which philosophers still tussle: How can we know that future futures will be like past futures? They may be so, of course—but we may not *assume* that they will for the sake of *proving* that they will.[8]

9, 10, and 11. The Appeals to Emotion, to Pity, and to Force: Arguments *ad Populum, ad Misericordiam,* and *ad Baculum*

These three fallacies, although common enough, are also so evidently fallacious as to require little explanation here. In each case the premises are plainly not relevant to the conclusion, but are deliberately chosen as instruments with which to manipulate the beliefs of the listener or reader.

The argument *ad populum,* the appeal to emotion, is the device of every propagandist and every demagogue. It is fallacious because it replaces the laborious task of presenting evidence and rational argument with expressive language and other devices calculated to excite enthusiasm, excitement, anger or hate. The speeches of Adolph Hitler, which brought his German listeners to a state of patriotic frenzy, may be taken as a classic example. Love of country is an honorable emotion; the use of that love to manipulate one's audience is intellectually disreputable—hence the saying (itself manifesting the fallacy of converse accident) that "patriotism is the last refuge of a scoundrel."

Those who rely most heavily upon arguments *ad populum* are now to be found in advertising agencies, where the use of that fallacy has been elevated almost to the status of a fine art. Every attempt is made to associate some product being advertised with things of which we can be expected to approve strongly, or which excite us favorably. The breakfast cereal is associated with trim youthfulness, athletic prowess, and vibrant good health; whiskey is associated with luxury and achievement, and beer with high adventure; the automobile to be sold is associated with romance, riches and sex. Every device, appealing to sight and sound and smell, is brought to bear: the men who use the advertised product are clear-eyed, broad-shouldered and distinguished; the women are slim, lovely, very well-dressed—or hardly dressed at all. Advertisers, as we know well, often sell us daydreams and delusions of grandeur. So clever and persistent are the ballyhoo artists of our time that all of us are influenced in spite of our resolution to resist. In one way or another the hucksters penetrate our consciousness, even our subconscious

[8]See David Hume, "Sceptical Doubts Concerning the Operations of the Understanding," in *An Enquiry Concerning Human Understanding* (1747), Section IV.

thoughts, manipulating us to their purposes with relentless appeals to emotions of every kind.

Of course, the mere association of the product and the emotion is, by itself, no argument—but an argument *ad populum* commonly lies not far beneath the surface. When advertisers make claims about their product designed to win our emotional approval, and when it is suggested that we ought to make the purchase *because* the item in question is "new" or "sexy" or "best-selling," or is associated with wealth or power—the implicit claim that this conclusion follows from those premises is plainly fallacious. The widespread appeal of certain products does not prove them to be satisfactory; the popular acceptance of a policy does not show it to be wise; the fact that a great many people hold a given opinion does not prove it to be true. Bertrand Russell has condemned such argument in language almost too vigorous:

> The fact that an opinion has been widely held is no evidence whatever that it is not utterly absurd; indeed in view of the silliness of the majority of mankind, a wide-spread belief is more likely to be foolish than sensible.[9]

The argument *ad misericordiam*, the appeal to pity, may be viewed as a special case of the appeal to emotion, in which the altruism and mercy of the audience are the special emotions appealed to. When civil damages are sought, in court, for injury allegedly the fault of the defendant, the plaintiff's attorney will often arrange to have his client's injury exhibited to the jury in the most heart-rending way. Jury sympathy for a defendant has no bearing whatever upon the guilt or innocence of the accused—but no defense attorney will fail to appeal to the pity of the jury to the extent circumstances allow. Sometimes that appeal will be made obliquely. At his trial in Athens Socrates refers with disdain to other defendants who have appeared before their juries accompanied by their children and families, seeking to be acquitted by evoking pity—whereupon Socrates then continues:

> . . . I, who am probably in danger of my life, will do none of these things. The contrast may occur to his [each juror's] mind, and he may be set against me, and vote in anger because he is displeased at me on this account. Now if there be such a person among you—mind, I do not say that there is—to him I may fairly reply: My friend, I am a man, and like other men, a creature of flesh and blood, and not 'of wood or stone' as Homer says; and I have a family, yes, and sons, O Athenians, three in number, one almost a man, and two others who are still young; and yet I will not bring any of them here to petition you for acquittal.[10]

There are many ways to pull heart strings, and virtually all will be tried. The argument *ad misericordiam* is ridiculed in the story of the trial of a youth accused of the murder of his mother and father with an ax. Confronted with overwhelming proof of his guilt, he pleaded for leniency on the grounds that he was an orphan.

---

[9]Bertrand Russell, *Marriage and Morals* (New York: Horace Liveright, 1929), p. 58.
[10]Plato, *Apology*, No. 34; Jowett Translation, Vol. I, p. 417.

The argument *ad baculum*, the appeal to force to cause the acceptance of some conclusion, seems at first to be so obvious a fallacy as to need no discussion at all. The use or threat of "strong-arm methods" to coerce opponents would seem to be a last resort—a useful expedient when evidence or rational methods fail. "Might makes right" is hardly a subtle principle.

But, in fact, there are occasions when arguments *ad baculum* are employed with considerable subtlety. The arguer may not threaten directly, and yet may convey a veiled threat, or a possible threat in a form calculated to win the assent (or at least the support) of those imperiled. While Edward Meese, then Attorney General in the Reagan administration, was under strong attack in the press for misconduct, the White House Chief of Staff, Howard Baker, opened one meeting of his staff (according to a report in *The Washington Post*) by saying:

> The President continues to have confidence in the Attorney General and I have confidence in the Attorney General and you ought to have confidence in the Attorney General, because we work for the President and because that's the way things are. And if anyone has a different view of that, or any different motive, ambition, or intention, he can tell me about it because we're going to have to discuss your status.[11]

One may say that nobody is fooled by argument of this sort; the threatened party may *behave* appropriately, but need not, in the end, accept the *truth* of the conclusion insisted upon. To this it was answered, by philosophers of twentieth-century Italian fascism, that real persuasion can come through many different instruments—of which reason is one and the blackjack is another. But once the opponent is truly persuaded, they held, the instrument of persuasion may be forgotten. That fascist view appears to guide many of the governments of the globe to this day; but the argument *ad baculum*— reliance upon the blackjack, or upon the threat of force in any form—is by reason unacceptable. The appeal to force is the abandonment of reason.

X. Irrelevant Conclusion—*Ignoratio Elenchi*

The fallacy of *ignoratio elenchi* is committed when an argument purporting to establish a particular conclusion is instead directed to proving a different conclusion. The premises "miss the point"—the reasoning may seem plausible in itself, and yet the argument misfires as a defense of the conclusion in dispute. Arguments in the sphere of social legislation frequently commit this fallacy; a program of a particular kind, designed to achieve some larger objective that is widely shared, is supported by premises that do give reason to share the larger end, but tell us nothing relevant about the specific program under consideration. Sometimes this is deliberate; sometimes it is the result of passionate concern for the larger objective, which blinds some advocates of the more specific proposal to the irrelevance of their premises.

[11]"White House Orders Silence on Meese," *The Honolulu Advertiser*, April 29, 1988, p. D-1.

For example: Particular tax reforms are sometimes defended by emphasizing the need to reduce budget deficits—when the real issue is the fairness or yield of the specific tax measure proposed; special programs to support the building industry, or the automobile industry, are defended with premises that may support the need for assistance, but do not support the need for the kind or amount of assistance the program at issue would provide. When the issue is the wisdom of developing a new and very expensive weapon system, the premises will miss the point if they simply underscore the need for a strong national defense. Whether the weapon system proposed is the one we really need and want is likely to be the real question. Objectives that are stated in very general terms—national security, good housing, a balanced budget—are easy to endorse; the hard questions are likely to be: Will this particular measure promote the end sought, and if so, will it do so better— more efficiently or more effectively—than the available alternatives? Bypassing these questions, by obscuring the issue with attractive generalizations about some larger or different end, commits the *ignoratio elenchi*.

How do such arguments ever fool anyone? They do so in several ways, and in fact are very common. They entrap as a result of inattention; by urging with enthusiasm the need for the objective actually defended by the premisses, the advocate often succeeds in transferring that enthusiasm, in the minds of his audience, to the specific means fallaciously supported. The *ignoratio elenchi* is also effective as a rhetorical device when it is framed in highly emotional language, thus concealing the misfire with an *ad populum* appeal. But emotion is not the essence of this fallacy; even if the language used be cool and neutral, it is an *ignoratio elenchi* when its real thrust is a conclusion different from the one at issue in the argument.

It may be said that every Fallacy of Relevance (except the begging of the question) is, in a sense, an *ignoratio elenchi*. But as we use this term, it is the fallacy in which the argument misses the point without necessarily making one of those mistakes—of false cause, or misplaced authority, or *ad hominem* attack, etc.—that characterize the other fallacies based on irrelevance.

The term *non sequitur* is also often applied to arguments that commit a Fallacy of Relevance (again except for those that commit a *petitio principii*). It means simply that the stated conclusion does not follow from its premiss or premisses. Here is a recent example:

> "Veterans have always had a strong voice in our government," he [President Reagan] said all too accurately, adding the non sequitur: "It's time to give them the recognition they so rightly deserve."[12]

And a well-known conservative political commentator, condemning the illogic as well as the immorality of a recent book defending pederasty, gives another illustration of the *non sequitur*.

> "It is time. . . . " This incantation moves the modern mind: Change is natural, therefore change is progressive, therefore the natural progression of mankind is

[12]"The Department of Fat," *The New Republic*, January 4, 1988, p. 7

through expanding "emancipation" from "taboos" and other "hang-ups" that inhibit "self-fulfillment." The non sequiturs clang together like empty freight cars on a railroad to barbarism."[13]

EXERCISES

I. Identify the Fallacies of Relevance in the following passages and explain how each specific passage involves that fallacy or fallacies.

★ 1. All of us cannot be famous, because all of us cannot be well known.
—JESSE JACKSON, quoted by Elizabeth Drew, "A Political Journal,"
The New Yorker, March 12, 1984, p. 140

2. The sage expresses joy at things which properly call for joy, and anger at things which properly call for anger. Therefore the joy and anger of the sage are not connected with his mind, but with things.
—CH'ENG HAO, quoted in Fung Yu-lan, *A History of Chinese Philosophy*

3. As an academic, Professor Benedict J. Kerkvliet has given himself away as biased and unscientific . . . it is pathetic to see Professor Kerkvliet, a non-Filipino, deploring political and social conditions in a foreign country like the Philippines when his own country calls for social and moral regeneration.
—VINCENTE ROMERO, Consul General, Philippine consulate general,
letter to the editor, *The Honolulu Advertiser*, December 5, 1974

4. Why do I know more than other people? Why, in general, am I so clever? I have never pondered over questions that are not really questions. I have never wasted my strength.   —FRIEDRICH NIETZSCHE, *Ecce Homo*

★ 5. The Inquisition must have been justified and beneficial, if whole peoples invoked and defended it, if men of the loftiest souls founded and created it severally and impartially, and its very adversaries applied it on their own account, pyre answering to pyre.   —BENEDETTO CROCE, *Philosophy of the Practical*

6. "I'm all for women having equal rights," said Bullfight Association president Paco Camino. "But I repeat, women shouldn't fight bulls because a bullfighter is and should be a man."   —*San Francisco Chronicle*, March 28, 1972

7. In that melancholy book *The Future of an Illusion*, Dr. Freud, himself one of the last great theorists of the European capitalist class, has stated with simple clarity the impossibility of religious belief for the educated man of today.
—JOHN STRACHEY, *The Coming Struggle for Power*

8. "But I observe," says Cleanthes, "with regard to you, Philo, and all speculative sceptics, that your doctrine and practice are as much at variance in the most abstruse points of theory as in the conduct of common life."
—DAVID HUME, *Dialogues Concerning Natural Religion*

9. On the Senate floor in 1950, Joe McCarthy announced that he had penetrated "Truman's iron curtain of secrecy." He had 81 case histories of persons whom he considered to be Communists in the State Department. Of Case 40, he said, "I do not have much information on this except the general statement of

---

[13]George F. Will, "The Incest Lobby," in *The Pursuit of Virtue and Other Tory Notions* (New York: Simon and Schuster, Inc., 1982), pp 65–66.

the agency that there is nothing in the files to disprove his Communist connections."   —RICHARD H. ROVERE, *Senator Joe McCarthy*

★ 10. When Rodger Babson, whose prediction of the great stock market crash brought him renown, became ill with tuberculosis, he returned to his home in Massachusetts rather than follow his doctor's advice to remain in the West. During the freezing winter he left the windows open, wore a coat with a heating pad in back, and had his secretary wear mittens and hit the typewriter keys with rubber hammers. Babson got well and attributed his cure to fresh air. Air from pine woods, according to Babson, has chemical or electrical qualities (or both) of great medicinal value.

—MARTIN GARDNER, *Fads and Fallacies in the Name of Science*

11. According to R. Grunberger, author of *A Social History of the Third Reich,* published in Britain, the Nazis used to send the following notice to German readers who let their subscriptions lapse: "Our paper certainly deserves the support of every German. We shall continue to forward copies of it to you, and hope that you will not want to expose yourself to unfortunate consequences in the case of cancellation."   —*Parade,* May 9, 1971

12. . . . it is only when it is believed that I could have acted otherwise that I am held to be morally responsible for what I have done. For a man is not thought to be morally responsible for an action that it was not in his power to avoid.
—ALFRED J. AYER, "Freedom and Necessity," *Polemic,* No. 5, 1946

13. But can you doubt that air has weight when you have the clear testimony of Aristotle affirming that all the elements have weight including air, and excepting only fire?   —GALILEO GALILEI, *Dialogues Concerning Two New Sciences*

14. There is no such thing as a leaderless group. Though the style and function of leadership will differ with each group and situation, a leader or leaders will always emerge in a task-oriented group or the task is simply never accomplished.
—*Ms,* September 1976

★ 15. I testify unto every man that heareth the words of the prophecy of this book, If any man shall add unto these things, God shall add unto him the plagues that are written in this book: And if any man shall take away from the words of the book of this prophecy, God shall take away his part out of the book of life, and out of the holy city, and *from* the things which are written in this book.
—Revelation 22:18–19

16. Benjamin Fernandez, a candidate for the Republican presidential nomination, was born in a converted boxcar in Kansas City, to Mexican immigrants, 53 years ago. When asked why he is a Republican, he says that when he was in college in California, someone told him the Republican Party was the party of rich people. "And I said, 'Sign me up! I've had enough poverty.' "
—GEORGE F. WILL, *Washington Post,* August 23, 1979

17. Like an armed warrior, like a plumed knight, James G. Blaine marched down the halls of the American Congress and threw his shining lances full and fair against the brazen foreheads of every defamer of his country and maligner of its honor.

For the Republican party to desert a gallant man now is worse than if an army should desert their general upon the field of battle.
—ROBERT G. INGERSOLL, nominating speech at the
Republican National Convention, 1876

18. For, if the distinction of degrees is infinite, so that there is among them no degree than which no higher can be found, our course of reasoning reaches this conclusion: that the multitude of natures themselves is not limited by any bounds. But only an absurdly foolish man can fail to regard such a conclusion as absurdly foolish. There is, then, necessarily some nature which is so superior to some nature or natures, that there is none in comparison with which it is ranked as inferior.   —ST. ANSELM, *Monologium*, Chapter VI

19. A press release from the National Education Association (NEA) distributed in November begins with the following statement: "America's teachers see smaller classes as the most critical element in doing a better job, a survey by the NEA indicates." . . .

But the NEA, of course, is interested in having as many teachers in the schools as possible. For example, in a 3,000-pupil school system with 30 pupils assigned to each class, the teaching staff would be approximately 100. But if class size were changed to 25 the total number of teachers would rise to 120. And in a time of shrinking enrollments, that is a way to keep teachers on the public payroll. . . .

It is unfortunate that an organization with the professional reputation the National Education Association enjoys should be so self-serving.

   —CYNTHIA PARSONS, *Christian Science Monitor Service*, February 1976

★ 20. I was seven years old when the first election campaign, which I can remember, took place in my district. At that time we still had no political parties, so the announcement of this campaign was received with very little interest. But popular feeling ran high when it was disclosed that one of the candidates was "the Prince." There was no need to add Christian and surname to realize which Prince was meant. He was the owner of the great estate formed by the arbitrary occupation of the vast tracts of land reclaimed in the previous century from the Lake of Fucino. About eight thousand families (that is, the majority of the local population) are still employed today in cultivating the estate's fourteen thousand hectares. The Prince was deigning to solicit "his" families for their vote so that he could become their deputy in parliament. The agents of the estate, who were working for the Prince, talked in impeccably liberal phrases: "Naturally," said they, "naturally, no one will be forced to vote for the Prince, that's understood; in the same way that no one, naturally, can force the Prince to allow people who don't vote for him to work on his land.

   —IGNAZIO SILONE, *The God That Failed*

21. The following is quoted from F. L. Wellman, *The Art of Cross Examination* (New York: Macmillan Publishing Company, Inc., 1946). The conclusion here, it should be noted, is implied rather than explicitly drawn.

A very well-known doctor had given important testimony in a case where his most intimate friend appeared as opposing counsel. These two men—doctor and lawyer—stood equally high in their respective professions, and had been close friends for many years and were frequent dinner companions at one another's homes, with their wives and children. In fact, they had practically grown up together. The lawyer knew that his friend had testified to his honest opinion, which no amount of cross-examination could weaken. He therefore confined himself to the following few interrogations; and, fearing that he could not keep a straight face while he put his questions, he avoided facing the witness at all, keeping his face turned toward a side window.

Q. Doctor, you say you are a practicing physician. Have you practiced your profession in the City of Chicago for any length of time?"

A. "Yes, I have been in practice here in Chicago now for about forty years."

Q. "Well, doctor, during that time I presume you have had occasion to treat some of our most prominent citizens. Have you not?"

A. "Yes, I think I have."

Q. "By any chance, doctor, were you ever called as a family physician to prescribe for the elder Marshall Field?"

A. "Yes, I was his family physician for a number of years."

Q. "By the way, I haven't heard of him lately. Where is he now?" (Still looking out of the window.)

A. "He is dead."

Q. "Oh—I'm sorry. Were you ever the family physician to the elder Mr. McCormick?"

A. "Yes, also for many years."

Q. "Would you mind my asking where he is now?"

A. "He is dead."

Q. "Oh—I'm sorry."

Then he proceeded in the same vein to make inquiries about eight or ten of the leading Chicago citizens whom he knew his friend had attended, all of whom were dead, and having exhausted the list he sat down quietly amid the amused chuckles of the jurors with the comment: "I don't think it is necessary to ask you any more questions. Please step down."

II. Identify any Fallacies of Relevance in the following passages and explain how the argument in question involves that fallacy.

★ 1. The story is told about Wendell Phillips, the abolitionist, who one day found himself on the same train with a group of Southern clergymen on their way to a conference. When the Southerners learned of Phillips's presence, they decided to have some fun at his expense. One of them approached and said, "Are you Wendell Phillips?"

"Yes, sir," came the reply.

"Are you the great abolitionist?"

"I am not great, but I am an abolitionist."

"Are you not the one who makes speeches in Boston and New York against slavery?"

"Yes, I am."

"Why don't you go to Kentucky and make speeches there?"

Phillips looked at his questioner for a moment and then said, "Are you a clergyman?"

"Yes, I am," replied the other.

"Are you trying to save souls from hell?"

"Yes."

"Well—why don't you go there?"

2. . . . we must accept the traditions of the men of old time who affirm themselves to be the offspring of the gods—that is what they say—and they must surely have known their own ancestors. How can we doubt the word of the children of the gods?   —PLATO, *Timaeus*

3. The Master said, [the good man] does not grieve that other people do not recognize his merits. His only anxiety is lest he should fail to recognize theirs.
                                    —CONFUCIUS, *The Analects*

4. However, it matters very little now what the king of England either says or does; he hath wickedly broken through every moral and human obligation, trampled nature and conscience beneath his feet, and by a steady and constitutional spirit of insolence and cruelty procured for himself an universal hatred.

—THOMAS PAINE, *Common Sense*

★ 5. Just as some penalty deters a prospective offender by making the prospect of crime less attractive, so does a more severe penalty make crime still less attractive, and so less likely to occur. Because death is perceived by most potential law breakers as the maximum feasible penalty, it is probably the most effective deterrent force. —FRANK G. CARRINGTON, *Neither Cruel Nor Unusual*

6. In a motion picture featuring the famous French comedian Sacha Guitry some thieves are arguing over division of seven pearls worth a king's ransom. One of them hands two to the man on his right, then two to the man on his left. "I," he says, "will keep three." The man on his right says, "How come you keep three?" "Because I am the leader." "Oh. But how come you are the leader?" "Because I have more pearls."

7. Although physicians and hospital administrators are often blamed for the rising cost of medical care, the fact is that the character of hospital services has changed. New surgical techniques like transplantation, new kinds of equipment like the CAT Scanner and new diagnostic and therapeutic modes that are prolonging life for patients with once-terminal diseases have increased the costs of hospital care.

—GERALDINE ALPERT and MARSHA HURST, "A Plague on Our Hospitals," *The Nation*, June 14, 1980

8. While General Grant was winning battles in the West, President Lincoln received many complaints about Grant's being a drunkard. When a delegation told him one day that Grant was hopelessly addicted to whiskey, the President is said to have replied: "I wish General Grant would send a barrel of whiskey to each of my other Generals!"

9. The free market . . . responds to shortages by increases in prices. But it spurs others to enter that area because of the lure of profit, and thus benefits the consumer as the price comes down when supply increases.

—JOHN HOSPERS, "Free Enterprise as the Embodiment of Justice"

★ 10. Kenneth Robinson, when he was Great Britain's minister of health, told Parliament that Scientology was "potentially harmful" and "a potential menace."
Elliott, the local minister of the Church of Scientology, was asked to comment on those criticisms. Of the remarks made before Parliament, he said: "I am afraid Mr. Robinson has since suffered two demotions and was just in the last few weeks quietly released from the Wilson Administration altogether."

—*Honolulu Advertiser*, November 22, 1969

11. To put it briefly, then, we can maintain that natural reason cannot prove that the resurrection is necessary, neither by way of *a priori* reasons such as those based on the notion of the intrinsic principle in man, nor by *a posteriori* arguments, for instance, by reason of some operation or perfection fitting to man. Hence we hold the resurrection to be certain on the basis of faith alone.

—DUNS SCOTUS, *Oxford Commentary on the Sentences of Peter Lombard*

12. To the industrial democracies peace appears as a naturally attainable condition; it is the composition of differences, the absence of struggle. To the Soviet

leaders, by contrast, struggle is ended not by compromise but by the victory of one side. Permanent peace, according to Communist theory, can be achieved only by abolishing the class struggle and the class struggle can be ended only by a Communist victory. Hence, any Soviet move, no matter how belligerent, advances the cause of peace, while any capitalist policy, no matter how conciliatory, serves the ends of war.   —HENRY KISSINGER, *White House Years*

13. . . . it is impossible to talk or think at all without employing general concepts: without them, cognition and language are impossible.
                    —DANIEL CALLAHAN, "The WHO Definition of 'Health,' "
                         The Hastings Center Studies, Vol. 1, No. 3, 1973

14. ". . . I've always reckoned that looking at the new moon over your left shoulder is one of the carelessest and foolishest things a body can do. Old Hank Bunker done it once, and bragged about it; and in less than two years he got drunk and fell off of the shot tower, and spread himself out so that he was just a kind of a layer, as you may say; and they slid him edgeways between two barn doors for a coffin, and buried him so, so they say, but I didn't see it. Pap told me. But anyway it all come of looking at the moon that way, like a fool."
                    —MARK TWAIN, *The Adventures of Huckleberry Finn*

★ 15. Mr. Quintus Slide was now, as formerly, the editor of the *People's Banner*, but a change had come over the spirit of his dream. His newspaper was still the *People's Banner*, and Mr. Slide still professed to protect the existing rights of the people, and to demand new rights for the people. But he did so as a Conservative. . . . It became Mr. Slide's duty to speak of men as heaven-born patriots whom he had designated a month or two since as bloated aristocrats and leeches fattened on the blood of the people. Of course remarks were made by his brethren of the press, —remarks which were intended to be very unpleasant. One evening newspaper took the trouble to divide a column of its own into double columns, printing on one side of the inserted line remarks made by the *People's Banner* in September respecting the Duke of ———, and the Marquis of ———, and Sir ———, which were certainly very harsh; and on the other side remarks equally laudatory as to the characters of the same titled politicians. But a journalist, with the tact and experience of Mr. Quintus Slide, knew his business too well to allow himself to be harassed by any such small stratagem as that. He did not pause to defend himself, but boldly attacked the meanness, the duplicity, the immorality, the grammar, the paper, the type, and the wife of the editor of the evening newspaper. In the storm of wind in which he rowed it was unnecessary for him to defend his own conduct. "And then," said he at the close of a very virulent and successful article, "the hirelings of ——— dare to accuse me of inconsistency!" The readers of the *People's Banner* all thought that their editor had beaten his adversary out of the field.   —ANTHONY TROLLOPE, *Phineas Redux*

16. Nietzsche was personally more philosophical than his philosophy. His talk about power, harshness, and superb immorality was the hobby of a harmless young scholar and constitutional invalid.
                    —GEORGE SANTAYANA, *Egotism in German Philosophy*

17. Appeals are riskless for the defendant: penalties cannot be increased nor partial acquittals overturned. The prosecution cannot appeal. This makes it safe for judges to help produce acquittals if they so want. At any rate, they become defense-minded: if a judge errs against the defendant, an appeal is likely and he may be overruled. If he errs against the prosecution, the judge is safe. No appeal

is possible. Hence, when in doubt, it is in the judge's interest to rule for the defense.   —ERNEST VAN DEN HAAG, *Punishing Criminals*

18. When you spend the money you yourself have worked to earn, you are likely to exercise some care in how you spend it; you know that it will take lots of work to replace what you spend.

—JOHN HOSPERS, "Free Enterprise as the Embodiment of Justice"

19. If we must not act save on a certainty, we ought not to act on religion, for it is not certain.   —BLAISE PASCAL, *Pensées*

★ 20. There is no such thing as knowledge which cannot be carried into practice, for such knowledge is really no knowledge at all.

—WANG SHOU-JEN, *Record of Instructions*

21. ANYTUS: "Socrates, I think that you are too ready to speak evil of men: and, if you will take my advice, I would recommend you to be careful. Perhaps there is no city in which it is not easier to do men harm than to do them good, and this is certainly the case at Athens, as I believe that you know."

—PLATO, *Meno*

3.3 *Fallacies of Ambiguity*

Arguments sometimes fail because their formulation contains ambiguous words or phrases, whose meanings shift and change within the course of the argument, thus rendering it fallacious. These are the fallacies of ambiguity— *sophisms*, as they are sometimes called—and while they are often crude and easily detected, they can at times prove subtle and dangerous. Five varieties are distinguished below.

1. Equivocation

Most words have more than one literal meaning, and most of the time we have no difficulty in keeping these meanings apart, using the context and our good sense in reading and listening. Sometimes the several meanings of a word of phrase become confused—accidentally or deliberately—and in such a case the word is being used *equivocally*. If we do that in the context of an argument, we commit the fallacy of equivocation.

Sometimes the equivocation is obvious, absurd, and used in a joking line or passage. Lewis Carroll's account of the adventures of Alice in *Through the Looking Glass* is replete with clever and amusing equivocations. One of them goes like this:

"Who did you pass on the road?" the King went on, holding his hand out to the messenger for some hay.
"Nobody," said the messenger.
"Quite right," said the King; "this young lady saw him too. So of course Nobody walks slower than you."

The equivocation here is more subtle and complex than at first it may appear. The first use of the word "nobody" (meaning "no person") is replaced by the second use of it, as a name, "Nobody." Then the name is used again, but as having a characteristic—not being passed on the road—derived from the first use of the word. The witty conclusion is then drawn using the word once again to mean "no person." Lewis Carroll, of course, was a very accomplished logician!

Equivocal arguments are always fallacious, but they are not alway silly or comic—as will be seen in the example discussed in the following excerpt from *An Atheist's Values*, by Richard Robinson:

> There is an ambiguity in the phrase "have faith in" that helps to make faith look respectable. When a man says that he has faith in the president he is assuming that it is obvious and known to everybody that there is a president, that the president exists, and he is asserting his confidence that the president will do good work on the whole. But, if a man says he has faith in telepathy, he does not mean that he is confident that telepathy will do good work on the whole, but that he believes that telepathy really occurs sometimes, that telepathy exists. Thus the phrase "to have faith in x" sometimes means to be confident that good work will be done by x, who is assumed or known to exist, but at other times means to believe that x exists. Which does it mean in the phrase "have faith in God"? It means ambiguously both; and the selfevidence of what it means in the one sense recommends what it means in the other sense. If there is a perfectly powerful and good god it is self-evidently reasonable to believe that he will do good. In this sense "have faith in God" is a reasonable exhortation. But it insinuates the other sense, namely "believe that there is a perfectly powerful and good god, no matter what the evidence." Thus the reasonableness of trusting God if he exists is used to make it seem also reasonable to believe that he exists.

There is a special kind of equivocation that deserves special mention. This has to do with "relative" terms, which have different meanings in different contexts. For example, the word "tall" is a relative word; a tall man and a tall building are in quite different categories. A tall man is one who is taller than most men, a tall building is one that is taller than most buildings. Certain forms of argument that are valid for nonrelative terms break down when relative terms are substituted for them. The argument "an elephant is an animal; therefore a gray elephant is a gray animal" is perfectly valid. The word "gray" is a nonrelative term. But the argument "an elephant is an animal; therefore a small elephant is a small animal" is ridiculous. The point here is that "small" is a relative term: a small elephant is a very large animal. The fallacy is one of equivocation on the relative term "small." Not all equivocation on relative terms is so obvious, however. The word "good" is a relative term and is frequently equivocated on when it is argued, for example, that so-and-so is a good general and would therefore be a good president, or is a good scholar and must therefore be a good teacher.

2. Amphiboly

The Fallacy of Amphiboly occurs in arguing from premises whose formulations are ambiguous because of their grammatical construction. A statement is amphibolous when its meaning is indeterminate because of the loose or awkward way in which its words are combined. An amphibolous statement may be true on one interpretation and false on another. When it is stated as premiss with the interpretation that makes it true, and a conclusion is drawn from it on the interpretation that makes it false, then the Fallacy of Amphiboly has been committed.

Amphibolous utterances were the chief stock in trade of the ancient oracles. Croesus, the King of Lydia, is said to have consulted the Oracle of Delphi before beginning his war with the kingdom of Persia. "If Croesus went to war with Cyrus," came the oracular reply, "he would destroy a mighty kingdom." Delighted with this prediction, which he took to mean that he would destroy the mighty kingdom of Persia, he attacked, and was crushed by Cyrus, king of the Persians. His life having been spared, he complained bitterly to the Oracle, whose priests pointed out in reply that the Oracle had been entirely right: in going to war Croesus *had* destroyed a mighty kingdom—his own! Amphibolous statements make dangerous premisses. They are, however, seldom encountered in serious discussion.

What grammarians call "dangling" participles and phrases often present amphiboly of an entertaining sort, as in "The farmer blew out his brains after taking affectionate farewell of his family with a shotgun." And tid-bits in *The New Yorker* make acid fun of writers and editors who overlook careless amphiboly:

"Leaking badly, manned by a skeleton crew, one infirmity after another over-takes the little ship." (The *Herald Tribune*, Book Section)
Those game little infirmities!   —*The New Yorker*, November 8, 1958

3. Accent

An argument may prove deceptive, and invalid, when the shift of meaning within it arises from changes in the emphasis given to its words or parts. When a premiss relies for its apparent meaning upon one possible emphasis, but a conclusion is drawn from it which relies upon the meaning of the same words accented differently, the Fallacy of Accent is committed.

Consider, as illustration, the different meanings that can be given to the statement

We should not speak ill of our friends.

At least five distinct meanings—or more?—can be given to those eight words, depending upon which one of them is emphasized. When read without any undue stresses, the injunction is perfectly sound. If the conclusion is drawn from it, however, that we should feel free to speak ill of someone who is *not* our friend, then this conclusion follows only if the premiss has the meaning it acquires when its last word is accented. But when its last word is accented, it is no longer acceptable as a moral law, it has a different meaning, and it is in fact a different premiss. The argument is a case of the Fallacy of Accent. So too would be the argument that drew from the same premiss the conclusion that we are free to *work* ill upon our friends if only we do it silently. And similarly with the other fallacious inferences that suggest themselves. In the same light vein, depending upon how it is accented, the statement

Woman without her man would be lost

would be perfectly acceptable to either sex. But to infer the statement with one accent from the statement accented differently would be an instance of the Fallacy of Accent.

Accent is sometimes deliberately used in a seriously damaging way in quoting an author or document, by inserting (or deleting) italics to change the meaning of what had originally been written. Or, construing the Fallacy of Accent more broadly, distortion may be produced simply by pulling a quoted passage out of its context. Often a phrase or passage can be understood correctly only in its context, which makes clear the *sense* in which it is intended. The original author may have ironically meant the reverse of what the words appear to say.

Sometimes one discovers the deliberate omission, within a quotation, of a qualification made by the author, or of associated words that greatly change the meaning of the original. In a critical essay about conservative thinkers Sidney Blumenthal wrote (in 1985) about one such thinker, Gregory A. Fossedal, that "On the right, Fossedal is widely regarded as his generation's most promising journalist. . . ." A 1989 advertisement for a later book by Mr. Fossedal contained several "blurbs," including this one attributed to Mr. Blumenthal: "Many consider Fossedal the most promising journalist of his generation." The omission of the critic's phrase "on the right" very greatly distorts the sense of the original passage, leading the reader to draw a mistaken conclusion about the critic's judgment of the author. Mr. Blumenthal was understandably infuriated.[14]

Similarly, a theater critic who says of a new play that it is far from the funniest appearing on Broadway this year, may find himself quoted in an ad for the play, ". . . funniest appearing on Broadway this year"! To avoid such distortions, and the fallacies of accent that may be built upon them, the responsible writer must be scrupulously accurate in quotation, always indicating whether italics were in the original, indicating (with dots) whether passages have been omitted, and so on.

Physical devices are frequently used to mislead with accent, in print and with pictures. Sensational words in large letters, qualified sharply by other words in much smaller letters, appear in the headings of newspaper reports

---

[14]"You Write the Facts, I'll Write the Blurbs," *The New York Times*, April 18, 1989, p. 10. The original passage appeared in *The Washington Post*, November 22, 1985; the offending advertisement appeared in *The New Republic*, in March 1989. Mr. Fossedal subsequently apologized to Mr. Blumenthal.

so as to suggest fallacious arguments, deliberately, to the mind of the reader. For this reason one is well advised, before signing any contract, to give careful attention to the "small print." In political propaganda the misleading choice of a sensational heading, or the use of a clipped photograph, in what purports to be a factual report, will use accent shrewdly to encourage conclusions known by the propagandist to be false. An account that may not be an outright lie, may yet distort by accent in ways that are deliberately manipulative or dishonest.

In advertising such practices are not rare. A remarkably low price often appears in very large letters, followed by "and up" in tiny print. Wonderful bargains in airplane fares are followed by an asterisk, with a distant footnote explaining that that price is available only three months in advance for flights on Thursdays following a full moon, or that there may be other "applicable restrictions." Costly items with well-known brand names are advertised at very low price, with a small note elsewhere in the ad that "prices listed are for limited quantities in stock." Readers drawn into the store but unable to make the purchase at the advertised price may have been deliberately tricked. Accented passages, by themselves, are not strictly fallacies; they become embedded in fallacies when one interpretation of a phrase, flowing from its accent, is relied upon to draw a conclusion (e.g., that the plane ticket or brand item can be advantageously purchased at the listed price) that is not correct when account is taken of the misleading accent.

Even the literal truth can be used, by manipulating its placement, to deceive with accent. Disgusted with his first mate who was repeatedly inebriated on duty, the captain of a ship noted in the ship's log-book, almost every day, that "The mate was drunk today." The angry mate took his revenge. Keeping the log himself on a day the captain was ill, the mate recorded: "The captain was sober today."

4 and 5. Composition and Division

4. Composition

The term "Fallacy of Composition" is applied to both of two closely related types of invalid argument. The first may be described as reasoning fallaciously from the attributes of the parts of a whole to the attributes of the whole itself. A particularly flagrant example would be to argue that since every part of a certain machine is light in weight, the machine "as a whole" is light in weight. The error here is manifest when we consider that a very heavy machine may consist of a very large number of lightweight parts. Not all examples of this kind of fallacious composition are so obvious, however. Some are misleading. One may hear it seriously argued that since each scene of a certain play was a model of artistic perfection, the play as a whole was artistically perfect. But this is as much a Fallacy of Composition as it would be to argue that since every ship is ready for battle, the whole fleet must be ready for battle.

The other type of Composition Fallacy is strictly parallel to that just described. Here the fallacious reasoning is from attributes of the individual elements or members of a collection to attributes of the collection or totality of those elements. For example, it would be fallacious to argue that, because a bus uses more gasoline than an automobile, therefore all buses use more gasoline than all automobiles. This version of the Fallacy of Composition turns on a confusion between the "distributive" and the "collective" use of general terms. Thus although college students may enroll in no more than six different classes each semester, it is also true that college students enroll in hundreds of different classes each semester. This verbal conflict is easily resolved. It is true of college students, distributively, that each of them may enroll in no more than six classes each semester. This is a distributive use of the term in that we are speaking of college students taken singly, or severally. But it is true of college students, collectively, that they enroll in hundreds of different classes each semester. This is a collective use of the term in that we are speaking of college students all together, as a collection or totality. Thus buses use more gasoline than automobiles, distributively, but collectively automobiles use more gasoline than buses, because there are so many more of them.

This second kind of Composition Fallacy may be defined as the invalid inference that what may truly be predicated of a term distributively may also be truly predicated of the term collectively. Thus the atomic bombs dropped during World War II did more damage than did the ordinary bombs dropped—but only distributively. The matter is exactly reversed when the two kinds of bombs are considered collectively, because there were so many more bombs of the conventional type dropped than atomic ones. Ignoring this distinction in an argument would permit the Fallacy of Composition.

These two varieties of composition, although parallel, are really distinct, because of the difference between a mere collection of elements and a whole constructed out of those elements. Thus a mere collection of parts is no machine; a mere collection of bricks is neither a house nor a wall. A whole like a machine, a house, or a wall has its parts organized or arranged in certain definite ways. And since organized wholes and mere collections are distinct, so are the two versions of the Composition Fallacy, one proceeding invalidly to wholes from their parts, the other proceeding invalidly to collections from their members or elements.

5. Division

The Fallacy of Division is simply the reverse of the Fallacy of Composition. In it the same confusion is present but the inference proceeds in the opposite direction. As in the case of composition, two varieties of the Fallacy of Division may be distinguished. The first kind of division consists in arguing fallaciously that what is true of a whole must also be true of its parts. To argue that since a certain corporation is very important and Mr. Doe is an official of that corporation, therefore Mr. Doe is very important, is to commit the Fallacy of Division. This first variety of the Division Fallacy would be committed in any such argument, as in going from the premiss that a certain machine is heavy, or complicated, or valuable, to the conclusion that this or any other part of the machine must be heavy, or complicated, or valuable. To argue that a student must have a large room because it is located in a large dormitory would be still another instance of the first kind of Fallacy of Division.

The second type of Division Fallacy is committed when one argues from the attributes of a collection of elements to the attributes of the elements themselves. To argue that since university students study medicine, law, engineering, dentistry, and architecture, therefore each, or even any, university student studies medicine, law, engineering, dentistry, and architecture, would be to commit the second kind of Division Fallacy. It is true that university students, collectively, study all these various subjects, but false that university students, distributively, do so. Instances of this variety of the Fallacy of Division often look like valid arguments, for what is true of a class distributively is certainly true of each and every member. Thus the argument

> Dogs are carnivorous.
> Afghan hounds are dogs.
> Therefore Afghan hounds are carnivorous.

is perfectly valid. But although it closely resembles the foregoing, the argument

> Dogs are frequently encountered in the streets.
> Afghan hounds are dogs.
> Therefore Afghan hounds are frequently encountered in the streets.

is invalid, committing the Fallacy of Division. Some instances of division are obviously jokes, as when the classical example of valid argumentation

> Humans are mortal.
> ~~Socrates is a human.~~
> Therefore Socrates is mortal.

is parodied by the fallacious

> American Indians are disappearing.
> That man is an American Indian.
> Therefore that man is disappearing.

The old riddle "Why do white sheep eat more than black ones?" turns on the confusion involved in the Fallacy of Division. For the answer, "Because there are more of them," treats collectively what seemed to be referred to distributively in the question.

There are resemblances between the fallacies of Division and Accident, and also between the fallacies of Composition and Converse Accident. But these likenesses are only superficial, and an explanation of the real differences between the members of the two pairs will be helpful in understanding the errors committed in all four.

If we were to infer, from looking at one or two parts of a large machine, that because they happen to be well designed, every one of its many parts is well designed, we would commit the fallacy of Converse Accident—for what is true about one or two surely may not be true of all. If we were to examine every single part and find each carefully made, and from that infer that the entire machine was carefully made, we would also reason fallaciously, because however carefully the parts were produced, they may have been *assembled* awkwardly or carelessly. But here the fallacy is one of Composition. In Converse Accident one argues that some atypical members of a class have a specified attribute, and therefore that all members of the class, distributively, have that attribute; in Composition one argues that since each and every member of the class has that attribute, the class *itself* (collectively) has that attribute. The difference is great. In Converse Accident all predications are distributive, whereas in Composition the mistaken inference is from distributive to collective predication.

Similarly, Division and Accident are two distinct fallacies; their superficial resemblance hides the same kind of underlying difference. In Division we argue (mistakenly) that since the class itself has a given attribute, each of its members does also. Thus it is the fallacy of Division to conclude that because an army as a whole is nearly invincible, each of its units is nearly invincible. But in Accident we argue (also mistakenly) that because some rule applies in general there are no special circumstances in which it might not. Thus we commit the fallacy of Accident when we insist that a person should be fined for ignoring a "no swimming" sign when jumping into the water to rescue someone from drowning.

Ambiguity—a shift in the meanings of the terms used—lies at the heart of the fallacies of Composition and Division, as it does also at the heart of Equivocation, and Amphiboly and Accent. Wherever the words or phrases used may mean one thing in one part of the argument, and another thing in another part, and those meanings are deliberately or accidentally confounded, we may anticipate serious logical mistakes.

EXERCISES

I. Identify the Fallacies of Ambiguity in the following passages and explain how each specific passage involves that fallacy or fallacies.

*   1. Robert Toombs is reputed to have said, just before the Civil War, "We could lick those Yankees with cornstalks." When he was asked after the war what had gone wrong, he is reputed to have said, "It's very simple. Those damyankees refused to fight with cornstalks."

—E. J. KAHN, JR., "Profiles (Georgia)," *The New Yorker*, February 13, 1978

2. If the parts of the Universe are not accidental, how can the whole Universe be considered as the result of chance? Therefore the existence of the Universe is not due to chance. —MOSES MAIMONIDES, *The Guide for the Perplexed*

3. And to judge still better of the minute perceptions which we cannot distinguish in the crowd. I am wont to make use of the example of the roar or noise of the sea which strikes one when on its shore. To understand this noise as it is made, it would be necessary to hear the parts which compose this whole, i.e., the noise of each wave, although each of these little noises . . . would not be noticed if the wave which makes it were alone. For it must be that we are affected a little by the motion of this wave, and that we have some perception of each one of these noises, small as they are; otherwise we would not have that of a hundred thousand waves, since a hundred thousand nothings cannot make something. —GOTTFRIED LEIBNIZ, *New Essays Concerning Human Understanding*

4. . . . since it is impossible for an animal or plant to be indefinitely big or small, neither can its parts be such, or the whole will be the same.
—ARISTOTLE, *Physics*

* 5. Israeli Prime Minister Menachem Begin, who says he is giving away his $82,000 share of the Nobel Prize money, is perhaps the poorest head of government in the developed world. —*New Haven Register.*
Just give the news, please. —*The New Yorker*, March 5, 1979

6. . . . each person's happiness is a good to that person, and the general happiness, therefore, a good to the aggregate of all persons.
—JOHN STUART MILL, *Utilitarianism*

7. If the man who turnips cries
   Cry not when his father dies,
   'Tis a proof that he had rather
   Have a turnip than his father. —MRS. PIOZZI, *Anecdotes of Samuel Johnson*

8. Fallaci wrote her: "You are a bad journalist because you are a bad woman."
—ELIZABETH PEER, "The Fallaci Papers," *Newsweek*, December 1, 1980

9. A Worm-eating Warbler was discovered by Hazel Miller in Concord, while walking along the branch of a tree, singing, and in good view.
—*New Hampshire Audubon Quarterly*
That's our Hazel—surefooted, happy, and with just a touch of the exhibitionist.
—*The New Yorker*, July 2, 1979

* 10. . . . the universe is spherical in form . . . because all the constituent parts of the universe, that is the sun, moon, and the planets appear in this form.
—NICOLAUS COPERNICUS, "The New Idea of the Universe"

II. Identify any Fallacies of Ambiguity in the following passages and explain how the argument in question involves that fallacy.

* 1. Seeing that eye and hand and foot and every one of our members has some obvious function, must we not believe that in like manner a human being has a function over and above these particular functions?
—ARISTOTLE, *Nicomachean Ethics*

2. If there is a God, He is infinitely incomprehensible, since, having neither parts nor limits, He has no affinity to us. —BLAISE PASCAL, *Pensées*

3. Medical care is certainly very expensive, and therefore, for this reason alone, not equally available to all.

—LEON R. KASS, "The Pursuit of Health and the Right to Health," *The Public Interest*, Summer 1975

4. . . . a community should be governed by men and women who are elected by and responsible to the majority. Since judges are, for the most part, not elected, and since they are not, in practice, responsible to the electorate in the way legislators are, it seems to compromise that proposition when judges make law. —RONALD DWORKIN, *Taking Rights Seriously*

* 5. I've looked everywhere in this area for an instruction book on how to play the concertina without success.

—MRS. F. M., Myrtle Beach, S.C., *Charlotte* (N.C.) *Observer*.
You need no instruction. Just plunge ahead boldly.

—*The New Yorker*, February 21, 1977

6. . . . if your job is dirty or dangerous, we would ordinarily say you deserve a higher wage for performing it; and since people will not go into that line of work without additional incentive, the wages (on the free market) are indeed higher for such work.

—JOHN HOSPERS, Free Enterprise as the Embodiment of Justice"

7. No man will take counsel, but every man will take money: therefore money is better than counsel. —JONATHAN SWIFT

8. Beliefs transcending all possible tests by observation, self-observation, experiment, measurement, or statistical analysis are recognized as theological or metaphysical and therefore devoid of the type of meaning that we all associate with the knowledge-claims of common sense or factual science.

—HERBERT FEIGL, "Naturalism and Humanism," *American Quarterly*, Vol. 1, 1949

9. To press forward with a properly ordered wage structure in each industry is the first condition for curbing competitive bargaining; but there is no reason why the process should stop there. What is good for each industry can hardly be bad for the economy as a whole. —*Twentieth Century Socialism*

* 10. But space is nothing but a relation. For, in the first place, any space must consist of parts; and if the parts are not spaces, the whole is not space.

—F. H. BRADLEY, *Appearance and Reality*

11. Since it is the *understanding* that sets man above the rest of sensible beings, and gives him all the advantage and dominion which he has over them; it is certainly a subject, even for its nobleness, worth our labour to inquire into.

—JOHN LOCKE, *An Essay Concerning Human Understanding*

12. Tzu-kung said, "The gentleman is judged wise by a single word he utters; equally, he is judged foolish by a single word he utters. That is why one really must be careful of what one says." —CONFUCIUS, *The Analects*

13. Improbable events happen almost every day, but what happens almost every day is a very probable event. Therefore improbable events are very probable events.

14. Statutes and common law rules are often vague and must be interpreted before they can be applied to novel cases. Some cases, moreover, raise issues so

novel that they cannot be decided even by stretching or reinterpreting existing rules. So judges must sometimes make new law, either covertly or explicitly.
—RONALD DWORKIN, *Taking Rights Seriously*

* 15. All phenomena in the universe are saturated with moral values. And, therefore, we can come to assert that the universe for the Chinese is a moral universe. —THOME H. FANG, *The Chinese View of Life*

3.4 *Avoiding Fallacies*

Fallacies are pitfalls into which any of us may stumble in our reasoning. Just as danger signals are erected to warn travelers away from hazards on their route, so the labels for fallacies presented in this chapter may be regarded as so many danger signals posted to keep us away from the widespread quagmires of incorrect argument. Understanding these errors to which we are all prone, and developing the ability to analyze them and to name them, may very well help us to keep from becoming their victims. But there is no mechanical test for the fallacies, no sure way to avoid the traps that they set up.

To avoid the Fallacies of Relevance requires constant intellectual vigilance; we must be aware of the many different ways in which irrelevance can intrude. Our study of the various uses of language, in Chapter 2, will be helpful in this connection. A realization of the flexibility of language and the multiplicity of its uses will help to keep us from mistaking expressive uses of language for its informative uses. Sensitive to the weave of different functions, we are less likely to receive an exhortation to approve some proposition as though it were an argument that supports the truth of that proposition, or to treat an attack upon the speaker as an argument against his views.

It is when the gap between premises and conclusion is great, the error in reasoning blatant, that we are most likely to call the blunder a *non sequitur*. In a speech in Chicago in 1854, Abraham Lincoln said:

> It was a great trick among some public speakers to hurl a naked absurdity at his audience, with such confidence that they should be puzzled to know if the speaker didn't see some point of great magnitude in it which entirely escaped their observation. A neatly varnished sophism would be readily penetrated, but a great, rough, *non sequitur* was sometimes twice as dangerous as a well polished fallacy.[15]

But the Fallacies of Ambiguity, unlike the "great rough *non sequitur*," are often subtle. Words are slippery; most of them have a variety of different senses or meanings, which may be confused in fallacious reasoning. To avoid the various Fallacies of Ambiguity we must have and keep the meanings of our terms clearly in mind. One way to accomplish this is by defining the key terms that we use. Ambiguity can be avoided by the careful definition of terms, thereby warding off inadvertent shifts in meaning by ourselves, and

[15]Roy R. Bassler, ed., *The Collected Works of Abraham Lincoln* (New Brunswick, N.J.: Rutgers University Press, 1953), Vol. II, p. 283.

blocking the sometimes deliberate manipulation of meanings by others. For this reason *definition* is a matter of importance for the student of logic—and it is the topic to which our next chapter is devoted.

EXERCISES

Among the following passages identify those in which there is a fallacy; if there is a fallacy, analyze it, give its kind (whether of relevance or ambiguity) and its specific name, and explain the occurrence of that fallacy in the passage.

★ 1. Agatha Christie's second husband, Max Mallowan, was a distinguished archaeologist. Christie was once asked how she felt about being married to a man whose primary interest lay in antiquities.

"An archaeologist is the best husband any woman can have," she said. "The older she gets, the more interested he is in her."

— *The Honolulu Star-Bulletin*, November 23, 1987

2. After deciding to sell his home in Upland, California, novelist Whitney Stine pounded a 'For Sale' sign into his front yard. But he deliberately waited to do so until 2:22 P.M. one Thursday. The house sold three days later for his asking price—$238,000. And Mr. Stine credits the quick sale to the advice of his astrologer, John Bradford, whom he has consulted for 12 years in the sale of five houses.

"He always tells me the exact time to put out the sign according to the phases of the moon, and the houses have always sold within a few months," Mr. Stine says.   —"Thinking of Buying or Selling a House? Ask Your Astrologer," *The Wall Street Journal*, October 12, 1986

3. If you hold that nothing is self-evident, I will not argue with you for it is clear that you are a quibbler and are not to be convinced.

—DUNS SCOTUS, *Oxford Commentary on the Sentences of Peter Lombard*

4. . . . the greatest thing by far is to be a master of metaphor. It is the one thing that cannot be learned from others; and it is also a sign of genius, since a good metaphor implies an intuitive perception of the similarity in dissimilars.

—ARISTOTLE, *Poetics*, 22, 1459ᵃ 5–7

★ 5. Analysis . . . is the operation which reduces the object to elements already known, that is, to elements common both to it and other objects. To analyze, therefore, is to express a thing as a function of something other than itself.

—HENRI BERGSON, *An Introduction to Metaphysics*

6. Order is indispensable to justice because justice can be achieved only by means of a social and legal order.

—ERNEST VAN DEN HAAG, *Punishing Criminals*

7. The classic trap for any revolutionary is always "What's your alternative?" But even if you *could* provide the interrogator with a blueprint, this does not mean he would use it; in most cases he is not sincere in wanting to know.

—SHULAMITH FIRESTONE, *The Dialectic of Sex: The Case for Feminist Revolution*

8. William Butler, chief counsel for the Environmental Defense Fund, which led the attack on DDT between 1966 and 1972, repeats the argument today: "You can't prove a negative. . . . You can't say something doesn't exist because there's

always a chance that it does exist but nobody has seen it. Therefore you can't say something doesn't cause cancer because there's always the chance that it does cause cancer but it hasn't showed up yet. . . ."

—WILLIAM TUCKER, "Of Mice and Men," *Harper's Magazine*

9. When we had got to this point in the argument, and every one saw that the definition of justice had been completely upset, Thrasymachus, instead of replying to me, said: "Tell me, Socrates, have you got a nurse?"

"Why do you ask such a question," I said, "when you ought rather to be answering?"

"Because she leaves you to snivel, and never wipes your nose; she has not even taught you to know the shepherd from the sheep."   —PLATO, *Republic*

★ 10. Which is more useful, the Sun or the Moon? The Moon is more useful since it gives us light during the night, when it is dark, whereas the Sun shines only in the daytime, when it is light anyway.

—GEORGE GAMOW (inscribed in the entry hall of the Hayden Planetarium, New York City)

11. Most men marry a younger spouse and therefore it is not surprising that few men have married as teenagers in the past or today.

—P. LINDSAY CHASE LANSDALE and MARIS A. VINOVSKIS, "Should We Discourage Teenage Marriage?" *The Public Interest*, No. 87, Spring 1987, p. 24

12. Time heals all wounds. Time is money. Therefore money heals all wounds.

—"Ask Marilyn," *Parade*, April 12, 1987

13. Revelation is a communication of something which the person to whom that thing is revealed did not know before. For if I have done a thing or seen it done, it needs no revelation to tell me I have done it or seen it, or to enable me to tell it or to write it. Revelation, therefore, cannot be applied to anything done upon earth, of which man himself is the actor or the witness; and consequently, all the historical and anecdotal parts of the Bible, which is almost the whole of it, is not within the meaning and compass of the word revelation, and therefore is not the word of God.   —THOMAS PAINE, *The Age of Reason*, Part I, p. 13

14. Families are the means by which wealth is passed from one generation to another. Families that remain intact accumulate wealth. By contrast, single-parent families seem to accumulate little or no wealth. When last measured, black female heads of households with income under $11,000 had a median net worth of minus $18.   —DANIEL PATRICK MOYNIHAN, "Half the Nation's Children: Born Without a Fair Chance," *The New York Times*, September 25, 1988

★ 15. An outstanding person is always "out of step" in some respects. If he were entirely "in step" he would be no different from anyone else and hence, by definition, not outstanding.

—EDWARD SHILS, "More at Home Than out of Step," *The American Scholar*, Autumn 1987, p. 577

16. Mysticism is one of the great forces of the world's history. For religion is nearly the most important thing in the world, and religion never remains for long altogether untouched by mysticism.

—JOHN MCTAGGART ELLIS MCTAGGART, "Mysticism," *Philosophical Studies*

17. Mr. Stace says that my writings are "extremely obscure," and this is a matter as to which the author is the worst of all possible judges. I must therefore

accept his opinion. As I have a very intense desire to make my meaning plain, I regret this.

—BERTRAND RUSSELL, "Reply to Criticisms," in P. A. Schilpp, ed., *The Philosophy of Bertrand Russell* (Evanston, Ill.: The Library of Living Philosophers, Inc.), p. 707

18. For the benefit of those representatives who have not been here before this year, it may be useful to explain that the item before the General Assembly is that hardy perennial called the "Soviet item." It is purely a propaganda proposition, not introduced with a serious purpose of serious action, but solely as a peg on which to hang a number of speeches with view to getting them into the press of the world. This is considered by some to be very clever politics. Others, among whom the present speaker wishes to be included, consider it an inadequate response to the challenge of the hour.

—HENRY CABOT LODGE, speech to the United Nations General Assembly, November 30, 1953

19. The war-mongering character of all this flood of propaganda in the United States is admitted even by the American Press. Such provocative and slanderous aims clearly inspired today's speech by the United States Representative, consisting only of impudent slander against the Soviet Union, to answer which would be beneath our dignity. The heroic epic of Stalingrad is impervious to libel. The Soviet people in the battles at Stalingrad saved the world from the fascist plague and that great victory which decided the fate of the world is remembered with recognition and gratitude by all humanity. Only men dead to all shame could try to cast aspersions on the shining memory of the heroes of that battle.

—BARANOVSKY, speech to the United Nations General Assembly, November 30, 1953

★ 20. "We just don't know what the distribution of quality [in day care centers] is," says Dr. Alfred Kahn. . . . "And about 90 percent of the family day care in this country is underground. It's not licensed, it's not regulated, and you have to assume that a lot of it is very low quality. We have some excellent care, and the research shows that either kids gain or aren't hurt by day care. However, the research hasn't gone into places that aren't licensed and aren't standardized, so I would have to guess that there are a lot of terrible things out there."

—*The New York Times*, September 3, 1984

21. If Utilitarianism be true it would be one's duty to try to increase the numbers of a community, even though one reduced the average total happiness of the members, so long as the total happiness in the community would be in the least increased. It seems perfectly plain to me that this kind of action, so far from being a duty, would quite certainly be wrong.

—C. D. BROAD, *Five Types of Ethical Theory*, p. 250

22. I also admit that there are people for whom even the reality of the external world and the identifications leading to it constitute a grave problem. My answer is that I do not address *them*, but that I presuppose a minimum of reason in my readers.   —PAUL FEYERABEND, "Materialism and the Mind-Body Problem," *The Review of Metaphysics*

23. Whether we are to live in a future state, as it is the most important question which can possibly be asked, so it is the most intelligible one which can be expressed in language.   —JOSEPH BUTLER, "Of Personal Identity"

24. Furthermore, all philosophers commonly assign ''rational'' as the difference that properly defines man, meaning by ''rational'' that the intellective soul is an essential part of man. In fact, to put it briefly, no philosopher of any note can be found to deny this except that accursed Averroes in his commentary on De anima, Bk III, where his fantastic conception, intelligible neither to himself nor to others, assumes the intellective part of man to be a sort of separate substance united to man through the medium of sense images.

      —DUNS SCOTUS, *Oxford Commentary on the Sentences of Peter Lombard*

★ 25. Thomas Carlyle said of Walt Whitman that he thinks he is a big poet because he comes from a big country.

      —ALFRED KAZIN, ''The Haunted Chamber,'' *The New Republic,*
      June 23, 1986, p. 39.

4

Definition

Nothing new can ever be learned by analyzing definitions. Nevertheless, our existing beliefs can be set in order by this process, and order is an essential element of intellectual economy, as of every other. It may be acknowledged, therefore, that the books are right in making familiarity with a notion the first step toward clearness of apprehension, and the defining of it the second.
—CHARLES SANDERS PEIRCE

It is certainly praiseworthy to try to make clear to oneself as far as possible the sense one associates with a word. But here we must not forget that not everything can be defined.

—GOTTLOB FREGE

Since all terms that are defined are defined by means of other terms, it is clear that human knowledge must always be content to accept some terms as intelligible without definition, in order to have a starting-point for its definitions.

—BERTRAND RUSSELL

4.1 *Disputes, Verbal Disputes, and Definitions*

When two parties disagree—as we saw in Section 2.5—the disagreement may be about the facts, or it may be in their feelings about the facts. We called these disagreements in *belief* and disagreements in *attitude*. And of course the parties may disagree both in belief and in attitude. Genuine disagreements of either kind will not be resolved by definitions. Sometimes, however, a dispute arises when there is no genuine disagreement in either belief or attitude, the parties being in conflict only because they do not realize that they are using an ambiguous word or phrase in different senses. Such disputes we call *merely verbal*. They are not always easy to spot—but once recognized they can be resolved fairly easily by specifying the different senses in which the ambiguous term is being used.

Language is the principal tool with which we communicate; but when words are used carelessly or mistakenly what was intended to advance mutual understanding may in tact hinder it; our instrument becomes our burden. This can happen when the words used in discussion are *ambiguous,* or excessively *vague,* or *imprecise,* or *emotionally loaded.* Often much more than merely verbal issues are at stake. But sometimes the conflict turns on an unsuspected difference in the ways the parties are using some key term whose different senses are equally legitimate but must not be confused. Then it is useful to be able to specify or explain the different senses of the ambiguous term.

We distinguish three different kinds of disputes. The first is the obviously genuine variety, in which the parties explicitly and unambiguously disagree—either in their attitudes toward something, or in their beliefs about some question of fact. When the Yankees win the World Series, one party may say "That's great!" while another replies, "That's awful!" Nothing is likely to resolve that disagreement in attitude, but there is no argument about who won. Or one party may maintain that the Pacific entrance to the Panama Canal is farther east than the Atlantic entrance while the other party denies it; attitudes are not involved, and a good map will probably settle the controversy. A factual dispute may be *about* words—how a word is spelled, or pronounced, or used; or it may be *about* attitudes—for example, whether some third party is unfriendly or only shy. Facts may be linguistic or psychological as well as geographical or physical, and beliefs about such facts will vary. But a dispute of this first kind always involves some *genuine* disagreement, either in attitude or in belief.

A second kind of dispute is one that is merely verbal—where the presence of an ambiguous key term in the disputants' formulations of their beliefs conceals the fact that there is no real disagreement between them. A now classic example of such a dispute was given by William James in the second lecture in *Pragmatism.* He wrote:

> Some years ago, being with a camping party in the mountains, I returned from a solitary ramble to find every one engaged in a ferocious metaphysical dispute. The *corpus* of the dispute was a squirrel—a live squirrel supposed to be clinging to one side of a tree trunk; while over against the tree's opposite side a human being was imagined to stand. This human witness tries to get sight of the squirrel by moving rapidly round the tree, but no matter how fast he goes, the squirrel moves as fast in the opposite direction, and always keeps the tree between himself and the man, so that never a glimpse of him is caught. The resultant metaphysical problem is this: *Does the man go round the squirrel or not?* He goes round the tree, sure enough, and the squirrel is on the tree; but does he go round the squirrel? In the unlimited leisure of the wilderness, discussion had been worn threadbare. Everyone had taken sides and was obstinate; and the number on both sides were even. Each side, when I appeared, therefore appealed to me to make it a majority.[1]

Of course it is not hard to see—and this is James's point in telling the story—that between the two parties in this dispute there was no genuine disagreement. Attitudes toward the squirrel and the tree were neutral, and

[1]William James, *Pragmatism* (New York: Longmans, Green and Co., Inc., 1907).

all disputants fully understood and agreed upon all the facts of the case given. What then was at issue? In this case—as in other cases, sometimes—no more than words. James continues:

> "Which party is right," I said, "depends on what you practically mean by 'going round' the squirrel. If you mean passing from the north of him to the east, then to the south, then to the west, and then to the north of him again, obviously the man does go round him, for he occupies these successive positions. But if on the contrary you mean being first in front of him, then on the right of him, then behind him, then on his left, and finally in front again, it is quite obvious that the man fails to go round him, for by the compensating movements the squirrel makes, he keeps his belly turned toward the man all the time, and his back turned away. Make the distinction, and there is no occasion for any further dispute. You are both right and both wrong according as you conceive the verb 'go round' in one practical fashion or the other."[2]

No new facts were required to resolve this dispute, and none could possibly have helped to do so. What was needed was just what James supplied, a distinction between different meanings of a key term in the argument. With alternative definitions of the term "go round" the dispute evaporates; the disagreement was never genuine. Wherever disputes are *merely* verbal, we can resolve them by supplying the definitions that eliminate the critical ambiguity. In such circumstances we are exhibiting the fact that the parties are not truly opposed to one another; they may simply be defending *different* propositions using the *same* word or words in different senses or with different meanings, or they may be defending the *same* proposition using *different* words. Once the different meanings have been identified, and with them the different propositions that result from using them, nothing remains at issue between the parties.

But sometimes it happens that, while confusion stems in part from the parties' mutual misunderstanding of their uses of words or phrases, more is involved in the dispute than words alone. This third kind of dispute may be said to be apparently verbal but really genuine. In such a conflict, resolving the ambiguity will not settle the dispute, for there remains some genuine disagreement—possibly in belief, but more likely in attitude—that lies between them.

To illustrate: Two parties may dispute whether a given film, in which explicit sexual activity is depicted, should be banned as "pornography." One party insists that its explicitness makes it pornography, and wicked; the other party insists that in the light of its sensitivity and aesthetic merit it is true art and not pornography at all. These parties plainly disagree about the meaning of the word "pornography"—but if that verbal issue were cleared up, and some definition of pornography were accepted by both, thus eliminating all dispute over that verbal matter, it is very likely that they would remain in genuine disagreement in attitude toward that film.

These three kinds of disputes, then, can be summarily described as follows:

[2]Ibid.

In an obviously genuine dispute there is no ambiguity present and the disputers do disagree, in belief or attitude. In a merely verbal dispute there is ambiguity present, but no genuine disagreement at all. And in an apparently verbal dispute that is really genuine there is ambiguity present *and* the disputers disagree in attitude.

EXERCISE

I. Identify three disagreements in current political or social controversy which exhibit the features described in this section:

(1) a disagreement that is genuine.
(2) a disagreement that is merely verbal.
(3) a disagreement that is apparently verbal but really genuine.

Explain the disagreements in each case.

4.2 *Kinds of Definition and the Resolution of Disputes*

We have seen in the preceding section that definitions, by exposing and eliminating ambiguities, can effectively resolve disputes that are merely verbal. We also noted in Section 3.3 that to expose and avoid the fallacies of ambiguity, definition may be essential. Now we examine the *kinds* of definition, to see how definitions work in avoiding or correcting mistakes in reasoning.

Note first that definitions are always of symbols, for only symbols have meanings for definitions to explain. We can define the word "chair," since it has a meaning; but a chair itself we cannot define. We can sit on a chair, or paint it, or burn it, or describe it—but we cannot define it, since the chair itself is not a symbol that has a meaning to explain. Of course in expressing definitions we sometimes talk about the symbol, and sometimes about the thing referred to by the symbol. Thus we can equally well say either

> The word "triangle" means a plane figure enclosed by three straight lines.

or

> A triangle is (by definition) a plane figure enclosed by three straight lines.

Two technical terms are common and useful. The symbol being defined is called the *definiendum*; the symbol or group of symbols being used to explain the meaning of the definiendum is called the *definiens*. It would be a mistake to say that the definiens is the meaning of the definiendum; rather, it is another symbol, or group of symbols that, according to the definition, *has the same meaning* as the definiendum.

The principal use of definition, in reasoning, is the elimination of ambiguity. To this end, two kinds of definition are commonly used, the *stipulative* and the *lexical*.

1. Stipulative Definitions

One who introduces a new symbol has complete freedom to stipulate what meaning is to be given to it; the definition that arises from the deliberate assignment of a meaning is properly called *stipulative*. The term newly defined need not itself be entirely novel; it may be new only in the context in which the defining takes place. What are here called stipulative definitions have sometimes been referred to as "nominal" or "verbal" definitions.

New terms may be introduced by stipulation for a variety of reasons. Convenience is one reason; a single word may serve as "short for" many words in a cable code or message. Secrecy is another reason; the stipulation may be understood only by the sender and the receiver of the message. Economy in expression is a third reason; in the sciences especially there are many advantages to introducing a new and technical symbol defined to mean what would otherwise require a long sequence of familiar words for its expression. By doing so, the scientist economizes the space required for writing out reports and theories, and also the time involved. More important, there is a reduction in the amount of attention or mental energy required, for when a sentence or equation grows too long, its sense cannot easily be "taken in." Consider the economy on all counts achieved by the introduction of the exponent in mathematics. What is now written quite briefly as

$$A^{12} = B$$

would, prior to the adoption of the special symbol for exponentiation, have had to be expressed either by

$$A \times A \times A \times A \times A \times A \times A \times A \times A \times A \times A \times A = B$$

or by a sentence of ordinary language instead of a mathematical equation.

There is still another reason for the scientist's introduction of new symbols. The emotive suggestions of familiar words are often disturbing to one interested only in their literal or informative meanings. The introduction of new symbols, explicitly defined as having the same literal meanings as familiar ones, will free the investigator from the distraction of the latter's emotive associations. This advantage accounts for the presence of some curious words in modern psychology, such as Spearman's "g factor," for example, which is intended to convey the same descriptive meaning as the word "intelligence" but to share none of its emotional significance. And for the new terminology to be learned and used, the new symbols must have their meanings explained by definitions.

New words have also sometimes been introduced in philosophy to facilitate a neutral analysis of controversial matters. To refer narrowly to the content of sensory experience some recent philosophers have introduced the word "sensum" stipulatively, thus bypassing a venerable dispute over whether our experience of physical objects is direct or indirect. And the American philosopher, Charles Sanders Peirce, one of the originators of the philosophical movement called pragmatism, after becoming bitter about the careless way in which that word had been used, stipulated that his own view would henceforth be known as "pragmaticism"—which he said was a word ugly enough that no one would want to steal it!

A stipulative definition is neither true nor false, neither accurate nor inaccurate; in this respect it differs sharply from a dictionary definition. A symbol defined by a stipulative definition did not have that meaning prior to being given it by the definition. Hence its definition cannot be regarded as a statement or report that the definiendum and the definiens have the same meaning. They actually will have the same meaning for anyone who accepts the definition, but that is a consequence of the definition rather than a fact asserted by it. A stipulative definition should be regarded as a proposal or resolution to use the definiendum to mean what is meant by the definiens, or as a request or instruction to do so. In this sense a stipulative definition is directive rather than informative. Proposals may be rejected, requests refused, instructions disobeyed—but they are neither true nor false. So it is with stipulative definitions.

Of course, stipulative definitions may be evaluated on other grounds. A stipulation may be unusable because very obscure, or too complex. The stipulation itself may be arbitrary—as when the mathematician Edward Kasner stipulated that the number 1 followed by 100 zeros is to be called a "googol"— but whether that stipulation is clear or unclear, advantageous or disadvantageous, or serves the purposes for which it was introduced, are matters of fact. Stipulative definitions are not normally productive in resolving genuine disagreements; but by clarifying informative discourse, and by reducing the emotive role of language, they can help to avoid fruitless verbal conflict.

2. Lexical Definitions

Where the purpose of a definition is to eliminate ambiguity or to increase the vocabulary of the person for whom it is constructed, then if the term being defined is not new but has an established usage, the definition is *lexical* rather than stipulative. A lexical definition does not give its definiendum a meaning it hitherto lacked, but reports a meaning the definiendum already has. It is clear that a lexical definition may be either true or false. Thus the definition

> The word "mountain" means a large mass of earth or rock rising to a considerable height above the surrounding country.

is true; it is a true report of how English-speaking people use the word "mountain" (i.e., of what they mean by it). On the other hand, the definition

> The word "mountain" means a plane figure enclosed by three straight lines.

is false, being a false report of how English-speaking people use the word "mountain."

Here lies the important difference between stipulative and lexical definitions. Because a stipulative definition's definiendum has no meaning apart from or prior to the definition introducing it, that definition cannot be false (or true). But because the definiendum of a lexical definition *does* have a prior and independent meaning, its definition is either true or false, depending upon whether that meaning is correctly or incorrectly reported. What we are calling lexical definitions have sometimes been referred to as "real" definitions.

One point should be made clear, however, concerning the question of "existence." Whether a definition is stipulative or lexical has nothing to do with the question of whether the definiendum names any "real" or "existent" thing. The definition

> The word "unicorn" means an animal like a horse but having a single straight horn projecting from its forehead.

is a "real" or lexical definition, and a true one, because the definiendum is a word with long-established usage and means exactly what is meant by the definiens. Yet the definiendum does not name or denote any existent, since there are no unicorns.

A qualification must be made at this point, for in asserting that lexical definitions of the kind illustrated were true or false, we were oversimplifying a complex situation. The fact is that many words are used in different ways, not because they have a plurality of standard meanings, but through what we should call error. Not all instances of erroneous word usage are as funny as those of Sheridan's Mrs. Malaprop when she gives the order to "illiterate him . . . from your memory" or uses the phrase "as headstrong as an allegory on the banks of the Nile." Some words are used by many people in ways that might be called erroneous or mistaken, but which are better described as unorthodox. Any definition of a word that ignores the way in which it is used by any sizable group of speakers is not true to actual usage and is, therefore, not quite correct.

Word usage is a statistical matter, and any definition of a word whose usage is subject to this kind of variation must not be a simple statement of "the meaning" of the term, but a statistical description of the various meanings of the term, as determined by the uses it has in actual speech. The need for lexical statistics cannot be evaded by reference to "correct" usage, for that too is a matter of degree, being measured by the number of "first-rate" authors whose usages of a given term are in agreement. Moreover, literary and academic vocabularies tend to lag behind the growth of living language. Unorthodox usages have a way of becoming catholic, so definitions that report only the meanings countenanced by an academic aristocracy are likely to be very misleading. Of course, the notion of statistical definitions is utopian, but dictionaries approximate it more or less by indicating which meanings are "archaic" or "obsolete" and which are "colloquial" or "slang." With the foregoing as qualification, we may repeat that lexical definitions are true or false, in the sense of being true to actual usage or failing to be true to it.

3. Precising Definitions

Confusion in argument can arise from *vagueness* as well as from ambiguity. The users of a term may, in a sense, know its meaning, yet remain unsure of the limits of its applicability. Vagueness and ambiguity are different. A term is ambiguous in a given context when it has more than one distinct meaning and the context does not make clear which is intended. A term is vague when there exist "borderline cases" such that it cannot be determined whether the term should be applied to them or not. Most words have some degree of vagueness; and of course a single term may exhibit both failings. In heated controversies—such as that over the morality of abortion, for example—key phrases like "right to life," or "right to choose," or "human infant" may be both ambiguous and vague.

Under some circumstances difficulties like these can assume great practical importance. A fairly recent newspaper headline read:

WHAT IS OBSCENITY?
Lack of a Definition
Stymies a Crackdown
Against Smut Dealers[3]

Another example of the importance of precision in definition arises from the fact that persons may be used as sources for organ donation only after they are declared *dead*. When the brain is dead the person is dead, but the term "brain death" was long used imprecisely. This is because there are two divisions of the brain, higher and lower; the higher brain may be permanently destroyed, with it all sensation and all awareness, while the lower brain, or brain stem, continues to function. A precise and well-understood definition of "death" was badly needed. That definition was recently formulated by the President's Commission for the Study of Ethical Problems in Medicine:

An individual who has sustained either
(1) irreversible cessation of circulatory and respiratory functions, or (2) irreversible cessation of all functions of the entire brain, including the brain stem, is dead.[4]

This definition has subsequently been incorporated into the Uniform Determination of Death Act, adopted by most of the States. A precise legal defi-

---

[3]Headline in *The Wall Street Journal*, August 19, 1970, p. 1.
[4]President's Commission for the Study of Ethical Problems in Medicine, *Summing Up*, Washington, D.C., 1983, p. 16.

nition of death, supplemented by measuring techniques for determining when brain activity has ceased, was essential to protect transplant surgeons from criminal or civil liability.

To eliminate the troublesome vagueness of the term "brain death" it was not possible to appeal to ordinary usage. Ordinary usage was not sufficiently clear on the matter, and if it had been, the term would not have been vague. To reach a decision about borderline cases ordinary usage must often be transcended; a definition that can help to decide borderline cases will go beyond the report of normal usage. Such a definition may be called a *precising definition*.

A precising definition thus differs from both stipulative and lexical definitions. It differs from a stipulative definition because its definiendum is not a new term, but one whose usage is established, although vague. The makers of a precising definition, therefore, are not free to assign any meaning they choose to the definiendum. They must remain true to established usage, so far as that is possible. The aim is to make a known term more precise. At the same time they must go beyond established usage if the vagueness of the definiendum is to be reduced. Exactly how they go beyond, just how they fill the gaps or resolve the conflicts of established usage, is partly a matter of stipulation, but not completely so.

Legal decisions often involve precising definitions in which certain statutory terms are clarified to cover or specifically to exclude the case at issue. But judges will not decide such matters arbitrarily. They will normally present arguments to justify their decisions in such matters. This shows that they do not regard their precising definitions as *mere* stipulations, even in those areas not covered by precedent or established usage. Instead, they seek to be guided in part by the supposed intentions of the legislators who enacted the law, and in part by what the public, subject to the law, may be expected to understand its terms to mean. In North Carolina the sale of a motor vehicle has long been subject to taxation at a special rate, much lower than the regular sales tax. This problem arose: is a yacht a motor vehicle? The Supreme Court of that state, formulating its definition of "motor vehicle" precisely, has decided that it is not; on the sale of yachts, therefore, the higher sales tax must be collected.[5] Precise definitions may be required in order that laws can be enforced fairly.

Legislatures will therefore commonly preface the formulation of a new law with a section called "definitions"—in which it is specified how the key terms used in that statute are to be understood. The meanings specified will be as close as possible to the lexical, but where ordinary usage would leave troubling uncertainties, future disputes will be avoided so far as possible by means of stipulated precision. Without precising definitions disagreement concerning the just application of laws (and other sorts of rules, in the workplace, and elsewhere) would be unending. Indeed, appellate courts some-

---

[5]*The Wall Street Journal*, March 16, 1966, p. 1.

times strike down a statute simply because its terms are so vague that those who are governed by it could not be expected to understand the limits of its applicability, and therefore could not be expected to be able to obey the law itself.

4. Theoretical Definitions

It is in connection with theoretical definitions that most "disputing over definitions" occurs. A *theoretical definition* of a term is a definition that attempts to formulate a theoretically adequate or scientifically useful description of the objects to which the term applies. To propose a theoretical definition is tantamount to proposing the acceptance of a theory—and theories, as the name suggests, are notoriously debatable. Here one definition is replaced by another as our knowledge and theoretical understanding increase. At one time physicists defined "heat" to mean a subtle imponderable fluid; now they define it as a form of energy possessed by a body by virtue of the irregular motion of its molecules. Physicists have given different theoretical definitions of "heat" at different times because they accepted different theories of heat at those different times.

Theoretical definitions have a major role in philosophy as well as in the sciences. Socrates (as represented in the writings of Plato) was continually seeking definitions. But plainly Socrates was not after a mere report about how people used juicy words like "justice" or "courage." And arbitrary stipulations about their meanings interested him not at all. Even precising definitions were not his chief object, since borderline cases were rarely emphasized by him. Socrates' target was much larger: a theory within which a fully adequate definition of important terms—"knowledge" and "temperance" and "love" and the like—might be stated. Philosophers disputing today with Plato's accounts, or with one another, are surely not seeking to resolve merely verbal matters; they are seeking, as scientists seek, to construct theoretical definitions; with such definitions, it is claimed, disagreements and misunderstandings about other facts, physical or political or moral, may be effectively resolved.

5. Persuasive Definitions

Finally, definitions may be formulated and used persuasively, to resolve disputes by influencing the attitudes, or stirring the emotions, of readers or hearers. These we call *persuasive* definitions. We have seen in Chapter 2 that language can function both informatively and expressively. The kinds of definition discussed thus far are all concerned with the informative use of language; but sometimes we define terms in ways deliberately calculated to affect feelings, and indirectly, to alter conduct. This was well illustrated during hearings, held by the Hawaiian state legislature, on a proposal to abolish the state's law against abortion. Under the heading "Defining Abortion a

Tricky Business" the following story appeared in a Honolulu newspaper:

> Amidst the emotional debate on the abortion issue at the State Legislature, humor still lives.
>
> Anonymous legislative staffers this week drafted and circulated to legislators a proposed "general response to constituent letters on abortion." It goes like this:
>
> "Dear Sir:
>
> "You ask me how I stand on abortion. Let me answer forthrightly and without equivocation.
>
> "If by abortion you mean the murdering of defenseless human beings; the denial of rights to the youngest of our citizens; the promotion of promiscuity among our shiftless and valueless youth and the rejection of Life, Liberty and the Pursuit of Happiness—then, Sir, be assured that I shall never waver in my opposition, so help me God.
>
> "But, Sir, if by abortion you mean the granting of equal rights to all our citizens regardless of race, color or sex; the elimination of evil and vile institutions preying upon desperate and hopeless women; a chance to all our youth to be wanted and loved; and, above all, that God-given right for all citizens to act in accordance with the dictates of their own conscience—then, Sir, let me promise you as a patriot and a humanist that I shall never be persuaded to forego my pursuit of these most basic human rights.
>
> "Thank you for asking my position on this most crucial issue and let me again assure you of the steadfastness of my stand.
>
> "Mahalo and Aloha Nui."[6]

Persuasive definitions are common in political argument. From the left we encounter "socialism" defined as *democracy extended to the economic field,* and from the right we hear "capitalism" defined as *freedom in the economic sphere.* There is little doubt what purposes are served by the emotive language in each of these definitions. But manipulation can also be more subtle; emotive coloration may be slyly injected into the language of a definition that purports to be accurate, and that appears on the surface to be objective. As we seek to distinguish good reasoning from bad, we must be on our guard against persuasive definitions.

EXERCISES

I. Five types of definitions are discussed in this section:

Lexical definitions
Stipulative definitions
Precising definitions
Theoretical definitions
Persuasive definitions

Find two examples of each type, and explain the purposes they are intended to serve.

II. Discuss each of the following disputes. If it is obviously genuine, indicate each of the disputers' positions with respect to the proposition at issue. If it is

---

[6]"Thanks and Much Love," *The Honolulu Advertiser,* February 14, 1970.

merely verbal, resolve it by explaining the different senses attached by the disputers to the key word or phrase that is used ambiguously. If it is an apparently verbal dispute that is really genuine, locate the ambiguity and explain the real disagreement involved.

★ 1. DAYE: Pete Rose was the greatest hitter in the history of baseball. He got more hits than any other major league player.
KNIGHT: No, Hank Aaron deserves that title. He hit more home runs than any other major league player.

2. DAYE: Despite their great age, the plays of Sophocles are enormously relevant today. They deal with eternally recurring problems and values such as love and sacrifice, the conflict of generations, life and death, as central today as they were over two thousand years ago.
KNIGHT: I don't agree with you at all. Sophocles has nothing to say about the pressing and immediate issues of our time: inflation, unemployment, the population explosion, and the energy crisis. His plays have no relevance for today.

3. DAYE: Bob Jones is certainly a wonderful father to his children. He provides a beautiful home in a fine neighborhood, buys them everything they need or want, and has made ample provision for their education.
KNIGHT: I don't think Bob Jones is a good father at all. He is so busy getting and spending that he has no time to be with his children. They hardly know him except as somebody who pays the bills.

4. DAYE: Amalgamated General Corporation's earnings were higher than ever last year, I see by reading their annual report.
KNIGHT: No, their earnings were really much lower than in the preceding year, and they have been cited by the SEC for issuing a false and misleading report.

★ 5. DAYE: Business continues to be good for National Conglomerate, Inc. Their sales so far this year are 25 percent higher than they were at this time last year.
KNIGHT: No, their business is not so good now. Their profits so far this year are 30 percent lower than they were last year at this time.

6. DAYE: Ann is an excellent student. She takes a lively interest in everything and asks very intelligent questions in class.
KNIGHT: Ann is one of the worst students I've ever seen. She never gets her assignments in on time.

7. DAYE: Tom did it of his own free will. No pressure was brought to bear on him, no threats were made, no inducements were offered, there was no hint of force. He deliberated about it and made up his own mind.
KNIGHT: That is impossible. Nobody has free will, because everything anyone does is inevitably determined by heredity and environment according to inexorable causal laws of nature.

8. DAYE: Professor Graybeard is one of the most productive scholars at the university. His bibliography of publications is longer than those of any of his colleagues.
KNIGHT: I wouldn't call him a productive scholar. He is a great teacher, but he has never produced any new ideas or discoveries in his entire career.

9. DAYE: Betty finally got rid of that old Chevy of hers and bought herself a new car. She's driving a Buick now.

   KNIGHT: No, Betty didn't buy herself a new car. That Buick is a good three years old.

★ 10. DAYE: Dick finally got rid of that old Ford of his and bought himself a new car. He's driving a Pontiac now.

   KNIGHT: No, Dick didn't buy himself a new car. It's his roommate's new Pontiac that he's driving.

11. DAYE: Helen lives a long way from campus. I walked out to see her the other day, and it took me nearly two hours to get there.

   KNIGHT: No, Helen doesn't live such a long way from campus. I drove her home last night, and we reached her place in less than ten minutes.

12. DAYE: Senator Gray is a fine man and a genuine liberal. He votes for every progressive measure that comes before the legislature.

   KNIGHT: He is no liberal, in my opinion—the old skinflint contributes less money to worthy causes than any other man in his income bracket.

13. DAYE: The University of Winnemac overemphasizes athletics, for it has the largest college stadium in the world and has constructed new sports buildings instead of badly needed classroom space.

   KNIGHT: No, the University of Winnemac does not overemphasize athletics. Its academic standards are very high, and it sponsors a wide range of extracurricular activities for students in addition to its athletic program.

14. DAYE: It was in bad taste to serve roast beef at the banquet. There were Hindus present, and it is against their religion to eat beef.

   KNIGHT: Bad taste nothing! That was the tastiest meal I've had in a long time. I think it was delicious!

★ 15. DAYE: There are less than 8 million unemployed persons in this country, according to the Bureau of Labor Statistics.

   KNIGHT: Oh no, there are over fifteen times that number of unemployed. The President's Economic Report states that there are 100 million employed in this country, and the Census Bureau reports a total population of over 230 million. So the government's figures reveal that there are over 130 million unemployed persons in this country.

16. DAYE: The average intelligence of college graduates is higher than that of college freshmen, because it takes more intelligence to graduate from college than to be admitted to college.

   KNIGHT: No, the average intelligence of college graduates is not higher than that of college freshmen, because every college graduate was once a college freshman and a person's intelligence does not change from year to year.

17. DAYE: A tree falling in a wilderness with nobody around to hear will produce no sound. There can be no auditory sensation unless someone actually senses it.

   KNIGHT: No, whether anyone is there to hear it or not, the crash of a falling tree will set up vibrations in the air and will therefore produce a sound in any event.

18. DAYE: I see by the financial pages that money is much more plentiful than it was six months ago.

KNIGHT: That can't be true. I read a government report just yesterday to the effect that more old currency has been destroyed at the mint during the last half year than has been replaced. Money is therefore less plentiful, not more so.

19. DAYE: Mr. Green is a real Christian. He speaks well of everyone and is never too busy to give friendly assistance to anyone who is in need.

KNIGHT: I wouldn't call Green a Christian—he spends his Sundays working in his yard or playing out on the golf course, never showing his face in church from one end of the year to the other!

20. DAYE: Don't ask your wife about it. You ought to use your own judgment.

KNIGHT: I will use my own judgment, and in my judgment I should ask my wife.

4.3 *Denotation (Extension) and Connotation (Intension)*

A definition states the *meaning* of a term, but there are different senses of the word "meaning." Earlier we distinguished the descriptive or literal meaning of a term from its expressive meaning. Now we look more closely at literal meaning, and especially at the literal meaning of *general terms*—class terms that may be applicable to more than one object. In reasoning the definition of general terms is of special importance.

The general term "planet" applies in the same sense equally to Mercury, Venus, Earth, Mars, Jupiter, and so on. In one sense these various objects are meant by the word; the collection of the planets constitutes its meaning. If I say that all planets have elliptical orbits, part of what I assert is that Mars has an elliptical orbit, and another part is that Venus has an elliptical orbit, and so on. The meaning of the term "planet"—in this important sense—consists of the objects to which the term may be correctly applied. This sense of "meaning" is called the *extensional* or *denotative* meaning of the term. A general term, or class term, denotes the several objects to which it may correctly be applied. The collection of these objects constitutes the extension or denotation of the term.

To understand the meaning of a general term is to know how to apply it correctly—but to do this it is not necessary to know all of the objects to which it may be correctly applied. All the objects within the extension of a given term have some common attributes or characteristics that lead us to use the same term to denote them. Therefore we may know the meaning of a term without knowing its extension. "Meaning," in this second sense, supposes some *criterion for deciding*, of any given object, whether it falls within the extension of that term. This sense of "meaning" is called the *intensional* or *connotative* meaning of the term. The totality of attributes shared by all and only those objects within a term's extension is called the intension, or connotation of that term.

Thus we see that every general or class term has both an intensional, or connotative meaning, and an extensional, or denotative meaning. The *intension* of the general term "skyscraper" consists of the attributes common and peculiar to all buildings over a certain height. The *extension* of the term "skyscraper" is the class that contains the Empire State Building, the World Trade Center, the Sears Tower, and so on—the collection of the objects to which the term applies.

Sometimes it is alleged that the extension of a term changes from time to time, although its intension does not. The extension of the term "person," it is said, for example, changes continually as people die and babies are born. This claim flows from a confusion. The term "person," conceived as denoting *all* persons, the dead as well as the unborn, does not have a changing extension. The varying extension is that of the term "living person." But the term "living person" has the sense of "person living now" in which the word "now" refers to the fleeting, changing present. Therefore the intension of the term "living person" is also different at different times. It is thus clear that any term with a changing extension must have a changing intension also. One is as constant as the other; when the intension of a term is fixed, the extension is fixed also.

Note that the extension of a term is determined by its intension, but that the reverse is not true. The intension of the term "equilateral triangle" is the attribute of being a plane figure enclosed by three straight lines of equal length. The extension of "equilateral triangle" is the class of all those objects and only those objects which have this attribute. Now the term "equiangular triangle" has a different intension, connoting the attribute of being a plane figure enclosed by three straight lines that intersect each other to form equal angles. Of course the extension of the term "equiangular triangle" is exactly the same as the extension of the term "equilateral triangle." Thus, to identify the extension of one of these terms leaves uncertain the intension of the class; intension is not determined by extension. But intension must determine extension. So terms may have different intensions and yet the same extension; but terms with different extensions cannot possibly have the same intension.

When attributes are added to the intension of a term we say that the intension *increases*. In the following sequence of terms, the intension of each is included within the intension of the term following it: "person," "living person," "living person over twenty years old," "living person over twenty years old having red hair." The intensions of each is greater than the intentions of those preceding it in the sequence; the terms are arranged in order of *increasing intension*. But if we turn to the extensions of those terms, we find the reverse to be the case. The extension of "person" is greater than that of "living person," and so on—the terms are arranged in order of *decreasing extension*. Some logicians have been led to formulate a "law of inverse variation," asserting that extension and intension always vary inversely with each other. This is suggestive, but not entirely correct. We could construct a series of terms in order of increasing intension, where the extension does not decrease, but remains the same. Consider this series: "living person," "living person with a spinal column," "living person with a spinal column less than one thousand years old," "living person with a spinal column less than one thousand years old who has not read all the books in the Library of Congress." These terms are clearly in order of increasing intension, but the extension of each of them is the same, not decreasing at all. The correct, amended "law" asserts that if terms are arranged in order of increasing intension, their extensions will be in nonincreasing order; that is, if the extensions vary, they will vary inversely with the intensions.

Our distinction between intension and extension, and the recognition that extensions may be empty, can be used to resolve the ambiguity of some occurrences of the term "meaning." Thus we can expose the following fallacy of equivocation:

> The word "God" is not meaningless and therefore has a meaning. But by definition the word "God" means a supremely good and omnipotent being. Therefore, that supremely good and omnipotent being, God, must exist.

The equivocation here is on the words "meaning" and "meaningless." The word "God" is not meaningless, and so there is an intension or connotation that is its meaning in one sense. But it does not follow simply from the fact that a term has connotation that it denotes anything. The distinction between intension and extension is an old one, but it is still valuable and important.[7]

In earlier sections we have examined the *kinds* of definitions, and their *uses*—lexical and stipulative definitions to eliminate or avoid ambiguity, precising definitions to diminish vagueness, and so on. In the sections that follow we will examine *techniques* for constructing definitions. Some definitions approach a general term through its extension, or denotation, while other definitions approach it through its intension, or connotation. We shall see that each approach has both advantages and disadvantages.

EXERCISES

I. Arrange each of the following groups of terms in order of increasing intension.

★ 1. animal, feline, lynx, mammal, vertebrate, wildcat.

2. alcoholic beverage, beverage, champagne, fine white wine, white wine, wine.

3. athlete, ball player, baseball player, fielder, infielder, shortstop.

---

[7]The useful distinction between intension and extension was introduced and emphasized by St. Anselm of Canterbury (1033–1109), who is best known for his "ontological argument," to which the preceding fallacious argument has little if any resemblance. See Jan Pinborg, *Logik und Semantik im Mittelalter. Ein Uberblick mit einem Nachwort von Helmut Kohlenberger* (Stuttgart-Bad Cannstatt: Friedrich Frommann Verlag, 1972), and Wolfgang L. Gombocz, "Logik und Existenz in Mittelalter," *Philosophische Rundschau*, Heft 3/4, 1977.

4. cheese, dairy product, Limburger, milk derivative, soft cheese, strong soft cheese.

5. integer, number, positive integer, prime, rational number, real number.

II. Divide the following list of terms into five groups of five terms each, arranged in order of increasing intension.

aquatic animal, beast of burden, beverage, brandy, cognac, domestic animal, filly, fish, foal, game fish, horse, instrument, liquid, liquor, musical instrument, muskellunge, parallelogram, pike, polygon, quadrilateral, rectangle, square, Stradivarius, string instrument, violin.

4.4 *Extension, and Denotative Definitions*

Denotative definitions rely upon techniques that identify the extension of the general term being defined. The most obvious way to instruct someone about the extension of a term is to give examples of objects denoted by it. This technique is often used, and is often very effective. It has certain limitations, however, that ought to be recognized.

It was noted in the preceding section (using the examples of "equilateral triangle" and "equiangular triangle") that two terms with different meanings—that is, different intensions—may have exactly the same extensions. Therefore, even if we could give a complete enumeration of the objects denoted by one of those two general terms, this denotative definition would fail to distinguish it from the other term that denotes the same objects. The two terms are not synonyms—but the denotative definition cannot make the distinction between them.

By itself this is not a troubling limitation, however, because very few terms can have their extensions completely enumerated. To enumerate all the infinitely many numbers denoted by the term "number" is absolutely impossible. To enumerate all the literally astronomical number of objects denoted by the term "star," even if their number is finite, is a practical impossibility. And for most other general terms complete enumeration is practically out of the question.

Thus denotative definitions must generally be restricted to partial enumerations of the objects denoted—and that is a limitation giving rise to serious difficulties. Any given object—say, the man John Doe—has many, many attributes, and is therefore included in the extensions of many, many different general terms. Therefore, when given as an example in a denotative definition of one term, it will be just as appropriately mentioned as an example in a denotative definition of many other terms. John Doe is an example of "man," of "animal," of "mammal"—perhaps also of "husband," and "father," and "student," and so on. Mentioning him, therefore, cannot help to distinguish between the meanings of any of these terms. And even if we give two examples, or three, or four, the same difficulty is confronted. In defining the term "skyscraper" we may use the obvious examples of the Empire State, Chrysler, and Woolworth buildings—but these three serve equally well as examples of the denotation of the terms "great structures of the twentieth century," "expensive pieces of real estate in Manhattan," or "landmarks in New York City," and so on. Yet each of these general terms denotes objects not denoted by the others—so using partial enumeration we could not even distinguish among terms that have different extensions. Introducing "negative instances" (e.g., "not the Taj Mahal," "not the Pentagon," etc.) may help to specify the meaning of the definiendum, but the negative instances also must remain incomplete, and the basic limitation remains.

We may seek to provide examples not by mentioning one case at a time, but by mentioning whole groups of members. Using this technique—definition by subclasses—it is sometimes possible to achieve a complete enumeration. Thus we might define "vertebrate" to mean amphibians and birds and fishes and mammals and reptiles. Definition by enumeration—whether complete or partial, whether by individual class members or by subclasses—has some psychological merits, but it is logically inadequate to specify completely the meaning of the terms being defined.

A special kind of definition by example is called *ostensive* or *demonstrative* definition. Instead of naming or describing the objects denoted by the term being defined, as in the ordinary sort of denotative definition, an ostensive definition refers to the examples by means of pointing, or some other gesture. An example of an ostensive definition would be: the word "desk" means *this*, accompanied by a gesture such as pointing a finger in the direction of a desk.

Ostensive definitions have all the limitations mentioned in the preceding discussion, and some limitations peculiar to themselves. There is a relatively trivial geographical limitation; one can indicate only what is visible, and so cannot ostensively define the word "skyscraper" in a country village, or ostensively define the word "mountain" while on a prairie. More seriously, gestures are invariably ambiguous. To point to a desk is also to point to a part of it, and also to its color, and its size, and its shape and material, and so on—in fact, to everything that lies in the general direction of the desk, including the wall behind it or the garden beyond.

This ambiguity can be resolved only by adding some descriptive phrase to the definiens, which results in what may be called a quasi-ostensive definition, as for example: "The word 'desk' means this *article of furniture* (accompanied by an appropriate gesture)." But this sort of addition defeats the purpose that ostensive definitions have been claimed to serve. Ostensive definitions have been alleged by some to be the "primary" or "primitive" definitions, in the sense that it is (allegedly) in this way that we first learn the meanings of words, and that other definitions rely upon the meanings of words first learned in this way. But that claim of primacy is mistaken, since the significance of gestures themselves must be learned. When a finger is pointed to the side of a baby's crib, the attention of the baby, if attracted at all, is as likely to be attracted to the finger as to the thing pointed at. And the same difficulty arises if we seek to define gestures with other gestures. To understand the definition of any sign, some signs must already be understood. The primary way of learning to use language is by observation and imitation, not by definition.

One might construe the phrase "ostensive definition" very broadly, as some logicians have done, so as to include the process of "frequently hearing the word when the object it denotes is present." But such a process would not be a definition at all, as we have been using the term here. It would be the primitive, pre-definitional way of learning to use language.

Finally, there are words which, although perfectly meaningful, do not denote anything at all, and therefore *cannot* be defined denotatively. When we say, for example, that there are no unicorns, we are asserting that the term "unicorn" does not denote, that it has an "empty" extension. Such terms do more than exhibit a limitation of denotative definition; they show that "meaning" really pertains more to intension than to extension. For although the term "unicorn" has an empty extension, this is certainly not to say that the term "unicorn" is meaningless. It does not denote anything because there are no unicorns; but if the term "unicorn" were meaningless, it would also be meaningless to say that "There are no unicorns." But this statement is very far from meaningless; we fully understand its meaning, and it *is* true. Clearly, intension is the real key to definition, and to it we turn in the following section.

EXERCISES

I. Define the following terms by example, enumerating three examples for each term.

★	1. actor		2. boxer
	3. composer		4. dramatist
★	5. element		6. flower
	7. general (officer)		8. harbor
	9. inventor		10. poet

II. For each of the terms in Exercise I, find a nonsynonymous general term that your three examples serve equally well to illustrate.

4.5 *Intension, and Connotative Definition*

The intension or connotation of a term, we have said, consists of the attributes shared by *all* the objects denoted by the term, and shared *only* by those objects. Thus, if the attributes that define "chair" are being a single raised seat, and having a back, then every chair is a single raised seat with a back, and only chairs are single raised seats with backs. It is a confusing fact that the word "connotation" has other uses, in which it sometimes refers to the total significance of a word, emotive as well as descriptive, and sometimes to its emotive meaning alone. Thus a person who is cold and harsh may be described as not human—where the word "human" is plainly being used to communicate an attitude or feeling, rather than to provide a biological classification. In such uses "connotation" refers to more than intension, but in logic we use the word "connotation" in the stricter sense. In our usage connotation and intension are part of the informative significance of the term only.

Even with this restriction, three different senses of "connotation" must be distinguished: the *subjective*, the *objective*, and the *conventional*. The subjective connotation of a word for a speaker is the set of all attributes the speaker believes possessed by objects denoted by that word. But this set plainly varies from individual to individual and even from time to time for the same individual—and thus cannot serve the purposes of definition. It is the public meanings of words, not their private interpretations, in which we are interested. The objective connotation (or intension) of a word is the total set of characteristics shared by all the objects in the word's extension. Thus, the term "circle" may have, within its objective connotation, a universal feature of circles—say, that a circle encloses a greater area than any other closed plane figure having an equal perimeter—that many who use the word are completely unaware of. It would require complete omniscience to know all the attributes shared by the objects denoted by the term, and since no one has that omniscience, the objective connotation cannot be the public meaning in whose explanation we are interested.

We do communicate with one another, and we understand the terms we use—hence plainly there must be connotations publicly available, neither subjective nor objective in the senses explained. Terms have stable meanings because we have *agreed to use the same criterion for deciding of any object whether it is part of the term's extension.* Thus, what makes a thing a circle, conventionally, is its being a closed plane curve, all points of which are equidistant from a point within called the center. This criterion is established by convention—and this meaning is its conventional connotation or conventional intension. For purposes of definition this is the important sense of intension, since it is both public and does not require omniscience to use. Normally, the term "connotation" is used to mean "conventional connotation," and the term "intension" is used to mean "conventional intension." This will be our usage, unless otherwise specified.

How does one actually go about defining a word? What techniques does one use to identify its conventional intension, the agreed-upon set of attributes common and peculiar to objects denoted by the word? Several ways of doing this are common.

The simplest and most frequently used—but one having limited power—is that of providing another word, whose meaning is already understood, which has the same meaning as the word being defined. Two words with the same meaning are called "synonyms," so a definition of this sort is called a *synonymous* definition. Dictionaries, especially smaller ones, rely heavily on this method of defining terms. Thus, a pocket dictionary may define "adage" as meaning proverb, "bashful" as meaning shy, and so on. Synonymous definitions are particularly useful, often essential, when it is the meanings of words in a foreign language that need explanation. In French, *chat* means cat; in Spanish, *amigo* means friend, and so on. Learning the vocabulary of a foreign language depends upon definitions using synonyms.

This is a good method of defining terms; it is easy, efficient, and helpful—but its limitations are serious. Many words have no exact synonyms, and hence synonymous definitions are often less than fully accurate, and can mislead. From this realization comes the Italian proverb: *"Traduttore, traditore"*—"Translator, traitor."

A more serious limitation of synonymous definitions is this: where the concept connoted by the word is not understood, every synonym will be as puzzling to the hearer or reader as the definiendum itself. In such cases more needs to be done than provide an alternative word. Thus, synonymous definitions are virtually useless in the construction of precising or of theoretical definitions, as those were explained in Section 4.2.

Operational definition—a term first used by the Nobel prize-winning physicist P. W. Bridgeman in his influential book *The Logic of Modern Physics* (1927)—has been introduced by some scientists to tie the definiendum to some describable set of actions or operations. For example: "space" and "time," after the success and widespread acceptance of Einstein's theory of relativity, could not be defined in the abstract way that Newton had used. It was then proposed to define them operationally—that is, by means of the operations used in measuring distances and durations. An operational definition of a term states that the term is correctly applied to a given case if and only if the performance of specified operations in that case yield a specified result. The numerical value given for length would then be operationally defined by reference to the results of specified measuring procedures, and so on. Only public and repeatable operations are referred to in the definiens of an operational definition.

Some social scientists have sought to incorporate this relatively new technique of defining into their disciplines also, to avoid the confusion and disagreement that have surrounded more traditional definitions of some key terms. Thus, for example, some psychologists have sought to replace abstract definitions of "sensation," and "mind" by operational definitions referring exclusively to behavior or to physiological observations; reliance upon operational definitions in psychology and other social sciences has tended to be associated with behaviorism. Extreme empiricists have sometimes insisted that a term is meaningful only if it is susceptible of operational definition—but to evaluate such claims is beyond the scope of this book.

Where a synonymous definition is unavailable, and an operational definition is inappropriate, we can often use a definition by genus and difference to explain the conventional intension of a term. This method is also called "definition by division," "analytical definition," "definition *per genus et differentiam*," or simply "connotative definition." It would be wrong to say, as some do, that this is the only "genuine" kind of definition, but it is the technique more widely applicable than any other.

The possibility of defining terms by genus and difference depends upon the fact that some attributes are complex—that is, they are analyzable into two or more other attributes. This complexity and analyzability can best be explained in terms of classes.

Classes having members may have their memberships divided into sub-classes. For example, the class of all triangles may be divided into three nonempty subclasses: equilateral triangles, isosceles triangles, and scalene triangles. The terms "genus" and "species" are often used in this connection: the class whose membership is divided into subclasses is the *genus,* the various subclasses are *species.* As used here, the words "genus" and "species" are *relative* terms, like parent and offspring. Just as the same persons may be parents in relation to their children and offspring in relation to their parents, so one and the same class may be a genus in relation to its own subclasses, and a species in relation to some larger class of which it is a subclass. Thus the class of all triangles is a genus relative to the species *scalene triangle* and a species relative to the genus *polygon.* The logician's use of the words "genus" and "species" as relative terms is different from the biologist's use of them as absolute terms, and the two should not be confused.

Since a class is a collection of entities having some common characteristic, all the members of a given genus will have some characteristic in common. Thus all members of the genus *polygon* share the characteristic of being closed plane figures bounded by straight line segments. This genus may be divided into different species or subclasses such that all the members of each subclass have some further attribute in common shared by no member of any other subclass. The genus polygon is divided into *triangles, quadrilaterals, pentagons, hexagons,* and so on. Each species of the genus polygon differs from all the rest; the specific difference between members of the subclass hexagon and the members of any other subclass is that only members of the subclass of hexagons have precisely six sides. In general: all members of all species of a given genus share some attribute that makes them members of the genus, but the members of any one species share some further attribute that differentiates them from the members of every other species of that genus. The characteristic that serves to distinguish them is called the *specific difference.* Thus, having six sides is the specific difference between the species *hexagon* and all other species of the genus *polygon.*

In this sense the attribute of being a hexagon is analyzable into the attribute of being a polygon and the attribute of having six sides. To someone who did not know the meaning of the word "hexagon" or of any synonym of it, but who did know the meanings of the words "polygon," "sides," and "six," the meaning of the word "hexagon" could be explained by means of a *definition by genus and difference*:

> The word "hexagon" means polygon having six sides.

The ancient definition of the word "human" as meaning "rational animal" is another example of definition by genus and difference. Here the genus is animal; the species human is subsumed under it, differentiated from all other species of animals by rationality. Thus, one defines a term by genus and difference in two steps: first a genus must be named—the genus of which the species designated by the definiendum is a subclass; then the specific difference must be named—the attribute that distinguishes the members of that species from members of all other species in that genus. Of course, in the definition of "human" just mentioned, we could regard "rational" as the genus and "animal" as the difference, as well as the other way around. The order is not absolute from the point of view of logic, although there may be extralogical reasons for considering one as genus rather than the other.

The method of definition by genus and difference also has limitations, of which two may be mentioned briefly. First, the method is applicable only to words that connote complex attributes. If there are any simple, *unanalyzable* attributes, then the words connoting them cannot be defined by genus and difference. Some have suggested that the sensed qualities of specific shades of colors are examples of simple attributes of this kind. Whether or not there are any such unanalyzable attributes remains an open question, but if there are, they limit the applicability of definition by genus and difference. Another limitation has to do with words connoting *universal* attributes—such as the words "being," "entity," "existent," "object," or the like. These cannot be defined by the method of genus and difference because the class of all entities, for example, is not a species of some broader genus; a universal class would constitute the very highest class, or *summum genus,* as it is called. The same applies to words for ultimate metaphysical categories, such as "substance" or "attribute." These limitations, however, are of little practical importance in appraising this method of definition.

Connotative definitions, especially definitions by genus and difference, can serve any of the purposes for which definitions are constructed: they may help to eliminate ambiguity, to reduce vagueness, to explain theoretically, and even to influence attitudes. They may also be used simply to increase and enrich the vocabulary of those to whom they are provided. In Section 4.2 we noted that, in achieving these different objectives, five different types of definition may be distinguished: lexical, stipulative, precising, theoretical, and persuasive. For each of these kinds the techniques of connotative definition may be used.

EXERCISES

I. Give synonymous definitions for each of the following terms.

★ 1. absurd   2. buffoon
   3. cemetery   4. dictator
★ 5. egotism   6. feast
   7. garret   8. hasten
   9. infant   ★ 10. jeopardy
  11. kine   12. labyrinth
  13. mendicant   14. novice
★ 15. omen   16. panacea
  17. quack   18. rostrum
  19. scoundrel   20. tepee

II. Construct definitions for the following terms by matching the definiendum with an appropriate genus and difference.

		Definiens	
Definiendum		*(Genus)*	*(Difference)*
★ 1. bachelor		1. offspring	1. female
2. banquet		2. horse	2. male
3. boy		3. man	3. married
4. brother		4. meal	4. unmarried
★ 5. child		5. parent	5. very large
6. foal		6. sheep	6. very small
7. daughter		7. sibling	7. young
8. ewe		8. woman	
9. father			
★ 10. giant			
11. girl			
12. husband			
13. lamb			
14. mare			
★ 15. midget			
16. mother			
17. pony			
18. ram			
19. sister			
★ 20. snack			
21. son			
22. spinster			
23. stallion			
24. wife			

4.6 *Rules for Definition by Genus and Difference*

Certain rules have traditionally been laid down for definition by genus and difference. They do not constitute a recipe that will enable us to construct good connotative definitions without having to think, but they are useful as criteria for appraising definitions once they are proposed. There are five such rules, which are intended to apply primarily to lexical definitions.

Rule 1: A definition should state the essential attributes of the species.

As stated, this rule is somewhat cryptic, because in itself a species has just those attributes that it has, and none is more "essential" than any other. But if we understand the rule properly, as dealing with terms, it becomes clear. We distinguished earlier between the objective connotation of a term and its conventional connotation, the latter being those attributes whose possession constitutes the conventional criterion by which we decide whether an object is denoted by the term. Thus is it part of the objective connotation of "circle" to enclose a greater area than any other plane closed figure of equal perimeter. But to define the word "circle" by this attribute would be to violate the spirit or the intention of our first rule, because it is not *the* attribute that people have agreed to mean by that word. The conventional connotation is the attribute of being a closed plane curve, all points of which are equidistant from a given point called the center. To define it in these terms would be to state its "essence" and thus to conform to this first rule. In our present terminology, perhaps a better way to phrase the rule would be "A definition should state the conventional connotation of the term being defined."

It should be kept in mind that the conventional connotation of a term need not be an intrinsic characteristic of the things denoted by it, but might well have to do with the origin of those things, the relations they have to other things, or the uses to which they are put. Thus the word "Stradivarius," which denotes a number of violins, need not connote any actual physical characteristic shared by all those violins and not possessed by any other, but rather has the conventional connotation of being a violin made in the Cremona workshop of Antonio Stradivari. Again, governors are not physically or mentally different from all other persons; they simply are related differently to their fellow citizens. Finally, the word "shoe" cannot be defined exclusively in terms of the shapes or materials of the things denoted by it; its definition must include reference to the use to which those things are put, as outer coverings for the foot.

Rule 2: A definition must not be circular.

If the definiendum itself appears in the definiens, the definition can explain the meaning of the term being defined only to those who already understand it. So if a definition is circular it must fail in its purpose, which is to explain the meaning of the definiendum. Here is an example, from a recent book entitled *Compulsive Gamblers*:

A compulsive gambler is a person who gambles compulsively.[8]

When applied to definition by genus and difference, this principle also rules out the use (in the definiens) of any synonym of the definiendum. For if a synonym is assumed to be understood, one could as well have given a synonymous definition instead of using the more powerful but more complicated technique of definition by genus and difference. Rule 2 is usually understood to forbid the use of antonyms as well as synonyms.

Rule 3: A definition must be neither too broad nor too narrow.

[8]Jay Livingston, *Compulsive Gamblers* (New York: Harper & Row, Publishers, Inc., 1974) p. 2.

The definiens should not denote more things than are denoted by the definiendum, nor fewer things either. This is an easy rule to understand, but a difficult one to follow.

When Plato's successors in the Academy at Athens at last settled on the definition of "man" as "featherless biped," their critic Diogenes plucked a chicken and threw it over the wall into the Academy. A featherless biped was before them—but one that was assuredly not a man. That definiens was too broad. Legend has it that to narrow it they added to the definiens the phrase "with broad nails."

When certain items are customarily, but not necessarily, made of a given stuff, it is a temptation to make that stuff part of the definition. It would be quite incorrect to define the word "shoe" as a leather covering for the foot—for shoes may be made of wood or canvas also, and that definition would be too narrow. Finding or constructing the definiens that has precisely the correct breadth to explain the definiendum can prove very challenging.

Of course, in constructing a stipulative definition Rule 3 cannot be violated, since in such cases the definiendum has no meaning apart from the definiens provided. And in any case if Rule 1 is fully observed (the essence of the definiendum stated in the definiens) Rule 3 will have been obeyed, since the conventional connotation of the term can be neither too broad nor too narrow.

Rule 4: A definition must not be expressed in ambiguous, obscure, or figurative language.

Ambiguous terms in the definiens will obviously prevent the definition from performing its function of explaining the definiendum. Obscure terms will also defeat that purpose, but obscurity is a relative matter. Words obscure to children are reasonably clear to most adults; words obscure to amateurs may be perfectly familiar to professionals. A "dynatron oscillator" means *a circuit that employs a negative-resistance, volt-ampere curve to produce an alternating current.*[9] While this is terribly obscure to the ordinary person, the language is perfectly intelligible to the students of electrical engineering for whom the definition was written, and is justifiably technical. But to use obscure language in non-technical matters is often a futile attempt to explain the unknown by the still more unknown.

A good example of self-defeating obscurity is found in Herbert Spencer's definition of "evolution" as

> An integration of matter and concomitant dissipation of motion, during which the matter passes from an indefinite, incoherent homogeneity to a definite, coherent heterogeneity, and during which the retained motion undergoes a parallel transformation.

[9] W. G. Dow, *Fundamentals of Engineering Electronics* (New York: John Wiley & Sons, Inc., 1937), p. 331.

Another example of obscurity in definition often cited is Dr. Samuel John-son's celebrated second definition of the word "net" as meaning "anything made with interstitial vacuities."

Figurative or metaphorical language used in the definiens may give some feeling for the use of the term being defined, but cannot give a clear expla-nation of what the definiendum means. Bread may be "the staff of life" — but the meaning of the word is hardly explained in such a definition. Fig-urative definitions may serve as humor, as in the definition of "wedding ring" as "a matrimonial tourniquet designed to stop circulation" or the def-inition of "discretion" as "something that comes to people after they are too old for it to do them any good." Persuasive definitions may rely upon fig-urative language, as in the definition of "prejudice" as "being down on what you aren't up on." But any definition that contains figurative language, how-ever entertaining or persuasive, cannot serve as a serious explanation of the precise meaning of the term to be defined.

Rule 5: A definition should not be negative where it can be affirma-tive.

A definition should explain what a term does mean rather than what it does not mean. For the vast majority of terms there are far too many things that they do *not* mean for any negative definition possibly to cover. To define "couch" as "a piece of furniture that is neither a bed nor a chair" is to fail miserably to explain its meaning, for there are very many other kinds of furniture not meant by the word "couch."

Some terms are essentially negative in meaning and so *require* negative definitions. The word "orphan" means a child who does not have parents; the word "bald" means the state of not having hair on one's head, and so on. Sometimes there is no basis for choosing between affirmative and nega-tive definitions; we may define "drunkard" as one who drinks excessively, and about equally well as one who is not temperate in drink. But even where negatives are appropriately used, the genus must first be affirmatively men-tioned; then, sometimes, the species can be characterized negatively by re-jecting all other species of the genus named. But it will be rare that there are few enough species that they may be conveniently mentioned and rejected in a negative definition. And even when that is possible—as when we define "scalene triangle" as a triangle that is neither equilateral nor isosceles—we will comply far better with Rule 1 if we affirmatively identify the attribute—having sides of unequal length—that mark off the class of scalene triangles. We certainly cannot define the word "quadrilateral" as a polygon that is neither a triangle, nor a pentagon, nor a hexagon, nor . . . because there are too many alternative species of the genus polygon to be excluded. In general, affirmative definitions are much to be preferred over negative ones.

For most purposes, connotative definitions are much superior to denotative definitions; and of all connotative definitions, those constructed by genus and difference are usually most effective and most helpful in reasoning and in other informative uses of language.

EXERCISES

I. Construct a definition by genus and difference for each of the terms in Exercise I on page 150.

II. Criticize the following in terms of the rules for definition by genus and difference. After identifying the difficulty (or difficulties), state the rule (or rules) violated. If the definition is either too narrow or too broad, explain why.

★ 1. A teacher is a person who gives instruction to children.

   2. Knowledge is true opinion.   —PLATO, *Theaetetus*

   3. Life is the art of drawing sufficient conclusions from insufficient premises.
                                          —SAMUEL BUTLER, *Notebooks*

   4. "Base" means that which serves as a base.
                          —CH'ENG WEI-SHIH LUN, quoted in Fung Yu-Lan,
                                          A History of Chinese Philosophy

★ 5. Alteration is combination of contradictorily opposed determinations in the existence of one and the same thing   —IMMANUEL KANT, *Critique of Pure Reason*

   6. Honesty is the habitual absence of the intent to deceive.

   7. Hypocrisy is the homage that vice pays to virtue.
                          —FRANCOIS, Duc de la Rochefoucauld

   8. The word *body*, in the most general acceptation, signifieth that which filleth, or occupieth some certain room, or imagined place; and dependeth not on the imagination, but is a real part of that we call the universe.
                                          —THOMAS HOBBES, *Leviathan*

   9. A painting is a picture drawn on canvas with a brush.

★ 10. "Cause" means something that produces an effect.

   11. War . . . is an act of violence intended to compel our opponent to fulfil our will.   —CARL VON CLAUSEWITZ, *On War*

   12. A raincoat is an outer garment of plastic that repels water.

   13. A hazard is anything that is dangerous.
                          —*Safety with Beef Cattle*, published by the
                          Occupational Safety and Health Administration, 1976

   14. To sneeze [is] to emit wind audibly by the nose.
                                          —SAMUEL JOHNSON, *Dictionary*

★ 15. A bore is a person who talks when you want him to listen.
                                          —AMBROSE BIERCE

   16. Art is a human activity having for its purpose the transmission to others of the highest and best feelings to which men have risen.
                                          —COUNT LYOF TOLSTOI, *What Is Art?*

17. Murder is when a person of sound memory and discretion unlawfully killeth any reasonable creature in being, and under the king's peace, with malice aforethought, either express or implied.   —EDWARD COKE, *Institutes*

18. A cloud is a large semi-transparent mass with a fleecy texture suspended in the atmosphere whose shape is subject to continual and kaleidoscopic change.
—U. T. PLACE, "Is Consciousness a Brain Process?"
The British Journal of Psychology, February 1956

19. Freedom of choice. The human capacity to choose freely between two or more genuine alternatives or possibilities, such choosing being always limited both by the past and by the circumstances of the immediate present.
—CORLISS LAMONT, *Freedom of Choice Affirmed*

★ 20. Health is a state of complete physical, mental, and social well-being and not merely the absence of disease or infirmity.
—World Health Organization, definition of "health"

21. By analysis, we mean analyzing the contradictions in things.
—MAO TSETUNG, *Quotations from Chairman Mao*

22. Noise is any unwanted signal.
—VICTOR E. RAGOSINE, "Magnetic Recording,"
Scientific American, Vol. 222, February 1970

23. To explain (explicate, *explicare*) is to strip reality of the appearances covering it like a veil, in order to see the bare reality itself.
—PIERRE DUHEM, *The Aim and Structure of Physical Theory*

24. The Master said, Yu, shall I teach you what knowledge is? When you know a thing, to recognize that you know it, and when you do not know a thing, to recognize that you do not know it. That is knowledge.
—CONFUCIUS, *The Analects*

25. Opportunity cost is the economic expression of the familiar idea that you can't have your cake and eat it too.   —DANIEL B. SUITS, *Principles of Economics*

III. Discuss the following definitions.

★ 1. Faith is the substance of things hoped for, the evidence of things not seen.
—Hebrews 11:1

2. "Faith is when you believe something that you know ain't true."
—Definition attributed to a schoolboy by William James in
"The Will to Believe"

3. Faith may be defined briefly as an illogical belief in the occurrence of the improbable.   —H. L. MENCKEN

4. Poetry is simply the most beautiful, impressive, and widely effective mode of saying things.   —MATTHEW ARNOLD

★ 5. Poetry is the record of the best and happiest moments of the happiest and best minds.   —PERCY BYSSHE SHELLEY, *The Defence of Poetry*

6. A cynic is a man who knows the price of everything and the value of nothing.   —OSCAR WILDE, *Lady Windermere's Fan*

7. Conscience is an inner voice that warns us somebody is looking.
—H. L. MENCKEN

8. A sentimentalist is a man who sees an absurd value in everything and doesn't know the market price of a single thing.

—OSCAR WILDE, *Lady Windermere's Fan*

9. "The true," to put it very briefly, is only the expedient in the way of our thinking, just as "the right" is only the expedient in the way of our behaving.

—WILLIAM JAMES, "Pragmatism's Conception of Truth"

★ 10. To be conceited is to tend to boast of one's own excellences, to pity or ridicule the deficiencies of others, to daydream about imaginary triumphs, to reminisce about actual triumphs, to weary quickly of conversations which reflect unfavorably upon oneself, to lavish one's society upon distinguished persons and to economize in association with the undistinguished.

—GILBERT RYLE, *The Concept of Mind*

11. Economics is the science which treats of the phenomena arising out of the economic activities of men in society.

—J. N. KEYNES, *Scope and Methods of Political Economy*

12. Justice is doing one's own business, and not being a busybody.

—PLATO, *Republic*

13. What, then, is the government? An intermediate body established between the subjects and the sovereign for their mutual correspondence, charged with the execution of the laws and with the maintenance of liberty both civil and political.

—JEAN JACQUES ROUSSEAU, *The Social Contract*

14. By good, I understand that which we certainly know is useful to us.

—BARUCH SPINOZA, *Ethics*

★ 15. Political power, then, I take to be a right of making laws with penalties of death, and consequently all less penalties, for the regulating and preserving of property, and of employing the force of the community in the execution of such laws, and in defense of the commonwealth from foreign injury, and all this only for the public good.   —JOHN LOCKE, *Essay Concerning Civil Government*

16. And what, then, is belief? It is the demi-cadence which closes a musical phrase in the symphony of our intellectual life.

—CHARLES SANDERS PEIRCE, "How to Make Our Ideas Clear"

17. Political power, properly so called, is merely the organized power of one class for oppressing another.

—KARL MARX and FRIEDRICH ENGELS, *The Communist Manifesto*

18. Grief for the calamity of another is *pity*; and ariseth from the imagination that the like calamity may befall himself.   —THOMAS HOBBES, *Leviathan*

19. We see that all men mean by justice that kind of state of character which makes people disposed to do what is just and makes them act justly and wish for what is just.   —ARISTOTLE, *Nichomachean Ethics*

★ 20. Inquiry is the controlled or directed transformation of an indeterminate situation into one that is so determimate in its constituent distinctions and relations as to convert the elements of the original situation into a unified whole.

—JOHN DEWEY, *Logic: The Theory of Inquiry*

21. A fanatic is one who can't change his mind and won't change the subject.

—WINSTON CHURCHILL

22. Fanaticism consists in redoubling your efforts when you have forgotten your aim. —GEORGE SANTAYANA, *The Life of Reason*, Vol. 1

23. Happiness is the satisfaction of all our desires, *extensively*, in respect of their manifoldness, *intensively*, in respect of their degree, and *potensively*, in respect of their duration. —IMMANUEL KANT, *Critique of Pure Reason*

24. A tragedy is the imitation of an action that is serious and also, as having magnitude, complete in itself; in language with pleasurable accessories, each kind brought in separately in the parts of the work; in a dramatic, not in a narrative form; with incidents arousing pity and fear, wherewith to accomplish its catharsis of such emotions. —ARISTOTLE, *Poetics*

★ 25. "Then," I said, "your people don't understand the difference between liberty and license."
He reported my remark, and again there was a long, very long, general discussion, which the interpreter summed up.
"True," he said, "We don't know the difference between liberty and—what is it?—license. In fact, we never heard of license. We would like you to tell us what is liberty and what is license. And what is the difference?"
"The distinction in America is very important," I said, trying to think quick of a definition, which came to me at last. "Liberty," I defined, "liberty is the right of any proper person—I mean anybody in a good social position—to say anything whatsoever that everybody believes."
The interpreter translated, and I expected his hearers to laugh. But no, they threshed out my definition in all sobriety at great length with never a smile, and the conclusion interpreted was: "Yes. We understand that. And now what is that other thing—license?"
"License," I said, "is not a right. It is an impertinence. License is the impudence of some son-of-a-gun, who has no right to live on earth anyhow, to say some damned thing that is true." —LINCOLN STEFFENS, *Autobiography*

26. . . . the frequently celebrated female intuition . . . is after all only a faculty for observing tiny insignificant aspects of behavior and forming an empirical conclusion which cannot be syllogistically examined.
—GERMAINE GREER, *The Female Eunuch*

27. Patriotism is loyalty to the civic group to which one belongs by birth or other group bond. —W. G. SUMNER, *Folkways*

28. Within the context of these considerations, let me now proceed to suggest a definition of Religion and to offer as well two corollary definitions that grow out of the basic definition. I suggest the following: *Religion* is a "complete system of human communication" (or a "form of life") showing in primarily "commissive," "behabitive," and "exercitive" modes how a community comports itself when it encounters an "untranscendable negation of . . . possibilities."
—GERALD JAMES LARSON, "Prolegomenon to a Theory of Religion," *Journal of the American Academy of Religion*

29. Robert Frost, the distinguished New England poet, used to define a liberal as someone who refuses to take his own side in an argument.
—"Dreaming of JFK," *The Economist*, March 17, 1984, p. 25

* 30. The meaning of a word is what is explained by the explanation of the meaning. —LUDWIG WITTGENSTEIN, *Philosophical Investigations*, No. 560, p. 149e

PART TWO

Deduction

5

Categorical Propositions

*Like Molière's M. Jourdain who found that he had long been speaking prose,
I found that I had long been forming propositions. I said to myself, "Yes, I
form propositions when my tongue does more than wag. I form them out of
terms. I say something about something. Therefore I ought to be able, in
serious talk, to pinpoint those two parts of my proposition. I ought to know
exactly what I am talking about, and exactly what I am saying about it."*
—A. A. LUCE

5.1 *Categorical Propositions and Classes*

The preceding chapters have dealt, for the most part, with the topic of language and its influence on argumentation. We turn now to that special kind of argument called deduction. A deductive argument is one whose premisses are claimed to provide conclusive grounds for the truth of its conclusion. Every deductive argument is either valid or invalid: valid if it is impossible for its premisses to be true without its conclusion being true also, invalid otherwise. The theory of deduction is intended to explain the relationship between premisses and conclusion of a valid argument and to provide techniques for the appraisal of deductive arguments, that is, for discriminating between valid and invalid deductions.

Informal fallacies were discussed at length in Chapter 3. But even where no informal fallacy is involved, a deductive argument may be invalid rather than valid; so further techniques for appraising such arguments must be devised. The classical or Aristotelian[1] study of deduction focused on arguments containing only propositions of a special kind, called "categorical prop-

---

[1]So called after Aristotle (384–322 B.C.), one of the greatest philosophers of ancient Greece. After studying for twenty years in Plato's Academy, he became tutor to Alexander the Great. Later he founded his own school, the Lyceum, where he contributed to nearly every field of human knowledge. After Aristotle's death his treatises on reasoning were grouped together and came to be called the *Organon*. The word "logic" did not acquire its modern meaning until the second century A.D., but the subject matter of logic was determined by the content of the *Organon*.

ositions." In the argument

> No athletes are vegetarians.
> All football players are athletes.
> _____
> Therefore no football players are vegetarians.

both premises and the conclusion are *categorical* propositions. Propositions of this kind can be analyzed as being about classes, affirming or denying that a class *S* is included in a class *P*, either in whole or in part. The premises and conclusion of the preceding argument are about the class of all athletes, the class of all vegetarians, and the class of all football players.

Classes were mentioned briefly in the preceding chapter, where a *class* was explained to be the collection of all objects that have some specified characteristic in common. There are various ways in which classes may be related to each other. If every member of one class is also a member of a second class, then the first class is said to be included or contained in the second. If some but perhaps not all members of one class are also members of another, then the first class may be said to be partially contained in the second class. Of course, there are pairs of classes having no members in common, such as the class of all triangles and the class of all circles. These various different relationships between classes are affirmed or denied by categorical propositions.

There are just four different *standard forms* of categorical propositions. They are illustrated by the four following propositions:

1. All politicians are liars.
2. No politicians are liars.
3. Some politicians are liars.
4. Some politicians are not liars.

The first is a universal affirmative proposition. It is about two classes, the class of all politicians and the class of all liars, saying that the first class is included or contained in the second, which means that every member of the first class is also a member of the second class. In the present example, the subject term "politicians" designates the class of all politicians, and the predicate term "liars" designates the class of all liars. Any universal affirmative proposition may be written schematically as

$$\text{All } S \text{ is } P.$$

where the letters *S* and *P* represent the subject and predicate terms, respectively. The name "universal affirmative" is appropriate because the proposition affirms that the relationship of class inclusion holds between the two classes and says that the inclusion is complete or universal: all members of *S* are said to be members of *P* also.

The second example

No politicians are liars.

is a universal negative proposition. It denies of politicians universally that they are liars. Concerned with two classes, it says that the first class is excluded from the second—wholly excluded—which is to say that there is no member of the first class that is also a member of the second. Any universal negative proposition may be written schematically as

No *S* is *P*

where, again, the letters *S* and *P* represent the subject and predicate terms. The name "universal negative" is appropriate because the proposition denies that the relation of class inclusion holds between the two classes, and denies it universally: no members at all of *S* are members of *P*.

The third example

Some politicans are liars.

is a particular affirmative proposition. Clearly what the present example affirms is that some members of the class of all politicians are (also) members of the class of all liars. But it does not affirm this of politicians universally: not all politicians universally are said to be liars but, rather, some particular politician or politicians. This proposition neither affirms nor denies that *all* politicians are liars; it makes no pronouncement on the matter. It does not literally say that some politicians are *not* liars, although in some contexts it might be taken to suggest it. The literal, minimal interpretation of the present proposition is that the class of politicians and the class of liars have some member or members in common. For definiteness, we adopt that minimal interpretation here.

The word "some" is indefinite. Does it mean "at least one," or "at least two," or "at least a hundred"? Or how many? For the sake of definiteness, although this may depart from ordinary usage in some cases, it is customary to regard the word "some" as meaning "at least one." Thus a particular affirmative proposition, written schematically as

Some *S* is *P*.

is interpreted as saying that at least one member of the class designated by the subject term *S* is also a member of the class designated by the predicate term *P*. The name "particular affirmative" is appropriate because the proposition affirms that the relationship of class inclusion holds, but does not affirm it of the first class universally, but only partially, of some particular member or members of the first class.

The fourth example

> Some politicians are not liars.

is a particular negative proposition. This example, like the one preceding it, is particular in that it does not refer to politicians universally but only to some particular member or members of that class. But unlike the former, it does not affirm that the particular members of the first class referred to are included in the second class: this is precisely what is denied. A particular negative proposition, schematically written as

> Some *S* is not *P*.

says that at least one member of the class designated by the subject term *S* is excluded from the whole of the class designated by the predicate term *P*.

It was traditionally held that all deductive arguments were analyzable in terms of these four standard forms of categorical propositions, and a considerable amount of theory was built up around them. Not all standard-form categorical propositions are as simple and straightforward as the examples considered thus far. Although the subject and predicate terms of a standard-form categorical proposition designate classes, they may be quite complicated expressions instead of single words. For example, the proposition

> All candidates for the position are persons of honor and integrity

has as its subject and predicate terms, respectively, the phrases "candidates for the position" and "persons of honor and integrity."

EXERCISES

Identify the subject and predicate terms and name the form of each of the following propositions.

★ 1. Some historians are extremely gifted writers whose works read like first-rate novels.

2. No athletes who have ever accepted pay for participating in sports are amateurs.

3. No dogs that are without pedigrees are candidates for blue ribbons in official dog shows sponsored by the American Kennel Society.

4. All satellites that are presently in orbits less than ten thousand miles high are very delicate devices that cost many thousands of dollars to manufacture.

★ 5. Some members of families that are rich and famous are not persons of either wealth or distinction.

6. Some paintings produced by artists who are universally recognized as masters are not works of genuine merit that either are or deserve to be preserved in museums and made available to the public.

7. All drivers of automobiles that are not safe are desperadoes who threaten the lives of their fellows.

8. Some politicians who could not be elected to the most minor positions are appointed officials in our government today.

9. Some drugs that are very effective when properly administered are not safe remedies that all medicine cabinets should contain.

10. No people who have not themselves done creative work in the arts are responsible critics on whose judgment we can rely.

5.2 *Quality, Quantity, and Distribution*

Every standard-form categorical proposition is said to have both a *quality* and and a *quantity*. The quality of a proposition is *affirmative* or *negative* according to whether class inclusion (complete or partial) is affirmed or denied by the proposition. Thus both universal affirmative and particular affirmative propositions are affirmative in quality, while universal negative and particular negative propositions are both negative. It is customary to use the letters *A, E, I,* and *O* as names for the four standard forms of categorical propositions: universal affirmative, universal negative, particular affirmative, and particular negative, respectively. The letter names are presumed to come from the Latin words "AffIrmo" and "nEgO," which mean "I affirm" and "I deny," respectively.

The quantity of a proposition is universal or particular according to whether the proposition refers to all members or only to some members of the class designated by its subject term. Thus the *A* and *E* propositions are universal in quantity, whereas the *I* and *O* propositions are particular in quantity. We observe that the names "universal affirmative," "universal negative," "particular affirmative," and "particular negative" uniquely describe each of the four standard forms by mentioning first its quantity and then its quality.

Every standard-form categorical proposition begins with one of the words "all," "no," or "some." These words show the quantity of the proposition, and they are called the "quantifiers." The first two indicate that the proposition is universal, the third that it is particular. In addition to expressing the universal quantity, the quantifier "no" serves to indicate the negative quality of the *E* proposition.

Between the subject and predicate terms of every standard-form categorical proposition occurs some form of the verb "to be" (accompanied by the word "not" in the case of the *O* proposition). This serves to connect the subject and predicate terms, and is called the "copula." In the schematic formulations given in the preceding section, only "is" and "is not" appear, but depending upon how the proposition is worded otherwise, some other form of the verb "to be" may be more appropriate. For example, in the following three propositions

Some Roman emperors were monsters.
All communists are fanatics.
Some soldiers will not be heroes.

"were," "are," and "will not be" serve as copulas. The general skeleton or schema of a standard-form categorical proposition consists of four parts: first the quantifier, then the subject term, next the copula, and finally the predicate term. This schema may be written as

Quantifier (subject term) copula (predicate term).

On the class interpretation, the subject and predicate terms of a standard-form categorical proposition designate classes of objects, and the proposition is regarded as being about these classes. Propositions may refer to classes in different ways, of course. A proposition may refer to *all* members of a class, or it may refer to only *some* members of that class. Thus the proposition

All senators are citizens.

refers to or is about *all* senators, but does not refer to all citizens. It asserts that each and every member of the class of senators is a citizen, but it makes no assertion about all citizens. It does not affirm that each and every citizen is a senator, but it does not deny it either. Any *A* proposition, of this form,

All *S* is *P*.

is thus seen to refer to *all* members of the class designated by its subject term *S*, but does not refer to all members of the class designated by its predicate term *P*.

The technical term "distribution" is introduced to characterize the ways in which terms can occur in categorical propositions. A proposition *distributes* a term if it refers to all members of the class designated by the term. As we have seen, the subject term of an *A* proposition is *distributed in* (or *by*) that proposition, whereas its predicate term is *undistributed in* (or *by*) it. Let us examine the other standard-form categorical propositions to see which terms are distributed or undistributed in them.

An *E* proposition, such as

No athletes are vegetarians.

asserts of each and every athlete that he or she is not a vegetarian. The whole of the class of athletes is said to be excluded from the class of vegetarians. All members of the class designated by its subject term are referred to by an *E* proposition, which is therefore said to distribute its subject term. On the other hand, in asserting that the whole class of athletes is excluded from the class of vegetarians, it is also asserted that the whole class of vegetarians is excluded from the class of athletes. The given proposition clearly asserts of each and every vegetarian that he or she is not an athlete. An *E* proposition, therefore, refers to all members of the class designated by its predicate term, and is said to distribute its predicate term also. *E* propositions distribute both their subject and predicate terms.

The situation is different with respect to *I* propositions. Thus

Some soldiers are cowards.

makes no assertion about *all* soldiers and makes no assertion about all cowards either. It says nothing about each and every soldier, nor about each and every coward. Neither class is said to be either wholly included or wholly excluded from the other. Both subject and predicate terms are undistributed in any particular affirmative proposition.

The particular negative or *O* proposition is similar in that it too does not distribute its subject term. Thus the proposition

Some horses are not thoroughbreds.

says nothing about *all* horses but refers to *some* members of the class designated by the subject term. It says of this part of the class of all horses that it is excluded from the class of all thoroughbreds, that is, from the *whole* of the latter class. Given the particular horses referred to, it says that each and every member of the class of thoroughbreds is *not* one of those particular horses. When something is said to be excluded from a class, the whole of the class is referred to; as when a person is excluded from a country, all parts of that country are forbidden to that person. The particular negative proposition does distribute its predicate term, but not its subject term.

We may summarize these remarks on distribution as follows. Universal propositions, both affirmative and negative, distribute their subject terms, whereas particular propositions, whether affirmative or negative, do not distribute their subject terms. Thus the *quantity* of any standard-form categorical proposition determines whether its *subject* term is distributed or undistributed. Affirmative propositions, whether universal or particular, do not distribute their predicate terms, whereas negative propositions, both universal and particular, do distribute their predicate terms. Thus the *quality* of any standard-form categorical proposition determines whether its predicate term is distributed or undistributed.

The following diagram summarizes this information and may be useful in helping the student to remember which propositions distribute which of their terms.

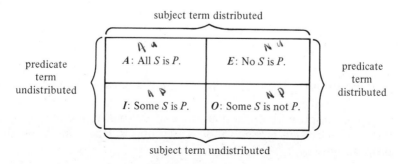

EXERCISES

Name the quality and quantity of each of the following propositions and state whether their subject and predicate terms are distributed or undistributed.

★ 1. Some presidential candidates will be sadly disappointed people.

2. All persons arrested in the Watergate burglary were dupes of the Nixon "law and order" administration.

3. Some recently identified unstable elements were not entirely accidental discoveries.

4. Some members of the military–industrial complex are mild-mannered people to whom violence is abhorrent.

★ 5. No leader of the feminist movement is a major business executive.

6. All hard-line advocates of law and order at any cost are people who will be remembered, if at all, only for having failed to understand the major social pressures of the late twentieth century.

7. Some recent rulings of the Supreme Court were politically motivated decisions that flouted the entire history of American legal practice.

8. No harmful pesticides or chemical defoliants were genuine contributions to the long-range agricultural goals of the nation.

9. Some advocates of major political, social, and economic reforms are not responsible people who have a stake in maintaining the status quo.

10. All new labor-saving devices are major threats to the trade union movement.

5.3 *The Traditional Square of Opposition*

Standard-form categorical propositions having the same subject and predicate terms may differ from each other in quality or in quantity or in both. This kind of differing was given the technical name "opposition" by older logicians, and certain important truth relations were correlated with the various kinds of opposition. Two propositions are *contradictories* if one is the denial or negation of the other, that is, if they cannot both be true *and* they cannot both be false. It is clear that two standard-form categorical propositions having the same subject and predicate terms but differing from each other *both* in quantity and in quality are contradictories. Thus the *A* and *O* propositions

All judges are lawyers.

and

Some judges are not lawyers.

which are opposed both in quantity and in quality, are obviously contradictories. Exactly one is true, and exactly one is false. Similarly, the *E* and *I* propositions

No politicians are idealists.

and

Some politicians are idealists.

are opposed both in quantity and quality and are contradictories. Schematically we may say that the contradictory of "All *S* is *P*" is "Some *S* is not *P*," and the contradictory of "No *S* is *P*" is "Some *S* is *P*"; *A* and *O* are contradictories, as are *E* and *I*.

Two propositions are said to be *contraries* if they cannot both be true, that is, if the truth of either one entails that the other is false. Thus "Alice is older than Betty" and "Betty is older than Alice" are contraries: if either one is true then the other must be false. But they are not contradictories: both would be false if Alice and Betty were exactly the same age. Two propositions are contraries if they cannot both be true, although they might both be false. The traditional or Aristotelian account of categorical propositions held that universal propositions having the same subject and predicate terms but differing in quality were contraries.[2] Thus, it was urged, *A* and *E* propositions such as

All poets are idlers.

and

No poets are idlers.

cannot both be true, although both might be false, and are therefore to be regarded as contraries.

It is obvious that this claim that *A* and *E* propositions are contraries is *not* correct if either the *A* or the *E* proposition is a necessary, that is, a logical or mathematical truth, such as "All squares are rectangles" or "No squares are circles." For if a proposition is necessarily true, that is, cannot possibly be false, it cannot have a contrary, because propositions that are contraries *can* both be false. A proposition that is neither necessarily true nor necessarily false is said to be *contingent*. The claim that *A* and *E* propositions having the same subject and predicate terms are contraries can be correct if both are contingent propositions, and we shall assume that they are in the remainder of this chapter.[3]

Two propositions are said to be *subcontraries* if they cannot both be false, although they might both be true. The same traditional account held that

---

[2]This traditional view will be examined critically in Section 5.5.

[3]That the complications in this account are required has been cogently argued by Professor David H. Sanford in his article "Contraries and Subcontraries," in *NOÛS*, Vol. 2, No. 1, February 1968, pp. 95–96.

particular propositions having the same subject and predicate terms but differing in quality were subcontraries. It was affirmed that *I* and *O* propositions such as

Some diamonds are precious stones.

and

Some diamonds are not precious stones.

could both be true, but could not both be false, and must therefore be regarded as subcontraries.

It is obvious that this claim that *I* and *O* propositions are subcontraries is *not* correct if either the *I* or the *O* proposition is necessarily false, for example, "Some squares are circles" or "Some squares are not rectangles." For if a proposition is necessarily false, that is, cannot possibly be true, it cannot have a subcontrary, because propositions that are subcontraries *can* both be true. However, if both the *I* and *O* are contingent propositions then they can both be true, and we shall assume that they are contingent in the remainder of this chapter.[4]

Thus far the examples of opposition between propositions have been such as to suggest disagreement. But "opposition" in the present context is a technical term and applies even where disagreement in the ordinary sense is not present. Thus where two propositions, again having the same subject and predicate terms, agree in quality and differ only in quantity, there is *opposition* even though there is no disagreement implied. In such cases the truth of the particular proposition was asserted to follow from or to be implied by the truth of the universal. Thus from the truth of an *A* proposition, such as

All spiders are eight-legged animals.

the truth of the corresponding *I* proposition

Some spiders are eight-legged animals.

was supposed to follow. And from the truth of an *E* proposition, such as

No spiders are insects.

the truth of the corresponding *O* proposition

Some spiders are not insects.

was supposed to follow. The opposition between a universal proposition and its corresponding particular (i.e., the particular proposition having the same

[4]Ibid.

subject and predicate terms and the same quality as the universal) was named *subalternation*. In this situation the universal proposition is called the *superaltern* and the particular is referred to either as the *subalternate* or simply as the *subaltern*. In subalternation, it was held, the *superaltern* implies the *subaltern*. The implication does not hold from the subaltern to superaltern, for such subalterns as

Some animals are cats.

and

Some animals are not cats.

are both true while their superalterns are clearly both false.

These various kinds of opposition were represented by a diagram called the *Square of Opposition,* which is reproduced as Figure 1.

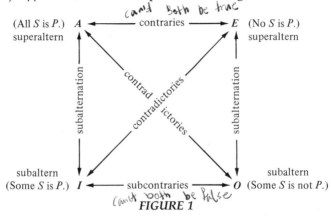

FIGURE 1

The relationships diagrammed by this Square of Opposition were believed to provide a logical basis for validating certain rather elementary forms of argument. In this connection it is customary to distinguish between *mediate* and *immediate* inference. Any inference is the drawing of a conclusion from one or more premisses. Where there is more than one premiss involved, as in a syllogism, which has two premisses, the inference is said to be *mediate*— presumably because the conclusion is supposed to be drawn from the first premiss through the *mediation* of the second. Where a conclusion is drawn from only one premiss, there is no such *mediation,* and the inference is said to be *immediate*. The information embodied in the traditional Square of Opposition clearly provides a basis for a number of immediate inferences. Thus if an *A* proposition is taken as premiss, then according to the Square of Opposition one can validly infer that the corresponding *O* proposition (i.e., the *O* proposition having the same subject and predicate terms as the *A*) is false. And from the same premiss one can immediately infer that the corresponding *I* proposition is true. Of course, from the truth of an *I* proposition the truth of its corresponding *A* proposition does not follow, but the falsehood of the corresponding *E* proposition does. The traditional Square of Opposition provides the basis for a considerable number of such immediate inferences. Given the truth or falsehood of any one of the four standard-form categorical propositions, the truth or falsehood of some or all of the others can be inferred immediately. The immediate inferences based on the traditional Square of Opposition may be listed as follows:

A being given as true: *E* is false, *I* is true, *O* is false.
E being given as true: *A* is false, *I* is false, *O* is true.
I being given as true: *E* is false, while *A* and *O* are undetermined.
O being given as true: *A* is false, while *E* and *I* are undetermined.
A being given as false: *O* is true, while *E* and *I* are undetermined.
E being given as false: *I* is true, while *A* and *O* are undetermined.
I being given as false: *A* is false, *E* is true, *O* is true.
O being given as false: *A* is true, *E* is false, *I* is true.

EXERCISES

What can be inferred about the truth or falsehood of the remaining propositions in each of the following sets: (1) if we assume the first to be true? (2) If we assume it to be false?

★ 1. a. All successful executives are intelligent people.
    b. No successful executives are intelligent people.
    c. Some successful executives are intelligent people.
    d. Some successful executives are not intelligent people.

2. a. No animals with horns are carnivores.
    b. Some animals with horns are carnivores.
    c. Some animals with horns are not carnivores.
    d. All animals with horns are carnivores.

3. a. Some uranium isotopes are highly unstable substances.
    b. Some uranium isotopes are not highly unstable substances.
    c. All uranium isotopes are highly unstable substances.
    d. No uranium isotopes are highly unstable substances.

4. a. Some college professors are not entertaining lecturers.
    b. All college professors are entertaining lecturers.
    c. No college professors are entertaining lecturers.
    d. Some college professors are entertaining lecturers.

5.4 *Further Immediate Inferences*

There are other kinds of immediate inference in addition to those associated with the traditional Square of Opposition. In this section we shall present three of these other types. The first kind of immediate inference proceeds by simply interchanging the subject and predicate terms of the proposition. It is called *conversion* and is perfectly valid in the case of *E* and *I* propositions.

Clearly, "No men are angels" can be uttered to make the same assertion as "No angels are men," and either can be validly inferred from the other by the immediate inference called conversion. Just as clearly, "Some writers are women" and "Some women are writers" are logically equivalent, so by conversion either can validly be inferred from the other. One standard-form categorical proposition is said to be the *converse* of another when it is formed by simply interchanging the subject and predicate terms of that other proposition. Thus "No idealists are politicians" is the converse of "No politicians are idealists," and each can validly be inferred from the other by conversion.

But the converse of an *A* proposition does not in general follow validly from that *A* proposition. Thus if our original proposition is "All dogs are animals," its converse "All animals are dogs," does not follow from the original proposition at all, the original being true while its converse is false. Traditional logic recognized this fact, of course, but asserted that something *like* conversion was valid for *A* propositions. We have already remarked in Section 5.3 on the traditional Square of Opposition that the subaltern *I* proposition (Some *S* is *P*) can validly be inferred from its superaltern *A* proposition (All *S* is *P*). The *A* proposition says something about *all* members of *S*, but the *I* proposition makes a more limited claim, about only *some* members of *S*. We have just seen that conversion of an *I* proposition is perfectly valid. So given the *A* proposition (All *S* is *P*), its subaltern (Some *S* is *P*) can validly be inferred by subalternation, and from that subaltern the proposition (Some *P* is *S*) can validly be inferred by conversion. So by a combination of subalternation and conversion (Some *P* is *S*) can validly be inferred from (All *S* is *P*). This pattern of inference was called "conversion by limitation" (or *per accidens*). It proceeds by interchanging subject and predicate terms and changing the quantity of the proposition from universal to particular. Thus it was claimed that from the premiss "All dogs are animals" the conclusion "Some animals are dogs" could validly be inferred, the inference being called *conversion by limitation*. This type of conversion will be considered further in the next section.

Finally, it should be observed that converting an *O* proposition is not in general valid. For the true *O* proposition "Some animals are not dogs" has as its converse the false proposition "Some dogs are not animals." We see, then, that an *O* proposition and its converse are not in general equivalent.

The term "convertend" is used to refer to the premiss of an immediate inference by conversion, and the conclusion is called the "converse." The following table was traditionally held to give a complete picture of valid conversions:

Conversions

Convertend	Converse
A: All *S* is *P*	*I:* Some *P* is *S* (by limitation)
E: No *S* is *P*	*E:* No *P* is *S*
I: Some *S* is *P*	*I:* Some *P* is *S*
O: Some *S* is not *P*	(not valid)

The converse of a given proposition contains exactly the same terms as the given proposition (their order being reversed) and has the same quality.

The next type of immediate inference to be discussed is called "obversion." Before explaining it, we shall find it helpful to return briefly to the notion of a "class" and to introduce some new ideas which enable us to discuss obversion more easily. A class is the collection of all objects having a certain common attribute that we refer to as the *class-defining characteristic*. Thus the class of all humans is the collection of all things which have the characteristic of being human, and its class-defining characteristic is the attribute of being human. The class-defining characteristic need not be a "simple" attribute in any sense, for *any* attribute determines a class. Thus the complex attribute of being left-handed and red-headed and a student determines a class—the class of all left-handed, red-headed students.

Every class has associated with it a *complementary class*, or *complement*, which is the collection of all things that do *not* belong to the original class. Thus the complement of the class of all people is the class of all things that are *not* people. The class-defining characteristic of the complementary class is the (negative) attribute of *not being a person*. The complement of the class of all people contains no people, but contains everything else: shoes and ships and sealing wax, and cabbages—but no kings, since kings are people. It is sometimes convenient to speak of the complement of the class of all persons as "the class of all nonpersons." The complement of the class designated by the term S is then designated by the term non-S, and we may speak of the term non-S as being the complement of the term S. We are using the word "complement" in two senses: one the sense of class complement, the other the sense of the complement of a term. The two senses, although different, are very closely connected. One term is the (term) complement of another just in case the first term designates the (class) complement of the class designated by the second term. It should be noted that just as a class is the (class) complement of its own complement, a term is the (term) complement of its own complement. A sort of "double negative" rule is involved here, so that we need not have strings of "non's" prefixed to a term. Thus we should write the complement of the term "voter" as "nonvoter," but we should write the complement of the latter term simply as "voter" rather than "nonnonvoter." One must be careful not to mistake contrary terms for complementary terms, as in identifying "cowards" and "nonheroes." The terms "coward" and "hero" are contraries in that no person can be both a coward and a hero, but not everyone—and certainly not everything—need be either one or the other. Thus the complement of the term "winner" is not "loser," but "nonwinner," for although not everything—or even everyone—is either a winner or a loser, absolutely everything is either a winner or a nonwinner.

Now that we understand what is meant by the complement of a term, the process of obversion is easy to describe. In *obversion*, the subject term remains unchanged, and so does the quantity of the proposition being obverted. To obvert a proposition, we change its quality and replace the predicate term by its complement. Thus the A proposition

All residents are voters.

has as its obverse the *E* proposition

No residents are nonvoters.

These two propositions, it is clear, are logically equivalent, so either one can validly be inferred from the other. Obversion is a valid immediate inference when applied to *any* standard-form categorical proposition. Thus the *E* proposition

No umpires are partisans.

has as its obverse the logically equivalent *A* proposition

All umpires are nonpartisans.

Similarly, the obverse of the *I* proposition

Some metals are conductors.

is the *O* proposition

Some metals are not nonconductors.

And finally the *O* proposition

Some nations were not belligerents.

has as its obverse the *I* proposition

Some nations were nonbelligerents.

The term *obvertend* is used to refer to the premiss of an immediate inference by obversion, and the conclusion is called the *obverse*. Every standard-form categorical proposition is logically equivalent to its obverse, so obversion is a valid form of immediate inference for any standard-form categorical proposition. To obtain the obverse of a proposition, we leave the quantity and the subject term unchanged, change the quality of the proposition, and replace the predicate term by its complement. The following table gives a complete picture of all valid obversions:

Obversions

Obvertend	Obverse
A: All S is P	*E:* No S is non-P
E: No S is P	*A:* All S is non-P
I: Some S is P	*O:* Some S is not non-P
O: Some S is not P	*I:* Some S is non-P

The third variety of immediate inference to be discussed introduces no new principles, for it can be reduced, in a sense, to the first two. To form the *contrapositive* of a given proposition we replace its subject term by the complement of its predicate term and replace its predicate term by the complement of its subject term. Thus the contrapositive of the *A* proposition

All members are voters.

is the *A* proposition

All nonvoters are nonmembers.

That these two are logically equivalent will be evident upon a moment's reflection, and from this it is clear that contraposition is a valid form of immediate inference when applied to *A* propositions. Contraposition introduces nothing new, for we can get from any *A* proposition to its contrapositive by first obverting it, next applying conversion, and then applying obversion again. Thus, beginning with "All *S* is *P*," we obvert it to obtain "No *S* is non-*P*," which converts validly to "No non-*P* is *S*," whose obverse is "All non-*P* is non-*S*." Thus the contrapositive of any *A* proposition is the obverse of the converse of the obverse of that proposition.

Contraposition is most useful in working with *A* propositions, but it is a valid form of immediate inference when applied to *O* propositions also. Thus the contrapositive of the *O* proposition

Some students are not idealists.

is the somewhat cumbersome *O* proposition

Some nonidealists are not nonstudents.

which is logically equivalent to the first. Their logical equivalence can be shown by deriving the contrapositive a step at a time through obverting, converting, and then obverting again, as in the following schematic derivation: "Some *S* is not *P*" obverts to "Some *S* is non-*P*," which converts to "Some non-*P* is *S*," which obverts to "Some non-*P* is not non-*S*" (the contrapositive).

Contraposition is not, in general, valid for *I* propositions. This can be seen by noting that the true *I* proposition

Some citizens are nonlegislators.

has as its contrapositive the false proposition

Some legislators are noncitizens.

The reason that contraposition is not generally valid when applied to *I* propositions can be seen when we attempt to derive the contrapositive of an *I* proposition by successively obverting, converting, and obverting. The obverse of the *I* proposition "Some *S* is *P*" is the *O* proposition "Some *S* is not non-*P*," whose converse does not in general follow validly from it.

The contrapositive of the *E* proposition "No *S* is *P*" is "No non-*P* is non-*S*," which does not in general follow validly from the original, as can be seen by observing that the *E* proposition

No wrestlers are weaklings.

which is true, has as its contrapositive the false proposition

No nonweaklings are nonwrestlers.

If we attempt to derive the contrapositive of an *E* proposition by successive obversion, conversion, and obversion, we find the reason for this invalidity. The obverse of the *E* proposition "No *S* is *P*" is the *A* proposition "All *S* is non-*P*," and in general it cannot validly be converted except *by limitation*. If we do convert it by limitation to obtain "Some non-*P* is *S*," then the latter can be obverted to obtain "Some non-*P* is not non-*S*," which we may call the contrapositive by limitation. This type of contraposition will be considered further in the next section.

Thus we see that contraposition is a valid form of immediate inference only when applied to *A* and *O* propositions. Contraposition is not valid at all for *I* propositions, and for *E* propositions only by limitation. This may also be presented in the form of a table:

Contraposition

Premiss	Contrapositive
A: All *S* is *P*	*A:* All non-*P* is non-*S*
E: No *S* is *P*	*O:* Some non-*P* is not non-*S* (by limitation)
I: Some *S* is *P*	(not valid)
O: Some *S* is not *P*	*O:* Some non-*P* is not non-*S*

There are many other types of immediate inference that have been classified and given special names, but since they involve no new principles we shall not discuss them here.

Some questions about the relations between propositions are best answered by explaining the various immediate inferences that can be drawn from one or the other of them. For example, given that the proposition "All surgeons are physicians" is true, what can be said about the truth or falsehood of the proposition "No nonsurgeons are nonphysicians"? Here one useful procedure is to draw as many valid inferences from the *given* proposition as you can, to see if the problematic proposition—or its contradictory or contrary—follows validly from the one given as true. In this example, given that "All *S* is *P*" we validly infer its contrapositive "All non-*P* is non-*S*," from which conversion by limitation gives us "Some non-*S* is non-*P*," which is, according to the traditional logic, a valid consequence of the given proposition and is therefore true. But by the Square of Opposition it is the contradictory of the problematic proposition "no non-*S* is non-*P*," which is thus no longer problematic but known to be false.

As was pointed out in Section 1.7, although a valid argument whose premisses are true *must* have a true conclusion, a valid argument whose premisses are false *can* have a true conclusion. Examples of the latter come easily to mind for conversion by limitation, contraposition by limitation, and subalternation in the Square of Opposition. Thus from the false premiss "All animals are cats," the true proposition "Some animals are cats" follows by subalternation. And from the false proposition "All parents are students," conversion by limitation yields the true proposition "Some students are parents." So if a proposition is given to be false and the question is raised about the truth or falsehood of *another* (somehow related) proposition, the recommended procedure is to begin drawing immediate inference either from the contradictory of the proposition given to be false or from the problematic proposition itself. For the contradictory of a false proposition must be true, and all valid inferences from it will also be true propositions. And if the problematic proposition can be shown to imply the proposition that is given to be false, it must itself be false.

EXERCISES

I. State the converses of the following propositions and indicate which of them are equivalent to the given propositions.

★ 1. No people who are considerate of others are reckless drivers who pay no attention to traffic regulations.

2. All graduates of West Point are commissioned officers in the U.S. Army.

3. Some European cars are overpriced and underpowered automobiles.

4. No reptiles are warm-blooded animals.

5. Some professional wrestlers are elderly persons who are incapable of doing an honest day's work.

II. State the obverses of the following propositions.

★ 1. Some college athletes are professionals.

2. No organic compounds are metals.

3. Some clergymen are not abstainers.

4. No geniuses are conformists.

5. All objects suitable for boat anchors are objects weighing at least fifteen pounds.

III. State the contrapositives of the following propositions and indicate which of them are equivalent to the given propositions.

⋆ 1. All journalists are pessimists.

2. Some soldiers are not officers.

3. All scholars are nondegenerates.

4. All things weighing less than fifty pounds are objects not more than four feet high.

5. Some noncitizens are not nonresidents.

IV. If "All socialists are pacifists" is true, what may be inferred about the truth or falsehood of the following propositions?

⋆ 1. Some nonpacifists are not nonsocialists.

2. No socialists are nonpacifists.

3. All nonsocialists are nonpacifists.

4. No nonpacifists are socialists.

* 5. No nonsocialists are nonpacifists.

6. All nonpacifists are nonsocialists.

7. No pacifists are nonsocialists.

8. Some socialists are not pacifists.

9. All pacifists are socialists.

10. Some nonpacifists are socialists.

V. If "No scientists are philosophers" is true, what may be inferred about the truth or falsehood of the following propositions?

⋆ 1. No nonphilosophers are scientists.

2. Some nonphilosophers are not nonscientists.

3. All nonscientists are nonphilosophers.

4. No scientists are nonphilosophers.

⋆ 5. No nonscientists are nonphilosophers.

6. All philosophers are scientists.

7. Some nonphilosophers are scientists.

8. All nonphilosophers are nonscientists.

9. Some scientists are not philosophers.

10. No philosophers are nonscientists.

VI. If "Some saints were martyrs" is true, what may be inferred about the truth or falsehood of the following propositions?

⋆ 1. All saints were martyrs.

2. Some nonmartyrs were not nonsaints.

3. No nonsaints were martyrs.

4. Some nonmartyrs were saints.

⋆ 5. Some martyrs were not nonsaints.

6. No martyrs were nonsaints.

7. Some nonsaints were not nonmartyrs.

8. All martyrs were saints.

9. No saints were martyrs.

★ 10. All martyrs were nonsaints.

11. Some nonsaints were not martyrs.

12. No nonmartyrs were saints.

13. No saints were nonmartyrs.

14. Some nonmartyrs were nonsaints.

★ 15. No martyrs were saints.

16. Some nonsaints were nonmartyrs.

17. No nonmartyrs were nonsaints.

18. Some nonsaints were martyrs.

19. All nonmartyrs were saints.

★ 20. Some saints were not nonmartyrs.

21. Some martyrs were not saints.

22. No nonsaints were nonmartyrs.

23. Some martyrs were saints.

24. Some saints were nonmartyrs.

★ 25. All nonmartyrs were nonsaints.

26. All saints were nonmartyrs.

27. Some saints were not martyrs.

28. All nonsaints were nonmartyrs.

29. Some martyrs were nonsaints.

30. All nonsaints were martyrs.

31. Some nonmartyrs were not saints.

VII. If "Some merchants are not pirates" is true, what may be inferred about the truth or falsehood of the following propositions?

★ 1. Some nonpirates are not nonmerchants.

2. No nonmerchants are pirates.

3. No pirates are nonmerchants.

4. All merchants are nonpirates.

★ 5. All nonpirates are nonmerchants.

6. No merchants are pirates.

7. Some pirates are merchants.

8. No nonmerchants are nonpirates.

9. All nonpirates are merchants.

★ 10. All nonmerchants are pirates.

11. Some pirates are not nonmerchants.

12. No nonpirates are nonmerchants.

13. Some merchants are pirates.

14. Some pirates are not merchants.

★ 15. No nonpirates are merchants.

16. All pirates are nonmerchants.
17. Some merchants are not nonpirates.
18. Some nonpirates are nonmerchants.
19. Some merchants are nonpirates.
★ 20. Some nonpirates are merchants.
21. Some nonmerchants are not pirates.
22. Some nonmerchants are not nonpirates.
23. All nonmerchants are nonpirates.
24. Some nonmerchants are pirates.
★ 25. Some pirates are nonmerchants.
26. No merchants are nonpirates.
27. Some nonpirates are not merchants.
28. All merchants are pirates.
29. No pirates are merchants.
30. Some nonmerchants are nonpirates.
31. All pirates are merchants.

5.5 *Existential Import*

A proposition is said to have "existential import" if it is typically uttered to assert the existence of objects of some specified kind. For example, the proposition "There are books on my desk" has existential import, whereas the proposition "There are no unicorns" does not. It seems clear, especially in the light of our discussion of the word "some" in the first section of this chapter, that particular propositions have existential import. The *I* proposition "Some soldiers are heroes" says that there exists at least one soldier who is a hero. And the *O* proposition "Some soldiers are not heroes" says that there exists at least one soldier who is not a hero. Both particular propositions say that the classes designated by their subject terms are not empty; that is, they do have members.

Apparent exceptions to this view are such statements as "Some ghosts appear in Shakespeare's plays" and "Some Greek gods are described in the *Iliad*." These statements are true despite the fact that there are neither ghosts nor Greek gods. But a little thought will reveal that these apparent exceptions are formulated in a misleading fashion. These statements do not really affirm the existence of ghosts or of Greek gods; they say only that there are certain *other* propositions that are affirmed or implied in Shakespeare's plays and in the *Iliad*. The propositions of Shakespeare and Homer may not be true, but it is certainly true that their writings contain or imply them. And that is all that is affirmed by the apparent exceptions. Outside these fairly uncommon literary or mythological contexts, *I* and *O* propositions do have existential import as explained in the preceding paragraph.

If we grant that *I* and *O* propositions have existential import, then the traditional Square of Opposition would require that *A* and *E* propositions have existential import also. For if *I* follows validly from the corresponding *A* by subalternation, and if *I* asserts existence, then *A* must assert existence also. Similarly, *E* must have existential import if *O* does. (The existential import of *A* and *E* also follows from that of *I* and *O* if we grant the validity of conversion by limitation of *A* and of contraposition by limitation of *E*.)

A difficulty arises at this point. If corresponding *A* and *O* propositions have existential import, then both could be false. If "All inhabitants of Mars are blond" and "Some inhabitants of Mars are not blond" both assert that there exist inhabitants of Mars, then they are both false if Mars is uninhabited. And if corresponding *A* and *O* propositions can both be false, then they are not contradictories. It would seem, then, that there is something wrong with the traditional Square of Opposition. If it is correct in what it says about superalterns *A* and *E* implying subalterns *I* and *O*, then it is clearly mistaken in holding corresponding *A* and *O* propositions to be contradictories. It must also be mistaken in holding *I* and *O* to be subcontraries.

One can defend or rehabilitate the traditional Square of Opposition, as well as conversion by limitation and contraposition by limitation, through introducing the notion of a *presupposition*. We have already encountered this notion in discussing complex questions in Section 3.2. Some (complex) questions are properly answered "yes" or "no" only if it is presupposed that a definite answer has already been given to a prior question. Thus an answer "yes" or "no" can reasonably be given to the question "Did you spend the money you stole?" only if one grants the presupposition that you did steal some money. Similarly, the four standard-form categorical propositions may be said to presuppose that the classes to which they refer do have members. That is, questions of their truth or falsehood, and of the logical relations holding among them, are admissible only if it is presupposed that the existential question has already been answered in the affirmative. If we make the blanket presupposition that all classes designated by our terms (and their complements) do have members, then conversion and contraposition by limitation are valid, and all of the relationships set forth in the traditional Square of Opposition do hold: *A* and *E* are contraries, *I* and *O* are subcontraries, subalterns follow validly from their superalterns, and *A* and *O* are contradictories, as are *E* and *I*.

The existential presupposition necessary and sufficient for the correctness of the traditional Aristotelian logic is in close accord with ordinary English usage in many cases. Suppose, for example, someone were to assert that "All the apples in the barrel are Jonathans," and we look in the barrel and find it empty. Ordinarily we should not take that to make the proposition true, nor to make it false. We would be more inclined to point out that there are no apples in the barrel, indicating that in this particular case the existential presupposition was mistaken.

There are, however, several objections to making this blanket existential presupposition. In the first place, although it preserves the traditional relations among categorical propositions, it does so at the cost of cutting down on their power to formulate assertions. The existential presupposition makes it impossible for any standard-form categorical proposition to deny the existence of members of the classes designated by its terms. In the second place, the existential presupposition is not in *complete* accord with ordinary usage. For example, the proposition "All trespassers will be prosecuted," far from presupposing that the class of trespassers has members, is ordinarily intended to ensure that the class remain empty. And in the third place, we often wish to reason without making any presuppositions about existence. In physics, for instance, Newton's First Law of Motion asserts that every body not acted upon by external forces perseveres in its state of rest or of uniform motion in a straight line. Yet no physicist would want to presuppose that there actually are any bodies not acted upon by external forces.

On the basis of such objections as these, modern logicians decline to make this blanket existential presupposition, even though their decision forces them to give up some of the traditional Aristotelian logic. In contrast to the traditional or Aristotelian interpretation, the modern treatment of standard-form categorical propositions is called Boolean,[5] after the English mathematician and logician George Boole (1815–1864), one of the founders of modern symbolic logic.

On the Boolean interpretation, *I* and *O* propositions have existential import, so where the class *S* is empty the propositions "Some *S* is *P*" and "Some *S* is not *P*" are both false. The universal propositions *A* and *E* are still taken to be the contradictories of the *O* and *I* propositions, respectively. Where *S* is an empty class, both particular propositions are false, and their contradictories "All *S* is *P*" and "No *S* is *P*" are both true. On the Boolean interpretation, universal propositions are understood as having no existential import. However, a universal proposition formulated in ordinary English that is intended to assert existence can be represented in Boolean terms. This is accomplished by using two propositions, the Boolean nonexistential universal and the corresponding existential particular.

We shall adopt the Boolean interpretation in all that follows. This means that *A* and *E* propositions can both be true, and are therefore not contraries, and that *I* and *O* propositions can both be false, and are therefore not subcontraries. Moreover, since *A* and *E* can be true while *I* and *O* are false, inferences based on subalternation are not in general valid. The diagonal (contradictory) relations are all that remain of the traditional Square of Opposition. Obversion remains valid when applied to any proposition, but conversion (and contraposition) by limitation is rejected as not generally valid. Conversion remains valid for *E* and *I* propositions, and contraposition remains valid for *A* and *O* propositions.

---

[5]Bertrand Russell refers to it as "Peano's interpretation," in "The Existential Import of Propositions," *Mind*, n.s., Vol. 14, July 1905, pp. 398–401, reprinted in Douglas Lackey, ed., *Essays in Analysis* (New York: George Braziller, Inc., 1973), pp. 98–102.

If it is not asserted explicitly that a class has members, it is a mistake to assume that it has. Any argument that turns on this mistake will be said to commit the Fallacy of Existential Assumption or, more briefly, the Existential Fallacy.

EXERCISES

In the light of the preceding discussion of existential import, explain at which step (or steps) the following arguments commit the Existential Fallacy.

★   **I.**   (1) No mathematician is one who has squared the circle;
        therefore, (2) No one who has squared the circle is a mathematician;
        therefore, (3) All who have squared the circle are nonmathematicians;
        therefore, (4) Some nonmathematician is one who has squared the circle.

   II.   (1) No citizen is one who has succeeded in accomplishing the impossible;
        therefore, (2) No one who has succeeded in accomplishing the impossible is a citizen;
        therefore, (3) All who have succeeded in accomplishing the impossible are noncitizens;
        therefore, (4) Some who have succeeded in accomplishing the impossible are noncitizens;
        therefore, (5) Some noncitizen is one who has succeeded in accomplishing the impossible.

   III.   (1) No acrobat is one who can lift himself by his own bootstraps;
        therefore, (2) No one who can lift himself by his own bootstraps is an acrobat;
        therefore, (3) Some one who can lift himself by his own bootstraps is not an acrobat. (From which it follows that there is at least one being who can lift himself by his own bootstraps.)

   IV.   (1) It is true that: *No unicorns are animals found in the Bronx Zoo;*
        therefore, (2) It is false that: *All unicorns are animals found in the Bronx Zoo;*
        therefore, (3) It is true that: *Some unicorns are not animals found in the Bronx Zoo.* (From which it follows that there exists at least one unicorn.)

   V.   (1) It is false that: *Some mermaids are members of college sororities;*
        therefore, (2) It is true that: *Some mermaids are not members of college sororities.* (From which it follows that there exists at least one mermaid.)

5.6 *Symbolism and Diagrams for Categorical Propositions*

Since the Boolean interpretation of categorical propositions depends heavily upon the notion of an empty class, it is convenient to have a special symbol to represent it. The zero symbol, 0, is used for this purpose. To say that the class designated by the term S has no members, we write an equals sign between S and 0. Thus the equation $S = 0$ says that there are no S's, or that S has no members.

To say that the class designated by S does have members is to deny that S is empty. To assert that there are S's is to deny the proposition symbolized by $S = 0$. We symbolize that denial by drawing a slanting line through the equality sign. Thus the inequality $S \neq 0$ says that there are S's, by denying that S is empty.

Standard-form categorical propositions refer to two classes; so the equations that represent them are somewhat more complicated. Where each of two classes is already designated by a symbol, the class of all things that belong to both of them can be represented by juxtaposing the symbols for the two original classes. For example, if the letter S designates the class of all satires and the letter P designates the class of all poems, then the class of all things that are both satires and poems is represented by the symbol SP, which thus designates the class of all satiric poems (or poetic satires). The common part or common membership of two classes is called the product or intersection of the two classes. The *product* of two classes is the class of all things that belong to both of them. The product of the class of all Americans and the class of all composers is the class of all American composers. (One must be on guard against certain oddities of the English language here. For example, the product of the class of all Spaniards and the class of all dancers is not the class of all Spanish dancers, for a Spanish dancer is not a dancer who is Spanish, but any person who performs Spanish dances. Similarly, with abstract painters, English majors, antique dealers, and so on.)

This new notation permits us to symbolize E and I propositions as equations and inequalities. The E proposition "No S is P" says that no members of the class S are members of the class P; that is, there are no things that belong to both classes. This can be rephrased by saying that the product of the two classes is empty, which is symbolized by the equation $SP = 0$. The I proposition "Some S is P" says that at least one member of S is also a member of P. This means that the product of the classes S and P is not empty and is symbolized by the inequality $SP \neq 0$.

To symbolize A and O propositions, it is convenient to introduce a new method of representing class complements. The complement of the class of all soldiers is the class of all things that are not soldiers, the class of all nonsoldiers. Where the letter S symbolizes the class of all soldiers, we symbolize the class of all nonsoldiers by $\bar{S}$ (*read* "S bar"), the symbol for the original class with a bar above it. The A proposition "All S is P" says that all members of the class S are also members of the class P, that is, that there are no members of the class S which are not members of P or (by obversion) that "No S is non-P." This, like any other E proposition, says that the product of the classes designated by its subject and predicate terms is empty. It is symbolized by the equation $S\bar{P} = 0$. The O proposition "Some S is not P" obverts to the logically equivalent I proposition "Some S is non-P," which is symbolized by the inequality $S\bar{P} \neq 0$.

In their symbolic formulations, the interrelations among the four standard-form categorical propositions appear very clearly. It is obvious that the *A* and *O* propositions are contradictories when they are symbolized as $S\overline{P} = 0$ and $S\overline{P} \neq 0$, and it is equally obvious that the *E* and *I* propositions, $SP = 0$ and $SP \neq 0$ are contradictories. The Boolean Square of Opposition may be represented as shown in Figure 2.

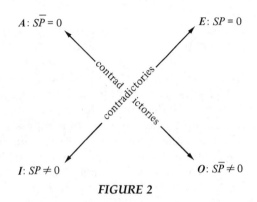

A: $S\overline{P} = 0$ *E*: $SP = 0$

I: $SP \neq 0$ *O*: $S\overline{P} \neq 0$

FIGURE 2

Propositions can be expressed diagrammatically by diagramming the classes to which they refer. We represent a class by a circle labeled with the term that designates the class. Thus the class *S* is diagrammed as in Figure 3.

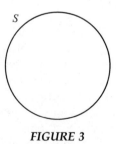

S

FIGURE 3

This diagram is of a class, not a proposition. It represents the class *S*, but says nothing about it. To diagram the proposition that *S* has no members, or that there are no *S*'s, we shade all of the interior of the circle representing *S*—indicating in this way that it contains nothing, but is empty. To diagram the proposition that there are *S*'s, which we interpret as saying that there is at least one member of *S*, we place an *x* anywhere in the interior of the circle representing *S*—indicating in this way that there is something inside it, that it is not empty. Thus the two propositions "There are no *S*'s" and "There are *S*'s" are represented by the two diagrams in Figure 4.

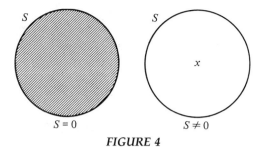

FIGURE 4

It should be noted in passing that the circle that diagrams the class S will also, in effect, diagram the class $\overline{S}$, for just as the interior of the circle represents all members of S, so the exterior of the circle represents all members of $\overline{S}$.

To diagram a standard-form categorical proposition, not one but two circles are required. The skeleton or framework for diagramming any standard-form proposition whose subject and predicate terms are abbreviated by S and P is constructed by drawing two intersecting circles, as in Figure 5.

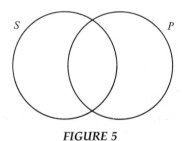

FIGURE 5

This figure diagrams the two classes of S and P, but diagrams no proposition concerning them. It does not affirm that either or both have members, nor does it deny that they have. As a matter of fact, there are more than two classes diagrammed by the two intersecting circles. The part of the circle labeled S that does not overlap the circle labeled P diagrams all S's that are not P's and can be thought of as representing the product of the classes S and $\overline{P}$. We may label it $S\overline{P}$. The overlapping part of the two circles represents the product of the classes S and P and diagrams all things belonging to both of them. It is labeled SP. The part of the circle labeled P that does not overlap the circle labeled S diagrams all P's that are not S's and represents the product of the class $\overline{S}$ and P. It is labeled $\overline{S}P$. Finally, the part of the diagram external to both circles represents all things that are neither in S nor in P; it diagrams the fourth class $\overline{S}\overline{P}$, so labeled. With these labels inserted, Figure 5 becomes Figure 6.

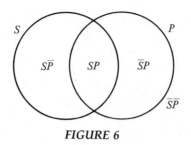

FIGURE 6

This diagram can be interpreted in terms of the various different classes determined by the class of all Spaniards (*S*) and the class of all painters (*P*). *SP* is the product of these two classes, containing all those things and only those things that belong to both of them. Every member of *SP* must be a member of both *S* and *P*; every member must be both a Spaniard and a painter. This product class *SP* is the class of all Spanish painters, which contains, among others, Velásquez and Goya. *SP̄* is the product of the first class and the complement of the second, containing all those things and only those things that belong to the class *S* but not to the class *P*. It is the class of all Spaniards who are not painters, all Spanish nonpainters, and it will contain neither Velásquez nor Goya, but it will include both the novelist Cervantes and the dictator Franco, among many others. *S̄P* is the product of the second class and the complement of the first, and is the class of all painters who are not Spaniards. This class *S̄P* of all non-Spanish painters includes, among others, both the Dutch painter Rembrandt and the French painter Rosa Bonheur. Finally, *S̄P̄* is the product of the complements of the two original classes. It contains all those things and only those things that are neither Spaniards nor painters. It is a very large class indeed, containing not merely English admirals and Swiss mountain climbers, but such things as the Mississippi River and Mount Everest. All these classes are diagrammed in Figure 6, where the letters *S* and *P* are interpreted as in the present paragraph.

By shading or inserting *x*'s in various parts of this picture we can diagram any one of the four standard-form categorical propositions. To diagram the *A* proposition "All *S* is *P*," symbolized as *SP̄* = 0, we simply shade out the part of the diagram that represents the class *SP̄*, thus indicating it has no members, or is empty. To diagram the *E* proposition "No *S* is *P*," symbolized as *SP* = 0, we shade out that part of the diagram which represents the class *SP*, to indicate that it is empty. To diagram the *I* proposition "Some *S* is *P*," symbolized *SP* ≠ 0, we insert an *x* into that part of the diagram which represents the class *SP*. This insertion indicates that the class product is not empty but has at least one member. Finally, for the *O* proposition "Some *S* is not *P*," symbolized *SP̄* ≠ 0, we insert an *x* into that part of the diagram which represents the class *SP̄*, to indicate that it is not empty but has at least one member. Placed side by side, diagrams for the four standard-form categorical propositions display their different meanings very clearly, as shown in Figure 7.

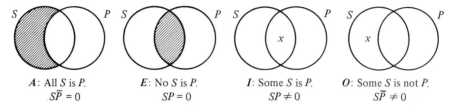

A: All S is P.	E: No S is P.	I: Some S is P.	O: Some S is not P.
$S\overline{P} = 0$	$SP = 0$	$SP \neq 0$	$S\overline{P} \neq 0$

FIGURE 7

One aspect of these Venn Diagrams [named for the English mathematician and logician John Venn (1834–1923), who introduced them] must be emphasized. The bare two-circle diagram, labeled but not otherwise marked, represents classes but diagrams no proposition. That a space is left blank signifies nothing—neither that there are nor that there are not members of the class represented by that space. Propositions are diagrammed only by those diagrams in which a part has been shaded out or in which an x has been inserted.

We have constructed diagrammatic representations for "No S is P" and "Some S is P," and since these are logically equivalent to their converses "No P is S" and "Some P is S," the diagrams for the latter have already been shown. To diagram the A proposition "All P is S," symbolized as $P\overline{S} = 0$, within the same framework we must shade out the part of the diagram which represents the class $P\overline{S}$. It should be obvious that the class $P\overline{S}$ is the same as the class $\overline{S}P$, if not immediately, then by considering that every object that belongs to the class of all painters and the class of all non-Spaniards must (also) belong to the class of all non-Spaniards and the class of all painters— all painting non-Spaniards are non-Spanish painters, and vice versa. And to diagram the O proposition "Some P is not S," symbolized by $P\overline{S} \neq 0$, we insert an x into the part of the diagram which represents the class $P\overline{S}$ ($= \overline{S}P$). Diagrams for these propositions then appear as shown in Figure 8.

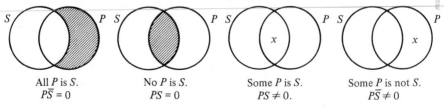

All P is S.	No P is S.	Some P is S.	Some P is not S.
$P\overline{S} = 0$	$PS = 0$	$PS \neq 0$.	$P\overline{S} \neq 0$

FIGURE 8

This further adequacy of the two-circle diagrams is mentioned because in the following chapter it will be important to be able to use a given pair of overlapping circles with given labels, say, S and M, to diagram any standard-form categorical proposition containing S and M as its terms, regardless of the order in which they occur in it.

The Venn Diagrams constitute an *iconic* representation of the standard-form categorical propositions, in which spatial inclusions and exclusions correspond to the nonspatial inclusions and exclusions of classes. They not only provide an exceptionally clear method of notation, but also are the basis of the simplest and most direct method of testing the validity of categorical syllogisms, as will be explained in the following chapter.

EXERCISES

Express each of the following propositions as equations or inequalities, representing each class by the first letter of the English term designating it and symbolize them by means of Venn Diagrams.

★   1. Some sculptors are painters.

  2. No peddlers are millionaires.

  3. All merchants are speculators.

  4. Some musicians are not pianists.

★   5. No shopkeepers are members.

  6. Some political leaders of high reputation are scoundrels.

  7. All physicians licensed to practice in this state are medical college graduates who have passed special qualifying examinations.

  8. Some stockbrokers who advise their customers about making investments are not partners in companies whose securities they recommend.

  9. All puritans who reject all useless pleasure are strangers to much that makes life worth living.

★ 10. No modern paintings are photographic likenesses of their objects.

 11. Some student activists are middle-aged men and women striving to recapture their lost youth.

 12. All medieval scholars were pious monks living in monasteries.

 13. Some state employees are not public-spirited citizens.

 14. No magistrates subject to election and recall will be punitive tyrants.

★ 15. Some patients exhibiting all the symptoms of schizophrenia are manic-depressives.

 16. Some passengers on the new large jet airplanes are not satisfied customers.

 17. Some priests are militant advocates of radical social change.

 18. Some stalwart defenders of the existing order are not members of political parties.

 19. No pipelines laid across foreign territories are safe investments.

 20. All pornographic films are menaces to civilization and decency.

6

Categorical Syllogisms

*I consider the invention of the form of syllogisms one of the most beautiful,
and also one of the most important, made by the human mind.*
                                                    —GOTTFRIED LEIBNIZ

*Fallacious and misleading arguments are most easily detected if set out in
correct syllogistic form.*
                                                    —IMMANUEL KANT

6.1 *Standard-Form Categorical Syllogisms*

A *syllogism* is a deductive argument in which a conclusion is inferred from
two premisses. A *categorical syllogism* is a deductive argument consisting of
three categorical propositions that contain exactly three terms, each of which
occurs in exactly two of the constituent propositions. A categorical syllogism
is said to be in *standard form* when its premisses and conclusion are all
standard-form categorical propositions and are arranged in a specified
standard order. To specify that order, it will be useful to explain the logician's
special names for the terms and premisses of categorical syllogisms. For brevity, in this chapter we shall refer to categorical syllogisms simply as syllogisms, even though there are other kinds of syllogisms that will be discussed
in later chapters.

The conclusion of a standard-form syllogism is a standard-form categorical
proposition that contains two of the syllogism's three terms. The term that
occurs as the predicate of the conclusion is called the *major* term of the syllogism, and the term that occurs as the subject term of the conclusion is
called the *minor* term of the syllogism. Thus in the standard-form syllogism

> No heroes are cowards.
> Some soldiers are cowards.
> Therefore some soldiers are not heroes.

the term "soldiers" is the *minor term* and the term "heroes" is the *major term.*
The third term of the syllogism, which does not occur in the conclusion,

appearing instead in both premisses, is called the middle term. In our example, the term "cowards" is the *middle term.*

The major and minor terms of a standard-form syllogism each occur in a
different one of the premisses. The premiss containing the major term is
called the major premiss, and the premiss containing the minor term is called
the minor premiss. In the syllogism just stated, the major premiss is "No
heroes are cowards," and the minor premiss is "Some soldiers are cowards."

Now the other defining characteristic of a standard-form syllogism can be
stated. It is that the major premiss is stated first, the minor premiss second,
and the conclusion last. It should be emphasized that the major premiss is
not defined in terms of its position, but as the premiss that contains the
major term (which is by definition the predicate term of the conclusion). And
the minor premiss is not defined in terms of its position, but as the premiss
that contains the minor term (which is defined as the subject term of the
conclusion).

The *mood* of a standard-form syllogism is determined by the forms of the
standard-form categorical propositions it contains. It is represented by three
letters, the first of which names the form of the syllogism's major premiss,
the second that of the minor premiss, and the third that of the conclusion.
For example, in the case of the preceding syllogism, since its major premiss
is an *E* proposition, its minor premiss an *I* proposition, and its conclusion
an *O* proposition, the mood of the syllogism is *EIO*.

But the mood of a standard-form syllogism does not completely characterize its form. Consider the two following syllogisms:

> All great scientists are college graduates.
> Some professional athletes are college graduates
> _____
> Therefore some professional athletes are great scientists.

and

> All artists are egotists.
> Some artists are paupers.
> _____
> Therefore some paupers are egotists.

Both are of mood *AII*, but they are of different forms. We can bring out the
difference in their forms most clearly by displaying their logical "skeletons,"
abbreviating the minor terms by *S*, the major terms by *P*, the middle terms
by *M*, and using the three-dot symbol "∴" for "therefore." The forms or
"skeletons" of these two syllogisms are

All *P* is *M*.	All *M* is *P*.
Some *S* is *M*.	Some *M* is *S*.
_____	_____
∴ Some *S* is *P*.	∴ Some *S* is *P*.

In the first the middle term is the predicate term of both premises, while in the second the middle term is the subject term of both premises. These examples show that although the form of a syllogism is partially described by stating its mood, syllogisms having the same mood may differ in their forms, depending upon the relative positions of their middle terms.

The form of a syllogism may be completely described, however, by stating its mood and *figure,* where the figure indicates the position of the middle term in the premises. It is clear that there are four possible different figures that syllogisms may have. The middle term may be the subject term of the major premiss and the predicate term of the minor premiss, or it may be the predicate term of both premises, or it may be the subject term of both premisses, or it may be the predicate term of the major premiss and the subject term of the minor premiss. These different possible positions of the middle term constitute the first, second, third, and fourth figures, respectively. They are schematized in the following array, where only the relative positions of the terms are shown, and reference to mood is suppressed by not representing either quantifiers or copulas:

$M - P$	$P - M$	$M - P$	$P - M$
$S - M$	$S - M$	$M - S$	$M - S$
$\therefore S - P$	$\therefore S - P$	$\therefore S - P$	$\therefore S - P$
First Figure	*Second Figure*	*Third Figure*	*Fourth Figure*

We give a complete description of the form of any standard-form syllogism by naming its mood and figure. Thus any syllogism of mood *AOO* in the second figure (named more briefly as *AOO − 2*) will have the form

All *P* is *M*.
Some *S* is not *M*.

$\therefore$ Some *S* is not *P*.

Abstracting from the infinite variety of their possible subject matters, we obtain many different forms of standard-form syllogisms. Were we to list all possible different moods, beginning with *AAA, AAE, AAI, AAO; AEA, AEE, AEI, AEO; AIA, . . . ,* and continuing through, by the time we reached *OOO* sixty-four different moods would have been enumerated. And since each mood can occur with each of the four different figures, there must be 256 distinct forms that standard-form syllogisms may assume. Only a few of them are valid, however.

EXERCISES

Rewrite each of the following syllogisms in standard form and name its mood and figure. (Procedure: First, identify the conclusion; second, note its predicate term, which is the major term of the syllogism; third, identify the major premiss, which is the premiss containing the major term; fourth, verify that the other premiss is the minor premiss through its containing the syllogism's minor term, which is the subject term of the conclusion; fifth, rewrite the argument in standard form, with the major premiss first, the minor premiss second, and the conclusion third; sixth, name the mood and figure of the syllogism.)

★ 1. No nuclear-powered submarines are commercial vessels, so no warships are commercial vessels, since all nuclear-powered submarines are warships.

2. Some evergreens are objects of worship, because all fir trees are evergreens, and some objects of worship are fir trees.

3. All artificial satellites are important scientific achievements; therefore some important scientific achievements are not American inventions, inasmuch as some artificial satellites are not American inventions.

4. No television stars are certified public accountants, but all certified public accountants are people of good business sense; it follows that no television stars are people of good business sense.*S* *P*

★ 5. Some conservatives are not advocates of high tariff rates, because all advocates of high tariff rates are Republicans, and some Republicans are not conservatives.

6. All hi-fi sets are expensive and delicate mechanisms, but no expensive and delicate mechanisms are suitable toys for children; consequently no hi-fi sets are suitable toys for children.

7. All juvenile delinquents are maladjusted individuals, and some juvenile delinquents are products of broken homes; hence some maladjusted individuals are products of broken homes.

8. No stubborn individuals who never admit a mistake are good teachers, so, since some well-informed people are stubborn individuals who never admit a mistake, some good teachers are not well-informed people.

9. All proteins are organic compounds, whence all enzymes are proteins, as all enzymes are organic compounds.

10. No sports cars are vehicles intended to be driven at moderate speeds, but all automobiles designed for family use are vehicles intended to be driven at moderate speeds, from which it follows that no sports cars are automobiles designed for family use.

6.2 *The Formal Nature of Syllogistic Argument*

The form of a syllogism is, from the point of view of logic, its most important aspect. The validity or invalidity of a syllogism (whose constituent propositions are all contingent) depends exclusively upon its form and is completely independent of its specific content or subject matter. Thus any syllogism of form $AAA-1$

All M is P.
All S is M.

∴ All S is P.

is a valid argument, regardless of its subject matter. That is, no matter what terms are substituted in this form or skeleton for the letters *S*, *P*, and *M*, the resulting argument will be valid. If we substitute the terms "Athenians," "humans," and "Greeks" for those letters, we obtain the valid argument

> All Greeks are humans.
> All Athenians are Greeks.
> _____
> Therefore all Athenians are humans.

And if we substitute the terms "soaps," "water-soluble substances," and "sodium salts" for the letters *S*, *P*, and *M* in the same form, we obtain

> All sodium salts are water-soluble substances.
> All soaps are sodium salts.
> _____
> Therefore all soaps are water-soluble substances.

which is also valid.

A valid syllogism is a formally valid argument, valid by virtue of its form alone. This implies that if a given syllogism is valid, *any other syllogism of the same form will also be valid.* And if a syllogism is invalid, *any other syllogism of the same form will also be invalid.*[1] The common recognition of this fact is attested by the frequent use of "logical analogies" in argumentation. Suppose that we were presented with the argument

> All liberals are proponents of national health insurance.
> Some members of the administration are proponents of national health insurance.
> _____
> Therefore some members of the administration are liberals.

and felt (justifiably) that regardless of the truth or falsehood of its constituent propositions, the argument was invalid. By far the best way of exposing its fallacious character would be to construct another argument having exactly the same form but whose invalidity was immediately apparent. We might seek to expose the given argument by replying, "You might as well argue

_____

[1]Here we assume that the constituent propositions are themselves contingent, that is, neither logically true (e.g., all easy chairs are chairs) nor logically false (e.g., some easy chairs are not chairs). For if it contained either a logically false premise or a logically true conclusion, then the argument would be valid regardless of its syllogistic form—valid in that it would be logically impossible for its premisses to be true and its conclusion false. We also assume that the only logical relations among the terms of the syllogism are those asserted or entailed by its premisses. The point of these restrictions is to limit our considerations in this chapter and the next to syllogistic arguments alone and to exclude other kinds of arguments whose validity turns on more complex logical considerations not appropriately introduced at this place.

that

> All rabbits are very fast runners.
> Some horses are very fast runners.
> _____
> Therefore some horses are rabbits.

And you cannot seriously defend this argument," we might continue, "because here there is no question about the facts. The premises are known to be true and the conclusion is known to be false. Your argument is of the same pattern as this analogous one about horses and rabbits. It is invalid— so *your* argument is invalid." Here is an excellent method of arguing; the logical analogy is one of the most powerful weapons that can be used in debate.

Underlying the method of logical analogy is the fact that the validity or invalidity of such arguments as the categorical syllogism is a purely formal matter. Any fallacious argument can be proved invalid by finding a second argument that has exactly the same form and is known to be invalid by the fact that its premises are known to be true while its conclusion is known to be false. (It should be remembered that an invalid argument may very well have a true conclusion—that an argument is invalid simply means that its conclusion is not logically implied or necessitated by its premises.)

However, this method of testing the validity of arguments has serious limitations. Sometimes a logical analogy is difficult to "think up" on the spur of the moment. And there are far too many invalid forms of argument for us to prepare and try to remember refuting analogies of each of them in advance. Moreover, although being able to think of a logical analogy with true premisses and false conclusions proves its form to be invalid, not being able to think of one does not prove the form valid, for it may only reflect the limitations of our thinking. There may be an invalidating analogy even though we are not able to think of it. A more effective method of establishing the formal validity or invalidity of syllogisms is required. It is to the explanation of effective methods of testing syllogisms that the remaining sections of this chapter are devoted.

EXERCISES

Refute any of the following arguments that are invalid by the method of constructing logical analogies.

★ 1. All business executives are active opponents of increased corporation taxes, for all active opponents of increased corporation taxes are members of the chamber of commerce, and all members of the chamber of commerce are business executives.

2. No medicines that can be purchased without a doctor's prescription are habit-forming drugs, so some narcotics are not habit-forming drugs, since some narcotics are medicines that can be purchased without a doctor's prescription.

3. No Republicans are Democrats, so some Democrats are wealthy stockbrokers, since some wealthy stockbrokers are not Republican.

4. No college graduates are persons having an IQ of less than 70, but all persons having an IQ of less than 70 are morons, so no college graduates are morons.

★ 5. All fireproof buildings are structures that can be insured at special rates, so some structures that can be insured at special rates are not wooden houses, since no wooden houses are fireproof buildings.

6. All blue-chip securities are safe investments, so some stocks that pay a generous dividend are safe investments, since some blue-chip securities are stocks that pay a generous dividend.

7. Some pediatricians are not specialists in surgery, so some general practitioners are not pediatricians, since some general practitioners are not specialists in surgery.

8. No intellectuals are successful politicians, because no shy and retiring people are successful politicians, and some intellectuals are shy and retiring people.

9. All trade union executives are labor leaders, so some labor leaders are conservatives in politics, since some conservatives in politics are trade union executives.

10. All new automobiles are economical means of transportation, and all new automobiles are status symbols; therefore some economical means of transportation are status symbols.

6.3 *Venn Diagram Technique for Testing Syllogisms*

In the preceding chapter the employment of two-circle Venn Diagrams to represent standard-form categorical propositions was explained. To test a categorical syllogism by the method of Venn Diagrams it is necessary to represent both of its premises in one diagram. Here we are required to draw *three* overlapping circles, for the two premises of a standard-form syllogism contain three different terms, minor term, major term, and middle term, which we abbreviate as *S*, *P*, and *M*, respectively. We first draw two circles just as for the diagramming of a single proposition, and then we draw a third circle beneath, overlapping both of the first two. We label the three circles *S*, *P*, and *M*, in that order. Just as one circle labeled *S* diagrammed both the class *S* and the class $\bar{S}$; and as two overlapping circles labeled *S* and *P* diagrammed four classes: *SP*, $S\bar{P}$, $\bar{S}P$, and $\bar{S}\bar{P}$; so three overlapping circles labeled *S*, *P*, and *M* diagram eight classes: $SP\bar{M}$, *SPM*, $\bar{S}P\bar{M}$, $\bar{S}PM$, *SPM*, $\bar{S}PM$, $\bar{S}\bar{P}M$, and $\bar{S}\bar{P}\bar{M}$. These are represented by the eight parts into which the three circles divide the plane, as shown in Figure 9, on page 198.

This can be interpreted in terms of the various different classes determined by the class of all Swedes (*S*), the class of all peasants (*P*), and the class of all musicians (*M*). *SPM* is the product of these three classes, which is the class of all Swedish peasant musicians. $SP\bar{M}$ is the product of the first two and the complement of the third, which is the class of all Swedish peasants

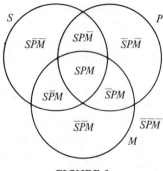

FIGURE 9

who are not musicians. $S\overline{P}M$ is the product of the first and third and the complement of the second: the class of all Swedish musicians who are not peasants. $S\overline{PM}$ is the product of the first and the complement of the others: the class of all Swedes who are neither peasants nor musicians. Next, $\overline{S}PM$ is the product of the second and third classes with the complement of the first: the class of all peasant musicians who are not Swedes. $\overline{S}P\overline{M}$ is the product of the second class with the complements of the other two: the class of all peasants who are neither Swedes nor musicians. $\overline{SP}M$ is the product of the third class and the complements of the first two: the class of all musicians who are neither Swedes nor peasants. Finally, $\overline{SPM}$ is the product of the complements of the three original classes: the class of all things that are neither Swedes nor peasants nor musicians.

If we focus our attention on just the two circles labeled P and M, it is clear that by shading out or inserting an x we can diagram any standard-form categorical proposition whose two terms are P and M, regardless of which is the subject term and which the predicate. Thus, to diagram the proposition "All M is P" ($M\overline{P} = 0$), we shade out all of M that is not contained in (or overlapped by) P. This area, it is seen, includes both the portions labeled $S\overline{P}M$ and $\overline{SP}M$. The diagram then becomes Figure 10.

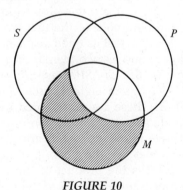

FIGURE 10

And if we focus our attention on just the two circles *S* and *M*, by shading out or inserting an *x* we can diagram any standard-form categorical proposition whose terms are *S* and *M*, regardless of the order in which they appear in it. To diagram the proposition "All *S* is *M*" ($S\overline{M} = 0$), we shade out all of *S* that is not contained in (or overlapped by) *M*. This area, it is seen, includes both the portions labeled $S\overline{P}\overline{M}$ and $SP\overline{M}$. The diagram for this proposition will appear as Figure 11.

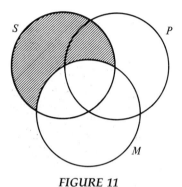

FIGURE 11

Now the advantage of having three circles overlapping is that it allows us to diagram two propositions together—on condition, of course, that only three different terms occur in them. Thus diagramming both "All *M* is *P*" and "All *S* is *M*" at the same time gives us Figure 12.

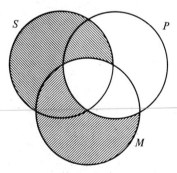

FIGURE 12

This is the diagram for both premisses of the syllogism *AAA* – **1**:

> All *M* is *P*.
> All *S* is *M*.
> —————————
> ∴ All *S* is *P*.

Now this syllogism is valid if and only if the two premisses imply or entail the conclusion—that is, if together they say what is said by the conclusion. Consequently, diagramming the premisses of a valid argument should suffice to diagram its conclusion also, with no further marking of the circles needed. To diagram the conclusion "All S is P" is to shade out both the portion labeled $S\overline{P}\,\overline{M}$ and the portion labeled $S\overline{P}M$. Inspecting the diagram that represents the two premisses, we see that it does diagram the conclusion also. And from this fact we can conclude that $AAA-1$ is a valid syllogism.

Let us now apply the Venn Diagram test to an obviously invalid syllogism:

All dogs are mammals.
All cats are mammals.

Therefore all cats are dogs.

Diagramming both premisses gives us Figure 13.

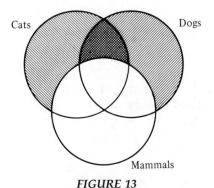

FIGURE 13

In this diagram, where S designates the class of all cats, P the class of all dogs, and M the class of all mammals, the portions $S\overline{P}\,\overline{M}$, $SP\overline{M}$, and $\overline{S}P\overline{M}$ have been shaded out. But the conclusion has not been diagrammed, because the part $S\overline{P}M$ has been left unshaded, and to diagram the conclusion *both* $S\overline{P}\,\overline{M}$ and $S\overline{P}M$ must be shaded. Thus we see that diagramming both the premisses of a syllogism of form $AAA-2$ does *not* suffice to diagram its conclusion, which proves that the conclusion says something more than is said by the premisses, which shows that the premisses do not imply the conclusion. But an argument whose premisses do not imply its conclusion is invalid, and so our diagram proves the given syllogism to be invalid. (It proves, in fact, that *any* syllogism of the form $AAA-2$ is invalid.)

When we use a Venn Diagram to test a syllogism with one universal premiss and one particular premiss, it is advisable to diagram the universal premiss first. Thus in testing the $AII-3$ syllogism

All artists are egotists.
Some artists are paupers.

Therefore some paupers are egotists.

we should diagram the universal premiss "All artists are egotists" before inserting an *x* to diagram the particular premiss "Some artists are paupers." Properly diagrammed, the premisses appear as in Figure 14.

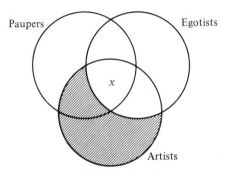

FIGURE 14

Had we tried to diagram the particular premiss first, before the region $S\overline{P}M$ was shaded out along with $\overline{S}\overline{P}M$ in diagramming the universal premiss, we should not have known whether to insert an *x* in SPM or in $S\overline{P}M$ or in both. And had we put it in $S\overline{P}M$ or on the line separating it from SPM, the subsequent shading of $S\overline{P}M$ would have obscured the information the diagram was intended to contain. Now that the information contained in the premisses has been inserted into the diagram, we examine it to see whether the conclusion has already been diagrammed. For the conclusion "Some paupers are egotists" to be diagrammed, an *x* must appear somewhere in the overlapping part of the circles labeled "paupers" and "egotists." This overlapping part consists of both of the regions $SP\overline{M}$ and SPM, which together constitute SP. There is an *x* in the region SPM, so there *is* an *x* in the overlapping part SP. What the conclusion of the syllogism says is diagrammed by the diagramming of its premisses; therefore the syllogism is valid.

Let us consider still another example, the discussion of which will bring out a further important point about the use of Venn Diagrams. In testing the argument

All great scientists are college graduates.
Some professional athletes are college graduates.

Therefore some professional athletes are great scientists.

after diagramming the universal premiss first in Figure 15 by shading out both regions $SP\overline{M}$ and $\overline{S}P\overline{M}$, we may still be puzzled about where to put the

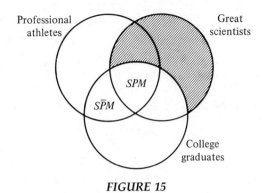

FIGURE 15

x required to diagram the particular premiss. That premiss is "Some professional athletes are college graduates," so an *x* must be inserted somewhere in the overlapping part of the two circles labeled "professional athletes" and "college graduates." That overlapping part, however, contains two regions: *SPM* and *SP̄M*. In which of these should an *x* be placed? The premisses do not tell us, and if we made an arbitrary decision to place it in one rather than the other, we should be inserting more information into the diagram than the premisses warrant—which would spoil the diagram's use as a test for validity. Placing *x*'s in each of them would also go beyond what the premisses assert. By placing an *x* on the line that divides the overlapping region *SM* into the two parts *SPM* and *SP̄M* we can diagram exactly what the second premiss asserts without adding anything to it. Placing an *x* on the line between two regions indicates that there is something that belongs in one of them, but does not indicate which one. The completed diagram of both premisses should be as in Figure 16.

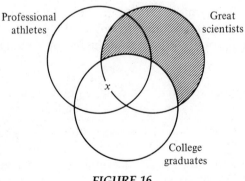

FIGURE 16

Inspecting this diagram of the premises to see whether the conclusion of the syllogism has already been diagrammed in it, we find that it has not been. For the conclusion "Some professional athletes are great scientists" to be diagrammed, an x would have to occur in the overlapping part of the two upper circles, either in $S\overline{P}M$ or in SPM. The first of these is shaded out and certainly contains no x. The diagram does not show an x in SPM either. True, there must be a member of *either* SPM or $S\overline{P}M$, but the diagram does not tell us that it is in the former rather than the latter, and so, for all the premises tell us, the conclusion may be false. We do not know that the conclusion *is* false, but only that it is not asserted or implied by the premises. The latter is enough, however, to let us know that the argument is invalid. The diagram suffices to show not merely that the given syllogism is invalid, but that *all* syllogisms of the form $AII - 2$ are invalid.

The general technique of using Venn Diagrams to test the validity of any standard-form syllogism may be summarily described as follows. First, label the circles of a three-circle Venn Diagram with the syllogism's three terms. Next, diagram both premises, diagramming the universal one first if there is one universal and one particular, being careful in diagramming a particular proposition to put an x on a line if the premises do not determine on which side of the line it should go. Finally, inspect the diagram to see whether or not the diagram of the premises contains a diagram of the conclusion: if it does, the syllogism is valid, if it does not, the syllogism is invalid.

What is the theoretical basis for using Venn Diagrams to distinguish valid from invalid syllogism? The answer to this question divides into two parts. The first has to do with the formal nature of syllogistic argument as explained in Section 6.2. It was there shown that one legitimate test of the validity or invalidity of a given syllogism is to establish the validity or invalidity of a different syllogism having exactly the same form. This technique is basic to the use of Venn Diagrams. The explanation of how they serve this purpose constitutes the second part of the answer to our question.

Ordinarily, a syllogism will be about classes of objects that are not all present, such as the class of all musicians, or great scientists, or sodium salts, or the like. The relations of inclusion or exclusion among such classes may be reasoned about and may be empirically discoverable in the course of sci-entific investigation. But they are certainly not open to direct inspection, since not all members of the classes involved are ever present at one time to be inspected. We can, however, examine situations of our own making in which the only classes concerned will contain by their very definitions only things that are present and directly open to inspection. And we can argue syllo-gistically about such situations of our own making. Venn Diagrams are de-vices for expressing standard-form categorical propositions, but they are also situations of our own making, patterns of graphite or ink on paper or mounds of chalk raised on blackboards. And the propositions they express can be interpreted as referring to the diagrams themselves. An example can help make this clear. Suppose we have a particular syllogism whose terms denote various kinds of people, successful, interested in their work, able to concentrate, who may be scattered widely over all parts of the world:

All successful people are people who are keenly interested in their work.

No people who are keenly interested in their work are people whose attention is easily distracted when they are working.

Therefore no people whose attention is easily distracted when they are working are successful people.

Its form is *AEE* − **4**, and it may be schematized as

All *P* is *M*.
No *M* is *S*.

∴ No *S* is *P*.

We may test it by constructing the Venn Diagram shown in Figure 17, with its regions $SP\overline{M}$ and $\overline{S}P\overline{M}$ shaded out to express the first premiss, and $\overline{S}PM$ and SPM shaded out to express the second premiss.

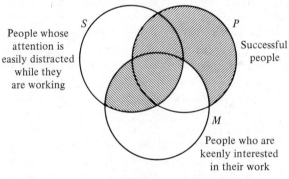

People whose attention is easily distracted while they are working — *S*

Successful people — *P*

M — People who are keenly interested in their work

FIGURE 17

Examining the diagram, we find that *SP* (which consists of the regions SPM and $SP\overline{M}$) has been shaded out, so the syllogism's conclusion has already been diagrammed. Now how does this tell us that the given syllogism is valid? That syllogism concerns large classes of remote objects: there are many people whose attention is easily distracted while they are working, and they are scattered far and wide. However, we can construct a syllogism of the same form dealing with objects which are immediately present and directly available for our inspection. These objects are the points within the unshaded portions of the circles labeled *S*, *P*, and *M* in our Venn Diagram. Here is the new syllogism:

All points within the unshaded part of the circle labeled *P* are points within the unshaded part of the circle labeled *M*.

No points within the unshaded part of the circle labeled *M* are points within the unshaded part of the circle labeled *S*.

Therefore no points within the unshaded part of the circle labeled *S* are points within the unshaded part of the circle labeled *P*.

This new syllogism refers to nothing remote, but is about the parts of a situation we ourselves have created—the Venn Diagram we have drawn. All the parts and all the possibilities of inclusion and exclusion among these classes are immediately present to us and directly open to inspection. We can literally see all the possibilities here and know that, since all the points of *P* are also points of *M*, and since *M* and *S* have no points in common, *S* and *P* cannot possibly have any points in common. Since it refers only to classes of points in the diagram, the new syllogism is literally seen to be valid by looking at the things it talks about. Since the original syllogism about classes of people has exactly the same form as this second one, by the formal nature of syllogistic argument the original syllogism is also seen to be valid. The explanation is exactly the same for Venn Diagram proofs of the invalidity of invalid syllogisms—there too we test the original syllogism indirectly by directly testing a second syllogism having exactly the same form but referring to the diagram that exhibits that form.

EXERCISES

I. Test the validity of each of the following syllogistic forms by means of a Venn Diagram.

★ 1. *AEE* − 1
    3. *OAO* − 3
★ 5. *EIO* − 4
    7. *AOO* − 1
    9. *EIO* − 3
  11. *AOO* − 3
  13. *IAI* − 1
  15. *EIO* − 1

    2. *EIO* − 2
    4. *AOO* − 4
    6. *OAO* − 2
    8. *EAE* − 3
  10. *IAI* − 4
★ 12. *EAE* − 1
  14. *OAO* − 4

II. Put each of the following syllogisms into standard form, name its mood and figure, and test its validity by means of a Venn Diagram.

★ 1. Some reformers are fanatics, so some idealists are fanatics, since all reformers are idealists.

2. Some philosophers are mathematicians; hence some scientists are philosophers, since all scientists are mathematicians.

3. Some mammals are not horses, for no horses are centaurs, and all centaurs are mammals.

4. Some neurotics are not parasites, but all criminals are parasites; it follows that some neurotics are not criminals.

★ 5. All underwater craft are submarines; therefore no submarines are pleasure vessels, since no pleasure vessels are underwater craft.

6. No criminals were pioneers, for all criminals are unsavory persons, and no pioneers were unsavory persons.

7. No musicians are astronauts, all musicians are baseball fans; consequently no astronauts are baseball fans.

8. Some Christians are not Methodists, for some Christians are not Protestants, and some Protestants are not Methodists.

9. No people whose primary interest is in winning elections are true liberals, and all active politicians are people whose primary interest is in winning elections, which entails that no true liberals are active politicians.

10. No weaklings are labor leaders, because no weaklings are true liberals, and all labor leaders are true liberals.

6.4 *Rules and Fallacies*

There are many ways in which a syllogism may fail to establish its conclusion. Just as travel is facilitated by the mapping of highways and the labeling of otherwise tempting roads as "dead ends," so cogency of argument is made more easily attainable by setting forth certain rules that enable the reasoner to avoid fallacies. The advantage of having a clearly stated set of easily applied rules is manifest. Any given standard-form syllogism can be evaluated by observing whether the rules are violated or not. In the present section six rules for standard-form syllogisms are presented.

Rule 1: A valid standard-form categorical syllogism must contain exactly three terms, each of which is used in the same sense throughout the argument.

The conclusion of a categorical syllogism asserts that a certain relation holds between two terms. It is clear that the conclusion is justified only if the premises assert the relationship of each of the conclusion's terms to the same third term. Were these not asserted by the premises, no connection between the two terms of the conclusion would be established, and the conclusion would not be implied by the premises. Three terms must be involved in every valid categorical syllogism; no more and no less. Any categorical syllogism that contains more than three terms is invalid, and is said to commit the Fallacy of Four Terms (in Latin, *quaternio terminorum*).[2]

If a term is used in different senses in the argument, it is being used equivocally, and the fallacy committed is that of *equivocation*.[3] An example is

---

[2]Even where it contains as many as five or six different terms, the same name is applied to the fallacy.

[3]Discussed in Chapter 3, pages 113–114.

the following rather silly argument whose premisses are drawn from different writers.

> Power tends to corrupt . . .[4]
> Knowledge is power.[5]
> Therefore knowledge tends to corrupt.

This syllogism appears to have only three terms, but there are really four, since one of them, the middle term "power," is used in different senses in the two premisses. To reveal the argument's invalidity we need only note that the word "power" in the first premiss means "the possession of control or command over people," whereas the word "power" in the second premiss means "the ability to control *things*." When the term in question is understood in the same sense throughout the argument, one or the other premiss becomes patently false.

Arguments of this sort are more common than one might suspect. It is generally the middle term whose meaning is shifted—in one direction to connect it with the minor term, in a different direction to relate it to the major term. But this connects the two terms of the conclusion with two different terms, so the relationship asserted by the conclusion is not established. Although it is sometimes called the Fallacy of the Ambiguous Middle, that name is not generally applicable, since one of the other terms may have its meaning shifted instead, which would involve the same error.

As we defined the term "categorical syllogism" at the beginning of this chapter, every syllogism by its very definition contains three terms. And the Fallacy of Equivocation was already explained and warned against in Chapter 3. But the term "syllogism" is sometimes defined more broadly than in the present book, and Rule 1 is part of the traditional logic of the syllogism. In the present context it may be regarded simply as a reminder to make sure that the argument being appraised really is a syllogism. And the "Fallacy of Four Terms" is our label for a syllogism that commits the fallacy of equivocation.

The next two rules deal with distribution. As was explained in Section 5.2, a term is distributed in a proposition when the proposition refers to all members of the class designated by that term; otherwise the term is said to be undistributed in (or by) that proposition.

Rule 2: In a valid standard-form categorical syllogism, the middle term must be distributed in at least one premiss.

Consider the following argument, referred to by the historian Barbara W. Tuchman, as an "unconscious syllogism:"

[4]John Emerich Edward Dalberg-Acton, letter to Bishop Mandell Creighton, April 5, 1887.
[5]Francis Bacon, *Meditationes Sacrae.*

Russians were revolutionists;
Anarchists were revolutionists;
_____
ergo, Anarchists were Russians.[6]

which is logically equivalent to the following standard-form categorical syllogism:

All Russians were revolutionists;
All Anarchists were revolutionists;
_____
Therefore Anarchists were Russians.

The middle term "revolutionists" is not distributed in either premiss, and this violates Rule 2. Any syllogism that violates Rule 2 is said to commit the Fallacy of the Undistributed Middle. It should be clear by the following considerations that any syllogism that violates this rule is invalid. The conclusion of any syllogism asserts a connection between two terms. The premisses justify asserting such a connection only if they assert that each of the two terms is connected with a third term in such a way that the first two are appropriately connected with each other through or by means of the third. For the two terms of the conclusion really to be connected through the third, at least one of them must be related to the *whole* of the class designated by the third or middle term. Otherwise, each may be connected with a different part of that class, and not necessarily connected with each other at all. This is obviously what occurs in the example. Russians are included in part of the class of revolutionists, and Anarchists are included in part of the class of revolutionists. But different parts of that class may be (and, in this case, are) involved, so the middle term does not connect the syllogism's major and minor terms. For it to connect them, *all* the class designated by it must be referred to in at least one premiss, which is to say that in a valid syllogism the middle term must be distributed in at least one premiss.

Rule 3: In a valid standard-form categorical syllogism, if either term is distributed in the conclusion, then it must be distributed in the premisses.

A valid argument is one whose premisses logically imply or entail its conclusion. The conclusion of a valid argument cannot go beyond or assert any more than is (implicitly) contained in the premisses. If the conclusion does illegitimately "go beyond" what is asserted by the premisses, the argument is invalid. It is an "illicit process" for the conclusion to say more about its terms than the premisses do. A proposition that distributes one of its terms says more about the class designated by that term than it would if the term were undistributed by it. To refer to *all* members of a class is to say more about it (apart from questions of existence) than is said when only some of

[6]Barbara W. Tuchman, *The Proud Tower* (New York: The Macmillan Company, 1966), p. 129.

its members are referred to. Therefore when the conclusion of a syllogism distributes a term that was undistributed in the premisses, it says more about it than the premisses warrant, and the syllogism is invalid. Such an illicit process can occur in the case of either the major or the minor term. There are, then, two different ways in which Rule 3 may be broken. Special names have been given to the two fallacies involved.

When a syllogism contains its major term undistributed in the major premiss but distributed in the conclusion, the argument is said to commit the Fallacy of Illicit Process of the Major Term (or, more briefly, the Illicit Major). An example of this fallacy is

> All dogs are mammals.
> No cats are dogs.
> ———————————————
> Therefore no cats are mammals.

The conclusion makes an assertion about *all* mammals, saying that all of them are excluded from the class of cats. But the premisses make no assertion about *all* mammals; so the conclusion illicitly goes beyond what the premisses assert. Since "mammals" is the major term, the fallacy here is an Illicit Major.

When a syllogism contains its minor term undistributed in its minor premiss but distributed in its conclusion, the argument commits the Fallacy of Illicit Process of the Minor Term (more briefly called the Illicit Minor). An example of this fallacy is

> All communists are subversive elements.
> All communists are critics of the present administration.
> ———————————————————————————————
> Therefore all critics of the present administration are subversive elements.

The conclusion here makes an assertion about *all* critics of the present administration. But the premisses make no assertion about *all* such critics; so the conclusion illicitly goes beyond what the premisses warrant. Since it goes beyond the premisses in what it says about the minor term, the fallacy is an Illicit Minor.

The next two rules are called Rules of Quality because they refer to the ways in which the negative quality of one or both premisses restricts the kinds of conclusions that validly may be inferred.

Rule 4: No standard-form categorical syllogism having two negative premisses is valid.

We can see that this rule must be obeyed when we recall what negative propositions assert. Any negative proposition (*E* or *O*) denies class inclusion, asserting that all or some of one class is excluded from the whole of the other.

Where *S*, *P*, and *M* are the minor, major, and middle terms, respectively, two negative premisses can assert only that *S* is wholly or partially excluded from all or part of *M*, and that *P* is wholly or partially excluded from all or part of *M*. But these conditions may very well obtain no matter how *S* and *P* are related, whether by inclusion or exclusion, partial or complete. Therefore from two negative premisses no relationship whatever between *S* and *P* can validly be inferred. Any syllogism that breaks Rule 4 is said to commit the Fallacy of Exclusive Premisses.

Rule 5: *If either premiss of a valid standard-form categorical syllogism is negative, the conclusion must be negative.*

An affirmative conclusion asserts that one class is either wholly or partly contained in a second. This can be justified only by premisses that assert the existence of a third class that contains the first and is itself contained in the second. In other words, to entail an affirmative conclusion, both premisses must assert class inclusion. But class inclusion can be stated only by affirmative propositions. So an affirmative conclusion logically follows only from two affirmative premisses. Hence, if either premiss is negative, the conclusion cannot be affirmative but must be negative also. Arguments breaking this rule are so implausible that they are very seldom encountered in serious discussions. Any syllogism that breaks Rule 5 may be said to commit the Fallacy of Drawing an Affirmative Conclusion from a Negative Premiss.

Some lists of syllogistic rules also include the converse of Rule 5: "If the conclusion of a valid standard-form categorical syllogism is negative, at least one premiss must be negative." This additional rule is explained on much the same grounds that were appealed to in discussing Rule 5. If the conclusion is negative, it *denies* inclusion. But affirmative premisses *assert* inclusion; hence they cannot entail a negative conclusion. This additional rule is both necessary and sufficient to complete the traditional or Aristotelian account of the categorical syllogism, which paid no attention to the problem of existential import. But on the Boolean interpretation, which pays particular attention to the problem of existential import, a separate syllogistic rule—Rule 6—is required. And the usual formulation of such a rule suffices—in the presence of the other rules—to prevent syllogisms with affirmative premisses and a negative conclusion. See Exercise IV-7 on page 213.

Our sixth and final rule concerns existential import. It is

Rule 6: *No valid standard-form categorical syllogism with a particular conclusion can have two universal premisses.*

To break this rule is to go from premisses having no existential import to a conclusion that does. A particular proposition asserts the existence of objects of a specified kind, so to infer it from two universal premisses that do not assert the existence of anything at all is clearly to go beyond what is warranted by the premisses. An example of a syllogism that breaks this rule is

> All household pets are domestic animals.
> No unicorns are domestic animals.
> _____
> Therefore some unicorns are not household pets.

On the traditional interpretation, which did attribute existential import to universal propositions, such arguments were said to have "weakened conclusions," because the "stronger" conclusion "No unicorns are household pets" might equally well have been inferred. But the latter is not stronger, it is simply different. The syllogism with the same premisses and the universal conclusion is perfectly valid. But the given syllogism is invalid, because its conclusion asserts that there are unicorns (a false proposition), whereas its premisses do not assert the existence of unicorns (or of anything at all). Being universal propositions, they are without existential import. The conclusion would follow validly if to the two universal premisses were added the additional premiss "There are unicorns." But the resulting argument, although perfectly valid, would have three premisses and would therefore not be a syllogism. Any syllogism that violates Rule 6 may be said to commit the Existential Fallacy. The six rules here presented are intended to apply only to standard-form categorical syllogisms. Within this area they provide an adequate test for the validity of any argument. If a standard-form categorical syllogism violates any of these rules, it is invalid, whereas if it conforms to all of them it is valid.

EXERCISES

I. Name the fallacies committed and the rules broken by invalid syllogisms of the following forms.

★ 1. *AAA* – 2   2. *EAA* – 1
   3. *IAO* – 3   4. *OEO* – 4
★ 5. *AAA* – 3   6. *IAI* – 2
   7. *OAA* – 4   8. *EAO* – 4
   9. *OAI* – 3   ★ 10. *IEO* – 1
  11. *EAO* – 1   12. *AII* – 2
  13. *EEE* – 1   14. *OAO* – 2
  15. *IAA* – 3

II. Name the fallacies committed and the rules broken by any of the following syllogisms that are invalid.

★ 1. All textbooks are books intended for careful study.
        Some reference books are books intended for careful study.
        _____
        Therefore some reference books are textbooks.

   2. All criminal actions are wicked deeds.
        All prosecutions for murder are criminal actions.
        _____
        Therefore all prosecutions for murder are wicked deeds.

3. No tragic actors are idiots.
   Some comedians are not idiots.

   Therefore some comedians are not tragic actors.

4. Some parrots are not pests.
   All parrots are pets.

   Therefore no pets are pests.

★ 5. All perceptual motion devices are 100 percent efficient machines.
   All 100 percent efficient machines are machines with frictionless bearings.

   Therefore some machines with frictionless bearings are perpetual motion devices.

6. Some good actors are not powerful athletes.
   All professional wrestlers are powerful athletes.

   Therefore all professional wrestlers are good actors.

7. Some diamonds are precious stones.
   Some carbon compounds are not diamonds.

   Therefore some carbon compounds are not precious stones.

8. Some diamonds are not precious stones.
   Some carbon compounds are diamonds.

   Therefore some carbon compounds are not precious stones.

9. All people who are most hungry are people who eat most.
   All people who eat least are people who are most hungry.

   Therefore all people who eat least are people who eat most.

10. Some spaniels are not good hunters.
    All spaniels are gentle dogs.

    Therefore no gentle dogs are good hunters.

III. Name the fallacies committed and the rules broken by any of the following syllogisms that are invalid.

★ 1. All chocolate eclairs are fattening foods, because all chocolate eclairs are rich desserts, and some fattening foods are not rich desserts.

2. All inventors are people who see new patterns in familiar things, so all inventors are eccentrics, since all eccentrics are people who see new patterns in familiar things.

3. Some snakes are not dangerous animals, but all snakes are reptiles, therefore some dangerous animals are not reptiles.

4. Some foods that contain iron are toxic substances, for all fish containing mercury are foods that contain iron, and all fish containing mercury are toxic substances.

★ 5. All opponents of basic economic and political changes are outspoken critics of the liberal leaders of Congress, and all right-wing extremists are opponents of basic economic and political changes. It follows that all outspoken critics of the liberal leaders of Congress are right-wing extremists.

6. No writers of lewd and sensational articles are honest and decent citizens, but some journalists are not writers of lewd and sensational articles; consequently some journalists are honest and decent citizens.

7. All supporters of popular government are democrats, so all supporters of popular government are opponents of the Republican Party, inasmuch as all Democrats are opponents of the Republican Party.

8. No coal tar derivatives are nourishing foods, because all artificial dyes are coal tar derivatives, and no artificial dyes are nourishing foods.

9. No coal tar derivatives are nourishing foods, because no coal tar derivatives are natural grain products, and all natural grain products are nourishing foods.

10. All people who live in London are people who drink tea, and all people who drink tea are people who like it. We may conclude, then, that all people who live in London are people who like it.

IV. Answer the following questions by appealing to the six rules. (Make sure you consider all possible cases.)

★ 1. Can any standard-form categorical syllogism be valid that contains exactly three terms, each of which is distributed in both of its occurrences?

2. In what mood or moods, if any, can a first figure standard-form categorical syllogism with a particular conclusion be valid?

3. In what figure or figures, if any, can the premisses of a valid standard-form categorical syllogism distribute both major and minor terms?

4. In what figure or figures, if any, can a valid standard-form categorical syllogism have two particular premisses?

★ 5. In what figure or figures, if any, can a valid standard-form categorical syllogism have only one term distributed, and that one only once?

6. In what mood or moods, if any, can a valid standard-form categorical syllogism have just two terms distributed, each one twice?

7. In what mood or moods, if any, can a valid standard-form categorical syllogism have two affirmative premisses and a negative conclusion?

8. In what figure or figures, if any, can a valid standard-form categorical syllogism have a particular premiss and a universal conclusion?

9. In what mood or moods, if any, can a second figure standard-form categorical syllogism with a universal conclusion be valid?

10. In what figure or figures, if any, can a valid standard-form categorical syllogism have its middle term distributed in both premisses?

11. Determine by a process of elimination which of the 256 forms of standard-form categorical syllogism are valid.

12. Can a valid standard-form categorical syllogism have a term distributed in a premiss that appears undistributed in the conclusion?

7

Arguments in Ordinary Language

The value, therefore, of the syllogistic form and of the rules for using it correctly does not consist in their being the form and the rules according to which our reasonings are necessarily, or even usually, made, but in their furnishing us with a mode in which those reasonings may always be represented and which is admirably calculated, if they are inconclusive, to bring their inconclusiveness to light.

—JOHN STUART MILL

7.1 *Reducing the Number of Terms in a Syllogistic Argument*

In the preceding chapter we presented two different tests to distinguish valid from invalid categorical syllogisms. Such tests as these are applicable only to categorical syllogisms that are in *standard form*. A standard-form categorical syllogism can be thought of as being "chemically pure," free from all obscurities and irrelevancies. Needless to say, of course, arguments do not always occur thus refined in a "state of nature."

We introduce the term "syllogistic argument" to refer to any argument that is either a standard-form categorical syllogism or can be reformulated as a standard-form categorical syllogism without any loss or change of meaning. The process of reformulating a syllogistic argument as a standard-form categorical syllogism will be called translation or reduction to standard form, and the resulting standard-form categorical syllogism will be called a standard-form translation of the given syllogistic argument.

Syllogistic arguments are fairly common, but they usually appear in a guise far different from the stilted and artificial standard form to which the tests of the preceding chapter can be directly applied. They take on such varied shapes that to devise special logical tests for all of them would require a hopelessly complicated logical apparatus. The combined interests of logical simplicity and adequacy to arguments stated in ordinary language require that we perform two tasks. First, easily applicable tests must be devised by which we can distinguish valid from invalid standard-form categorical syllogisms. This has already been done. And, second, the techniques of translating syllogistic arguments of *any* form into standard form must be understood and mastered. When these are both accomplished, *any* syllogistic argument may be tested: first, by translating it into standard form and, second, by applying to its standard form translation one of the tests described in the preceding chapter.

Apart from the relatively minor question of the order in which its premises and conclusion happen to be stated, a syllogistic argument may deviate from standard form in either or both of two ways. Its component propositions may not all be standard-form categorical propositions. Or its component propositions may be standard-form categorical propositions that apparently involve more than three terms. In the latter case, the argument is not to be rejected out of hand as invalid through committing the Fallacy of Four Terms. It is frequently possible to translate such an argument into a logically equivalent standard-form syllogism that contains only three terms and is perfectly valid.

(1) Such translation often can be effected simply by eliminating synonyms. Thus, before attempting to apply Venn Diagrams or the Syllogistic Rules to the argument

> No wealthy persons are vagrants.
> All lawyers are rich people.
> ___
> Therefore no attorneys are tramps.

we should eliminate the synonymous terms occurring in it. When that is done, the argument translates into

> No wealthy persons are vagrants.
> ~~All lawyers are wealthy persons.~~
> ___
> Therefore no lawyers are vagrants.

In this standard form *EAE*-1 the argument is easily seen to be valid.

Sometimes, however, the simple elimination of synonyms will not suffice. Consider, the following argument, all of whose propositions are standard-form categorical propositions:

> All mammals are warm-blooded animals.
> No lizards are warm-blooded animals.
> ___
> Therefore all lizards are nonmammals.

Were we to apply to this argument the six rules explained in Chapter 6, we should judge it to be invalid on more than one count. For one thing, it contains four terms: "mammals," "warm-blooded animals," "lizards," and "nonmammals." And for another, it has an affirmative conclusion drawn from a negative premiss. But it is nevertheless perfectly valid, as students can probably see for themselves. Because it has four terms, it is not a standard-form categorical syllogism, and the rules are not directly applicable to it. To test it by the Syllogistic Rules presented in the preceding chapter, we must first translate it into standard form. To do so we reduce the number of its terms to three, which is easily accomplished by simply obverting the conclusion. Performing this obversion, we obtain a standard-form translation of the original argument

> All mammals are warm-blooded animals.
> No lizards are warm-blooded animals.
> ———————————————————
> Therefore no lizards are mammals.

which is logically equivalent to it, having identically the same premisses and a logically equivalent conclusion. This standard-form translation conforms to all the Syllogistic Rules, and is thus known to be valid.

The latter is not the only standard-form translation of the given argument, although it is the most easily obtainable. A different (but logically equivalent) standard-form translation can be obtained by taking the contrapositive of the first premiss and obverting the second, leaving the conclusion unchanged. This would yield

> All non (warm-blooded animals) are nonmammals.
> All lizards are non (warm-blooded animals).
> ———————————————————
> Therefore all lizards are nonmammals.

which is also valid by the rules. There is no unique standard-form translation of a given syllogistic argument, but if any one is valid, all of the others must be valid also.

(2) Any syllogistic argument containing four terms can be reduced to standard form (or translated into a logically equivalent standard-form categorical syllogism) *if* one of its four terms is the complement of one of the other three. And any containing five (or six) terms can be reduced to standard form if two (or three) of its terms are the complements of two (or three) of the others. These reductions are all effected by means of valid immediate inferences: conversion, obversion, and contraposition.

Syllogistic arguments whose constituent propositions are all in standard form may contain as many as half a dozen different terms and may require the drawing of more than one immediate inference for their reduction to standard form. An example of a six-term syllogistic argument that is perfectly valid is the following:

> No nonresidents are citizens.
> All noncitizens are nonvoters.
>
> Therefore all voters are residents.

There are alternative ways of reducing this argument to a standard-form syllogism. One method, perhaps the most natural and obvious, requires the use of all three types of immediate inference. Converting and then obverting the first premiss and taking the contrapositive of the second premiss yields the standard-form categorical syllogism

> All citizens are residents.
> All voters are citizens.
>
> Therefore all voters are residents.

which is easily proved valid by either of the methods set forth in the preceding chapter.

EXERCISES

Translate the following syllogistic arguments into standard form and test their validity by one of the methods of Chapter 6.

★ 1. Some preachers are persons of unfailing vigor. No preachers are nonintellectuals. Therefore some intellectuals are persons of unfailing vigor.

2. Some metals are rare and costly substances, but no welder's materials are nonmetals; hence some welder's materials are rare and costly substances.

3. Some Oriental nations are nonbelligerents, since all belligerents are allies either of the United States or of the Soviet Union, and some Oriental nations are not allies either of the United States or of the Soviet Union.

4. Some nondrinkers are athletes, because no drinkers are persons in perfect physical condition, and some people in perfect physical condition are not nonathletes.

★ 5. All things inflammable are unsafe things, so all things that are safe are nonexplosives, since all explosives are flammable things.

6. All worldly goods are changeable things, for no worldly goods are things immaterial, and no material things are unchangeable things.

7. All those who are neither members nor guests of members are those who are excluded; therefore no nonconformists are either members or guests of members, for all those who are included are conformists.

8. All mortals are imperfect beings, and no humans are immortals, whence it follows that all perfect beings are nonhumans.

9. All things present are nonirritants; therefore no irritants are invisible objects, because all visible objects are absent things.

10. All useful things are objects no more than six feet long, since all difficult things to store are useless things, and no objects over six feet long are easy things to store.

7.2 *Translating Categorical Propositions into Standard Form*

The somewhat stilted **A, E, I,** and **O** forms are not the only ones in which categorical propositions may be expressed. Many syllogistic arguments contain nonstandard-form propositions. To reduce these arguments to standard form requires that their constituent propositions be translated into standard form. But ordinary language is too rich and multiform to permit a complete set of rules for such translation. In every case the crucial element is the ability to understand the given nonstandard-form proposition. We can, however, note a number of conventional techniques that are often useful. These must be regarded as guides rather than as rules, of course. Nine methods of dealing with various nonstandard-form propositions will be described in the present section.

(1) We ought first to mention singular propositions, such as "Socrates is a philosopher" and "This table is not an antique." These do not affirm or deny the inclusion of one class in another but, rather, affirm or deny that a specified individual or object belongs to a class. A singular proposition, however, can be interpreted as a proposition dealing with classes and their interrelations in the following way. To every individual object there corresponds a unique *unit class* (one-membered class) whose only member is that object itself. Then to assert that an object s belongs to a class P is logically equivalent to asserting that the unit class S containing just that object s is wholly included in the class P. And to assert that an object s does *not* belong to a class P is logically equivalent to asserting that the unit class S containing just that object s is wholly excluded from the class P. It is customary to make this interpretation automatically without any notational adjustment. Thus it is customary to take any affirmative singular proposition of the form "s is P" as if it were already expressed as the logically equivalent A proposition "All S is P," and similarly understand any negative singular proposition "s is not P" as an alternative formulation of the logically equivalent E proposition "No S is P"—in each case understanding "S" to designate the unit class whose only member is the object s. Thus no explicit translations have been provided for singular propositions; they have usually been classified as A and E propositions as they stand. As Kant remarked, "Logicians are justified in saying that, in the employment of judgments in syllogisms, singular judgments can be treated like those that are universal."[1]

---

[1] Immanuel Kant's *Critique of Pure Reason,* trans. N. K. Smith, p. 107. But compare Bertrand Russell's *My Philosophical Development,* p. 66.

The situation, however, is not quite so simple. If singular propositions are treated mechanically as *A* and *E* propositions in syllogistic arguments, and those arguments have their validity checked by Venn Diagrams or the Rules of the preceding chapter, serious difficulties arise.

In some cases obviously valid two-premiss arguments containing singular propositions translate into valid categorical syllogisms, as when

All *H* is *M*.	goes into the obviously valid	All *H* is *M*.
s is an *H*.	*AAA*–1 categorical syllogism	All *S* is *H*.
∴ *s* is an *M*.		∴ All *S* is *M*.

But in other cases obviously valid two-premiss arguments containing singular propositions translate into categorical syllogisms that are *invalid*, as when

s is *M*.	goes into the invalid	All *S* is *M*.
s is *H*.	*AAI*–3 categorical syllogism	All *S* is *H*.
∴ Some *H* is *M*.·		∴ Some *H* is *M*.

which violates Rule 6 and commits the Existential Fallacy.

On the other hand, if we translate singular propositions into particular propositions, there is the same kind of difficulty. In some cases obviously valid two-premiss arguments containing singular propositions translate into valid categorical syllogisms, as when

All *H* is *M*.	goes into the obviously valid	All *H* is *M*.
s is an *H*.	*AII*–1 categorical syllogism	Some *S* is *H*.
∴ *s* is an *M*.		∴ Some *S* is *M*.

But in other cases obviously valid two-premiss arguments containing singular propositions translate into categorical syllogisms that are *invalid*, as when

s is *M*.	goes into the invalid	Some *S* is *M*.
s is *H*.	*III*–3 categorical syllogism	Some *S* is *H*.
∴ Some *H* is *M*.		∴ Some *H* is *M*.

which violates Rule 2 and commits the Fallacy of the Undistributed Middle.

The difficulty arises from the fact that a singular proposition contains more information than is contained in any single one of the four standard-form categorical propositions. If "*s* is *P*" is construed as "All *S* is *P*," then what is lost is the existential import of the singular proposition, the fact that *S* is not empty. But if "*s* is *P*" is construed as "Some *S* is *P*," then what is lost is the universal aspect of the singular proposition, which distributes its subject term, the fact that *all S* is *P*.

The solution to the difficulty is to construe singular propositions as conjunctions of standard-form categorical propositions. An affirmative singular proposition is equivalent to the conjunction of the related **A** and **I** categorical propositions. Thus "*s* is *P*" is equivalent to "All *S* is *P*" *and* "Some *S* is *P*."

A negative singular proposition is equivalent to the conjunction of the related *E* and *O* categorical propositions. Thus "*s* is not *P*" is equivalent to "No *S* is *P*" *and* "Some *S* is not *P*." Venn Diagrams for affirmative and negative singular propositions are shown in Figure 18.

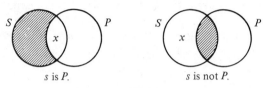

s is P.   s is not P.

FIGURE 18

And in applying the Syllogistic Rules to evaluate a syllogistic argument containing singular propositions, we must take account of *all* the information contained in those singular propositions, both distribution and existential import.

Provided that we keep in mind the existential import of singular propositions when we invoke the Syllogistic Rules or apply Venn Diagrams to test the validity of syllogistic arguments, it is acceptable practice to regard singular propositions as Universal (*A* or *E*) Propositions.

(2) The first group of categorical propositions that require translation into standard form contains those that have adjectives or adjectival phrases as predicates rather than substantives or class *terms*. For example, "Some flowers are beautiful" and "No warships are available for active duty" deviate from standard form only in that their predicates "beautiful" and "available for active duty" designate attributes rather than classes. But every attribute *determines* a class, the class of things having that attribute; so to every such proposition corresponds a logically equivalent proposition that is in standard form. To the two examples cited correspond the *I* and *E* propositions "Some flowers are beauties" and "No warships are things available for active duty." Where a categorical proposition is in standard form except that it has an adjectival predicate instead of a predicate term, the translation into standard form is made by replacing the adjectival predicate with a term designating the class of all objects of which the adjective may truly be predicated.

(3) Next we turn to categorical propositions whose main verbs are other than the standard-form copula "to be." Examples of this type are "All people desire recognition" and "Some people drink." The usual method of translating such a statement into standard form is to regard all of it except the subject term and quantifier as naming a class-defining characteristic and replace it by a standard copula and a term designating the class determined by that class-defining characteristic. Thus the two examples cited translate into the standard-form categorical propositions "All people are desirers of recognition" and "Some people are drinkers."

(4) Another type of statement easily put into standard form is that in which the standard-form ingredients are all present but not arranged in standard-form order. Two examples of this kind are "Racehorses are all thorough-breds" and "All is well that ends well." In such cases we first decide which is the subject term and then rearrange the words to express a standard-form categorical proposition. It is clear that the preceding two statements translate into the *A* propositions "All racehorses are thoroughbreds" and "All things that end well are things that are well."

(5) Many categorical propositions have their quantities indicated by words other than the standard-form quantifiers "all," "no," and "some." State-ments involving the words "every" and "any" are very easily translated. The propositions "Every dog has his day" and "Any contribution will be appre-ciated" reduce to "All dogs are creatures that have their days" and "All contributions are things that are appreciated." Similar to "every" and "any" are "everything" and "anything." Paralleling these, but clearly restricted to classes of persons, are "everyone," "anyone," "whoever," "whoso," "who," "one who," and the like. These should occasion no difficulty. The gram-matical particles "a," "an," and "the" can also serve to indicate quantity. The first two sometimes mean "all" and in other contexts mean "some." Thus "A bat is a mammal" and "An elephant is a pachyderm" are reasonably interpreted as meaning "All bats are mammals" and "All elephants are pachyderms." But "A bat flew in the window" and "An elephant escaped" quite clearly do not refer to all bats or all elephants, but are properly reduced to "Some bats are creatures that flew in the window" and "Some elephants are creatures that escaped." The word "the" may be used to refer either to a particular individual or to all the members of a class. But there is little or no danger of ambiguity here, for such a statement as "The whale is a mam-mal" translates in almost any context into the *A* proposition "All whales are mammals," whereas the singular proposition "The first president was a mil-itary hero" is already in standard form as an *A* proposition (with existential import) as discussed in the first part of this section.

On the other hand, although affirmative statements beginning with "Every" and "Any" are translated into "All *S* is *P*," negative statements beginning with "Not every" and "Not any" are quite different. "Not every *S* is *P*" means that *some S is not* P, whereas "Not any *S* is *P*" means that *no* S *is* P.

(6) Categorical propositions involving the words "only" or "none but" are often called "exclusive" propositions, because in general they assert that the predicate applies exclusively to the subject named. Examples of such usages are "Only citizens can vote" and "None but the brave deserve the fair." The first translates into the standard-form categorical proposition "All those who can vote are citizens," and the second into the standard-form categorical proposition "All those who deserve the fair are those who are brave." So-called exclusive propositions, beginning with "only" or "none but," translate

into *A* propositions whose subject and predicate terms are the same, respectively, as the predicate and subject terms of the exclusive proposition. There are contexts in which "Only *S* is *P*" or "None but *S*'s are *P*'s" are intended not merely to express that "All *P* is *S*" but also to suggest either that "All *S* is *P*" or that "Some *S* is *P*." This is not always the case, however. Where context helps to determine meaning, attention must be paid to it, of course. But in the absence of such additional information, the suggested translations are adequate.

(7) Some categorical propositions contain no words at all to indicate quantity; for example, "Dogs are carnivorous" and "Children are present." Where there is no quantifier, what the sentence is intended to express may be doubtful. We may be able to determine its meaning only by examining the context in which it occurs. The two examples cited are reasonably clear, however. In the first it is probable that *all* dogs are referred to, whereas in the second it is more likely that only *some* children are intended. The standard-form translation of the first is "All dogs are carnivores"; that of the second, "Some children are beings who are present."

(8) Next we may consider briefly some propositions that do not resemble standard-form categorical propositions at all but *can* be translated into standard form. Some examples are "Not all children believe in Santa Claus," "There are white elephants," "There are no pink elephants," and "Nothing is both round and square." A moment's thought about these propositions suffices to show that they are logically equivalent to, and therefore translate into, the following standard-form propositions: "Some children are not believers in Santa Claus," "Some elephants are white things," "No elephants are pink things," and "No round objects are square objects."

(9) It must be recognized that many propositions mention "quantity" more specifically than standard-form propositions do. This specification is accomplished by the use of numerical or quasi-numerical quantifiers such as "one," "two," "three," . . . , "many," "a few," "most," and so on. But arguments which depend for their validity upon numerical or quasi-numerical information are *asyllogistic* and hence require a more complicated analysis than that which is contained in the simple theory of the categorical syllogism.

Some quasi-numerical quantifiers, however, occur in arguments that lend themselves to syllogistic analysis. These include "almost all," "not quite all," "all but a few," "almost everyone." Propositions in which these phrases appear as quantifiers are "exceptive" propositions, which (like singular propositions) make two assertions rather than one. They are of the same type as explicitly *exceptive* propositions like "All except employees are eligible," "All but employees are eligible," and "Employees alone are not eligible." Each of these logically equivalent propositions asserts not merely that *all nonemployees are eligible* but also (at least in the usual context) that *no employees are eligible*. Where "employees" is abbreviated by *S* and "eligible persons" by *P*, these two propositions can be written as "All non-*S* is *P*" and "No *S* is *P*." These are clearly independent and together assert that *S* and *P* are complementary classes.

Each of these exceptive propositions is compound, and therefore cannot be translated into a single standard-form categorical proposition, but rather into an explicit conjunction of two standard-form categoricals. Thus the three propositions about eligibility translate identically into "All nonemployees are eligible persons and no employees are eligible persons." Also compound are the following exceptive propositions with quasi-numerical quantifiers: "Almost all students were at the dance," "Not quite all students were at the dance," "All but a few students were at the dance," and "Only some students were at the dance." Each of these affirms that *some students were at the dance* and denies that *all students were at the dance*. The quasi-numerical information they present is irrelevant from the point of view of syllogistic inference, and all are translated indifferently as "Some students are persons who were at the dance and some students are not persons who were at the dance."

Because exceptive propositions are not categorical propositions but conjunctions, arguments containing them are not syllogistic arguments as we are using that term. But they may nevertheless be susceptible to syllogistic analysis and appraisal. How an argument containing an exceptive proposition should be tested depends upon the exceptive proposition's position in the argument. If it is a premiss, then the argument may have to be given two separate tests. For example, consider the argument

> Everyone who saw the game was at the dance.
> Not quite all the students were at the dance.
> ___
> So some students didn't see the game.

Its first premiss and its conclusion are categorical propositions, which are easily translated into standard form. But its second premiss is an exceptive proposition, not simple but compound. To discover whether or not its premisses imply its conclusion, one first tests the syllogism composed of the first premiss of the given argument, the first half of its second premiss, and its conclusion. In standard form, we have

> All persons who saw the game are persons who were at the dance.
> Some students are persons who were at the dance.
> ___
> Therefore some students are not persons who saw the game.

The standard-form categorical syllogism is of form *AIO*–2 and violates Rule 2, committing the Fallacy of the Undistributed Middle. But the original argument is not yet proved to be invalid, because the syllogism just tested contains only part of the premisses of the original argument. One now has the task of testing the categorical syllogism composed of the first premiss and the conclusion of the original argument together with the second half of the second premiss. In standard form we have

> All persons who saw the game are persons who were at the dance.
> Some students are not persons who were at the dance.
> _____
> Therefore some students are not persons who saw the game.

This standard-form categorical syllogism is of a different form, *AOO–2*, and is easily shown to be valid. Hence the original argument is valid, for the conclusion is the same, and the premisses of the original argument include the premisses of this valid standard-form syllogism. Thus to test the validity of an argument one of whose premisses is an exceptive proposition may require the testing of two different standard-form categorical syllogisms. If the premisses of an argument are both categorical propositions, and its conclusion is exceptive, then we know it to be invalid, for although the two categorical premisses may imply one or the other half of the compound conclusion, they cannot imply them both. Finally, if an argument contains exceptive propositions as both premisses and conclusion, all possible syllogisms constructable out of the original argument may have to be tested in order to determine its validity. Enough has been explained to enable the student to cope with such situations.

It is important to acquire facility at translating nonstandard-form propositions into standard form, for the tests of validity that we have developed can be applied directly only to standard-form categorical syllogisms.

EXERCISES

Translate the following into standard-form categorical propositions.

★ 1. Roses are fragrant.
   2. Orchids are not fragrant.
   3. Many a person has lived to regret a misspent youth.
   4. Not everyone worth meeting is worth having as a friend.
★ 5. If it's a Junko, it's the best that money can buy.
   6. If it isn't a real Havana, it isn't a Ropo.
   7. Nothing is both safe and exciting.
   8. Only brave people have ever won the Congressional Medal of Honor.
   9. Good counselors are not universally appreciated.
★ 10. He sees not his shadow who faces the sun.
  11. To hear her sing is an inspiration.
  12. He who takes the sword shall perish by the sword.
  13. Only members can use the front door.
  14. Pledges can use only the side door.
★ 15. The Young Turks support no candidate of the Old Guard.

16. The party regulars support any candidate of the Old Guard.
17. They also serve who only stand and wait.
18. Happy indeed is she who knows her own limitations.
19. A thing of beauty is a joy forever.
★ 20. He prayeth well who loveth well.
21. All that glitters is not gold.
22. None think the great unhappy but the great.
23. He jests at scars that never felt a wound.
24. Whatsoever a man soweth, that shall he also reap.
25. A soft answer turneth away wrath.

7.3 *Uniform Translation*

For a syllogistic argument to be tested, it must be expressed in propositions that together contain exactly three terms. Sometimes this aim is difficult to accomplish and requires a more subtle approach than that suggested in the preceding sections. Consider the proposition "The poor always ye have with you." It clearly does not assert that *all* the poor are with you, or even that *some* (particular) poor are *always* with you. There are alternative methods of reducing this proposition to standard form, but one perfectly natural route is by way of the key word "always." This word means "at all times" and suggests the standard-form categorical proposition "All times are times when ye have the poor with you." The word "times," which appears in both the subject and predicate terms, may be regarded as a *parameter*, that is, an auxiliary symbol which is of aid in expressing the original assertion in standard form.

Care should be taken not to introduce and use parameters in a mechanical, unthinking fashion. One must always be guided by an understanding of the proposition to be translated. Thus the proposition "Smith always wins at billiards" pretty clearly does not assert that Smith is incessantly, at all times, winning at billiards! It is more reasonable to interpret it as meaning that Smith wins at billiards whenever he plays. And so understood, it translates directly into "All times when Smith plays billiards are times when Smith wins at billiards." Not all parameters need be "temporal." To translate some propositions into standard form, the words "places" and "cases" can be introduced as parameters. Thus "Where there is no vision the people perish" and "Jones loses a sale whenever he is late" translate into "All places where there is no vision are places where the people perish" and "All cases in which Jones is late are cases in which Jones loses a sale."

The introduction of parameters is often necessary for the *uniform translation* of all three constituent propositions of a syllogistic argument into standard form. Since a categorical syllogism contains exactly three terms, to test a syllogistic argument we must translate its constituent propositions into standard-form categorical propositions that contain just three terms. The elimination of synonyms and the applications of conversion, obversion, and contraposition were already discussed in Section 7.1. However, there are many syllogistic arguments that cannot have the number of their terms reduced to three either by eliminating synonyms or by applying conversion, obversion, or contraposition. Here uniform translation requires the introduction of a parameter—the same parameter—into all three of the constituent propositions. Consider the following argument:

Soiled paper plates are scattered only where careless people have picnicked.
There are soiled paper plates scattered about here.

Therefore careless people must have been picnicking here.

This argument is perfectly valid, but before it can be proved valid by our diagrams or rules, its premisses and conclusion must be translated into standard-form categorical propositions involving only three terms. The second premiss and the conclusion might be translated most naturally into "Some soiled paper plates are things that are scattered about here" and "Some careless people are those who have been picnicking here." But these two statements contain four different terms. To reduce the given argument to standard form we begin with the first premiss, which requires a parameter for its standard-form expression, and then use the same parameter in translating the second premiss and the conclusion into standard form. The word "where" in the first premiss suggests that the parameter "places" can be used. If this parameter is used to obtain uniform standard-form translations of all three propositions, the argument translates into

All places where soiled paper plates are scattered are places where careless people have picnicked.
This place is a place where soiled paper plates are scattered.

Therefore this place is a place where careless people have picnicked.

This standard-form categorical syllogism has mood and figure *AAA–1* and has already been proved valid.

The notion of standardizing expressions through the use of a parameter is not an altogether easy one to grasp, but some syllogistic arguments cannot be translated into standard-form categorical syllogisms by any other method. Another example may help to make clear the technique involved. Let us take the argument

The hounds bay wherever a fox has passed, so the fox must have taken another path, since the hounds are quiet.

First, we must understand what is asserted in the given argument. We may take the statement that the hounds are quiet as asserting that the hounds are not baying here and now. This step is part of the necessary process of eliminating synonyms, since the first assertion makes explicit reference to the baying of hounds. And in the same manner we may understand the conclusion that the fox must have taken another path as asserting that the fox did not pass here. The word "wherever" in the first assertion should suggest that the parameter "places" can be used in its translation. The standard-form translation thus arrived at is

> All places where a fox has passed are places where the hounds bay.
> This place is not a place where the hounds bay.
>
> Therefore this place is not a place where a fox has passed.

This standard-form categorical syllogism has mood and figure *AEE–2*, and its validity is easy to establish.

EXERCISES

I. Translate the following propositions into standard form using parameters where necessary.

★ 1. He groans whenever he is reminded of his loss.

2. She never drives her car to work.

3. He walks where he chooses.

4. He always orders the most expensive item on the menu.

★ 5. She does not give her opinion unless she is asked to do so.

6. She tries to sell life insurance wherever she may happen to be.

7. His face gets red when he gets angry.

8. If he is asked to say a few words, he talks for hours.

9. Error of opinion may be tolerated where reason is left free to combat it.

10. People are never so likely to settle a question rightly as when they discuss it freely.

II. Translate each of the following arguments into standard form; name the mood and figure of its standard-form translation; test its validity by a Venn Diagram; and if it is invalid, name the fallacy it commits.

★ 1. Since all knowledge comes from sensory impressions and since there's no sensory impression of substance itself, it follows logically that there is no knowledge of substance.

—ROBERT M. PIRSIG, *Zen and the Art of Motorcycle Maintenance*

2. . . . no names come in contradictory pairs; but all predicables come in contradictory pairs; therefore no name is a predicable.

—PETER THOMAS GEACH, *Reference and Generality*

3. Everyone who smokes marijuana goes on to try heroin. Everyone who tries heroin becomes hopelessly addicted to it. Therefore everyone who smokes marijuana becomes hopelessly addicted to it.

4. A body on which a freely swinging pendulum of fixed length has periods of oscillation which decrease slightly with increasing latitude from the equator to both poles is an oblate spheroid slightly flattened at the poles.

But the earth is a body on which a freely swinging pendulum of fixed length has periods of oscillation which decrease slightly with increasing latitude from the equator to both poles.

Therefore the earth is an oblate spheroid slightly flattened at the poles.

—W. A. WALLACE, *Einstein, Galileo, and Aquinas: Three Views of Scientific Method*

★ 5. Barcelona Traction was unable to pay interest on its debts; bankrupt companies are unable to pay interest on their debts; therefore, Barcelona Traction must be bankrupt.

—JOHN BROOKS, "Annals of Finance," *The New Yorker*, May 28, 1979

6. Barry Goldwater to the contrary notwithstanding, extremism in defense of liberty, or virtue, or whatever is *always* a vice—because extremism is but another name for fanaticism which is a vice by definition.

—IRVING KRISTOL, "The Environmentalist Crusade," *The Wall Street Journal*, December 16, 1974

7. When teachers' values conflict with social norms, particularly those of the local community or with those of administrators or students or other teachers, a pervasive tension marks their professional life. . . .

In a pluralistic society dedicated, in principle at least, to respect for differences among people and to universal education for all, teachers' values will inevitably be in conflict with those of some segment or segments of the community in which they teach. Therefore, tension is a fact of professional life in our public schools.

—DAVID W. ADAMS, "Tired and Frustrated Teachers," *Today's Education*, Vol. 64, No. 1, January–February 1975

8. All syllogisms having two negative premises are invalid. Some valid syllogisms are sound. Therefore some unsound arguments are syllogisms having two negative premises.

9. Any two persons who contradict each other cannot both be lying. Hence the first and third natives cannot both be lying, since they contradict each other.

★ 10. Not all is gold that glitters, for some base metals glitter, and gold is not a base metal.

11. All who are inebriated are undependable, so all who are dependable are nonalcoholics, since all alcoholics are ebriated.

12. Where there's smoke there's fire, so there's no fire in the basement, because there's no smoke there.

13. It seems that mercy cannot be attributed to God. For mercy is a kind of sorrow, as Damascene says. But there is no sorrow in God; and therefore there is no mercy in Him.

—THOMAS AQUINAS, *Summa Theologica*, I, Question 21, Article 3

14. . . . because intense heat is nothing else but a particular kind of painful sensation; and pain cannot exist but in a perceiving being; it follows that no intense heat can really exist in an unperceiving corporeal substance.

—GEORGE BERKELEY, *Three Dialogues Between Hylas and Philonous, In Opposition to Sceptics and Atheists*

★ 15. Only those who ignore the facts are likely to be mistaken. No one who is truly objective is likely to be mistaken. Hence no one who ignores the facts is truly objective.

16. All bridge players are people. All people think. Therefore all bridge players think.   —OSWALD and JAMES JACOBY, "Jacoby on Bridge," *Ann Arbor News,*
November 5, 1966

17. Whenever I'm in trouble, I pray. And since I'm always in trouble, there is not a day when I don't pray.
—ISAAC BASHEVIS SINGER, interview in *The New York Times*

18. The after-image is not in physical space. The brain-process is. So the after-image is not a brain-process.
—J. J. C. SMART, "Sensations and Brain Processes," *Philosophical Review,*
April 1959

19. It must have rained lately, because the fish are not biting, and fish never bite after a rain.

★ 20. . . . it is obvious that irrationals are uninteresting to engineers, since they are concerned only with approximations, and all approximations are rational.
—G. H. HARDY, *A Mathematician's Apology*

21. All practice is theory; all surgery is practice; ergo, all surgery is theory.
—LANFRANC, *Chirurgia magna*

22. Since then to fight against neighbors is an evil, and to fight against the Thebans is to fight against neighbors, it is clear that to fight against the Thebans is an evil.   —ARISTOTLE, *Prior Analytics*

23. According to Aristotle, none of the products of Nature are due to chance. His proof is this: That which is due to chance does not reappear constantly nor frequently, but all products of Nature reappear either constantly or at least frequently.   —MOSES MAIMONIDES, *The Guide for the Perplexed*

24. She told me that she had a very simple attitude toward her students which was in fact no different from her feelings about people in general. That was, all her life she'd spoken only to people who were ladies and gentlemen. Since none of the students of 9D were ladies and gentlemen, she never spoke to them, never had, and never would.   —JAMES HERNDON, *The Way It Spozed to Be*

★ 25. Not all who have jobs are temperate in their drinking. Only debtors drink to excess. So not all the unemployed are in debt.

26. It will be a good game tomorrow, for the conference title is at stake, and no title contest is ever dull.

27. Bill didn't go to work this morning, because he wore a sweater, and he never wears a sweater to work.

28. Cynthia must have complimented Henry, because he is cheerful whenever Cynthia compliments him, and he's cheerful now.

29. Every boy who meets Alice falls in love with her. Every boy who dates Betty meets Alice. Therefore every boy who dates Betty falls in love with her.

★ 30. There must be a strike at the factory, for there is a picket line there, and pickets are present only at strikes.

31. As epidemiologists often point out, epidemiology is not merely the study of epidemics of infectious disease; it is the broad examination of the rates and

patterns of disease in the community. By almost any standard drug abuse can be regarded as a disease; accordingly it can be profitably investigated by the methods of epidemiology.

—"Science and the Citizen," *Scientific American*, Vol. 232, No. 2, February 1975

32. And no man can be a rhapsode who does not understand the meaning of the poet. For the rhapsode ought to interpret the mind of the poet to his hearers, but how can he interpret him well unless he knows what he means?

—PLATO, *Ion*

33. Since morals, therefore, have an influence on the actions and affections, it follows, that they cannot be deriv'd from reason; and that because reason alone, as we have already prov'd, can never have any such influence.

—DAVID HUME, *A Treatise of Human Nature*

34. Any argument worthy of logical recognition must be such as would occur in ordinary discourse. Now it will be found that no argument occurring in ordinary discourse is in the fourth figure. Hence, no argument in the fourth figure is worthy of logical recognition.

★ 35. All valid syllogisms distribute their middle terms in at least one premiss, so this syllogism must be valid, for it distributes its middle term in at least one premiss.

36. The express train alone does not stop at this station, and as the last train did not stop, it must have been the express train.

37. No valid syllogisms have two negative premisses. No syllogisms on this page are invalid. Therefore no syllogisms on this page have two negative premisses.

38. All invalid syllogisms commit an illicit process of their major terms, but this syllogism is valid, so this syllogism does not commit an illicit process of its major term.

39. There are plants growing here, and since vegetation requires water, water must be present.

★ 40. No one present is out of work. No members are absent. Therefore all members are employed.

41. The competition is stiff, for there is a great deal of money involved, and there is never easy competition where much money is at stake.

42. There are handsome men, but only man is vile, so it is false that nothing is both vile and handsome.

43. Also, what is simple cannot be separated from itself. The soul is simple; therefore, it cannot be separated from itself.

—DUNS SCOTUS, *Oxford Commentary on the Sentences of Peter Lombard*

44. All that glitters is not gold, so gold is not the only precious metal, since only precious metals glitter.

★ 45. Although he complains whenever he is sick, his health is excellent, so he won't complain.

46. No sane witnesses incriminate themselves. But some witnesses criminate themselves. So some witnesses are insane.

47. We . . . define a metaphysical sentence as a sentence which purports to express a genuine proposition, but does, in fact, express neither a tautology nor

an empirical hypothesis. And as tautologies and empirical hypotheses form the entire class of significant propositions, we are justified in concluding that all metaphysical assertions are nonsensical.

—ALFRED J. AYER, *Language, Truth, and Logic*

48. This syllogism is valid, for all invalid syllogisms commit an illicit process, and this syllogism commits no illicit process.

49. All who were penniless were convicted. Some of the guilty were acquitted. Therefore some who had money were not innocent.

50. All buildings over three hundred feet tall are skyscrapers, but not all examples of modern architecture are buildings over three hundred feet tall, since skyscrapers are not the only examples of modern architecture.

7.4 *Enthymemes*

Syllogistic arguments occur frequently, but their premisses and conclusions are not always stated explicitly. Often only part of the argument is expressed, the rest being "understood." Thus one may justify the conclusion that "Jones is a citizen" by mentioning only the one premiss: "Jones is a native-born American." As stated, the argument is incomplete, but the missing premiss is easily supplied from the Constitution of the United States. Were the missing premiss to be stated, the completed argument would appear as

> All native-born Americans are citizens.
> Jones is a native-born American.
> _____
> Therefore Jones is a citizen.

Fully stated, the argument is a categorical syllogism of form *AAA–1* and is perfectly valid. An argument that is stated incompletely, part being "understood" or only "in the mind," is called an *enthymeme*. An incompletely stated argument is characterized as *enthymematic*.

In everyday discourse, and even in science, many inferences are expressed enthymematically. The reason is easy to understand. A large body of propositions can be presumed to be common knowledge, and many speakers and writers save themselves trouble by not repeating well-known and perhaps trivially true propositions that their hearers or readers can perfectly well be expected to supply for themselves. Moreover, it is not at all unusual for an argument to be *rhetorically* more powerful and persuasive when stated enthymematically than when enunciated in complete detail. As Aristotle wrote in his *Rhetoric*, "Speeches that . . . rely on Enthymemes excite the louder applause."

Because it is incomplete, an enthymeme must have its suppressed parts taken into account when the question arises of testing its validity. When a necessary premiss is missing, without that premiss the inference is invalid. But where the unexpressed premiss is easily supplied, in all fairness it ought to be included as part of the argument in appraising it. In such a case one assumes that the maker of the argument did have more "in mind" than was stated explicitly. In most cases there is no difficulty in supplying the tacit premiss that the speaker intended but did not express. A cardinal principle in supplying suppressed premisses is that the proposition must be one that speakers can safely presume their hearers to accept as true. Thus it would be foolish to suggest taking the conclusion itself as a suppressed premiss, for if the arguer could have expected the auditors to accept that proposition as a premiss, without proof, it would have been idle to present it to them as conclusion of an argument.

Any kind of argument can be expressed enthymematically, but the kinds of enthymemes that have been most extensively studied are incompletely expressed syllogistic arguments. We confine our attention to these in the remainder of this section. Enthymemes have traditionally been divided into different "orders," according to which part of the syllogism is left unexpressed. A *first-order* enthymeme is one in which the syllogism's major premiss is not stated. The preceding example is of the first order. A *second-order* enthymeme is one in which only the major premiss and the conclusion are stated, the minor premiss being suppressed. An example of this type is "All students are opposed to the new regulations, so all sophomores are opposed to them." Here the minor premiss is easily supplied, being the obviously true proposition "All sophomores are students." A *third-order* enthymeme is one in which both premisses are stated, but the conclusion is left unexpressed. An example of this type is the following:

> Our ideas reach no farther than our experience: we have no experience of divine attributes and operations: I need not conclude my syllogism: you can draw the inference yourself.[2]

Another example of the same type is the argument "No true Christian is vain, but some churchgoers are vain." If the context is such that the intended conclusion is "Some churchgoers are not true Christians," then the argument is valid. But if the speaker was intending to establish the conclusion that "Some true Christians are not churchgoers," then his enthymeme is invalid, committing the Fallacy of Illicit Process of the Major Term. Here the context is decisive. But in other cases a third-order enthymeme may be invalid regardless of context. Where both premisses are negative, or where both premisses are particular propositions, or where their common term is undistributed, no syllogistic conclusion follows validly, so such enthymemes are invalid in any context.

In testing an enthymeme for validity, two steps are involved. The first is to supply the missing parts of the argument; the second is to test the resulting syllogism. If one of the premisses is missing, it may be that only the addition of an implausible proposition as premiss will make the argument valid, while with any plausible proposition added the argument is invalid. Pointing this

[2]David Hume, *Dialogues Concerning Natural Religion*, Pt. II.

out is a legitimate criticism of an enthymematic argument. Of course, an even more crushing objection is to show that *no* additional premiss, no matter how implausible, can turn the enthymeme into a valid categorical syllogism.

It should be observed that no new logical principles need be introduced in dealing with enthymemes. They are ultimately tested by the same methods that apply to standard-form categorical syllogisms. The difference between enthymemes and syllogisms is rhetorical rather than logical.

EXERCISES

Name the order and discuss the correctness of each of the following enthymemes. Write the arguments in standard form, adding a missing premiss or conclusion to make the completed argument valid—if possible—and using parameters if necessary.

★ 1. The American people are well-mannered, and no well-mannered people is "alienated."   —HENRY FAIRLIE, *Washington Post Service*, March 28, 1976

2. The soul through all her being is immortal, for that which is ever in motion is immortal.   —PLATO, *Phaedrus*

3. Abraham Beame . . . campaigned for mayor—as has been mentioned in recent weeks more often and with more irony than he might have wished—on the slogan "If you don't know the buck, you don't know the job—and Abe knows the buck."   —*The New Yorker*, August 26, 1974

4. Although these textbooks purport to be a universal guide to learning of great worth and importance—there is a single clue that points to another direction. In the six years I taught in city and country schools, no one ever stole a textbook.

—W. RON JONES, *Changing Education*, Vol. 5, No. 4, Winter–Spring 1974

★ 5. As a matter of fact, man, like woman, is flesh, therefore passive, the plaything of his hormones and of the species, the restless prey of his desires.

—SIMONE DE BEAUVOIR, *The Second Sex*

6. Leslie Cole is well groomed, and we know what that implies because all successful people are well-groomed.

7. . . . I am an Idealist, since I believe that all that exists is spiritual.

—JOHN MCTAGGART ELLIS MCTAGGART, *Philosophical Studies*

8. Mary attended the opera, so her lamb must have attended the opera too.

9. However, the legal propriety of Manchester's book is at this writing before the courts and is accordingly not an appropriate subject for discussion.

—ARNOLD L. FAIN, "The Legal Right to Privacy,"
Saturday Review, January 21, 1967

★ 10. I do not believe we can have any freedom at all in the philosophical sense, for we act not only under external compulsion but also by inner necessity.

—ALBERT EINSTEIN

11. All physicians are college graduates, so all members of the American Medical Association must be college graduates.

12. Small countries tend to remember history especially well, since it often turns out badly for them.   —MARC FALCOFF, "Semper Fidel,"
The New Republic, July 3, 1989, p. 39.

13. It must have rained lately, because the fish just aren't biting.

14. Yond' Cassius has a lean and hungry look . . . such men are dangerous.
—WILLIAM SHAKESPEARE, *Julius Caesar,* I, ii

★ 15. Henry is interested only in making money, but you cannot serve both God and Mammon!

16. The Adamsons can't have a telephone, because their name isn't listed in the phone book.

17. No enthymemes are complete, so this argument is incomplete.

18. He would not take the crown
Therefore 'tis certain he was not ambitious.
—WILLIAM SHAKESPEARE, *Julius Caesar,* III, ii

19. Any reader who completes this argument is a good student, for it is difficult.

★ 20. He knows his own child, so he must be a wise father.

21. . . . we possess some immaterial knowledge. No sense knowledge, however, can be immaterial; therefore, etc.
—DUNS SCOTUS, *Oxford Commentary on the Sentences of Peter Lombard*

22. It could hardly be denied that a tax laid specifically on the exercise of these freedoms would be unconstitutional. Yet the license tax imposed by this ordinance is in substance just that.   —MR. JUSTICE DOUGLAS, for the Court,
Murdock v. *Commonwealth of Pennsylvania,* 319 U.S. 105 (1943)

23. He who is without sin should cast the first stone. There is no one here who does not have a skeleton in his closet. I know, and I know them by name.
—REP. ADAM CLAYTON POWELL, speech in the
United States House of Representatives, 1967

24. Only demonstrative proof should be able to make you abandon the theory of the Creation; but such a proof does not exist in Nature.
—MOSES MAIMONIDES, *The Guide for the Perplexed*

★ 25. Achilles is brave so he must be deserving of the fair.

26. Man tends to increase at a greater rate than his means of subsistence; consequently he is occasionally subject to a severe struggle for existence.
—CHARLES DARWIN, *The Descent of Man*

27. No internal combustion engines are free from pollution; but no internal combustion engine is completely efficient. You may draw your own conclusion.

28. A nation without a conscience is a nation without a soul. A nation without a soul is a nation that cannot live.   —WINSTON CHURCHILL

29. Liberty means responsibility. That is why most men dread it.
—GEORGE BERNARD SHAW, *Maxims for Revolutionists*

★ 30. It is always possible to pretend to motives and abilities other than one's real ones, or to pretend to strengths of motives and levels of ability other than their real strengths and levels. The theatre could not exist, if it was not possible to make such pretences and to make them efficiently.

—GILBERT RYLE, *The Concept of Mind*

31. Douglas A. Fraser, president of the United Auto Workers union, summarized Carter's problems:

"If you look back in history, any time we (Democrats) were successful in politics we had the issues of high unemployment, high interest rates and high inflation. We don't have those issues this time. Our historical, traditional issues now belong to the Republican Party."

—ROBERT G. KAISER, "Inflation Drop Follows President's Game Plan," *Washington Post Service*, June 8, 1980

32. Productivity is desirable because it betters the condition of the vast majority of the people. . . .

—STEPHEN MILLER, "Adam Smith and the Commercial Republic," *The Public Interest*, Fall 1980

33. Advertisements perform a vital function in almost any society, for they help to bring buyers and sellers together.

—BURTON M. LEISER, *Liberty, Justice, and Morals*

34. Logic is a matter of profound human importance precisely because it is empirically founded and experimentally applied.

—JOHN DEWEY, *Reconstruction in Philosophy*

35. *Iphigeneia at Aulis* is a tragedy because it demonstrates inexorably how human character, with its itch to be admired (*philotimia* in Greek), combines with the malice of heaven to produce wars which no one in his right mind would want and which turn out to be utterly disastrous for everybody.

—GEORGE E. DIMOCK, JR., Introduction to *Iphigeneia at Aulis* by Euripides

36. . . . the law does not expressly permit suicide, and what it does not expressly permit it forbids.   —ARISTOTLE, *Nichomachean Ethics*

37. The man who says that all things come to pass by necessity cannot criticize one who denies that all things come to pass by necessity: for he admits that this too happens of necessity.   —EPICURUS, Fragment XL, Vatican Collection

7.5 *Sorites*

There are occasions when a single categorical syllogism will not suffice for drawing a desired conclusion from a group of premisses. Thus from the premisses

> All diplomats are tactful.
> Some government officials are diplomats.
> All government officials are people in public life.

one cannot draw the conclusion

> Some people in public life are tactful.

by a single syllogistic inference. Yet the indicated conclusion is entailed by the stated premisses. To derive it requires two syllogisms rather than one. A stepwise process of argumentation must be resorted to, where each step is a separate categorical syllogism. When stated explicitly, the required argument will be

> All diplomats are tactful individuals.
> Some government officials are diplomats.
> _____
> Therefore some government officials are tactful individuals.
> All government officials are people in public life.
> _____
> Therefore some people in public life are tactful individuals.

The present argument is not a syllogism but a *chain* of categorical syllogisms, connected by the conclusion of the first, which is a premiss of the second. This chain has only two links, but more extended arguments may consist of a greater number. Since a chain is no stronger than its weakest link, an argument of this type is valid if, and only if, all its constituent syllogisms are valid.

Where such an argument is expressed enthymematically, with only the premisses and the final conclusion stated, it is called a "sorites." Sorites may have three, four, or *any* number of premisses. Some are very lengthy indeed. The following example is due to the philosopher Gottfried Leibniz:

> The human soul is a thing whose activity is thinking. A thing whose activity is thinking is one whose activity is immediately apprehended, and without any representation of parts therein. A thing whose activity is immediately apprehended without any representation of parts therein is a thing whose activity does not contain parts. A thing whose activity does not contain parts is one whose activity is not motion. A thing whose activity is not motion is not a body. What is not a body is not in space. What is not in space is insusceptible of motion. What is insusceptible of motion is indissoluble (for dissolution is a movement of parts). What is indissoluble is incorruptible. What is incorruptible is immortal. Therefore the human soul is immortal.[3]

This sorites contains no less than ten premisses. Any sorites may be tested by making its intermediate conclusions or steps explicit and testing separately the various categorical syllogisms thus obtained. If we ignore the possibility that an equivocation is present, then the validity of Leibniz's sorites is easily verified.

It will be convenient, in connection with the exercises provided for this section, to say that a sorites is in standard form when all of its propositions are in standard form, when each term occurs exactly twice, and when every proposition (except the last) has a term in common with the proposition which immediately follows it. Thus one standard-form translation of Lewis

---

[3]From H. W. B. Joseph, *An Introduction to Logic* (New York: Oxford University Press, 1906, 1916).

Carroll's sorites

> (1) Every one who is sane can do Logic.
> (2) No lunatics are fit to serve on a jury.
> (3) None of your sons can do Logic.
>
> ———
>
> Therefore none of your sons is fit to serve on a jury.

is

> (2') All persons fit to serve on a jury are sane persons.
> (1') All sane persons are persons who can do Logic.
> (3') No sons of yours are persons who can do Logic.
>
> ———
>
> Therefore no sons of yours are persons fit to serve on a jury.

It can be tested by stating the suppressed subconclusion explicitly, and then testing the resulting categorical syllogisms.

EXERCISES

I. Translate each of the following sorites into standard form and test its validity.[4]

★ 1. (1) Babies are illogical.
   (2) Nobody is despised who can manage a crocodile.
   (3) Illogical persons are despised.

   Therefore babies cannot manage crocodiles.

2. (1) No experienced person is incompetent.
   (2) Jenkins is always blundering.
   (3) No competent person is always blundering.

   Therefore Jenkins is inexperienced.

3. (1) The only books in this library that I do not recommend for reading are unhealthy in tone.
   (2) The bound books are all well written.
   (3) All the romances are healthy in tone.
   (4) I do not recommend you to read any of the unbound books.

   Therefore all the romances in this library are well written.

4. (1) Only profound scholars can be dons at Oxford.
   (2) No insensitive souls are great lovers of music.
   (3) No one whose soul is not sensitive can be a Don Juan.
   (4) There are no profound scholars who are not great lovers of music.

   Therefore all Oxford dons are Don Juans.

---

[4]All the following exercises except 4 and 6 under I are taken, with little or no modification, from Lewis Carroll's *Symbolic Logic.*

5. (1) No interesting poems are unpopular among people of real taste.
   (2) No modern poetry is free from affectation.
   (3) All your poems are on the subject of soap bubbles.
   (4) No affected poetry is popular among people of real taste.
   (5) Only a modern poem would be on the subject of soap bubbles.

   Therefore all your poems are uninteresting.

6. (1) None but writers are poets.
   (2) Only military officers are astronauts.
   (3) Whoever contributes to the new magazine is a poet.
   (4) Nobody is both a military officer and a writer.

   Therefore not one astronaut is a contributor to the new magazine.

   II. Each of the following sets of propositions can serve as premises for a valid sorites. For each, find the conclusion and establish the argument as valid.

★ 1. (1) No one takes in the *Times* unless he is well educated.
   (2) No hedgehogs can read.
   (3) Those who cannot read are not well educated.

2. (1) All puddings are nice.
   (2) This dish is a pudding.
   (3) No nice things are wholesome.

3. (1) The only articles of food that my doctor allows me are such as are not very rich.
   (2) Nothing that agrees with me is unsuitable for supper.
   (3) Wedding cake is always very rich.
   (4) My doctor allows me all articles of food that are suitable for supper.

4. (1) All my daughters are slim.
   (2) No child of mine is healthy who takes no exercise.
   (3) All gluttons who are children of mine are fat.
   (4) No son of mine takes any exercise.

5. (1) When I work a Logic example without grumbling, you may be sure it is one that I can understand.
   (2) These sorites are not arranged in regular order, like the examples I am used to.
   (3) No easy example ever makes my head ache.
   (4) I can't understand examples that are not arranged in regular order, like those I am used to.
   (5) I never grumble at an example, unless it gives me a headache.

7.6 *Disjunctive and Hypothetical Syllogisms*

A syllogism is a deductive argument consisting of two premises and a conclusion. There are different kinds of syllogisms, taking their names from the kinds of propositions they contain. Thus the categorical syllogism is so called because it contains categorical propositions exclusively. Other kinds of propositions occur in other kinds of syllogisms.

We may think of categorical propositions as *simple*, in contrast to *compound* propositions that contain other propositions as components. The first kind of compound proposition to be considered is the *disjunctive* (or *alternative*) proposition, an example of which is "Either Fido ran away or Fido got hit by a car." Its two component propositions are "Fido ran away" and "Fido got hit by a car." The disjunctive proposition, or disjunction, contains two component propositions, which are its disjuncts. The disjunction does not categorically affirm the truth of either one of its disjuncts, but says that at least one of them is true, allowing for the possibility that both may be true.

If we have a disjunction as one premiss, and as another premiss the denial or contradictory of one of its two disjuncts, then we can validly infer that the disjunction's other disjunct is true. Any argument of this form is a valid disjunctive syllogism, for example,

> Either Fido ran away or Fido got hit by a car.
> Fido did not run away.
> Therefore Fido got hit by a car.

As we use the term in this section, not every disjunctive syllogism is valid. For example, the argument

> Either Fido ran away or Fido got hit by a car.
> Fido ran away.
> Therefore Fido did not get hit by a car.

may be classified as an invalid disjunctive syllogism. It bears a superficial resemblance to the preceding example, but it is easily seen to be fallacious. Consistently with the premisses, Fido might have run away *and* got hit by a car. The truth of one disjunct of a disjunction does not imply the falsehood of the other disjunct, since both disjuncts of a disjunction can be true. Hence we have a valid disjunctive syllogism only where the categorical premiss contradicts one disjunct of the disjunctive premiss and the conclusion affirms the other disjunct of the disjunctive premiss.

An objection might be raised at this point, based on such an argument as the following:

> Either Smith is in New York or Smith is in Paris.
> Smith is in New York.
> Therefore Smith is not in Paris.

Here the categorical premiss affirms one disjunct of the stated disjunction, and the conclusion contradicts the other disjunct, yet the conclusion seems to follow validly. Closer analysis shows, however, that the stated disjunction plays no role in the argument. The conclusion follows enthymematically from the categorical premiss, with the unexpressed additional premiss being the obviously true proposition that "Smith can't be both in New York and in

Paris," which can be stated in disjunctive form as

> Either Smith is not in New York or Smith is not in Paris.

When this tacit premiss is supplied, and the superfluous original disjunction is discarded, the resulting argument is easily seen to be a valid disjunctive syllogism. The apparent exception is not really an exception, and the objection is groundless.

The second kind of compound proposition to be considered is the *conditional* (or *hypothetical*) proposition, an example of which is "If the first native is a politician, then the first native lies." A conditional proposition contains two component propositions: the one following the "if" is the *antecedent*, and the one following the "then" is the *consequent*. A syllogism that contains conditional propositions exclusively is called a *pure hypothetical syllogism*, for example,

> If the first native is a politician, then he lies.
> If he lies, then he denies being a politician.
> Therefore if the first native is a politician, then he denies being a politician.

In this argument it can be observed that the first premiss and the conclusion have the same antecedent, that the second premiss and the conclusion have the same consequent, and that the consequent of the first premiss is the same as the antecedent of the second premiss. It should be clear that any pure hypothetical syllogism whose premisses and conclusion have their component parts so related is a valid argument.

A syllogism having one conditional premiss and one categorical premiss is called a *mixed hypothetical syllogism*. There are two valid forms of the mixed hypothetical syllogism that have been given special names. The first is illustrated by

> If the second native told the truth, then only one native is a politician.
> The second native told the truth.
> Therefore only one native is a politician.

Here the categorical premiss affirms the antecedent of the conditional premiss, and the conclusion affirms its consequent. Any argument of this form is valid and is said to be in the *affirmative mood* or *modus ponens* (from the Latin *ponere*, meaning "to affirm"). One must not confuse the valid form *modus ponens* with the clearly invalid form displayed by the following argument:

> If Bacon wrote *Hamlet*, then Bacon was a great writer.
> Bacon was a great writer.
> Therefore Bacon wrote *Hamlet*.

This argument differs from *modus ponens* in that its categorical premiss affirms the consequent, rather than the antecedent, of the conditional premiss. Any argument of this form is said to commit the <u>Fallacy of Affirming the Conse</u>quent.

The other valid form of mixed hypothetical syllogism is illustrated by

> If the one-eyed prisoner saw two red hats, then he could tell the color of the hat on his own head.
> The one-eyed prisoner could not tell the color of the hat on his own head.
> Therefore the one-eyed prisoner did not see two red hats.

Here the categorical premiss denies the consequent of the conditional premiss, and the conclusion denies its antecedent. Any argument of this form is valid, and is said to be in the form *modus tollens* (from the Latin *tollere*, meaning "to deny"). One must not confuse the valid form *modus tollens* with the clearly invalid form displayed by the following argument:

> If Carl embezzled the college funds, then Carl is guilty of a felony.
> Carl did not embezzle the college funds.
> Therefore Carl is not guilty of a felony.

This argument differs from *modus tollens* in that its categorical premiss denies the antecedent, rather than the consequent, of the conditional premiss. Any argument of this form is said to commit the <u>Fallacy of Denying the Anteced</u>ent.

EXERCISES

Identify the form and discuss the validity or invalidity of each of the following arguments.

★ 1. If a man could not have done otherwise than he in fact did, then he is not responsible for his action. But if determinism is true, it is true of every action that the agent could not have done otherwise. Therefore, if determinism is true, no one is ever responsible for what he does.
—WINSTON NESBITT and STEWART CANDLISH, "Determinism and the Ability to Do Otherwise," *Mind*, July 1978

2. I can't have anything more to do with the operation. If I did, I'd have to lie to the Ambassador. And I can't do that.
—HENRY BROMELL, "I Know Your Heart, Marco Polo," *The New Yorker*, March 6, 1978

3. "J. J.," I replied, "If it was any of your business, I would have invited you. It is not, and so I did not." —PAUL ERDMAN, *The Crash of '79*

4. Men, it is assumed, act in economic matters only in response to pecuniary compensation or to force. Force in the modern society is largely, although by no

means completely, obsolete. So only pecuniary compensation remains of importance.   —JOHN KENNETH GALBRAITH, *The New Industrial State*

★ 5. If each man had a definite set of rules of conduct by which he regulated his life he would be no better than a machine. But there are no such rules, so men cannot be machines.
—A. M. TURING, "Computing Machinery and Intelligence," *Mind*, Vol. 59, 1950

6. Smith is the fireman or Smith is the engineer. Smith is not the fireman. Therefore Smith is the engineer.

7. If the first native is a politician, then the first native denied being a politician. The first native denied being a politician. Therefore the first native is a politician.

8. If the first native denied being a politician, then the second native told the truth. If the second native told the truth, then the second native is not a politician. Therefore if the first native denied being a politician, then the second native is not a politician.

9. If Mr. Jones lived in Chicago, then Jones is the brakeman. Mr. Jones lives in Chicago. Therefore Jones is the brakeman.

★ 10. If the second native told the truth, then the first native denied being a politician. If the third native told the truth, then the first native denied being a politician. Therefore if the second native told the truth, then the third native told the truth.

11. If Robinson is the brakeman, then Mr. Robinson lives in Chicago. Mr. Robinson does not live in Chicago. Therefore Robinson is not the brakeman.

12. If Robinson is the brakeman, then Smith is the engineer. Robinson is not the brakeman. Therefore Smith is not the engineer.

13. If Mr. Jones is the brakeman's next-door neighbor, then $20,000 is exactly divisible by 3. But $20,000 is not exactly divisible by 3. Therefore Mr. Jones is not the brakeman's next-door neighbor.

14. If the one-eyed prisoner does not know the color of the hat on his own head, then the blind prisoner cannot have on a red hat. The one-eyed prisoner does not know the color of the hat on his own head. Therefore the blind prisoner cannot have on a red hat.

★ 15. Mr. Smith is the brakeman's next-door neighbor or Mr. Robinson is the brakeman's next-door neighbor. Mr. Robinson is not the brakeman's next-door neighbor. Therefore Mr. Smith is the brakeman's next-door neighbor.

16. If all three prisoners have on white hats, then the one-eyed prisoner does not know the color of the hat on his own head. The one-eyed prisoner does not know the color of the hat on his own head. Therefore all three prisoners have on white hats.

17. Mr. Robinson lives in Detroit or Mr. Robinson lives in Chicago. Mr. Robinson lives in Detroit. Therefore Mr. Robinson does not live in Chicago.

18. The stranger is either a knave or a fool. The stranger is a knave. Therefore the stranger is no fool.

19. If this syllogism commits the Fallacy of Affirming the Consequent, then it

is invalid. This syllogism does not commit the Fallacy of Affirming the Consequent. Therefore this syllogism is valid.

★ 20. If the first native is a politician, then the third native tells the truth. If the third native tells the truth, then the third native is not a politician. Therefore if the first native is a politician, then the third native is not a politician.

21. Mankind, he said, judging by their neglect of him, have never, as I think, at all understood the power of Love. For if they had understood him they would surely have built noble temples and altars, and offered solemn sacrifices in his honor; but this is not done. —PLATO, *Symposium*

22. I have already said that he must have gone to King's Pyland or to Capleton. He is not at King's Pyland, therefore he is at Capleton.
—A. CONAN DOYLE, *Silver Blaze*

23. If Pluto, according to Halliday's calculations, had a diameter of more than 4,200 miles, then an occultation would have occurred at McDonald [Observatory at Fort Davis, Texas], and the records clearly indicated that it did not. Thus Pluto must be that size or smaller; it cannot be larger.
—THOMAS D. NICHOLSON, "The Enigma of Pluto,"
Natural History, Vol. 76, March 1967

24. If then, it is agreed that things are either the result of coincidence or for an end, and these cannot be the result of coincidence or spontaneity, it follows that they must be for an end. —ARISTOTLE, *Physics*

★ 25. There is no case known (neither is it, indeed, possible) in which a thing is found to be the efficient cause of itself; for so it would be prior to itself, which is impossible.   —THOMAS AQUINAS, *Summa Theologica,* I, Question 2, Article 3

26. Either wealth is an evil or wealth is a good; but wealth is not an evil; therefore wealth is a good.   —SEXTUS EMPIRICUS, *Against the Logicans*

27. And certainly if its essence and power are infinite, its goodness must be infinite, since a thing whose essence is finite has finite goodness.
—ROGER BACON, *The Opus Majus*

28. I *do* know that this pencil exists; but I could not know this, if Hume's principles were true; *therefore,* Hume's principles, one or both of them, are false.
—GEORGE EDWARD MOORE, *Some Main Problems of Philosophy*

29. A theoryless position is possible only if there are no theories of evidence. But there are theories of evidence. Therefore, a theoryless position is impossible.
—HENRY W. JOHNSTONE, JR., "The Law of Non-contradiction,"
Logique et Analyse, n.s. Vol. 3, 1960

★ 30. It is clear that we mean something, and something different in each case, by such words [as *substance, cause, change,* etc.]. If we did not we could not use them consistently, and it is obvious that on the whole we do consistently apply and withhold such names.   —C. D. BROAD, *Scientific Thought*

31. If number were an idea, then arithmetic would be psychology. But arithmetic is no more psychology than, say, astronomy is. Astronomy is concerned, not with ideas of the planets, but with the planets themselves, and by the same token the objects of arithmetic are not ideas either.
—GOTTLOB FREGE, *The Foundations of Arithmetic*

32. If error were something positive, God would be its cause, and by Him it would continually be procreated (per Prop. 12). [All existing things are conserved by God's power alone.] But this is absurd (per Prop. 13). [God is never a deceiver, but in all things is perfectly true.] Therefore error is nothing positive. Q. E. D.
—BARUCH SPINOZA, *The Principles of Philosophy Demonstrated by the Method of Geometry*

33. . . . If a mental state is to be identical with a physical state, the two must share all properties in common. But there is one property, spatial localizability, that is not so shared; that is, physical states and events are located in space, whereas mental events and states are not. Hence, mental events and states are different from physical ones.
—JAEGWON KIM, "On the Psycho-physical Identity Theory," *American Philosophical Quarterly*, 1966

34. When we regard a man as morally responsible for an act, we regard him as a legitimate object of moral praise or blame in respect of it. But it seems plain that a man cannot be a legitimate object of moral praise or blame for an act unless in willing the act he is in some important sense a "free" agent. Evidently free will in some sense, therefore, is a pre-condition of moral responsibility.
—C. ARTHUR CAMPBELL, *In Defence of Free Will*

★ 35. Syllogism [is] not the great instrument of reason . . . if syllogisms must be taken for the only proper instrument and means of knowledge; it will follow, that before Aristotle there was not one man that did or could know anything by reason; and that since the invention of syllogisms there is not one of ten thousand that doth.
But God has not been so sparing to men to make them barely two-legged creatures, and left it to Aristotle to make them rational.
—JOHN LOCKE, *An Essay Concerning Human Understanding*

36. "It's going to be a very cold winter for housing and for the economy in general," said Michael Sumichrast, chief economist for the National Association of Home Builders.
"You cannot have a general economic recovery without housing doing reasonably well and housing will not be doing reasonably well."
—UPI report, November 18, 1980

37. In spite of the popularity of the finite-world picture, however, it is open to a devastating objection. In being finite the world must have a limiting boundary, such as Aristotle's outermost sphere. That is impossible, because a boundary can only separate one part of space from another. This objection was put forward by the Greeks, reappeared in the scientific skepticism of the early Renaissance and probably occurs to any schoolchild who thinks about it today. If one accepts the objection, one must conclude that the universe is infinite.
—J. J. CALLAHAN, "The Curvature of Space in a Finite Universe," *Scientific American*, August 1976

38. If he prayed for Stalin—prayed that Stalin should mend his ways—then Stalin might become commendable, and if he was commendable, Vadim would logically be obliged to revere him. But all he could ever do was hate the monster, so he must *not* pray for him, otherwise he would face a terrible dilemma.
—WILLIAM F. BUCKLEY, JR., *Who's on First?*

39. Total pacifism might be a good principle if everyone were to follow it. But not everyone does, so it isn't.   —GILBERT HARMAN, *The Nature of Morality*

7.7 *The Dilemma*

The dilemma, a common form of argument in ordinary language, is a legacy from older times when logic and rhetoric were more closely connected than they are today. From the strictly logical point of view, the dilemma is not of special interest or importance. But rhetorically the dilemma is perhaps the most powerful instrument of persuasion ever devised. It is a devastating weapon in controversy.

Today one says somewhat loosely that a person is in a dilemma when the person must choose between two alternatives, both of which are bad or unpleasant. More picturesquely such a person is described as being "impaled on the horns of a dilemma." Traditionally, a dilemma is an argument intended to put one's opponent in just that kind of position. In debate, one uses a dilemma to offer alternative positions to one's adversary, from which a choice must be made, and then to prove that no matter which choice is made, the adversary is committed to an unacceptable conclusion. Thus in a debate on a proposed protective tariff bill, an opponent of the measure may argue as follows:

> If the proposed tariff produces scarcity, it will be injurious; and if it does not produce scarcity, it will be useless. It will either produce scarcity or else it won't. Therefore the proposed tariff will either be injurious or useless.

Such an argument is designed to push the adversaries (in this case the sponsors of the bill) into a corner and there annihilate them. The second premiss, which offers the alternatives, is a disjunction. The first premiss, which asserts that both of the alternatives have certain undesirable consequences, consists of two conditional propositions linked by a conjunction, for example, "and," "but," or "though." The conclusion of a dilemma may be another disjunction, offering alternatives, or it may be a categorical proposition. In the former case the dilemma is said to be "complex," in the latter case "simple." A dilemma need not have an unpleasant conclusion. An example of one with a happy conclusion is provided by the following *simple* dilemma:

> If the blest in heaven have no desires, they will be perfectly content; so they will, if their desires are fully gratified; but either they will have no desires, or have them fully gratified; therefore they will be perfectly content.

The premisses of a dilemma need not be stated in any special order: the disjunctive premiss, which offers the alternatives, may either precede or follow the other. And the consequences of those alternatives may be stated either in a conjunctive proposition or in separate propositions. A dilemmatic argument is often stated enthymematically: its conclusion is generally so obvious that it scarcely needs to be spelled out. This is illustrated in the following passage dealing with the Emancipation Proclamation, which freed the slaves in the Confederacy. It occurred in a letter from Abraham Lincoln to James C. Conkling, dated August 26, 1863:

> But the proclamation, as law, either is valid, or is not valid. If it is not valid, it needs no retraction. If it is valid, it cannot be retracted, any more than the dead can be brought to life.

Because of its importance in debate, a number of ways of evading or refuting the conclusion of a dilemma have been given special names. They are all picturesque, relating to the fact that a dilemma has two (or more) "horns." The three ways of defeating or refuting a dilemma are known as "going (or escaping) between the horns," "taking (or grasping) it by the horns," and "rebutting it by means of a counterdilemma." It should be borne in mind that these are not ways to prove the dilemma invalid but, rather, are ways of avoiding its conclusion without challenging the formal validity of the argument.

One escapes between the horns of a dilemma by rejecting its disjunctive premiss. This method is often the easiest way to evade the conclusion of a dilemma, for unless one half of the disjunction is the explicit contradictory of the other, the disjunction may very well be false. One justification sometimes offered for giving grades to students is that recognizing good work will stimulate the student to study harder. Students may criticize this theory, using the following dilemma.

> If students are fond of learning, they need no stimulus, and if they dislike learning, no stimulus will be of any avail. But any student is either fond of learning or dislikes it. Therefore a stimulus is either needless or of no avail.

This argument is formally valid, but we can evade its conclusion by *going between the horns*. The disjunctive premiss is false, for students have all kinds of attitudes toward learning: some may be fond of it, many dislike it, but many are indifferent. And for them a stimulus may be both needed and of some avail. It should be remembered that going between the horns does not prove the conclusion to be false but shows merely that the argument does not provide adequate grounds for accepting that conclusion.

Where the disjunctive premiss is unassailable, as when the alternatives exhaust the possibilities, it is impossible to escape between the horns. Another method of evading the conclusion must be sought. One such method is to *grasp the dilemma by the horns*, which involves rejecting the premiss that is a conjunction. To deny a conjunction, we need only deny one of its parts. When we grasp the dilemma by the horns, we attempt to show that at least one of the conditionals is false. Consider again the dilemma attacking the protective tariff. The proponent of the tariff bill might grasp the dilemma by the horns and argue that, even if the proposed tariff were to produce scarcity, it would not be injurious. After all, a scarcity would stimulate domestic production, thus giving the country increased employment and more highly developed industry. Were any scarcity produced, the proponent might argue, it would be only temporary, and, far from being injurious, it would be highly beneficial. Of course there may be more to be said, but the original dilemma has been grasped firmly by the horns.

Rebutting a dilemma by means of a counterdilemma is the most entertaining and ingenious method of all; but it is seldom cogent, for reasons that will appear presently. To rebut a given dilemma, one constructs another dilemma whose conclusion is opposed to the conclusion of the original. *Any* counterdilemma may be used in rebuttal, but ideally it should be built up out of the same ingredients (categorical propositions) that the original dilemma contained.

A classical example of this elegant kind of rebuttal concerns the following argument of an Athenian mother attempting to persuade her son not to enter politics:

If you say what is just, men will hate you; and if you say what is unjust, the gods will hate you; but you must either say the one or the other; therefore you will be hated.

Her son rebutted the dilemma with the following one:

If I say what is just, the gods will love me; and if I say what is unjust, men will love me. I must say either the one or the other. Therefore I shall be loved!

In public discussion, where the dilemma is one of the strongest of the weapons of controversy, a rebuttal like this, which derives an opposite conclusion from almost the same premises, marks the absolute zenith of rhetorical skill. But if we examine the dilemma and rebutting counterdilemma more closely, we see that their conclusions are not as opposed as they might at first appear.

The conclusion of the first dilemma is that the son will be hated (by men or by the gods), whereas that of the rebutting dilemma is that the son will be loved (by gods or by men). But these two conclusions are perfectly compatible. The rebutting counterdilemma serves merely to establish a conclusion different from that of the original. Both conclusions may very well be true together, so no refutation has been accomplished. But in the heat of controversy analysis is unwelcome; and if such a rebuttal occurred in a public debate, the average audience would overwhelmingly agree that the rebuttal completely demolished the original argument.

That this sort of rebuttal does not refute, but only directs attention to a different aspect of the same situation, is perhaps more clearly shown in the case of the following little dilemma, advanced by an "optimist":

If I work, I earn money; and if I am idle, I enjoy myself. Either I work or I am idle. Therefore either I earn money or I enjoy myself.

A "pessimist" might offer the following counterdilemma:

> If I work, I don't enjoy myself; and if I am idle, I don't earn money. Either I work or I am idle. Therefore either I don't earn money or I don't enjoy myself.

These conclusions represent merely different ways of viewing the same facts; they do not constitute a disagreement over what the facts are.

No discussion of dilemmas would be complete unless it mentioned the celebrated lawsuit between Protagoras and Euathlus. Protagoras was a teacher who lived in Greece during the fifth century B.C. He taught many subjects but specialized in the art of pleading before juries. Euathlus wanted to become a lawyer, but, not being able to pay the required tuition, he made an arrangement according to which Protagoras would teach him but not receive payment until Euathlus won his first case. When Euathlus finished his course of study, he delayed going into practice. Tired of waiting for his money, Protagoras brought suit against his former pupil for the tuition money that was owed. Unmindful of the adage that the lawyer who tries his own case has a fool for a client, Euathlus decided to plead his own case in court. When the trial began, Protagoras presented his side of the case in a crushing dilemma:

> If Euathlus loses this case, then he must pay me (by the judgment of the court); if he wins this case, then he must pay me (by the terms of the contract). He must either lose or win this case. Therefore Euathlus must pay me.

The situation looked bad for Euathlus, but he had learned well the art of rhetoric. He offered the court the following counterdilemma in rebuttal:

> If I win this case, I shall not have to pay Protagoras (by the judgment of the court); if I lose this case, I shall not have to pay Protagoras (by the terms of the contract, for then I shall not yet have won my first case). I must either win or lose this case. Therefore I do not have to pay Protagoras!

Had you been the judge, how would you have decided?

It is to be noted that the conclusion of Euathlus' rebutting dilemma is *not* compatible with the conclusion of Protagoras' original dilemma. One conclusion is the explicit denial of the other. But it is a rare case in which a rebuttal stands in this relation to the dilemma against which it is directed. When it does so, the premises involved are themselves inconsistent, and it is this implicit contradiction that the two dilemmas serve to make explicit.

EXERCISES

Discuss the various arguments that might be offered to refute each of the following.

★ 1. If we interfere with the publication of false and harmful doctrines, we shall be guilty of suppressing the liberties of others, whereas if we do not interfere with the publication of such doctrines, we run the risk of losing our own liberties. We must either interfere or not interfere with the publication of false and harmful doctrines. Hence we must either be guilty of suppressing the liberties of others or else run the risk of losing our own liberties.

2. Circuit Courts are useful, or they are not useful. If useful, no State should be denied them; if not useful, no State should have them. Let them be provided for all, or abolished as to all.
—ABRAHAM LINCOLN, annual message to Congress, December 3, 1861

3. If you tell me what I already understand, you do not enlarge my understanding, whereas if you tell me something that I do not understand, then your remarks are unintelligible to me. Whatever you tell me must be either something I already understand or something that I do not understand. Hence whatever you say either does not enlarge my understanding or else is unintelligible to me.

4. If what you say does not enlarge my understanding, then what you say is without value to me; and if what you say is unintelligible to me, then it is without value to me. Whatever you say either does not enlarge my understanding or else is unintelligible to me. Therefore nothing you say is of any value to me.

★ 5. If the conclusion of a deductive argument goes beyond the premises, then the argument is invalid; while if the conclusion of a deductive argument does not go beyond the premises, then the argument brings nothing new to light. The conclusion of a deductive argument must either go beyond the premises or not go beyond them. Therefore deductive arguments are either invalid or else they bring nothing new to light.

6. If a deductive argument is invalid, it is without value, whereas a deductive argument that brings nothing new to light is also without value. Deductive arguments are either invalid or else they bring nothing new to light. Therefore deductive arguments are without value.

7. If the general was loyal, he would have obeyed his orders; and if he was intelligent, he would have understood them. The general either disobeyed his orders or else he did not understand them. Therefore the general must have been either disloyal or unintelligent.

8. If he was disloyal, then his dismissal was justified; and if he was unintelligent, then his dismissal was justified. He was either disloyal or unintelligent. Therefore his dismissal was justified.

9. If the several nations keep the peace, the United Nations is unnecessary; while if the several nations go to war, the United Nations will have been unsuccessful in its purpose of preventing war. Now either the several nations keep the peace or they go to war. Hence the United Nations is unnecessary or unsuccessful.

★ 10. If people are good, laws are not needed to prevent wrongdoing, whereas if people are bad, laws will not succeed in preventing wrongdoing. People are either good or bad. Therefore either laws are not needed to prevent wrongdoing or laws will not succeed in preventing wrongdoing.

11. Archbishop Morton, Chancellor under Henry VII, was famous for his method of extracting "contributions" to the king's purse. A person who lived extravagantly was forced to make a large contribution, because it was obvious that he could afford it. Someone who lived modestly was forced to make a large contribution because it was clear that he must have saved a lot of money on living expenses. Whichever way he turned he was said to be "caught on Morton's fork."

—DOROTHY HAYDEN, *Winning Declarer Play*

12. If any member of our party is guilty in that matter, you know it or you do not know it. If you do know it, you are inexcusable for not designating the man and proving the fact. If you do not know it, you are inexcusable for asserting it, and especially for persisting in the assertion after you have tried and failed to make the proof.

—ABRAHAM LINCOLN, address at Cooper Institute,
New York City, February 27, 1860

13. There is a dilemma to which every opposition to successful iniquity must, in the nature of things, be liable. If you lie still, you are considered as an accomplice in the measures in which you silently acquiesce. If you resist, you are accused of provoking irritable power to new excesses. The conduct of a losing party never appears right.

—EDMUND BURKE, *A Letter to a Member of the National Assembly*

14. And we seem unable to clear ourselves from the old dilemma. If you predicate what is different, you ascribe to the subject what it is *not*; and if you predicate what is *not* different, you say nothing at all.

—F. H. BRADLEY, *Appearance and Reality*

★ 15. All political action aims at either preservation or change. When desiring to preserve, we wish to prevent a change to the worse; when desiring to change, we wish to bring about something better. All political action is then guided by some thought of better and worse.   —LEO STRAUSS, *What Is Political Philosophy?*

16. If a thing moves, it moves either in the place where it is or in that where it is not; but it moves neither in the place where it is (for it remains therein) nor in that where it is not (for it does not exist therein); therefore nothing moves.

—SEXTUS EMPIRICUS, *Against the Physicists*

17. And what a life should I lead, at my age, wandering from city to city, ever changing my place of exile, and always being driven out! For I am quite sure that wherever I go, there, as here, the young men will flock to me; and if I drive them away, their elders will drive me out at their request; and if I let them come, their fathers and friends will drive me out for their sakes.   —PLATO, *Apology*

18. If Socrates died, he died either when he was living or when he was dead. But he did not die while living; for assuredly he was living, and as living he had not died. Nor when he died; for then he would be twice dead. Therefore Socrates did not die.   —SEXTUS EMPIRICUS, *Against the Physicists*

19. Inevitably, the use of the placebo involved built-in contradictions. A good patient—doctor relationship is essential to the process, but what happens to that

relationship when one of the partners conceals important information from the other? If the doctor tells the truth, he destroys the base on which the placebo rests. If he doesn't tell the truth, he jeopardizes a relationship built on trust.

—NORMAN COUSINS, *Anatomy of an Illness*

★ 20. The "paradox of analysis," which postulates the dilemma that an analysis is either a mere synonym and hence trivial, or more than a synonym and hence false, has its equivalent in Linguistic Philosophy: a neologism can either be accounted for in existing terms, in which case it is redundant, or it cannot, in which case it has not "been given sense."   —ERNEST GELLNER, *Words and Things*

21. In discussing Allan Bloom's *The Closing of the American Mind,* an enormously successful, best-selling book whose message is that "Our culture is going downhill. Thought has been vanquished." along with several other widely selling books with much the same message, all of which received much critical acclaim, the reviewer wrote: ". . . if the books really are good, then the public, far from being boorish and uncultivated, knows how to appreciate quality—and the books' central argument is false. On the other hand, if the argument is true, and the public can appreciate only books aimed at its own low level and the mass media can glorify nothing but marketability, then these books do not embody the high culture they extol, and are therefore not good."

—TZVETAN TODOROV, "The Philosopher and the Everyday,"
The New Republic, September 14 and 21, 1987, p. 34

22. The dilemma of permissible novelty is interesting . . . we may put it thus: for an interpretation to be valuable, it must do more than merely duplicate the ideas of the thinker being interpreted. Yet if it is to be just, it cannot deviate significantly from the original formulation.

—GEORGE KIMBALL PLOCHMAN, Foreword to
Frege's Logical Theory by Robert Sternfeld

23. The decision of the Supreme Court in *U.S.* v. *Nixon* (1974) handed down the first day of the Judiciary committee's final debate was critical. If the President defied the order, he would be impeached. If he obeyed the order, it was increasingly apparent, he would be impeached on the evidence.

—VICTORIA SCHUCK, "Watergate," *The Key Reporter,*
Vol. 41, No. 2, Winter 1975–1976

24. Kamisar . . . seeks to impale the advocates of euthanasia on an old dilemma. Either the victim is not yet suffering pain, in which case his consent is merely an uninformed and anticipatory one—and he cannot bind himself by contract to be killed in the future—or he is crazed by pain and stupefied by drugs, in which case he is not of sound mind.

—GLANVILLE WILLIAMS, " 'Mercykilling' Legislation—A Rejoinder,"
Minnesota Law Review, Vol. 43, No. 1, 1958

25. If we are to have peace, we must not encourage the competitive spirit, whereas if we are to make progress, we must encourage the competitive spirit. We must either encourage or not encourage the competitive spirit. Therefore we shall either have no peace or make no progress.

26. The argument under the present head may be put into a very concise form, which appears altogether conclusive. Either the mode in which the federal government is to be constructed will render it sufficiently dependent on the people, or it will not. On the first supposition, it will be restrained by that dependence

from forming schemes obnoxious to their constituents. On the other supposition, it will not possess the confidence of the people, and its schemes of usurpation will be easily defeated by the State governments, who will be supported by the people.   —JAMES MADISON, *The Federalist Papers*, Number 46

27. Does the gentleman from Coles know that there is a statute standing in full force, making it highly penal, for an individual to loan money at a higher rate of interest than twelve per cent? If he does not he is too ignorant to be placed at the head of the committee which his resolution proposes; and if he does, his neglect to mention it shows him to be too uncandid to merit the respect or confidence of any one.

   —ABRAHAM LINCOLN, speech in the Illinois legislature, January 11, 1837

28. . . . a man cannot enquire either about that which he knows, or about that which he does not know; for if he knows, he has no need to enquire; and if not, he cannot; for he does not know the very subject about which he is to enquire.

   —PLATO, *Meno*

29. Dissidents confined to asylums are caught up in an insoluble dilemma. "If you recant, they say, it proves that he was crazy. If you refuse to recant, and protest, they say that it proves he is still crazy."

   —LEWIS H. GANN, "Psychiatry: Helpful Servant or Cruel Master?"
   The Intercollegiate Review, Spring–Summer, 1982, p. 109

30. We tell clients to try to go through the entire first interview without even mentioning money. If you ask for a salary that is too high, the employer concludes that he can't afford you. If you ask for one that is too low, you're essentially saying, "I'm not competent enough to handle the job that you're offering."

   —JAMES CHALLENGER, "What to Do—and Not to Do—When Job Hunting,"
   U.S. News & World Report, August 6, 1984, pp. 63–66

31. "Pascal's wager," justifiably famous in the history of religion and also of betting, had nothing to do with making sacrifices for a good cause. Pascal was arguing that agnostics—people unsure of God's existence—are best off betting that He does exist. If He does but you end up living as an unbeliever, then you could be condemned to spend eternity in the flames of Hell. If, on the other hand, He doesn't exist but you live as a believer, you suffer no corresponding penalty for being in error. Obviously, then, bettors on God start out with a big edge.   —DANIEL SELIGMAN, "Keeping Up," *Fortune*, January 7, 1985, p. 104

8

Symbolic Logic

There is no royal road to logic, and really valuable ideas can only be had at the price of close attention.
—CHARLES SANDERS PEIRCE

Because language is misleading, as well as because it is diffuse and inexact when applied to logic (for which it was never intended), logical symbolism is absolutely necessary to any exact or thorough treatment of our subject.
—BERTRAND RUSSELL

In order to avoid the inadequacies of the natural languages for purposes of logical analysis, it is necessary first to translate into a more exact notation.
—ALONZO CHURCH

8.1 *The Value of Special Symbols*

Arguments presented in English or any other natural language are often difficult to appraise because of the vague and equivocal nature of the words used, the ambiguity of their construction, the misleading idioms they may contain, their potentially confusing metaphorical style, and the distraction due to whatever emotive significance they may express. These topics were discussed at length in Part One. Even after these difficulties are resolved, there still remains the problem of determining the validity or invalidity of the argument. To avoid those peripheral difficulties, it is convenient to set up an *artificial symbolic language*, free from such defects, in which statements and arguments can be formulated.

Some of the advantages of a technical vocabulary for a science have already been mentioned in Chapter 4. The use of a special logical notation is not peculiar to modern logic. Aristotle, the ancient founder of the subject, used variables to facilitate his own work. Although the difference in this respect between modern and classical logic is not one of kind but of degree, the difference in degree is tremendous. The greater extent to which modern logic has developed its own special technical language has made it immeasurably more powerful a tool for analysis and deduction. The special symbols of modern logic help us to exhibit with greater clarity the logical structures of propositions and arguments whose forms may tend to be obscured by the unwieldiness of ordinary language.

A further value of the logician's special symbols is the aid they give in the actual use and manipulation of statements and arguments. The situation here is comparable to that which led to the replacement of Roman numerals by the Arabic notation. We all know that Arabic numerals are clearer and more easily comprehended than the older Roman numerals which they displaced. But the real superiority of Arabic numerals is revealed only in computation. Any student can easily multiply 113 by 9. But to multiply CXIII by IX is a more difficult task, and the difficulty increases as larger and larger numbers are considered.[1] Similarly, the drawing of inferences and the appraisal of arguments is greatly facilitated by the adoption of a special logical notation. To quote Alfred North Whitehead, one of the great contributors to the advance of symbolic logic,

> . . . by the aid of symbolism, we can make transitions in reasoning almost mechanically by the eye, which otherwise would call into play the higher faculties of the brain.[2]

From this point of view, paradoxically enough, logic is not concerned with developing our powers of thought but with developing techniques that permit us to accomplish some tasks without having to think so much.

8.2 *The Symbols for Conjunction, Negation, and Disjunction*

In this chapter we shall be concerned with relatively simple arguments such as

> The blind prisoner has a red hat or the blind prisoner has a white hat.
> The blind prisoner does not have a red hat.
> Therefore the blind prisoner has a white hat.

and

> If Mr. Robinson is the brakeman's next-door neighbor, then Mr. Robinson lives halfway between Detroit and Chicago.
> Mr. Robinson does not live halfway between Detroit and Chicago.
> Therefore Mr. Robinson is not the brakeman's next-door neighbor.

---

[1]There is much evidence that even the ancient Romans did not use their numerals in computation. Instead they utilized "counting boards," a Western version of the Oriental abacus. See Karl Menninger, *Number Words and Number Symbols* (Cambridge, Mass.: MIT Press, 1969).

[2]A. N. Whitehead, *An Introduction to Mathematics* (New York: Oxford University Press, 1911).

Every argument of this general type contains at least one compound statement. In studying such arguments we divide all statements into two general
categories, simple and compound. A *simple* statement is one that does not
contain any other statement as a component. For example, "Charlie's neat"
is a simple statement. A *compound* statement is one that does contain another
statement as a component. For example, "Charlie's neat and Charlie's sweet"
is a compound statement, for it contains two simple statements as components. Of course the components of a compound statement may themselves
be compound.

The notion of a component of a statement is fairly straightforward, although it is not exactly the same as "a part that is itself a statement." For
example, the last four words of the statement "The man who shot Lincoln
was an actor" could indeed be regarded as a statement in their own right.
But this statement is not a *component* of the larger statement of which those
four words are a part. For a part of a statement to be a component of that
statement two conditions must be satisfied: first, the part must be a statement
in its own right, and, second, if the part is replaced in the larger statement
by any other statement, the result of that replacement will be meaningful.
Although the first condition is satisfied in the example given, the second is
not. For if the part "Lincoln was an actor" is replaced by "there are lions in
Africa," the result is the nonsensical expression "The man who shot there
are lions in Africa."[3]

1. Conjunction

There are several types of compound statements, each requiring its own
logical notation. The first type of compound statement to be considered is
the *conjunction*. We can form the conjunction of two statements by placing
the word "and" between them: the two statements so combined are called
conjuncts. Thus the compound statement "Charlie's neat and Charlie's sweet"
is a conjunction, whose first conjunct is "Charlie's neat" and whose second
conjunct is "Charlie's sweet."

The word "and" is a short and convenient word, but it has other uses
besides that of connecting statements. For example, the statement "Lincoln
and Grant were contemporaries" is *not* a conjunction but a simple statement
expressing a relationship. To have a unique symbol whose only function is
to connect statements conjunctively, we introduce the dot "•" as our symbol
for conjunction. Thus the previous conjunction can be written as "Charlie's
neat • Charlie's sweet." More generally, where p and q are any two statements whatever, their conjunction is written $p \cdot q$.

---

[3]For this more complicated but more satisfactory account of compound and component statements we thank Professor C. Mason Myers of Northern Illinois University, Professor Alex Blum
of Bar-Ilan University (who sent independent personal communications), and Professor James
A. Martin of the University of Wyoming, for his "How Not to Define Truth-Functionality,"
Logique et Analyse, Vol. 14, No. 52, 1970, pp. 476–482.

We know that every statement is either true or false. Therefore, we say, every statement has a *truth value*—where the truth value of a true statement is *true* and the truth value of a false statement is *false*. Using this concept of "truth value" we can divide compound statements into two distinct categories, according to whether or not the truth value of the compound statement is determined wholly by the truth values of its components, or determined by anything other than the truth values of its components.

We apply this distinction to conjunctions. The truth value of the conjunction of two statements is determined wholly and entirely by the truth values of its two conjuncts. If both its conjuncts are true, the conjunction is true; otherwise it is false. For this reason a conjunction is said to be a *truth-functional* compound statement, and its conjuncts are said to be *truth-functional* components of it.

Not every compound statement is truth-functional, however. For example, the truth value of the compound statement "Othello believes that Desdemona loves Cassio" is not in any way determined by the truth value of its component simple statement "Desdemona loves Cassio," for it could be true that Othello believes that Desdemona loves Cassio regardless of whether she does so or not. So the component "Desdemona loves Cassio" is not a truth-functional component of the statement "Othello believes that Desdemona loves Cassio," and the latter is not a truth-functional compound statement.

For our present purposes we define a component of a compound statement to be a *truth-functional component* of it provided that, if the component is replaced in the compound by any different statements having the same truth value as each other, the different compound statements produced by those replacements will also have the same truth values as each other. And now a compound statement we define to be a *truth-functional compound statement* if all of its components are truth-functional components of it.[4]

Here we shall be concerned only with those compound statements that are truth-functionally compound. In the remainder of this book, therefore, we shall use the term "simple statement" to refer to any statement that is not truth-functionally compound.

A conjunction is a truth-functional compound statement, so our dot symbol is a *truth-functional connective*. Given any two statements, p and q, there are only four possible sets of truth values they can have. These four possible cases, and the truth value of the conjunction in each, can be displayed as follows:

> where p is true and q is true, $p \cdot q$ is true;
> where p is true and q is false, $p \cdot q$ is false;
> where p is false and q is true, $p \cdot q$ is false;
> where p is false and q is false, $p \cdot q$ is false.

[4]Somewhat more complicated definitions have been proposed by Professor David H. Sanford in his "What Is a Truth Functional Component?" *Logique et Analyse*, Vol. 14, No. 52, 1970, pp. 483–486.

If we represent the truth values "true" and "false" by the capital letters **T** and **F**, the determination of the truth value of a conjunction by the truth values of its conjuncts can be represented more briefly and more clearly by means of a truth table as

p	q	$p \cdot q$
T	T	T
T	F	F
F	T	F
F	F	F

This truth table can be taken as defining the dot symbol, since it explains what truth values are assumed by $p \cdot q$ in every possible case.

We shall find it convenient to abbreviate simple statements by capital letters, generally using for this purpose a letter that will help us remember which statement it abbreviates. Thus we should abbreviate "Charlie's neat and Charlie's sweet" as $N \cdot S$. Some conjunctions both of whose conjuncts have the same subject term—for example, "Byron was a great poet and Byron was a great adventurer"—are more briefly and perhaps more naturally stated in English by placing the "and" between the predicate terms and not repeating the subject term, as in "Byron was a great poet and a great adventurer." For our purposes we regard the latter as formulating the same statement as the former, and symbolize either one indifferently as $P \cdot A$. If both conjuncts of a conjunction have the same predicate term, as in "Lewis was a famous explorer and Clark was a famous explorer," again the conjunction would usually be stated in English by placing the "and" between the subject terms and not repeating the predicate, as in "Lewis and Clark were famous explorers." Either formulation is symbolized as $L \cdot C$.

As shown by the truth table defining the dot symbol, a conjunction is true if and only if both of its conjuncts are true. But the word "and" has another use in which it signifies not *mere* (truth-functional) conjunction but has the sense of "and subsequently," meaning temporal succession. Thus the statement "Jones entered the country at New York and went straight to Chicago" is significant and might be true, whereas "Jones went straight to Chicago and entered the country at New York" is hardly intelligible. And there is quite a difference between "He took off his shoes and got into bed" and "He got into bed and took off his shoes." Consideration of such examples emphasizes the desirability of having a special symbol with an exclusively truth-functional conjunctive use.

It should be remarked that the English words "but," "yet," "also," "still," "although," "however," "moreover," "nevertheless," and so on, and even the comma and the semicolon, can also be used to conjoin two statements into a single compound statement, and in their conjunctive sense they can all be represented by the dot symbol.

2. Negation

The *negation* (or contradictory or denial) of a statement in English is often formed by inserting a "not" into the original statement. Alternatively, one can express the negation of a statement in English by prefixing to it the phrase "it is false that" or "it is not the case that." It is customary to use the symbol "~" (called a *curl* or, less frequently, a *tilde*) to form the negation of a statement. Thus where M symbolizes the statement "All humans are mortal," the various statements "Not all humans are mortal," "Some humans are not mortal," "It is false that all humans are mortal," "It is not the case that all humans are mortal," are all indifferently symbolized as ~M. More generally, where p is any statement whatever, its negation is written ~p. It is obvious that the curl is a truth-functional operator. The negation of any true statement is false, and the negation of any false statement is true. This fact can be presented very simply and clearly by means of a truth table:

p	~p
T	F
F	T

This truth table may be regarded as the definition of the negation symbol "~."

3. Disjunction

The disjunction (or *alternation*) of two statements is formed in English by inserting the word "or" between them. The two component statements so combined are called *disjuncts* (or *alternatives*). The English word "or" is ambiguous, having two related but distinguishable meanings. One of them is exemplified in the statement "Premiums will be waived in the event of sickness or unemployment," for the intention here is obviously that premiums are waived not only for sick persons and for unemployed persons, but also for persons who are *both* sick *and* unemployed. This sense of the word "or" is called *weak* or *inclusive*. An inclusive disjunction is true in case one or the other or both disjuncts are true; only if both disjuncts are false is their inclusive disjunction false. The inclusive "or" has the sense of "either, possibly both." Where precision is at a premium, as in contracts and other legal documents, this sense is made explicit by the use of the phrase "and/or."

The word "or" is also used in a *strong* or *exclusive* sense, in which the meaning is not "at least one" but "at least one and at most one." Where a restaurant lists "salad or dessert" on its table d'hôte menu, it is clearly meant that, for the stated price of the meal, the diner may have one or the other *but not both*. Where precision is at a premium and the exclusive sense of "or" is intended, the phrase "but not both" is usually added.

We interpret the inclusive disjunction of two statements as an assertion that at least one of the statements is true, and their exclusive disjunction as an assertion that at least one of the statements is true but not both are true. We observe here that the two kinds of disjunction have a part of their meanings in common. This partial common meaning, that at least one of the disjuncts is true, is the *whole* meaning of the inclusive "or" and a *part* of the meaning of the exclusive "or."

Although disjunctions are stated ambiguously in English, they are unambiguous in Latin. The Latin language has two different words corresponding to the two different senses of the English word "or." The Latin word *vel* signifies weak or inclusive disjunction, and the Latin word *aut* corresponds to the word "or" in its strong or exclusive sense. It is customary to use the initial letter of the word *vel* to stand for "or" in its weak, inclusive sense. Where p and q are any two statements whatever, their weak or inclusive disjunction is written $p \vee q$. Our symbol for inclusive disjunction (called a *wedge*, or, less frequently, a *vee*) is also a truth-functional connective. A weak disjunction is false only in case both of its disjuncts are false. We may regard the wedge as being defined by the following truth table:

p	q	$p \vee q$
T	T	T
T	F	T
F	T	T
F	F	F

The first specimen argument presented in this section was a Disjunctive Syllogism.[5]

The blind prisoner has a red hat or the blind prisoner has a white hat.
The blind prisoner does not have a red hat.
Therefore the blind prisoner has a white hat.

Its form is characterized by saying that its first premiss is a disjunction; its second premiss is the negation of the first disjunct of the first premiss; and its conclusion is the same as the second disjunct of the first premiss. It is evident that the Disjunctive Syllogism, so defined, is valid on either interpretation of the word "or," that is, regardless of whether an inclusive or exclusive disjunction is intended.[6] Since the typical valid argument that has a disjunction for a premiss is, like the Disjunctive Syllogism, valid on either interpretation of the word "or," a simplification may be effected by translating the English word "or" into our logical symbol "v"—*regardless of which meaning of the English word "or" is intended.* In general, only a close examination of the context or an explicit questioning of the speaker or writer can reveal which sense of "or" is intended. This problem, at best difficult and

---

[5]A *syllogism* is a deductive argument consisting of two premises and a conclusion.
[6]The student should note that the term "Disjunctive Syllogism" is being used in a narrower sense here than it was in the preceding chapter.

often impossible to resolve, can be avoided if we agree to treat *any* occurrence of the word "or" as inclusive. On the other hand, if it is explicitly stated that the disjunction is intended to be exclusive, by means of the added phrase "but not both," for example, we have the symbolic machinery to formulate that additional sense, as will be shown directly.

Where both disjuncts have either the same subject term or the same predicate term, it is often natural to compress the formulation of their disjunction in English by so placing the "or" that there is no need to repeat the common part of the two disjuncts. Thus "Either Smith is the owner or Smith is the manager" might equally well be stated as "Smith is either the owner or the manager," and either one is properly symbolized as $O \lor M$. And "Either Red is guilty or Butch is guilty" would often be stated as "Either Red or Butch is guilty," either one being symbolized as $R \lor B$. It should be remarked that the word "unless" can also be used to form the disjunction of two statements. Thus "The picnic will be held unless it rains" and "Unless it rains the picnic will be held" can equally well be stated as "Either the picnic will be held or it rains," and symbolized as $R \lor P$.

4. Punctuation

In English, punctuation is absolutely required if complicated statements are to be clear. A great many different punctuation marks are used, without which many sentences would be highly ambiguous. For example, quite different meanings attach to "The teacher says John is a fool," when it is given different punctuations. Other sentences require punctuation for their very intelligibility, as, for example, "Jill where Jack had had had had had had had had had had the teacher's approval." Punctuation is equally necessary in mathematics. In the absence of a special convention, no number is uniquely denoted by $2 \times 3 + 5$, although when it is made clear how its constituents are to be grouped, it denotes either 11 or 16: the first when punctuated $(2 \times 3) + 5$, the second when punctuated $2 \times (3 + 5)$. Punctuation is needed in both mathematics and English for ambiguity to be avoided and meaning made clear.

Punctuation is also required in the language of symbolic logic, for compound statements may themselves be compounded together into more complicated ones. Thus $p \cdot q \lor r$ is ambiguous: it might mean the conjunction of p with the disjunction of q with r, or it might mean the disjunction whose first disjunct is the conjunction of p and q and whose second disjunct is r. We distinguish between these two different senses by punctuating the given formula as $p \cdot (q \lor r)$ or else as $(p \cdot q) \lor r$. In symbolic logic parentheses, brackets, and braces are used as punctuation marks. That the different ways of punctuating the original formula do make a difference can be seen by considering the case in which p is false and q and r are both true. In this case the second punctuated formula is true (since its second disjunct is true), whereas the first one is false (since its first conjunct is false). Here the difference in punctuation makes all the difference between truth and falsehood, for different punctuations can assign different truth values to the ambiguous $p \cdot q \lor r$.

The word "either" has a variety of different meanings and uses in English. It has conjunctive force in the sentence "There is danger on either side." More often it is used to introduce the first disjunct in a disjunction, as in "Either the blind prisoner has a red hat or the blind prisoner has a white hat." There it contributes to the rhetorical balance of the sentence, but it does not affect its meaning. Perhaps the most important use of the word "either" is to punctuate a compound statement. Thus the sentence

> The organization will meet on Thursday and Alice will be elected or the election will be postponed.

can have its ambiguity resolved in one direction by placing the word "either" at its beginning, or in the other direction by inserting the word "either" before the name "Alice." Such punctuation is effected in our symbolic language by parentheses. The ambiguous formula $p \cdot q \lor r$ discussed in the preceding paragraph corresponds to the ambiguous sentence just examined. The two different punctuations of the formula correspond to the two different punctuations of the sentence effected by the two different insertions of the word "either."

The negation of a disjunction is often formed by use of the phrase "neither–nor." Thus the statement "Either Fillmore or Harding was the greatest American president" can be contradicted by the statement "Neither Fillmore nor Harding was the greatest American president." The disjunction would be symbolized as $F \lor H$, and its negation as either $\sim(F \lor H)$ or as $(\sim F) \cdot (\sim H)$. (The logical equivalence of these two symbolic formulas will be discussed in Section 8.5.) It should be clear that to deny a disjunction stating that one or another statement is true requires that both be stated to be false.

The word "both" in English plays several roles. One is a matter of emphasis. To say that "Both Lewis and Clark were famous explorers" is merely to state more emphatically that "Lewis and Clark were famous explorers." But the word "both" also has a punctuational use, comparable to that of "either." We remarked in the preceding paragraph that "Both . . . and . . . are not . . ." can be used to make the same statement as "Neither . . . nor . . . is. . . ." The *order* of the words "both" and "not" is very important. There is considerable difference between

> Jane and Dick will not both be elected.

and

> Jane and Dick will both not be elected.

The first denies the conjunction $J \cdot D$ and is symbolized as $\sim(J \cdot D)$. The second says that each one will not be elected, and is symbolized as $(\sim J) \cdot (\sim D)$.

In the interest of brevity, that is, to decrease the number of parentheses required, it is convenient to establish the convention that in any formula the negation symbol will be understood to apply to the smallest statement that the punctuation permits. Without this convention the formula $\sim p$ v q is ambiguous, meaning either $(\sim p)$ v q or $\sim(p$ v $q)$. But by our convention we take it to mean the first of these alternatives, for the curl *can* (and therefore by our convention *does*) apply to the first component, p, rather than to the larger formula p v q.

Given a set of punctuation marks for our symbolic language, it is possible to write not merely conjunctions, negations, and weak disjunctions in it, but exclusive disjunctions as well. The exclusive disjunction of p and q asserts that at least one of them is true but not both are true, which is written quite simply as $(p$ v $q)$ • $\sim(p$ • $q)$.

The word "unless" is also used in English to form the disjunction of two statements. Thus "The picnic will be held unless it rains" and "Unless it rains the picnic will be held" can equally well be stated as "Either the picnic will be held or it rains," and symbolized as P v R.

Any compound statement constructed from simple statements using only the truth-functional connectives dot, curl, and wedge, has its truth value completely determined by the truth or falsehood of its component simple statements. If we know the truth values of simple statements, the truth value of any truth-functional compound of them is easily calculated. In working with such compound statements, we always begin with their inmost components and work outward. For example, if A and B are true and X and Y are false statements, we calculate the truth value of the compound statement $\sim[\sim(A \cdot X) \cdot (Y$ v $\sim B)]$ as follows. Since X is false, the conjunction $A \cdot X$ is false, and so its negation $\sim(A \cdot X)$ is true. B is true; so its negation $\sim B$ is false, and since Y is false also, the disjunction of Y with $\sim B$, Y v $\sim B$, is false. The bracketed formula $[\sim(A \cdot X) \cdot (Y$ v $\sim B)]$ is the conjunction of a true with a false statement and is therefore false. Hence its negation, which is the entire statement, is true. Such a stepwise procedure always enables us to determine the truth value of a compound statement from the truth values of its components.

EXERCISES

I. Which of the following statements are true?

★ 1. Rome is the capital of Italy v Rome is the capital of Spain.

2. $\sim$(London is the capital of England • Stockholm is the capital of Norway).

3. $\sim$London is the capital of England • $\sim$Stockholm is the capital of Norway.

4. $\sim$(Rome is the capital of Spain v Paris is the capital of France).

★ 5. $\sim$Rome is the capital of Spain v $\sim$Paris is the capital of France.

6. London is the capital of England v $\sim$London is the capital of England.

7. Stockholm is the capital of Norway • $\sim$Stockholm is the capital of Norway.

8. (Paris is the capital of France • Rome is the capital of Spain) v (Paris is the capital of France • ~Rome is the capital of Spain).

9. (London is the capital of England v Stockholm is the capital of Norway) • (~Rome is the capital of Italy • ~Stockholm is the capital of Norway).

★ 10. Rome is the capital of Spain v ~(Paris is the capital of France • Rome is the capital of Spain).

11. Rome is the capital of Italy • ~(Paris is the capital of France v Rome is the capital of Spain).

12. ~(~Paris is the capital of France • ~Stockholm is the capital of Norway).

13. ~[~(~Rome is the capital of Spain v ~Paris is the capital of France) v ~(~Paris is the capital of France v Stockholm is the capital of Norway)].

14. ~[~(~London is the capital of England • Rome is the capital of Spain) • ~(Rome is the capital of Spain • ~Rome is the capital of Spain)].

★ 15. ~[~(Stockholm is the capital of Norway v Paris is the capital of France) v ~(~London is the capital of England • ~Rome is the capital of Spain)].

16. Rome is the capital of Spain v (~London is the capital of England v London is the capital of England).

17. Paris is the capital of France • ~(Paris is the capital of France • Rome is the capital of Spain).

18. London is the capital of England • ~(Rome is the capital of Italy • Rome is the capital of Italy).

19. (Stockholm is the capital of Norway v ~Paris is the capital of France) v ~(~Stockholm is the capital of Norway • ~London is the capital of England).

★ 20. (Paris is the capital of France v ~Rome is the capital of Spain) v ~(~Paris is the capital of France • ~Rome is the capital of Spain).

21. ~[~(Rome is the capital of Spain • Stockholm is the capital of Norway) v ~(~Paris is the capital of France v ~Rome is the capital of Spain)].

22. ~[~(London is the capital of England • Paris is the capital of France) v ~(~Stockholm is the capital of Norway v ~Paris is the capital of France)].

23. ~[(~Paris is the capital of France v Rome is the capital of Italy) • ~(~Rome is the capital of Italy v Stockholm is the capital of Norway)].

24. ~[(~Rome is the capital of Spain v Stockholm is the capital of Norway) • ~(~Stockholm is the capital of Norway v Paris is the capital of France)].

25. ~[(~London is the capital of England • Paris is the capital of France) v ~(~Paris is the capital of France • Rome is the capital of Spain)].

II. If *A*, *B*, and *C* are true statements and *X*, *Y*, and *Z* are false statements, which of the following are true?

★ 1. ~*A* v *B*
    2. ~*B* v *X*

    3. ~*Y* v *C*
    4. ~*Z* v *X*

★ 5. (*A* • *X*) v (*B* • *Y*)
    6. (*B* • *C*) v (*Y* • *Z*)

    7. ~(*C* • *Y*) v (*A* • *Z*)
    8. ~(*A* • *B*) v (*X* • *Y*)

9. ~(X • Z) v (B • C)

★ 10. ~(X • ~Y) v (B • ~C)

11. (A v X) • (Y v B)

12. (B v C) • (Y v Z)

13. (X v Y) • (X v Z)

14. ~(A v Y) • (B v X)

★ 15. ~(X v Z) • (~X v Z)

16. ~(A v C) v ~(X • ~Y)

17. ~(B v Z) • ~(X v ~Y)

18. ~[(A v ~C) v (C v ~A)]

19. ~[(B • C) • ~(C • B)]

★ 20. ~[(A • B) v ~(B • A)]

21. [A v (B v C)] • ~[(A v B) v C]

22. [X v (Y • Z)] v ~[(X v Y) • (X v Z)]

23. [A • (B v C)] • ~[(A • B) v (A • C)]

24. ~{[(~A • B) • (~X • Z)] • ~[(A • ~B) v ~(~Y • ~Z)]}

25. ~{~[(B • ~C) v (Y • ~Z)] • [(~B v X) v (B v ~Y)]}

III. If *A* and *B* are known to be true and *X* and *Y* are known to be false, but the truth values of *P* and *Q* are not known, of which of the following statements can you determine the truth values?

★ 1. A v P

2. Q • X

3. Q v ~X

4. ~B • P

★ 5. P v ~P

6. ~P v (Q v P)

7. Q • ~Q

8. P • (~P v X)

9. ~(P • Q) v P

★ 10. ~Q • [(P v Q) • ~P]

11. (P v Q) • ~(Q v P)

12. (P • Q) • (~P v ~Q)

13. ~P v [~Q v (P • Q)]

14. P v ~(~A v X)

★ 15. P • [~(P v Q) v ~P]

16. ~(P • Q) v (Q • P)

17. ~[~(~P v Q) v P] v P

18. (~P v Q) • ~[~P v (P • Q)]

19. (~A v P) • (~P v Y)

★ 20. ~[P v (B • Y)] v [(P v B) • (P v Y)]

21. [P v (Q • A)] • ~[(P v Q) • (P v A)]

22. [P v (Q • X)] • ~[(P v Q) • (P v X)]

23. ~[~P v (~Q v X)] v [~(~P v Q) v (~P v X)]

24. ~[~P v (~Q v A)] v [~(~P v Q) v (~P v A)]

25. ~[(P • Q) v (Q • ~P)] • ~[(P • ~Q) v (~Q • ~P)]

IV. Using the letters *E, I, J, L,* and *S* to abbreviate the simple statements "Egypt's food shortage worsens," "Iran raises the price of oil," "Jordan requests more American aid," "Libya raises the price of oil," and "Saudi Arabia buys five hundred more warplanes," symbolize the following:

★ 1. Iran raises the price of oil but Libya does not raise the price of oil.

2. Either Iran or Libya raises the price of oil.

3. Iran and Libya both raise the price of oil.

4. Iran and Libya do not both raise the price of oil.

★ 5. Iran and Libya both do not raise the price of oil.

6. Iran or Libya raises the price of oil but they do not both do so.

7. Saudi Arabia buys five hundred more warplanes and either Iran raises the price of oil or Jordan requests more American aid.

8. Either Saudi Arabia buys five hundred more warplanes and Iran raises the price of oil or Jordan requests more American aid.

9. It is not the case that Egypt's food shortage worsens, and Jordan requests more American aid.

★ 10. It is not the case that either Egypt's food shortage worsens or Jordan requests more American aid.

11. Either it is not the case that Egypt's food shortage worsens or Jordan requests more American aid.

12. It is not the case that both Egypt's food shortage worsens and Jordan requests more American aid.

13. Jordan requests more American aid unless Saudi Arabia buys five hundred more warplanes.

14. Unless Egypt's food shortage worsens, Libya raises the price of oil.

★ 15. Iran won't raise the price of oil unless Libya does so.

16. Unless both Iran and Libya raise the price of oil neither of them does.

17. Libya raises the price of oil and Egypt's food shortage worsens.

18. It is not the case that neither Iran nor Libya raises the price of oil.

19. Egypt's food shortage worsens and Jordan requests more American aid, unless both Iran and Libya do not raise the price of oil.

★ 20. Either Iran raises the price of oil and Egypt's food shortage worsens or it is not the case both that Jordan requests more American aid and that Saudi Arabia buys five hundred more warplanes.

21. Either Egypt's food shortage worsens and Saudi Arabia buys five hundred more warplanes or either Jordan requests more American aid or Libya raises the price of oil.

22. Saudi Arabia buys five hundred more warplanes and either Jordan requests more American aid or both Libya and Iran raise the price of oil.

23. Either Egypt's food shortage worsens or Jordan requests more American aid, but neither Libya nor Iran raises the price of oil.

24. Egypt's food shortage worsens, but Saudi Arabia buys five hundred more warplanes and Libya raises the price of oil.

25. Libya raises the price of oil and Egypt's food shortage worsens; however, Saudi Arabia buys five hundred more warplanes and Jordan requests more American aid.

8.3 *Conditional Statements and Material Implication*

Where two statements are combined by placing the word "if" before the first and inserting the word "then" between them, the resulting compound statement is a *conditional* (also called a *hypothetical*, an *implication*, or an *implicative statement*). In a conditional, the component statement between the "if" and the "then" is called the *antecedent* (or the *implicans* or—rarely—the *protasis*), and the component statement that follows the "then" is the *consequent* (or the *implicate* or—rarely—the *apodosis*). For example, "If Mr. Jones is the brakeman's next-door neighbor, then Mr. Jones earns exactly three times as much as the brakeman" is a conditional statement in which "Mr. Jones is the brakeman's next-door neighbor" is the antecedent, and "Mr. Jones earns exactly three times as much as the brakeman" is the consequent.

A conditional statement asserts that in any case in which its antecedent is true, its consequent is true also. It does not assert that its antecedent is true, but only that if its antecedent is true, its consequent is true also. It does not assert that its consequent is true, but only that its consequent is true if its antecedent is true. The essential meaning of a conditional statement is the relationship asserted to hold between its antecedent and consequent, in that order. To understand the meaning of a conditional statement, then, we must understand what the relationship of implication is.

The possibility suggests itself that perhaps "implication" has more than one meaning. We found it useful to distinguish different senses of the word "or" before introducing a special logical symbol to correspond exactly to a single one of the meanings of the English word. Had we not done so, the ambiguity of the English would have infected our logical symbolism and prevented it from achieving the clarity and precision aimed at. It will be equally useful to distinguish the different senses of "implies" or "if–then" before introducing a special logical symbol in this connection.

Let us begin by listing a number of different conditional statements, each of which seems to assert a different type of implication, and to each of which corresponds a different sense of "if–then."

A. If all humans are mortal and Socrates is a human, then Socrates is mortal.
B. If Leslie is a bachelor, then Leslie is unmarried.
C. If this piece of blue litmus paper is placed in acid, then this piece of blue litmus paper will turn red.
D. If State loses the homecoming game, then I'll eat my hat.

Even a casual inspection of these four conditional statements reveals that they are of quite different types. The consequent of *A* follows logically from its antecedent, whereas the consequent of *B* follows from its antecedent by the very definition of the term "bachelor," which means unmarried man. The consequent of *C* does not follow from its antecedent either by logic alone or by the definition of its terms; the connection must be discovered empirically, for the implication stated here is causal. Finally, the consequent of *D* does not follow from its antecedent either by logic or by definition, nor is there any causal law involved—in the usual sense of the term. Most causal laws, those discovered in physics and chemistry, for example, describe what happens in the world regardless of the hopes or desires of men. There is no such law connected with statement *D*, of course. That statement reports a decision of the speaker to behave in the specified way under the specified circumstances.

The four conditional statements examined in the preceding paragraph are different in that each asserts a different type of implication between its antecedent and consequent. But they are not completely different; all assert types of implication. Is there any identifiable common meaning, any partial meaning that is common to these admittedly different types of implication, although perhaps not the whole or complete meaning of any one of them?

The search for a common partial meaning takes on an added significance when we recall our procedure in working out a symbolic representation for the English word "or." In that case we proceeded as follows. First, we emphasized the difference between the two senses of that word, contrasting inclusive with exclusive disjunction. The inclusive disjunction of two statements was observed to mean that at least one of the statements is true, and the exclusive disjunction of two statements was observed to mean that at least one of the statements is true but not both are true. Second, we noted that these two types of disjunction had a common *partial* meaning. This partial common meaning, that at least one of the disjuncts is true, was seen to be the *whole* meaning of the weak, inclusive "or," and a *part* of the meaning of the strong, exclusive "or." We then introduced the special symbol "v" to represent this common partial meaning (which was the entire meaning of "or" in its inclusive sense). Third, we noted that the symbol representing the common partial meaning was an adequate translation of either sense of the word "or" for the purpose of retaining the Disjunctive Syllogism as a valid form of argument. It was admitted that translating an exclusive "or" into the symbol "v" ignored and lost part of the word's meaning. But the part of its meaning that is preserved by this translation is all that is needed for the Disjunctive Syllogism to remain a valid form of argument. Since the Disjunctive Syllogism is typical of arguments involving disjunction with which we are here concerned, this partial translation of the word "or," which may abstract from its "full" or "complete" meaning in some cases, is wholly adequate for our present purposes.

Now we wish to follow the same pattern again, this time in connection with the English phrase "if–then." The first part is already accomplished: we have already emphasized the differences among some four senses of the "if–then" phrase, corresponding to four different types of implication. We are now ready for the second step, which is to discover a sense that is at least a part of the meaning of all four different types of implication.

One way of approaching this problem is to ask what circumstances would suffice to establish the falsehood of a given conditional statement. Let us consider another example. Under what circumstances should we agree that the conditional statement

If this piece of blue litmus paper is placed in that solution, then this piece of blue litmus paper will turn red.

is false? There are, of course, many ways of investigating the truth of such a statement, and not all of them involve actually placing this piece of blue litmus paper in the solution. Some other chemical indicator might be used, and if it showed the solution to be acid, this would confirm the given conditional as true, since we know that blue litmus paper always turns red in acid. On the other hand, if it showed the solution to be alkaline, this would tend to show that the given conditional was false. It is important to realize that this conditional does not assert that any blue litmus paper is actually placed in the solution, or that any litmus paper actually turns red. It asserts merely that if this piece of blue litmus paper is placed in the solution, then this piece of blue litmus paper will turn red. It is proved false in case this piece of blue litmus paper is actually placed in the solution and does not turn red. The acid test, so to speak, of the falsehood of a conditional statement is available when its antecedent is true, for if its consequent is false while its antecedent is true, the conditional itself is thereby proved false.

Any conditional statement "if p then q" is known to be false in case the conjunction $p \cdot \sim q$ is known to be true, that is, in case its antecedent is true and its consequent is false. For a conditional to be true, then, the indicated conjunction must be false, that is, its negation $\sim(p \cdot \sim q)$ must be true. In other words, for any conditional "If p then q" to be true, $\sim(p \cdot \sim q)$, the negation of the conjunction of its antecedent with the negation of its consequent, must also be true. We may, then, regard $\sim(p \cdot \sim q)$ as a part of the meaning of "If p then q."

Every conditional statement means to deny that its antecedent is true and its consequent false, but this need not be the whole of its meaning. A conditional such as A on page 266 also asserts a logical connection between its antecedent and consequent, one like B asserts a definitional connection, C a causal connection, D a decisional connection. But no matter what type of implication is asserted by a conditional statement, part of its meaning is the negation of the conjunction of its antecedent with the negation of its consequent.

We now introduce a special symbol to represent this common partial meaning of the "if–then" phrase. We define the new symbol "$\supset$" (called a *horseshoe*) by taking $p \supset q$ as an abbreviation of $\sim(p \cdot \sim q)$. The exact significance of the "$\supset$" symbol can be indicated by means of a truth table:

p	q	$\sim q$	$p \cdot \sim q$	$\sim(p \cdot \sim q)$	$p \supset q$
T	T	F	F	T	T
T	F	T	T	F	F
F	T	F	F	T	T
F	F	T	F	T	T

Here the first two columns are the guide columns; the third is filled in by reference to the second, the fourth by reference to the first and third, the fifth by reference to the fourth, and the sixth is identically the same as the fifth by definition.

The symbol "⊃" is not to be regarded as denoting *the* meaning of "if–then," or standing for *the* relation of implication. That would be impossible, for there is no single meaning of "if–then"; there are several meanings. There is no unique relation of implication to be thus represented; there are several different implication relations. Nor is the symbol "⊃" to be regarded as somehow standing for *all* the meanings of "if–then." These are all different, and any attempt to abbreviate all of them by a single logical symbol would render that symbol multiply ambiguous—as ambiguous as the English phrase "if–then" or the English word "implication." The symbol "⊃" is completely unambiguous. What $p \supset q$ abbreviates is $\sim(p \cdot \sim q)$, whose meaning is included in the meanings of each of the various kinds of implications considered, but which does not constitute the entire meaning of any of them.

We can consider the symbol "⊃" as representing another kind of implication, and it will be expedient to do so, since a convenient way to read $p \supset q$ is "if p then q." But it is not the same kind of implication as any of those mentioned earlier. It is called *material implication* by logicians, who in giving it a special name admit that it is a special notion, not to be confused with other, more usual, types of implication.

Not all conditional statements in English need assert one of the four types of implication previously considered. Material implication constitutes a fifth type that may be asserted in ordinary discourse. Consider the remark "If Hitler was a military genius, then I'm a monkey's uncle." It is quite clear that it does not assert logical, definitional, or causal implication. It should also be apparent that it cannot represent a decisional implication, since it scarcely lies in the speaker's power to make the consequent true. No "real connection," whether logical, definitional, or causal, obtains between antecedent and consequent here. A conditional of this sort is often used as an emphatic or humorous method of denying its antecedent. The consequent of such a conditional is usually a statement which is obviously or ludicrously false. And since no true conditional can have both its antecedent true and its consequent false, to affirm such a conditional amounts to denying that its antecedent is true. The full meaning of the present conditional seems to be the denial that "Hitler was a military genius" is true when "I'm a monkey's uncle" is false. And since the latter is so obviously false, the conditional must be understood to deny the former.

No "real connection" between antecedent and consequent is suggested by a *material implication*. All it asserts is that as a matter of fact it is not the case that the antecedent is true when the consequent is false. It should be noted that the material implication symbol is a truth-functional connective, like the symbols for conjunction and disjunction. As such, it is defined by the truth table

p	q	$p \supset q$
T	T	T
T	F	F
F	T	T
F	F	T

The strangeness that sometimes attaches to the horseshoe symbol "⊃" as defined by the given truth table can be dissipated at least in part by the following considerations. Because the number 2 is smaller than the number 4 (written symbolically as $2 < 4$), it follows that *any* number smaller than 2 is smaller than 4. The conditional formula

$$\text{If } x < 2 \text{ then } x < 4$$

is true for any number x whatsoever. If we focus on the numbers 1, 3, and 4 and replace the number variable x in the preceding conditional formula by each of them in turn, we can make the following observations. In

$$\text{If } 1 < 2 \text{ then } 1 < 4$$

both antecedent and consequent are true, and of course the conditional is true. In

$$\text{If } 3 < 2 \text{ then } 3 < 4$$

the antecedent is false and the consequent is true, and of course the conditional is again true. In

$$\text{If } 4 < 2 \text{ then } 4 < 4$$

both antecedent and consequent are false, but the conditional remains true. These three cases correspond to the first, third, and fourth rows of the table defining the horseshoe symbol "⊃." So there is nothing particularly remarkable or surprising that a conditional should be true where both antecedent and consequent are true, where the antecedent is false and the consequent is true, or where antecedent and consequent are both false. Of course there is no number that is smaller than 2 but not smaller than 4; that is, there is no true conditional statement with true antecedent and false consequent. This is exactly what the defining truth table for "⊃" lays down.

Now we propose to translate any occurrence of the "if–then" phrase into our logical symbol "⊃." This proposal means that in translating conditional statements into our symbolism we treat them all as merely material implications. Of course many, if not most, conditional statements assert more than a merely material implication to hold between their antecedents and consequents. So our proposal amounts to suggesting that we ignore, or throw away, or "abstract from" part of the meaning of a conditional statement when we translate it into our symbolic language. How can this proposal be justified?

The previous proposal to translate both inclusive and exclusive disjunctions by means of the "v" symbol was justified on the grounds that the validity of the Disjunctive Syllogism was preserved even if the additional meaning that attaches to the exclusive "or" was ignored. Our present proposal to translate all conditional statements into the merely material implication symbolized by "⊃" is to be justified in exactly the same way. Many arguments contain conditional statements of various different kinds, but the validity of all valid arguments of the general type with which we will be concerned is preserved even if the additional meanings of their conditional statements are ignored. This remains to be proved, of course, and will occupy our attention in the next section.

Conditional statements can be formulated in a variety of ways. The statement

> If he has a good lawyer then he will be acquitted.

can equally well be stated without using the word "then" as

> If he has a good lawyer he will be acquitted.

Antecedent and consequent can have their order reversed, provided that the "if" still directly precedes the antecedent, as

> He will be acquitted if he has a good lawyer.

It should be clear that in any of the above the word "if" can be replaced by such phrases as "in case," "provided that," "given that," or "on condition that" without any change in meaning. Minor adjustments in the phrasings of antecedent and consequent permit such alternative phrasings of the same conditional as

> That he has a good lawyer implies that he will be acquitted.

or

> His having a good lawyer entails his acquittal.

A shift from active to passive voice accompanies a reversal of order of antecedent and consequent to yield the logically equivalent

> His being acquitted is implied (or entailed) by his having a good lawyer.

Any of these is symbolized as $L \supset A$.

The notions of necessary and sufficient conditions provide other formulations of conditional statements. For any specified event there are many circumstances necessary for its occurrence. Thus, for a car to run, it is necessary that there be gas in its tank, its spark plugs properly gapped, its oil pump working, and so on. So if the event occurs every one of the conditions necessary for its occurrence must be fulfilled. Hence to say

That there is gas in its tank is a necessary condition for the car to run.

can equally well be stated as

The car runs only if there is gas in its tank.

which is another way of saying that

If the car runs then there is gas in its tank.

Any of these is symbolized as $R \supset G$, and in general, "q is a necessary condition for p" and "p only if q" are symbolized as $p \supset q$.

For a specified situation there are many alternative circumstances any one of which is sufficient to produce that situation. Thus, for a purse to contain over a dollar, it would be sufficient for it to contain one hundred and one pennies, twenty-one nickels, eleven dimes, five quarters, and so on. If any one of these circumstances obtains, the specified situation will be realized. Hence to say "That the purse contains five quarters is a sufficient condition for it to contain over a dollar" is to say the same as "If the purse contains five quarters then it contains over a dollar." In general, "p is a sufficient condition for q" is symbolized as $p \supset q$.

If p is a sufficient condition for q, we have $p \supset q$, and q must be a necessary condition for p. If p is a necessary condition for q, we have $q \supset p$, and q must be a sufficient condition for p. Hence if p is necessary and sufficient for q, then q is sufficient and necessary for p (or we could say that q is necessary and sufficient for p, since conjunction is commutative). Not every statement containing the word "if" is a conditional. None of the following statements is a conditional: "There is food in the refrigerator if you want some," "Your table is ready, if you please," "There is a message for you if you're interested," "The meeting will be held even if no permit is obtained." The presence or absence of particular words is never decisive. In every case one must understand what a given sentence means and then restate that meaning in a symbolic formula.

There is no necessary or logical relation between the words "if" and "iffy," though there is often a suggestion that what is preceded by the word "if" is somewhat doubtful. That is illustrated by the following anecdote:

> . . . George Bernard Shaw once sent Winston Churchill two tickets for the opening night of one of his new plays, noting, "Bring a friend—if you have one"; to which Churchill wrote back to say that he was otherwise engaged opening night, but would appreciate tickets for the second performance, "if there is one."[7]

---

[7]Aristides, "The Gentle Art of the Resounding Put-Down," *The American Scholar*, Summer 1987, p. 313.

EXERCISES

I. If *A*, *B*, and *C* are true statements and *X*, *Y*, *Z* are false statements, determine which of the following are true.

★ 1. $A \supset B$ 　　　　　　　　　　　　2. $A \supset X$

3. $B \supset Y$ 　　　　　　　　　　　　4. $Y \supset Z$

★ 5. $(A \supset B) \supset Z$ 　　　　　　　　6. $(X \supset Y) \supset Z$

7. $(A \supset B) \supset C$ 　　　　　　　　8. $(X \supset Y) \supset C$

9. $A \supset (B \supset Z)$ 　　　　　　★ 10. $X \supset (Y \supset Z)$

11. $[(A \supset B) \supset C] \supset Z$ 　　　　12. $[(A \supset X) \supset Y] \supset Z$

13. $[A \supset (X \supset Y)] \supset C$ 　　　　14. $[A \supset (B \supset Y)] \supset X$

★ 15. $[(X \supset Z) \supset C] \supset Y$ 　　　　16. $[(Y \supset B) \supset Y] \supset Y$

17. $[(A \supset Y) \supset B] \supset Z$

18. $[(A \cdot X) \supset C] \supset [(A \supset C) \supset X]$

19. $[(A \cdot X) \supset C] \supset [(A \supset X) \supset C]$

★ 20. $[(A \cdot X) \supset Y] \supset [(X \supset A) \supset (A \supset Y)]$

21. $[(A \cdot X) \lor (\sim A \cdot \sim X)] \supset [(A \supset X) \cdot (X \supset A)]$

22. $\{[A \supset (B \supset C)] \supset [(A \cdot B) \supset C]\} \supset [(Y \supset B) \supset (C \supset Z)]$

23. $\{[(X \supset Y) \supset Z] \supset [Z \supset (X \supset Y)]\} \supset [(X \supset Z) \supset Y]$

24. $[(A \cdot X) \supset Y] \supset [(A \supset X) \cdot (A \supset Y)]$

25. $[A \supset (X \cdot Y)] \supset [(A \supset X) \lor (A \supset Y)]$

II. If *A* and *B* are known to be true, and *X* and *Y* are known to be false, but the truth values of *P* and *Q* are not known, of which of the following statements can you determine the truth values?

★ 1. $P \supset A$ 　　　　　　　　　　　2. $X \supset Q$

3. $(Q \supset A) \supset Z$ 　　　　　　　4. $(P \cdot A) \supset B$

★ 5. $(P \supset P) \supset X$ 　　　　　　　6. $(X \supset Q) \supset X$

7. $X \supset (Q \supset X)$ 　　　　　　　8. $(P \cdot X) \supset Y$

9. $[P \supset (Q \supset P)] \supset Y$ 　　★ 10. $(Q \supset Q) \supset (A \supset X)$

11. $(P \supset X) \supset (X \supset P)$ 　　　12. $(P \supset A) \supset (B \supset X)$

13. $(X \supset P) \supset (B \supset Y)$ 　　　14. $[(P \supset B) \supset B] \supset B$

★ 15. $[(X \supset Q) \supset Q] \supset Q$ 　　　16. $(P \supset X) \supset (\sim X \supset \sim P)$

17. $(X \supset P) \supset (\sim X \supset Y)$ 　　18. $(P \supset A) \supset (A \supset \sim B)$

19. $(P \supset Q) \supset (P \supset Q)$ 　　★ 20. $(P \supset \sim\sim P) \supset (A \supset \sim B)$

21. $\sim(A \cdot P) \supset (\sim A \lor \sim P)$ 　　22. $\sim(P \cdot X) \supset \sim(P \lor \sim X)$

23. $(X \lor Q) \supset (\sim X \cdot \sim Q)$

24. $[P \supset (A \lor X)] \supset [(P \supset A) \supset X]$

25. $[Q \lor (B \cdot Y)] \supset [(Q \lor B) \cdot (Q \lor Y)]$

III. Symbolize the following, using capital letters to abbreviate the simple statements involved.

★ 1. If Argentina mobilizes then if Brazil protests to the U.N. then Chile will call for a meeting of all the Latin American States.

2. If Argentina mobilizes then either Brazil will protest to the U.N. or Chile will call for a meeting of all the Latin American States.

3. If Argentina mobilizes then Brazil will protest to the U.N. and Chile will call for a meeting of all the Latin American States.

4. If Argentina mobilizes then Brazil will protest to the U.N., and Chile will call for a meeting of all the Latin American States.

★ 5. If Argentina mobilizes and Brazil protests to the U.N. then Chile will call for a meeting of all the Latin American States.

6. If either Argentina mobilizes or Brazil protests to the U.N. then Chile will call for a meeting of all the Latin American States.

7. Either Argentina will mobilize or if Brazil protests to the U.N. then Chile will call for a meeting of all the Latin American States.

8. If Argentina does not mobilize then either Brazil will not protest to the U.N. or Chile will not call for a meeting of all the Latin American States.

9. If Argentina does not mobilize then neither will Brazil protest to the U.N. nor will Chile call for a meeting of all the Latin American States.

★ 10. It is not the case that if Argentina mobilizes then both Brazil will protest to the U.N. and Chile will call for a meeting of all the Latin American States.

11. If it is not the case that Argentina mobilizes then Brazil will not protest to the U.N., and Chile will call for a meeting of all the Latin American States.

12. Brazil will protest to the U.N. if Argentina mobilizes.

13. Brazil will protest to the U.N. only if Argentina mobilizes.

14. Chile will call for a meeting of all the Latin American States only if both Argentina mobilizes and Brazil protests to the U.N.

★ 15. Brazil will protest to the U.N. only if either Argentina mobilizes or Chile calls for a meeting of all the Latin American States.

16. Argentina will mobilize if either Brazil protests to the U.N. or Chile calls for a meeting of all the Latin American States.

17. Brazil will protest to the U.N. unless Chile calls for a meeting of all the Latin American States.

18. If Argentina mobilizes, then Brazil will protest to the U.N. unless Chile calls for a meeting of all the Latin American States.

19. Brazil will not protest to the U.N. unless Argentina mobilizes.

★ 20. Unless Chile calls for a meeting of all the Latin American States, Brazil will protest to the U.N.

21. Argentina's mobilizing is a sufficient condition for Brazil to protest to the U.N.

22. Argentina's mobilizing is a necessary condition for Chile to call for a meeting of all the Latin American States.

23. If Argentina mobilizes and Brazil protests to the U.N. then both Chile and the Dominican Republic will call for a meeting of all the Latin American States.

24. If Argentina mobilizes and Brazil protests to the U.N. then either Chile or the Dominican Republic will call for a meeting of all the Latin American States.

25. If neither Chile nor the Dominican Republic calls for a meeting of all the Latin American States, then Brazil will not protest to the U.N. unless Argentina mobilizes.

8.4 *Argument Forms and Arguments*

In this section we specify more precisely what is meant by the term "valid." We relate our formal definition to more familiar and intuitive notions by considering the method of refutation by logical analogy.[8] Presented with the argument

> If Bacon wrote the plays attributed to Shakespeare, then Bacon was a great writer.
> Bacon was a great writer.
> Therefore Bacon wrote the plays attributed to Shakespeare.

we may agree with the premises but disagree with the conclusion, judging the argument to be invalid. One way of providing invalidity is by the method of logical analogy. "You might as well argue," we could retort, "that

> If Washington was assassinated, then Washington is dead.
> Washington is dead.
> Therefore Washington was assassinated.

And you cannot seriously defend this argument," we should continue, "because here the premises are known to be true and the conclusion known to be false. This argument is obviously invalid; your argument is of the *same form*; so yours is invalid also." This type of refutation is very effective.

Let us examine more closely the method of refutation by logical analogy, for it points the way to an excellent general technique for testing arguments. To prove the invalidity of an argument, it suffices to formulate another argument that (1) has exactly the same form as the first and (2) has true premisses and a false conclusion. This method is based upon the fact that validity and invalidity are purely *formal* characteristics of arguments, which is to say that any two arguments having exactly the same form are either both valid

---

[8]Just as in discussing the categorical syllogism in Section 6.2.

or both invalid, regardless of any differences in the subject matter with which they are concerned.[9]

A given argument exhibits its form very clearly when the simple statements that appear in it are abbreviated by capital letters. Thus we may abbreviate the statements "Bacon wrote the plays attributed to Shakespeare," "Bacon was a great writer," "Washington was assassinated," and "Washington is dead" by the letters B, G, A, and D, respectively, and using the familiar three dot symbol "$\therefore$" for "therefore," symbolize the two preceding arguments as

$$
\begin{array}{ccc}
B \supset G & & A \supset D \\
G & \text{and} & D \\
\therefore B & & \therefore A
\end{array}
$$

So written, their common form is easily seen.

If we are interested in discussing forms of arguments rather than particular arguments having those forms, we need some method of symbolizing argument forms themselves. To achieve such a method, we introduce the notion of a *variable*. In the preceding sections we used capital letters to symbolize particular simple statements. To avoid confusion, we use small, or lowercase, letters from the middle part of the alphabet $p, q, r, s, \ldots$ as *statement variables*. A statement variable, as we shall use the term, is simply a letter for which, or in place of which, a statement may be substituted. Compound statements as well as simple statements may be substituted for statement variables.

We define an "argument form" as any array of symbols containing statement variables but no statements, such that when statements are substituted for the statement variables—the same statement being substituted for the same statement variable throughout—the result is an argument. For definiteness, we establish the convention that in any argument form p shall be the first statement variable that occurs in it, q shall be the second, r the third, and so on. Thus the expression

$$
\begin{array}{c}
p \supset q \\
q \\
\therefore p
\end{array}
$$

is an argument form, for when the statements B and G are substituted for the statement variables p and q, respectively, the result is the first argument of this section. If the statements A and D are substituted for the variables p and q, the result is the second argument. Any argument that results from the substitution of statements for statement variables in an argument form

[9]Here we assume that the simple statements involved are neither logically true (e.g., "All chairs are chairs") nor logically false (e.g., "Some chairs are nonchairs"). We also assume that the only logical relations among the simple statements involved are those asserted or entailed by the premises. The point of these restrictions is to limit our considerations in this chapter and the next to truth-functional arguments alone and to exclude other kinds of arguments whose validity turns on more complex logical considerations not appropriately introduced at this place.

is called a *substitution instance* of that argument form. It is clear that any substitution instance of an argument form may be said to have that form, and that any argument which has a certain form is a substitution instance of that form.

For any argument there are usually several argument forms that have the given argument as a substitution instance. For example, the first argument of this section

$$B \supset G$$
$$G$$
$$\therefore B$$

is a substitution instance of each of the four argument forms

$p \supset q$	$p \supset q$	$p \supset q$	p
q	r	r	q
$\therefore p$	$\therefore p$	$\therefore s$	$\therefore r$

Thus we obtain the given argument by substituting B for p and G for q in the first argument form; by substituting B for p and G for both q and r in the second; B for both p and s, and G for both q and r in the third; and $B \supset G$ for p, G for q, and B for r in the fourth. Of these four argument forms, the first corresponds more closely to the structure of the given argument than do the others. It does so because the given argument results from the first argument form by substituting a different simple statement for each different statement variable in it. We call the first argument form "the specific form" of the given argument. Our definition of "the specific form" of a given argument is the following: in case an argument is produced by substituting a different simple statement for each different statement variable in an argument form, that argument form is *the specific form* of that argument. For any given argument, there is a unique argument form that is *the specific form* of that argument.

The technique of refutation by logical analogy can now be described more precisely. If the specific form of a given argument has any substitution instance whose premises are true and whose conclusion is false, then the given argument is invalid. We may define the term "invalid" as applied to argument forms as follows: an argument form is invalid if and only if it has at least one substitution instance with true premises and a false conclusion. Refutation by logical analogy is based on the fact that any argument whose specific form is an *invalid argument form* is an *invalid argument*. Any argument form that is not invalid must be valid. Hence an argument form is valid if and only if it has *no* substitution instances with true premises and a false conclusion. And since validity is a formal notion, an argument is valid if and only if the specific form of that argument is a valid argument form.

A given argument is proved invalid if a refuting analogy for it can be found, but "thinking up" such refuting analogies may not always be easy. Happily, it is not necessary, because for arguments of this type there is a simpler, purely mechanical test based upon the same principle. Given any argument, we test the specific form of that argument, for its validity or invalidity determines the validity or invalidity of the argument.

To test an argument form, we examine all possible substitution instances of it to see if any of them have true premises and false conclusions. Of course any argument form has infinitely many substitution instances, but we need not worry about having to examine them one at a time. Because we are interested only in the truth or falsehood of their premises and conclusions, we need consider only the truth values involved. The arguments that concern us here contain only simple statements and compound statements that are built up out of simple statements by means of the truth-functional connectives symbolized by the dot, curl, wedge, and horseshoe. Hence we obtain all possible substitution instances whose premises and conclusions have different truth values by examining all possible different arrangements of truth values for the statements that can be substituted for the different statement variables in the argument form to be tested.

Where an argument form contains just two different statement variables p and q, all of its substitution instances are the result of either substituting true statements for both p and q, or a true statement for p and a false one for q, or a false one for p and a true one for q, or false statements for both p and q. These different cases are assembled most conveniently in the form of a truth table. To decide the validity of the argument form

$$p \supset q$$
$$q$$
$$\therefore p$$

we construct the following truth table:

p	q	$p \supset q$
T	T	T
T	F	F
F	T	T
F	F	T

Each row of this table represents a whole class of substitution instances. The T's and F's in the two initial or guide columns represent the truth values of the statements substituted for the variables p and q in the argument form. We fill in the third column by referring back to the initial or guide columns and the definition of the horseshoe symbol. The third column heading is the first "premiss" of the argument form, the second column is the second "premiss," and the first column is the "conclusion." In examining this truth table, we find that in the third row there are T's under both premises and an F under the conclusion, which indicates that there is at least one substitution instance of this argument form which has true premises and a false conclusion. This row suffices to show that the argument form is invalid. Any argument of this specific form (that is, any argument the specific argument form of which is the given argument form) is said to commit the Fallacy of Affirming the Consequent, since its second premiss affirms the consequent of its conditional first premiss.

Until you become quite familiar with this use of truth tables to establish the validity or invalidity of argument forms, a slightly more complicated version might be easier to use. After each of the premisses and the conclusion has had the column under it filled in properly with **T**'s and **F**'s, all of the premisses—in the order in which they occur in the argument—should be written again, followed immediately by the conclusion, and the columns under them filled in with **T**'s and **F**'s again. The expanded truth table will appear as

p	q	$p \supset q$	q	p
T	T	T	T	T
T	F	F	F	T
F	T	T	T	F
F	F	T	F	F

In this table it is easier to see that there is a row (the third) in which all premisses are **T** and the conclusion is **F**, which establishes the invalidity of the argument form in question.

To show the validity of the Disjunctive Syllogism form

$$p \lor q$$
$$\sim p$$
$$\therefore q$$

we construct the following different truth table:

p	q	$p \lor q$	$\sim p$
T	T	T	F
T	F	T	F
F	T	T	T
F	F	F	T

Here too the initial or guide columns have written under them all possible different truth values of statements that may be substituted for the variables p and q. We fill in the third column by referring back to the first two and the fourth by reference to the first alone. Now the third row is the only one in which **T**'s appear under both premisses (the third and fourth columns), and there a **T** appears under the conclusion also (the second column). The truth table thus shows that the argument form has no substitution instance having true premisses and a false conclusion, and thereby proves the validity of the argument form being tested.

Here the longer truth table is only very slightly longer than the given one. Indeed, only one more column is needed, headed by the conclusion *q*. The longer truth table is

p	*q*	*p* ∨ *q*	~*p*	*q*
T	T	T	F	T
T	F	T	F	F
F	T	T	T	T
F	F	F	T	F

and we "read the validity" of the argument form directly from the last three columns of the table.

The truth table technique provides a completely mechanical method for testing the validity of any argument of the general type here considered. We are now in a position to justify our proposal to translate any occurrence of the "if–then" phrase into our material implication symbol "⊃." In the preceding section the claim was made that all valid arguments of the general type with which we are here concerned that involve "if–then" statements remain valid when those statements are interpreted as affirming merely material implications. Truth tables can be used to substantiate this claim, and will justify our translation of "if–then" into the horseshoe symbol.

The simplest type of intuitively valid argument involving a conditional statement is illustrated by the argument

If the second native told the truth, then only one native is a politician.
The second native told the truth.
Therefore only one native is a politician.

The specific form of this argument, known as *modus ponens*, is

$$p \supset q$$
$$p$$
$$\therefore q$$

and is proved valid by the following truth table:

p	*q*	*p* ⊃ *q*
T	T	T
T	F	F
F	T	T
F	F	T

Here the two premisses are represented by the third and first columns, and the conclusion is represented by the second. Only the first row represents substitution instances in which both premisses are true, and the T in the second column shows that in these arguments the conclusion is true also. This truth table establishes the validity of any argument of form *modus ponens*.

Here the longer truth table appears as

p	q	$p \supset q$	p	q
T	T	T	T	T
T	F	F	T	F
F	T	T	F	T
F	F	T	F	F

and we read the validity of *modus ponens* directly from the last three columns.

Another common type of intuitively valid argument contains conditional statements exclusively and is called a "Hypothetical Syllogism."[10] An example is

> If the first native is a politician, then the first native lies.
> If the first native lies, then the first native denies being a politician.
> Therefore if the first native is a politician, then the first native denies being a politician.

The specific form of this argument is

$$p \supset q$$
$$q \supset r$$
$$\therefore p \supset r$$

Since it contains three distinct statement variables, the truth table here must have three initial or guide columns and will require eight rows for the listing of all possible substitution instances. Besides the initial columns, three additional columns are required, two for the premisses, the third for the conclusion. The table appears as

p	q	r	$p \supset q$	$q \supset r$	$p \supset r$
T	T	T	T	T	T
T	T	F	T	F	F
T	F	T	F	T	T
T	F	F	F	T	F
F	T	T	T	T	T
F	T	F	T	F	T
F	F	T	T	T	T
F	F	F	T	T	T

In constructing it, we fill in the fourth column by referring back to the first and second, the fifth by reference to the second and third, and the sixth by

[10]Called a "pure Hypothetical Syllogism" in Chapter 7.

reference to the first and third. Examining the completed table, we observe that the premisses are true only in the first, fifth, seventh and eighth rows and that in all of these the conclusion is true also. This truth table establishes the validity of the argument form and proves that the Hypothetical Syllogism also remains valid when its conditional statements are translated by means of the horseshoe symbol.

Enough examples have been provided to illustrate the proper use of the truth table technique for testing arguments. And perhaps enough have been given to show that the validity of any valid argument involving conditional statements is preserved when its conditionals are translated into merely material implications. Any doubts that remain can be allayed by the reader's providing, translating, and testing his or her own examples.

As more complicated argument forms are considered, larger truth tables are required to test them, for a separate initial or guide column is required for each different statement variable in the argument form. Only two are required for a form with just two variables, and that table will have four rows. But three initial columns are required for a form with three variables, like the Hypothetical Syllogism, and such truth tables will have eight rows. To test the validity of an argument form such as that of the Constructive Dilemma,

$$(p \supset q) \bullet (r \supset s)$$
$$p \lor r$$
$$\therefore q \lor s$$

which contains four distinct statement variables, a truth table with four initial columns and sixteen rows is required. In general, to test an argument form containing n distinct statement variables requires a truth table with n initial columns and 2^n rows.

The first argument form that we proved invalid,

$$p \supset q$$
$$q$$
$$\therefore p$$

bears a superficial resemblance to the valid argument form *modus ponens*, and was labeled the Fallacy of Affirming the Consequent. Another invalid form that has been given a special name is

$$p \supset q$$
$$\sim p$$
$$\therefore \sim q$$

which is the Fallacy of Denying the Antecedent, and whose invalidity is readily established by means of truth tables. The latter fallacy bears a superficial resemblance to the valid argument form

$$p \supset q$$
$$\sim q$$
$$\therefore \sim p$$

called *modus tollens.*

As was pointed out on page 277, a given argument can be a substitution instance of several different argument forms. A given valid argument like the Disjunctive Syllogism on page 259, which may be symbolized as

$$R \vee W$$
$$\sim R$$
$$\therefore W$$

is a substitution instance of the valid argument form

$$p \vee q$$
$$\sim p$$
$$\therefore q$$

but is also a substitution instance of the invalid argument form

$$p$$
$$q$$
$$\therefore r$$

There is no reason why an invalid argument form cannot have a valid argument as a substitution instance. But the specific form of a valid argument must be a valid argument form. Thus the first argument form is valid and is the specific form of the given valid argument. But the second argument form is invalid and therefore cannot be the specific form of the given valid argument.

On the other hand, a valid argument form can have *only* valid arguments as substitution instances. This is proved by the truth table proof of validity for the valid argument form, which shows that there is no possible substitution instance of it that has true premises and false conclusion.

It should be emphasized that, although a valid argument form has only valid arguments as substitution instances, an invalid argument form can have both valid and invalid substitution instances. So to prove that a given argument is invalid, we must prove that *the specific form* of that argument is invalid.

EXERCISES

I. On the pages immediately following will be found a group of arguments (Group A, lettered a–o) and a group of argument forms (Group B, numbered 1–24). For each of the arguments (in Group A) indicate which of the argument forms (in Group B), if any, have the given argument as a substitution instance. In addition, for each given argument (in Group A) indicate which of the argument forms (in Group B), if any, is the specific form of that argument.

Group A—Arguments

★ a. $A \cdot B$
   $\therefore A$

b. $C \supset D$
   $\therefore C \supset (C \cdot D)$

c. E
   $\therefore E \vee F$

d. $G \supset H$
   $\sim H$
   $\therefore \sim G$

★ e. I
   J
   $\therefore I \cdot J$

f. $(K \supset L) \cdot (M \supset N)$
   $K \vee M$
   $\therefore L \vee N$

g. $O \supset P$
   $\sim O$
   $\therefore \sim P$

h. $Q \supset R$
   $Q \supset S$
   $\therefore R \vee S$

i. $T \supset U$
   $U \supset V$
   $\therefore V \supset T$

★ j. $(W \cdot X) \supset (Y \cdot Z)$
   $\therefore (W \cdot X) \supset [(W \cdot X) \cdot (Y \cdot Z)]$

m. $[G \supset (G \cdot H)] \cdot [H \supset (H \cdot G)]$
   $\therefore G \supset (G \cdot H)$

k. $A \supset B$
   $\therefore (A \supset B) \vee C$

n. $(I \vee J) \supset (I \cdot J)$
   $\sim (I \vee J)$
   $\therefore \sim (I \cdot J)$

l. $(D \vee E) \cdot \sim F$
   $\therefore D \vee E$

o. $(K \supset L) \cdot (M \supset N)$
   $\therefore K \supset L$

Group B—Argument Forms

★ 1. $p \supset q$
   $\therefore \sim q \supset \sim p$

2. $p \supset q$
   $\therefore \sim p \supset \sim q$

3. $p \cdot q$
   $\therefore p$

4. p
   $\therefore p \vee q$

★ 5. p
   $\therefore p \supset q$

6. $p \supset q$
   $\therefore p \supset (p \cdot q)$

7. $(p \vee q) \supset (p \cdot q)$
   $\therefore (p \supset q) \cdot (q \supset p)$

8. $p \supset q$
   $\sim p$
   $\therefore \sim q$

9. $p \supset q$
   $\sim q$
   $\therefore \sim p$

★ 10. p
   q
   $\therefore p \cdot q$

11. $p \supset q$
   $p \supset r$
   $\therefore q \vee r$

12. $p \supset q$
   $q \supset r$
   $\therefore r \supset p$

13. $p \supset (q \supset r)$
   $p \supset q$
   $\therefore p \supset r$

14. $p \supset (q \cdot r)$
   $(q \vee r) \supset \sim p$
   $\therefore \sim p$

★ 15. $p \supset (q \supset r)$
   $q \supset (p \supset r)$
   $\therefore (p \vee q) \supset r$

16. $(p \supset q) \cdot (r \supset s)$
   $p \vee r$
   $\therefore q \vee s$

17. $(p \supset q) \cdot (r \supset s)$
   $\sim q \vee \sim s$
   $\therefore \sim p \vee \sim s$

18. $p \supset (q \supset r)$
   $q \supset (r \supset s)$
   $\therefore p \supset s$

19. $p \supset (q \supset r)$
   $(q \supset r) \supset s$
   $\therefore p \supset s$

★ 20. $(p \supset q) \cdot [(p \cdot q) \supset r]$
   $p \supset (r \supset s)$
   $\therefore p \supset s$

21. $(p \vee q) \supset (p \cdot q)$
   $\sim(p \vee q)$
   $\therefore \sim(p \cdot q)$

22. $(p \vee q) \supset (p \cdot q)$
   $p \cdot q$
   $\therefore p \vee q$

23. $(p \cdot q) \supset (r \cdot s)$
   $\therefore (p \cdot q) \supset [(p \cdot q) \cdot (r \cdot s)]$

24. $(p \supset q) \cdot (r \supset s)$
   $\therefore p \supset q$

II. Use truth tables to prove the validity or invalidity of each of the argument forms in Group B, above.

III. Use truth tables to determine the validity or invalidity of each of the following arguments.

★ 1. $(A \vee B) \supset (A \cdot B)$
   $A \vee B$
   $\therefore A \cdot B$

2. $(C \vee D) \supset (C \cdot D)$
   $C \cdot D$
   $\therefore C \vee D$

3. $E \supset F$
   $F \supset E$
   $\therefore E \vee F$

4. $(G \vee H) \supset (G \cdot H)$
   $\sim(G \cdot H)$
   $\therefore \sim(G \vee H)$

★ 5. $(I \vee J) \supset (I \cdot J)$
   $\sim(I \vee J)$
   $\therefore \sim(I \cdot J)$

6. $K \vee L$
   K
   $\therefore \sim L$

7. $M \vee (N \cdot \sim N)$
   M
   $\therefore \sim(N \cdot \sim N)$

8. $(O \vee P) \supset Q$
   $Q \supset (O \cdot P)$
   $\therefore (O \vee P) \supset (O \cdot P)$

9. $(R \vee S) \supset T$
   $T \supset (R \cdot S)$
   $\therefore (R \cdot S) \supset (R \vee S)$

10. $U \supset (V \vee W)$
   $(V \cdot W) \supset \sim U$
   $\therefore \sim U$

IV. Use truth tables to determine the validity or invalidity of each of the following arguments.

★ 1. If Albania managers to free itself from Chinese influence then both Bulgaria and Czechoslovakia will adopt more liberal policies. But Bulgaria will not adopt a more liberal policy. Therefore Albania will not manage to free itself from Chinese influence.

2. If Denmark drifts further to the left then if Estonia continues to be a puppet of Soviet Russia then Finland must become increasingly subservient to Soviet Russia. Estonia will continue to be a puppet of Soviet Russia. So if Denmark drifts further to the left then Finland must become increasingly subservient to Soviet Russia.

3. If Greece strengthens her democratic institutions then Hungary will pursue a more independent policy. If Greece strengthens her democratic institutions then the Italian Communist Party will attract fewer and fewer voters. Hence if Hungary pursues a more independent policy then the Italian Communist Party will attract fewer and fewer voters.

4. If Japan continues to export capital then either Korea or Laos will become rapidly industrialized. Korea will not become rapidly industrialized. It follows

that if Japan continues to export capital then Laos will become rapidly industrialized.

★ 5. If Montana suffers a severe drought then if Nevada has its normal light rainfall then Oregon's water supply will be greatly reduced. Nevada does have its normal light rainfall. So if Oregon's water supply is greatly reduced then Montana suffers a severe drought.

6. If equality of opportunity is to be achieved then those people previously disadvantaged should now be given special opportunities. If those people previously disadvantaged should now be given special opportunities then some people receive preferential treatment. If some people receive preferential treatment then equality of opportunity is not to be achieved. Therefore equality of opportunity is not to be achieved.

7. If terrorists' demands are met then lawlessness will be rewarded. If terrorists' demands are not met then innocent hostages will be murdered. So either lawlessness will be rewarded or innocent hostages will be murdered.

8. If people are entirely rational then either all of a person's actions can be predicted in advance or the universe is essentially deterministic. Not all of a person's actions can be predicted in advance. Thus if the universe is not essentially deterministic then people are not entirely rational.

9. If oil consumption continues to grow then either oil imports will increase or domestic oil reserves will be depleted. If oil imports increase and domestic oil reserves are depleted then the nation will soon be bankrupt. Therefore if oil consumption continues to grow then the nation will soon be bankrupt.

10. If oil consumption continues to grow then oil imports will increase and domestic oil reserves will be depleted. If either oil imports increase or domestic oil reserves are depleted then the nation will soon be bankrupt. Therefore if oil consumption continues to grow then the nation will soon be bankrupt.

8.5 *Statement Forms, Material Equivalence, and Logical Equivalence*

1. Statement Forms and Statements

We now make explicit a notion tacitly assumed in the preceding section, the notion of a *statement form*. There is an exact parallel between the relation of argument to argument form, on the one hand, and the relation of statement to statement form, on the other. The definition of "statement form" makes this evident: "a statement form is any sequence of symbols containing statement variables but no statements, such that when statements are substituted for the statement variables—the same statement being substituted for the same statement variable throughout—the result is a statement." Thus $p \lor q$ is a statement form, for when statements are substituted for the variables p and q a statement results. Since the resulting statement is a disjunction, $p \lor q$ is called a *disjunctive statement form*. Analogously, $p \cdot q$ and $p \supset q$ are called *conjunctive* and *conditional statement forms*, and $\sim p$ is called a *negation form* or *denial form*. Just as any argument of a certain form is said to be a substitution instance of that argument form, so any statement of a certain form is said to be a substitution instance of that statement form. And just as we distinguished *the specific form* of a given argument, so we distinguish *the specific form* of a given statement as that statement form from which the statement results by substituting a different *simple* statement for each different statement variable. Thus *p* v *q* is *the specific form* of the statement "The blind prisoner has a red hat or the blind prisoner has a white hat."

2. Tautologous, Contradictory, and Contingent Statement Forms

It is perfectly natural to feel that although the statements "Lincoln was assassinated" (symbolized as *L*) and "Either Lincoln was assassinated or else he wasn't" (symbolized as *L* v ~*L*) are both *true*, they are true "in different ways," or have "different kinds" of truth. Similarly, it is perfectly natural to feel that although the statements "Washington was assassinated" (symbolized as *W*) and "Washington was both assassinated and not assassinated" (symbolized as *W* • ~*W*) are both *false*, they are false "in different ways," or have "different kinds" of falsehood. While not pretending to give any kind of psychological explanation of these "feelings," we can nevertheless point out certain logical differences to which they are probably appropriate.

The statement *L* is true and the statement *W* is false; these are historical facts. There is no logical necessity about them. Events might have occurred differently, and the truth values of such statements as *L* and *W* must be discovered by an empirical study of history. But the statement *L* v ~*L*, although true, is not a truth of history. There is logical necessity here, events could not have been such as to make it false, and its truth can be known independently of any particular empirical investigation. The statement *L* v ~*L* is a logical truth, a formal truth, true in virtue of its form alone. It is a substitution instance of a statement form *all* of whose substitution instances are true statements.

A statement form that has only true substitution instances is called a *tautologous* statement form, or a *tautology*. To show that the statement form *p* v ~*p* is a tautology, we construct the following truth table:

p	~*p*	*p* v ~*p*
T	F	T
F	T	T

There is only one initial or guide column to this truth table, since the form under consideration contains only one statement variable. Consequently, there are only two rows, which represent all possible substitution instances. There are only T's in the column under the statement form in question, and this fact shows that all of its substitution instances are true. Any statement that is a substitution instance of a tautologous statement form is true in virtue of its form and is itself said to be tautologous, or a tautology.

A statement form that has only false substitution instances is said to be *self-contradictory,* or a *contradiction,* and is logically false. The statement form $p \cdot \sim p$ is self-contradictory, for in its truth table only **F**'s occur under it, signifying that all of its substitution instances are false. Any statement, such as $W \cdot \sim W$, which is a substitution instance of a self-contradictory statement form, is false in virtue of its form and is itself said to be self-contradictory, or a contradiction.

Statement forms that have both true and false statements among their substitution instances are called *contingent* statement forms. Any statement whose specific form is contingent is called a contingent statement.[11] Thus p, $\sim p$, $p \cdot q$, $p \vee q$, and $p \supset q$ are all contingent statement forms. And such statements as L, $\sim L$, $L \cdot W$, $L \vee W$, and $L \supset W$ are contingent statements, since their truth values are dependent or contingent on their contents rather than on their forms alone.

Not all statement forms are so obviously tautological or self-contradictory or contingent as the simple examples cited. For example, the statement form $[(p \supset q) \supset p] \supset p$ is not at all obvious, though its truth table will show it to be a tautology. It even has a special name, "Peirce's Law."

3. Material Equivalence

Two statements are said to be *materially equivalent,* or *equivalent in truth value,* when they are either both true or both false. This notion is expressed by the symbol "$\equiv$." Material equivalence is a truth function and can be defined by the following truth table:

p	q	$p \equiv q$
T	T	T
T	F	F
F	T	F
F	F	T

Whenever two statements are materially equivalent, they materially imply each other. This is easily verified by a truth table. Hence the symbol "$\equiv$" may be read "if and only if." A statement of the form $p \equiv q$ is called a *biconditional,* and the form is also called a *biconditional.*

4. Logical Equivalence

The notion of "logical equivalence" is both more important and more complicated. In dealing with truth-functional compound statements we give the following definition: two statements are *logically equivalent* when the (state-

---

[11]It will be recalled that we are assuming here that no simple statements are either logically true or logically false. Only contingent simple statements are admitted here. See footnote 9 on page 276.

ment) of their material equivalence is a tautology. Thus the "principle of double negation," expressed as the biconditional $p \equiv \sim\sim p$, is proved to be tautologous by the following truth table:

p	$\sim p$	$\sim\sim p$	$p \equiv \sim\sim p$
T	F	T	T
F	T	F	T

which proves the logical equivalence of $p \sim\sim p$.

The difference between logical equivalence on the one hand and material equivalence on the other hand is very great and very important. Two statements are logically equivalent only when it is absolutely impossible for the two statements to have different truth values. Therefore, logically equivalent statements have the same meaning, and may be substituted for one another in any truth-functional context without changing the truth value of that context. But two statements are materially equivalent (even if they have no factual connections with one another) if they merely happen to have the same truth value. Statements that are merely materially equivalent, therefore, certainly may not be substituted for one another.

5. De Morgan's Theorems

There are two logical equivalences (i.e., logically true biconditionals) of some intrinsic interest and importance that express the interrelations among conjunction, disjunction, and negation. Since the disjunction $p \vee q$ asserts merely that *at least one* of its two disjuncts is *true*, it is not contradicted by asserting that *at least one is false*, but only by asserting that *both* are false. Thus asserting the negation of the disjunction $p \vee q$ is logically equivalent to asserting the conjunction of the negations of p and of q. In symbols we have the biconditional $\sim(p \vee q) \equiv (\sim p \cdot \sim q)$, whose logical truth is established by the following truth table:

p	q	$p \vee q$	$\sim(p \vee q)$	$\sim p$	$\sim q$	$\sim p \cdot \sim q$	$\sim(p \vee q) \equiv (\sim p \cdot \sim q)$
T	T	T	F	F	F	F	T
T	F	T	F	F	T	F	T
F	T	T	F	T	F	F	T
F	F	F	T	T	T	T	T

Similarly, since asserting the conjunction of p and q asserts that *both* are *true*, to contradict it we need merely assert that *at least one* is *false*. Thus asserting the negation of the conjunction $p \cdot q$ is logically equivalent to asserting the disjunction of the negations of p and of q. In symbols we have the biconditional $\sim(p \cdot q) \equiv (\sim p \vee \sim q)$, which is easily proved to be a tautology. These two tautologous biconditionals are known as De Morgan's Theorems, having been stated by the mathematician and logician Augustus De Morgan

(1806–1871). De Morgan's Theorems can be given a combined formulation in English as

The negation of the $\begin{Bmatrix} \text{disjunction} \\ \text{conjunction} \end{Bmatrix}$ of two statements is logically

equivalent to the $\begin{Bmatrix} \text{conjunction} \\ \text{disjunction} \end{Bmatrix}$ of the negations of the two statements.

6. The Definition of Material Implication

Earlier (in Section 8.3) we defined material implication, the horseshoe, by treating $p \supset q$ as simply an abbreviated way of saying $\sim(p \cdot \sim q)$. That is, p materially implies q, we said, simply means (by definition) that it is not the case that p is true while q is false. The definiendum in this definition, $\sim(p \cdot \sim q)$ is plainly the denial of a conjunction. And by De Morgan's Theorem we know that any such denial is logically equivalent to the disjunction of the denials of the conjuncts; that is, we know that $\sim(p \cdot \sim q)$ is logically equivalent to $\sim p \vee \sim\sim q$; and this expression in turn (using the principle of double negation) is logically equivalent to $\sim p \vee q$. Logically equivalent expressions mean the same thing, and therefore the original definiendum of the horseshoe, $\sim(p \cdot \sim q)$, may be replaced, with no change of meaning, by the simpler expression, $\sim p \vee q$. The resulting definition of material implication: $p \supset q$ is logically equivalent to $\sim p \vee q$, is the one most commonly used, and we will find that it is extremely useful.

Finally, there is an important relationship between tautologies and valid arguments. To every argument there corresponds a conditional statement whose antecedent is the conjunction of the argument's premises and whose consequent is the argument's conclusion. Thus to any argument of the form

$$p \supset q$$
$$p$$
$$\therefore q$$

corresponds a conditional statement of the form $[(p \supset q) \cdot p] \supset q$. It is clear that a truth table that proves an argument form valid will also show its corresponding conditional statement form to be tautologous. An argument form is valid if and only if its truth table has a **T** under the conclusion in every row in which there are **T**'s under all of its premises. But an **F** can occur in the column headed by the corresponding conditional statement form only in a row in which there are **T**'s under all the premises and an **F** under the conclusion. Hence only **T**'s will occur under a conditional that corresponds to a valid argument. Thus for every valid argument of the truth-functional variety discussed in the present chapter, the statement that the conjunction of its premises implies its conclusion is a tautology. And for every invalid argument of the truth-functional variety, the statement that the conjunction of its premises implies its conclusion is either contingent or contradictory.

EXERCISES

I. For each statement in the left-hand column indicate which, if any, of the statement forms in the right-hand column have the given statement as a substitution instance, and indicate which, if any, is the specific form of the given statement.

★ 1. $A \text{ v } B$ a. $p \cdot q$
   2. $C \cdot {\sim}D$ b. $p \supset q$
   3. ${\sim}E \supset (F \cdot G)$ c. $p \text{ v } q$
   4. $H \supset (I \cdot J)$ d. $p \cdot {\sim}q$
★ 5. $(K \cdot L) \text{ v } (M \cdot N)$ e. $p \equiv q$
   6. $(O \text{ v } P) \supset (P \cdot Q)$ f. $(p \supset q) \text{ v } (r \cdot s)$
   7. $(R \supset S) \text{ v } (T \cdot {\sim}U)$ g. $[(p \supset q) \supset r] \supset s$
   8. $V \supset (W \text{ v } {\sim}W)$ h. $[(p \supset q) \supset p] \supset p$
   9. $[(X \supset Y) \supset X] \supset X$ i. $(p \cdot q) \text{ v } (r \cdot s)$
  10. $Z \equiv {\sim}{\sim}Z$ j. $p \supset (q \text{ v } {\sim}r)$

II. Use truth tables to characterize the following statement forms as tautologous, self-contradictory, or contingent.

★ 1. $[p \supset (p \supset q)] \supset q$ 2. $p \supset [p \supset q) \supset q]$
   3. $(p \cdot q) \cdot (p \supset {\sim}q)$ 4. $p \supset [{\sim}p \supset (q \text{ v } {\sim}q)]$
★ 5. $p \supset [p \supset (q \cdot {\sim}q)]$ 6. $(p \supset p) \supset (q \cdot {\sim}q)$
   7. $[p \supset (q \supset r)] \supset [(p \supset q) \supset (p \supset r)]$
   8. $[p \supset (q \supset p)] \supset [(q \supset q) \supset {\sim}(r \supset r)]$
   9. $\{[(p \supset q) \cdot (r \supset s)] \cdot (p \text{ v } r)\} \supset (q \text{ v } s)$
  10. $\{[(p \supset q) \cdot (r \supset s)] \cdot (q \text{ v } s)\} \supset (p \text{ v } r)$

III. Use truth tables to decide which of the following biconditionals are tautologies.

★ 1. $(p \supset q) \equiv ({\sim}q \supset {\sim}p)$ 2. $(p \supset q) \equiv ({\sim}p \supset {\sim}q)$
   3. $[(p \supset q) \supset r] \equiv [(q \supset p) \supset r]$ 4. $[p \supset (q \supset r)] \equiv [q \supset (p \supset r)]$
★ 5. $p \equiv [p \cdot (p \text{ v } q)]$ 6. $p \equiv [p \text{ v } (p \cdot q)]$
   7. $p \equiv [p \cdot (p \supset q)]$ 8. $p \equiv [p \cdot (q \supset p)]$
   9. $p \equiv [p \text{ v } (p \supset q)]$ ★ 10. $(p \supset q) \equiv [(p \text{ v } q) \equiv q]$
  11. $p \equiv [p \text{ v } (q \cdot {\sim}q)]$ 12. $p \equiv [p \cdot (q \cdot {\sim}q)]$
  13. $p \equiv [p \cdot (q \text{ v } {\sim}q)]$ 14. $p \equiv [p \text{ v } (q \text{ v } {\sim}q)]$
★ 15. $[p \cdot (q \text{ v } r)] \equiv [(p \cdot q) \text{ v } (p \cdot r)]$
  16. $[p \cdot (q \text{ v } r)] \equiv [(p \text{ v } q) \cdot (p \text{ v } r)]$
  17. $[p \text{ v } (q \cdot r)] \equiv [(p \cdot q) \text{ v } (p \cdot r)]$

18. $[p \lor (q \cdot r)] \equiv [(p \lor q) \cdot (p \lor r)]$
19. $[(p \cdot q) \supset r] \equiv [p \supset (q \supset r)]$
20. $[(p \supset q) \cdot (q \supset p)] \equiv [(p \cdot q) \lor (\sim p \cdot \sim q)]$

8.6 *The Paradoxes of Material Implication*

There are two forms of statements, $p \supset (q \supset p)$ and $\sim p \supset (p \supset q)$, that are easily proved to be tautologies. Trivial as these statement forms may be in their symbolic formulation, when stated in ordinary English they seem surprising and even paradoxical. The first may be stated as "If a statement is true then it is implied by any statement whatever." Since it is true that the earth is round, it follows that "The moon is made of green cheese implies that the earth is round"; and this is very curious indeed, especially since it also follows that "The moon is *not* made of green cheese implies that the earth is round." The second tautology may be stated as "If a statement is false then it implies any statement whatever." Since it is false that the moon is made of green cheese, it follows that "The moon is made of green cheese implies that the earth is round"; and this is all the more curious when we realize that it also follows that "The moon is made of green cheese implies that the earth is *not* round."

These seem paradoxical because we believe that the shape of the earth and the matter of the moon are utterly irrelevant to each other, and we believe further that no statement, true or false, can really imply any other statement, false or true, to which it is utterly irrelevant. And yet truth tables establish that a false statement implies any statement, and that a true statement is implied by any statement. This paradox is easily resolved, however, when we acknowledge the ambiguity of the word "implies." In several senses of the word "implies" it is perfectly true that no contingent statement can imply any other contingent statement with unrelated subject matter. It is true in the case of *logical* implication and of *definitional* and *causal* implications. It may even be true of *decisional* implications, although here the notion of *relevance* may have to be construed more broadly.

But subject matter or *meaning* is strictly irrelevant to *material implication*, which is a truth function. Only truth and falsehood are relevant here. There is nothing paradoxical in stating that any disjunction is true which contains at least one true disjunct, and this fact is all that is asserted by statements of the forms $p \supset (\sim q \lor p)$ and $\sim p \supset (\sim p \lor q)$, which are logically equivalent to the "paradoxical" ones. We have already given a justification of treating material implication as *a* sense of "if–then," and of the logical expediency of translating *every* occurrence of "if–then" into the "$\supset$" notation. That justification was the fact that translating "if–then" into the "$\supset$" preserves the validity of all valid arguments of the type with which we are concerned in this part of our logical studies. There are other proposed symbolizations, adequate to other types of implication, but they belong to more advanced parts of logic, beyond the scope of this book.

8.7 *The Three "Laws of Thought"*

Those who have defined logic as the science of the laws of thought have often gone on to assert that there are exactly three fundamental or basic laws of thought necessary and sufficient for thinking to follow if it is to be "correct." These have traditionally been called the Principle of Identity, the Principle of Contradiction (sometimes the Principle of Noncontradiction), and the Principle of Excluded Middle. There are alternative formulations of these principles, appropriate to different contexts. The formulations appropriate here are the following:

> The Principle of Identity asserts that *if any statement is true, then it is true.*
>
> The Principle of Contradiction asserts that *no statement can be both true and false.*
>
> The Principle of Excluded Middle asserts that *any statement is either true or false.*

In the terminology of the present chapter, we may rephrase them as follows. The Principle of Identity asserts that every statement of the form $p \supset p$ is true, that is, that every such statement is a tautology. The Principle of Contradiction asserts that every statement of the form $p \cdot \sim p$ is false, that is, that every such statement is self-contradictory. The Principle of Excluded Middle asserts that every statement of the form $p \vee \sim p$ is true, that is, that every such statement is a tautology.

Objections have been made to these principles from time to time, but for the most part the objections seem to be based upon misunderstandings. The Principle of Identity has been criticized on the grounds that things change, for what was true, say, of the United States when it consisted of the thirteen original tiny states is no longer true of the United States today with its fifty states. In one sense of the word "statement" this observation is correct; but that sense is not the one with which logic is concerned. Those "statements" whose truth values change with time are *elliptical* or incomplete formulations of propositions that do not change, and it is the latter with which logic deals. Thus the sentence "There are only thirteen states in the United States" may be regarded as an elliptical or partial formulation of "There were only thirteen states in the United States *in 1790*," which is just as true in the twentieth century as it was in 1790. When we confine our attention to *complete* or *nonelliptical* formulations, the Principle of Identity is perfectly true and unobjectionable.

The Principle of Contradiction has been criticized by Hegelians, General Semanticists, and Marxists, on the grounds that there are contradictions, or situations in which contradictory or conflicting forces are at work. That there are situations containing conflicting forces must be admitted: this is as true in the realm of mechanics as in the social and economic spheres. But it is a loose and inconvenient terminology to call these conflicting forces "contradictory." The heat applied to a contained gas, which tends to make it expand,

and the container, which tends to keep it from expanding, may be described as conflicting with each other, but neither is the negation or denial or contradictory of the other. The private owner of a large factory, which requires thousands of laborers working together for its operation, may oppose and be opposed by the labor union that could never have been organized if its members had not been brought together to work in that factory; but neither owner nor union is the negation or denial or contradictory of the other. When understood in the sense in which it is intended, the Principle of Contradiction is unobjectionable and perfectly true.

The Principle of Excluded Middle has been the object of more attacks than either of the other principles. It has been urged that its acceptance leads to a "two-valued orientation," which implies, among other things, that everything is either white or black, with any middle ground excluded. But although the statement "this is black" cannot be jointly true along with the statement "this is white" (where the word "this" refers to exactly the same thing in both statements), one is not the denial or contradictory of the other. Admittedly they cannot both be true, but they can both be false. They are contrary, but not contradictory. The negation or contradictory of "this is white," is "$\sim$ this is white," and one of these statements must be true—if the word "white" is used in precisely the same sense in both statements. When restricted to statements containing completely unambiguous and perfectly precise terms, the Principle of Excluded Middle also is perfectly true.

Although the three principles are true, it may be doubted that they have the privileged and fundamental status traditionally assigned them. The first and third are not the only forms of tautologies, and the explicit contradiction $p \cdot \sim p$ is not the only contradictory form of statement. Yet the three Laws of Thought *can* be regarded as having a certain fundamental status in relation to truth tables. As we fill in subsequent columns by referring back to the initial columns, we are guided by the Principle of Identity: if a **T** has been placed under a symbol in a certain row, then in filling in other columns under expressions containing that symbol, when we come to that row we consider that symbol still to be assigned a **T**. In filling out the initial columns, in each row we put either a **T** or an **F**, being guided by the Principle of Excluded Middle; and nowhere do we put both **T** and **F** together, being guided by the Principle of Contradiction. The three Laws of Thought can be regarded as the basic principles governing the construction of truth tables.

Still, it should be remarked that when one attempts to set up logic as a system, the three laws are not merely no more "important" or "fruitful" than any others, but there are other tautologies that are more fruitful for purposes of deduction—and hence more important—than the three principles discussed. A treatment of this point, however, lies beyond the scope of this book.[12]

---

[12]For further discussion of these matters, the interested reader can consult I. M. Copi and J. A. Gould, eds., *Readings on Logic*, Part 3, 2nd ed. (New York: Macmillan Publishing Company, 1972); and I. M. Copi and J. A. Gould, eds., *Contemporary Philosophical Logic*, Part 8 (New York: St. Martin's Press, Inc., 1978).

9

The Method of Deduction

For as one may feel sure that a chain will hold when he is assured that each separate link is of good material and that it clasps the two neighboring links, viz., the one preceding and the one following it, so we may be sure of the accuracy of the reasoning when the matter is good, that is to say, when nothing doubtful enters into it, and when the form consists in a perpetual concatenation of truths which allows of no gap.

—GOTTFRIED LEIBNIZ

It cannot be demanded that we should prove everything, because that is impossible; but we can require that all propositions used without proof be expressly declared to be so. . . . Furthermore I demand—and in this I go beyond Euclid—that all of the methods of inference used must be specified in advance.

—GOTTLOB FREGE

9.1 *Formal Proof of Validity*

In theory, truth tables are adequate to test the validity of any argument of the general type here considered. But in practice they grow unwieldy as the number of component statements increases. A more efficient method of establishing the validity of an extended argument is to deduce its conclusion from its premises by a sequence of elementary arguments each of which is known to be valid. This technique accords fairly well with ordinary methods of argumentation.

Consider, for example, the following argument:

If Anderson was nominated, then she went to Boston.
If she went to Boston, then she campaigned there.
If she campaigned there, she met Douglas.
Anderson did not meet Douglas.
Either Anderson was nominated or someone more eligible was selected.
Therefore someone more eligible was selected.

Its validity may be intuitively obvious, but let us consider the matter of proof. The discussion will be facilitated by translating the argument into our symbolism as

$$A \supset B$$
$$B \supset C$$
$$C \supset D$$
$$\sim D$$
$$A \lor E$$
$$\therefore E$$

To establish the validity of this argument by means of a truth table would require one with thirty-two rows, since there are five different simple statements involved. But we can prove the given argument valid by deducing its conclusion from its premisses by a sequence of just four elementary valid arguments. From the first two premisses $A \supset B$ and $B \supset C$ we validly infer $A \supset C$ by a Hypothetical Syllogism. From $A \supset C$ and the third premiss $C \supset D$ we validly infer $A \supset D$ by another Hypothetical Syllogism. From $A \supset D$ and the fourth premiss $\sim D$ we validly infer $\sim A$ by *modus tollens*. And from $\sim A$ and the fifth premiss $A \lor E$, by a Disjunctive Syllogism we validly infer E, the conclusion of the original argument. That the conclusion can be deduced from the five premisses of the original argument by four elementary valid arguments proves the original argument to be valid. Here the elementary valid argument forms Hypothetical Syllogism (H.S.), *modus tollens* (M.T.), and Disjunctive Syllogism (D.S.) are used as *rules of inference* in accordance with which conclusions are validly inferred or deduced from premisses.

A more formal proof of validity is given by writing the premisses and the statements that we deduce from them in a single column, and setting off in another column, to the right of each such statement, its "justification," or the reason we can give for including it in the proof. It is convenient to list all the premisses first and to write the conclusion slightly to one side, separated by a diagonal line from the premisses. The diagonal line automatically labels all statements above it as premisses. If all the statements in the column are numbered, the "justification" for each statement consists of the numbers of the preceding statements from which it is inferred, together with the abbreviation for the rule of inference by which it follows from them. The formal proof is written as

1. $A \supset B$
2. $B \supset C$
3. $C \supset D$
4. $\sim D$
5. $A \lor E \mathbin{/} \therefore E$
6. $A \supset C$ \hspace{2cm} 1,2, H.S.

7. $A \supset D$ 6,3, H.S.
8. $\sim A$ 7,4, M.T.
9. E 5,8, D.S.

We define a *formal proof* that a given argument is valid to be a sequence of statements each of which is either a premiss of that argument or follows from preceding statements of the sequence by an elementary valid argument, and the last statement in the sequence is the conclusion of the argument whose validity is being proved.

We define an *elementary valid argument* to be any argument that is a substitution instance of an elementary valid argument form. One matter to be emphasized is that *any* substitution instance of an elementary valid argument form is an elementary valid argument. Thus the argument

$$(A \cdot B) \supset [C \equiv (D \text{ v } E)]$$
$$A \cdot B$$
$$\therefore C \equiv (D \text{ v } E)$$

is an elementary valid argument because it is a substitution instance of the elementary valid argument form *modus ponens* (M.P.). It results from

$$p \supset q$$
$$p$$
$$\therefore q$$

by substituting $A \cdot B$ for p and $C \equiv (D \text{ v } E)$ for q and is therefore of that form even though *modus ponens* is not *the specific form* of the given argument.

Modus ponens is a very elementary valid argument form indeed, but what *other* valid argument forms are to be included as Rules of Inference? We begin with a list of just nine Rules of Inference to be used in constructing formal proofs of validity:

Rules of Inference

1. *Modus Ponens* (M.P.)
$$p \supset q$$
$$p$$
$$\therefore q$$

2. *Modus Tollens* (M.T.)
$$p \supset q$$
$$\sim q$$
$$\therefore \sim p$$

3. *Hypothetical Syllogism* (H.S.)
$$p \supset q$$
$$q \supset r$$
$$\therefore p \supset r$$

4. *Disjunctive Syllogism* (D.S.)
$$p \text{ v } q$$
$$\sim p$$
$$\therefore q$$

5. *Constructive Dilemma* (C.D.)
$$(p \supset q) \cdot (r \supset s)$$
$$p \text{ v } r$$
$$\therefore q \text{ v } s$$

6. *Absorption* (Abs.)
$$p \supset q$$
$$\therefore p \supset (p \cdot q)$$

7. *Simplification* (Simp.)

$p \cdot q$
$\therefore p$

8. *Conjunction* (Conj.)

p
q
$\therefore p \cdot q$

9. *Addition* (Add.)

p
$\therefore p \vee q$

These nine Rules of Inference correspond to elementary argument forms whose validity is easily established by truth tables. With their aid, formal proofs of validity can be constructed for a wide range of more complicated arguments. The names listed are for the most part standard, and the use of their abbreviations permits formal proofs to be set down with a minimum of writing.

EXERCISES

I. For each of the following elementary valid arguments state the Rule of Inference by which its conclusion follows from its premiss or premisses.

★ 1. $(A \cdot B) \supset C$
  $\therefore (A \cdot B) \supset [(A \cdot B) \cdot C]$

2. $(D \vee E) \cdot (F \vee G)$
  $\therefore D \vee E$

3. $H \supset I$
  $\therefore (H \supset I) \vee (H \supset \sim I)$

4. $\sim(J \cdot K) \cdot (L \supset \sim M)$
  $\therefore \sim(J \cdot K)$

★ 5. $[N \supset (O \cdot P)] \cdot [Q \supset (O \cdot R)]$
  $N \vee Q$
  $\therefore (O \cdot P) \vee (O \cdot R)$

6. $(X \vee Y) \supset \sim(Z \cdot \sim A)$
  $\sim\sim(Z \cdot \sim A)$
  $\therefore \sim(X \vee Y)$

7. $(S \equiv T) \vee [(U \cdot V) \vee (U \cdot W)]$
  $\sim(S \equiv T)$
  $\therefore (U \cdot V) \vee (U \cdot W)$

8. $\sim(B \cdot C) \supset (D \vee E)$
  $\sim(B \cdot C)$
  $\therefore D \vee E$

9. $(F \equiv G) \supset \sim(G \cdot \sim F)$
  $\sim(G \cdot \sim F) \supset (G \supset F)$
  $\therefore (F \equiv G) \supset (G \supset F)$

★ 10. $\sim(H \cdot \sim I) \supset (H \supset I)$
   $(I \equiv H) \supset \sim(H \cdot \sim I)$
   $\therefore (I \equiv H) \supset (H \supset I)$

11. $(A \supset B) \supset (C \vee D)$
   $A \supset B$
   $\therefore C \vee D$

12. $[E \supset (F \equiv \sim G)] \vee (C \vee D)$
   $\sim[E \supset (F \equiv \sim G)]$
   $\therefore C \vee D$

13. $(C \vee D) \supset [(J \vee K) \supset (J \cdot K)]$
   $\sim[(J \vee K) \supset (J \cdot K)]$
   $\therefore \sim(C \vee D)$

14. $\sim[L \supset (M \supset N)] \supset \sim(C \vee D)$
   $\sim[L \supset (M \supset N)]$
   $\therefore \sim(C \vee D)$

★ 15. $(J \supset K) \cdot (K \supset L)$
   $L \supset M$
   $\therefore [(J \supset K) \cdot (K \supset L)] \cdot (L \supset M)$

16. $N \supset (O \vee P)$
   $Q \supset (O \vee R)$
   $\therefore [Q \supset (O \vee R)] \cdot [N \supset (O \vee P)]$

17. $(S \supset T) \supset (U \supset V)$
   $\therefore (S \supset T) \supset [(S \supset T) \cdot (U \supset V)]$

18. $(W \cdot {\sim}X) \equiv (Y \supset Z)$
    $\therefore [(W \cdot {\sim}X) \equiv (Y \supset Z)] \vee (X \equiv {\sim}Z)$
19. $[(H \cdot {\sim}I) \supset C] \cdot [(I \cdot {\sim}H) \supset D]$
    $(H \cdot {\sim}I) \vee (I \cdot {\sim}H)$
    $\therefore C \vee D$
20. $[(O \supset P) \supset Q] \supset {\sim}(C \vee D)$
    $(C \vee D) \supset [(O \supset P) \supset Q]$
    $\therefore (C \vee D) \supset {\sim}(C \vee D)$

II. Each of the following is a formal proof of validity for the indicated argument. State the "justification" for each line that is not a premiss.

★ 1.
1. $A \cdot B$
2. $(A \vee C) \supset D \ / \ \therefore A \cdot D$
3. A
4. $A \vee C$
5. D
6. $A \cdot D$

3.
1. $I \supset J$
2. $J \supset K$
3. $L \supset M$
4. $I \vee L \ / \ \therefore K \vee M$
5. $I \supset K$
6. $(I \supset K) \cdot (L \supset M)$
7. $K \vee M$

★ 5.
1. $Q \supset R$
2. ${\sim}S \supset (T \supset U)$
3. $S \vee (Q \vee T)$
4. ${\sim}S \ / \ \therefore R \vee U$
5. $T \supset U$
6. $(Q \supset R) \cdot (T \supset U)$
7. $Q \vee T$
8. $R \vee U$

7.
1. $(A \vee B) \supset C$
2. $(C \vee B) \supset [A \supset (D \equiv E)]$
3. $A \cdot D \ / \ \therefore D \equiv E$
4. A
5. $A \vee B$
6. C
7. $C \vee B$
8. $A \supset (D \equiv E)$
9. $D \equiv E$

9.
1. $I \supset J$
2. $I \vee ({\sim}{\sim}K \cdot {\sim}{\sim}J)$
3. $L \supset {\sim}K$
4. ${\sim}(I \cdot J) \ / \ \therefore {\sim}L \vee {\sim}J$
5. $I \supset (I \cdot J)$
6. ${\sim}I$
7. ${\sim}{\sim}K \cdot {\sim}{\sim}J$

2.
1. $(E \vee F) \cdot (G \vee H)$
2. $(E \supset G) \cdot (F \supset H)$
3. ${\sim}G \ / \ \therefore H$
4. $E \vee F$
5. $G \vee H$
6. H

4.
1. $N \supset O$
2. $(N \cdot O) \supset P$
3. ${\sim}(N \cdot P) \ / \ \therefore {\sim}N$
4. $N \supset (N \cdot O)$
5. $N \supset P$
6. $N \supset (N \cdot P)$
7. ${\sim}N$

6.
1. $W \supset X$
2. $(W \supset Y) \supset (Z \vee X)$
3. $(W \cdot X) \supset Y$
4. ${\sim}Z \ / \ \therefore X$
5. $W \supset (W \cdot X)$
6. $W \supset Y$
7. $Z \vee X$
8. X

8.
1. $F \supset {\sim}G$
2. ${\sim}F \supset (H \supset {\sim}G)$
3. $({\sim}I \vee {\sim}H) \supset {\sim}{\sim}G$
4. ${\sim}I \ / \ \therefore {\sim}H$
5. ${\sim}I \vee {\sim}H$
6. ${\sim}{\sim}G$
7. ${\sim}F$
8. $H \supset {\sim}G$
9. ${\sim}H$

8. ${\sim}{\sim}K$
9. ${\sim}L$
10. ${\sim}L \vee {\sim}J$

10.　1. $(L \supset M) \supset (N \equiv O)$
　　　2. $(P \supset {\sim}Q) \supset (M \equiv {\sim}Q)$
　　　3. $\{[P \supset {\sim}Q) \mathbin{v} (R \equiv S)] \cdot (N \mathbin{v} O)\} \supset [(R \equiv S) \supset (L \supset M)]$
　　　4. $(P \supset {\sim}Q) \mathbin{v} (R \equiv S)$
　　　5. $N \mathbin{v} O$ / $\therefore (M \equiv {\sim}Q) \mathbin{v} (N \equiv O)$
　　　6. $[(P \supset {\sim}Q) \mathbin{v} (R \equiv S)] \cdot (N \mathbin{v} O)$
　　　7. $(R \equiv S) \supset (L \supset M)$
　　　8. $(R \equiv S) \supset (N \equiv O)$
　　　9. $[(P \supset {\sim}Q) \supset (M = {\sim}Q)] \cdot [(R \equiv S) \supset (N \equiv O)]$
　　10. $(M \equiv {\sim}Q) \mathbin{v} (N \equiv O)$

III. For each of the following, adding just two statements to the premisses will produce a formal proof of validity. Construct a formal proof of validity for each of the following arguments.

★　1. A
　　　B / $\therefore (A \mathbin{v} C) \cdot B$

　　2. $D \supset E$
　　　$D \cdot F$ / $\therefore E$

　　3. G
　　　H / $\therefore (G \cdot H)) \mathbin{v} I$

　　4. $J \supset K$
　　　J / $\therefore K \mathbin{v} L$

★　5. $M \mathbin{v} N$
　　　${\sim}M \cdot {\sim}O$ / $\therefore N$

　　6. $P \cdot Q$
　　　R / $\therefore P \cdot R$

　　7. $S \supset T$
　　　${\sim}T \cdot {\sim}U$ / $\therefore {\sim}S$

　　8. $V \mathbin{v} W$
　　　${\sim}V$ / $\therefore W \mathbin{v} X$

　　9. $Y \supset Z$
　　　Y / $\therefore Y \cdot Z$

★　10. $A \supset B$
　　　$(A \cdot B) \supset C$ / $\therefore A \supset C$

　11. $D \supset E$
　　　$(E \supset F) \cdot (F \supset D)$ / $\therefore D \supset F$

　12. $(G \supset H)) \cdot (I \supset J)$
　　　G / $\therefore H) \mathbin{v} J$

　13. ${\sim}(K \cdot L)$
　　　$K \supset L$ / $\therefore {\sim}K$

　14. $(M \supset N) \cdot (M \supset O)$
　　　$N \supset O$ / $\therefore M \supset O$

★　15. $(P \supset Q) \cdot (R \supset S)$
　　　$(P \mathbin{v} R) \cdot (Q \mathbin{v} R)$ / $\therefore Q \mathbin{v} S$

　16. $(T \supset U) \cdot (T \supset V)$
　　　T / $\therefore U \mathbin{v} V$

　17. $(W \mathbin{v} X) \supset Y$
　　　W / $\therefore Y$

　18. $(Z \cdot A) \supset (B \cdot C)$
　　　$Z \supset A$ / $\therefore Z \supset (B \cdot C)$

　19. $D \supset E$
　　　$[D \supset (D \cdot E)] \supset (F \supset {\sim}G)$ / $\therefore F \supset {\sim}G$

★　20. $({\sim}H) \mathbin{v} I) \mathbin{v} J$
　　　${\sim}({\sim}H) \mathbin{v} I)$ / $\therefore J \mathbin{v} {\sim}H)$

　21. $(K \supset L) \supset M$
　　　${\sim}M \cdot {\sim}(L \supset K)$ / $\therefore {\sim}(K \supset L)$

　22. $(N \supset O) \supset (P \supset Q)$
　　　$[P \supset (N \supset O)] \cdot [N \supset (P \supset Q)]$ / $\therefore P \supset (P \supset Q)$

　23. $R \supset S$
　　　$S \supset (S \cdot R)$ / $\therefore [R \supset (R \cdot S)] \cdot [S \supset (S \cdot R)]$

　24. $[T \supset (U \mathbin{v} V)] \cdot [U \supset (T \mathbin{v} V)]$
　　　$(T \mathbin{v} U) \cdot (U \mathbin{v} V)$ / $\therefore (U \mathbin{v} V) \mathbin{v} (T \mathbin{v} V)$

★ 25. $(W \cdot X) \supset (Y \cdot Z)$
$\sim[(W \cdot X) \cdot (Y \cdot Z)]$
$/ \therefore \sim(W \cdot X)$

27. $(E \cdot F) \vee (G \supset H))$
$I \supset G$
$\sim(E \cdot F) / \therefore I \supset H$

29. $(M \supset N) \cdot (O \supset P)$
$N \supset P$
$(N \supset P) \supset (M \vee O) / \therefore N \vee P$

26. $A \supset B$
$A \vee C$
$C \supset D / \therefore B \vee D$

28. $J \vee \sim K$
$K \vee (L \supset J)$
$\sim J / \therefore L \supset J$

30. $Q \supset (R \vee S)$
$(T \cdot U) \supset R$
$(R \vee S) \supset (T \cdot U) / \therefore Q \supset R$

IV. For each of the following, adding just three statements to the premises will produce a formal proof of validity. Construct a formal proof of validity for each of the following arguments.

★ 1. $A \vee (B \supset A)$
$\sim A \cdot C / \therefore \sim B$

3. $(H \supset I) \cdot (H) \supset J)$
$H \cdot (I \vee J) / \therefore I \vee J$

★ 5. $N \supset [(N \cdot O) \supset P]$
$N \cdot O / \therefore P$

7. $T \supset U$
$V \vee \sim U$
$\sim V \cdot \sim W / \therefore \sim T$

9. $(A \vee B) \supset \sim C$
$C \vee D$
$A / \therefore D$

11. $(H) \supset I) \cdot (J \supset K)$
$K \vee H)$
$\sim K / \therefore I$

13. $(P \supset Q) \cdot (Q \supset P)$
$R \supset S$
$P \vee R / \therefore Q \vee S$

15. $(Z \cdot A) \supset B$
$B \supset A$
$(B \cdot A) \supset (A \cdot B) / \therefore (Z \cdot A) \supset (A \cdot B)$

2. $(D \vee E) \supset (F \cdot G)$
$D / \therefore F$

4. $(K \cdot L) \supset M$
$K \supset L / \therefore K \supset [(K \cdot L) \cdot M]$

6. $Q \supset R$
$R \supset S$
$\sim S / \therefore \sim Q \cdot \sim R$

8. $\sim X \supset Y$
$Z \supset X$
$\sim X / \therefore Y \cdot \sim Z$

★ 10. $E \vee \sim F$
$F \vee (E \vee G)$
$\sim E / \therefore G$

12. $L \vee (M \supset N)$
$\sim L \supset (N \supset O)$
$\sim L / \therefore M \supset O$

14. $(T \supset U) \cdot (V \supset W)$
$(U \supset X) \cdot (W \supset Y)$
$T / \therefore X \vee Y$

V. Construct a formal proof of validity for each of the following arguments.

★ 1. $A \supset B$
$A \vee (C \cdot D)$
$\sim B \cdot \sim E$
$\therefore C$

3. $(\sim M \cdot \sim N) \supset (O \supset N)$
$N \supset M$
$\sim M$
$\therefore \sim O$

2. $(F \supset G) \cdot (H) \supset I)$
$J \supset K$
$(F \vee J) \cdot (H) \vee L$
$\therefore G \vee K$

4. $(K \vee L) \supset (M \vee N)$
$(M \vee N) \supset (O \cdot P)$
K
$\therefore O$

★ 5. $(Q \supset R) \cdot (S \supset T)$
$(U \supset V) \cdot (W \supset X)$
$Q \vee U$
$\therefore R \vee V$

7. $A \supset B$
$C \supset D$
$A \vee C$
$\therefore (A \cdot B) \vee (C \cdot D)$

9. $J \supset K$
$K \vee L$
$(L \cdot {\sim}J) \supset (M \cdot {\sim}J)$
${\sim}K$
$\therefore M$

6. $W \supset X$
$(W \cdot X) \supset Y$
$(W \cdot Y) \supset Z$
$\therefore W \supset Z$

8. $(E \vee F) \supset (G \cdot H))$
$(G \vee H)) \supset I$
E
$\therefore I$

10. $(N \vee O) \supset P$
$(P \vee Q) \supset R$
$Q \vee N$
${\sim}Q$
$\therefore R$

VI. Construct a formal proof of validity for each of the following arguments, using the abbreviations suggested.

★ 1. If either Gertrude or Herbert wins, then both Jane and Kenneth lose. Gertrude wins. Therefore Jane loses. (G—Gertrude wins; H—Herbert wins; J—Jane loses; K—Kenneth loses.)

2. If Adams joins, then the club's social prestige will rise; and if Baker joins, then the club's financial position will be more secure. Either Adams or Baker will join. If the club's social prestige rises, then Baker will join; and if the club's financial position becomes more secure, then Wilson will join. Therefore either Baker or Wilson will join. (A—Adams joins; S—The club's social prestige rises; B—Baker joins; F—The club's financial position is more secure; W—Wilson joins.)

3. If Brown received the wire, then she took the plane; and if she took the plane, then she will not be late for the meeting. If the telegram was incorrectly addressed, then Brown will be late for the meeting. Either Brown received the wire or the telegram was incorrectly addressed. Therefore either Brown took the plane or she will be late for the meeting. (R—Brown received the wire; P—Brown took the plane; L—Brown will be late for the meeting; T—The telegram was incorrectly addressed.)

4. If Neville buys the lot, then an office building will be constructed; whereas if Payton buys the lot, then it quickly will be sold again. If Rivers buys the lot, then a store will be constructed; and if a store is constructed, then Thompson will offer to lease it. Either Neville or Rivers will buy the lot. Therefore either an office building or a store will be constructed. (N—Neville buys the lot; O—An office building will be constructed; P—Payton buys the lot; Q—The lot quickly will be sold again; R—Rivers buys the lot; S—A store will be constructed; T—Thompson will offer to lease it.)

★ 5. If rain continues, then the river rises. If rain continues and the river rises, then the bridge will wash out. If continuation of rain would cause the bridge to wash out, then a single road is not sufficient for the town. Either a single road is sufficient for the town or the traffic engineers have made a mistake. Therefore the traffic engineers have made a mistake. (C—Rain continues; R—The river rises; B—The bridge washes out; S—A single road is sufficient for the town; M—The traffic engineers have made a mistake.)

6. If Jacobson goes to the meeting, then a complete report will be made; but if Jacobson does not go to the meeting, then a special election will be required.

If a complete report is made, then an investigation will be launched. If Jacobson's going to the meeting implies that a complete report will be made, and the making of a complete report implies that an investigation will be launched, then either Jacobson goes to the meeting and an investigation is launched or Jacobson does not go to the meeting and no investigation is launched. If Jacobson goes to the meeting and an investigation is launched, then some members will have to stand trial. But if Jacobson does not go to the meeting and no investigation is launched, then the organization will disintegrate very rapidly. Therefore either some members will have to stand trial or the organization will disintegrate very rapidly. (J—Jacobson goes to the meeting; R—A complete report is made; E—A special election is required; I—An investigation is launched; T—Some members have to stand trial; D—The organization disintegrates very rapidly.)

7. If Ann is present, then Bill is present. If Ann and Bill are both present, then either Charles or Doris will be elected. If either Charles or Doris is elected, then Elmer does not really dominate the club. If Ann's presence implies that Elmer does not really dominate the club, then Florence will be the new president. So Florence will be the new president. (A—Ann is present; B—Bill is present; C—Charles will be elected; D—Doris will be elected; E—Elmer really dominates the club; F—Florence will be the new president.)

8. If Mr. Jones is the brakeman's next-door neighbor, then Mr. Jones's annual earnings are exactly divisible by 3. If Mr. Jones's annual earnings are exactly divisible by 3, then \$20,000 is exactly divisible by 3. But \$20,000 is not exactly divisible by 3. If Mr. Robinson is the brakeman's next-door neighbor, then Mr. Robinson lives halfway between Detroit and Chicago. If Mr. Robinson lives in Detroit, then he does not live halfway between Detroit and Chicago. Mr. Robinson lives in Detroit. If Mr. Jones is not the brakeman's next-door neighbor, then either Mr. Robinson or Mr. Smith is the brakeman's next-door neighbor. Therefore Mr. Smith is the brakeman's next-door neighbor. (J—Mr. Jones is the brakeman's next-door neighbor; E—Mr. Jones's annual earnings are exactly divisible by 3; T—\$20,000 is exactly divisible by 3; R—Mr. Robinson is the brakeman's next-door neighbor; H—Mr. Robinson lives halfway between Detroit and Chicago; D—Mr. Robinson lives in Detroit; S—Mr. Smith is the brakeman's next-door neighbor.)

9. If Mr. Smith is the brakeman's next-door neighbor, then Mr. Smith lives halfway between Detroit and Chicago. If Mr. Smith lives halfway between Detroit and Chicago, then he does not live in Chicago. Mr. Smith is the brakeman's next-door neighbor. If Mr. Robinson lives in Detroit, then he does not live in Chicago. Mr. Robinson lives in Detroit. Mr. Smith lives in Chicago or else either Mr. Robinson or Mr. Jones lives in Chicago. If Mr. Jones lives in Chicago, then the brakeman is Jones. Therefore the brakeman is Jones. (S—Mr. Smith is the brakeman's next-door neighbor; W—Mr. Smith lives halfway between Detroit and Chicago; L—Mr. Smith lives in Chicago; D—Mr. Robinson lives in Detroit; I—Mr. Robinson lives in Chicago; C—Mr. Jones lives in Chicago; B—The brakeman is Jones.)

10. If Smith once beat the fireman at billiards, then Smith is not the fireman. Smith once beat the fireman at billiards. If the brakeman is Jones, then Jones is not the fireman. The brakeman is Jones. If Smith is not the fireman and Jones is not the fireman, then Robinson is the fireman. If the brakeman is Jones and Robinson is the fireman, then Smith is the engineer. Therefore Smith is the en-

gineer. (*O*—Smith once beat the fireman at billiards; *M*—Smith is the fireman; *B*—The brakeman is Jones; *N*—Jones is the fireman; *F*—Robinson is the fireman; *G*—Smith is the engineer.)

9.2 *The Rule of Replacement*

There are many valid truth-functional arguments whose validity cannot be proved using only the nine Rules of Inference given thus far. For example, to construct a formal proof of validity for the obviously valid argument

$$A \supset B$$
$$C \supset {\sim}B$$
$$\therefore A \supset {\sim}C$$

additional rules are required.

In any truth-functional compound statement, if a component statement in it is replaced by another statement having the same truth value, the truth value of the compound statement will remain unchanged. But the only compound statements that concern us here are truth-functional compound statements. We may accept, therefore, as an additional principle of inference, the Rule of Replacement, which permits us to infer from any statement the result of replacing any component of that statement by any other statement *logically* equivalent to the component replaced. Using the Principle of Double Negation (D.N.), which asserts that p is logically equivalent to ${\sim}{\sim}p$, we can infer from $A \supset {\sim}{\sim}B$ any of the following:

$$A \supset B, \; {\sim}{\sim}A \supset {\sim}{\sim}B, \; {\sim}{\sim}(A \supset {\sim}{\sim}B), \; \text{or } A \supset {\sim}{\sim}{\sim}{\sim}B$$

by Replacement.

To make the new rule definite, we list a number of tautologous or logically true biconditionals with which it can be used. These biconditionals provide additional Rules of Inference to be used in proving the validity of extended arguments. We number them consecutively after the first nine Rules already stated.

Rule of Replacement: *Any of the following logically equivalent expressions may replace each other wherever they occur:*

---

10. *De Morgan's Theorems* (De M.): ${\sim}(p \cdot q) \equiv ({\sim}p \vee {\sim}q)$
                                                ${\sim}(p \vee q) \equiv ({\sim}p \cdot {\sim}q)$
11. *Commutation* (Com.): $(p \vee q) \equiv (q \vee p)$
                                                $(p \cdot q) \equiv (q \cdot p)$
12. *Association* (Assoc.): $[p \vee (q \vee r)] \equiv [(p \vee q) \vee r]$
                                             $[p \cdot (q \cdot r)] \equiv [(p \cdot q) \cdot r]$

13. *Distribution* (Dist.):
$$[p \bullet (q \vee r)] \equiv [(p \bullet q) \vee (p \bullet r)]$$
$$[p \vee (q \bullet r)] \equiv [(p \vee q) \bullet (p \vee r)]$$

14. *Double Negation* (D.N.):
$$p \equiv \sim\sim p$$

15. *Transposition* (Trans.):
$$(p \supset q) \equiv (\sim q \supset \sim p)$$

16. *Material Implication* (Impl.):
$$(p \supset q) \equiv (\sim p \vee q)$$

17. *Material Equivalence* (Equiv.):
$$(p \equiv q) \equiv [(p \supset q) \bullet (q \supset p)]$$
$$(p \equiv q) \equiv [(p \bullet q) \vee (\sim p \bullet \sim q)]$$

18. *Exportation* (Exp.):
$$[(p \bullet q) \supset r] \equiv [p \supset (q \supset r)]$$

19. *Tautology* (Taut.):[1]
$$p \equiv (p \vee p)$$
$$p \equiv (p \bullet p)$$

The process of replacement is very different from that of substitution: we substitute statements for statement variables, whereas we replace statements by other statements. In moving from a statement form to a substitution instance of it, or from an argument form to a substitution instance of it, we can substitute any statement for any statement variable, provided that if a statement is substituted for one occurrence of a statement variable it must be substituted for every other occurrence of that statement variable. But in moving from one statement to another by way of replacement, we can replace a component of the first only by a statement certified to be logically equivalent to that component by one of the logical equivalences 10 through 19, and we can replace one occurrence of that component without having to replace any other occurrence of it.

These nineteen Rules of Inference are somewhat redundant, in the sense that they do not constitute a bare minimum which would suffice for the construction of formal proofs of validity for extended arguments. For example, *modus tollens* could be dropped from the list without any real weakening of our proof apparatus, for any line depending upon *modus tollens* can be justified by appealing to other rules in the list instead. Thus in the first formal proof given in this chapter on pages 296–297.

1. $A \supset B$
2. $B \supset C$
3. $C \supset D$
4. $\sim D$
5. $A \vee E$ / $\therefore E$
6. $A \supset C$ 1,2, H.S.
7. $A \supset D$ 6,3, H.S.
8. $\sim A$ 7,4, M.T.
9. E 5,8, D.S.

[1]It should be noted that the word "tautology" is used in three different senses: (1) a statement form all of whose substitution instances are true, (2) a statement whose specific form is a tautology in sense (1), and (3) the particular logical equivalences numbered 19 in our list of Rules of Inference.

line 8, $\sim\!A$, was deduced from lines 4 and 7, $\sim\!D$ and $A \supset D$, by *modus tollens*, but if *modus tollens* were eliminated as a Rule of Inference we could still deduce $\sim\!A$ from $A \supset D$ and $\sim\!D$. This could be done by inserting the intermediate line $\sim\!D \supset \sim\!A$, which follows from $A \supset D$ by the Principle of Transposition (Trans.), and then obtaining $\sim\!A$ from $\sim\!D \supset \sim\!A$ and $\sim\!D$ by *modus ponens* (M.P.). But *modus tollens* is such a commonly used and intuitively obvious Rule of Inference that it has been included anyway. Others of the nineteen are also redundant in this same sense.

The list of nineteen Rules of Inference is characterized not only by redundancy, but also by a certain sort of deficiency. For example, although the argument

$$A \vee B$$
$$\sim\!B$$
$$\therefore A$$

is intuitively valid, its form

$$p \vee q$$
$$\sim\!q$$
$$\therefore p$$

has not been included as a Rule of Inference. The conclusion A does not follow from the premises $A \vee B$ and $\sim\!B$ by any single Rule of Inference, although it can be deduced from them by two Rules of Inference. A formal proof of validity for the given argument can be written as

1. $A \vee B$
2. $\sim\!B$ / $\therefore A$
3. $B \vee A$ 1, Com.
4. A 3,2, D.S.

We could eliminate the indicated deficiency by adding another rule to our list, but if we made additions for all such cases we should end up with a list that was much longer and therefore less manageable.

The present list of nineteen Rules of Inference constitutes a *complete* system of truth-functional logic, in the sense that it permits the construction of a formal proof of validity for *any* valid truth-functional argument.[2]

The notion of *formal proof* is an *effective* notion, which means that it can be decided quite mechanically, in a finite number of steps, whether or not a given sequence of statements constitutes a formal proof (with reference to a given list of Rules of Inference). No thinking is required, either in the sense of thinking about what the statements in the sequence "mean" or in the sense of using logical intuition to check any step's validity. Only two things

---

[2] A method of proving this kind of completeness for a set of rules of inference can be found in I. M. Copi, *Symbolic Logic*, 5th ed. (New York: Macmillan Publishing Company, 1979), Chapter 8. See also John A. Winnie, "The Completeness of Copi's System of Natural Deduction," *Notre Dame Journal of Formal Logic*, Vol. 11, No. 3, July 1970, pp. 379–382.

are required, of which the first is the ability to see that a statement occurring in one place is precisely the same as a statement occurring in another, for we must be able to check that some statements in the proof are premises of the argument being proved valid and that the last statement in the proof is the conclusion of that argument. The second thing required is the ability to see whether a given statement has a certain pattern or not, that is, to see if it is a substitution instance of a given statement form.

Thus any question about whether the preceding sequence of statements is a formal proof of validity can easily be settled in a completely mechanical fashion. That lines 1 and 2 are the premises and line 4 is the conclusion of the given argument is obvious on inspection. That 3 follows from preceding lines by one of the given Rules of Inference can be decided in a finite number of steps—even where the notation "1, Com." is not written at the side. The explanatory notation in the second column is a help and should always be included, but it is not, strictly speaking, a necessary part of the proof itself. At every line, there are only finitely many preceding lines and only finitely many Rules of Inference or reference forms to be consulted. Although time consuming, it can be verified by inspection and comparison of shapes that 3 does not follow from 1 and 2 by *modus ponens,* or by *modus tollens,* or by a Hypothetical Syllogism, . . . , and so on, until in following this procedure we come to the question of whether or not 3 follows from 1 by the Principle of Commutation, and there we see, simply by looking at the forms, that it does. In the same way the legitimacy of *any* statement in *any* formal proof can be tested in a finite number of steps, none of which involves anything more than comparing forms or shapes. It is to preserve this effectiveness that we require that only one step should be taken at a time. One might be tempted to shorten a proof by combining steps, but the space and time saved are negligible. More important is the effectiveness we achieve by taking each step by means of one single Rule of Inference at a time.

Although a formal proof of validity is effective in the sense that it can be mechanically decided of any given sequence whether it is a proof, *constructing* a formal proof is not an effective procedure. In this respect formal proofs differ from truth tables. The use of truth tables is completely mechanical: given any argument of the sort with which we are now concerned, we can always construct a truth table to test its validity by following the simple rules of procedure set forth in the preceding chapter. But we have no effective or mechanical rules for the construction of formal proofs. Here we must think or "figure out" where to begin and how to proceed. Nevertheless, proving an argument valid by constructing a formal proof of its validity is much easier than the purely mechanical construction of a truth table with perhaps hundreds or even thousands of rows.

There is an important difference between the first nine and the last ten Rules of Inference. The first nine rules can be applied only to whole lines of a proof. Thus in a formal proof of validity the statement A can be inferred from the statement $A \cdot B$ by Simplification only if $A \cdot B$ constitutes a whole line. It is obvious that A cannot be inferred validly either from $(A \cdot B) \supset C$

or from $C \supset (A \cdot B)$, because the latter two statements can be true while A is false. And the statement $A \supset C$ does not follow from the statement $(A \cdot B) \supset C$ by Simplification or by any other Rule of Inference. It does not follow at all, for if A is true and B and C are both false, $(A \cdot B) \supset C$ is true but $A \supset C$ is false. Again, although $A \vee B$ follows from A by Addition, we cannot infer $(A \vee B) \supset C$ from $A \supset C$ by Addition or by any other Rule of Inference. For if A and C are both false and B is true, $A \supset C$ is true but $(A \vee B) \supset C$ is false. On the other hand, any of the last ten Rules can be applied either to whole lines or to parts of lines. Not only can the statement $A \supset (B \supset C)$ be inferred from the whole line $(A \cdot B) \supset C$ by Exportation, but from the line $[(A \cdot B) \supset C] \vee D$ we can infer $[A \supset (B \supset C)] \vee D$ by Exportation. By Replacement, logically equivalent expressions can replace each other wherever they occur, even where they do not constitute whole lines of a proof. But the first nine Rules of Inference can be used only with whole lines of a proof serving as premises.

Although we have no purely mechanical rules for constructing formal proofs, some rough-and-ready rules of thumb or hints on procedure may be suggested. The first is simply to begin deducing conclusions from the given premises by the given Rules of Inference. As more and more of these subconclusions become available as premises for further deductions, the greater is the likelihood of being able to see how to deduce the conclusion of the argument to be proved valid. Another hint is to try to eliminate statements that occur in the premises but not in the conclusion. Such elimination can proceed, of course, only in accordance with the Rules of Inference. But the Rules contain many techniques for eliminating statements. Simplification is such a rule, whereby the right-hand conjunct can be dropped from a whole line that is a conjunction. And Commutation is a rule that permits switching the left-hand conjunct of a conjunction over to the right-hand side, from which it can be dropped by Simplification. The "middle" term q can be eliminated by a Hypothetical Syllogism given two statements of the patterns $p \supset q$ and $q \supset r$. Distribution is a useful rule for transforming a disjunction of the pattern $p \vee (q \cdot r)$ into the conjunction $(p \vee q) \cdot (p \vee r)$, whose right-hand conjunct can then be eliminated by Simplification. Another rule of thumb is to introduce by means of Addition a statement that occurs in the conclusion but not in any premiss. Another method is to work backward from the conclusion by looking for some statement or statements from which it can be deduced, and then trying to deduce those intermediate statements from the premises. There is, however, no substitute for practice as a method of acquiring facility in constructing formal proofs.

EXERCISES

I. For each of the following arguments state the Rule of Inference by which its conclusion follows from its premiss.

★ 1. $(A \supset B) \cdot (C \supset D)$
    $\therefore (A \supset B) \cdot (\sim D \supset \sim C)$

2. $(E \supset F) \cdot (G \supset \sim H)$
    $\therefore (\sim E \vee F) \cdot (G \supset \sim H)$

3. $[I \supset (J \supset K)] \cdot (J \supset \sim I)$
   $\therefore [(I \cdot J) \supset K] \cdot (J \supset \sim I)$

★ 5. $O \supset [(P \supset Q) \cdot (Q \supset P)]$
   $\therefore O \supset (P \equiv Q)$

7. $(T \vee \sim U) \cdot [(W \cdot \sim V) \supset \sim T]$
   $\therefore (T \vee \sim U) \cdot [W \supset (\sim V \supset \sim T)]$

8. $(X \vee Y) \cdot (\sim X \vee \sim Y)$
   $\therefore [(X \vee Y) \cdot \sim X] \vee [(X \vee Y) \cdot \sim Y]$

9. $Z \supset (A \supset B)$
   $\therefore Z \supset (\sim\sim A \supset B)$

★ 10. $[C \cdot (D \cdot \sim E)] \cdot [(C \cdot D) \cdot \sim E]$
   $\therefore [(C \cdot D) \cdot \sim E] \cdot [(C \cdot D) \cdot \sim E]$

11. $(\sim F \vee G) \cdot (F \supset G)$
   $\therefore (F \supset G) \cdot (F \supset G)$

12. $(H \supset \sim I) \supset (\sim I \supset \sim J)$
   $\therefore (H \supset \sim I) \supset (J \supset I)$

13. $(\sim K \supset L) \supset (\sim M \vee \sim N)$
   $\therefore (\sim K \supset L) \supset \sim (M \cdot N)$

14. $[(\sim O \vee P) \vee \sim Q] \cdot [\sim O \vee (P \vee \sim Q)]$
   $\therefore [\sim O \vee (P \vee \sim Q)] \cdot [\sim O \vee (P \vee \sim Q)]$

★ 15. $[(R \vee \sim S) \cdot \sim T] \vee [(R \vee \sim S) \cdot U]$
   $\therefore (R \vee \sim S) \cdot (\sim T \vee U)$

16. $[V \supset \sim (W \vee X)] \supset (Y \vee Z)$
   $\therefore \{[V \supset \sim (W \vee X)] \cdot [V \supset \sim (W \vee X)]\} \supset (Y \vee Z)$

17. $[(\sim A \cdot B) \cdot (C \vee D)] \vee [\sim (\sim A \cdot B) \cdot \sim (C \vee D)]$
   $\therefore (\sim A \cdot B) \equiv (C \vee D)$

18. $[\sim E \vee (\sim\sim F \supset G)] \cdot [\sim E \vee (F \supset G)]$
   $\therefore [\sim E \vee (F \supset G)] \cdot [\sim E \vee (F \supset G)]$

19. $[H \cdot (I \vee J)] \vee [H \cdot (K \supset \sim L)]$
   $\therefore H \cdot [(I \vee J) \vee (K \supset \sim L)]$

20. $(\sim M \vee \sim N) \supset (O \supset \sim\sim P)$
   $\therefore \sim (M \cdot N) \supset (O \supset \sim\sim P)$

4. $[L \supset (M \vee N)] \vee [L \supset (M \vee N)]$
   $\therefore L \supset (M \vee N)$

6. $\sim (R \vee S) \supset (\sim R \vee \sim S)$
   $\therefore (\sim R \cdot \sim S) \supset (\sim R \vee \sim S)$

II. Each of the following is a formal proof of validity for the indicated argument. State the "justification" for each line that is not a premiss.

★ 1. 1. $A \supset B$
   2. $C \supset \sim B$ / $\therefore A \supset \sim C$
   3. $\sim\sim B \supset \sim C$
   4. $B \supset \sim C$
   5. $A \supset \sim C$

2. 1. $(D \cdot E) \supset F$
   2. $(D \supset F) \supset G$ / $\therefore E \supset G$
   3. $(E \cdot D) \supset F$
   4. $E \supset (D \supset F)$
   5. $E \supset G$

3. 1. $(H \vee I) \supset [J \cdot (K \cdot L)]$
   2. I / $\therefore J \cdot K$
   3. $I \vee H$
   4. $H \vee I$
   5. $J \cdot (K \cdot L)$
   6. $(J \cdot K) \cdot L$
   7. $J \cdot K$

4. 1. $(M \vee N) \supset (O \cdot P)$
   2. $\sim O$ / $\therefore \sim M$
   3. $\sim O \vee \sim P$
   4. $\sim (O \cdot P)$
   5. $\sim (M \vee N)$
   6. $\sim M \cdot \sim N$
   7. $\sim M$

★ 5.   1. $(Q \lor \sim R) \lor S$
     2. $\sim Q \lor (R \cdot \sim Q)$
     $/ \therefore R \supset S$
     3. $(\sim Q \lor R) \cdot (\sim Q \lor \sim Q)$
     4. $(\sim Q \lor \sim Q) \cdot (\sim Q \lor R)$
     5. $\sim Q \lor \sim Q$
     6. $\sim Q$
     7. $Q \lor (\sim R \lor S)$
     8. $\sim R \lor S$
     9. $R \supset S$

   7.   1. $Y \supset Z$
     2. $Z \supset [Y \supset (R \lor S)]$
     3. $R \equiv S$
     4. $\sim (R \cdot S) \ / \therefore \sim Y$
     5. $(R \cdot S) \lor (\sim R \cdot \sim S)$
     6. $\sim R \cdot \sim S$
     7. $\sim (R \lor S)$
     8. $Y \supset [Y \supset (R \lor S)]$
     9. $(Y \cdot Y) \supset (R \lor S)$
     10. $Y \supset (R \lor S)$
     11. $\sim Y$

   9.   1. $(D \cdot E) \supset \sim F$
     2. $F \lor (G \cdot H))$
     3. $D \equiv E \ / \therefore D \supset G$
     4. $(D \supset E) \cdot (E \supset D)$
     5. $D \supset E$
     6. $D \supset (D \cdot E)$
     7. $D \supset \sim F$
     8. $(F \lor G) \cdot (F \lor H))$
     9. $F \lor G$
     10. $\sim\sim F \lor G$
     11. $\sim F \supset G$
     12. $D \supset G$

   6.   1. $T \cdot (U \lor V)$
     2. $T \supset [U \supset (W \cdot X)]$
     3. $(T \cdot V) \supset \sim (W \lor X)$
     $/ \therefore W \equiv X$
     4. $(T \cdot U) \supset (W \cdot X)$
     5. $(T \cdot V) \supset (\sim W \cdot \sim X)$
     6. $[(T \cdot U) \supset (W \cdot X)] \cdot$
         $[(T \cdot V) \supset (\sim W \cdot \sim X)]$
     7. $(T \cdot U) \lor (T \cdot V)$
     8. $(W \cdot X) \lor (\sim W \cdot \sim X)$
     9. $W \equiv X$

   8.   1. $A \supset B$
     2. $B \supset C$
     3. $C \supset A$
     4. $A \supset \sim C \ / \therefore \sim A \cdot \sim C$
     5. $A \supset C$
     6. $(A \supset C) \cdot (C \supset A)$
     7. $A \equiv C$
     8. $(A \cdot C) \lor (\sim A \cdot \sim C)$
     9. $\sim A \lor \sim C$
     10. $\sim (A \cdot C)$
     11. $\sim A \cdot \sim C$

   10.   1. $(I \lor \sim\sim J) \cdot K$
     2. $[\sim L \supset \sim (K \cdot J)] \cdot$
         $[K \supset (I \supset \sim M)]$
     $/ \therefore \sim (M \cdot \sim L)$
     3. $[(K \cdot J) \supset L] \cdot$
         $[K \supset (I \supset \sim M)]$
     4. $[(K \cdot J) \supset L] \cdot$
         $[(K \cdot I) \supset \sim M]$
     5. $(I \lor J) \cdot K$
     6. $K \cdot (I \lor J)$
     7. $(K \cdot I) \lor (K \cdot J)$
     8. $(K \cdot J) \lor (K \cdot I)$
     9. $L \lor \sim M$
     10. $\sim M \lor L$
     11. $\sim M \lor \sim\sim L$
     12. $\sim (M \cdot \sim L)$

III. For each of the following, adding just two statements to the premisses will produce a formal proof of validity. Construct a formal proof of validity for each of the following arguments.

★ 1. $A \supset \sim A \ / \therefore \sim A$

   3. $E \ / \therefore (E \lor F) \cdot (E \lor G)$

★ 5. $\sim K \lor (L \supset M) \ / \therefore (K \cdot L) \supset M$

   7. $Q \supset [R \supset (S \supset T)]$
     $Q \supset (Q \cdot R) \ / \therefore Q \supset (S \supset T)$

   2. $B \cdot (C \cdot D) \ / \therefore C \cdot (D \cdot B)$

   4. $H \lor (I \cdot J) \ / \therefore H \lor I$

   6. $(N \cdot O) \supset P \ / \therefore (N \cdot O) \supset$
     $[N \cdot (O \cdot P)]$

   8. $U \supset \sim V$
     $V \ / \therefore \sim U$

9. $W \supset X$
   $\sim Y \supset \sim X$ / $\therefore W \supset Y$

★ 10. $Z \supset A$
   $\sim A \lor B$ / $\therefore Z \supset B$

11. $C \supset \sim D$
   $\sim E \supset D$ / $\therefore C \supset \sim\sim E$

12. $F \equiv G$
   $\sim(F \cdot G)$ / $\therefore \sim F \cdot \sim G$

13. $H \supset (I \cdot J)$
   $I \supset (J \supset K)$ / $\therefore H \supset K$

14. $(L \supset M) \cdot (N \supset M)$
   $L \lor N$ / $\therefore M$

★ 15. $(O \lor P) \supset (Q \lor R)$
   $P \lor O$ / $\therefore Q \lor R$

16. $(S \cdot T) \lor (U \cdot V)$
   $\sim S \lor \sim T$ / $\therefore U \cdot V$

17. $(W \cdot X) \supset Y$
   $(X \supset Y) \supset Z$ / $\therefore W \supset Z$

18. $(A \lor B) \supset (C \lor D)$
   $\sim C \cdot \sim D$ / $\therefore \sim(A \lor B)$

19. $(E \cdot F) \supset (G \cdot H)$
   $F \cdot E$ / $\therefore G \cdot H$

★ 20. $I \supset [J \lor (K \lor L)]$
   $\sim[(J \lor K) \lor L]$ / $\therefore \sim I$

21. $(M \supset N) \cdot (\sim O \lor P)$
   $M \lor O$ / $\therefore N \lor P$

22. $(\sim Q \supset \sim R) \cdot (\sim S \supset \sim T)$
   $\sim\sim(\sim Q \lor \sim S)$ / $\therefore \sim R \lor \sim T$

23. $\sim[(U \supset V) \cdot (V \supset U)]$
   $(W \equiv X) \supset (U \equiv V)$
   / $\therefore \sim(W \equiv X)$

24. $(Y \supset Z) \cdot (Z \supset Y)$
   / $\therefore (Y \cdot Z) \lor (\sim Y \cdot \sim Z)$

★ 25. $A \lor B$
   $C \lor D$ / $\therefore [(A \lor B) \cdot C] \lor$
   $[(A \lor B) \cdot D]$

26. $[(E \lor F) \cdot (G \lor H)] \supset (F \cdot I)$
   $(G \lor H) \cdot (E \lor F)$ / $\therefore F \cdot I$

27. $(J \cdot K) \supset [(L \cdot M) \lor (N \cdot O)]$
   $\sim(L \cdot M) \cdot \sim(N \cdot O)$ / $\therefore \sim(J \cdot K)$

28. $(P \supset Q) \supset [(R \lor S) \cdot (T \equiv U)]$
   $(R \lor S) \supset [(T \equiv U) \supset Q]$ / $\therefore (P \supset Q) \supset Q$

29. $[V \cdot (W \lor X)] \supset (Y \supset Z)$
   $\sim(Y \supset Z) \lor (\sim W \equiv A)$ / $\therefore [V \cdot (W \lor X)] \supset (\sim W \equiv A)$

30. $\sim[(B \supset \sim C) \cdot (\sim C \supset B)]$
   $(D \cdot E) \supset (B \equiv \sim C)$ / $\therefore \sim(D \cdot E)$

IV. For each of the following, adding just three statements to the premises will produce a formal proof of validity. Construct a formal proof of validity for each of the following arguments.

★ 1. $\sim A \supset A$ / $\therefore A$

2. $\sim B \lor (C \cdot D)$ / $\therefore B \supset C$

3. $E \lor (F \cdot G)$ / $\therefore E \lor G$

4. $H \cdot (I \cdot J)$ / $\therefore J \cdot (I \cdot H)$

★ 5. $[(K \lor L) \lor M] \lor N$
   / $\therefore (N \lor K) \lor (L \lor M)$

6. $O \supset P$
   $P \supset \sim P$ / $\therefore \sim O$

7. $Q \supset (R \supset S)$
   $Q \supset R$ / $\therefore Q \supset S$

8. $T \supset U$
   $\sim(U \lor V)$ / $\therefore \sim T$

9. $W \cdot (X \lor Y)$
   $\sim W \lor \sim X$ / $\therefore W \cdot Y$

★ 10. $(Z \lor A) \lor B$
   $\sim A$ / $\therefore Z \lor B$

11. $(C \lor D) \supset (E \cdot F)$
   $D \lor C$ / $\therefore E$

12. $G \supset H$
   $H \supset G$ / $\therefore (G \cdot H) \lor (\sim G \cdot \sim H)$

13. $(I \supset J) \cdot (K \supset L)$
   $I \lor (K \cdot M)$ / $\therefore J \lor L$

14. $(N \cdot O) \supset P$
   $(\sim P \supset \sim O) \supset Q$ / $\therefore N \supset Q$

15. $[R \supset (S \supset T)] \cdot [(R \cdot T) \supset U]$
   $R \cdot (S \lor T)$ / $\therefore T \lor U$

V. The exercises in this set represent frequently recurring patterns of inference found in longer formal proofs of validity. Familiarity with them will be useful in subsequent work. Construct a formal proof of validity for each of the following arguments.

★ 1. $\sim A$
    $\therefore A \supset B$

2. C
   $\therefore D \supset C$

3. $E \supset (F \supset G)$
   $\therefore F \supset (E \supset G)$

4. $H \supset (I \cdot J)$
   $\therefore H \supset I$

★ 5. $K \supset L$
    $\therefore K \supset (L \vee M)$

6. $N \supset O$
   $\therefore (N \cdot P) \supset O$

7. $(Q \vee R) \supset S$
   $\therefore Q \supset S$

8. $T \supset U$
   $T \supset V \; / \therefore T \supset (U \cdot V)$

9. $W \supset X$
   $Y \supset X$
   $\therefore (W \vee Y) \supset X$

10. $Z \supset A$
    $Z \vee A$
    $\therefore A$

VI. Construct a formal proof of validity for each of the following arguments.

★ 1. $A \supset \sim B$
    $\sim(C \cdot \sim A)$
    $\therefore C \supset \sim B$

2. $(D \cdot \sim E) \supset F$
   $\sim(E \vee F)$
   $\therefore \sim D$

3. $(G \supset \sim H) \supset I$
   $\sim(G \cdot H)$
   $\therefore I \vee \sim H$

4. $(J \vee K) \supset \sim L$
   L
   $\therefore \sim J$

★ 5. $[(M \cdot N) \cdot O] \supset P$
    $Q \supset [(O \cdot M) \cdot N]$
    $\therefore \sim Q \vee P$

6. $R \vee (S \cdot \sim T)$
   $(R \vee S) \supset (U \vee \sim T)$
   $\therefore T \supset U$

7. $(\sim V \supset W) \cdot (X \supset W)$
   $\sim(\sim X \cdot V)$
   $\therefore W$

8. $[(Y \cdot Z) \supset A] \cdot [(Y \cdot B) \supset C]$
   $(B \vee Z) \cdot Y$
   $\therefore A \vee C$

9. $\sim D \supset (\sim E \supset \sim F)$
   $\sim(F \cdot \sim D) \supset \sim G$
   $\therefore G \supset E$

★ 10. $[H \vee (I \vee J)] \supset (K \supset J)$
    $L \supset [I \vee (J \vee H)]$
    $\therefore (L \cdot K) \supset J$

11. $M \supset N$
    $M \supset (N \supset O)$
    $\therefore M \supset O$

12. $(P \supset Q) \cdot (P \vee R)$
    $(R \supset S) \cdot (R \vee P)$
    $\therefore Q \vee S$

13. $T \supset (U \cdot V)$
    $(U \vee V) \supset W$
    $\therefore T \supset W$

14. $(X \vee Y) \supset (X \cdot Y)$
    $\sim(X \vee Y)$
    $\therefore \sim(X \cdot Y)$

★ 15. $(Z \supset Z) \supset (A \supset A)$
    $(A \supset A) \supset (Z \supset Z)$
    $\therefore A \supset A$

16. $\sim B \vee [(C \supset D) \cdot (E \supset D)]$
    $B \cdot (C \vee E)$
    $\therefore D$

17. $\sim F \vee \sim[\sim(G \cdot H) \cdot (G \vee H)]$
    $(G \supset H) \supset [(H \supset G) \supset I]$
    $\therefore F \supset (F \cdot I)$

18. $J \vee (\sim J \cdot K)$
    $J \supset L$
    $\therefore (L \cdot J) \equiv J$

19. $(M \supset N) \cdot (O \supset P)$
  $\sim N \text{ v } \sim P$
  $\sim(M \cdot O) \supset Q$
  $\therefore Q$

20. $(R \text{ v } S) \supset (T \cdot U)$
  $\sim R \supset (V \supset \sim V)$
  $\sim T$
  $\therefore \sim V$

VII. Construct a formal proof of validity for each of the following arguments, in each case using the suggested notation.

★ 1. Either the manager didn't notice the change or else he approves of it. He noticed it all right. So he must approve of it. (*N, A*)

2. The oxygen in the tube either combined with the filament to form an oxide or else it vanished completely. The oxygen in the tube could not have vanished completely. Therefore the oxygen in the tube combined with the filament to form an oxide. (*C, V*)

3. If a political leader who sees her former opinions to be wrong does not alter her course, she is guilty of deceit; and if she does alter her course, she is open to a change of inconsistency. She either alters her course or she doesn't. Therefore either she is guilty of deceit or else she is open to a charge of inconsistency. (*A, D, I*)

4. It is not the case that she either forgot or wasn't able to finish. Therefore she was able to finish. (*F, A*)

★ 5. If the litmus paper turns red, then the solution is acid. Hence if the litmus paper turns red, then either the solution is acid or something is wrong somewhere. (*R, A, W*)

6. She can have many friends only if she respects them as individuals. If she respects them as individuals, then she cannot expect them all to behave alike. She does have many friends. Therefore she does not expect them all to behave alike. (*F, R, E*)

7. If the victim had money in his pockets, then robbery wasn't the motive for the crime. But robbery or vengeance was the motive for the crime. The victim had money in his pockets. Therefore vengeance must have been the motive for the crime. (*M, R, V*)

8. Napoleon is to be condemned if he usurped power that was not rightfully his own. Either Napoleon was a legitimate monarch or else he usurped power that was not rightfully his own. Napoleon was not a legitimate monarch. So Napoleon is to be condemned. (*C, U, L*)

9. If we extend further credit on the Wilkins account, they will have a moral obligation to accept our bid on their next project. We can figure a more generous margin of profit in preparing our estimates if they have a moral obligation to accept our bid on their next project. Figuring a more generous margin of profit in preparing our estimates will cause our general financial condition to improve considerably. Hence a considerable improvement in our general financial condition will follow from our extension of further credit on the Wilkins account. (*C, M, P, I*)

★ 10. If the laws are good and their enforcement is strict, then crime will diminish. If strict enforcement of laws will make crime diminish, then our problem is a practical one. The laws are good. Therefore our problem is a practical one. (*G, S, D, P*)

11. Had Roman citizenship guaranteed civil liberties, then Roman citizens would have enjoyed religious freedom. Had Roman citizens enjoyed religious freedom, there would have been no persecution of the early Christians. But the early Christians were persecuted. Hence Roman citizenship could not have guaranteed civil liberties. (*G, F, P*)

12. If the first disjunct of a disjunction is true, the disjunction as a whole is true. Therefore if both the first and second disjuncts of the disjunction are true, then the disjunction as a whole is true. (*F, W, S*)

13. If the new courthouse is to be conveniently located, it will have to be situated in the heart of the city; and if it is to be adequate to its function, it will have to be built large enough to house all the city offices. If the new courthouse is situated in the heart of the city and is built large enough to house all the city offices, then its cost will run to over a million dollars. Its cost cannot exceed a million dollars. Therefore either the new courthouse will have an inconvenient location or it will be inadequate to its function. (*C, H, A, L, O*)

14. Jones will come if she gets the message, provided that she is still interested. Although she didn't come, she is still interested. Therefore she didn't get the message. (*C, M, I*)

★ 15. If the Mosaic account of the cosmogony is strictly correct, the sun was not created till the fourth day. And if the sun was not created till the fourth day, it could not have been the cause of the alternation of day and night for the first three days. But either the word "day" is used in Scripture in a different sense from that in which it is commonly accepted now or else the sun must have been the cause of the alternation of day and night for the first three days. Hence it follows that either the Mosaic account of the cosmogony is not strictly correct or else the word "day" is used in Scripture in a different sense from that in which it is commonly accepted now. (*M, C, A, D*)

16. If the teller or the cashier had pushed the alarm button, the vault would have locked automatically and the police would have arrived within three minutes. Had the police arrived within three minutes, the robbers' car would have been overtaken. But the robbers' car was not overtaken. Therefore the teller did not push the alarm button. (*T, C, V, P, O*)

17. If people are always guided by their sense of duty, they must forego the enjoyment of many pleasures; and if they are always guided by their desire for pleasure, they must often neglect their duty. People are either always guided by their sense of duty or always guided by their desire for pleasure. If people are always guided by their sense of duty, they do not often neglect their duty; and if they are always guided by their desire for pleasure, they do not forego the enjoyment of many pleasures. Therefore people must forego the enjoyment of many pleasures if and only if they do not often neglect their duty. (*D, F, P, N*)

18. Although world population is increasing, agricultural production is declining and manufacturing output remains constant. If agricultural production declines and world population increases then either new food sources will become available or else there will be a radical redistribution of food resources in the world unless human nutritional requirements diminish. No new food sources will become available, yet neither will family planning be encouraged nor will human nutritional requirements diminish. Therefore there will be a radical redistribution of food resources in the world. (*W, A, M, N, R, H, P*)

19. Either the robber came in the door, or else the crime was an inside one and one of the servants is implicated. The robber could come in the door only if the latch had been raised from the inside; but one of the servants is surely implicated if the latch was raised from the inside. Therefore one of the servants is implicated. (*D, I, S, L*)

★ 20. If I pay the tailor, I won't have any money left. I can take my girl to the dance only if I have money. She'll be unhappy unless I take her to the dance. But if I don't pay the tailor, he won't let me have my suit; and without the suit I certainly can't take my girl to the dance. I must either pay the tailor or not pay him. So my girl is bound to be unhappy! (*P, M, D, U, S*)

21. If you study the humanities then you will develop an understanding of people, and if you study the sciences then you will develop an understanding of the world about you. So if you study either the humanities or the sciences then you will develop an understanding either of people or of the world about you. (*H, P, S, W*)

22. If you study the humanities then you will develop an understanding of people, and if you study the sciences then you will develop an understanding of the world about you. So if you study both the humanities and the sciences then you will develop an understanding both of people and of the world about you. (*H, P, S, W*)

23. If you have free will then your actions are not determined by any antecedent events. If you have free will then if your actions are not determined by any antecedent events then your actions cannot be predicted. If your actions are not determined by any antecedent events then if your actions cannot be predicted then the consequences of your actions cannot be predicted. Therefore if you have free will then the consequences of your actions cannot be predicted. (*F, A, P, C*)

24. Socrates was a great philosopher. Therefore either Socrates was happily married or else he wasn't. (*G, H*)

25. If either Socrates was happily married or else he wasn't, then Socrates was a great philosopher. Therefore Socrates was a great philosopher. (*H, G*)

9.3 *Proof of Invalidity*

For an invalid argument there is, of course, no formal proof of validity. But if we fail to discover a formal proof of validity for a given argument, this failure does not prove that the argument is invalid and that no such proof can be constructed. It may mean only that we have not tried hard enough. Our inability to find a proof of validity may be caused by the fact that the argument is not valid, but it may be caused instead by our own lack of ingenuity—as a consequence of the noneffective character of the process of proof construction. Not being able to construct a formal proof of its validity does not prove an argument to be invalid. What *does* constitute a proof that a given argument is invalid?

The method about to be described is closely related to the truth table method, although it is a great deal shorter. It will be helpful to recall how an invalid argument form is proved invalid by a truth table. If a single case (row) can be found in which truth values are assigned to the statement variables in such a way that the premisses are made true and the conclusion false, then the argument form is invalid. If we can somehow make an assignment of truth values to the simple component statements of an argument that will make its premisses true and its conclusion false, then making that assignment will suffice to prove the argument invalid. To make such an assignment is, in effect, what the truth table does. But if we can make such an assignment of truth values without actually constructing the whole truth table, a certain amount of work will be eliminated.

Consider the argument

If the governor favors public housing, then he is in favor of restricting the scope of private enterprise.
If the governor were a pinko-radical, then he would be in favor of restricting the scope of private enterprise.
Therefore if the governor favors public housing, then he is ia pinko-radical.

This is symbolized as

$$F \supset R$$
$$P \supset R$$
$$\therefore F \supset P$$

and we can prove it invalid without having to construct a complete truth table. First we ask, What assignment of truth values is required to make the conclusion false? It is clear that a conditional is false only if its antecedent is true and its consequent false. Hence assigning the truth value "true" to F and "false" to P will make the conclusion $F \supset P$ false. Now if the truth value "true" is assigned to R, both premisses are made true, because a conditional is true whenever its consequent is true. We can say, then, that if the truth value "true" is assigned to F and to R, and the truth value "false" is assigned to P, the argument will have true premisses and a false conclusion and is thus proved to be invalid.

This method of proving invalidity is an alternative to the truth table method of proof. The two methods are closely related, however, and the essential connection between them should be noticed. In effect, what we did when we made the indicated assignment of truth values was to construct one row of the given argument's truth table. The relationship can perhaps be seen more clearly when the truth value assignments are written out horizontally:

F	R	P	$F \supset R$	$P \supset R$	$F \supset P$
true	true	false	true	true	false

in which form they constitute one row (the second) of the truth table for the given argument. An argument is proved invalid by displaying at least one row of its truth table in which all its premisses are true but its conclusion is false. Consequently we need not examine *all* rows of its truth table to discover an argument's invalidity: the discovery of a single row in which its premisses are all true and its conclusion false will suffice. The present method of proving invalidity is a method of constructing such a row without having to construct the entire truth table.

The present method is shorter than writing out an entire truth table, and the amount of time and work saved is proportionally greater for arguments involving a greater number of component simple statements. For arguments with a considerable number of premisses, or with premisses of considerable complexity, the needed assignment of truth values may not be so easy to make. It may be desirable to assign some truth values to make some premisses true before choosing an assignment to make the conclusion false. A certain amount of trial and error may be necessary. But it will generally be shorter and easier than writing out a complete truth table.

EXERCISES

Prove the invalidity of each of the following by the method of assigning truth values.

★ 1. $A \supset B$
$C \supset D$
$A \vee D$
$\therefore B \vee C$

2. $\sim(E \cdot F)$
$(\sim E \cdot \sim F) \supset (G \cdot H)$
$H \supset G$
$\therefore G$

3. $I \vee \sim J$
$\sim(\sim K \cdot L)$
$\sim(\sim I \cdot \sim L)$
$\therefore \sim J \supset K$

4. $M \supset (N \vee O)$
$N \supset (P \vee Q)$
$Q \supset R$
$\sim(R \vee P)$
$\therefore \sim M$

★ 5. $S \supset (T \supset U)$
$V \supset (W \supset X)$
$T \supset (V \cdot W)$
$\sim(T \cdot X)$
$\therefore S \equiv U$

6. $A \equiv (B \vee C)$
$B \equiv (C \vee A)$
$C \equiv (A \vee B)$
$\sim A$
$\therefore B \vee C$

7. $D \supset (E \vee F)$
$G \supset (H \vee I)$
$\sim E \supset (I \vee J)$
$(I \supset G) \cdot (\sim H \supset \sim G)$
$\sim J$
$\therefore D \supset (G \vee I)$

8. $K \supset (L \cdot M)$
$(L \supset N) \vee \sim K$
$O \supset (P \vee \sim N)$
$(\sim P \vee Q) \cdot \sim Q$
$(R \vee \sim P) \vee \sim M$
$\therefore K \supset R$

9. $(S \supset T) \cdot (T \supset S)$
$(U \cdot T) \vee (\sim T \cdot \sim U)$
$(U \vee V) \vee (S \vee T)$
$\sim U \supset (W \cdot X)$
$(V \supset \sim S) \cdot (\sim V \supset \sim Y)$
$X \supset (\sim Y \supset \sim X)$
$(U \vee S) \cdot (V \vee Z)$
$\therefore X \cdot Z$

10. $A \supset (B \supset \sim C)$
$(D \supset B) \cdot (E \supset A)$
$F \vee C$
$G \supset \sim H$
$(I \supset G) \cdot (H \supset J)$
$I \equiv \sim D$
$(B \supset H) \cdot (\sim H \supset D)$
$\therefore E \equiv F$

9.4 *Inconsistency*

If no truth value assignment can be given to the component simple statements of an argument that makes its premises true and its conclusion false, then the argument must be valid. Although this follows from the definition of "validity," it has a curious consequence. Consider the following argument, whose premises appear to be totally irrelevant to its conclusion:

If the airplane had engine trouble, it would have landed at Bridgeport.
If the airplane did not have engine trouble, it would have landed at Cleveland.
The airplane did not land at either Bridgeport or Cleveland.
Therefore the airplane must have landed in Denver.

and its symbolic translation:

$$A \supset B$$
$$\sim A \supset C$$
$$\sim (B \lor C)$$
$$\therefore D$$

Any attempt to assign truth values to its component simple statements in such a way as to make the conclusion false and the premises all true is doomed to failure. If we ignore the conclusion and concentrate our attention upon the other part of the objective, that of making all the premises true by an assignment of truth values to their component simple statements, we are bound to fail even here, in this apparently less ambitious project.

The reason the premises cannot be made true and the conclusion false is that the premises cannot possibly be made true in any case by *any* truth value assignment. No truth value assignment can make the premises true because they are inconsistent with each other. Their conjunction is *self-contradictory*, being a substitution instance of a self-contradictory statement form. Were we to construct a truth table for the given argument, we should find that in every row at least one of the premises is false. Because there is no row in which the premises are all true, there is no row in which the premises are all true and the conclusion false. Hence the truth table for this argument would establish its validity. Its validity can also be established by the following formal proof:

1. $A \supset B$
2. $\sim A \supset C$
3. $\sim (B \lor C) \; / \therefore D$
4. $\sim B \cdot \sim C$ 3, De M.
5. $\sim B$ 4, Simp.

6. ~*A*   1,5, M.T.
7. *C*   2,6, M.P.
8. ~*C* • ~*B*   4, Com.
9. ~*C*   8, Simp.
10. *C* v *D*   7, Add.
11. *D*   10,9, D.S.

In this proof the lines from 1 through 9 are devoted to making explicit the inconsistency that was implicitly contained in the premisses. That inconsistency emerges in lines 7 and 9, which assert *C* and ~*C*, respectively. Once this explicit contradiction is achieved, the conclusion follows swiftly by the Principle of Addition and the Disjunctive Syllogism.

Thus we see that if a set of premisses is inconsistent, those premisses will validly yield *any* conclusion, no matter how irrelevant. The essence of the matter is more simply shown in the case of the following argument, whose openly inconsistent premisses allow us validly to infer an irrelevant and fantastic conclusion:

> Today is Sunday. Today is not Sunday.
> Therefore the moon is made of green cheese.

In symbols, we have

1. *S*
2. ~*S* / ∴ *M*

The formal proof of its validity is almost immediately obvious:

3. *S* v *M*   1, Add.
4. *M*   3,2, D.S.

What is wrong here? How can such meager and even inconsistent premisses make any argument in which they occur valid? It should be noted first that, if an argument is valid because of an inconsistency in its premisses, it cannot possibly be a sound argument. If premisses are inconsistent with each other, they cannot possibly all be true. No conclusion can be established to be true by an argument with inconsistent premisses, because its premisses cannot possibly be true themselves.

The present situation is closely related to the so-called paradox of material implication. In discussing the latter, we observed that the statement form $\sim p \supset (p \supset q)$ is a tautology, having all its substitution instances true. Its formulation in English asserts that "If a statement is false then it materially implies any statement whatever," which is easily proved by means of truth tables. What has been established in the present discussion is that the argument form

$$p$$
$$\sim p$$
$$\therefore q$$

is valid. We have proved that *any argument with inconsistent premisses is valid, regardless of what its conclusion may be*. It may be established either by a truth table or by the kind of formal proof given.

The premisses of a valid argument imply its conclusion not merely in the sense of "material" implication, but *logically* or "strictly." In a valid argument, it is logically impossible for the premisses to be true when the conclusion is false. And this situation obtains whenever it is logically impossible for the premisses to be true, even when the question of the truth or falsehood of the conclusion is ignored. Its analogy with the corresponding property of material implication has led some writers on logic to call this a "paradox of strict implication." In view of the logician's technical definition of "validity," however, it does not seem to be especially paradoxical. The alleged paradox arises primarily from treating a technical term as if it were a term of ordinary, everyday language.

The foregoing discussion helps to explain why consistency is so highly prized. One reason, of course, is that inconsistent statements cannot both be true. This fact underlies the strategy of cross-examination, where an attorney may seek to maneuver a hostile witness into contradicting himself. If testimony affirms incompatible or inconsistent assertions, it cannot all be true, and the witness's credibility is destroyed—or at least shaken. But another reason why inconsistency is so repugnant is that any and every conclusion follows logically from inconsistent statements taken as premisses. Inconsistent statements are not "meaningless," their trouble is just the opposite. They mean too much—they mean everything, in the sense of implying everything. And if *everything* is asserted, half of what is asserted is surely *false*, because every statement has a denial.

The preceding discussion incidentally provides us with an answer to the old riddle: What happens when an irresistible force meets an immovable object? The description involves a contradiction. For an irresistible force to meet an immovable object, both must exist. There must be an irresistible force and there must also be an immovable object. But if there is an irresistible force there can be no immovable object. Here is the contradiction made explicit: there is an immovable object, and there is no immovable object. Given these inconsistent premisses, *any* conclusion may validly be inferred. So the correct answer to the question "What happens when an irresistible force meets an immovable object?" is "Everything!"

EXERCISES

I. For each of the following, either construct a formal proof of validity or prove invalidity by the method of assigning truth values to the simple statements involved.

★ 1. $(A \supset B) \cdot (C \supset D)$
   $\therefore (A \cdot C) \supset (B \vee D)$

2. $(E \supset F) \cdot (G \supset H)$
   $\therefore (E \vee G) \supset (F \cdot H)$

3. $I \supset (J \vee K)$
   $(J \cdot K) \supset L$
   $\therefore I \supset L$

4. $M \supset (N \cdot O)$
   $(N \vee O) \supset P$
   $\therefore M \supset P$

★ 5. $[(X \cdot Y) \cdot Z] \supset A$
   $(Z \supset A) \supset (B \supset C)$
   B
   $\therefore X \supset C$

6. $[(D \vee E) \cdot F] \supset G$
   $(F \supset G) \supset (H \supset I)$
   H
   $\therefore D \supset I$

7. $(J \cdot K) \supset (L \supset M)$
   $N \supset {\sim}M$
   ${\sim}(K \supset {\sim}N)$
   ${\sim}(J \supset {\sim}L)$
   $\therefore {\sim}J$

8. $(O \cdot P) \supset (Q \supset R)$
   $S \supset {\sim}R$
   ${\sim}(P \supset {\sim}S)$
   ${\sim}(O \supset Q)$
   $\therefore {\sim}O$

9. $T \supset (U \cdot V)$
   $U \supset (W \cdot X)$
   $(T \supset W) \supset (Y \equiv Z)$
   $(T \supset U) \supset {\sim}Y$
   ${\sim}Y \supset ({\sim}Z \supset X)$
   $\therefore X$

10. $A \supset (B \cdot C)$
   $B \supset (D \cdot E)$
   $(A \supset D) \supset (F \equiv G)$
   $A \supset (B \supset {\sim}F)$
   ${\sim}F \supset ({\sim}G \supset E)$
   $\therefore E$

II. For each of the following, either construct a formal proof of validity or prove invalidity by the method of assigning truth values to the simple statements involved.

★ 1. If the linguistics investigators are correct, then if more than one dialect was present in Ancient Greece, then different tribes came down at different times from the North. If different tribes came down at different times from the North, they must have come from the Danube River Valley. But archeological excavations would have revealed traces of different tribes there if different tribes had come down at different times from the North, and archeological excavations have revealed no such traces there. Hence if more than one dialect was present in Ancient Greece, then the linguistics investigators are not correct. (C, M, D, V, A)

2. If there are the ordinary symptoms of a cold and the patient has a high temperature, then if there are tiny spots on his skin, he has measles. Of course the patient cannot have measles if his record shows that he has had them before. The patient does have a high temperature and his record shows that he has had measles before. Besides the ordinary symptoms of a cold, there are tiny spots on his skin. I conclude that the patient has a viral infection. (O, T, S, M, R, V)

3. If God were willing to prevent evil, but unable to do so, he would be impotent; if he were able to prevent evil, but unwilling to do so, he would be malevolent. Evil can exist only if God is either unwilling or unable to prevent it. There is evil. If God exists, he is neither impotent nor malevolent. Therefore God does not exist. (W, A, I, M, E, G)

4. If I buy a new car this spring or have my old car fixed, then I'll get up to Canada this summer and stop off in Duluth. I'll visit my parents if I stop off in Duluth. If I visit my parents, they'll insist upon my spending the summer with them. If they insist upon my spending the summer with them, I'll be there till autumn. But if I stay there till autumn, then I won't get to Canada after all! So I won't have my old car fixed. (N, F, C, D, V, I, A)

★ 5. If Smith is intelligent and studies hard, then she will get good grades and pass her courses. If Smith studies hard but lacks intelligence, then her efforts will be appreciated; and if her efforts are appreciated, then she will pass her courses. If Smith is intelligent, then she studies hard. Therefore Smith will pass her courses. (*I, S, G, P, A*)

6. If there is a single norm for greatness of poetry, then Milton and Edgar Guest cannot both be great poets. If either Pope or Dryden is regarded as a great poet, then Wordsworth is certainly no great poet; but if Wordsworth is no great poet, then neither is Keats nor Shelley. But after all, even though Edgar Guest is not, Dryden and Keats are both great poets. Hence there is no single norm for greatness of poetry. (*N, M, G, P, D, W, K, S*)

7. If the butler were present, he would have been seen; and if he had been seen, he would have been questioned. If he had been questioned, he would have replied; and if he had replied, he would have been heard. But the butler was not heard. If the butler was neither seen nor heard, then he must have been on duty; and if he was on duty, he must have been present. Therefore the butler was questioned. (*P, S, Q, R, H, D*)

8. If the butler told the truth, then the window was closed when he entered the room; and if the gardener told the truth, then the automatic sprinkler system was not operating on the evening of the murder. If the butler and the gardener are both lying, then a conspiracy must exist to protect someone in the house and there would have been a little pool of water on the floor just inside the window. We know that the window could not have been closed when the butler entered the room. There was a little pool of water on the floor just inside the window. So if there is a conspiracy to protect someone in the house, then the gardener did not tell the truth. (*B, W, G, S, C, P*)

9. Their chief would leave the country if she feared capture, and she would not leave the country unless she feared capture. If she feared capture and left the country, then the enemy's espionage network would be demoralized and powerless to harm us. If she did not fear capture and remained in the country, it would mean that she was ignorant of our own agents' work. If she is really ignorant of our agents' work, then our agents can consolidate their positions within the enemy's organization; and if our agents can consolidate their positions there, they will render the enemy's espionage network powerless to harm us. Therefore the enemy's espionage network will be powerless to harm us. (*L, F, D, P, I, C*)

★ 10. If the investigators of extrasensory perception are regarded as honest, then considerable evidence for extrasensory perception must be admitted; and the doctrine of clairvoyance must be considered seriously if extrasensory perception is tentatively accepted as a fact. If considerable evidence for extrasensory perception is admitted, then it must be tentatively accepted as a fact and an effort must be made to explain it. The doctrine of clairvoyance must be considered seriously if we are prepared to take seriously that class of phenomena called occult; and if we are prepared to take seriously that class of phenomena called occult, a new respect must be paid to mediums. If we pursue the matter further, then if a new respect must be paid to mediums, we must take seriously their claims to communicate with the dead. We do pursue the matter further, but still we are practically committed to believing in ghosts if we take seriously the mediums' claims to communicate with the dead. Hence if the investigators of extrasensory perception are regarded as honest, we are practically committed to believing in ghosts. (*H, A, C, F, E, O, M, P, D, G*)

11. If we buy a lot then we will build a house. If we buy a lot then if we build a house then we will buy furniture. If we build a house then if we buy furniture then we will buy dishes. Therefore if we buy a lot then we will buy dishes. (L, H, F, D)

12. If your prices are low then your sales will be high, and if you sell quality merchandise then your customers will be satisfied. So if your prices are low and you sell quality merchandise, then your sales will be high and your customers satisfied. (L, H, Q, S)

13. If your prices are low then your sales will be high, and if you sell quality merchandise then your customers will be satisfied. So if either your prices are low or you sell quality merchandise, then either your sales will be high or your customers will be satisfied. (L, H, Q, S)

14. If Jordan joins the alliance then either Algeria or Syria boycotts it. If Kuwait joins the alliance then either Syria or Iraq boycotts it. Syria does not boycott it. Therefore if neither Algeria nor Iraq boycotts it then neither Jordan nor Kuwait joins the alliance. (J, A, S, K, I)

★ 15. If either Jordan or Algeria joins the alliance then if either Syria or Kuwait boycotts it then although Iraq does not boycott it Yemen boycotts it. If either Iraq or Morocco does not boycott it then Egypt will join the alliance. Therefore if Jordan joins the alliance then if Syria boycotts it then Egypt will join the alliance. (J, A, S, K, I, Y, M, E)

16. If the President cuts social security benefit payments he will lose the support of the senior citizens, and if he cuts defense spending then he will lose the support of the conservatives. If the President loses the support of either the senior citizens or the conservatives then his influence in the Senate will diminish. But his influence in the Senate will not diminish. Therefore the President will not cut either social security benefits or defense spending. (B, S, D, C, I)

17. If inflation continues then the interest rate will remain high. If inflation continues then if the interest rates remain high then business activity will decrease. If interest rates remain high then if business activity decreases then unemployment will rise. So if unemployment rises then inflation will continue. (I, H, D, U)

18. If taxes are reduced then inflation will rise, but if the budget is balanced then unemployment will increase. If the President keeps his campaign promises then either taxes are reduced or the budget is balanced. Therefore if the President keeps his campaign promises then either inflation will rise or unemployment will increase. (T, I, B, U, K)

19. Weather predicting is an exact science. Therefore either it will rain tomorrow or it won't. (W, R)

20. If either it will rain tomorrow or it won't rain tomorrow then weather predicting is an exact science. Therefore weather predicting is an exact science. (R, W)

1 0

Quantification Theory

Frege's . . . discovery of quantification, the deepest single technical advance ever made in logic.

—MICHAEL DUMMETT

10.1 *Singular Propositions*

The logical techniques of the two preceding chapters permit us to discriminate between valid and invalid arguments of one certain type. Arguments of that type are roughly characterized as those whose validity depends only upon the ways in which simple statements are truth-functionally combined into compound statements. There are, however, other types of arguments to which the validity criteria of the two preceding chapters do not apply. An example of a different type is the obviously valid argument

> All humans are mortal.
> Socrates is human.
> Therefore Socrates is mortal.

Were we to apply to this argument the evaluation methods previously introduced, we would symbolize it as

$$A$$
$$H$$
$$\therefore M$$

But in this notation it appears to be invalid. The techniques of symbolic logic presented thus far cannot be applied to arguments of this new type. The validity of the given argument does not depend upon the way in which simple statements are compounded, for no compound statements occur in it. Its validity depends rather upon the inner logical structure of the noncompound statements involved. To formulate methods for testing the validity of arguments of this new sort, techniques for describing and symbolizing noncompound statements by reference to their inner logical structure must be devised.[1]

The simplest kind of noncompound statement is illustrated by the second premiss of the preceding argument, "Socrates is human." Statements of this kind have traditionally been called *singular propositions*. An (affirmative) singular proposition asserts that a particular individual has a specified attribute. In the present example, ordinary grammar and traditional logic would agree in classifying "Socrates" as the *subject* term and "human" as the *predicate* term. The subject term denotes a particular individual and the predicate term designates some attribute the individual is said to have.

It is clear that one and the same subject term can occur in different singular propositions. Thus we have the term "Socrates" as subject term in each of the following: "Socrates is mortal," "Socrates is fat," "Socrates is wise," and "Socrates is beautiful." Of these, some are true (the first and third) and some are false (the second and fourth).[2] It is also clear that one and the same predicate term can occur in different singular propositions. Thus we have the term "human" as predicate term in each of the following: "Aristotle is human," "Brazil is human," "Chicago is human," and "Dorothy is human." Of course, some are true (the first and fourth) and some are false (the second and third).

It should be clear from the foregoing that the word "individual" is used to refer not only to persons, but to any *thing*—such as a country, a city, or in fact anything of which an attribute such as *human* or *mortal* can be meaningfully predicated. In all the examples given thus far the predicate term has been an *adjective*. From the point of view of grammar the distinction between adjective and noun is of considerable importance. But in the present chapter the difference is not significant, and we do not distinguish between "Socrates is mortal" and "Socrates is a mortal," or between "Socrates is wise" and "Socrates is a wise individual." A predicate may be either an adjective or a noun, or even a verb, as in "Aristotle writes," which can alternatively be expressed as "Aristotle is a writer."

Assuming that we can distinguish between individuals that have attributes and the attributes that they have, we introduce and use two different kinds of symbols for referring to them. In the following discussion we will use small or lowercase letters from *a* through *w* to denote individuals. These

---

[1]It was to arguments of this type that the classical or Aristotelian logic was primarily devoted, as described in Chapters 5 and 6. The older methods, however, do not possess the generality or power of the newer symbolic logic and cannot be extended to cover all asyllogistic inference.

[2]Here we shall follow the custom of ignoring the time factor, and will use the verb "is" in the tenseless sense of "is, will be, or has been." Where considerations of time change are crucial, the somewhat more complicated symbolism of the logic of relations is required for an adequate treatment.

symbols are *individual constants.* In any particular context in which they occur, each will designate one particular individual throughout the whole of that context. It will usually be convenient to denote an individual by the first letter of its (or his or her) name. Thus in the present context we should use the letters *s, a, b, c, d* to denote the individuals Socrates, Aristotle, Brazil, Chicago, and Dorothy, respectively. We shall use capital letters to symbolize attributes, and it will be convenient to use the same guiding principles here, using the letters *H, M, F, W, B* to symbolize the attributes of being human, of being mortal, of being fat, of being wise, and of being beautiful, respectively.

Having two groups of symbols, one for individuals and one for attributes of individuals, we adopt the convention that writing an attribute symbol immediately to the left of an individual symbol will symbolize the singular proposition affirming that the individual named has the attribute specified. Thus the singular proposition "Socrates is human" will be symbolized as *Hs.* The other singular propositions mentioned involving the predicate "human" are symbolized as *Ha, Hb, Hc,* and *Hd.* All of them, it will be observed, have a certain common pattern, not to be symbolized as *H* by itself but, rather, as *H−,* where the "−" indicates that to the right of the predicate symbol another symbol, an individual symbol, occurs. Instead of using the dash symbol ("−") as a place marker, it is customary to use the letter *x* (which is available since only the letters *a* through *w* are used as individual constants). We use *Hx* [sometimes written *H(x)*] to symbolize the common pattern of all singular propositions that attribute "being human" to an individual. The letter *x,* called an individual variable, is a mere *place marker,* serving to indicate where the various letters *a* through *w*—our individual constants—may be written for singular propositions to result.

The various singular propositions *Ha, Hb, Hc, Hd* are either true or false; but *Hx* is neither true nor false, not being a statement or proposition at all. The expression *Hx* is a propositional function, which may be defined as an expression that (1) contains an individual variable and (2) becomes a statement when an individual constant is substituted for the individual variable.[3] Individual constants are to be thought of as proper names of individuals. Any singular proposition is a *substitution instance* of a propositional function, the result of substituting an individual constant for the individual variable in that propositional function. Ordinarily, a propositional function will have some true substitution instances and some false substitution instances. The propositional functions considered thus far, that is, *Hx, Mx, Fx,* and *Wx,* are all of this kind. We shall call these propositional functions "simple predicates," to distinguish them from the more complex propositional functions introduced in the following sections. A *simple predicate,* then, is a propositional function having some true and some false substitution instances, each of which is an affirmative singular proposition.

[3]Some writers have regarded "propositional functions" as the meanings of such expressions, but here we define them to be the expressions themselves.

10.2 *Quantification*

The substitution of individual constants for individual variables is not the only way that propositions can be obtained from propositional functions. Propositions may also be obtained by the process called generalization or quantification. Predicate terms occur frequently in propositions other than singular ones. Thus the propositions "Everything is mortal" and "Something is beautiful" contain predicate terms, but are not singular propositions, since they do not contain the names of any particular individuals. Indeed, they do not refer specifically to *any* particular individuals, being *general* propositions.

The first may be expressed in various ways that are logically equivalent: either as "All things are mortal" or as

Given any individual thing whatever, it is mortal.

In the latter formulation, the word "it" is a relative pronoun, referring back to the word "thing" that precedes it in the statement. Using the letter x, our individual variable, in place of the pronoun "it" and its antecedent, we may rewrite the first general proposition as

Given any x, x is mortal.

Or, using the notation introduced in the preceding section, we may write

Given any x, Mx.

Although the propositional function Mx is not a proposition, here we have an expression containing it that *is* a proposition. The phrase "Given any x" is customarily symbolized by "(x)," which is called the universal quantifier. Our first general proposition may be completely symbolized as

$$(x)Mx$$

The second general proposition, "Something is beautiful," may also be expressed as

There is at least one thing that is beautiful.

In the latter formulation, the word "that" is a relative pronoun referring back to the word "thing." Using our individual variable x in place of both the pronoun "that" and its antecedent, we may rewrite the second general proposition as

There is at least one x such that x is beautiful.

Or, using the notation at hand, we may write

There is at least one *x* such that *Bx*.

Just as before, although *Bx* is a propositional function, we have here an expression containing it that is a proposition. The phrase "there is at least one *x* such that" is customarily symbolized by "$(\exists x)$," which is called the existential quantifier. The second general proposition may be completely symbolized as

$$(\exists x)Bx$$

Thus we see that propositions may be formed from propositional functions either by *instantiation*, that is, by substituting an individual constant for its individual variable, or by *generalization*, that is, by placing a universal or existential quantifier before it. It is clear that the universal quantification of a propositional function is true if and only if all of its substitution instances are true, and that the existential quantification of a propositional function is true if and only if it has at least one true substitution instance. If we grant that there is at least one individual, then every propositional function has at least one substitution instance. That substitution instance is not necessarily true, of course. Under this assumption, if the universal quantification of a propositional function is true, then its existential quantification is true also.

All the propositional functions mentioned thus far have had only affirmative singular propositions as substitution instances. But not all propositions are affirmative. The denial of the affirmative singular proposition "Socrates is mortal" is the negative singular proposition "Socrates is not mortal." In symbols we have *Ms* and ~*Ms*. The first is a substitution instance of the propositional function *Mx*. The second can be regarded as a substitution instance of the propositional function ~*Mx*. Here we enlarge our conception of propositional functions beyond the simple predicates introduced in the preceding section to permit them to contain the negation symbol "~." Thus the general proposition

Nothing is perfect.

can be paraphrased as

Everything is imperfect.

or as

Given any individual thing whatever, it is not perfect.

which can be rewritten as

Given any *x*, *x* is not perfect.

Now symbolizing the attribute of being perfect by the letter P and using the notation already introduced, we have

$$(x)\sim Px$$

Now the further connections between universal and existential quantification can be illustrated. The (universal) general proposition "Everything is mortal" is denied by the (existential) general proposition "Something is not mortal." These are symbolized as $(x)Mx$ and $(\exists x)\sim Mx$, respectively. Since one is the denial of the other, the biconditionals

$$[\sim(x)Mx] \equiv [(\exists x)\sim Mx] \quad \text{and} \quad [(x)Mx] \equiv [\sim(\exists x)\sim Mx]$$

are logically true. Similarly, the (universal) general proposition "Nothing is mortal" is denied by the (existential) general proposition "Something is mortal." These are symbolized as $(x)\sim Mx$ and $(\exists x)Mx$, respectively. Since one is the denial of the other, the further biconditionals

$$[\sim(x)\sim Mx] \equiv [(\exists x)Mx] \quad \text{and} \quad [(x)\sim Mx] \equiv [\sim(\exists x)Mx]$$

are logically true also. If we use the Greek letter *phi* to represent any simple predicate whatsoever, the relations between universal and existential quantification can be set down as follows:

$$[(x)\phi x] \equiv [\sim(\exists x)\sim \phi x]$$
$$[(\exists x)\phi x] \equiv [\sim(x)\sim \phi x]$$
$$[(x)\sim \phi x] \equiv [\sim(\exists x)\phi x]$$
$$[(\exists x)\sim \phi x] \equiv [\sim(x)\phi x]$$

More graphically, the general connections between universal and existential quantification can be described in terms of the square array shown in Figure 19.

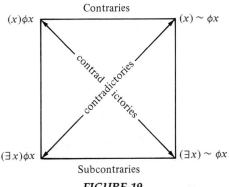

FIGURE 19

Continuing to assume the existence of at least one individual, we can say that the two top propositions are *contraries,* that is, they might both be false but cannot both be true; the two bottom propositions are *subcontraries,* that is, they can both be true but cannot both be false; propositions that are at opposite ends of the diagonals are *contradictories,* of which one must be true and the other false; and finally, on each side, the truth of the lower proposition is implied by the truth of the proposition directly above it.

10.3 *Traditional Subject–Predicate Propositions*

The four types of general propositions traditionally emphasized in the study of logic are illustrated by the following:

All humans are mortal.
No humans are mortal.
Some humans are mortal.
Some humans are not mortal.

These have been classified as "universal affirmative," "universal negative," "particular affirmative," and "particular negative," respectively, and their types abbreviated as *A, E, I,* and *O,* again respectively.[4]

In symbolizing these propositions by means of quantifiers, we are led to a further enlargement of our conception of a propositional function. Turning first to the *A* proposition, we proceed by means of successive paraphrasings, beginning with

Given any individual thing whatever, if it is human then it is mortal.

The two instances of the relative pronoun "it" clearly refer back to their common antecedent, the word "thing." As in the early part of the preceding section, since the three words have the same (indefinite) reference, they can be replaced by the letter "*x*," and the proposition rewritten as

Given any *x*, if *x* is human then *x* is mortal.

Now using our previously introduced notation for "if–then," we can rewrite the preceding as

Given any *x*, *x* is human $\supset$ *x* is mortal.

Finally, using our now familiar notation for propositional functions and quan-

---

[4]An account of their traditional analysis and nomenclature is presented in Chapter 5.

tifiers, the original A proposition is expressed as

$$(x)(Hx \supset Mx)$$

Our symbolic translation of the A proposition appears as the universal quantification of a new kind of propositional function. The expression $Hx \supset Mx$ is a propositional function that has as its substitution instances neither affirmative nor negative singular propositions, but conditional statements whose antecedents and consequents are singular propositions having the same subject term. Among the substitution instances of the propositional function $Hx \supset Mx$ are the conditional statements $Ha \supset Ma$, $Hb \supset Mb$, $Hc \supset Mc$, $Hd \supset Md$, and so on. There are also propositional functions whose substitution instances are conjunctions of singular propositions having the same subject terms. Thus the conjunctions $Ha \cdot Ma$, $Hb \cdot Mb$, $Hc \cdot Mc$, $Hd \cdot Md$, and so on, are substitution instances of the propositional function $Hx \cdot Mx$. There are also propositional functions such as $Wx \vee Bx$, whose substitution instances are disjunctions such as $Wa \vee Ba$ and $Wb \vee Bb$. In fact, any truth-functionally compound statement whose simple component statements are singular propositions all having the same subject term can be regarded as a substitution instance of a propositional function containing some or all of the various truth-functional connectives dot, wedge, horseshoe, three-bar equivalence, and curl, in addition to the simple predicates Ax, Bx, Cx, Dx, $\ldots$. In our translation of the A proposition as $(x)(Hx \supset Mx)$ the parentheses serve as punctuation marks. They indicate that the universal quantifier (x) "applies to" or "has within its scope" the entire (complex) propositional function $Hx \supset Mx$.

Before going on to discuss the other traditional forms of categorical propositions, it should be observed that our symbolic formula (x) $(Hx \supset Mx)$ translates not only the standard-form proposition "All H's are M's," but any other English sentence having the same meaning. There are many ways in English of saying the same thing—a partial list of them may be set down as "H's are M's," "An H is an M," "Every H is M," "Each H is M," "Any H is M," "No H's are not M," "Everything that is H is M," "Anything that is H is M," "If anything is H, it is M," "If something is H, it is M," "Whatever is H is M," "H's are all M's," "Only M's are H's," "None but M's are H's," "Nothing is an H unless it is an M," and "Nothing is an H but not an M." Some English idioms are a little misleading in using a temporal term when no reference to time is intended. Thus the proposition "H's are always M's" is ordinarily understood to mean simply that *all* H's are M's. Again, the same meaning may be expressed by the use of abstract nouns: "Humanity implies (or entails) mortality" is correctly symbolized as an A proposition. That the language of symbolic logic has a single expression for the common meaning of a considerable number of English sentences may be regarded as an advantage of symbolic logic over English for cognitive or informative purposes—although admittedly a disadvantage from the point of view of rhetorical power or poetic expressiveness.

The *E* proposition "No humans are mortal" may be successively para-phrased as

Given any individual thing whatever, if it is human then it is not mortal.
Given any *x*, if *x* is human then *x* is not mortal.
Given any *x*, *x* is human ⊃ *x* is not mortal.

and finally as

$$(x)(Hx \supset \sim Mx)$$

The preceding symbolic translation expresses not only the traditional *E* form in English, but also such diverse ways of saying the same thing as "There are no *H*'s that are *M*," "Nothing is both an *H* and an *M*," "*H*'s are never *M*," and so on.

Similarly, the *I* proposition "Some humans are mortal" may be successively paraphrased as

There is at least one thing that is human and mortal.
There is at least one *x* such that *x* is human and *x* is mortal.
There is at least one *x* such that *x* is human • *x* is mortal.

and then as

$$(\exists x)(Hx \cdot Mx)$$

Finally, the *O* proposition "Some humans are not mortal" is successively paraphrased as

There is at least one thing that is human but not mortal.
There is at least one *x* such that *x* is human and *x* is not mortal.
There is at least one *x* such that *x* is human • ~*x* is mortal.

and completely symbolized as

$$(\exists x)(Hx \cdot \sim Mx)$$

Where the Greek letters *phi* (φ) and *psi* (ψ) are used to represent any predicates whatever, the four general subject–predicate propositions of traditional logic may be represented in a square array as shown in Figure 20. Of these, the *A* and the *O* are "contradictories," each being the denial of the other; *E* and *I* are also contradictories.

It might be thought that an *I* proposition follows from its corresponding *A* proposition, and an *O* from its corresponding *E*; but this is not so. An *A* proposition may very well be true while its corresponding *I* proposition is

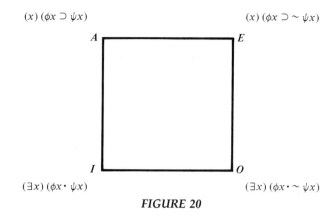

$(x)(\phi x \supset \psi x)$ $(x)(\phi x \supset \sim \psi x)$

$(\exists x)(\phi x \cdot \psi x)$ $(\exists x)(\phi x \cdot \sim \psi x)$

FIGURE 20

false. Where ϕx is a propositional function that has no true substitution instances, then no matter what kinds of substitution instances the propositional function ψx may have, the universal quantification of the (complex) propositional function $\phi x \supset \psi x$ will be true. For example, consider the propositional function "x is a centaur," which we abbreviate as Cx. Because there are no centaurs, every substitution instance of Cx is false, that is, $Ca, Cb, Cc, \ldots$ are all false. Hence every substitution instance of the complex propositional function $Cx \supset Bx$ will be a conditional statement whose antecedent is false. The substitution instances $Ca \supset Ba, Cb \supset Bb, Cc \supset Bc, \ldots$ are therefore all true, because any conditional statement asserting a material implication must be true if its antecedent is false. Because all its substitution instances are true, the universal quantification of the propositional function $Cx \supset Bx$, which is the A proposition $(x)(Cx \supset Bx)$, is true. But the corresponding I proposition $(\exists x)(Cx \cdot Bx)$ is false, because the propositional function $Cx \cdot Bx$ has no true substitution instances. That $Cx \cdot Bx$ has no true substitution instances follows from the fact that Cx has no true substitution instances. The various substitution instances of $Cx \cdot Bx$ are $Ca \cdot Ba, Cb \cdot Bb, Cc \cdot Bc, \ldots$, each of which is a conjunction whose first conjunct is false, because $Ca, Cb, Cc, \ldots$ are all false. Because all its substitution instances are false, the existential quantification of the propositional function $Cx \cdot Bx$, which is the I proposition $(\exists x)(Cx \cdot Bx)$, is false. Hence an A proposition may be true while its corresponding I proposition is false. If the propositional function Bx is replaced by the propositional function $\sim Bx$ in the preceding discussion, it will then establish that an E proposition may be true while its corresponding O proposition is false.

If we make the general assumption that there is at least one individual, then $(x)(Cx \supset Bx)$ does imply $(\exists x)(Cx \supset Bx)$. But the latter is not an I proposition. The I proposition "Some centaurs are beautiful" is symbolized as $(\exists x)(Cx \cdot Bx)$, which says that there is at least one centaur that is beautiful. But what is symbolized as $(\exists x)(Cx \supset Bx)$ can be rendered in English as "there is at least one thing such that if it is a centaur then it is beautiful." It does not say that there is a centaur, but only that there is an individual which is either not a centaur or is beautiful. And this proposition would be false in only two possible cases: first, if there were no individuals at all; and, second, if all individuals were centaurs and none of them was beautiful. We rule out the first case by making the explicit (and obviously true) assumption that there is at least one individual in the universe. And the second case is so extremely unplausible that any proposition of the form $(\exists x)(\phi x \supset \psi x)$ is bound to be quite trivial—in contrast to the significant I form $(\exists x)(\phi x \cdot \psi x)$. The foregoing should make clear that, although in English the A and I propositions "All humans are mortal" and "Some humans are mortal" differ only in their initial words "all" and "some," their difference in meaning is not confined to the matter of universal versus existential quantification, but goes deeper than that. The propositional functions quantified to yield A and I propositions are not just differently quantified, they are different propositional functions, one containing "$\supset$," the other "$\cdot$." In other words, A and I propositions are not so much alike as they appear in English. Their differences are brought out very clearly in the notation of propositional functions and quantifiers.

The four logical equivalences listed on page 329, together with the various logical equivalences accompanying the Rule of Replacement in Chapter 9, provide us with methods of replacing a given formula by a simpler formula logically equivalent to the given one. The kind of simplification intended here is achieved by shifting negation signs until they no longer apply to compound expressions but apply only to simple predicates. Thus the formula

$$\sim(\exists x)(Fx \cdot \sim Gx)$$

can be successively rewritten. First, by appealing to the third logical equivalence on page 329, it is transformed into

$$(x)\sim(Fx \cdot \sim Gx)$$

Then using De Morgan's Theorem it becomes

$$(x)(\sim Fx \ \text{v} \sim \sim Gx)$$

Next the Principle of Double Negation gives us

$$(x)(\sim Fx \ \text{v} \ Gx)$$

And finally, by invoking the definition of Material Implication, the original formula is rewritten as the A proposition

$$(x)(Fx \supset Gx)$$

A formula in which negation signs apply only to simple predicates is sometimes called a *normal form formula*.

Before turning to the topic of inferences involving noncompound statements, the reader should acquire some practice in translating noncompound statements from English into our logical symbolism. The English language has so many irregular or idiomatic constructions that there can be no simple rules for translating an English sentence into logical notation. What is required in each case is that the meaning of the sentence be understood and then restated in terms of propositional functions and quantifiers.

EXERCISES

I. Translate each of the following into the logical notation of propositional functions and quantifiers, in each case using the abbreviations suggested, and having each formula begin with a quantifier, *not* with a negation symbol.

★ 1. Bats are mammals. (*Bx: x* is a bat; *Mx: x* is a mammal.)

2. Sparrows are not mammals. (*Sx: x* is a sparrow; *Mx: x* is a mammal.)

3. Reporters are present. (*Rx: x* is a reporter; *Px: x* is present.)

4. Nurses are always considerate. (*Nx: x* is a nurse; *Cx: x* is considerate.)

★ 5. Diplomats are not always rich. (*Dx: x* is a diplomat; *Rx: x* is rich.)

6. Ambassadors are always dignified. (*Ax: x* is an ambassador; *Dx: x* is dignified.)

7. No boy scout ever cheats. (*Bx: x* is a boy scout; *Cx: x* cheats.)

8. Only licensed physicians can charge for medical treatment. (*Lx: x* is a licensed physician; *Cx: x* can charge for medical treatment.)

9. Snake bites are sometimes fatal. (*Sx: x* is a snake bite; *Fx: x* is fatal.)

★ 10. The common cold is never fatal. (*Cx: x* is a common cold; *Fx: x* is fatal.)

11. A child pointed his finger at the emperor. (*Cx: x* is a child; *Px: x* pointed his finger at the emperor.)

12. Not all children pointed their fingers at the emperor. (*Cx: x* is a child; *Px: x* pointed his finger at the emperor.)

13. All that glitters is not gold. (*Gx: x* glitters; *Ax: x* is gold.)

14. None but the brave deserve the fair. (*Bx: x* is brave; *Dx: x* deserves the fair.)

★ 15. Only citizens of the United States can vote in U.S. elections. (*Cx: x* is a citizen of the United States; *Vx: x* can vote in U.S. elections.)

16. Citizens of the United States can vote only in U.S. elections. (*Ex: x* is an election in which citizens of the United States can vote; *Ux: x* is a U.S. election.)

17. There are honest politicians. (*Hx: x* is honest; *Px: x* is a politician.)

18. Not every applicant was hired. (*Ax: x* is an applicant; *Hx: x* was hired.)

19. Not any applicant was hired. (*Ax: x* is an applicant; *Hx: x* was hired.)

20. Nothing of importance was said. (*Ix: x* is of importance; *Sx: x* was said.)

II. For each of the following find a normal form formula logically equivalent to the given one.

★ 1. ~(x)(Ax ⊃ Bx)   2. ~(x)(Cx ⊃ ~Dx)

    3. $\sim(\exists x)(Ex \cdot Fx)$ 4. $\sim(\exists x)(Gx \cdot \sim Hx)$
★ 5. $\sim(x)(\sim Ix \text{ v } Jx)$ 6. $\sim(x)(\sim Kx \text{ v } \sim Lx)$
    7. $\sim(\exists x)[\sim(Mx \text{ v } Nx)]$ 8. $\sim(\exists x)[\sim(Ox \text{ v } \sim Px)]$
    9. $\sim(\exists x)[\sim(\sim Qx \text{ v } Rx)]$ 10. $\sim(x)[\sim(Sx \cdot \sim Tx)]$
   11. $\sim(x)[\sim(\sim Ux \cdot \sim Vx)]$ 12. $\sim(\exists x)[\sim(\sim Wx \text{ v } Xx)]$

10.4 *Proving Validity*

If we wish to construct formal proofs of validity for arguments whose validity
turns upon the inner structures of noncompound statements occurring in
them, we must expand our list of Rules of Inference. Only four additional
rules are required, and they will be introduced in connection with arguments
for which they are needed. Let us consider the first argument cited in the
present chapter: "All humans are mortal. Socrates is human. Therefore Socrates is mortal." It is symbolized as

$$(x)(Hx \supset Mx)$$
$$Hs$$
$$\therefore Ms$$

The first premiss affirms the truth of the universal quantification of the
propositional function $Hx \supset Mx$. Since the universal quantification of a propositional function is true if and only if all of its substitution instances are
true, from the first premiss we can infer any desire substitution instance of
the propositional function $Hx \supset Mx$. In particular we can infer the substitution instance $Hs \supset Ms$. From that and the second premiss Hs, the conclusion
Ms follows directly by *modus ponens*.

If we add to our list of Rules of Inference the principle that any substitution
instance of a propositional function can validly be inferred from its universal
quantification, then we can give a formal proof of the validity of the given
argument by reference to the expanded list of elementary valid argument
forms. This new Rule of Inference is the Principle of Universal Instantiation[5]
and is abbreviated as **"UI."** Using the Greek letter *nu* (ν) to represent any
individual symbol whatever, we state the new rule as

UI: $\dfrac{(x)(\phi x)}{\therefore \phi \nu}$ (where ν is any individual symbol)

A formal proof of validity may now be written as

        1. $(x)(Hx \supset Mx)$
        2. Hs / $\therefore Ms$
        3. $Hs \supset Ms$ 1, **UI**
        4. Ms 3,2, M.P.

[5]This rule and the three following are variants of rules for "natural deduction" that were
devised independently by Gerhard Gentzen and Stanislaw Jaskowski in 1934.

The addition of **UI** strengthens our proof apparatus considerably, but more is required. The need for additional rules governing quantification arises in connection with arguments like "All humans are mortal. All Greeks are human. Therefore all Greeks are mortal." The symbolic translation of this argument is

$$(x)(Hx \supset Mx)$$
$$(x)(Gx \supset Hx)$$
$$\therefore (x)(Gx \supset Mx)$$

Here both premises and conclusion are general propositions rather than singular ones, universal quantifications of propositional functions rather than substitution instances of them. From the two premises, by **UI**, we may validly infer the following pairs of conditional statements:

$$\left\{ \begin{array}{l} Ga \supset Ha \\ Ha \supset Ma \end{array} \right\}, \left\{ \begin{array}{l} Gb \supset Hb \\ Hb \supset Mb \end{array} \right\}, \left\{ \begin{array}{l} Gc \supset Hc \\ Hc \supset Mc \end{array} \right\}, \left\{ \begin{array}{l} Gd \supset Hd \\ Hd \supset Md \end{array} \right\}, \ldots$$

and by successive uses of the principle of the Hypothetical Syllogism we may validly infer the conclusions:

$$Ga \supset Ma, \quad Gb \supset Mb, \quad Gc \supset Mc, \quad Gd \supset Md, \ldots$$

If $a, b, c, d, \ldots$ are all the individuals there are, it follows that from the truth of the premises one can validly infer the truth of all substitution instances of the propositional function $Gx \supset Mx$. Since the universal quantification of a propositional function is true if and only if all its substitution instances are true, we can go on to infer the truth of $(x)(Gx \supset Mx)$, which is the conclusion of the given argument.

The preceding paragraph may be thought of as containing an *informal* proof of the validity of the given argument, in which the principle of the Hypothetical Syllogism and two principles governing quantification are appealed to. But it describes indefinitely long sequences of statements: the lists of all substitution instances of the two propositional functions quantified universally in the premises, and the list of all substitution instances of the propositional function whose universal quantification is the conclusion. A *formal* proof cannot contain such indefinitely, perhaps even infinitely long sequences of statements, so some method must be sought for expressing those indefinitely long sequences in some finite, definite fashion.

A method for doing this is suggested by a common technique of elementary mathematics. A geometer, seeking to prove that *all* triangles possess a certain attribute, may begin with the words "Let *ABC* be any arbitrarily selected triangle." Then the geometer begins to reason about the triangle *ABC*, and establishes that it has the attribute in question. From this he concludes that *all* triangles have that attribute. Now what justifies his final conclusion? Granted of the particular triangle *ABC* that *it* has the attribute, why does it follow that *all* triangles do? The answer to this question is easily given. If no assumption other than its triangularity is made about the triangle *ABC*, then the symbol "*ABC*" can be taken as denoting any triangle you please. Then the geometer's argument establishes that *any* triangle has the attribute in question, and if *any* triangle has it, then *all* triangles do. We wish now to introduce a notation analogous to the geometer's in talking about "any arbitrarily selected triangle *ABC*." This will avoid the pretense of listing an indefinite or infinite number of substitution instances of a propositional function, for instead we shall talk about *any* substitution instance of the propositional function.

We shall use the (hitherto unused) lowercase letter *y* to denote *any arbitrarily selected* individual. We shall use it in a way similar to that in which the geometer used the letters *ABC*. Since the truth of *any* substitution instance of a propositional function follows from its universal quantification, we can infer the substitution instance that results from replacing *x* by *y*, where *y* denotes "any arbitrarily selected" individual. Thus we may begin our formal proof of the validity of the given argument as follows:

1. $(x)(Hx \supset Mx)$
2. $(x)(Gx \supset Hx) / \therefore (x)(Gx \supset Mx)$
3. $Hy \supset My$ 1, **UI**
4. $Gy \supset Hy$ 2, **UI**
5. $Gy \supset My$ 4,3, H.S.

From the premises we have deduced the statement $Gy \supset My$, which in effect, since *y* denotes "any arbitrarily selected individual," asserts the truth of *any* substitution instance of the propositional function $Gx \supset Mx$. Since *any* substitution instance is true, all substitution instances must be true, and hence the universal quantification of that propositional function is true also. We may add this principle to our list of Rules of Inference, stating it as "From the substitution instance of a propositional function with respect to the name of *any arbitrarily selected* individual, one can validly infer the universal quantification of that propositional function." Since this new principle permits us to *generalize,* that is, to go from a special substitution instance to a generalized or universally quantified expression, we refer to it as the Principle of Universal Generalization and abbreviate it as **"UG."** It is stated as

UG: $\dfrac{\phi y}{\therefore (x)(\phi x)}$ (Where *y* denotes "any arbitrarily selected individual")

The sixth and final line of the formal proof already begun may now be written (and justified) as

6. $(x)(Gx \supset Mx)$ 5, **UG**

Let us review the preceding discussion. In the geometer's proof the only assumption made about *ABC* is that it is a triangle; hence what is proved true of *ABC* is proved true of *any* triangle. In our proof the only assumption made about *y* is that it is an individual; hence what is proved true of *y* is proved true of *any* individual. The symbol *y* is an individual symbol, but it is a very special one. It is typically introduced into a proof by using **UI**. And only its presence permits the use of **UG**.

Another argument the demonstration of whose validity requires the use of **UG** as well as **UI** is "No humans are perfect. All Greeks are humans. Therefore no Greeks are perfect." The formal proof of its validity is

1. $(x)(Hx \supset {\sim}Px)$
2. $(x)(Gx \supset Hx) / \therefore (x)(Gx \supset {\sim}Px)$
3. $Hy \supset {\sim}Py$ 1, **UI**
4. $Gy \supset Hy$ 2, **UI**
5. $Gy \supset {\sim}Py$ 4,3, H.S.
6. $(x)(Gx \supset {\sim}Px)$ 5, **UG**

There may seem to be some artificiality about the foregoing. It may be urged that distinguishing carefully between $(x)(\phi x)$ and ϕy, so they are not identified but must be inferred from each other by **UI** and **UG**, is to insist upon a distinction without a difference. But there is certainly a *formal* difference between them. The statement $(x)(Hx \supset Mx)$ is a noncompound statement, whereas $Hy \supset My$ is compound, being a conditional. From the two noncompound statements $(x)(Gx \supset Hx)$ and $(x)(Hx \supset Mx)$ no relevant inference can be drawn by means of the original list of nineteen Rules of Inference. But from the compound statements $Gy \supset Hy$ and $Hy \supset My$ the indicated conclusion $Gy \supset My$ follows by a Hypothetical Syllogism. The principle of **UI** is used to get from noncompound statements, to which our earlier Rules of Inference do not usefully apply, to compound statements, to which they *can* be applied to derive the desired conclusion. The quantification principles thus augment our logical apparatus to make it capable of validating arguments essentially involving noncompound (generalized) propositions as well as the other (simpler) kind of argument discussed in our earlier chapters. On the other hand, in spite of this formal difference, there must be a logical equivalence between $(x)(\phi x)$ and ϕy, or the rules **UI** and **UG** would not be valid. Both the difference and the logical equivalence are important for our purpose of validating arguments by reference to a list of Rules of Inference. The addition of **UI** and **UG** to our list strengthens it considerably.

The list must be expanded further when we turn to arguments involving existential propositions. A convenient example with which to begin is, "All criminals are vicious. Some humans are criminals. Therefore some humans are vicious." It is symbolized as

$(x)(Cx \supset Vx)$
$(\exists x)(Hx \cdot Cx)$
$\therefore (\exists x)(Hx \cdot Vx)$

The existential quantification of a propositional function is true if and only if it has at least one true substitution instance. Hence whatever attribute may be designated by ϕ, $(\exists x)(\phi x)$ says that there is at least one individual that has the attribute ϕ. If an individual constant (other than the special symbol y) is used nowhere earlier in the context, we may use it to denote either the individual that has the attribute ϕ or some one of the individuals that have ϕ, if there are several. Knowing that there is such an individual, say, a, we know that ϕa is a true substitution instance of the propositional function ϕx. Hence we add to our list of Rules of Inference this principle: From the existential quantification of a propositional function we may infer the truth of its substitution instance with respect to any individual constant (other than y) that occurs nowhere earlier in that context. The new Rule of Inference is the principle of Existential Instantiation and is abbreviated as **"EI."** It is stated as

EI: $\begin{array}{l} (\exists x)(\phi x) \\ \therefore\ \phi \nu \end{array}$ [where ν is any individual constant (other than y) having no previous occurrence in the context]

Granted the additional Rule of Inference **EI**, we may begin a demonstration of the validity of the stated argument

1. $(x)(Cx \supset Vx)$
2. $(\exists x)(Hx \cdot Cx)/\therefore (\exists x)(Hx \cdot Vx)$
3. $Ha \cdot Ca$ 2, **EI**
4. $Ca \supset Va$ 1, **UI**
5. $Ca \cdot Ha$ 3, Com.
6. Ca 5, Simp.
7. Va 4,6, M.P.
8. Ha 3, Simp.
9. $Ha \cdot Va$ 8,7, Conj.

Thus far we have deducted $Ha \cdot Va$, which is a substitution instance of the propositional function whose existential quantification is asserted by the conclusion. Since the existential quantification of a propositional function is true if and only if it has at least one true substitution instance, we add to our list of Rules of Inference the principle that from any true substitution instance of a propositional function we may validly infer the existential quantification of that propositional function. This fourth and final Rule of Inference is the Principle of Existential Generalization, abbreviated as **"EG"** and stated as

EG: $\begin{array}{l} \phi \nu \\ \therefore (\exists x)(\phi x) \end{array}$ (where ν is any individual symbol)

The tenth and final line of the demonstration already begun may now be written (and justified) as

10. $(\exists x)(Hx \cdot Vx)$ 9, **EG**

The need for the indicated restriction on the use of **EI** can be seen by considering the obviously invalid argument "Some alligators are kept in captivity. Some birds are kept in captivity. Therefore some alligators are birds." If we failed to heed the restriction on **EI** that a substitution instance of a propositional function inferred by it from the existential quantification of that propositional function can contain only an individual symbol (other than y) having no previous occurrence in the context, then we might proceed to construct a "proof" of validity for this invalid argument. Such an erroneous "proof" might proceed as follows:

1. $(\exists x)(Ax \cdot Cx)$
2. $(\exists x)(Bx \cdot Cx)/ \therefore (\exists x)(Ax \cdot Bx)$
3. $Aa \cdot Ca$ 1, **EI**
4. $Ba \cdot Ca$ 2, **EI** (wrong)
5. Aa 3, Simp.
6. Ba 4, Simp.
7. $Aa \cdot Ba$ 5,6 Conj.
8. $(\exists x)(Ax \cdot Bx)$ 7, **EG**

The error in this "proof" occurs at line 4. From the second premiss $(\exists x)(Bx \cdot Cx)$, we know that there is at least one thing that is both a bird and kept in captivity. *If* we were free to assign it the name a we could, of course, assert $Ba \cdot Ca$. But we are not free to make any such assignment of "a," for it has already been preempted in line 3 to serve as name for an alligator that is kept in captivity. To avoid errors of this sort, we must obey the indicated restriction whenever we use **EI**. The preceding discussion should make clear that in any demonstration requiring the use of both **EI** and **UI**, **EI** should always be used first.

For more complicated modes of argumentation, especially those that involve relations, certain additional restrictions must be placed on our four quantification rules. But for arguments of the present sort, traditionally called categorical syllogisms, the present restrictions are sufficient to prevent mistakes.

EXERCISES

I. Construct a formal proof of validity for each of the following arguments.

★ 1. $(x)(Ax \supset \sim Bx)$
$(\exists x)(Cx \cdot Ax)$
$\therefore (\exists x)(Cx \cdot \sim Bx)$

2. $(x)(Dx \supset \sim Ex)$
$(x)(Fx \supset Ex)$
$\therefore (x)(Fx \supset \sim Dx)$

3. $(x)(Gx \supset Hx)$
$(x)(Ix \supset \sim Hx)$
$\therefore (x)(Ix \supset \sim Gx)$

4. $(\exists x)(Jx \cdot Kx)$
$(x)(Jx \supset Lx)$
$\therefore (\exists x)(Lx \cdot \sim Kx)$

★ 5. $(x)(Mx \supset Nx)$
$(\exists x)(Mx \cdot Ox)$
$\therefore (\exists x)(Ox \cdot Nx)$

6. $(\exists x)(Px \cdot \sim Qx)$
$(x)(Px \supset Rx)$
$\therefore (\exists x)(Rx \cdot \sim Qx)$

7. $(x)(Sx \supset \sim Tx)$
$(\exists x)(Sx \cdot Ux)$
$\therefore (\exists x)(Ux \cdot \sim Tx)$

8. $(x)(Vx \supset Wx)$
$(x)(Wx \supset \sim Xx)$
$\therefore (x)(Xx \supset \sim Vx)$

9. $(\exists x)(Yx \cdot Zx)$
$(x)(Zx \supset Ax)$
$\therefore (\exists x)(Ax \cdot Yx)$

10. $(x)(Bx \supset \sim Cx)$
$(\exists x)(Cx \cdot Dx)$
$\therefore (\exists x)(Dx \cdot \sim Bx)$

11. $(x)(Fx \supset Gx)$
$(\exists x)(Fx \cdot \sim Gx)$
$\therefore (\exists x)(Gx \cdot \sim Fx)$

II. Construct a formal proof of validity for each of the following arguments, in each case using the suggested notations.

★ 1. No athletes are bookworms. Carol is a bookworm. Therefore Carol is not an athlete. (Ax, Bx, c)

2. All dancers are exuberant. Some fencers are not exuberant. Therefore some fencers are not dancers. (Dx, Ex, Fx)

3. No gamblers are happy. Some idealists are happy. Therefore some idealists are not gamblers. (Gx, Hx, Ix)

4. All jesters are knaves. No knaves are lucky. Therefore no jesters are lucky. (Jx, Kx, Lx)

★ 5. All mountaineers are neighborly. Some outlaws are mountaineers. Therefore some outlaws are neighborly. (Mx, Nx, Ox)

6. Only pacifists are Quakers. There are religious Quakers. Therefore pacifists are sometimes religious. (Px, Qx, Rx)

7. To be a swindler is to be a thief. None but the underprivileged are thieves. Therefore swindlers are always underprivileged. (Sx, Tx, Ux)

8. No violinists are not wealthy. There are no wealthy xylophonists. Therefore violinists are never xylophonists. (Vx, Wx, Xx)

9. None but the brave deserve the fair. Only soldiers are brave. Therefore the fair are deserved only by soldiers. $(Dx: x$ deserves the fair; $Bx: x$ is brave; $Sx: x$ is a soldier)

10. Everyone that asketh receiveth. Simon receiveth not. Therefore Simon asketh not. (Ax, Rx, s)

10.5 *Proving Invalidity*

To prove the invalidity of an argument involving quantifiers, we can use the method of refutation by logical analogy. For example, the argument "All communists are opponents of the administration; some delegates are opponents of the administration; therefore some delegates are communists" is proved invalid by the analogy "All cats are animals; some dogs are animals; therefore some dogs are cats"; which is obviously invalid, since its premises are known to be true and its conclusion known to be false. But such analogies are not always easy to devise. Some more nearly effective method of proving invalidity is desirable.

In the preceding chapter we developed a method of proving invalidity for arguments involving truth-functional compound statements. That method consisted of making truth value assignments to the component simple statements in arguments in such a way as to make the premises true and the conclusions false. That method can be adapted for arguments involving quantifiers. The adaptation involves our general assumption that there is at least one individual. For an argument involving quantifiers to be valid it must be impossible for its premises to be true and its conclusion false as long as there is at least one individual.

The general assumption that there is at least one individual is satisfied if there is exactly one individual, or exactly two individuals, or exactly three individuals, or. . . . If any one of these assumptions about the exact number of individuals is made, there is an equivalence between general propositions and truth-functional compounds of singular propositions. If there is exactly one individual, say, a, then

$$(x)(\phi x) \equiv \phi a \equiv (\exists x)(\phi x)$$

If there are exactly two individuals, say, a and b, then

$$(x)(\phi x) \equiv [\phi a \cdot \phi b] \qquad \text{and} \qquad (\exists x)(\phi x) \equiv [\phi a \text{ v } \phi b]$$

If there are exactly three individuals, say, a, b, and c, then

$$(x)(\phi x) \equiv [\phi a \cdot \phi b \cdot \phi c] \qquad \text{and} \qquad (\exists x)(\phi x) \equiv [\phi a \text{ v } \phi b \text{ v } \phi c]$$

In general, if there are exactly n individuals, say, a, b, c, . . . , n, then

$$(x)(\phi x) \equiv [\phi a \cdot \phi b \cdot \phi c \cdots \cdot \phi n] \qquad \text{and}$$
$$(\exists x)(\phi x) \equiv [\phi a \text{ v } \phi b \text{ v } \phi c \text{ v } \cdots \text{ v } \phi n]$$

These biconditionals are true as a consequence of our definitions of the universal and existential quantifiers. No use is made here of the four quantification rules explained in the preceding section.

An argument involving quantifiers is valid *if and only if* it is valid no matter how many individuals there are, provided there is at least one. So an argument involving quantifiers is proved invalid if there is a possible universe or *model* containing at least one individual such that the argument's premises are true and its conclusion false *of that model.* Consider the argument "All mercenaries are undependable. No guerrillas are mercenaries. Therefore no guerrillas are undependable." It may be symbolized as

$$(x)(Mx \supset Ux)$$
$$(x)(Gx \supset {\sim}Mx)$$
$$\therefore (x)(Gx \supset {\sim}Ux)$$

If there is exactly one individual, say, *a*, this argument is logically equivalent to

$$Ma \supset Ua$$
$$Ga \supset \sim Ma$$
$$\therefore Ga \supset \sim Ua$$

The latter can be proved invalid by assigning the truth value *true* to *Ga* and *Ua* and *false* to *Ma*. (This assignment of truth values is a shorthand way to describe the *model* in question as containing only the one individual *a* which is a guerrilla and undependable but is not a mercenary.) Hence the original argument is not valid for a model containing exactly one individual, and is therefore *invalid*. Similarly, we can prove the invalidity of the first argument mentioned in this section by describing a model containing exactly one individual *a* such that *Aa* and *Da* are assigned *truth* and *Ca* is assigned *falsehood*.[6]

Some arguments, for example,

$$(\exists x)Fx$$
$$\therefore (x)Fx$$

may be valid for any model in which there is exactly one individual, but invalid for a model containing two or more individuals. Such arguments must count as invalid also, because a valid argument must be valid regardless of how many individuals there are, so long as there is at least one. Another example of this kind of argument is "All collies are affectionate. Some collies are watchdogs. Therefore all watchdogs are affectionate." Its symbolic translation is

$$(x)(Cx \supset Ax)$$
$$(\exists x)(Cx \cdot Wx)$$
$$\therefore (x)(Wx \supset Ax)$$

For a model containing exactly one individual *a* it is logically equivalent to

$$Ca \supset Aa$$
$$Ca \cdot Wa$$
$$\therefore Wa \supset Aa$$

which is valid. But for a model containing two individuals *a* and *b* it is logically

---

[6]Here we assume that the simple predicates *Ax, Bx, Cx, Dx*, . . .occurring in our propositions are neither necessary, that is, logically true of all individuals (for example, *x* is identical with itself), nor impossible, that is, logically false of all individuals (for example, *x* is different from itself). We also assume that the only logical relations among the simple predicates involved are those asserted or logically implied by the premisses. The point of these restrictions is to permit us to assign truth values arbitrarily to the substitution instances of these simple predicates without any inconsistency—for a correct description of any model must of course be consistent.

equivalent to

$$(Ca \supset Aa) \cdot (Cb \supset Ab)$$
$$(Ca \cdot Wa) \text{ v } (Cb \cdot Wb)$$
$$\therefore (Wa \supset Aa) \cdot (Wb \supset Ab)$$

which is proved invalid by assigning *truth* to *Ca, Aa, Wa, Wb,* and *falsehood* to *Cb* and *Ab.* Hence the original argument is not valid for a model containing exactly two individuals, and is therefore *invalid.* For any invalid argument of this general type it is possible to describe a model containing some definite number of individuals for which its logically equivalent truth-functional argument can be proved invalid by the method of assigning truth values.

It should be emphasized again: In moving from a given argument involving general propositions to a truth-functional argument that for a specified model is logically equivalent to the given argument, no use is made of our four quantification rules. Instead, each statement of the truth-functional argument is logically equivalent to the corresponding general proposition of the given argument by way of biconditionals whose logical truth for the model in question follows from the very definitions of the universal and existential quantifiers.

The procedure for proving the invalidity of an argument containing general propositions is the following. First, consider a one-element model containing only the individual *a*. Then, write out the logically equivalent truth-functional argument for that model, which is obtained by moving from each general proposition (quantified propositional function) of the original argument to the substitution instance of that propositional function with respect to *a*. If the truth-functional argument can be proved invalid by assigning truth values to its component simple statements, that suffices to prove the original argument invalid. If that cannot be done, next consider a two-element model containing the individuals *a* and *b*. To obtain the logically equivalent truth-functional argument for this larger model one can simply join to each original substitution instance with respect to *a* a new substitution instance of the same propositional function with respect to *b*. This "joining" must be in accord with the logical equivalence stated on page 343; that is, where the original argument contains a universally quantified propositional function $(x)(\phi x)$, the new substitution instance ϕb is combined with the first substitution instance ϕa by conjunction ("•"), but where the original argument contains an existentially quantified propositional function $(\exists x)(\phi x)$, the new substitution instance ϕb is combined with the first substitution instance ϕa by disjunction ("v"). The preceding example illustrates this procedure. If the new truth-functional argument can be proved invalid by assigning truth values to its component simple statements, that suffices to prove the original argument invalid. If that cannot be done, next consider a three-element model containing the individuals *a, b,* and *c*. And so on. None of the immediately following exercises requires a model containing more than two elements, but some of those on pages 350–353 may require a three-element model. However, none of the exercises in this book requires a model containing more than three elements.

EXERCISES

I. Prove the invalidity of the following:

★ 1. $(\exists x)(Ax \cdot Bx)$
$(\exists x)(Cx \cdot Bx)$
∴ $(x)(Cx \supset {\sim}Ax)$

2. $(x)(Dx \supset {\sim}Ex)$
$(x)(Ex \supset Fx)$
∴ $(x)(Fx \supset {\sim}Dx)$

3. $(x)(Gx \supset Hx)$
$(x)(Gx \supset Ix)$
∴ $(x)(Ix \supset Hx)$

4. $(\exists x)(Jx \cdot Kx)$
$(\exists x)(Kx \cdot Lx)$
∴ $(\exists x)(Lx \cdot Jx)$

★ 5. $(\exists x)(Mx \cdot Nx)$
$(\exists x)(Mx \cdot Ox)$
∴ $(x)(Ox \supset Nx)$

6. $(x)(Px \supset {\sim}Qx)$
$(x)(Px \supset {\sim}Rx)$
∴ $(x)(Rx \supset {\sim}Qx)$

7. $(x)(Sx \supset {\sim}Tx)$
$(x)(Tx \supset Ux)$
∴ $(\exists x)(Ux \cdot {\sim}Sx)$

8. $(\exists x)(Vx \cdot {\sim}Wx)$
$(\exists x)(Wx \cdot {\sim}Xx)$
∴ $(\exists x)(Xx \cdot {\sim}Vx)$

9. $(\exists x)(Yx \cdot Zx)$
$(\exists x)(Ax \cdot Zx)$
∴ $(\exists x)(Ax \cdot {\sim}Yx)$

10. $(\exists x)(Bx \cdot {\sim}Cx)$
$(x)(Dx \supset {\sim}Cx)$
∴ $(x)(Dx \supset Bx)$

II. Prove the invalidity of the following, in each case using the suggested notation.

★ 1. All anarchists are bearded. All communists are bearded. Therefore all anarchists are communists. (Ax, Bx, Cx)

2. No diplomats are extremists. Some fanatics are extremists. Therefore some diplomats are not fanatics. (Dx, Ex, Fx)

3. All generals are handsome. Some intellectuals are handsome. Therefore some generals are intellectuals. (Gx, Hx, Ix)

4. Some journalists are not kibitzers. Some kibitzers are not lucky. Therefore some journalists are not lucky. (Jx, Kx, Lx)

★ 5. Some malcontents are noisy. Some officials are not noisy. Therefore no officials are malcontents. (Mx, Nx, Ox)

6. Some physicians are quacks. Some quacks are not responsible. Therefore some physicians are not responsible. (Px, Qx, Rx)

7. Some politicians are leaders. Some leaders are not orators. Therefore some orators are not politicians. (Px, Lx, Ox)

8. None but the brave deserve the fair. Every soldier is brave. Therefore none but soldiers deserve the fair. $(Dx:$ x deserves the fair; $Bx:$ x is brave; $Sx:$ x is a soldier)

9. If anything is metallic, then it is breakable. There are breakable ornaments. Therefore there are metallic ornaments. (Mx, Bx, Ox)

10. Only students are members. Only members are welcome. Therefore all students are welcome. (Sx, Mx, Wx)

10.6 *Asyllogistic Inference*

All the arguments considered in the preceding two sections were of the form traditionally called categorical syllogisms. These consist of two premises and a conclusion, each of which is analyzable either as a singular proposition or as one of the *A, E, I,* or *O* varieties. We turn now to the problem of evaluating somewhat more complicated arguments. These require no greater logical apparatus than has already been developed. Yet they are *asyllogistic* arguments and require a more powerful logic than was traditionally used in testing categorical syllogisms.

In this section we are still concerned with general propositions, formed by quantifying propositional functions that contain only a single individual variable. In the categorical syllogism, the only kinds of propositional functions quantified were of the forms $\phi x \supset \psi x$, $\phi x \supset \sim\psi x$, $\phi x \cdot \psi x$, and $\phi x \cdot \sim\psi x$. But now we shall be quantifying propositional functions with more complicated internal structures. An example will help make this clear. Consider the argument

> Hotels are both expensive and depressing.
> Some hotels are shabby.
> Therefore some expensive things are shabby.

This argument, for all its obvious validity, is not amenable to the traditional sort of analysis. True enough, it could be expressed in terms of *A* and *I* proportions by using the symbols *Hx, Bx, Sx,* and *Ex* to abbreviate the propositional functions "*x* is a hotel," "*x* is both expensive and depressing," "*x* is shabby," and "*x* is expensive," respectively.[7] Using these abbreviations, we might propose to symbolize the given argument as

$$(x)(Hx \supset Bx)$$
$$(\exists x)(Hx \cdot Sx)$$
$$\therefore (\exists x)(Ex \cdot Sx)$$

But forcing the argument into the straitjacket of the traditional *A* and *I* forms in this way obscures its validity. The argument in symbols is invalid, although the original argument is perfectly valid. The notation here obscures the logical connection between *Bx* and *Ex*. A more adequate analysis is obtained by using *Hx, Sx,* and *Ex,* as explained, plus *Dx* as an abbreviation for "*x* is depressing." By using these symbols, the original argument can be translated as

1. $(x)[Hx \supset (Ex \cdot Dx)]$
2. $(\exists x)(Hx \cdot Sx) \; / \therefore (\exists x)(Ex \cdot Sx)$

---

[7]This would, however, violate the restriction stated in footnote 6 on page 344.

Thus symbolized, a demonstration of its validity is easily constructed. One such demonstration proceeds as follows:

3. $Hw \cdot Sx$	2, **EI**
4. $Hw \supset (Ew \cdot Dw)$	1, **UI**
5. Hw	3, Simp.
6. $Ew \cdot Dw$	4,5, M.P.
7. Ew	6, Simp.
8. $Sw \cdot Hw$	3, Com.
9. Sw	8, Simp.
10. $Ew \cdot Sw$	7,9, Conj.
11. $(\exists x)(Ex \cdot Sx)$	10, **EG**

In symbolizing general propositions that result from quantifying more complicated propositional functions, care must be taken not to be misled by the deceptiveness of ordinary English. One cannot translate from English into our logical notation by following any formal or mechanical rules. In every case one must understand the meaning of the English sentence, and then symbolize that meaning in terms of propositional functions and quantifiers. Three locutions of ordinary English that are sometimes troublesome to students are the following.

First, it should be observed that a statement like "All athletes are either very strong or very quick" is *not* a disjunction, although it contains the connective "or." It definitely does *not* have the same meaning as "Either all athletes are very strong or all athletes are very quick." The former is properly symbolized—using obvious abbreviations—as

$$(x)[Ax \supset (Sx \text{ v } Qx)]$$

whereas the latter is symbolized as

$$(x)(Ax \supset Sx) \text{ v } (x)(Ax \supset Qx)$$

Second, it should be observed that a statement like "Oysters and clams are delicious," while it *can* be stated as the conjunction of two general propositions, "Oysters are delicious and clams are delicious," it can also be stated as a single noncompound general proposition, in which case the word "and" is properly symbolized by the "v" rather than by the "•." The stated proposition is symbolized as

$$(x)[Ox \text{ v } Cx) \supset Dx]$$

not as

$$(x)(Ox \cdot Cx) \supset Dx]$$

For to say that oysters and clams are delicious is to say that anything is delicious that is *either* an oyster *or* a clam, *not* to say that anything is delicious that is *both* an oyster *and* a clam.

Third, alternative ways of symbolizing *exceptive* propositions should be noted. Such propositions as:[8] "All except previous winners are eligible," "All but previous winners are eligible," "Previous winners alone are not eligible," are traditionally called exceptive propositions. Any proposition of this form may be translated as a conjunction of two general propositions, as, for example,

$$(x)(Px \supset \sim Ex) \cdot (x)(\sim Px \supset Ex)$$

It may also be translated as a noncompound general proposition that is the universal quantification of a propositional function containing the equivalence or biconditional symbol "$\equiv$." For the present example we have the translation

$$(x)(Ex \equiv \sim Px)$$

which can alternatively be rendered in English as "Anyone is eligible if and only if that person is not a previous winner." In general, exceptive propositions are most conveniently regarded as quantified biconditionals. It is clear that exceptive propositions are compound in the sense explained, but it may not be clear that a given sentence expresses an exceptive proposition. This question is one of interpreting or understanding the sentence, for which an examination of its context may be required.

We have seen that the expanded list of Rules of Inference that enabled us to demonstrate the validity of valid categorical syllogisms also suffices for the validation of asyllogistic arguments of the type described. The same method of describing possible nonempty universes or models that was used in proving syllogisms invalid also suffices to prove the invalidity of asyllogistic arguments of the present type. The following asyllogistic argument

Foremen and superintendents are either competent workers or relatives of the owner.
Anyone who dares to complain must be either a superintendent or a relative of the owner.
Foremen and foremen alone are competent workers.
Someone did dare to complain.
Therefore some superintendent is a relative of the owner.

---

[8]See the earlier discussion of exceptive propositions on pages 222–224.

may be symbolized as

$$(x)[(Fx \text{ v } Sx) \supset (Cx \text{ v } Rx)]$$
$$(x)[Dx \supset (Sx \text{ v } Rx)]$$
$$(x)(Fx \equiv Cx)$$
$$(\exists x)Dx$$
$$\therefore (\exists x)(Sx \cdot Rx)$$

and we can prove it invalid by describing a possible universe or model containing the single individual *a* and assigning the truth value *true* to *Ca*, *Da*, *Fa*, *Ra*, and the truth value *false* to *Sa*.

EXERCISES

I. Translate the following statements into logical symbolism, in each case using the abbreviations suggested.

★   1. Apples and oranges are delicious and nutritious. (*Ax*, *Ox*, *Dx*, *Nx*)

    2. Some foods are edible only if they are cooked. (*Fx*, *Ex*, *Cx*)

    3. No car is safe unless it has good brakes. (*Cx*, *Sx*, *Bx*)

    4. Any tall man is attractive if he is dark and handsome. (*Tx*, *Mx*, *Ax*, *Dx*, *Hx*)

★   5. A girl wins if and only if she is lucky. (*Gx*, *Wx*, *Lx*)

    6. A boy who wins if and only if he is lucky is not skillful. (*Bx*, *Wx*, *Lx*, *Sx*)

    7. Not all people who are wealthy are both educated and cultured. (*Px*, *Wx*, *Ex*, *Cx*)

    8. Not all tools that are cheap are either soft or breakable. (*Tx*, *Cx*, *Sx*, *Bx*)

    9. Any person is a coward who deserts. (*Px*, *Cx*, *Dx*)

    10. To achieve success, one must work hard if one goes into business, or study continuously if one enters a profession. (*Ax*: *x* achieves success; *Wx*: *x* works hard; *Bx*: *x* goes into business; *Sx*: *x* studies continuously; *Px*: *x* enters a profession)

II. For each of the following either construct a formal proof of validity or prove it invalid.

★   1. $(x)[(Ax \text{ v } Bx) \supset (Cx \cdot Dx)]$
      $\therefore (x)(Bx \supset Cx)$

    2. $(\exists x)\{(Ex \cdot Fx) \cdot [(Ex \text{ v } Fx) \supset (Gx \cdot Hx)]\}$
      $\therefore (x)(Ex \supset Hx)$

    3. $(x)\{[Ix \supset (Jx \cdot {\sim}Kx)] \cdot [Jx \supset (Ix \supset Kx)]\}$
      $(\exists x)[(Ix \cdot Jx) \cdot {\sim}Lx]$
      $\therefore (\exists x)(Kx \cdot Lx)$

    4. $(x)[(Mx \cdot Nx) \supset (Ox \text{ v } Px)]$
      $(x)[(Ox \cdot Px) \supset (Qx \text{ v } Rx)]$
      $\therefore (x)[(Mx \text{ v } Ox) \supset Rx]$

★ 5. $(\exists x)(Sx \cdot Tx)$
   $(\exists x)(Ux \cdot \sim Sx)$
   $(\exists x)(Vx \cdot \sim Tx)$
   $\therefore (\exists x)(Ux \cdot Vx)$

6. $(x)[Wx \supset (Xx \supset Yx)]$
   $(\exists x)[Xx \cdot (Zx \cdot \sim Ax)]$
   $(x)[(Wx \supset Yx) \supset (Bx \supset Ax)]$
   $\therefore (\exists x)(Zx \cdot \sim Bx)$

7. $(\exists x)[Cx \cdot \sim(Dx \supset Ex)]$
   $(x)[(Cx \cdot Dx) \supset Fx]$
   $(\exists x)[Ex \cdot \sim(Dx \supset Cx)]$
   $(x)(Gx \supset Cx)$
   $\therefore (\exists x)(Gx \cdot \sim Fx)$

8. $(x)(Hx \supset Ix)$
   $(x)[(Hx \cdot Ix) \supset Jx]$
   $(x)[\sim Kx \supset (Hx \vee Ix)]$
   $(x)[(Jx \vee \sim Jx) \supset (Ix \supset Hx)]$
   $\therefore (x)(Jx \vee Kx)$

9. $(x)\{(Lx \vee Mx) \supset \{[(Nx \cdot Ox) \vee Px] \supset Qx\}\}$
   $(\exists x)(Mx \cdot \sim Lx)$
   $(x)\{[(Ox \supset Qx) \cdot \sim Rx] \supset Mx\}$
   $(\exists x)(Lx \cdot \sim Mx)$
   $\therefore (\exists x)(Nx \supset Rx)$

10. $(x)[(Sx \vee Tx) \supset \sim(Ux \vee Vx)]$
    $(\exists x)(Sx \cdot \sim Wx)$
    $(\exists x)(Tx \cdot \sim Xx)$
    $(x)(\sim Wx \supset Xx)$
    $\therefore (\exists x)(Ux \cdot \sim Vx)$

III. For each of the following, either construct a formal proof of its validity or prove it invalid, in each case using the suggested notation.

★ 1. Acids and bases are chemicals. Vinegar is an acid. Therefore vinegar is a chemical. (Ax, Bx, Cx, Vx)

2. Teachers are either enthusiastic or unsuccessful. Teachers are not all unsuccessful. Therefore there are enthusiastic teachers. (Tx, Ex, Ux)

3. Argon compounds and sodium compounds are either oily or volatile. Not all sodium compounds are oily. Therefore some argon compounds are volatile. (Ax, Sx, Ox, Vx)

4. No employee who is either slovenly or discourteous can be promoted. Therefore no discourteous employee can be promoted. (Ex, Sx, Dx, Px)

★ 5. No employer who is either inconsiderate or tyrannical can be successful. Some employers are inconsiderate. There are tyrannical employers. Therefore no employer can be successful. (Ex, Ix, Tx, Sx)

6. There is nothing made of gold that is not expensive. No weapons are made of silver. Not all weapons are expensive. Therefore not everything is made of gold or silver. (Gx, Ex, Wx, Sx)

7. There is nothing made of tin that is not cheap. No rings are made of lead. Not everything is either tin or lead. Therefore not all rings are cheap. (*Tx, Cx, Rx, Lx*)

8. Some prize fighters are aggressive but not intelligent. All prize fighters wear gloves. Prize fighters are not all aggressive. Any slugger is aggressive. Therefore not every slugger wears gloves. (*Px, Ax, Ix, Gx, Sx*)

9. Some photographers are skillful but not imaginative. Only artists are photographers. Photographers are not all skillful. Any journeyman is skillful. Therefore not every artist is a journeyman. (*Px, Sx, Ix, Ax, Jx*)

10. A book is interesting only if it is well written. A book is well written only if it is interesting. Therefore any book is both interesting and well written if it is either interesting or well written. (*Bx, Ix, Wx*)

IV. Do the same for each of the following.

★ 1. All citizens who are not traitors are present. All officials are citizens. Some officials are not present. Therefore there are traitors. (*Cx, Tx, Px, Ox*)

2. Doctors and lawyers are professional people. Professional people and executives are respected. Therefore doctors are respected. (*Dx, Lx, Px, Ex, Rx*)

3. Only lawyers and politicians are members. Some members are not college graduates. Therefore some lawyers are not college graduates. (*Lx, Px, Mx, Cx*)

4. All cut-rate items are either shopworn or out of date. Nothing shopworn is worth buying. Some cut-rate items are worth buying. Therefore some cut-rate items are out of date. (*Cx, Sx, Ox, Wx*)

★ 5. Some diamonds are used for adornment. Only things worn as jewels or applied as cosmetics are used for adornment. Diamonds are never applied as cosmetics. Nothing worn as a jewel is properly used if it has an industrial application. Some diamonds have industrial applications. Therefore some diamonds are not properly used. (*Dx, Ax, Jx, Cx, Px, Ix*)

6. No candidate who is either endorsed by labor or opposed by the *Tribune* can carry the farm vote. No one can be elected who does not carry the farm vote. Therefore no candidate endorsed by labor can be elected. (*Cx, Lx, Ox, Fx, Ex*)

7. No metal is friable that has been properly tempered. No brass is properly tempered unless it is given an oil immersion. Some of the ash trays on the shelf are brass. Everything on the shelf is friable. Brass is a metal. Therefore some of the ash trays were not given an oil immersion. (*Mx: x* is metal; *Fx: x* is friable; *Tx: x* is properly tempered; *Bx: x* is brass; *Ox: x* is given an oil immersion; *Ax: x* is an ash tray; *Sx: x* is on the shelf.)

8. Anyone on the committee who knew the nominee would vote for the nominee if free to do so. Everyone on the committee was free to vote for the nominee except those who were either instructed not to by the party caucus or had pledged support to someone else. Everyone on the committee knew the nominee. No one who knew the nominee had pledged support to anyone else. Not everyone on the committee voted for the nominee. Therefore the party caucus had instructed some members of the committee not to vote for the nominee. (*Cx: x* is on the committee; *Kx: x* knows the nominee; *Vx: x* votes for the nominee; *Fx: x* is free to vote for the nominee; *Ix: x* is instructed by the party caucus not to vote for the nominee; *Px: x* had pledged support to someone else.)

9. All members of Beta Omicron are good dancers and please their dates. To please his date he must buy her a corsage if he takes her dancing, or some ice cream if he takes her to a movie. No good dancer takes his date to a movie if he can afford to take her dancing. Some members of Beta Omicron buy their dates ice cream instead of corsages. Therefore not all members of Beta Omicron can afford to take their dates dancing. (*Bx:* x is a member of Beta Omicron; *Gx:* x is a good dancer; *Px:* x pleases his date; *Cx:* x buys his date a corsage; *Dx:* x takes his date dancing; *Ix:* x buys his date ice cream; *Mx:* x takes his date to a movie; *Ax:* x can afford to take his date dancing.)

10. Some criminal robbed the Russell mansion. Whoever robbed the Russell mansion either had an accomplice among the servants or had to break in. To break in, one would either have to smash the door or pick the lock. Only an expert locksmith could have picked the lock. Had anyone smashed the door, he would have been heard. Nobody was heard. If the criminal who robbed the Russell mansion managed to fool the guard, he must have been a convincing actor. No one could rob the Russell mansion unless he fooled the guard. No criminal could be both an expert locksmith and a convincing actor. Therefore some criminal had an accomplice among the servants. (*Cx:* x is a criminal; *Rx:* x robbed the Russell mansion; *Sx:* x had an accomplice among the servants; *Bx:* x broke in; *Dx:* x smashed the door; *Px:* x picked the lock; *Lx:* x is an expert locksmith; *Hx:* x was heard; *Fx:* x fooled the guard; *Ax:* x is a convincing actor.)

11. If anything is expensive it is both valuable and rare. Whatever is valuable is both desirable and expensive. Therefore if anything is either valuable or expensive then it must be both valuable and expensive. (*Ex:* x is expensive; *Vx:* x is valuable; *Rx:* x is rare; *Dx:* x is desirable.)

12. Figs and grapes are healthful. Nothing healthful is either illaudable or jejune. Some grapes are jejune and knurly. Some figs are not knurly. Therefore some figs are illaudable. (*Fx:* x is a fig; *Gx:* x is a grape; *Hx:* x is healthful; *Ix:* x is illaudable; *Jx:* x is jejune; *Kx:* x is knurly.)

13. Figs and grapes are healthful. Nothing healthful is both illaudable and jejune. Some grapes are jejune and knurly. Some figs are not knurly. Therefore some figs are not illaudable. (*Fx:* x is a fig; *Gx:* x is a grape; *Hx:* x is healthful; *Ix:* x is illaudable; *Jx:* x is jejune; *Kx:* x is knurly.)

14. Gold is valuable. Rings are ornaments. Therefore gold rings are valuable ornaments. (*Gx:* x is gold; *Vx:* x is valuable; *Rx:* x is a ring; *Ox:* x is an ornament.)

15. Oranges are sweet. Lemons are tart. Therefore oranges and lemons are sweet or tart. (*Ox:* x is an orange; *Sx:* x is sweet; *Lx:* x is a lemon; *Tx:* x is tart.)

16. Socrates is mortal. Therefore everything is either mortal or not mortal. (*s:* Socrates; *Mx:* x is mortal.)

PART THREE

Induction

11

Analogy and Probable Inference

For when we determine a thing to be probably true, suppose that an event has or will come to pass, it is from the mind remarking in it a likeness to some other event, which we have observed has come to pass.
—JOSEPH BUTLER

In reality, all arguments from experience are founded on the similarity which we discover among natural objects, and by which we are induced to expect effects similar to those which we have found to follow from such objects.
—DAVID HUME

Though analogy is often misleading, it is the least misleading thing we have.
—SAMUEL BUTLER

Analogies prove nothing, that is quite true, but they can make one feel more at home.
—SIGMUND FREUD

11.1 *Argument by Analogy*

The preceding chapters have dealt with deductive arguments, which are valid if their premises establish their conclusions demonstratively, but invalid otherwise. Not all arguments are deductive, however. A great many arguments are not claimed to demonstrate the truth of their conclusions as following necessarily from their premises, but are intended merely to support their conclusions as probable, or probably true. Arguments of this latter kind are generally called *inductive,* and are radically different from the deductive variety. Of these nondeductive or inductive arguments, perhaps the type most commonly used is the argument by analogy. Two examples of analogical arguments are these:

1. . . . the first industrial revolution, the revolution of the "dark satanic mills," was the devaluation of the human arm by the competition of machinery. There is no rate of pay at which a United States pick-and-shovel laborer can live which is low enough to compete with the work of a steam shovel as an excavator. The modern industrial revolution [high speed electronic computers, so-called "thinking machines"] is similarly bound to devalue the human brain at least in its simpler and more routine decisions. Of course, just as the skilled carpenter, the skilled mechanic, the skilled dressmaker have in some degree survived the first industrial revolution, so the skilled scientist and the skilled administrator may survive the second.[1]

2. We may observe a very great similitude between this earth which we inhabit, and the other planets, Saturn, Jupiter, Mars, Venus, and Mercury. They all revolve round the sun, as the earth does, although at different distances and in different periods. They borrow all their light from the sun, as the earth does. Several of them are known to revolve around their axis like the earth, and by that means, must have a like succession of day and night. Some of them have moons, that serve to give them light in the absence of the sun, as our moon does to us. They are all, in their motions, subject to the same law of gravitation, as the earth is. From all this similitude, it is not unreasonable to think that those planets may, like our earth, be the habitation of various orders of living creatures. There is some probability in this conclusion from analogy.[2]

Most of our own everyday inferences are by analogy. Thus I infer that a new pair of shoes will wear well on the grounds that I got good wear from other shoes previously purchased from the same store. If a new book by a certain author is called to my attention, I infer that I will enjoy reading it on the basis of having read and enjoyed other books by that author. Analogy is at the basis of most of our ordinary reasonings from past experience to what the future will hold. Not an explicitly formulated argument, of course, but something very much like analogical inference is presumably involved in the conduct of the burned child who shuns the fire.

None of these arguments is certain or demonstratively valid. None of their conclusions follows with "logical necessity" from their premises. It is logically possible that what happened to skilled manual workers may not happen to skilled brain workers, that earth may be the only inhabited planet, that the new shoes may not wear well at all, and that I may find my favorite author's latest book to be intolerably dull. It is even logically possible that one fire may burn but not another. But then, no argument by analogy is *intended* to be mathematically certain. Analogical arguments are not to be classified as either valid or invalid. Probability is all that is claimed for them.

In addition to their frequent use in arguments, analogies are very often used nonargumentatively, and these different uses should not be confused. Since earliest times writers have made use of analogy for the purpose of

---

[1]N. Wiener, *Cybernetics* (The Technology Press, New York: John Wiley & Sons, Inc., and Hermann et Cie, 1948).

[2]Thomas Reid, *Essays on the Intellectual Powers of Man*, Essay I, Chapter 4.

lively description. The literary uses of analogy in metaphor and simile are tremendously helpful to the writer who strives to create a vivid picture in the reader's mind. For example,

> . . . the [history] books do not describe change or show the relationship between one kind of event and another. The nineteen-fifties texts are encyclopedias rather than history books. Their vast indexes contain references to everything under the sun, but there is no connection between one thing and another. Events stand isolated below headings of black type, like islands in some archipelago where no one has yet invented the canoe.[3]

Analogy is also used in explanation, where something unfamilar is made intelligible through being compared to something else, presumably more familiar, to which it has certain similarities. For example,

> Science is built up with facts, as a house is with stones. But a collection of facts is no more a science than a heap of stones is a house.[4]

The use of analogies in description and explanation is not the same as their use in argument, though in some cases it may not be easy to decide which use is intended.

Whether used argumentatively or otherwise, analogy is not difficult to define. To draw an analogy between two or more entities is to indicate one or more respects in which they are similar. This explains what an analogy is, but there is still the problem of characterizing an *argument by analogy*. We may approach this problem by examining a particular analogical argument and analyzing its structure. Let us take the simplest of the examples cited thus far, the argument that my new pair of shoes will wear well because my old shoes, which were purchased from the same store, have worn well. The two things said to be similar are the two pairs of shoes. There are three points of analogy involved: the respects in which the two entities are said to resemble each other are, first, in being shoes; second, in being purchased from the same store; and, third, in wearing well. The three points of analogy do not play identical roles in the argument, however. The first two occur in the premises, whereas the third occurs both in the premises and in the conclusion. In quite general terms, the given argument may be described as having premises that assert, first, that two things are similar in two respects and, second, that one of those things has a further characteristic, from which the conclusion is drawn that the other thing also has that further characteristic.

Not every analogical argument need concern exactly two things or exactly three different characteristics, of course. Thus the argument quoted from Reid draws analogies among six things (the then known planets) in some eight respects. Apart from these numerical differences, however, all analogical arguments have the same general structure or pattern. Every analogical inference proceeds from the similarity of two or more things in one or more

---

[3]Frances Fitzgerald, "Onward and Upward with the Arts (History Textbooks)," *The New Yorker*, February 26, 1979, pp. 70–71.

[4]Jules Henri Poincaré, *Science and Hypothesis.*

respects to the similarity of those things in some further respect. Schematically, where *a, b, c,* and *d* are any entities and P, Q, and R are any attributes or "respects," an analogical argument may be represented as having the form

> *a, b, c, d* all have the attributes P and Q.
> *a, b, c* all have the attribute R.
> Therefore *d* probably has the attribute R.

In identifying, and especially in appraising, analogical arguments, it will be found helpful to recast them into this form.

EXERCISES

All the following passages contain analogies. Distinguish those that contain analogical arguments from those that make nonargumentative uses of analogy.

★ 1. A Man ought no more to value himself for being wiser than a Woman, if he owes his Advantage to a better Education, than he ought to boast of his Courage for beating a Man when his hands were bound.
—MARY ASTELL, *An Essay in Defence of the Female Sex* (1721), quoted in Germaine Greer, *The Female Eunuch*

2. The brain secretes thought as the stomach secretes gastric juice, the liver bile, and the kidneys urine.   —KARL VOGT, *Köhlerglaube und Wissenschaft*

3. Marriage is in the same state as the Church: Both are becoming functionally defunct, as their preachers go about heralding a revival, eagerly chalking up converts in a day of dread. And just as God has been pronounced dead quite often but has this sneaky way of resurrecting himself, so everyone debunks marriage, yet ends up married.
—SHULAMITH FIRESTONE, *The Dialectic of Sex: The Case for Feminist Revolution*

4. Today . . . the project of interpretation is largely reactionary, stifling. Like the fumes of the automobile and of heavy industry which befoul the urban atmosphere, the effusion of interpretations of art today poisons our sensibilities. In a culture whose already classical dilemma is the hypertrophy of the intellect at the expense of energy and sensual capability, interpretation is the revenge of the intellect upon art.   —SUSAN SONTAG, *Against Interpretation*

★ 5. . . . . It astonishes me that the exploitation of women should be so readily accepted. When one thinks of the ancient democracies, deeply attached to the ideal of equality, it is difficult to see how they can possibly have thought the status of the slaves natural: anyone would suppose that the contradiction must have been glaringly obvious to them. Perhaps one day posterity will wonder with the same astonishment how the bourgeois or popular democracies of our day can conceivably have maintained a basic inequality between the two sexes, and have maintained it without the least qualm of conscience.
—SIMONE DE BEAUVOIR, *All Said and Done*

6. The famous chemist and biologist, Justus von Liebig, dismissed the germ theory with a shrug of the shoulders, regarding Pasteur's view that microbes could cause fermentation as ridiculous and naive as the opinion of a child "who

would explain the rapidity of the Rhine current by attributing it to the violent movement of the many millwheels at Maintz."

—RENÉ DUBOS, *Pasteur and Modern Science*

7. Thinking is an experimental dealing with small quantities of energy, just as a general moves miniature figures over a map before setting his troops in action.   —SIGMUND FREUD, *New Introductory Lectures on Psychoanalysis*

8. As in prospecting for gold, a scientist may dig with skill, courage, energy, and intelligence just a few feet away from a rich vein—but always unsuccessfully. Consequently in scientific research the rewards for industry, perseverance, imagination, and intelligence are highly uncertain.

—LAWRENCE S. KUBIE, "Some Unsolved Problems of the Scientific Career," *American Scientist*, Vol. 42, 1954

9. The methods and functions of discovery and proof in research are as different as are those of a detective and of a judge in a court of law. While playing the part of the detective the investigator follows clues, but having captured his alleged fact, he turns judge and examines the case by means of logically arranged evidence. Both functions are equally essential but they are different.

—W. I. B. BEVERIDGE, *The Art of Scientific Investigation*

★ 10. We have said that normal persons have little motivation to prompt special efforts at self-study. The same thing is true of arithmetic. If motivation were not supplied from parents and school pressure, there would be little learning of mathematics. By analogy, it seems possible that children could be motivated and trained to use their mental skills to solve emotional problems. They get almost no training in this important skill at the present time.

—JOHN DOLLARD and NEAL E. MILLER, *Personality and Psychotherapy*[5]

11. Perhaps the most startling discovery made in astronomy this century is that the universe is populated by billions of galaxies and that they are systematically receding from one another, like raisins in an expanding pudding.

—MARTIN J. REES and JOSEPH SILK, "The Origin of Galaxies," *Scientific American*, Vol. 221, No. 2, August 1969

12. Suppose that someone tells me that he has had a tooth extracted without an anaesthetic, and I express my sympathy, and suppose that I am then asked, "How do you know that it hurt him?" I might reasonably reply, "Well, I know that it would hurt me. I have been to the dentist and know how painful it is to have a tooth stopped [filled] without an anaesthetic, let alone taken out. And he has the same sort of nervous system as I have. I infer, therefore, that in these conditions he felt considerable pain, just as I should myself."

—ALFRED J. AYER, "One's Knowledge of Other Minds," *Theoria*, Vol. 19, 1953

13. The Feminists decided to examine the institution of marriage as it is set up by law in order to find out whether or not it did operate in women's favor. It became increasingly clear to us that the institution of marriage "protects" women in the same way that the institution of slavery was said to "protect" blacks—that is, that the word "protection" in this case is simply a euphemism for oppression.

—SHEILA CRONAN, "Marriage," in Anne Koedt, Ellen Levine, and Anita Rapone, eds., *Radical Feminism* (New York: Quadrangle/The New York Times Book Co., 1973)

[5]From John Dollard and Neal E. Miller, *Personality and Psychotherapy* (New York: McGraw-Hill Book Company, copyright 1950).

14. Wittgenstein used to compare thinking with swimming: just as in swimming our bodies have a natural tendency to float on the surface so that it requires great physical exertion to plunge to the bottom, so in thinking it requires great mental exertion to force our minds away from the superficial, down into the depth of a philosophical problem.   —GEORGE PITCHER, *The Philosophy of Wittgenstein*

15. One of the pleasures of science is to see two distant and apparently unrelated pieces of information suddenly come together. In a flash what one knows doubles or triples in size. It is like working on two large but separate sections of a jigsaw puzzle and, almost without realizing it until the moment it happens, finding that they fit into one.
    —JOHN TYLER BONNER, "Hormones in Social Amoebae and Mammals,"
    Scientific American, Vol. 221, No. 5, November 1969

16. Before getting down to the main subject of this book, our own planet, let us make a brief survey of the other members of the solar system and compare their physical properties with those of the Earth. This "comparative planetology," as it may be called, will help us to understand the characteristics of our own planet, much in the same way as comparative anatomy gives biologists a better understanding of the human organism by comparing it with those of mosquitoes and elephants.   —GEORGE GAMOW, *Biography of the Earth*

17. It is important that we make clear at this point what definition is and what can be attained by means of it. It seems frequently to be credited with a creative power; but all it accomplishes is that something is marked out in sharp relief and designated by a name. Just as the geographer does not create a sea when he draws boundary lines and says: the part of the ocean's surface bounded by these lines I am going to call the Yellow Sea, so too the mathematician cannot really create anything by his defining.   —GOTTLOB FREGE, *The Basic Laws of Arithmetic*

18. Children in school are like children at the doctor's. He can talk himself blue in the face about how much good his medicine is going to do them; all they think of is how much it will hurt or how bad it will taste. Given their own way, they would have none of it.
    So the valiant and resolute band of travelers I thought I was leading toward a much hoped-for destination turned out instead to be more like convicts in a chain gang, forced under threat of punishment to move along a rough path leading nobody knew where and down which they could see hardly more than a few steps ahead. School feels like this to children: it is a place where *they* make you go and where *they* tell you to do things and where *they* try to make your life unpleasant if you don't do them or don't do them right.
    —JOHN HOLT, *How Children Fail*

19. Look round the world: contemplate the whole and every part of it: you will find it to be nothing but one great machine, subdivided into an infinite number of lesser machines, which again admit of subdivisions, to a degree beyond what human senses and faculties can trace and explain. All these various machines, and even their most minute parts, are adjusted to each other with an accuracy, which ravishes into admiration all men, who have ever contemplated them. The curious adapting of means to ends, throughout all nature, resembles exactly, though it much exceeds, the production of human contrivance; of human design, thought, wisdom, and intelligence. Since therefore the effects resemble each other, we are led to infer, by all the rules of analogy, that the causes also

resemble; and that the Author of Nature is somewhat similar to the mind of men; though possessed of much larger faculties, proportioned to the grandeur of the work, which he has executed. By this argument *a posteriori*, and by this argument alone, do we prove at once the existence of a Deity, and his similarity to human mind and intelligence. —DAVID HUME, *Dialogues Concerning Natural Religion*

20. The semiconductor business has always been like a roller coaster ride. Chipmakers enjoy a couple of years of soaring sales—and then there's a gut-wrenching drop as supplies of their products momentarily outstrip demand.
—"High Technology," *Business Week*, January 14, 1985, p. 102

11.2 *Appraising Analogical Arguments*

Although no argument by analogy is ever deductively valid, in the sense of having its conclusion follow from its premises with logical necessity, some are more cogent than others. Analogical arguments may be appraised as establishing their conclusions as more or less probable. In this section we shall discuss some of the criteria that are applicable to arguments of this type.

(1) The first criterion relevant to the appraisal of an analogical argument is the *number of entities* between which the analogies are said to hold. This principle is deeply rooted in common sense. If I advise you not to send your shirts to such and such a laundry because I sent one there once and it came back ruined, you might caution me against jumping to conclusions and urge that they ought perhaps to be given another chance. On the other hand, if I give you the same advice and justify it by recounting four different occasions on which unsatisfactory work was done by them on my clothing and report further that our mutual friends Jones and Smith have also patronized them repeatedly with similarly unhappy results, these premises serve to establish the conclusion with much higher probability than did the first argument, which cited only a single instance. It should not be thought, however, that there is any simple numerical ratio between the number of instances and the probability of the conclusion. If I have known only one chow dog, and that one was ill tempered, that gives some probability to the conclusion that the next one I meet will be ill tempered also. On the other hand, if I have known ten chow dogs, all of them ill tempered, that gives considerably higher probability to the conclusion that the next one will also be ill tempered. But it by no means follows that the second argument's conclusion is *exactly ten times* as probable.

(2) A second criterion for appraising analogical arguments is the *number of respects* in which the things involved are said to be analogous. Take the example of the shoes again. That a new pair of shoes was purchased at the same store as an old pair that gave good wear is certainly a premiss from which it follows that the new shoes will probably give good wear also. But that same conclusion follows with greater probability if the premises assert not only that the shoes were purchased from the same store, but that they

were manufactured by the same company, that they were the highest-priced shoes in the store, that they are the same style, and that I plan to wear them in the same circumstances and activities. Again, it should not be thought that there is any simple numerical ratio between the number of points of resemblance asserted in the premisses and the probability of the conclusion.

(3) A third criterion by which analogical arguments may be judged is *the strength of their conclusions relative to their premisses.* If Jones has a new car and gets thirty miles to the gallon, from this Smith can infer with some probability that her new car, of the same make and model as Jones's, will also give good mileage. Smith can construct alternative arguments here, with the same premisses but different conclusions. If she draws the conclusion that her car will go over twenty-five miles to the gallon, that is very probable. If she infers that her car will go over twenty-nine miles to the gallon, her argument is not so strong; that is, there is less likelihood or probability of her conclusion being true. If she concludes, however, that her own car will give *exactly* thirty miles to the gallon, she has a very much weaker argument.

(4) A fourth criterion used in appraising analogical arguments has to do with *the number of disanalogies* or points of difference between the instances mentioned only in the premisses (more exactly, the instances mentioned in the second premiss of the form displayed on page 360) and the instance with which the conclusion is concerned. The conclusion of the preceding argument is made very doubtful if it is pointed out that Jones drives his car for the most part at a steady pace of about twenty-five miles per hour, while Smith habitually drives at speeds in excess of sixty miles per hour. This disanalogy between the instance in the premiss and that of the conclusion weakens the argument and greatly reduces the probability of its conclusion.

(5) Of course the larger the number of instances appealed to in the premisses, the less likely it is that they will *all* be disanalogous to the instance mentioned in the conclusion. To minimize disanalogies between the instances of the premisses and the instance of the conclusion, however, we need not enumerate more and more instances in the premisses. The same end can be achieved by taking instances in our premisses that are dissimilar to each other. The less similar the instances mentioned only in the premisses are to each other, the less likely it is for *all* of them to be dissimilar to the conclusion's instance. Our fifth criterion for appraising arguments by analogy, then, is that *the more dissimilar the instances mentioned only in its premisses, the stronger is the argument.*

This principle is just as often appealed to and just as commonly accepted as many of the others that have been mentioned. The conclusion that Jenny Jones, an entering freshman at State, will successfully finish her college education and receive a degree, can be established as highly probable on the grounds that ten other students who graduated from the same high school as Jenny Jones, and received grades there very similar to hers, have entered

State as freshmen and have successfully finished their college educations and received degrees. The argument is appreciably stronger if the ten other students mentioned in the premises do not resemble each other too closely. The argument is strengthened by pointing out that those ten other students did not all come from the same economic backgrounds, that they differ from each other in racial stock, in religious affiliation, and so on. Incidentally, the fifth criterion explains the importance of the first. The greater the number of instances appealed to, the greater the number of disanalogies likely to obtain among them. None of these five criteria is new or in any way startling. They are constantly used by us in appraising analogical arguments.

(6) There is just one criterion for arguments by analogy that remains to be discussed. Although last, it is definitely not least, being the most important of them all. The examples presented thus far have all been fairly good arguments, because their analogies have all been *relevant*. Thus in support of the conclusion that Smith's new car will give good mileage, we adduced as evidence the fact that Jones's new car, which is known to give good mileage, is the same make and model; that is, it has the same number of cylinders, the same body weight, and the same horsepower as Smith's. These are all *relevant* considerations. Contrast this argument with one that draws the same conclusion from different premises, from premises that assert nothing about cylinders, body weight, or horsepower, but affirm instead that the two cars have the same color, the same number of gauges on their dashboards, and the same style of upholstery in their interiors. The latter is a much weaker argument. But it cannot be judged so by any of the first five criteria mentioned. The two arguments appeal to the same number of instances and the same number of analogies. The reason why the first is a good argument and the second ridiculously bad is that the factors in the first are relevant to mileage, while those of the second are completely irrelevant.

The question of relevance is all important. An argument based on a single *relevant* analogy connected with a single instance will be more cogent than one that points out a dozen *irrelevant* points of resemblance between its conclusion's instance and over a score of instances enumerated in its premises. Thus a doctor's inference is sound when she reasons that Mr. Black will be helped by a specific drug on the grounds that Mr. White was helped by it when a blood test showed exactly the same type of germs in his system that are now in Mr. Black's. But it would be fantastic for her to draw the same conclusion from premises that assert that Smith, Jones, and Robinson were all helped by it and that they and Black all patronize the same tailor, drive the same make and model car, have the same number of children, had similar educations, and were all born under the same sign of the zodiac. The reason for the weakness of the second argument is that the points of resemblance cited are strictly irrelevant to the matter with which the conclusion is concerned.

Although there may be disagreement about what analogies are relevant for stated conclusions, that is, what attributes are relevant for proving the presence of certain other attributes in a given instance, it is doubtful that there is any disagreement about the *meaning* of relevance. An illustration given by Professor J. H. Wigmore in one of his important legal treatises is the following:

> To show that a certain boiler was not dangerously likely to explode at a certain pressure of steam, other instances of non-explosion of boilers at the same pressure would be relevant, provided the other boilers were substantially similar in type, age, and other circumstances affecting strength.[6]

Here we are given a criterion for relevance itself. An analogy is relevant to establishing the presence of a given attribute (strength, in Wigmore's illustration) provided that it is drawn with respect to *other circumstances affecting it*. One attribute or circumstance is relevant to another, for purposes of analogical argument, if the first affects the second, that is, if it has a *causal* or determining effect on that other.

The factor of relevance is to be explained in terms of causality. In an argument by analogy, the relevant analogies are those that deal with causally related attributes or circumstances. If my neighbor has her house insulated and her fuel bill goes down, then if I have my own house insulated, I can confidently expect my own fuel bill to decrease. The analogy is a good one, because insulation is relevant to the size of fuel bills, being causally connected with fuel consumption. Analogical arguments are highly probable whether they go from cause to effect or from effect to cause. They are even probable when the attribute in the premiss is neither cause nor effect of the conclusion's attribute, provided that both are effects of the same cause. Thus from the presence of some symptoms of a given disease, a doctor can predict other symptoms—not that either symptom is the cause of the other, but because they are jointly caused by one and the same infection.

To evaluate analogical arguments, then, requires some knowledge of causal connections. These are discovered only empirically, by observation and experiment. The theory of empirical investigation is the central concern of inductive logic, and to this topic we turn in the following chapters.

EXERCISES

I. Each of the following arguments by analogy has six additional premisses suggested for it. For each of these alternative premisses, decide whether its addition would make the resulting argument more or less probable.

★ 1. An investor has purchased one hundred shares of oil stock every December for the past five years. In every case the value of the stock has appreciated about 15 percent a year, and it has paid regular dividends of about 8 percent a year on the price at which she bought it. This December she decides to buy another

---

[6]John H. Wigmore, *Wigmore's Code of the Rules of Evidence in Trials at Law* (Boston: Little, Brown and Company, 1942).

hundred shares of oil stock, reasoning that she will probably receive modest earnings while watching the value of her new purchase increase over the years.

    a. Suppose that she had always purchased stock in eastern oil companies before and plans to purchase stock in an eastern oil company this year too.

    b. Suppose that she had purchased oil stocks every December for the past fifteen years instead of only five years.

    c. Suppose that the oil stocks previously purchased had gone up by 30 percent a year instead of only 15 percent.

    d. Suppose that her previous purchases of oil stock had been in foreign companies as well as in eastern, southern, and western American oil companies.

    e. Suppose that she learns that OPEC has decided to meet every month instead of every six months.

    f. Suppose that she discovers that tobacco stocks have just raised their dividend payments.

2. A faithful alumnus, heartened by State's winning its last four football games, decides to bet his money that State will win its next game too.

    a. Suppose that since the last game State's great triple-threat tailback was injured in practice and hospitalized for the remainder of the season.

    b. Suppose that two of the last four games were played away and that two of them were home games.

    c. Suppose that just before the game it is announced that a member of State's Chemistry Department has been awarded a Nobel Prize.

    d. Suppose that State had won its last six games instead of only four of them.

    e. Suppose that it has rained hard during each of the four preceding games and rain is forecast for next Saturday too.

    f. Suppose that each of the last four games had been won by a margin of at least four touchdowns.

3. Although she was bored by the last few foreign films she saw, Charlene agrees to go to see another one this evening, fully expecting to be bored again.

    a. Suppose that Charlene was also bored by the last few American movies she saw.

    b. Suppose that the star of this evening's film has recently been accused of bigamy.

    c. Suppose that the last few foreign films seen by Charlene were Italian and that tonight's film is also Italian.

    d. Suppose that Charlene was so bored by the other foreign films that she actually fell asleep during the performance.

    e. Suppose that the last few foreign films she saw included an Italian, a French, an English, and a Swedish film.

    f. Suppose that tonight's film is in color, whereas all of those she saw before were in black and white.

4. Bill has taken three history courses and found them very stimulating and valuable. So he signs up for another one, confidently expecting that it too will be worthwhile.

    a. Suppose that his previous history courses were in ancient history, modern European history, and American history.

b. Suppose that his previous history courses had all been taught by the same professor that is scheduled to teach the present one.

c. Suppose that his previous history courses all had been taught by Professor Smith and the present one is taught by Professor Jones.

d. Suppose that Bill had found his three previous history courses the most exciting intellectual experiences of his life.

e. Suppose that his previous history courses had all met at 9 A.M. and that the present one is scheduled to meet at 9 A.M. also.

f. Suppose that, in addition to the three history courses previously taken, Bill had also taken and enjoyed courses in anthropology, economics, political science, and sociology.

5. Dr. Brown has stayed at the Queen's Hotel every fall for the past six years on her annual visit to New York and has been quite satisfied with her accommodations there. On her visit to New York this fall she goes again to the Queen's Hotel confidently expecting to enjoy her stay there again.

a. Suppose that when she stayed at the Queen's Hotel before she had occupied a single room twice, shared a double room twice, and twice occupied a suite.

b. Suppose that last spring a new manager had been put in charge of the Queen's Hotel.

c. Suppose that she had occupied a suite on all of her previous trips and is assigned a suite this time too.

d. Suppose that on her previous trips she had come to New York by train, but this time she flew.

e. Suppose that, when she stayed at the Queen's Hotel before, her quarters had been the most luxurious she had ever known.

f. Suppose that she had stayed at the Queen's Hotel three times a year for the past six years.

II. Analyze the structures of the analogical arguments in the following passages and evaluate them in terms of the six criteria that have been explained.

★ 1. If you cut up a large diamond into little bits, it will entirely lose the value it had as a whole; and an army divided up into small bodies of soldiers, loses all its strength. So a great intellect sinks to the level of an ordinary one, as soon as it is interrupted and disturbed, its attention distracted and drawn off from the matter in hand: for its superiority depends upon its power of concentration—of bringing all its strength to bear upon one theme, in the same way as a concave mirror collects into one point all the rays of light that strike upon it.

—ARTHUR SCHOPENHAUER, "On Noise"

2. Every species of plant or animal is determined by a pool of germ plasm that has been most carefully selected over a period of hundreds of millions of years.

We can understand now why it is that mutations in these carefully selected organisms almost invariably are detrimental. The situation can be suggested by a statement made by Dr. J. B. S. Haldane: My clock is not keeping perfect time. It is conceivable that it will run better if I shoot a bullet through it; but it is much more probable that it will stop altogether. Professor George Beadle, in this connection, has asked: "What is the chance that a typographical error would improve *Hamlet?"*

—LINUS PAULING, *No More War!*

3. I think some of our schools should be less rigid than they still are and that teachers should not oppress their pupils in an authoritarian spirit as some of them still do. Yet it is essential for teachers to make clear what they expect of children. This is like giving a vine a pole on which to grow.

—BENJAMIN SPOCK, in *Today's Education*, Vol. 64, No. 1, January–February 1975

4. All the conspicuous features on the surface of the moon are the result of impacts. These features include not only the craters, which plainly advertise their origin, but also the great maria, or "seas," which are craters that filled with lava following the impact of very massive objects. Most of the impacts took place during a relatively brief period about four billion years ago, when debris left over from the formation of the solar system was swept up by the planets and their satellites. The earth probably received as heavy a pelting as the moon did, and it therefore must have been densely cratered.

—"Science and the Citizen," *Scientific American*, June 1976

★ 5. To the casual observer porpoises and sharks are kinds of fish. They are streamlined, good swimmers, and live in the sea. To the zoologist who examines these animals more closely, the shark has gills, cold blood, and scales; the porpoise has lungs, warm blood, and hair. The porpoise is fundamentally more like man than like the shark and belongs, with man, to the mammals—a group that nurses its young with milk. Having decided that the porpoise is a mammal, the zoologist can, without further examination, predict that the animal will have a four-chambered heart, bones of a particular type, and a certain general pattern of nerves and blood vessels. Without using a microscope the zoologist can say with reasonable confidence that the red blood cells in the blood of the porpoise will lack nuclei. This ability to generalize about animal structure depends upon a system for organizing the vast amount of knowledge about animals.

—RALPH BUCHSBAUM, *Animals Without Backbones*

6. The body is the substance of the soul; the soul is the functioning of the body. . . . The relationship of the soul to its substance is like that of sharpness to a knife, while the relationship of the body to its functioning is like that of a knife to sharpness. What is called sharpness is not the same as the knife, and what is called the knife is not the same as sharpness. Nevertheless, there can be no knife if the sharpness is discarded, nor sharpness if the knife is discarded. I have never heard of sharpness surviving if the knife is destroyed, so how can it be admitted that the soul can remain if the body is annihilated?

—FAN CHEN, *Essay on the Extinction of the Soul*, in Fung Yu-Lan, *A History of Chinese Philosophy*

7. If a single cell, under appropriate conditions, becomes a person in the space of a few years, there can surely be no difficulty in understanding how, under appropriate conditions, a cell may, in the course of untold millions of years, give origin to the human race. —HERBERT SPENCER, *Principles of Biology*

8. An electron is no more (and no less) hypothetical than a star. Nowadays we count electrons one by one in a Geiger counter, as we count the stars one by one on a photographic plate. In what sense can an electron be called more unobservable than a star? I am not sure whether I ought to say that I have seen an electron; but I have just the same doubt whether I have seen a star. If I have seen one, I have seen the other. I have seen a small disc of light surrounded by diffraction rings which has not the least resemblance to what a star is supposed

to be; but the name "star" is given to the object in the physical world which some hundreds of years ago started a chain of causation which has resulted in this particular light-pattern. Similarly in a Wilson expansion chamber I have seen a trail not in the least resembling what an electron is supposed to be; but the name "electron" is given to the object in the physical world which has caused this trail to appear. How can it possibly be maintained that a hypothesis is introduced in one case and not in the other?

—SIR ARTHUR EDDINGTON, *New Pathways in Science*

9. Just as the bottom of a bucket containing water is pressed more heavily by the weight of the water when it is full than when it is half empty, and the more heavily the deeper the water is, similarly the high places of the earth, such as the summits of mountains, are less heavily pressed than the lowlands are by the weight of the mass of the air. This is because there is more air above the lowlands than above the mountain tops; for all the air along a mountain side presses upon the lowlands but not upon the summit, being above the one but below the other.

—BLAISE PASCAL, *Treatise on the Weight of the Mass of the Air*

★ 10. The discovery of this remarkable weapon against disease dates back to 1929. It was purely accidental. Dr. Alexander Fleming, in St. Mary's Hospital, London, was growing colonies of bacteria on glass plates for certain bacteriological researches. One morning he noticed that a spot of mold had germinated on one of the plates. Such contaminations are not unusual, but for some reason, instead of discarding the impurity and starting fresh, Dr. Fleming decided to allow it to remain. He continued to culture the plate, and soon an interesting drama unfolded beneath his eyes. The area occupied by the bacteria was decreasing, that occupied by the mold was increasing, and presently the bacteria had vanished.

Dr. Fleming now took up this fungus for study on its own account. He recognized it as of the penicillium genus, and by deliberately introducing a particle into culture mediums where bacteria were growing, he found that quite a number of species wouldn't grow in its presence. . . . In his laboratory, whenever he wanted to get rid of a growth of gram-positive bacteria, Fleming would implant a little penicillium, and after that the microbes disappeared. . . . So the medical scientists began to speculate. Since the mold destroyed gram-positive organisms on a culture plate, could it be used to destroy gram-positive disease germs in the living body?   —GEORGE W. GRAY, *Science at War*

11. Now if we survey the universe, so far as it falls under our knowledge, it bears a great resemblance to an animal or organized body and seems actuated with a like principle of life and motion. A continual circulation of matter in it produces no disorder: a continual waste in every part is incessantly repaired; the closest sympathy is perceived throughout the entire system: and each part or member, in performing its proper offices, operates both to its own preservation and to that of the whole. The world, therefore, I infer, is an animal, and the Deity is the *soul* of the world, actuating it, and actuated by it.

DAVID HUME, *Dialogues Concerning Natural Religion*

12. One cannot require that everything shall be defined, any more than one can require that a chemist shall decompose every substance. What is simple cannot be decomposed, and what is logically simple cannot have a proper definition.

—GOTTLOB FREGE, "On Concept and Object"

13. And in truth, I am quite willing it should be known that the little I have hitherto learned is almost nothing in comparison with that of which I am ignorant and to the knowledge of which I do not despair of being able to attain; for it is much the same with those who gradually discover truth in the sciences, as with those who when growing rich find less difficulty in making great acquisitions, than they formerly experienced when poor in making acquisitions of much smaller amount. Or they may be compared to the commanders of armies, whose forces usually increase in proportion to their victories, and who need greater prudence to keep together the residue of their troops after a defeat than after a victory to take towns and provinces. —RENÉ DESCARTES, *A Discourse on Method*

14. Libel actions can survive the deaths of defamed persons, holds the New Jersey Supreme Court in allowing a widow to continue a suit filed by her husband. The court reasons that, if a claim for a broken leg can survive a person's death, one for a damaged name should also.
—"News-Lines," *U.S. News & World Report*, July 9, 1984

15. . . . The simplest form of the theological argument from design [was] once well known under the name "Paley's watch." Paley's form of it was just this: "If we found by chance a watch or other piece of intricate mechanism we should infer that it had been made by someone. But all around us we do find intricate pieces of natural mechanism, and the processes of the universe are seen to move together in complex relations; we should therefore infer that these too have a Maker."
—B. A. D. WILLIAMS, "Metaphysical Arguments," in D. F. Pears, ed.,
The Nature of Metaphysics

11.3 *Refutation by Logical Analogy*

There is a special kind of argument that uses an analogy to prove that another argument is wrong, or mistaken. It is intended to refute that other argument, not by showing that at least one of its premises is false (or mistaken) or by showing that it commits one of the fallacies discussed in Chapter 3, but by showing that the other argument's premises do not really support the conclusion that was claimed to follow from them. We have here a basic method of appraising an argument as unsatisfactory from a logical point of view.

Underlying this method of criticizing arguments is the fact that from the point of view of logic, the form of an argument is its most important aspect. This is certainly the case for arguments that are claimed to be absolutely demonstrative. There can be no question but that the world's oldest example of a valid deductive argument is absolutely demonstrative:

> All humans are mortal.
> Socrates is human.
> Therefore Socrates is mortal.

And any other argument that has exactly the same form (or shape, or pattern) is absolutely demonstrative also, as for example,

> All dogs are carnivorous.
> Fido is a dog.
> Therefore Fido is carnivorous.

This logical fact underlies the method of refutation by logical analogy. If a given argument has true premisses but a false conclusion, that is sufficient grounds for classifying it as invalid. But if we do not know whether its component propositions are true or false, we can prove it invalid by constructing a refuting analogy. A refuting analogy for a given argument is an argument of exactly the same form or pattern as the given argument, but whose premisses are known to be true and whose conclusion is known to be false. The refuting analogy is thus known to be invalid, and the given argument—since it has the same form—is also known to be invalid.

At the Mad Tea Party in Wonderland, Alice makes a logical mistake. The March Hare tells her: "you should say what you mean."

> "I do," Alice hastily replied; "at least—at least I mean what I say—that's the same thing, you know."
> "Not the same thing a bit!" said the Hatter. "Why, you might just as well say that 'I see what I eat' is the same thing as 'I eat what I see'!"
> "You might just as well say," added the March Hare, "that 'I like what I get' is the same thing as 'I get what I like'!"
> "You might just as well say," added the Dormouse, which seemed to be talking in its sleep, "that 'I breathe when I sleep' is the same thing as 'I sleep when I breathe'!"
> "It *is* the same thing with you," said the Hatter, and here the conversation dropped . . .[7]

Here Alice defended herself by arguing to the conclusion that "I say what I mean" from the premiss that "I mean what I say," on the grounds that they are "the same thing." But they are *not* the same thing, and Alice's premiss does *not* imply her conclusion. That is proved by the obviously invalid analogous arguments so scornfully offered by her disagreeable companions, whom Max Black characterized as being "infuriatingly logical."[8]

In the present case what signals that the Hatter and the March Hare and the Dormouse are offering refutations by logical analogy, is the phrase each of them uses: "you might just as well say." Nearly identical words introduced a much more serious refutation by logical analogy recently presented by a social scientist defending the depth of Islamic culture in the country of Chad:

> Chad [you say] has only an "Islamic overlay." One could as sensibly say that France has only a "Christian overlay."[9]

Other phrases often used with refuting analogies are "the same argument proves," "this is about as logical as arguing that," "I could use the same

---

[7]Lewis Carroll, *Alice's Adventures in Wonderland,* Chapter VII.
[8]Max Black, *Critical Thinking* (Englewood Cliffs, N.J.: Prentice-Hall, Inc., 1952), p. 43.
[9]Bassam K. Abed, in a letter to *The New York Times,* June 26, 1988, p. 26E.

reasoning to claim that," "the same methodology would lead to the conclusion that," where the refuting analogy is an argument of the same pattern as the one being refuted, but whose conclusion is known to be false although its premises are known to be true.

The method of refutation by logical analogy can be used with (almost) equally telling effect in criticizing an inductive argument, that is, one that is not claimed to be absolutely demonstrative. A great many arguments met with not only in daily life, but in scientific, legal, political, and economic discussions are inductive rather than deductive. An especially keen use of this method was made by Justice Clark in handing down a decision of the United States Supreme Court:

> It is urged that motion pictures do not fall within the First Amendment's aegis because their production, distribution, and exhibition is a large-scale business conducted for private profit. We cannot agree. That books, newspapers, and magazines are published and sold for profit does not prevent them from being a form of expression whose liberty is safeguarded by the First Amendment. We fail to see why operation for profit should have any different effect in the case of motion pictures.[10]

A recent refuting analogy, its thrust reinforced by additional analogical argument, is marked by a sharp interrogative:

> Mr. [Clifford A.] Wright says Israel is not a democracy because it gives Judaism a special status in the law. Really? Britain's blasphemy laws protect the beliefs of Christians only. Those laws do not vitiate Britain's claims to be a democracy, though arguably they make it a less perfect one. Israel still has universal suffrage, a multi-party system and a free press. To all but the blindly partisan, that looks rather like a democracy.[11]

EXERCISES

Each of the following is a refutation by logical analogy. In each identify the argument being refuted and the refuting analogy, and decide if they indeed have the same form or pattern.

★ 1. Bettelheim . . . is a true believer. "Psychoanalysis," he writes, "is beyond doubt the most valuable method of psychotherapy"; it is so because it is so difficult and time-consuming. The same argument proves that the Model T is the most valuable method of wheeled transportation . . .

—PETER S. PRESCOTT, review of Bruno Bettelheim, *Freud and Man's Soul,*
in *Newsweek*, January 10, 1983, p. 64

2. If widgets can be imported from Asia for a price reflecting labor costs of $1 an hour, then an hour spent making widgets adds a dollar of value to the economy. This is true no matter what American widget makers are being paid. If foreign widgets are excluded in order to protect the jobs of American widget makers getting $10 an hour, $1 of that $10 reflects their contribution to the econ-

---

[10]Mr. Justice Clark, for the Court, *Burstyn* v. *Wilson*, 43 U.S. 495 (1952).
[11]*The Economist*, July 15, 1989, p. 87.

omy and $9 is coming out of the pockets of other workers who have to pay more for widgets. Nice for widget makers, but perfectly futile from the perspective of net social welfare.

After all, if this economic alchemy really worked, we could shut our borders to all imports, pay one another $1,000 an hour, and we'd all be rich. It doesn't work that way.   —MICHAEL KINSLEY, "Keep Trade Free," *The New Republic*, Vol. 188, No. 14, April 11, 1983, p. 10

3. . . . one of the most misleading analogies today is the one that usually turns up for giving the vote to 18-year-olds. This argument asserts that 18-year-olds, being old enough to fight, are old enough to vote. True, only if you believe that fighting and voting are the same kind of thing, which I, for one, do not. Fighting requires strength, muscular coordination and, in a modern army, instant and automatic response to orders. Voting requires knowledge of men, history, reasoning power; it is essentially a deliberate activity. Army mules and police dogs are used to fight; nobody is interested in giving them the right to vote. This argument rests on a false analogy.

—RICHARD M. WEAVER, "A Responsible Rhetoric," *The Intercollegiate Review*, Vol. 12, No. 2, Winter 1976–77, pp. 86–87

4. The creationists frequently stress that we cannot explain everything. This comes oddly from a group that many conclude can explain nothing. It would be as foolish to discard evolutionary theory today because it cannot explain everything as it would be to disband the medical establishment because it cannot cure the common cold.   —JOHN A. MOORE, "Countering the Creationists," *Academe*, Vol. 68, No. 2, March–April 1982, p. 16

★ 5. . . . some people argue that there are many things wrong with society—some of which are increasingly conspicuous—and that since we have also had decades of uninterrupted growth the growth must be the cause of the various social and economic ills that we see around us. This is about as logical as arguing that all the ills of society must be caused by the fact that people spend more time these days in cleaning their teeth.

—WILFRED BECKERMAN, *Two Cheers for the Affluent Society* (New York: St. Martin's Press, Inc., 1974), p. 48

6. In your thought-provoking cover story about nuclear warfare . . . you said, "Deterrence has worked for 38 years." Has it? I could use the same reasoning to claim that my house has never been struck by lightning because I painted a face on the roof that frightens the lightning away. If something has never happened, we have no way of knowing what prevents it from happening. It is dangerous to award nuclear buildup a credit it may not deserve.

—GEORGE M. HIEBER, letter to the editor, *Newsweek*, December 19, 1983, p. 7

7. The critics of psychoanalysis argue that people who have been analyzed are "brainwashed" into "believing in" psychoanalysis. But the same could be said of people who have come to a sympathetic understanding of Beethoven's genius through learning to play his piano sonatas.

—JANET MALCOLM, "Annals of Scholarship (Psychoanalysis—Part I)," *The New Yorker*, December 5, 1983, p. 80

8. [A convicted murderer] . . . may file an infinite number of petitions alleging different violations (or, for that matter, the same ones); every petition, no matter how frivolous, will delay the execution for weeks or months, and its denial will be appealed, which takes even longer . . .

These nonstop legal proceedings have produced one of the most curious of the abolitionist arguments: death is not a practical sanction, for the inevitable litigation makes prohibitive its cost in time and money. In effect: I have poured glue in the works of your watch; it is therefore worthless, and you ought to throw it away.
  —JOSEPH W. BISHOP, JR., review of Ernest van den Haag and John P. Conrad, *The Death Penalty: A Debate*, in *Commentary*, February 1984, p. 70

9. When the film "Gandhi" opened, there was a brief flurry of interest in nonviolence, but even those people who gave the subject more than a moment's thought tended to reject it out of hand. It might have driven the British out of India, but would it suffice against a more brutal regime? One objection, though it was not always spoken, was that nonviolence wouldn't have worked against the Nazis. And that's right—it wouldn't have. The Nazis were brutal enough and strong enough—evil enough—to overwhelm anything save iron and lead. But to toss out an idea on those grounds is to allow Hitler's insanity to continue perverting our earth; one might as well scrap all cars too slow to win the Indy 500, or junk the Cuisinart because it won't chop firewood.
  —"The Talk of the Town," *The New Yorker*, December 12, 1983, p. 44

★ 10. Mr. Clark [William P. Clark, Secretary of the Interior] may be even less qualified to manage America's conservation lands than he was to manage foreign policy: Administration spokesmen have pointed out that Mr. Clark's father and grandfather were forest rangers—a proposition akin to claiming that someone should be Secretary of Transportation because he comes from a long line of cab drivers.   —"What Watt Wrought," *The New Republic*, December 26, 1983, p. 8

11. One of the great scandals of recent and current government rhetoric is that there has been a concerted attempt by the economic leadership to deny that budget deficits lead to inflation (or play anything more than a minimal role in inflation). The government consistently tries to maintain that *price increases* are the cause of inflation. This is like saying that meals cause hunger.
  —TOM BETHELL, "Fooling with the Budget," *Harper's*, October 1979, p. 44

12. Father was always a bit sceptical of this story, and of the new flying machines, otherwise he believed everything he read. Until 1909 no one in Lower Binfield believed that human beings would ever learn to fly. The official doctrine was that if God had meant us to fly He'd have given us wings. Uncle Ezekiel couldn't help retorting that if God had meant us to ride, He'd have given us wheels, but even he didn't believe in the new flying machines.
  —GEORGE ORWELL, *Coming Up for Air*

13. But the South were threatening to destroy the Union in the event of the election of a republican President, and were telling us that the great crime of having destroyed it will be upon us. This is cool. A highwayman holds a pistol to my ear, with "stand and deliver, or I shall kill you, and then you will be a murderer." To be sure the money which he demands is my own, and I have a clear right to keep it, but it is no more so than my vote, and the threat of death to extort my money, and the threat of destruction to the Union to exort my vote, can scarcely be distinguished in principle.
  —ABRAHAM LINCOLN, speech at Dover, New Hampshire, March 2, 1860, in Roy R. Basler, ed., *The Collected Works of Abraham Lincoln* (New Brunswick, N.J.: Rutgers University Press, 1953), Vol. III, p. 553

14. Dear Ann: I live in North Carolina and I sure wish you would quit trying to put the tobacco industry out of business. A lot of folks down here depend on it for a living.

Don't you know tobacco is a gift from God? He gave us the plant to be used and enjoyed. So lay off, lady. You are getting to be a real bore.

—*Raleigh Reader*

Dear Raleigh: Your argument is ridiculous. God also gave us poison ivy.

—ANN LANDERS column, *Honolulu Advertiser*, July 24, 1985, p. C-4.

★ 15. Many find it easier to lie to those they take to be untruthful themselves. It is as though a barrier had been let down. And to Augustine's argument that countering a lie with a lie is like countering sacrilege with sacrilege, they might answer: Such an analogy cannot be stretched to conclude that it is always wrong to repay lies in kind. They might advance another analogy—that between lying and the use of force—and ask: If at times force can be used to counter force, why should lies never be used to counter lies? And they might contend that just as someone forfeits his rights to noninterference by others, when he threatens them forcibly, so a liar has forfeited the ordinary right to be dealt with honestly.

—SISSELA BOK, *Lying: Moral Choice in Public and Private Life* (New York: Vintage Books, a division of Random House, 1979), pp. 132–133

1 2

Causal Connections: Mill's Methods of Experimental Inquiry

*For the induction which proceeds by simple enumeration is childish; its
conclusions are precarious, and exposed to peril from a contradictory
instance; and it generally decides on too small a number of facts, and on
those only which are at hand.*

—FRANCIS BACON

12.1 *The Meaning of "Cause"*

To exercise any measure of control over our environment, we must have
some knowledge of causal connections. Physicians have more power to cure
illnesses if they know what *causes* them, and they should understand the
effects (including the "side effects") of the drugs they administer. Since there
are several different meanings of the word "cause," we begin by distinguishing
them from one another.

It is a fundamental axiom in the study of nature that events do not just
happen, but occur only under certain conditions. It is customary to distinguish
between necessary and sufficient conditions for the occurrence of an
event. A *necessary* condition for the occurrence of a specified event is a circumstance
in whose absence the event cannot occur. For example, the presence
of oxygen is a necessary condition for combustion to occur: if combustion
occurs, then oxygen must have been present, for in the absence of
oxygen there can be no combustion.

Although it is a necessary condition, the presence of oxygen is not a sufficient
condition for combustion to occur. A *sufficient* condition for the occurrence
of an event is a circumstance in whose presence the event must
occur. The presence of oxygen is not a sufficient condition for combustion

because oxygen can be present without combustion occurring. On the other hand, for almost any substance there is some range of temperature such that *being in that range of temperature in the presence of oxygen* is a sufficient condition for combustion of that substance. It is obvious that there may be several *necessary* conditions for the occurrence of an event, and that they must all be included in the sufficient condition.

The word "cause" is sometimes used in the sense of necessary condition and sometimes in the sense of sufficient condition. It is most often used in the sense of necessary condition when the problem at hand is the elimination of some undesirable phenomenon. To eliminate it, one need only find some condition that is necessary to its existence and then eliminate that condition. Thus a physician seeks to discover what kind of germ is the "cause" of a certain illness in order to cure the illness by prescribing a drug that will destroy those germs. The germs are said to be the cause of the disease in the sense of a necessary condition for it, since in their absence the disease cannot occur.

The word "cause" is used in the sense of sufficient condition when we are interested not in the elimination of something undesirable but rather in the production of something desirable. Thus a metallurgist seeks to discover the cause of strength in alloys in order to create stronger metals. The process of mixing and heating and cooling is said to be the cause of the strengthening in the sense of a sufficient condition, since such processing suffices to produce a stronger alloy.

In certain practical situations, the word "cause" is used in still a different sense. An insurance company might send investigators to determine the cause of a mysterious fire. If the investigators sent back a report that the fire was caused by the presence of oxygen in the atmosphere, they would not keep their jobs very long. And yet they would be right—in the sense of necessary condition—for had there been no oxygen present, there would have been no fire. But the insurance company did not have *that* sense in mind when it sent them to investigate. Nor is the company interested in the sufficient condition. If after several weeks the investigators reported that although they had proof that the fire was deliberately ignited by the policy-holder, they hadn't as yet been able to learn *all* the necessary conditions, and so hadn't been able to determine the cause (in the sense of sufficient condition), the company would recall the investigators and tell them to stop wasting their time and the company's money. The insurance company was using the word "cause" in another sense—what they wanted to find out was the incident or action that, in the presence of those conditions that usually prevail, made the difference between the occurrence or nonoccurrence of the event.

We may distinguish between two different subdivisions of this third sense of cause. These are traditionally characterized as the *remote* and the *proximate* causes. Where there is a causal sequence or chain of several events, *A* causing *B*, *B* causing *C*, *C* causing *D*, and *D* causing *E*, we can regard *E* as effect of any or of all of the preceding events. The nearest of them, *D*, is the proximate cause of *E*, and the others are more and more remote causes, *A* more remote than *B*, and *B* more remote than *C*. In this case the proximate cause was the policyholder's lighting the fire. But that action, and thus the fire, may have been caused by a need for money to cover losses in an investment in a cattle ranch, those losses occasioned by increased expenses brought about by soaring grain prices caused by a crop failure in India. The crop failure was a remote cause of the fire, but the insurance company would not have been interested in hearing that the mysterious fire was caused by an Indian crop failure.

There are several different senses of the term "cause," as we have seen. We can legitimately infer cause from effect only in the sense of necessary condition. And we can legitimately infer effect from cause only in the sense of sufficient condition. Where inferences are made both from cause to effect and from effect to cause, the term "cause" must be used in the sense of "necessary and sufficient condition." In this usage, cause is identified with sufficient condition, and sufficient condition is regarded as the conjunction of all necessary conditions. It should be clear that there is no single definition of "cause" that conforms to *all* of the different uses of that word.

On the conception of cause as necessary and sufficient condition there is a unique cause for any effect. That is not to say that the cause is simple: it may be extremely complex, involving a great many factors, all of which must be present for the effort to occur. But there is only one such complex, on this view, that can produce the effect in question. This conception runs counter to the commonsense opinion that a given phenomenon may have been the result of alternative causes. If a person's death occurs, it may have been caused by heart failure, or by poisoning, by a bullet, by a traffic accident, or by any of the hundreds of other circumstances that are capable, as we say, of causing death. But the view that there may be a "plurality of causes" of a single kind of effect conflicts with the notion that a cause is a *necessary* and sufficient condition for its effect. If there can be a plurality of causes, then inferences from effects to their causes are not possible. The doctrine of plurality of causes is very widely accepted indeed. A crop failure may be caused by drought or by excessive rainfall or by grasshoppers.

It should not be concluded, however, that interpreting cause as a necessary and sufficient condition is mistaken and unfruitful. Any farmer would agree that there are different kinds of crop failures, and the kind produced by drought could not possibly have been caused by excessive rainfall or grasshoppers. If an effect is specified with sufficient precision, the apparent plurality of causes tends to disappear. True enough, "death in general" may be caused by a plurality of alternative circumstances, but a specific kind of death, that induced, say, by strychnine poisoning, could not possibly have resulted from a coronary thrombosis. The unique cause of death is frequently discovered by postmortem examinations, where an autopsy reveals the particular kind of death with enough specificity to permit an inference that *the* cause of the death in question was one thing rather than any other. The doctrine of plurality of causes may be rejected, then, for in every case in which it is thought that alternative circumstances might have caused a given phenomenon, it is probable that a further specification or more precise description of that phenomenon would make the apparent plurality of causes disappear.

We need not rule out plurality of causes in an *a priori* fashion. We may regard the doctrine of uniqueness of cause as itself the result of an inductive generalization. In every case of alleged plurality of causes encountered thus far, the apparent plurality vanishes when the effect in question is more precisely specified. From this fact we can conclude with probability that in every case a more precise specification of the effect will decrease the number of alternative circumstances that might have caused that effect. And so we can accept, not as necessarily true *a priori*, but as highly probable on the evidence, the working hypothesis that every effect of a specific kind has a single and unique kind of cause.

An even stronger case can be made against the doctrine of plurality of causes. We may quote in this connection William James's dictum that *every difference must make a difference*. If two circumstances can result in the same kinds of effects, it is proper to regard them as being themselves of the same kind. If their effects are no different, then they are not really different from each other. Ordinarily we pay attention only to those differences that are important to us and ignore those in which we have no interest. Certainly their effects are of greatest moment in distinguishing circumstances as being of the same or of different kinds. If all their effects are the same—that is, if they do not differ in any "important" respects—then the circumstances are also "the same," whereas if their effects are significantly different, this difference is the basis on which we distinguish them as different circumstances. If we agree that *every difference must make a difference*, then we shall reject the doctrine of plurality of causes.

On the other hand, there is much to be said for the commonsense view. If we consider certain types of effects, it seems plausible that alternative antecedent circumstances might equally well have produced them. Thus a solution of sugar in water would not be any different whether the sugar or the water was placed in the container first. To provide an adequate discussion of this issue, however, lies far beyond the scope of the present book.

Every use of the word "cause," whether in everyday life or in science, involves or presupposes the doctrine that cause and effect are *uniformly* connected. We admit that a particular circumstance caused a particular effect only if we agree that any other circumstance of that type will—if the attendant circumstances are sufficiently similar—cause another effect of the same kind as the first. In other words, similar causes produce similar effects. Part of the very meaning of the word "cause" as used today is that every occurrence of a cause producing an effect is an *instance* or *example* of the general causal law that such circumstances are *always* accompanied by such phenomena. Thus we are willing to relinquish a belief that circumstance C was the cause of effect E in one particular case if it can be shown that the same (type of) circumstance was present in another situation which was the same as the first except that the effect E *did not occur* in the latter.

Since a general causal law is implied by every assertion that a particular circumstance was the cause of a particular phenomenon, there is an element of generality ·in every such assertion. A causal law—as we shall use the term—asserts that such and such a circumstance is invariably attended by exactly the same kind of phenomenon, no matter when or where it occurs. Now how do we come to know such general truths? The causal relation is not a purely logical or deductive relationship; it cannot be discovered by any *a priori* reasoning. Causal laws can be discovered only *empirically*, by an appeal to experience. But our experiences are always of particular circumstances, particular phenomena, and particular sequences of them. We may observe several instances of a certain kind of circumstance (say, C), and every instance *that we observe* may be accompanied by an instance of a certain kind of phenomenon (say, P). These observations show us, of course, only that *some* cases of C are cases of P. How are we to get from this evidence to the general proposition that *all* cases of C are cases of P, which is involved in saying that C *causes P?*

The method of arriving at general or universal propositions from the particular facts of experience is called *inductive generalization.* From premises asserting that three particular pieces of blue litmus paper turned red when dipped in acid, we may draw either a particular conclusion about what will happen to a particular fourth piece of blue litmus paper if it is dipped in acid or a general conclusion about what happens to *every* piece of blue litmus paper dipped in acid. If we draw the first, we have an argument by analogy; the second is an inductive generalization. The structure of these two types of arguments may be analyzed as follows. The premises report a number of instances in which two attributes (or circumstances or phenomena) occur together. By analogy we may infer that a different particular instance of one attribute will also exhibit the other attribute. By inductive generalization we may infer that *every* instance of the one attribute will also be an instance of the other. An inductive generalization of the form

> Instance 1 of phenomenon E is accompanied by circumstance C.
> Instance 2 of phenomenon E is accompanied by circumstance C.
> Instance 3 of phenomenon E is accompanied by circumstance C.
> ....
>
> Therefore every instance of phenomenon E is accompanied by circumstance C.

is an induction by *simple enumeration.* An induction by simple enumeration is very similar to an argument by analogy, differing only in having a more general conclusion.

Simple enumeration is often used in establishing causal connections. Where a number of instances of a phenomenon are invariably accompanied by a certain type of circumstance, it is only natural to infer the existence of a causal relationship between them. Since the circumstance of dipping blue litmus paper in acid is accompanied in all observed instances by the phenomenon of the paper's turning red, we conclude that dipping blue litmus paper in acid is the *cause* of its turning red. Similarly, from the fact that a number of men contracted yellow fever after being bitten by mosquitoes that previously fed on yellow-fever patients, we may infer by simple enumeration that the bite of such a mosquito *causes* yellow-fever infection. The analogical character of such arguments is very apparent.

Because of the great similarity between argument by simple enumeration and argument by analogy, it should be clear that the same types of criteria apply to both. Some arguments by simple enumeration may establish their conclusions with a higher degree of probability than others. The greater the number of instances appealed to, the higher the probability of the conclusion. The various instances or cases of phenomenon E accompanied by circumstance C are often called *confirming instances* of the causal law asserting that C causes E. The greater the number of confirming instances, the higher the probability of the causal law—other things being equal. Thus the first criterion for analogical arguments applies directly to arguments by simple enumeration also.

Inductions by simple enumeration are frequently made, and are often very valuable and suggestive. But they are not very trustworthy. For example, consider the following argument:

> Tom broke a mirror and cut his hand, which was bad luck.
> Jane broke a mirror and then sprained her ankle, which was bad luck.
> Sally broke a mirror and then lost her purse, which was bad luck.
> _____
> Therefore breaking a mirror *causes* bad luck.

Most of us would be inclined to put very little trust in such an argument. Yet it is an argument by simple enumeration, appealing to three "confirming instances." Nevertheless, we should probably say that the three instances reported were coincidences rather than cases of a causal law. That is the chief weakness of arguments by simple enumeration. Their very nature prevents them from distinguishing between confirming instances of genuine causal laws, on the one hand, and mere accidents or coincidences, on the other.

Our criticism of the method of simple enumeration can be put in this way. A single negative or disconfirming instance will overthrow an alleged causal law (any exception obviously *disproves* a rule), whereas the method of simple enumeration takes no account of such exceptions. For an exception or negative instance is either one where C is present without E, or where E is present without C, but the only legitimate premises in an argument by simple enumeration are reports of instances in which both C and E are present. In other words, if we were to confine ourselves to simple enumeration arguments exclusively, we should look only for confirming instances and would tend to ignore any negative or disconfirming instances that might otherwise be found. For this reason, despite their fruitfulness and value in suggesting causal laws, inductions by simple enumeration are not at all suitable for *testing* causal laws. For the testing of causal laws, other types of inductive arguments have been devised, and to these we now turn.

12.2 *Mill's Methods*

His criticisms of induction by simple enumeration led the British philosopher Sir Francis Bacon (1561–1626) to recommend other types of inductive procedure. These were given their classic formulation by another British philosopher, John Stuart Mill (1806–1873), and have come to be called Mill's Methods of inductive inference. Mill formulated five of these "canons," as he called them, and they are known as the Method of Agreement, the Method of Difference, the Joint Method of Agreement and Difference, the Method of Residues, and the Method of Concomitant Variation. They will be presented here in that order.

1. Method of Agreement

The Method of Agreement is best introduced by way of an example. Suppose that some of the residents of a certain dormitory have become violently ill, suffering stomach distress and nausea, and that it is desired to determine the cause of this illness. Half a dozen of the affected students are interviewed to find out what they ate on the day the illness began. The first student ate soup, bread and butter, salad, vegetables, and canned pears; the second student ate soup, bread and butter, vegetables, and canned pears; the third student ate soup, a pork sandwich, salad, and canned pears; the fourth student ate bread and butter, salad, a pork sandwich, vegetables, and canned pears; the fifth student ate soup, salad, vegetables, and canned pears; and the sixth student ate bread and butter, vegetables, and canned pears. To make this information more readily available, we can set it down in the form of a table, using the capital letters *A, B, C, D, E, F* to denote the presence of the "antecedent circumstances" of having eaten soup, bread and butter, salad, pork sandwich, vegetables, and canned pears, respectively, and using the small letter *s* to denote the presence of the phenomenon of being sick. Where the six students are the six "instances" examined, our information can be represented as in the following table.

Instance	Antecedent Circumstances						Phenomenon
1	*A*	*B*	*C*		*E*	*F*	*s*
2	*A*	*B*			*E*	*F*	*s*
3	*A*		*C*	*D*		*F*	*s*
4		*B*	*C*	*D*	*E*	*F*	*s*
5	*A*		*C*		*E*	*F*	*s*
6		*B*			*E*	*F*	*s*

From these data we should naturally infer that the circumstance F could have been the cause of the phenomenon s, that is, that the illness was probably due to eating the particular canned pears served in the dormitory. As in any other inductive argument, these premises do not *prove* the conclusion, but they do establish it as probable by eliminating A, B, C, D, and E as possible causes, because s has been shown to occur in their absence. Any inference of this type is characterized as using the Method of Agreement. Mill's general formulation is this:

> If two or more instances of the phenomenon under investigation have only one circumstance in common, the circumstance in which alone all the instances agree, is the cause (or effect) of the given phenomenon.

Schematically, the Method of Agreement may be represented as follows, where capital letters represent circumstances and small letters denote phenomena:

$$A\ B\ C\ D \text{ occur together with } w\ x\ y\ z.$$
$$A\ E\ F\ G \text{ occur together with } w\ t\ u\ v.$$

Therefore *A* is the cause (or the effect) of *w*.

Another illustration of the use of the Method of Agreement can be drawn from a fairly recent innovation in dental hygiene. It was observed that the inhabitants of several cities enjoyed a much lower rate of dental decay than the national average, and some thought was given to discovering the cause of this happy phenomenon. It was found that the circumstances of these cities differed in many ways: in latitude and longitude, in elevation, in their types of economy, and so on. But one circumstance was common to all of them. This common circumstance was the presence of an unusually high percentage of fluorine in their water supplies, which meant that the diet of the inhabitants of these cities included an unusually large quantity of fluorine. It was inferred that the use of fluorine can cause a decrease in the incidence of dental decay, and acceptance of this conclusion has led to the adoption of fluorine treatments for this purpose in many other localities. Whenever we have found a single circumstance common to all instances of a given phenomenon, we believe ourselves to have discovered its cause.

A word should be said here about the limitations of the Method of Agreement. The available data in our first illustration of that method were remarkably well suited to the application of that method. But such convenient data may not always be available. For example, it might have been the case that all of the stricken students had eaten *both* salad and canned pears. In that case the Method of Agreement would have *eliminated* the soup, the bread and butter, the pork sandwiches, and the vegetables as possible causes of the illness, but would have left open the question as to whether it was the salad, the canned pears, or the combination of them that was responsible for the students' sickness. A different inductive method is required to establish the cause here, and it is provided by the second of Mill's Methods.

EXERCISES

Analyze each of the following arguments in terms of "circumstances" and "phenomena" to show how they follow the pattern of the Method of Agreement.

⋆ 1. Johnston compared the effects of smoking with those of hypodermically injected nicotine. The smokers almost invariably thought the sensation pleasant, although nonsmokers usually termed it "queer." Johnston, who gave himself 80 injections of 1.3 mg. of nicotine from three to four times a day, found that he preferred the hypodermic injections of nicotine to inhaling a cigarette. In his case, it would appear that nicotine was the major factor in the pleasant sensation due to smoking.   —ERNEST L. WYNDER, M.D., ed., *The Biologic Effect of Tobacco*

2. It is interesting to note that one of the frequent symptoms of extreme combat anxiety cases is an interference with speech that may run from complete muteness to hesitation and stuttering. Similarly, the sufferer from acute stage fright is unable to speak. Many animals tend to stop vocalizing when frightened, and it is obvious that this tendency is adaptive in preventing them from attracting the attention of their enemies. In the light of this evidence one might suspect that the drive of fear has an innate tendency to elicit the response of stopping vocal behavior.   —JOHN DOLLARD and NEAL E. MILLER, *Personality and Psychotherapy*[1]

3. He [Edward] Jenner kept neatly detailed records of his work, noting how Sarah Portlock, Mary Barge and Elizabeth Wynne, and Simon Nichols, Joseph Merret and William Rodway, had "taken" cowpox and how they showed immunity when he inoculated them with smallpox. He repeated his observations on others, and years passed as he accumulated page upon page of records of cowpox and smallpox. Eventually he was satisfied. He was convinced that the people who had taken cowpox were without exception immune to smallpox.

Jenner's crucial experiment was done in 1796. He took cowpox matter from the hands of Sarah Nelmes, dairymaid, and with it he vaccinated the arm of eight-year-old James Phipps. Two months later, Jenner inoculated Phipps with smallpox on both arms, and several months later he repeated the inoculation. There was neither fever nor pocks, only a trivial sore at the point of inoculation typical of immunity.   —A. L. BARON, *Man Against Germs*

4. A few years ago a small number of people living in various sections of the United States were inflicted with an identical disease. At about the same time the eyes of these individuals developed what the physician calls cataracts—small, irregular, opaque spots in the tissue of the lens. Cataracts interfere with the clear passage of light through the transparent medium of the eye lens. In severe cases they may block vision, visual acuity is lost and the lens must be removed. It turned out that all the individuals who developed these cataracts were physicists

---

[1]From John Dollard and Neal E. Miller, *Personality and Psychotherapy* (New York: McGraw-Hill Book Company, copyright 1950).

and that all of them had been connected with nuclear-energy projects during the war. While they worked with cyclotrons in atomic-energy laboratories they had been the targets of stray neutron rays. They were under medical supervision all during their work, but the density of the neutrons was thought to be entirely harmless. Several years later, however, they developed cataracts.

This case is one of the best examples of the insidiousness of nuclear radiation.
—HEINZ HABER, *Man in Space*

5. In 1951, Harris Isbell, at the Addiction Research Center of the U.S. Public Health Service Hospital for addicts in Lexington, Kentucky, reported on startling research. He had tested five volunteers, giving increasing doses of barbiturates over several months. Suddenly the drug was stopped. For about sixteen hours the men seemed well. Then four of them went into convulsions. All had a sense of impending doom; their hands shook; and several of the men lost as much as twelve pounds in a day and a half. Four became psychotic: One felt that his brain had slipped into his abdomen; another asserted that cotton was growing in his mouth. Isbell concluded that barbiturates were not only addictive, but he said, "The addiction is in fact far more dangerous than addiction to morphine."
—GAY GAER LUCE and JULIUS SEGAL, *Insomnia*

2. Method of Difference

The Method of Difference is often applicable to such cases as those described in our first illustration of the Method of Agreement. If on further investigation in the dormitory we found a student who, on the day that many had become ill, had eaten soup, bread and butter, salad, and vegetables only and had *not* become ill, we could profitably compare this case with that of the first student described. Denoting this last student as "instance n," and using the same abbreviations as in our first table, we can set down a new table as

Instance	Antecedent Circumstances					Phenomenon
1	A	B	C	E	F	s
n	A	B	C	E	—	—

From these new data we should again naturally infer that the circumstance F could have caused the phenomenon s; that is, the illness was probably due to eating the canned pears. Of course, the conclusion follows with probability rather than with certainty, but that is merely to say that the inference is inductive rather than deductive. Any inference of this type uses the Method of Difference, which was formulated by Mill in these words:

If an instance in which the phenomenon under investigation occurs and an instance in which it does not occur, have every circumstance in common save one, that one occurring only in the former, the circumstance in which alone the two instances differ, is the effect, or the cause, or an indispensable part of the cause, of the phenomenon.

Schematically, the Method of Difference may be represented as follows, where again capital letters represent circumstances and small letters denote phenomena:

$A\ B\ C\ D$ occur together with $w\ x\ y\ z$.
$\ B\ C\ D$ occur together with $\ x\ y\ z$.

Therefore A is the cause, or the effect, or an indispensable part of the cause, of w.

Strictly speaking, we should have inferred not that eating the canned pears was *the* cause of sickness but that eating the canned pears was "an indispensable part of the cause" of the sickness. This distinction is perhaps brought out more clearly in the case of a simple example. We might have two cigarette lighters in exactly the same condition except that the flint has been removed from one but not the other. The presence of the flint is the only circumstance in which they differ, and the phenomenon of lighting occurs in the one instance but not in the other, yet we should not say that the presence of flint was *the* cause, but rather *an indispensable part of the cause* of the lighting. Where it is known that the phenomenon occurs later in time than the circumstance, as when eating the canned pears was an antecedent circumstance, there need be no doubt as to which is cause and which effect, for an effect can never precede its cause.

A more serious illustration of the Method of Difference is provided by the following:

Experiments were devised to show that yellow fever was transmitted by the mosquito alone, all other reasonable opportunities for being infected being excluded. A small building was erected, all windows and doors and every other possible opening being absolutely mosquito-proof. A wire mosquito screen divided the room into two spaces. In one of these spaces fifteen mosquitoes, which had fed on yellow fever patients, were liberated. A non-immune volunteer entered the room with the mosquitoes and was bitten by seven mosquitoes. Four days later, he suffered an attack of yellow fever. Two other non-immune men slept for thirteen nights in the mosquito-free room without disturbances of any sort.

To show that the disease was transmitted by the mosquito and not through the excreta of yellow fever patients or anything which had come in contact with them, another house was constructed and made mosquito-proof. For 20 days, this house was occupied by three non-immunes, after the clothing, bedding and eating utensils and other vessels soiled with the discharge, blood and vomitus of yellow fever patients had been placed in it. The bed clothing which they used had been brought from the beds of the patients who had died of yellow fever, without being subjected to washing or any other treatment to remove anything with which it might have been soiled. The experiment was twice repeated by other non-immune volunteers. During the entire period all the men who occupied the house were strictly quarantined and protected from mosquitoes. None of those exposed to these experiments contracted yellow fever. That they were not immune was subsequently shown, since four of them became infected either by mosquito bites or the injection of blood from yellow fever patients.[2]

The preceding account contains three distinct uses of the Method of Difference. In the first paragraph, the reasoning involved may be schematized as follows, where A denotes the circumstance of being bitten by an infected mosquito; w denotes the phenomenon of suffering an attack of yellow fever; B, C, D denote the circumstances of living in the small building described; and x, y, z denote phenomena common to all the volunteers referred to

$$A\ B\ C\ D\text{\textemdash}\text{\textemdash}w\ x\ y\ z \text{ first nonimmune man.}$$
$$B\ C\ D\text{\textemdash}\text{\textemdash}\quad x\ y\ z \text{ second nonimmune man.}$$
$$B\ C\ D\text{\textemdash}\text{\textemdash}\quad x\ y\ z \text{ third nonimmune man.}$$

Therefore A is the cause of w.

The second paragraph involves a refinement on the preceding, for the infected mosquitoes, presumably, did not merely bite the first nonimmune man but in lighting on him deposited some matter picked up from the yellow-fever patients on whom they had previously fed. That it was the *bite* of the mosquito (A) that caused infection (w), rather than the circumstance (M) of coming into contact with what had been in contact with a yellow-fever patient, is established by the following pattern of argument:

$$B\ C\ D\ M\text{\textemdash}\text{\textemdash}\quad x\ y\ z\ t \text{ nonimmune men in house.}$$
$$A\ B\ C\ D\ M\text{\textemdash}\text{\textemdash}w\ x\ y\ z\ t \text{ same nonimmune men when subsequently}$$
bitten.

Therefore A (rather than M) is the cause of w.

The third pattern of argument found in the preceding account emerges when the first and second paragraphs are considered together. Here we focus our attention on two instances: first, the nonimmune man who was both bitten by a mosquito *and* thus brought into contact with matter from a yellow-fever patient, and, second, the nonimmune man who was not bitten but was nevertheless brought into contact with matter from a patient. Here the pattern emerges as

$$A\ M\text{\textemdash}\text{\textemdash}\text{\textemdash}w\ t.$$
$$M\text{\textemdash}\text{\textemdash}\text{\textemdash}\quad t.$$

Therefore A is the cause of w.

All these patterns exemplify the Method of Difference, which is thus seen to be a very pervasive type of experimental inference.

[2]Paul Henle and W. K. Frankena, *Exercises in Elementary Logic,* copyright 1940.

EXERCISES

Analyze each of the following arguments in terms of "circumstances" and "phenomena" to show how they follow the pattern of the Method of Difference.

★ 1. In 1861 Pasteur at last carried general conviction against spontaneous generation. He boiled meat broth in a flask with a very long thin neck until no bacteria were left. This was shown by the fact that he could now keep the broth in the flask for an indefinite period without change setting in, the narrow neck admitting nothing. Then he broke off the neck and in a few hours the liquid showed micro-organisms, and the meat was in full decay. That the air carried such organisms he proved by twice filtering it through sterile filters and showing that with the first filter, but not the second, he could set up putrefaction.

—H. T. PLEDGE, *Science Since 1500*

2. The primitive brain, as we saw in the planaria, served chiefly as a sensory relay—a center for receiving stimuli from the sense organs and then sending impulses down the nerve cord. This is also true of the nereis, for, if the brain is removed, the animal can still move in a coordinated way—and, in fact, it moves about more than usual. If it meets some obstacle, it does not withdraw and go off in a new direction but persists in its unsuccessful forward movements. This very unadaptive kind of behavior shows that in the normal nereis the brain has an important function which it did not have in flatworms—that of *inhibition* of movement in response to certain stimuli.

—RALPH BUCHSBAUM, *Animals Without Backbones*

3. It was assumed for a long time, by analogy with the mosquito and other bloodsucking vectors, that the virus of typhus was injected by the louse when sucking blood. But apparently this is not so. The infection is not in the saliva of the louse, as it probably is with the mosquito, but in the feces. The disease is thought to be spread through the feces coming into contact with scratches or abrasions in the skin, and scratching and louse infection are generally inseparable. This fact was first suggested in 1922 by the two workers who fed infected lice on a monkey, while taking great care that no feces from the lice should come in contact with the monkey's skin. They found that the monkey remained healthy.

—KENNETH M. SMITH, *Beyond the Microscope*

4. We have recently obtained conclusive experimental evidence that there can be no tooth decay without bacteria and a food supply for them. In germ-free laboratories at the University of Notre Dame and the University of Chicago, animals innocent of oral micro-organisms do not develop cavities. Where animals in normal circumstances average more than four cavities each, the germ-free rats show no signs of caries. At the Harvard School of Dental Medicine we have demonstrated the other side of the coin: that food debris also must be present. Rats that have plenty of bacteria in their mouths but are fed by tube directly to the stomach do not develop cavities. In a pair of rats joined by surgery so that they share a common blood circulation, the one fed by mouth develops tooth decay, the one fed by the tube does not.

—REIDER F. SOGNNAES, "Tooth Decay," *Scientific American,*
Vol. 197, No. 6. December 1957

5. Ignaz Semmelweis showed how the dreadful suffering and loss of life due to puerperal fever that was then the rule in the hospitals of Europe could be prevented.

In 1847 Semmelweis got the idea that the disease was carried to the women on the hands of the medical teachers and students coming direct from the post-mortem room. To destroy the "cadaveric material" on the hands he instituted a strict routine of washing the hands in a solution of chlorinated lime before the examination of the patients. As a result of this procedure, the mortality from puerperal fever in the first obstetric clinic of the General Hospital of Vienna fell immediately from 12 percent to 3 percent, and later almost to 1 percent.

— W. I. B. BEVERIDGE, *The Art of Scientific Investigation*

3. Joint Method of Agreement and Difference

The Joint Method of Agreement and Difference can be explained simply as the use of both the Method of Agreement and the Method of Difference in the same investigation. Its pattern is

A B C——*x y z*.	A B C——*x y z*.
A D E——*x t w*.	B C—— *y z*.

Therefore *A* is the effect, or the cause, or an indispensable part of the cause, of *x*.

Since each Method, used separately, affords some probability to the conclusion, their joint use as illustrated affords a higher probability to the conclusion. Although this interpretation would scarcely fit in with the view that the Joint Method is an additional and separate Method, it does reveal it as an extremely powerful pattern of inductive inference. Its use, in this form, is illustrated in Zeeman's report of his discovery of what has come to be known as Zeeman's Effect:

> In consequence of my measurements of Kerr's magneto-optical phenomena, the thought occurred to me whether the period of the light emitted by a flame might be altered when the flame was acted upon by magnetic force. It has turned out that such an action really occurs. I introduced into an oxyhydrogen flame, placed between the poles of a Ruhmkorff's electromagnet, a filament of asbestos soaked in common salt. The light of the flame was examined with a Rowland's grating. Whenever the circuit was closed both *D* lines were seen to widen.
>
> Since one might attribute the widening to the known effects of the magnetic field upon the flame, which would cause an alteration in the density and temperature of the sodium vapour, I had resort to a method of experimentation which is much more free from objection. Sodium was strongly heated in a tube of biscuit porcelain, such as Pringsheim used in his interesting investigations upon the radiation of gases. The tube was closed at both ends by plane parallel glass plates, whose effective area was 1 cm². The tube was placed horizontally between the poles, at right angles to the lines of force. The light of an arc lamp was sent through. The absorption spectrum showed both *D* lines. The tube was continuously rotated round its axis to avoid temperature variations. Excitation of the magnet caused

immediate widening of the lines. It thus appears very probable that the period of sodium light is altered in the magnetic field.[3]

The pattern of Zeeman's inference may be schematized by using the following symbols: A denotes the presence of a magnetic field, B denotes the presence of an open oxyhydrogen flame, C denotes the arc lamp illumination described, x denotes the widening of the D lines of the sodium spectrum, y denotes the usual effects of an open oxyhydrogen flame, and z denotes the usual effects of arc lamp illumination. The inference is now symbolized as

$$
\begin{array}{lll}
A\ B\text{———}x\ y. & A\ B\text{———}x\ y. & A\ C\text{———}x\ z. \\
A\ C\text{———}x\ z. & B\text{———}\ \ y. & C\text{———}\ \ z. \\
\end{array}
$$

Therefore A is the cause, or an indispensable part of the cause, of x.

Here the left-hand pair of premises yields the conclusion by the Method of Agreement, while the middle and right-hand pairs yield the conclusion by the Method of Difference, so the whole argument proceeds by the Joint Method.

EXERCISES

Analyze each of the following arguments in terms of "circumstances" and "phenomena" to show how they follow the pattern of the Joint Method of Agreement and Difference:

★ 1. Eijkman fed a group of chickens exclusively on white rice. They all developed polyneuritis and died. He fed another group of fowl unpolished rice. Not a single one of them contracted the disease. Then he gathered up the polishings from rice and fed them to other polyneuritic chickens, and in a short time the birds recovered. He had accurately traced the cause of polyneuritis to a faulty diet. For the first time in history, he had produced a food deficiency disease experimentally, and had actually cured it. It was a fine piece of work and resulted in some immediate remedial measures.   —BERNARD JAFFE, *Outposts of Science*[4]

2. An experiment by Greenspoon on the reinforcement of a response (1950) provides another clear example of direct, automatic, or, in other words, unconscious learning. He had his subjects sit facing away from him so that they could not see him. He asked them to say all the words they could think of, pronouncing them individually without using any sentences or phrases, and he recorded their responses on a tape recorder. The response he was reinforcing was that of saying plural nouns; he did this by saying "Mmm-hmm" immediately after the subject said a plural noun. In this case the response was a highly generalized part of language habits and the reinforcing value of the stimulus "Mmm-hmm" must have been acquired as a part of social learning.

---

[3]William Francis Magie, *A Source Book in Physics* (New York: McGraw-Hill Book Company, copyright 1935).

[4]Bernard Jaffe, *Outposts of Science*, copyright 1935, by Bernard Jaffe. Reprinted by permission of Simon and Schuster, Inc., New York.

Greenspoon found that during the "training" period the experimental group, to whom he said, "Mmm-hmm" after each plural noun, greatly increased the percentage of plural nouns spoken, while the control group, to whom nothing was said after plural nouns, showed no such increase. Furthermore this happened with subjects who on subsequent questioning showed that they had no idea what the purpose of the "Mmm-hmm" was and were completely unaware of the fact that they were increasing their percentage of plural nouns. This clearly demonstrates that the effect of a reinforcement can be entirely unconscious and automatic. Somewhat similar experiments have been performed by Thorndike (1932) and Thorndike and Rock (1934). A great deal of human learning seems to be of this direct, unconscious kind. Apparently many attitudes, prejudices, emotions, motor skills, and mannerisms are acquired in this way.

—JOHN DOLLARD and NEAL E. MILLER, *Personality and Psychotherapy*

3. So Metchnikoff, with Roux always being careful and insisting upon good check experiments—so Metchnikoff, after all of his theorizing about why we are immune, performed one of the most profoundly practical of all the experiments of microbe hunting. He sat himself down and invented the famous calomel ointment—that now is chasing syphilis out of armies and navies the world over. He took two apes, inoculated them with the syphilitic virus fresh from a man, and then, one hour later, he rubbed the grayish ointment into that scratch spot on one of his apes. He watched the horrid signs of the disease appear on the unanointed beast, and saw all signs of the disease stay away from the one that had got the calomel.

Then for the last time Metchnikoff's strange insanity got hold of him. He forgot his vows and induced a young medical student, Maisonneuve, to volunteer to be scratched with syphilis from an infected man. Before a committee of the most distinguished medical men of France, this brave Maisonneuve stood up, and into six long scratches he watched the dangerous virus go. It was a more severe inoculation than any man would ever get in nature. The results of it might make him a thing for loathing, might send him, insane, to his death. . . . For one hour Maisonneuve waited, then Metchnikoff, full of confidence, rubbed the calomel ointment into the wounds—but not into those which had been made at the same time on a chimpanzee and a monkey. It was a superb success, for Maisonneuve showed never a sign of the ugly ulcer, while the simians, thirty days afterwards, developed the disease—there was no doubt about it.

—PAUL DE KRUIF, *Microbe Hunters*[5]

4. The discovery was made in this way. I had dissected and prepared a frog . . . and while I was attending to something else, I laid it on a table on which stood an electrical machine at some distance from its conductor and separated from it by a considerable space. Now when one of the persons who were present touched accidentally and lightly the inner crural nerves of the frog with the point of a scalpel all the muscles of the legs seemed to contract again and again as if they were affected by powerful cramps. Another one who was there, who was helping us in electrical researches, thought that he had noticed that the action was excited when a spark was discharged from the conductor of the machine. Being astonished by this new phenomenon he called my attention to it, who at

that time had something else in mind and was deep in thought. Whereupon I was inflamed with an incredible zeal and eagerness to test the same and to bring to light what was concealed in it. I therefore myself touched one or the other nerve with the point of the knife and at the same time one of those present drew a spark. The phenomenon was always the same. Without fail there occurred lively contractions in every muscle of the leg at the same instant as that in which the spark jumped, as if the prepared animals was affected by tetanus.

With the thought that these motions might arise from the contact with the point of the knife, which perhaps caused the excited condition, rather than by the spark, I touched the same nerves again in the same way in other frogs with the point of the knife, and indeed with greater pressure, yet so that no one during this time drew off a spark. Now no motions could be detected. I therefore came to the conclusion that perhaps to excite the phenomenon there were needed both the contact of a body and the electric spark.

—LUIGI GALVANI, quoted in William Francis Magie, *A Source Book in Physics*

5. Pasteur . . . carried out at least one spectacular experiment having to do with the effect of temperature on susceptibility to infection. Puzzled by the fact that hens were refractory to anthrax, he had wondered whether this might not be explained by their body temperature, which is higher than that of animals susceptible to this disease. To test his hypothesis, he inoculated hens with anthrax bacilli and placed them in a cold bath to lower their body temperature. Animals so treated died the next day, showing numerous bacilli in their blood and organs. Another hen, similarly infected and maintained in the cold bath until the disease was in full progress, was then taken out of the water, dried, wrapped, and placed under conditions that allowed rapid return to normal body temperature. *Mirabile dictu*, this hen made a complete recovery. Thus, a mere fall of a few degrees in body temperature was sufficient to render birds almost as receptive to anthrax as were rabbits or guinea pigs.   RENÉ DUBOS, *Pasteur and Modern Science*

4. Method of Residues

In his statement of the Method of Residues, Mill varies his terminology slightly, referring not to *circumstances* and phenomena, but to *antecedents* and phenomena. Of course what he means is *antecedent circumstances*. Mill's formulation is

> Subduct from any phenomenon such part as is known by previous inductions to be the effect of certain antecedents, and the residue of the phenomenon is the effect of the remaining antecedents.

An illustration of this method is provided by the discovery of the planet Neptune:

> In 1821, Bouvard of Paris published tables of the motions of a number of planets, including Uranus. In preparing the latter he had found great difficulty in making an orbit calculated on the basis of positions obtained in the years after 1800 agree with one calculated from observations taken in the years immediately following discovery. He finally disregarded the older observations entirely and based his tables on the newer observations. In a few years, however, the positions calculated

from the tables disagreed with the observed positions of the planet and by 1844 the discrepancy amounted to 2 minutes of arc. Since all the other known planets agreed in their motions with those calculated for them, the discrepancy in the case of Uranus aroused much discussion.

In 1845, Leverrier, then a young man, attacked the problem. He checked Bouvard's calculations and found them essentially correct. Thereupon he felt that the only satisfactory explanation of the trouble lay in the presence of a planet somewhere beyond Uranus which was disturbing its motion. By the middle of 1846 he had finished his calculations. In September he wrote to Galle at Berlin and requested the latter to look for a new planet in a certain region of the sky for which some new star charts had just been prepared in Germany but of which Leverrier apparently had not as yet obtained copies. On the twenty-third of September Galle started the search and in less than an hour he found an object which was not on the chart. By the next night it had moved appreciably and the new planet, subsequently named Neptune, was discovered within 1° of the predicted place. This discovery ranks among the greatest achievements of mathematical astronomy.[6]

Here the phenomenon being investigated was the movement of Uranus. The part of the phenomenon known by previous inductions to be the effect of certain antecedents was a certain calculated orbit known to be the effect of the gravitational influence of the sun and the interior planets. The residue of the phenomenon was the perturbation in the calculated orbit. The remaining antecedent was the (hypothesized) planet Neptune, which was inferred to be the *cause* of the residue of the phenomenon by the Method of Residues.

Schematically, the Method of Residues can be represented as follows:

$A\ B\ C$——$x\ y\ z$.
B is known to be the cause of y.
C is known to be the cause of z.

Therefore A is the cause of x.

A simpler illustration of the use of this method is in the weighing of various types of cargo, especially that of trucks. The truck is weighed when empty and then weighed again when it has been loaded. The total phenomenon is the passage of the scale's pointer past the various numerals on its dial. The antecedents here are two: the truck and its cargo. The part of the phenomenon that consists of the scale's pointer moving up to the numeral that corresponds with the weight of the empty truck is known to be due to the truck alone. Then the residue of the phenomenon, the amount by which the scale's pointer moves beyond the numeral corresponding to the weight of the empty truck, is concluded to be the effect of the cargo, and therefore a measure of its weight.

The Method of Residues is sometimes said to be a strictly deductive pattern of inference and not inductive at all. It must be admitted that there are cer-

[6]Edward Arthur Fath, *The Elements of Astronomy* (New York: McGraw-Hill Book Company, 1934).

tainly differences between the other methods and the Method of Residues. Each of the other methods requires the examination of at least two instances, whereas the Method of Residues can be used with the examination of only one case. And none of the other Methods, as formulated by Mill, requires an appeal to any antecedently established causal laws, while the Method of Residues definitely does depend upon antecedently established causal laws. These differences are present, but they do not spell the difference between induction and deduction. For despite the presence of premises that state causal laws, a conclusion inferred by the Method of Residues is only probable, and cannot be *validly deduced* from its premises. Of course an additional premiss or two might serve to transform an inference by the Method of Residues into a valid deductive argument, but the same can be said for the other methods as well. There seems to be no basis for the claim that the Method of Residues is deductive rather than inductive.

EXERCISES

Analyze each of the following arguments in terms of "antecedents" and "phenomena" to show how they follow the pattern of the Method of Residues.

★ 1. Hoarders.

Is avarice a natural tendency or an acquired habit? Two Harvard psychologists have been investigating this question with rats. Louise C. Licklider and J. C. R. Licklider provided six rats with all the food they could eat and more. Their food after weaning consisted of pellets of Purina Laboratory Chow. Although none of the rats had ever experienced a food shortage, all immediately started hoarding pellets. Even after they had accumulated a hoard and the food-supply bin was empty, they kept coming back to hunt for more.

This behavior confirmed what previous investigators had found. But the Lickliders refined the experiment to try to unearth the rats' motives for hoarding. They covered half of the pellets with aluminum foil, thus eliminating their value as food. The experimenters discovered that four of the six avaricious rats actually preferred the worthless, inedible pellets in hoarding.

The rats were then put on short rations for six days. After this "deprivation period" they hoarded even more greedily and showed more interest in the plain food pellets, but some still hoarded foil-wrapped pellets and continued to prefer them.

The Lickliders conclude, in a report to the *Journal of Comparative and Clinical Psychology*: "The factors that lead to hoarding and that determine what is hoarded are by no means entirely alimentary. The initiation of hoarding seems to be for the rat, as for the human being, a complex motivational problem to which sensory and perceptual factors, rather than blood chemistry, hold the key."

—"Science and the Citizen," *Scientific American*, Vol. 183, No. 1, July 1950

2. In H. Davies' experiments on the decomposition of water by galvanism, it was found that besides the two components of water, oxygen and hydrogen, an acid and an alkali were developed at opposite poles of the machine. Since the theory of the analysis of water did not give reason to expect these products, their presence constituted a problem. Some chemists thought that electricity had the

power of producing these substances of itself. Davies conjectured that there might be some hidden cause for this part of the effect—the glass might suffer decomposition, or some foreign matter might be in the water. He then proceeded to investigate whether or not the diminution or total elimination of possible causes would change or eliminate the effect in question. Substituting gold vessels for glass ones, he found no change in the effect and concluded that glass was not the cause. Using distilled water, he found a decrease in the quantity of acid and alkali involved, yet enough remained to show that the cause was still in operation. He inferred that impurity of the water was not the sole cause, but was a concurrent cause. He then suspected that perspiration from the hands might be the cause, as it would contain salt which would decompose into acid and alkali under electricity. By avoiding such contact, he reduced the quantity of the effect still further, till only slight traces remained. These might be due to some impurity of the atmosphere decomposed by the electricity. An experiment determined this. The machine was put under an exhausted receiver and when it was thus secured from atmospheric influences, no acid or alkali was produced.

—G. GORE, *The Art of Scientific Discovery*

3. The return of the comet predicted by Professor Encke a great many times in succession, and the general good agreement of its calculated with its observed place during any one of its periods of visibility, would lead us to say that its gravitation toward the sun and planets is the sole and sufficient cause of all the phenomena of its orbital motion; but when the effect of this cause is strictly calculated and subducted from the observed motion, there is found to remain behind a *residual phenomenon*, which would never have been otherwise ascertained to exist, which is a small anticipation of the time of its re-appearance, or a diminution of its periodic time, which cannot be accounted for by gravity, and whose cause is therefore to be inquired into. Such an anticipation would be caused by the resistance of a medium disseminated through the celestial regions; and as there are other good reasons for believing this to be a *vera causa* (an actually existing antecedent), it has therefore been ascribed to such a resistance.

—SIR JOHN HERSCHEL, quoted in John Stuart Mill, *A System of Logic*

4. It was not merely the amount of water in circulation which was influenced by temperature. . . . It was the total amount of haemoglobin. The mystery was: "Whence came this outpouring of haemoglobin?" It was not credible that the bone-marrow could have provided the body with new corpuscles at the rate required. Moreover, there was no evidence of increase of immature corpuscles in circulation. . . .

The question then was forced upon us: Has the body any considerable but hidden store of haemoglobin which can be drawn upon in case of emergency? . . . In searching for a locality which might fulfill such a condition one naturally seeks in the first instance for some place where the red blood corpuscles are outside the circulatory system—some backwater outside the arteries, capillaries, and veins. There is only one such place of any considerable size in the body—that place is the spleen.   —JOSEPH BARCROFT, *The Lancet*, February 1925

5. It is no longer open to discussion that the air has weight. It is common knowledge that a balloon is heavier when inflated than when empty, which is proof enough. For if the air were light, the more the balloon was inflated, the lighter the whole would be, since there would be more air in it. But since, on the

contrary, when more air is put in, the whole becomes heavier, it follows that each part has a weight of its own, and consequently that the air has weight.

—BLAISE PASCAL, *Treatise on the Weight of the Mass of the Air*

5. Method of Concomitant Variation

At this point we may observe the common pattern that runs through all of the first four of Mill's Methods. In the Method of Agreement we eliminate as possible causes of a given phenomenon all those circumstances in whose absence the phenomenon can nevertheless occur, and the remaining circumstance is then inferred to be its cause. The essential character of that Method is thus seen to be eliminative. In the Method of Difference we exclude one of the circumstances that accompany a given phenomenon, while leaving the other circumstances the same. If the phenomenon is also removed thereby, we infer that the remaining circumstances can be eliminated as possible causes. Here we conclude that the one circumstance whose absence prevents the occurrence of the phenomenon in question is the cause of that phenomenon. The second Method also proceeds by elimination. The Joint Method of Agreement and Difference is easily shown to be essentially eliminative also, while the Method of Residues proceeds by eliminating as possible causes those antecedent circumstances whose effects have already been established by previous inductions.

There are situations, however, in which some circumstances cannot possibly be eliminated. Here none of the first four methods is applicable. One of Mill's own examples in discussing this problem concerns the cause of the phenomenon of the tides. We know that it is the gravitational attraction of the moon that causes the rise and fall of the tides, but this could not have been established by any of the first four Methods. The proximity of the moon at high tide is not the *only* circumstance present in all cases of high tide, for the fixed stars are also present and cannot be eliminated. Nor can the moon be removed from the heavens for the sake of applying the Method of Difference. The Joint Method is inapplicable, as is the Method of Residues. Of such situations, Mill writes

> But we have still a resource. Though we can not exclude an antecedent altogether, we may be able to produce, or nature may produce for us some modification in it. By a modification is here meant, a change in it not amounting to its total removal. . . . We can not try an experiment in the absence of the moon, so as to observe what terrestrial phenomena her annihilation would put an end to; but when we find that all the variations in the *position* of the moon are followed by corresponding variations in the time and place of high water, the place being always either the part of the earth which is nearest to, or that which is most remote from, the moon, we have ample evidence that the moon is, wholly or partially, the cause which determines the tides.[7]

[7]John Stuart Mill, *A System of Logic*, Book III. Chapter 8, Section 6.

The argument here proceeds according to what Mill named the Method of Concomitant Variation. The general statement of this Method is

> Whatever phenomenon varies in any manner whenever another phenomenon varies in some particular manner, is either a cause or an effect of that phenomenon, or is connected with it through some fact of causation.

If we use plus and minus signs to indicate the greater or lesser degree to which a varying phenomenon is present in a given situation, the Method of Concomitant Variation can be schematized as follows:

$$A \quad B \ C\text{———}x \quad y \ z.$$
$$A^+ \ B \ C\text{———}x^+ \ y \ z.$$
$$A^- \ B \ C\text{———}x^- \ y \ z.$$

Therefore A and x are causally connected.

This method is very widely used. A farmer establishes that there is a causal connection between the application of fertilizer to the ground and the size of the crop by applying different amounts to different parts of a field and noting that the parts to which more fertilizer has been applied yield a more abundant harvest. A merchant verifies the efficacy of advertising by running larger and smaller advertisements at different intervals and noting that business activity is increased during a period of intensive advertising. Here the phenomena are seen to vary *directly* with each other; that is, when one increases, the other increases also. However, the statement of the Method speaks of variation "in any manner," and in fact we infer a causal connection between phenomena that vary *inversely*, that is, phenomena such that when one increases the other *decreases*. Schematically, the Method of Concomitant Variation can also be represented as

$$A \quad B \ C\text{———}x \quad y \ z.$$
$$A^+ \ B \ C\text{———}x^- \ y \ z.$$
$$A^- \ B \ C\text{———}x^+ \ y \ z.$$

Therefore A and x are causally connected.

An example to illustrate this inverse variation is provided by economic phenomena: if the demand for a given type of goods remains constant, then any increase in the supply of those goods will be accompanied by a decrease in the price commanded by them. This concomitant variation is certainly part of the evidence for a causal connection between the supply and the price of a given commodity.

Mill's discussion of his own example is not altogether satisfactory. It may be objected that it is not the moon which is the cause of the tides, but the relative *position* of the moon. The moon itself is a circumstance that is never absent, but its occupation of this or that particular position is present only once every twenty-four hours, absent the rest of the time. Hence the Joint Method of Agreement and Difference is applicable to the situation and can perfectly well suffice to establish the causal connection between the position of the moon and the flow of the tides. The Method of Concomitant Variation is a new and important method, but its value was not adequately explained by Mill.

The other methods have an "all or nothing" character. Their use involves only the presence of a given circumstance, the occurrence or nonoccurrence of a given phenomenon. Thus the first four methods permit only a limited kind of evidence to be adduced in favor of causal laws. The Method of Concomitant Variation utilizes our ability to observe changes in the degree to which circumstances and phenomena are present and admits a vastly greater amount of data as evidence for the presence of causal connections. Its chief virtue lies in admitting more evidence, for thereby the new method widens the range of inductive inference.

The Method of Concomitant Variation is important as the first *quantitative* method of inductive inference, the preceding ones having all been qualitative. Its use, therefore, presupposes the existence of some method of measuring or estimating—even if only roughly—the degrees to which phenomena vary.

EXERCISES

Analyze each of the following arguments in terms of the variation of 'phenomena" to show how they follow the pattern of the Method of Concomitant Variation.

⋆ 1. In a *Harper's* article (October issue), the following observations on fuel–cancer relationships were attributed to Eugene J. Houdry, president of a firm that is developing a device for destroying harmful auto wastes: between 1940 and 1945 gasoline consumption in the United States dropped about 35 per cent because of wartime rationing, and in the same period lung cancer in U.S. white males dropped by approximately the same percentage; between 1914 and 1950 lung-cancer mortality increased nineteenfold and the rate of gasoline consumption also increased nineteenfold.   —*The New Yorker*, October 31, 1959

2. Careful studies have been made of the incidence of leukemia in the survivors of the atomic bombs burst over Hiroshima and Nagasaki. These survivors received exposures ranging from a few roentgens to 1000 roentgens or more.

They are divided into four groups. . . . The first group, *A*, consists of the estimated 1,870 survivors who were within 1 kilometer of the hypocenter (the point on the surface of the earth directly below the bomb when it exploded). There were very few survivors in this zone, and they received a large amount of radiation.

The second group, *B*, consists of the 13,730 survivors between 1.0 and 1.5 kilometers from the hypocenter, the third, *C*, of the 23,060 between 1.5 and 2.0 kilometers, and the fourth, *D*, of the 156,400 over 2.0 kilometers from the hypocenter.

The survivors of zones *A*, *B*, and *C* have been dying of leukemia during the period of careful study, the eight years from 1948 to 1955, at an average rate of about 9 per year . . . many more cases of leukemia occurred in the 15,600 survivors of zones *A* and *B* than in the 156,400 survivors of zone *D*, who received much less radiation. There is no doubt that the increased incidence is to be attributed to the exposure to radiation.

. . . The survivors of zone *A* received an estimated average of 650 roentgens, those of zone *B*, 250; those of zone *C*, 25, and of zone *D*, 2.5. . . . To within the reliability of the numbers, the incidence of leukemia in the three populations *A*, *B*, and *C* is proportional to the estimated dose of radiation, even for class *C*, in which the estimated dose is only 25 roentgens.

—LINUS PAULING, *No More War!*

3. Even as Banting was slaying dogs to save men, Evans was achieving a startling discovery in this field with another mysterious gland, *hypophysis cerebri*, commonly called the *pituitary*. This is a bit of an organ safely housed in a small pocket of bone attached to the base of the brain. Both Galen and Vesalius knew of this gland and thought it supplied the body with spit (in Latin, *sputus*). It is one of the most inaccessible glands in the living body. For many years, there appeared to be some connection between body growth and the functioning of this gland. In 1783 John Hunter had bargained with an undertaker for the body of an Irish giant of eight feet, four inches—Charles O'Brien, who had died at the age of twenty-two. The physician finally bought the body for twenty-five hundred dollars, and found a pituitary almost as large as a hen's egg. That of a normal adult man weighs hardly more than half a gram. A century later, *acromegaly*, an enlargement of the hands, feet, nose, lips, and jaw, was declared to be due to a tumor of the pituitary. The pituitary glands of dwarfs, some of them only eighteen inches high, all showed relatively small development or partial atrophy.

—BERNARD JAFFE, *Outposts of Science*

4. First Douglass attempted to get records of rainfall of this district as far back as possible, to test the correlation of moisture and the thickness of tree rings. Fortunately, temperature and rainfall measurements had been made and recorded at Whipple Barracks to the south of Flagstaff since 1867, and they were made available for his study. Then, in January, 1904, he visited the lumber yards of the Arizona Lumber and Timber Company and spent hours in the snow measuring the rings of many of their oldest trees. The president of the company became interested in the singular pastime of this strange hybrid of astronomer and politician, and had sections cut from the ends of scores of logs and stumps sent to Douglass for analysis. These pieces were carefully scraped with razor blades and brushed with kerosene for examination under the microscope. Every ring from the center of the tree to its bark was scrupulously scrutinized. To facilitate the dating of the rings, Douglass would make one pin prick to mark the last year of each decade, two to mark the middle year of each century, and three for the century year. Those cross sections which contained more than a thousand rings had an additional four pin pricks at the thousand-year tree-ring position. Douglass made tens of thousands of measurements, tabulated the data, drew curves and graphs, and as the average age of his trees was 348 years he was able to draw conclusions regarding the rainfall and tree-ring appearance of periods hundreds of years back.

Douglass found a striking correlation between tree growth and the recorded rainfall of the region. So accurate were his measurements and so apparently reliable his method that any marked peculiarity of any year could be identified with surprising ease and clarity in trees which often had grown more than four hundred miles apart. For example, the yellow pine ring of 1851 is small in trees which grew in regions between Santa Fe and Fresno because it represents a drought year. He could illustrate the accuracy of his technique in another way. He would pick out an old pine stump, study its rings, and then declare in what year the tree had been felled, much to the surprise of the owner of the land on which the tree had been cut. His tree time or "dendrochronology" was uncannily accurate.   —BERNARD JAFFE, *Outposts of Science*

5. For all the attention being directed toward heroin, cocaine and marijuana, the favorite mood-altering drug in the U.S., as it is in almost every human society, is alcohol. Its psychic effects, both pleasant and unpleasant, are well enough known. What is less well known is that alcohol, in different quantities for different people, is a toxic drug: its overconsumption taxes the body's economy, produces pathological changes in liver tissue and function and can cause disability and death. As the incidence of alcoholism has risen in the U.S. population, so has the incidence of cirrhosis of the liver, which in 1974 climbed past both arteriosclerosis and influenza and pneumonia to rank seventh among the leading causes of death; in some urban areas (including New York City) it is actually the third most frequent cause of death between the ages of 25 and 65.
    —CHARLES S. LIEBER, "The Metabolism of Alcohol," *Scientific American*,
    Vol. 234, No. 3, March 1976

12.3 *Criticisms of Mill's Methods*

There are two general types of criticism that can be made of Mill's Methods. The first is that the Methods fail to fulfill the claims made for them by Bacon and Mill; the second is that the five Methods, as stated, do not constitute an adequate or complete account of scientific method. We shall discuss these criticisms separately. Before we can state and evaluate the first criticism, we must report the claims that have been made for these methods and explain the motivations for those claims.

It is a truism today that knowledge is power, that an understanding of natural laws and causal connections is needed for humans to cope with their frequently hostile environment. Such understanding is not given to all people in the same degree. Beyond the more elementary cause-and-effect relations, such as those between fire and pain, or rainfall and harvest, the discovery of causal connections requires a rare and genuine insight. That is a sad truth, and like most sad truths, has often been denied. Devices have been sought that would permit *anyone* to discover causal connections, regardless of natural aptitudes or lack of them. These Methods have been hailed as just such a device; Bacon himself wrote that

> Our method of discovering the sciences is such as to leave little to the acuteness and strength of wit, and indeed rather to level wit and intellect. For as in the drawing of a straight line, or accurate circle by the hand, much depends on its

steadiness and practice, but if a ruler or compass be employed there is little occasion for either; so it is with our method.[8]

This claim has certainly not been fulfilled. Scores of competent scientists have been working for decades to discover the cause of cancer (or the causes of the various types of cancer), and Bacon's "method"—Mill's Methods—have been used, but so far with little success. There is no simple device or mechanical method for achieving scientific knowledge. In fact, the advance of empirical science has pushed the frontiers back so far that only those with the highest degree of "acuteness and strength of wit" can master enough of any field to approach the point from which new results can be sighted. Bacon's claim must be rejected as extravagant: his method simply cannot do what it is supposed to.

Mill himself made similar claims, extolling his Methods as adequate to serve two distinct functions. According to Mill, they are methods of *discovering* causal connections and also methods of *proving* or *demonstrating* the existence of particular causal connections. Mill's insistence upon the use of his Methods in discovering causal connections brought him into a long controversy with another nineteenth-century British philosopher, Dr. William Whewell, who minimized the value of Mill's Methods for discovery. In arguing against Whewell, Mill stated his view with great vigor:

> . . . Dr. Whewell's argument, if good at all, is good against all inferences from experience. In saying that no discoveries were ever made by the . . . Methods, he affirms that none were ever made by observation and experiment; for assuredly if any were, it was by processes reducible to one or other of those methods.[9]

Mill was convinced further that his Methods permitted the *demonstration* of causal connections:

> The business of Inductive Logic is to provide rules and models (such as the Syllogism and its rules are for ratiocination) to which if inductive arguments conform, those arguments are conclusive, and not otherwise. This is what the . . . Methods profess to be. . . .[10]

These are Mill's claims for his Methods: they are instruments for *discovery*, and they are rules for *proof.*

Let us examine first the doctrine that the Methods are instruments for discovery. We may begin with an example or two in which the scrupulous use of the Methods results in a more or less conspicuous failure to discover the cause of a given phenomenon. A favorite example used by critics of the Method of Agreement is the case of the Scientific Drinker, who was extremely fond of liquor and got drunk every night of the week. He was ruining his career and his health, and his few remaining friends pleaded with him to stop. Realizing himself that he could not go on, he resolved to conduct a careful experiment to discover the exact cause of his frequent inebriations.

---

[8]*Novum Organum,* Vol. 1, Section 61.
[9]*A System of Logic,* Book III, Chapter 9, Section 6.
[10]Ibid.

For five nights in a row he collected instances of the given phenomenon, the antecedent circumstances being, respectively, scotch and soda, bourbon and soda, brandy and soda, rum and soda, and gin and soda. Then using the Method of Agreement, he swore a solemn oath never to touch soda again!

Here is a case where the use of Mill's Method resulted in abysmal failure. The trouble here is not that the Method was not followed, for it was followed explicitly. The error, as we all can see, lay in a faulty analysis of the antecedent circumstances. Had the various liquors not been treated as so many different single circumstances but analyzed into their alcoholic contents plus their various other constituents, the Method of Agreement would have revealed, of course, that besides the soda, the alcohol too was a common circumstance, and then the Method of Difference would have sufficed to eliminate the soda and reveal the true cause. But how is one to know what kind of analysis to make of the antecedent circumstances? To make a correct analysis requires previous knowledge of causal laws, which must have been discovered by means other than Mill's Methods. Mill's Methods are not *sufficient* instruments for discovery, because their successful use requires a proper analysis of the factors of the antecedent circumstances, and the Methods themselves do not tell how to distinguish between a proper and an improper analysis.

Another objection to the view that Mill's Methods are sufficient instruments for discovery is illustrated by the following comment on an experiment that was interpreted as showing two things:

> (a) frustration leads to aggression and (b) aggression which arises in a group with strong in-group feeling will be expressed against an out-group.
>
> Thirty-one young men between the ages of eighteen and twenty years who worked in a camp were the subjects of this experiment. These young men looked forward to attending Bank Night in the theater in a nearby town, an event which was considered by them to be the most interesting one in the week. Interest in Bank Night was especially keen since one of them had won $200 the previous week. The conditions of the experiment were such, however, that the men missed this event. This then formed the frustrating circumstance. Instead of Bank Night there was "suddenly substituted" a "regime of testing." The tests were long and difficult.
>
> The 31 young men were called to the auditorium of the camp on the night in question. Without any forewarning as to what was in store for them, they were given a check list of twenty items pertaining to desirable and undesirable characteristics of two out-groups—Japanese and Mexicans. Half of the men rated the Japanese, the other half rated the Mexicans. The men were then given a series of tests which caused them to miss the truck to town. After the testing program, the half that rated the Japanese initially now rated the Mexicans, and likewise for the other half.
>
> The authors of the experiment concluded that the hypothesis that frustration leads to aggression was confirmed, because the young men became angry at the camp officials who ordered the tests and at the experimenters. With regard to the second hypothesis—that because of this aggression the men would rate the Japanese and Mexicans more unfavorably—the authors claim that the evidence pointed in the direction of confirming the hypothesis.

From the point of view of the young men, the procedure of suddenly giving a series of long, difficult, and boring examinations when it was probably well known that the night in question was one of significance to them must have seemed unjust. Why not some other time? Do not their rights merit consideration by the camp officials in setting plans? The aggressiveness of these young men probably represents a reaction to an unfair situation rather than to the mere fact of a frustrating circumstance. In this case, aggression serves to maintain a sense of dignity or individuality.[11]

The structure of the argument criticized in the preceding passage is clearly that of the Method of Difference.[12] There are thirty-one instances *after* the truck to town had been missed, in which the antecedent circumstance was frustration and the phenomena were aggression and more unfavorable ratings given the out-groups. And there are thirty-one instances *before* the truck had left, in which the antecedent circumstances did not include frustration and the phenomena included neither aggression nor so unfavorable a rating for the outgroups. Schematically, with A denoting frustration, B denoting the presence of the thirty-one men taking the tests, x denoting the phenomena of aggression and more unfavorable ratings for the outgroup, and y denoting the usual phenomena arising when such tests are administered, the experiment can be represented as

$$A \; B \text{———} x \; y.$$
$$\underline{B \text{———} \quad y.}$$

Therefore A causes x.

The criticism of this argument (regardless of whether one agrees or disagrees with the general point of view expressed) is perfectly straightforward. The inference is unsound, according to the critic, because *a relevant factor was ignored*. The relevant factor that the experimenters ignored is characterized by their critic as *unfairness* or *injustice*. The suggestion seems implicit here that, had the frustration been produced by natural or inevitable causes with which no human unfairness or injustice could be associated, neither aggression nor any lower ratings of outgroups would have occurred. Regardless of our own thoughts about the particular point at issue here, we should be able to see that the criticism is well taken. If a relevant circumstance is ignored, the Method of Difference is not properly applied; for according to its statement, that Method requires that the two or more instances "Have every circumstance in common save one."

It should be realized that this criticism is different from the one leveled at the Method of Agreement. There the problem was the correct analysis of the instances into a proper set of distinct circumstances. Here the criticism turns on relevant factors or circumstances being *omitted* rather than improperly

---

[11]Nicholas Pastore, "A Neglected Factor in the Frustration-Aggression Hypothesis: A Comment," *The Journal of Psychology*, Vol. 29, Part 2, April 1950.

[12]A more subtle analysis would show the Method of Concomitant Variation to be exemplified here also, but is not necessary for our purpose in this discussion.

analyzed. The problem of relevance, to which our discussion of analogical argument had previously led, arises once again. The Methods cannot be used unless all relevant circumstances are taken into account. But circumstances do not come wearing neat little tags marked "relevant" and "irrelevant." Questions of relevance are questions about *causal connectedness*, and at least some of these must be answered *before* Mill's Methods can be used. Hence Mill's Methods cannot be *the* methods for discovering causal connections, for some causal connections must be known prior to any application of those Methods.

It may be objected that what Mill's Methods call for is a consideration of *all* circumstances, rather than just the relevant ones, so that questions of relevance need not arise in the use of the Methods. True enough, Mill's statements of his Methods read "all" rather than "all relevant" circumstances. But if Mill is taken quite literally here, the situation is made worse instead of better so far as the use of his Methods is concerned. Consider the Method of Agreement. In its application we must verify that two or more instances of a phenomenon have only *one* circumstance in common. But the number of circumstances common to any two physical objects is probably unlimited, no matter how different they may appear. In our earlier example, in which the instances were two students living in the same dormitory who suffered digestive disturbances on the same day, what circumstances might be common here? Presumably they both are students, each has two legs, both are over ten years old, each has a nose, both are over three feet tall, each weighs less than four hundred pounds, and so on and on and on. It would be an unimaginative reasoner indeed who could ever stop and say that *all* common circumstances had been enumerated.

In the Method of Difference, two instances must "have every circumstance in common save one." Here the situation is even more hopeless, for it is extremely doubtful that *any* two things could differ in only one circumstance. Even of two peas in a pod, one must of necessity be either to the north or to the east or higher than the other, one must be closer to the stem, and it is highly probable that microscopic and chemical analysis would reveal many, many more differences between them. More devastating still is the fact that *all possible* circumstances in which they *might* differ must be examined to make sure that they do not differ in more than one of them, before the Method of Difference can legitimately be applied. No, to interpret Mill literally here would make the Methods hopelessly inapplicable. The Methods must be understood as referring to *relevant* circumstances alone. When so understood, the previous criticism is inescapable, and we must conclude that Mill's methods are not *the* methods for *discovering* causal laws.

So much for Mill's claim that the Methods are instruments for scientific discovery. Of his Methods, Mill wrote

> . . . but even if they were not methods of discovery, it would not be the less true that they are the sole methods of Proof.[13]

---

[13] *A System of Logic,* Book III, Chapter 9, Section 6.

Let us see whether or not this second claim is true. There are two reasons for denying that the Methods are *demonstrative*. In the first place, all the Methods proceed on the basis of antecedent hypotheses about which circumstances are causally relevant to the phenomenon under investigation. Since not all circumstances can be considered, attention must be confined to those believed to be possible causes. This prior judgment is liable to error, and if it is mistaken, the conclusion inferred by Mill's methods will be infected by that mistake. A variant of this same criticism has to do with the different ways in which even the relevant circumstances may be analyzed into separate factors. That analysis must be "correct" if the kind of mistake made by the Scientific Drinker is not to pervade all uses of Mill's Methods. Such analysis *must* be made prior to the use of the Methods, but since the analysis may be incorrect, the conclusion inferred may be incorrect also. This first criticism provides a strong reason for rejecting the claim that Mill's methods are methods of proof or demonstration.

The second criticism is even more damaging. It applies most obviously, perhaps, to the Method of Concomitant Variation. It may well be the case that in a number—even a very large number—of observed instances of two phenomena they are seen to vary concomitantly. Consider the following waggish magazine item:

> There have been seven presidential elections since 1952, and George L. Grassmuck, a political science professor at the University of Michigan, makes an interesting observation about them. Four of the elections were won by Republicans, and each G.O.P. victory occurred in a year in which an American League team won the World Series (1952, 1956, 1968, and 1972). The three Democratic wins occurred in years in which the Series went to National League clubs (1960, 1964, and 1976). These correlations suggest that baseball's October Classic could have important implications for this November's election. A victory in the World Series by, say, the Yankees presumably would portend a Reagan triumph. An Astro victory, on the other hand, would mean it's Carter again.
>
> It all seems pretty cut and dried.[14]

Such a correlation is clearly a mere coincidence rather than evidence of any causal connection between the two phenomena. Correlations, despite the great dependence of some of the social sciences upon them, are very often misleading. The danger of deception is attested by the common saying that there are three kinds of liars: liars, damn liars, and statistics. An observed correlation between two phenomena may be either a chance relationship peculiar to the *observed* instances, or it may be a regular, that is, lawful relationship of *all* instances of those phenomena. The greater the number of observed instances (and the greater the number of disanalogies among those instances), the higher the probability that the correlation is lawful rather than fortuitous. But no matter how great the number of observed instances, any inference from their relationship to the relationship of as yet unobserved

---

[14]Jerry Kirshenbaum, "Scorecard," *Sports Illustrated,* July 7, 1980, pp. 9–10.

instances will never be *certain*. It must be repeated that inductive inferences are never demonstrative.

This criticism applies with equal force to all of Mill's Methods. In the Method of Agreement, of all the circumstances explicitly taken into account, only one may accompany all the observed instances of the phenomenon under investigation. But the very next instance examined might *not* be accompanied by that circumstance. The greater the number of instances examined, the lower the probability of finding an exception; but so long as there are any unobserved instances, there is always the possibility that the inductive conclusion will be shown to be false by later investigation. The same remarks may be made of the Method of Difference, the Joint Method, and the Method of Residues. Moreover, since we rejected the possibility of a plurality of causes on the basis of arguments admitted to be at best merely probable, there is always the logical possibility that any particular phenomenon being investigated may have more than a single cause; if it has, none of the Methods will work. The plain fact is that there *is* a difference between deduction and induction. A valid deductive argument constitutes a proof or demonstration, but an inductive argument is at best highly probable. Therefore Mill's claim that his Methods are "methods of Proof" must be rejected along with his claim that they are "*the* methods of Discovery."

12.4 *Vindication of Mill's Methods*

The preceding criticisms are harsh; however, they were not directed against the Methods themselves, but rather against the too extravagant claims made for them. Mill's Methods are more limited instruments than Bacon and Mill conceived them to be, but within those limits they are indispensable. This is shown by the following considerations.

Since it is absolutely impossible to take *all* circumstances into account, Mill's Methods can be used only in conjunction with the *hypothesis* that the circumstances mentioned are the only relevant ones. Such a hypothesis amounts to saying that the only possible causes are the circumstances listed. Every experimental investigation of the cause of a phenomenon begins with some such hypothesis. If we are investigating the cause of phenomenon w, we may begin with the hypothesis that either A or B or C or D or E or F or G is the cause of w. Then the following two instances,

$$A\ B\ C\ D\text{——}w\ x\ y\ z.$$
$$A\ E\ F\ G\text{——}w\ t\ u\ v.$$

which by the Method of Agreement yield the inductive conclusion that A is the cause of w, yield that conclusion *deductively*, that is, *validly, in the presence of the stated hypothesis as an additional premiss*. The way in which the deduction proceeds is very simple. If G is the cause of w, then w cannot occur in the absence of G. But the first instance is a case in which w *does* occur in the absence of G. Therefore G is not the cause of w. The first instance also shows that neither E nor F is the cause of w, while the second instance shows that neither B nor C nor D is the cause of w. From the two instances, then, we can infer that neither B nor C nor D nor E nor F nor G is the cause of w, and from this conclusion together with the original hypothesis, it follows *validly* that A is the cause of w. Although the Method of Agreement cannot be used without a hypothesis of the type indicated, in the presence of that hypothesis it provides us with a valid deductive argument.

Exactly similar remarks can be made with respect to the other Methods. If we are attempting to determine the cause of phenomenon x by the Method of Difference, we may begin with the hypothesis that either A or B is the cause of x. Our instances here may be

$$A\ B \text{———} x\ y.$$
$$B \text{———} \quad y.$$

from which the conclusion that A is the cause of x follows inductively by the Method of Difference. In the second instance, circumstance B occurs without phenomenon x being present, which shows that B is not the cause of x. But by hypothesis, either A is the cause of x or B is the cause of x, so it follows validly that A is the cause of x. In every case, Mill's Methods cannot be used unless some hypothesis is made about possible causes. But in every such case, where the hypothesis is explicitly added as a premiss, the use of the Methods provides a deductive, rather than a merely inductive, argument. The conclusion, however, is not deduced from the particular facts or instances alone but depends upon that additional premiss whose status is merely *hypothetical*. To gain a clearer insight into the type of argument which emerges here, we must examine the nature of these additional hypothetical premisses.

What was referred to in the preceding paragraph as *the* hypothesis that either A or B is the cause of x may with advantage be divided into *two* hypotheses: one, that A is the cause of x, the other, that B is the cause of x. Then we can apply the Method of Difference by setting up a situation in which circumstance B is present but not A. If the phenomenon x does not appear when this is done, we have refuted the second of the two hypotheses, and only the first remains. In Section 12.2, it was observed that Mill's Methods are essentially eliminative, for their applications serve in each case to show that some particular circumstance is *not* the cause of a given phenomenon. We can rephrase this account in terms of alternative hypotheses, where each hypothesis states that some different circumstance is the cause of the phenomenon under investigation. Mill's Methods now appear as instruments for testing hypotheses. Their statements describe *the method of controlled experiment*, which is an absolutely indispensable weapon in the arsenal of modern science. An example or two should suffice to make this fact clear.

In a famous experiment conducted in the spring of 1881, Pasteur put to the test his hypothesis that anthrax vaccination produces immunity to the disease. That hypothesis had been ridiculed by the veterinarians, and the experiment was performed publicly under the auspices of the Agricultural Society of Melun.[15] At the farm of Pouilly-le-Fort, twenty-four sheep, one goat, and several cattle were given Pasteur's vaccination against anthrax, while twenty-four other sheep, one goat, and several other cattle were left unvaccinated. These unvaccinated animals constituted the "control group," being instances that were assumed to differ from the first group in only the one circumstance V (vaccination). After the vaccinations had been properly administered,

> . . . on the fateful thirty-first of May all of the forty-eight sheep, two goats, and several cattle—those that were vaccinated and those to which nothing whatever had been done—all of these received a surely fatal dose of virulent anthrax bugs.[16]

Then on the second day of June, at two o'clock, when Pasteur and his assistants came to inspect the animals they found that

> Not one of the twenty-four vaccinated sheep—though two days before millions of deadly germs had taken residence under their hides—not one of these sheep . . . had so much as a trace of fever. They ate and frisked about as if they had never been within a thousand miles of an anthrax bacillus.
> But the unprotected, the not vaccinated beasts—alas—there they lay in a tragic row, twenty-two out of twenty-four of them; and the remaining two were staggering about, at grips with that last inexplorable, always victorious enemy of all living things. Ominous black blood oozed from their mouths and noses.
> "See! There goes another one of those sheep that Pasteur did not vaccinate!" shouted an awed horse doctor.[17]

The pattern of Pasteur's experiment is the Joint Method of Agreement and Difference, and may be analyzed as follows. Where the phenomenon in question is immunity to anthrax, the vaccinated animals constitute some thirty instances that agree in only the one relevant circumstance of having been vaccinated, although they all exhibit the phenomenon of immunity. From a consideration of these instances, the inference can be drawn that vaccination causes immunity, and this follows by the pattern of the Method of Agreement. The Method of Difference is also exemplified here. The infected animals that sickened and died constituted thirty-odd instances in which the phenomenon of immunity did *not* occur; the one respect in which they differed from the equal number of immune animals was the vaccination administered to the others but not to them. From these facts, by the Method of Difference, the conclusion follows that Pasteur's vaccination does cause immunity. This account should make it clear that Mill's Methods do describe

---

[15]As recounted by Paul de Kruif in *Microbe Hunters*.

[16]Excerpted from *Microbe Hunters*, copyright 1926, 1954 by Paul de Kruif. Reprinted by permission of Harcourt Brace Jovanovich, Inc., and Jonathan Cape Ltd.

[17]Ibid., p. 162.

the general pattern of the modern scientific method of controlled experimentation.

It is obvious that the experiment *confirms* Pasteur's hypothesis. The newspaper reporter who was observing the experiment telegraphed his paper, the London *Times,* that "The experiment at Pouilly-le-Fort is a perfect, an unprecedented success."[18] The language used in his report was not too strong for the epoch-making event that it chronicled, but it was dangerously liable to misinterpretation. The experiment must not be thought of as providing a "proof" or "demonstration" of the truth of Pasteur's hypothesis, in the sense of a valid deductive argument. It rendered it highly probable, but there still remains a possibility that what happened was fortuitous rather than a genuine instance of the causal law stated by Pasteur. This type of possibility is illustrated by another, somewhat simpler experiment in which Pasteur participated.

Several years prior to the experiment reported, there had been

> . . . a great to-do about a cure for anthrax invented by the horse doctor, Louvrier, in the Jura mountains in the east of France. Louvrier had cured hundreds of cows who were at death's door, said the influential men of the district: it was time that this treatment received scientific approval. . . .
>
> Pasteur arrived there, escorted by his young assistants, and found that this miraculous cure consisted first, in having several farm hands rub the sick cow violently to make her as hot as possible; then long gashes were cut in the poor beast's skin and into these cuts Louvrier poured turpentine; finally the now bellowing and deplorably maltreated cow was covered—excepting her face!—with an inch thick layer of unmentionable stuff soaked in hot vinegar. This ointment was kept on the animal—who now doubtless wished she were dead—by a cloth that covered her entire body.
>
> Pasteur said to Louvrier: "Let us make an experiment. All cows attacked by anthrax do not die, some of them just get better by themselves; there is only one way to find out, Doctor Louvrier, whether or not it is your treatment that saves them."
>
> So four good healthy cows were brought, and Pasteur in the presence of Louvrier and a solemn commission of farmers, shot a powerful dose of virulent anthrax microbes into the shoulder of each one of these beasts: this stuff would have surely killed a sheep, it was enough to do to death a few dozen guineapigs. The next day Pasteur and the commission and Louvrier returned, and all the cows had large feverish swellings on their shoulders, their breath came in snorts—they were in a bad way, that was very evident.
>
> "Now, Doctor," said Pasteur, "choose two of these sick cows—we'll call them *A* and *B.* Give them your new cure, and we'll leave cows *C* and *D* without any treatment at all." So Louvrier assaulted poor *A* and *B* with his villainous treatment. The result was a terrible blow to the sincere would-be curer of cows, for one of the cows that Louvrier treated got better—but the other perished; and one of the creatures that had got no treatment at all, died—but the other got better.
>
> "Even this experiment might have tricked us, Doctor," said Pasteur. "If you had

[18]Ibid., p. 164.

given your treatment to cows *A* and *D* instead of *A* and *B*—we all would have thought you had really found a sovereign remedy for anthrax."[19]

This experiment involving four cows, two being given the alleged cure, the other two constituting the control group, served to refute the hypothesis that the horse doctor's treatment was a cure for anthrax. But Pasteur was right in remarking that had the cows been grouped differently, the experiment's results would have been deceptive. This remark emphasizes that the results of an experiment, even one that is carefully controlled and accords perfectly with Mill's Methods, are never demonstrative. A successful experiment (like Pasteur's own) *confirms* the hypothesis being tested, rendering it more probable, but never establishes its conclusion with *certainty*. Such qualifications are not intended to minimize the value of experimental investigation, but only to emphasize that its nature is inductive rather than deductive.

In concluding this chapter, we may summarize our discussion of Mill's Methods in these terms. Our need to control and understand the world in which we live leads us to search for causal connections between its various parts or aspects. Any assertion of a particular causal connection involves an element of generality, for to say that *C* is the cause of *E* is to say that *whenever* circumstance *C* occurs, *E* is sure to follow. Causal laws or general propositions are never *discovered* by Mill's Methods, nor are they ever established *demonstratively* by them. However, those Methods constitute the basic patterns for any attempt to confirm or disconfirm, by observation or experiment, a hypothesis asserting a causal connection. Experimental investigations cannot proceed without hypotheses, which are thus seen to play an all-important role in inductive logic. So important is the role of hypothesis in systematic empirical investigation that the formulation and testing of hypotheses can be regarded as *the* method of science. It is with science and hypothesis that our next chapter is concerned.

EXERCISES

Analyze each of the following arguments in terms of "circumstances" or "antecedents" and "phenomena" and indicate which of Mill's Methods are being used in each of them.

★ 1. On August 23, 1948, individual tagged fruits of Rome Beauty apples and adjacent spur leaves were sprayed at the Plant Industry Station, Beltsville, Maryland, with aqueous solutions of 2,4,5-T at 10-, 100-, and 200-ppm concentrations. Fruits that received either the 100- or the 200-ppm spray concentration developed red coloration and were maturing rapidly by September 13. This same stage of maturity on unsprayed fruits was not attained until one month later, October 12, the usual harvest date for this variety. At 10-ppm concentration, the spray had no observable effect. Measurements on fruit softening were made on September 27 with the aid of a fruit pressure tester. At this time the untreated fruits showed

[19]Ibid., pp. 149–150.

an average pressure reading of 25.9 lb., whereas the fruits sprayed with 10-, 100-, and 200-ppm concentrations of 2,4,5-T tested 24.8, 19.8, and 18.9 lb., respectively.

—P. C. MARTH et al., "Effect of 2,4,5,-Trichlorophenoxyacetic Acid on Ripening of Apples and Peaches," *Science*, Vol. 3, March 31, 1950

2. Repeated reports, before and after Kinsey, showed colleged-educated women to have a much lower than average divorce rate. More specifically, a massive and famous sociological study by Ernest W. Burgess and Leonard S. Cottrell indicated that women's chances of happiness in marriage increased as their career preparation increased. . . .

Among 526 couples, less than 10 percent showed "low" marital adjustment where the wife had been employed seven or more years, had completed college or professional training, and had not married before twenty-two. Where wives had been educated *beyond college*, less than 5 percent of marriages scored "low" in happiness. The following table shows the relationship between the marriage and the educational achievement of the wife.

Marriage Adjustment Scores at Different Educational Levels

Wife's Educational Level	Marital Adjustment Score			
	Very Low	Low	High	Very High
Graduate work	0.0	4.6	38.7	56.5
College	9.2	18.9	22.9	48.9
High school	14.4	16.3	32.2	37.1
Grades only	33.3	25.9	25.9	14.8

—BETTY FRIEDAN, *The Feminine Mystique*

3. Experiments which demonstrate the sense of smell are similar to those on color vision. First, it is necessary to determine if the insects react to odors. Sugar water is placed in small boxes, and, after bees have found them and are making trips to and from the hive, the box is substituted by one just like it, also containing sugar water, but sprinkled inside with flower extract. After the bees have made sufficient trips to get used to the scent, several new unscented boxes are placed beside a new scented one. When the bees return for more sugar, they buzz about the openings of the boxes but finally go inside the scented one. Further, when they are trained to go to one odor—say, rose—they will not go to another, such as lavender. That the sense organs are on the antennas is shown by removing parts or all of the antennas from bees trained to certain scented boxes. When the last eight segments are removed from each antenna, the bees cannot distinguish odors. That this result is not due to the shock of the operation is proved by a control experiment in which some bees are first trained to visit blue boxes for sugar water. Then their antennas are removed, and it is found that they still return to the correct boxes.   —RALPH BUCHSBAUM, *Animals Without Backbones*

4. It has long been assumed that a diet low in saturated fats (meaning mostly animal fats) can reduce the risk of cardiovascular disease. Direct evidence for this assumption, however, has been scarce. Such evidence is now provided by a study

made at a veterans' hospital in Los Angeles. The study shows that the incidence of cardiovascular disease in a group of 424 veterans with a diet high in unsaturated fats for eight years was 31.3 percent, whereas a control group of 422 men with a normal diet high in saturated fats had a cardiovascular disease rate of 47.7 percent.   —"Science and the Citizen," *Scientific American,*
Vol. 221, No. 3, September 1969

★ 5. On the 31st of August, 1909, Paul Ehrlich and Hata stood before a cage in which sat an excellent buck rabbit. Flourishing in every way was this rabbit, excepting for the tender skin of his scrotum, which was disfigured with two terrible ulcers, each bigger than a twenty-five-cent piece. Those sores were caused by the gnawing of the pale spirochete of the disease that is the reward of sin. They had been put under the skin of that rabbit by S. Hata a month before. Under the microscope—it was a special one built for spying just such a thin rogue as that pale microbe—under this lens Hata put a wee drop of the fluid from these ugly sores. Against the blackness of the dark field of this special microscope, gleaming in a powerful beam of light that hit them sidewise, shooting backwards and forwards like ten thousand silver drills and augers, played myriads of these pale spirochetes. It was a pretty picture, to hold you there for hours, but it was sinister—for what living things can bring worse plague and sorrow to men?

Hata leaned aside. Paul Ehrlich looked down the shiny tube. Then he looked at Hata, and then at the rabbit.

"Make the injection," said Paul Ehrlich. And into the ear-vein of that rabbit went the clear yellow fluid of the solution of 606, for the first time to do battle with the disease of the loathsome name.

Next day there was not one of those spiral devils to be found in the scrotum of that rabbit. His ulcers? They were drying already! Good clean scabs were forming on them. In less than a month there was nothing to be seen but tiny scabs—it was like a cure of Bible times—no less! And a little while after that Paul Ehrlich could write:

"It is evident from these experiments that, if a large enough dose is given, the spirochetes can be destroyed *asbolutely and immediately with a single injection!*"
—PAUL DE KRUIF, *Microbe Hunters*[20]

6. . . . McLarty had reasoned that these physiological disorders were most probably caused by some mineral deficiency or mineral unbalance within the trees. Following up this line of reasoning, he injected severely affected apple trees with some thirty different chemicals. In these experiments, the dry test material was packed in holes drilled into the trunks of the trees. The holes were about one-half inch in diameter and two inches deep. After having been filled the holes were sealed with a commercial grafting compound. The dry materials were used because of the convenience of handling and also because greater amounts could be used without injury to the foliage. The following year the crop of two of the injected trees was practically free of the disorders, and it was noted that one of these trees had been injected with boric acid and the other with manganese borate. The trees injected with manganese compounds, other than the borate, showed no change. Following up this lead, forty trees were injected with either boric acid or borax in the fall of 1934. In the summer of 1935 every tree that had been injected the previous fall showed none of the diseases or a very low inci-

[20]Excerpted from *Microbe Hunters*, copyright 1926, 1954 by Paul de Kruif. Reprinted by permission of Harcourt Brace Jovanovich, Inc., and Jonathan Cape Ltd.

dence of them. Because of the great economic losses which many of the growers were suffering that year, the committee decided that it was well worthwhile to make an immediate recommendation that all affected trees be injected with boric acid crystals.

> —C. G. WOODBRIDGE, "The Role of Boron in the Agricultural Regions of the Pacific Northwest," *The Scientific Monthly,* Vol. 70, No. 2, February 1950

7. Over in Denmark Johannes Fibiger, a pathologist of the University of Copenhagen, had been working thirteen years on the problem of tuberculosis among laboratory animals. During a series of postmortem examinations of tubercular rats, he found three had suffered from stomach cancers. Fibiger knew enough about cancer to realize that he had come across a singular phenomenon. Rats rarely suffered from tumors of the stomach.

Fibiger made a visit to the dealer who had been supplying him with these rats, and on questioning found that those sent to his laboratory had all come from a sugar refinery. Was there anything peculiar about this refinery which could account for the unusually large percentage of stomach-cancerous rats from this spot? He investigated the place and found nothing unusual except a high infestation with cockroaches, which formed a fairly large part of the diet of its rats. Could he find some connection between roaches, rats, and cancer? Cancer as a disease of filth had been spoken about for years, and vermin were said to be responsible for the so-called "cancer houses," private homes from which emerged many a human cancer victim of the same family.

Fibiger planned a controlled experiment. He collected thousands of the refinery roaches and fed them to rats from another breeding establishment. The rats enjoyed this strange treatment, and for three years—that was the normal life span of his rodents—Fibiger remained skeptical. Then they died, and one by one he opened them up. To his astonishment, he found many stomach cancers. Fibiger made a careful microscopic study of the growths. He discovered that in every case they had formed around a parasitic worm, the same worm to which the roach had been host before it was fed to the rat. The larva of the worm coiled up in the muscles of the rat, later developing into an adult worm in the animal's stomach. Around this the tumorous growth had appeared. Fibiger had actually for the first time produced artificial cancer in a laboratory animal.

> —BERNARD JAFFE, *Outposts of Science*

8. It is not hard to demonstrate the key role that the love song plays in mating. Remove the male fly's wings and he will court with the same persistence as before, but his courtship is seldom successful. It is apparent that the male's wing display, at least, is a prerequisite to mating. Indeed, one species (*D. obscura*) sings no song and courts only by means of a silent wing display. This, however, is one of the few fruit fly species that will not mate in the dark. Since most species breed successfully at night, one must conclude that visual display alone is not enough to win female acceptance. The importance of sound to the female is also easy to demonstrate. Our colleague A. W. G. Manning has shown that when the antennae of a sexually responsive female are immobilized with glue, she ceases to be receptive.

> —H. C. BENNET-CLARK and A. W. EWING, "The Love Song of the Fruit Fly," *Scientific American,* Vol. 223, No. 1, July 1970

9. Effectiveness in the prevention of dental decay by the use of fluoride is well accepted. However, in many parts of the world resistance to fluoridation of

water supplies or the absence of a public water supply prevents the administration of this treatment. The addition of fluoride to a daily administered (by drop) solution of vitamins has been suggested as an alternate method.

Working in Stockholm through city child welfare centers, which are attended by about 85 percent of the city's children, Dr. Lennart Hamberg has conducted a study on the effectiveness of the addition of sodium fluoride to a solution of vitamin A and D drops. His findings are reported in the Feb. 27 *Lancet*. Of 705 children taking part in the experiment, 342 received the fluoride treatment and 363 were in a control group. All the children received yearly examinations from the time of their first birthday. After six years the fluoride group had up to 57 percent fewer decayed teeth.

Dr. Hamberg, of the department of pediatrics at the Karolinska Hospital in Stockholm, states that the simplicity, inexpensiveness and optional character of this method combine to make it far superior to all previous forms of fluoridation.
— *Science News*, Vol. 99, March 20, 1971

★ 10. One of the procedures which showed a high correlation with ulcers involved training the monkeys to avoid an electric shock by pressing a lever. The animal received a brief shock on the feet at regular intervals, say, every 20 seconds. It could avoid the shock if it learned to press the lever at least once in every 20-second interval. It does not take a monkey very long to master this problem; within a short time it is pressing the lever far oftener than once in 20 seconds. Only occasionally does it slow down enough to receive a shock as a reminder.

One possibility, of course, was that the monkeys which had developed ulcers under this procedure had done so not because of the psychological stress involved but rather as a cumulative result of the shocks. To test this possibility we set up a controlled experiment, using two monkeys in "yoked chairs" in which both monkeys received shocks but only one monkey could prevent them. The experimental or "executive" monkey could prevent shocks to himself and his partner by pressing the lever; the control monkey's lever was a dummy. Thus both animals were subjected to the same physical stress (i.e., both received the same number of shocks at the same time), but only the "executive" monkey was under the psychological stress of having to press the lever.

We placed the monkeys on a continuous schedule of alternate periods of shock-avoidance and rest, arbitrarily choosing an interval of six hours for each period. As a cue for the executive monkey we provided a red light which was turned on during the avoidance periods and turned off during the "off" hours. The animal soon learned to press its lever at a rate averaging between 15 and 20 times a minute during the avoidance periods, and to stop pressing the lever when the red light was turned off. These responses showed no change throughout the experiment. The control monkey at first pressed the lever sporadically during both the avoidance and rest sessions, but lost interest . . . within a few days.

After 23 days of a continuous six-hours-on, six-hours-off schedule the executive monkey died during one of the avoidance sessions. Our only advance warning had been the animal's failure to eat on the preceding day. It has lost no weight during the experiment, and it pressed the lever at an unflagging rate through the first two hours of its last avoidance session. Then it suddenly collapsed and had to be sacrificed. An autopsy revealed a large perforation in the wall of the duodenum — the upper part of the small intestine near its junction with the stomach, and a common site of ulcers in man. Microscopic analysis revealed both acute and chronic inflammation around this lesion. The control monkey, sacrificed in good health a few hours later, showed no gastrointestinal abnormalities. A second experiment using precisely the same procedure produced much the same results. This time the executive monkey developed ulcers in both the stomach and the duodenum; the control animal was again unaffected.

—JOSEPH V. BRADY, "Ulcers in 'Executive' Monkeys,"
Scientific American, Vol. 199, No. 4, October 1958

11. In a paper published June 26, 1914, attention was called to certain epidemiological observations relating to pellagra which appeared inexplicable on any theory of communicability. These observations showed that, at certain institutions at which pellagra was either epidemic or had long been endemic among the inmates, the nurses and attendants, drawn from the class economically and socially identical with that most afflicted in the population at large, appeared uniformly to be immune, although living in the same environment and under the same conditions as did the inmates. Neither "contact" nor insect transmission seemed capable of explaining such a phenomenon. It was suggested that the explanation was to be found in a difference, which was believed to exist, in the diet of the two groups of residents.

From a study of the dietaries of certain institutions in which pellagra prevailed the impression has been gained that cereals and vegetables formed a much greater proportion in them than they did in the dietaries of well-to-do people; that is, people who as a class are practically exempt from pellagra. It was suggested, therefore, that it might be well to attempt to prevent the disease by reducing the cereals, vegetables, and canned foods and increasing the fresh animal foods, such as fresh meats, eggs, and milk; in other words, by providing those subject to pellagra with a diet such as that enjoyed by well-to-do people, who as a group are practically free from the disease.

—JOSEPH GOLDBERGER, C. H. WARING, and DAVID G. WILLETS,
"The Prevention of Pellagra: A Test of Diet Among Institutional Inmates,"
Public Health Reports, Vol. 30, No. 43, October 22, 1915

12. Undoubtedly the outstanding point of departure of industrial social psychology was the series of studies performed in the Hawthorne plant of the Western Electric Company, starting in 1927. These were conducted by three Harvard professors, Elton Mayo, F. J. Roethlisberger, and T. N. Whitehead, and by W. J. Dickson of Western Electric. The original aim of the studies was to obtain concrete data on the effects of illumination, temperature, rest periods, hours of work, wage rate, etc., upon production. A group of six girls, average workers, were chosen for the experiment; their task was the assembly of telephone relays. Almost from the beginning, unexpected results appeared: The production rate kept going up whether rest periods and hours were increased or decreased! In each experimental period, whatever its conditions, output was higher than in the preceding one. The answer seemed to lie in a number of subtle social factors.

. . . As Homans summarizes it, the increase in the girls' output rate "could not be related to any change in their conditions of work, whether experimentally induced or not. It could, however, be related to what can only be spoken of as the development of an organized social group in a peculiar and effective relation with its supervisors."

—S. STANSFELD SARGENT and ROBERT C. WILLIAMSON, *Social Psychology*.
(Skeptics can have their skepticism reinforced by reading Alex Carey,
"The Hawthorne Studies: A Radical Criticism,"
American Sociological Review, Vol. 32, No. 3, June 1967)

13. When small fragments of tissue, removed from an organ, are cultivated like colonies of bacteria, they grow for a while, age, and die. What is the cause of death? Probably the waste products set free by the living cells. According to this hypothesis, the colonies of cells were washed frequently in a saline solution, and given proper food. A striking result was obtained. Aging and death were suppressed. The colonies originating from a fragment of tissue extirpated from a chick embryo nearly twenty-four years ago are still alive. Not only are they alive, but they grow as actively as on the first day. They double in size every forty-eight hours. Two important facts were brought to light by this experiment. First, removal of waste products and proper food prevent, in a colony of tissue cells, the occurrence of death. Second, the cells that build up the body are capable of unlimited multiplication. They are potentially immortal. Still more useful information can be obtained from viscera living outside of the body. An organ, such as the thyroid gland, ovary, testicle, spleen, etc., is placed in an apparatus recently invented by C. A. Lindbergh, where it is completely protected from bacterial infection. Through its arteries a nutrient fluid is caused to pulsate and circulate, just like the blood pumped by the heart through the whole body. Under these conditions, organs taken from dead animals not only survive, but also grow, and set free active substances in the circulating fluid. Thus, the mechanisms underlying the development, or the degeneration, of anatomical structures may be analyzed. The presence of certain chemical substances, and the lack of elimination of waste products are found to cause most of the alterations in the organs.
　　　　　　　　　　　　　　　　　　　　　　—ALEXIS CARREL, *The Mystery of Death*

14. The French historian Roustan asserts that the *philosophes* had a direct and strong influence upon the revolutionary development that exploded in 1789. Poverty, despair, and mistreatment inflamed the masses but without the intellectuals there would have been no revolution: the men of 1789 were not merely escaping starvation which had been an integral part of the national tradition. In 1753, eight hundred people died of hunger in one small community alone—more died in other cities. There were riots, but no revolution—the military won the day. It took almost forty years of education and propaganda on the part of the philosophers before the French could stand up and demand their rights and human dignity: " 'The spirit of the *philosophes* was the spirit of the Revolution.' "
　　　　　　　　　　　　　　　　　　　—GUNTER W. REMMLING, *Road to Suspicion*

15. M. Arago, having suspended a magnetic needle by a silk thread, and set it in vibration, observed that it came much sooner to a state of rest when suspended over a plate of copper, than when no such plate was beneath it. Now, in both cases there were two *verae causae* (antecedents known to exist) why it *should* come at length to rest, viz., the resistance of the air, which opposes, and at length destroys, all motions performed in it; and the want of perfect mobility in the silk thread. But the effect of these causes being exactly known by the observation made in the absence of the copper, and being thus allowed for and subducted, a residual phenomenon appeared, in the fact, that a retarding influence was exerted by the copper itself; and this fact, once ascertained, speedily led to the knowledge of an entirely new and unexpected class of relations.
　　　　　　　　　　　　　—JOHN STUART MILL, *A System of Logic*, Book III, Chapter 9

13

Science and Hypothesis

. . . every work of science great enough to be remembered for a few generations affords some exemplification of the defective state of the art of reasoning of the time when it was written; and each chief step in science has been a lesson in logic.

—CHARLES SANDERS PEIRCE

13.1 *The Values of Science*

Modern science came into existence only a few hundred years ago. Yet it has profoundly changed almost every aspect of life in the modern world. Improvements in farming and manufacturing, in communication and transportation, in health and hygiene, and in our standard of living generally, have all resulted from the application of scientific knowledge. Steam, water, and nuclear power have been harnessed to run our machinery. Rivers have been diverted to turn deserts into vineyards. These are but a few of the beneficent uses of science as a tool for ameliorating a hostile environment.

Much the same appraisal is well stated in the following passage:

> Science and technology have permitted enormous growth in the world population by improving man's ability to increase food production; to accommodate to harsh climates; to provide transportation and communication for the world's goods, services and ideas; to increase available resources and use them more effectively; and to live longer in better health.[1]

Some of the practical results of science, of course, are not so cheerful. The tremendous increase in the destructive power of weapons has made the risk of nuclear war a menace to civilization itself. And the very habitability of our planet is increasingly threatened by industrial, chemical, and automotive pollution. Yet, despite these unhappy aspects of scientific achievement, on the whole the development of science and its applications have benefited hu-

---

[1]Chauncey Starr, "The Growth of Limits," *Edison Electric Institute Symposium on Science, Technology and the Human Prospect*, April 1979.

manity. Terrible as recent wars have been, their toll of human life has been much smaller than that of the great plagues which formerly swept over Europe, decimating the population. And those plagues have been almost completely wiped out by modern medical science. The *practical* value of science lies in the easier and more abundant life made possible by technological advances based on scientific knowledge. The issue is clearly stated and cogently reasoned in the following passage:

> It's sometimes argued that there's no real progress; that a civilization that kills multitudes in mass warfare, that pollutes the land and oceans with ever larger quantities of debris, that destroys the dignity of individuals by subjecting them to a forced mechanized existence can hardly be called an advance over the simpler hunting and gathering and agricultural existence of prehistoric times. But this argument, though romantically appealing, doesn't hold up. The primitive tribes permitted far less individual freedom than does modern society. Ancient wars were committed with far less moral justification than modern ones. A technology that produces debris can find, and is finding, ways of disposing of it without ecological upset. And the school-book pictures of primitive man sometimes omit some of the detractions of his primitive life—the pain, the disease, famine, the hard labor needed just to stay alive. From that agony of bare existence to modern life can be soberly described only as upward progress, and the sole agent for this progress is quite clearly reason itself.[2]

Its applications are not the only value of science, however. Science is knowledge and thus an end in itself. The laws and principles discovered in scientific investigation have a value apart from any practical utility they may possess. This intrinsic value is the satisfaction of curiosity, the fulfillment of the desire to know. That human beings have such a desire has long been recognized. Aristotle wrote that ". . . to be learning something is the greatest of pleasures not only to the philosopher but also to the rest of mankind, however small their capacity for it."[3] If we consult the most distinguished of twentieth-century scientists, Albert Einstein, we are told that "There exists a passion for comprehension just as there exists a passion for music. That passion is rather common in children, but gets lost in most people later on. Without this passion, there would be neither mathematics nor natural science."[4] Scientific knowledge does not merely give us power to satisfy our practical needs; it is itself a direct satisfaction of a particular desire, the desire to know.

Some philosophers, to be sure, have denied the second of these values. They have challenged the notion of a purely disinterested desire for knowledge. People have only practical wants, they have said, and science is simply an instrument to be used for the control of nature. There can be no doubt

[2]Robert M. Pirsig, *Zen and the Art of Motorcycle Maintenance* (New York: William Morrow & Co., Inc., 1974); paperback (New York: Bantam Books, Inc., 1975), p. 121.

[3]*Poetics*, 1448[b], 14.

[4]Albert Einstein, "On the Generalized Theory of Gravitation," *Scientific American*, Vol. 182, No. 4, April 1950.

that its utility has profoundly stimulated the development of science. But when the great contributors to scientific progress are consulted about their own motives for research, their answers seldom mention this pragmatic or engineering aspect. Most answers to such questions are like that of Einstein:

> What, then, impels us to devise theory after theory? Why do we devise theories at all? The answer to the latter question is simply: because we enjoy "comprehending," i.e., reducing phenomena by the process of logic to something already known or (apparently) evident.[5]

These remarks of Einstein suggest a very fruitful conception of the nature of science.

The task of science, we all know, is to discover facts; but a haphazard collection of facts cannot be said to constitute a science. To be sure, some parts of science may focus on this or that particular fact. A geographer, for example, may be interested in the exact configuration of a particular coastline or a geologist in the rock strata in a particular locality. But in the more advanced sciences, bare descriptive knowledge of this or that particular fact is of little importance. The scientist is eager to search out more general truths, that particular facts illustrate and for which they are evidence. Isolated particular facts may be known—in a sense—by direct observation. That a particular released object falls, that this ball moves more slowly down an inclined plane than it did when dropped directly downward, that the tides ebb and flow, all these are matters of fact open to direct inspection. But scientists seek more than a mere record of such phenomena; they strive to *understand* them. To this end they seek to formulate general laws that state the patterns of all such occurrences and the systematic relationships between them. The scientist searches for natural laws that govern particular events, and for the fundamental principles that underlie them.

This preliminary exposition of the theoretical aims of science can perhaps be made clearer by means of an example. By careful observation and the application of geometrical reasoning to the data thus collected, the Italian physicist and astronomer Galileo (1564–1642) succeeded in formulating the laws of falling bodies, which gave a very general description of the behavior of bodies near the surface of the earth. At about the same time the German astronomer Kepler (1571–1630), basing his reasonings very largely on the astronomical data collected by Denmark's Tycho Brahe (1546–1601), formulated the laws of planetary motion describing the elliptical orbits traveled by the planets around the sun. Each of these two great scientists succeeded in unifying the various phenomena in his own field of investigation by formulating the interrelations between them: Kepler in celestial mechanics, Galileo in terrestrial mechanics. Their discoveries were great achievements, but they were, after all, separate and isolated. Just as separate particular facts challenge the scientist to unify and explain them by discovering their lawful connections, so a plurality of general laws challenges the scientist to unify

[5]Ibid.

and explain *them* by discovering a still more general principle that subsumes the several laws as special cases. In the case of Kepler's and Galileo's laws, this challenge was met by one of the greatest scientific geniuses of all time, Sir Isaac Newton (1642–1727). By his Theory of Gravitation and his three Laws of Motion, Newton unified and explained celestial and terrestrial mechanics, showing them both to be deducible within the framework of a single more fundamental *theory*. Scientists seek not merely to know what the facts are, but to explain them, and to this end they devise "theories." To understand exactly what is involved here, we must consider the general nature of explanation itself.

13.2 *Explanations: Scientific and Unscientific*

In everyday life it is the unusual or startling for which we demand explanations. An office boy may arrive at work on time every morning and no curiosity will be aroused. But let him come an hour late one day, and his employer will demand an *explanation*. What is it that is wanted when an explanation for something is requested? An example will help to answer this question. The office boy might reply that he had taken the seven-thirty bus to work as usual, but the bus had been involved in a traffic accident which entailed considerable delay. In the absence of any other transportation, the boy had had to wait a full hour for the bus to be repaired. This account would probably be accepted as a satisfactory explanation. It can be so regarded because from the statements that constitute the explanation the fact to be explained follows logically and no longer appears puzzling. An explanation is a group of statements or a story from which the thing to be explained can logically be inferred and whose acceptance removes or diminishes its problematic or puzzling character. Of course the inference of the fact as conclusion from the explanation as premiss might have to be enthymematic, where the "understood" additional premisses may be generally accepted causal laws,[6] or the conclusion may follow with probability rather than deductively. It thus appears that explanation and inference are very closely related. They are, in fact, the same process regarded from opposite points of view. Given certain premisses, any conclusion that can logically be inferred from them can be regarded as being explained by them. And given a fact to be explained, we say that we have found an explanation for it when we have found a set of premisses from which it can logically be inferred. As was indicated in our first chapter,[7] "*Q because P*" can express either an argument or an explanation.

Of course some proposed explanations are better than others. The chief criterion for evaluating explanations is *relevance*. If the tardy office boy had offered as explanation for his late arrival the fact that there is a war in Afghanistan or a famine in India, that would have been a very poor explanation,

[6]This complication will be considered further in Section 13.6.
[7]See pages 29–30.

or "no explanation at all." Such a story would have had "nothing to do with the case"; it would have been *irrelevant,* because from it the fact to be explained *cannot* be inferred. The relevance of a proposed explanation, then, corresponds exactly to the cogency of the argument by which the fact to be explained is inferred from the proposed explanation. Any acceptable explanation must be relevant, but not all stories that are relevant in this sense are acceptable explanations. There are other criteria for deciding the worth or acceptability of proposed explanations.

The most obvious requirement to propose is that the explanation be *true.* In the example of the office boy's lateness, the crucial part of his explanation was a particular fact, the traffic accident, of which he claimed to be an eyewitness. But the explanations of science are for the most part *general* rather than particular. The keystone of Newtonian Mechanics is the Law of Universal Gravitation, whose statement is

> Every particle of matter in the universe attracts every other particle with a force which is directly proportional to the product of the masses of the particles and inversely proportional to the square of the distance between them.

Newton's law is not directly verifiable in the same way as a bus accident. There is simply no way in which we can inspect *all* particles of matter in the universe and observe that they do attract each other in precisely the way that Newton's Law asserts. Few propositions of science are *directly* verifiable as true. In fact, none of the important ones are. For the most part they concern *unobservable* entities, such as molecules and atoms, electrons and protons, chromosomes and genes. Hence the proposed requirement of truth is not *directly* applicable to most scientific explanations. Before considering more useful criteria for evaluating scientific theories, it will be helpful to compare scientific with unscientific explanations.

Science is supposed to be concerned with facts, and yet in its further reaches we find it apparently committed to highly speculative notions far removed from the possibility of direct experience. How then are scientific explanations to be distinguished from those that are frankly mythological or superstitious? An unscientific "explanation" of the regular motions of the planets was the doctrine that each heavenly body was the abode of an "Intelligence" or "Spirit" that controlled its movement. A certain humorous currency was achieved during World War II by the unscientific explanation of certain aircraft failures as being due to "gremlins," invisible but mischievous little men who played pranks on aviators. The point to note here is that from the point of view of observability and direct verifiability, there is no great difference between modern scientific theories and the unscientific doctrines of mythology or theology. One can no more see or touch a Newtonian "particle," an atom, or electron than an "intelligence" or a "gremlin." What, then, are the differences between scientific and unscientific explanations?

There are two important and closely related differences between the kind of explanation sought by science and the kind provided by superstitions of various sorts. The first significant difference lies in the attitudes taken toward the explanations in question. The typical attitude of one who really *accepts* an unscientific explanation is *dogmatic*. The unscientific explanation is regarded as being absolutely true and beyond all possibility of improvement or correction. During the Middle Ages and the early modern period, the word of Aristotle was the ultimate authority to which scholars appealed for deciding questions of fact. However empirically and open mindedly Aristotle himself may have arrived at his views, they were accepted by some schoolmen in a completely different and unscientific spirit. One of the schoolmen to whom Galileo offered his telescope to view the newly discovered moons of Jupiter declined to look, being convinced that none could possibly be seen because no mention of them could be found in Aristotle's treatise on astronomy! Because unscientific beliefs are absolute, ultimate, and final, within the framework of any such doctrine or dogma there can be no rational method of ever considering the question of its truth. The scientist's attitude toward his explanations is altogether different. Every explanation in science is put forward tentatively and provisionally. Any proposed explanation is regarded as a mere hypothesis, more or less probable on the basis of the available facts or relevant evidence. It must be admitted that the scientist's vocabulary is a little misleading on this point. When what was first suggested as a "hypothesis" becomes well confirmed, it is frequently elevated to the position of a "theory." And when, on the basis of a great mass of evidence, it achieves well-nigh universal acceptance, it is promoted to the lofty status of a "law." This terminology is not always strictly adhered to: Newton's discovery is still called the "Law of Gravitation," whereas Einstein's contribution, which supersedes or at least improves on Newton's, is referred to as the "Theory of Relativity." The vocabulary of "hypothesis," "theory," and "law" is unfortunate, since it obscures the important fact that *all* of the general propositions of science are regarded as hypotheses, never as dogmas.

Closely allied with the difference in the way they are regarded is the second and more fundamental difference between scientific and unscientific explanations or theories. This second difference lies in the basis for accepting or rejecting the view in question. Many unscientific views are mere prejudices that their adherents could scarcely give any reason for holding. Since they are regarded as "certain," however, any challenge or question is likely to be regarded as an affront and met with abuse. If those who accept an unscientific explanation *can* be persuaded to discuss the basis for its acceptance, there are only a few grounds on which they will attempt to "defend" it. It is true because "we've always believed it" or because "everyone knows it." These all too familiar phrases express appeals to tradition or popularity rather than evidence. Or a questioned dogma may be defended on the grounds of revelation or authority. The absolute truth of their religious creeds and the absolute falsehood of all others have been revealed from on high, at various times, to Moses, to Paul, to Mohammed, to Joseph Smith, and to many others. That there are rival traditions, conflicting authorities, and revelations that contradict one another does not seem disturbing to those who have embraced an absolute creed. In general, unscientific beliefs are held independently of anything we should regard as *evidence* in their favor. Because they are *absolute,* questions of evidence for them are regarded as having little or no importance.

The case is quite different in the realm of science. Since every scientific explanation is regarded as a hypothesis, it is regarded as worthy of acceptance only to the extent that there is evidence for it. As a hypothesis, the question of its truth or falsehood is open, and there is continual search for more and more evidence to decide that question. The term "evidence" as used here refers ultimately to experience; *sensible* evidence is the ultimate court of appeal in verifying scientific propositions. Science is *empirical* in holding that sense experience is the *test of truth* for all its pronouncements. Consequently, it is of the essence of a scientific proposition that it be capable of being tested by observation.

Some propositions can be tested directly. To decide the truth or falsehood of the proposition that it is now raining outside, we need only glance out the window. To tell whether a traffic light shows green or red, all we have to do is to look at it. But the propositions offered by scientists as explanatory hypotheses are not of this type. Such general propositions as Newton's Laws or Einstein's Theory are not directly testable in this fashion. They can, however, be tested indirectly. The indirect method of testing the truth of a proposition is familiar to all of us, though we may not be familiar with this name for it. For example, if his employer had been suspicious of the office boy's explanation of his tardiness, she might have checked up on it by telephoning the bus company to find out whether an accident had really happened to the seven-thirty bus. If the bus company's report checked with the boy's story, this would serve to dispel the employer's suspicions; whereas if the bus company denied that an accident had occurred, it would probably convince the employer that her office boy's story was false. This inquiry would constitute an indirect test of the office boy's explanation.

The pattern of indirect testing or indirect verification consists of two parts. First, one deduces from the proposition to be tested one or more other propositions capable of being tested directly. Then, these conclusions are tested and are found to be either true or false. If the conclusions are false, any proposition that implies them must be false also. On the other hand, if the conclusions are true, that provides evidence for the truth of the proposition being tested, which is thus confirmed indirectly.

It should be noted that indirect testing is never demonstrative or certain. To deduce directly testable conclusions from a proposition usually requires additional premises. The conclusion that the bus company will confirm that its seven-thirty bus had an accident does not follow validly from the proposition that the seven-thirty bus did have an accident. Additional premises are needed, for example, that all accidents get reported to the company's office, that the reports are not mislaid or forgotten, and that the company does not make a policy of denying (or "covering up") its accidents. So the bus company's denying that an accident occurred would not prove the office boy's story to be false, for the discrepancy might be due to the falsehood of one of the other premisses mentioned. Those others, however, ordinarily have such a high degree of probability that a negative reply on the part of the bus company would render the office boy's story very doubtful indeed.

Similarly, establishing the truth of a conclusion does not demonstrate the truth of the premisses from which it was deduced. We know very well that a valid argument may have a true conclusion even though its premisses are not all true. In the present example, the bus company might confirm that an accident happened to the seven-thirty bus because of some mistake in their records, even though no accident had occurred. So the inferred conclusion might be true even though the premisses from which it was deduced were not. In the usual case, though, that is highly unlikely; so a successful or affirmative testing of a conclusion serves to corroborate the premisses from which it was deduced.

It must be admitted that every proposition, scientific or unscientific, that is a relevant explanation for any observable fact has *some* evidence in its favor, namely, the fact to which it is relevant. Thus the regular motions of the planets must be conceded to constitute evidence for the (unscientific) theory that the planets are inhabited by "intelligences" that cause them to move in just the orbits that are observed. The motions themselves are as much evidence for that myth as they are for Newton's or Einstein's theories. The difference lies in the fact that that is the *only* evidence for the unscientific hypothesis. Absolutely no other directly testable propositions can be deduced from the myth. On the other hand, a very large number of directly testable propositions can be deduced from the scientific explanations mentioned. Here, then, is *the* difference between scientific and unscientific explanations. A scientific explanation for a given fact will have directly testable propositions deducible from it, other than the one stating the fact to be explained. But an unscientific explanation will have no other directly testable propositions deducible from it. It is of the essence of a scientific proposition to be empirically verifiable.

It is clear that we have been using the term "scientific explanation" in a quite general sense. As here defined, an exploration may be scientific even though it is not a part of one of the various special sciences like physics or psychology. Thus the office boy's explanation of his tardiness would be classified as a scientific one, for it is testable, even if only indirectly. But had he offered as explanation the proposition that "God willed him to be late that morning, and God is omnipotent," the explanation would have been unscientific. For although his being late that morning is deducible from the proffered explanation, no other directly testable proposition is, and so the explanation is not even indirectly testable and hence is unscientific.

13.3 *Evaluating Scientific Explanations*

The question naturally arises as to how scientific explanations are to be evaluated, that is, judged as good or bad, or at least as better or worse. This question is especially important because there is usually more than a single scientific explanation for one and the same fact. A person's abrupt behavior may be explained either by the hypothesis that the person is shy or by the hypothesis that the person is unfriendly. In a criminal investigation, two different and incompatible hypotheses about the identity of the criminal may equally well account for the known facts. In the realm of science proper, that an object expands when heated is explained by both the caloric theory of heat and the kinetic theory. The caloric theory regarded heat as an invisible weightless fluid, called "caloric," with the power of penetrating, expanding, and dissolving bodies, or dissipating them in vapor. The kinetic theory, on the other hand, regards the heat of a body as consisting of random motions of the molecules of which the body is composed. These are *alternative* scientific explanations that serve equally well to explain some of the phenomena of thermal expansion. They cannot both be true, however, and the problem is to evaluate or choose between them.

What is wanted here is a list of conditions that a good hypothesis can be expected to fulfill. It must not be thought that such a list of conditions will provide a *recipe* by whose means anyone at all can construct good hypotheses. No one has ever pretended to lay down a set of rules for the invention or discovery of hypotheses. It is likely that none could ever be laid down, for that is the *creative* side of the scientific enterprise. Ability to create is a function of imagination and talent and cannot be reduced to a mechanical process. A great scientific hypothesis, with wide explanatory powers like those of Newton's or Einstein's, is as much the product of genius as a great work of art. There is no formula for discovering new hypotheses, but there are certain rules to which acceptable hypotheses can be expected to conform. These can be regarded as the criteria for evaluating hypotheses.

There are five criteria commonly used in judging the worth or acceptability of hypotheses. They may be listed as (1) relevance, (2) testability, (3) compatibility with previously well-established hypotheses, (4) predictive or explanatory power, and (5) simplicity. The first two have already been discussed, but we shall review them briefly here.

1. Relevance

No hypothesis is ever proposed for its own sake but is always intended as an explanation of some fact or other. Therefore it must be *relevant* to the fact it is intended to explain; that is, the fact in question must be *deducible* from the proposed hypothesis—either from the hypothesis alone or from it together with certain causal laws that may be presumed to have already been established as highly probable, or from these together with certain assumptions about particular initial conditions. A hypothesis that is not relevant to the fact it is intended to explain simply fails to explain it and can only be regarded as having failed to fulfill its intended function. A good hypothesis must be *relevant*.

The chief distinguishing characteristic of scientific hypotheses (as contrasted with unscientific ones) is that they are testable. That is, there must be the possibility of making observations that tend to confirm or disprove any scientific hypothesis. It need not be directly testable, of course. As has already been observed, most of the really important scientific hypotheses are formulated in terms of such unobservable entities as electrons or electromagnetic waves. As one research scientist has written,

> A physicist of this century, interested in the basic structure of matter, deals with radiation he cannot see, forces he cannot feel, particles he cannot touch.[8]

But there must be some way of getting from statements about such unobservables to statements about directly observable entities such as tables and chairs, or pointer readings, or lines on a photographic plate. In other words, there must be some connection between any scientific hypothesis and empirical data or facts of experience.

3. Compatibility with Previously Well-Established Hypotheses

The requirement that an acceptable hypothesis must be compatible or consistent with other hypotheses that have already been well confirmed is eminently reasonable. Science, in seeking to encompass more and more facts, aims at achieving a system of explanatory hypotheses. Of course, such a system must be self-consistent, for no self-contradictory set of propositions could possibly be true—or even intelligible. Ideally, the way in which scientists hope to make progress is by gradually expanding their hypotheses to comprehend more and more facts. For such progress to be made, each new hypothesis must be consistent with those already confirmed. Thus Leverrier's hypothesis that there was an additional but not yet charted planet beyond the orbit of Uranus was perfectly consistent with the main body of accepted astronomical theory. A new theory must fit with older theories if there is to be orderly progress in scientific inquiry.

It is possible, of course, to overestimate the importance of the third criterion. Although the ideal of science may be the gradual growth of theoretical knowledge by the addition of one new hypothesis after another, the actual history of scientific progress has not always followed that pattern. Many of the most important new hypotheses have been inconsistent with older theories and have in fact replaced them rather than fitted in with them. Einstein's Relativity Theory was of that sort, shattering many of the preconceptions of the older Newtonian theory. The phenomenon of radioactivity, first observed during the last decade of the nineteenth century, led to the overthrow—or at least the modification—of many cherished theories that had almost

---

[8]Lloyd Smith, "The Bevatron," *Scientific American*, Vol. 184, No. 2, February 1951.

achieved the status of absolutes. One of these was the Principle of the Conservation of Matter, which asserted that matter could be neither created nor destroyed. The hypothesis that radium atoms undergo spontaneous disintegration was inconsistent with that old, established principle—but it was the principle that was relinquished in favor of the newer hypothesis.

The foregoing is not intended to give the impression that scientific progress is a helter-skelter process in which theories are abandoned right and left in favor of newer and shinier ones. Older theories are not so much abandoned as corrected. Einstein himself always insisted that his own work was a modification rather than a rejection of Newton's. The Principle of the Conservation of Matter was modified by being absorbed into the more comprehensive Principle of the Conservation of Mass-Energy. Every established theory has been established through having proved adequate to explain a considerable mass of data, of observed facts. And it cannot be dethroned or discredited by any new hypothesis unless that new hypothesis can account for the same facts as well or even better. There is nothing capricious about the development of science. Every change represents an improvement, a more comprehensive and thus more adequate explanation of the way in which the world manifests itself in our experience. Where inconsistencies occur between hypotheses, the greater age of one does not automatically prove it to be correct and the newer one wrong. The *presumption* is in favor of the older one if it has already been extensively confirmed. But if the new one in conflict with it *also* receives extensive confirmation, considerations of age or priority are definitely irrelevant. Where there is a conflict between two hypotheses, we must turn to the observable facts to decide between them. Ultimately our last court of appeal in deciding between rival hypotheses is experience. What our third criterion, compatibility with previous well-established hypotheses, comes to is this: the totality of hypotheses accepted at any time should be consistent with each other,[9] and—other things being equal—of two new hypotheses, the one that fits in better with the accepted body of scientific theory is to be preferred. The question of what is involved in "other things being equal" takes us directly to our fourth criterion.

4. Predictive or Explanatory Power

By the predictive or explanatory power of a hypothesis is meant the range of observable facts that can be deduced from it. This criterion is related to, but different from, that of testability. A hypothesis is testable if *some* observable fact is deducible from it. If one of two testable hypotheses has a greater number of observable facts deducible from it than from the other, then it is said to have greater predictive or explanatory power. Thus, Newton's hypothesis of universal gravitation joined together with his three laws of motion

---

[9]Scientists may, however, consider and even use inconsistent hypotheses for years while awaiting the resolution of that inconsistency. This was for many years the situation with respect to the wave and the corpuscular theories of light.

had greater predictive power than did either Kepler's or Galileo's hypotheses, because all observable consequences of the last two were also consequences of the former, and the former had many more besides. An observable fact that can be deduced from a given hypothesis is said to be explained by it and also can be said to be *predicted* by it. The greater the predictive power of a hypothesis, the more it explains, and the better it contributes to our understanding of the phenomena with which it is concerned.

Our fourth criterion has a negative side that is of crucial importance. If a hypothesis is inconsistent with any well-attested fact of observation, the hypothesis is false and must be rejected. Where two different hypotheses are both relevant to explaining some set of facts and both are testable, and both are compatible with the whole body of already established scientific theory, it may be possible to choose between them by deducing from them incompatible propositions that are directly testable. If H_1 and H_2, two different hypotheses, entail incompatible consequences, it may be possible to set up a *crucial experiment* to decide between them. Thus if H_1 entails that under circumstance C phenomenon P will occur, while H_2 entails that under circumstance C phenomenon P will *not* occur, then all we need do to decide between H_1 and H_2 is to produce circumstance C and observe the presence or absence of phenomenon P. If P occurs, this is evidence *for H_1* and *against H_2*, while if P does not occur, this is evidence *against H_1* and *for H_2*.

This kind of crucial experiment to decide between rival hypotheses may not always be easy to carry out, for the required circumstance C may be difficult or impossible to produce. Thus the decision between Newtonian Theory and Einstein's General Theory of Relativity had to await a total eclipse of the sun—a situation or circumstance clearly beyond our power to produce. In other cases the crucial experiment may have to await the development of new instruments, either for the production of the required *circumstances,* or for the observation or measurement of the predicted phenomenon. Thus proponents of rival astronomical hypotheses must often bide their time while they await the construction of new and more powerful telescopes. The topic of crucial experiments will be discussed further in Section 13.6.

5. Simplicity

It sometimes happens that two rival hypotheses satisfy the first four criteria equally well. Historically, the most important pair of such hypotheses were those of Ptolemy (fl. 127–151) and Copernicus (1473–1543). Both were intended to explain all of the then known data of astronomy. According to the Ptolemaic theory, the earth is the center of the universe, and the heavenly bodies move about it in orbits that require a very complicated geometry of epicycles to describe. Ptolemy's theory was relevant, testable, and compatible with previously well-established hypotheses, satisfying the first three criteria perfectly. According to the Copernican theory, the sun rather than the earth is at the center, and the earth itself moves around the sun along with the other planets. Copernicus's theory too satisfied the first three criteria perfectly. With respect to the fourth criterion, that of predictive power, there was not a great deal of difference between the two theories. But with respect to the fifth criterion there was a very significant difference between the two rival hypotheses. Although both required the clumsy method of epicycles to account for the observed positions of the various heavenly bodies, *fewer* such epicycles were required within the Copernican theory. The Copernican system was therefore simpler, and this contributed greatly to its acceptance by all later astronomers.

The criterion of simplicity is a perfectly natural one to invoke. In ordinary life as well as in science, the simplest theory that fits all the available facts is the one we tend to accept. In court trials of criminal cases, the prosecution attempts to develop a hypothesis that includes the guilt of the accused and fits in with all the available evidence. Opposing the prosecuting attorney, the defense attorney seeks to set up a hypothesis that includes the innocence of the accused and also fits all the available evidence. Often both sides succeed, and then the case is usually decided—or *ought* to be decided—in favor of that hypothesis that is simpler or more "natural." Simplicity, however, is a very difficult term to define. Not all controversies are as straightforward as the Ptolemaic–Copernican one, in which the latter's greater simplicity consisted merely in requiring a smaller number of epicycles. And, of course, "naturalness" is an almost hopelessly deceptive term—for it seems much more "natural" to believe that the earth is still while the apparently moving sun really does move. The fifth and last criterion, simplicity, is an important and frequently decisive one, but it is difficult to formulate and not always easy to apply.

13.4 *The Detective as Scientist*

Now that we have stated and explained the criteria by which hypotheses are evaluated, we are in a position to describe the general pattern of scientific research. It will be helpful to begin by examining an illustration of that method. A perennial favorite in this connection is the detective, whose problem is not quite the same as that of the pure scientist, but whose approach and technique illustrate the method of science very clearly. The classical example of the astute detective who can solve even the most baffling mystery is A. Conan Doyle's immortal creation, Sherlock Holmes. Holmes, his stature undiminished by the passage of time, will be our hero in the following account.

1. The Problem

Some of our most vivid pictures of Holmes are those in which he is busy with magnifying glass and tape measure, searching out and finding essential clues that had escaped the attention of those stupid bunglers, the "experts" of Scotland Yard. Or those of us who are by temperament less vigorous may think back more fondly on Holmes the thinker,

. . . who, when he had an unsolved problem upon his mind, would go for days, and even for a week, without rest, turning it over, rearranging his facts, looking at it from every point of view until he had either fathomed it or convinced himself that his data were insufficient."[10]

At one such time, according to Dr. Watson,

He took off his coat and waistcoat, put on a large blue dressing-gown, and then wandered about the room collecting pillows from his bed and cushions from the sofa and armchairs. With these he constructed a sort of Eastern divan, upon which he perched himself cross-legged, with an ounce of shag tobacco and a box of matches laid out in front of him. In the dim light of the lamp I saw him sitting there, an old briar pipe between his lips, his eyes fixed vacantly upon the corner of the ceiling, the blue smoke curling up from him, silent, motionless, with the light shining upon his strong-set aquiline features. So he sat as I dropped off to sleep, and so he sat when a sudden ejaculation caused me to wake up, and I found the summer sun shining into the apartment. The pipe was still between his lips, the smoke still curled upward, and the room was full of a dense tobacco haze, but nothing remained of the heap of shag which I had seen upon the previous night.[11]

But such memories are incomplete. Holmes was not always searching for clues or pondering over solutions. We all remember those dark periods— especially in the earlier stories—when, much to the good Watson's annoyance, Holmes would drug himself with morphine or cocaine. That would happen, of course, between cases. For when there is no mystery to be unraveled, nobody in his right mind would go out to look for clues. Clues, after all, must be clues *for* something. Nor could Holmes, or anyone else, for that matter, engage in profound thought unless he had something to think about. Sherlock Holmes was a genius at solving problems, but even a genius must have a problem before he can solve it. All reflective thinking, and this term includes criminal investigation as well as scientific research, is a problem-solving activity, as John Dewey and other pragmatists have rightly insisted. There must be a problem felt before either the detective or the scientist can go to work.

Of course, the active mind sees problems where the dullard sees only familiar objects. One Christmas season Dr. Watson visited Holmes to find that the latter had been using a lens and forceps to examine "a very seedy and disreputable hard-felt hat, much the worse for wear, and cracked in several places."[12] After they had greeted each other, Holmes said of it to Watson, "I beg that you will look upon it not as a battered billycock but as an intellectual problem."[13] It so happened that the hat led them into one of their most interesting adventures, but it could not have done so had Holmes not seen a problem in it from the start. A problem may be characterized as a fact or group of facts for which we have no acceptable explanation, that

[10]A. Conan Doyle, *The Man with the Twisted Lip.*
[11]Ibid.
[12]A. Conan Doyle, *The Adventure of the Blue Carbuncle.*
[13]Ibid.

seem unusual, or that fail to fit in with our expectations or preconceptions. It should be obvious that *some* prior beliefs are required if anything is to appear problematic. If there are no expectations, there can be no surprises.

Sometimes, of course, problems came to Holmes already labeled. The very first adventure recounted by Dr. Watson began with the following message from Gregson of Scotland Yard:

> Mr. Dear Mr. Sherlock Holmes:
> There has been a bad business during the night at 3, Lauriston Gardens, off the Brixton Road. Our man on the beat saw a light there about two in the morning, and as the house was an empty one, suspected that something was amiss. He found the door open, and in the front room, which is bare of furniture, discovered the body of a gentleman, well dressed, and having cards in his pocket bearing the name of "Enoch J. Drebber, Cleveland, Ohio, USA." There had been no robbery, nor is there any evidence as to how the man met his death. There are marks of blood in the room, but there is no wound upon his person. We are at a loss as to how he came into the empty house; indeed, the whole affair is a puzzler. If you can come round to the house any time before twelve, you will find me there. I have left everything in statu quo until I hear from you. If you are unable to come, I shall give you fuller details, and would esteem it a great kindness if you would favour me with your opinion.
>
> Yours faithfully,
Tobias Gregson[14]

Here was a problem indeed. A few minutes after receiving the message, Sherlock Holmes and Dr. Watson "were both in a hansom, driving furiously for the Brixton Road."

2. Preliminary Hypotheses

On their ride out Brixton way, Holmes "prattled away about Cremona fiddles and the difference between a Stradivarius and an Amati." Dr. Watson chided Holmes for not giving much thought to the matter at hand, and Holmes replied: "No data yet. . . . It is a capital mistake to theorize before you have all the evidence. It biases the judgment."[15] This point of view was expressed by Holmes again and again. On one occasion he admonished a younger detective that "The temptation to form premature theories upon insufficient data is the bane of our profession."[16] Yet for all of his confidence about the matter, on this one issue Holmes was completely mistaken. Of course one should not reach a *final judgment* until a great deal of evidence has been considered, but this procedure is quite different from *not theorizing*. As a matter of fact, it is strictly impossible to make any serious attempt to collect evidence unless one *has* theorized beforehand. As Charles Darwin, the great biologist and author of the modern theory of evolution, observed,

> . . . all observation must be for or against some view, if it is to be of any service.

[14]A. Conan Doyle, *A Study in Scarlet.*
[15]Ibid.
[16]A. Conan Doyle, *The Valley of Fear.*

The point is that there are too many particular facts, too many data in the world, for anyone to try to become acquainted with them all. Everyone, even the most patient and thorough investigator, must pick and choose, deciding which facts to study and which to pass over. One must have some working hypothesis for or against which to collect relevant data. It need not be a *complete* theory, but at least the rough outline must be there. Otherwise how could one decide what facts to select for consideration out of the totality of all facts, which is too vast even to begin to sift?

Holmes's actions were wiser than his words in this connection. After all, the words were spoken in a hansom speeding toward the scene of the crime. If Holmes really had no theory about the matter, why go to Brixton Road? If facts and data were all that he wanted, any old facts and any old data, with no hypotheses to guide him in their selection, why should he have left Baker Street at all? There were plenty of facts in the rooms at 221-B Baker Street. Holmes might just as well have spent his time counting all the words on all the pages of all the books there, or perhaps making very accurate measurements of the distances between each separate pair of articles of furniture in the house. He could have gathered data to his heart's content and saved himself cab fare into the bargain!

It may be objected that the facts to be gathered at Baker Street have nothing to do with the case, whereas those awaiting Holmes at the scene of the crime were valuable clues for solving the problem. It was, of course, just this consideration that led Holmes to ignore the "data" at Baker Street and hurry away to collect those off Brixton Road. It must be insisted, however, that the greater relevance of the latter could not be *known* beforehand but only conjectured on the basis of previous experience with crimes and clues. In fact, a *hypothesis* led Holmes to look in one place rather than another for his facts, the hypothesis that there was a murder, that the crime was committed at the place where the body was found, and that the perpetrator had left some trace or clue. Some such hypothesis is always needed to guide an investigator in the search for relevant data, for in the absence of any preliminary hypothesis, there are simply too many facts in this world to examine. The preliminary hypothesis ought to be highly tentative, and it must be based on previous knowledge. But a preliminary hypothesis is as necessary as the existence of a problem for any serious inquiry to begin.

It must be emphasized that a preliminary hypothesis, as here conceived, need not be a complete solution to the problem. The hypothesis that the man was murdered by someone who had left some clues to his identity on or near the body of the victim was what led Holmes to Brixton Road. This hypothesis is clearly incomplete: it does not say who committed the crime, or how it was done, or why. Such a preliminary hypothesis may be very different from the final solution to the problem. It will never be complete: it may be a tentative explanation of only part of the problem. But however partial and however tentative, a preliminary hypothesis is required for any investigation to proceed.

3. Collecting Additional Facts

Every serious investigation begins with some fact or group of facts that strike the investigator as problematic and thus initiate the whole process of inquiry. The initial facts that constitute the problem are usually too meager to suggest a wholly satisfactory explanation for themselves, but they will suggest—to the competent investigator—some preliminary hypotheses that lead to the search for additional facts. These additional facts, it is hoped, will serve as clues to the final solution. The inexperienced or bungling investigator will overlook or ignore all but the most obvious of them; but the careful worker will aim at completeness in the examination of those additional facts to which the preliminary hypotheses had led. Holmes, of course, was the most careful and painstaking of investigators.

Holmes insisted on dismounting from the hansom a hundred yards or so from their destination and approached the house on foot, looking carefully at its surroundings and especially at the pathway leading up to it. When Holmes and Watson entered the house, they were shown the body by the two Scotland Yard operatives, Gregson and Lestrade. ("There is no clue," said Gregson. "None at all," chimed in Lestrade.) But Holmes had already started his own search for additional facts, looking first at the body:

> . . . his nimble fingers were flying here, there, and everywhere, feeling, pressing, unbuttoning, examining. . . . So swiftly was the examination made, that one would hardly have guessed the minuteness with which it was conducted. Finally, he sniffed the dead man's lips, and then glanced at the soles of his patent leather boots.[17]

Then, turning his attention to the room itself,

> . . . he whipped a tape measure and a large round magnifying glass from his pocket. With these two implements he trotted noiselessly about the room, sometimes stopping, occasionally kneeling, and once lying flat upon his face. So engrossed was he with his occupation that he appeared to have forgotten our presence, for he chattered away to himself under his breath the whole time, keeping up a running fire of exclamations, groans, whistles and little cries suggestive of encouragement and of hope. As I watched him I was irresistibly reminded of a pure-blooded, well-trained foxhound as it dashes backward and forward through the covert, whining in its eagerness, until it comes across the lost scent. For twenty minutes or more he continued his researches, measuring with the most exact care the distance between marks which were entirely invisible to me, and occasionally applying his tape to the walls in an equally incomprehensible manner. In one place he gathered up very carefully a little pile of gray dust from the floor and packed it away in an envelope. Finally he examined with his glass the word upon the wall, going over every letter of it, with the most minute exactness. This done, he appeared to be satisfied, for he replaced his tape and his glass in his pocket.

[17]A. Conan Doyle, *A Study in Scarlet.*

"They say that genius is an infinite capacity for taking pains," he remarked with a smile. "It's a very bad definition, but it does apply to detective work."[18]

One matter deserves to be emphasized very strongly. Steps 2 and 3 are not completely separable but are usually very intimately connected and interdependent. True enough, we require a preliminary hypothesis to begin any intelligent examination of facts, but the additional facts may themselves suggest new hypotheses, which may lead to new facts, which suggest still other hypotheses, which lead to still other additional facts, and so on. Thus having made his careful examination of the facts available in the house off Brixton Road, Holmes was led to formulate a further hypothesis that required the taking of testimony from the constable who found the body. The man was off duty at the moment and Lestrade gave Holmes the constable's name and address.

> Holmes took a note of the address.
> "Come along, Doctor," he said: "we shall go and look him up. I'll tell you one thing which may help you in the case," he continued, turning to the two detectives. "There has been murder done, and the murderer was a man. He was more than six feet high, was in the prime of his life, had small feet for his height, wore coarse, square-toed boots and smoked a Trichinopoly cigar. He came here with his victim in a four-wheeled cab, which was drawn by a horse with three old shoes and one new one on his off fore-leg. In all probability the murderer had a florid face, and the fingernails of his right hand were remarkably long. These are only a few indications, but they may assist you."
> Lestrade and Gregson glanced at each other with an incredulous smile.
> "If this man was murdered, how was it done?" asked the former.
> "Poison," said Sherlock Holmes curtly, and strode off.[19]

4. Formulating the Hypothesis

In any investigation the stage will be reached, sooner or later, at which the investigator—whether detective, scientist, or ordinary mortal—will begin to feel that all the facts needed for solving the problem are at hand. The investigator has the "2 and 2," so to speak, but the task still remains of "putting them together." At such a time Sherlock Holmes might sit up all night, consuming pipe after pipe of tobacco, trying to think things through. The result or end product of such thinking, if it is successful, is a hypothesis that accounts for all the data, both the original set of facts constituting the problem and the additional facts to which the preliminary hypotheses pointed. The actual discovery of such an explanatory hypothesis is a process of creation, in which imagination as well as knowledge is involved. Holmes, who was a genius at inventing hypotheses, described the process as reasoning "backward." As he put it,

[18]Ibid.
[19]Ibid.

Most people if you describe a train of events to them, will tell you what the result would be. They can put those events together in their minds, and argue from them that something will come to pass. There are few people, however, who, if you told them a result, would be able to evolve from their own inner consciousness what the steps were which led up to that result.[20]

Here is Holmes's description of the process of formulating an explanatory hypothesis. Whether his account is right or wrong, when a hypothesis has been proposed, its evaluation must be along the lines that were sketched in Section 13.3. Granted its relevance and testability, and its compatibility with other well-attested beliefs, the ultimate criterion for evaluating a hypothesis is its predictive power. As a more recent writer has put it,

> The formation of hypotheses is the most mysterious of all the categories of scientific method. Where they come from, no one knows. A person is sitting somewhere, minding his own business, and suddenly—flash!—he understands something he didn't understand before. Until it's tested the hypothesis isn't truth. For the tests aren't its source. Its source is somewhere else.[21]

5. Deducing Further Consequences

A really fruitful hypothesis will explain not only the facts that originally inspired it, but will explain many others in addition. A good hypothesis will point beyond the initial facts in the direction of new ones whose existence might otherwise not have been suspected. And, of course, the verification of those further consequences will tend to confirm the hypothesis that led to them. Holmes's hypothesis that the murdered man had been poisoned was soon put to such a test. A few days later the murdered man's secretary and traveling companion was also found murdered. Holmes asked Lestrade, who had discovered the second body, whether he had found anything in the room that could furnish a clue to the murderer. Lestrade answered, "Nothing," and went on to mention a few quite ordinary effects. Holmes was not satisfied and pressed him, asking, "And was there nothing else?" Lestrade answered, "Nothing of any importance," and named a few more details, the last of which was "a small chip ointment box containing a couple of pills." At this information,

> Sherlock Holmes sprang from his chair with an exclamation of delight.
> "The last link," he cried, exultantly. "My case is complete."
> The two detectives stared at him in amazement.
> "I have now in my hands," my companion said, confidently, "all the threads which have formed such a tangle. . . . I will give you a proof of my knowledge. Could you lay your hands upon those pills?"
> "I have them," said Lestrade, producing a small white box.[22]

---

[20]Ibid.
[21]Pirsig, *Zen and the Art of Motorcycle Maintenance*.
[22]A. Conan Doyle, *A Study in Scarlet*.

On the basis of his hypothesis about the original crime, Holmes was able to predict that the pills found at the scene of the second crime must contain poison. Here deduction has an essential role in the process of any scientific or inductive inquiry. The ultimate value of any hypothesis lies in its predictive or explanatory power, which means that additional facts must be deducible from an adequate hypothesis. From his theory that the first man was poisoned and that the second victim met his death at the hands of the same murderer, Holmes inferred that the pills found by Lestrade must be poison. His theory, however sure he may have felt about it, was only a theory and needed further confirmation. He obtained that confirmation by testing the consequences deduced from the hypothesis and finding them to be true. Having used deduction to make a prediction, his next step was to test it.

6. Testing the Consequences

The consequences of a hypothesis, that is, the predictions made on the basis of that hypothesis, may require various means for their testing. Some require only observation. In some cases, Holmes needed only to watch and wait— for the bank robbers to break into the vault, in the *Adventure of the Red-Headed League,* or for Dr. Roylott to slip a venomous snake through a dummy ventilator, in the *Adventure of the Speckled Band.* In the present case, however, an experiment had to be performed.

Holmes asked Dr. Watson to fetch the landlady's old and ailing terrier, which she had asked to have put out of its misery the day before. Holmes then cut one of the pills in two, dissolved it in a wineglass of water, added some milk, and

> . . . turned the contents of the wineglass into a saucer and placed it in front of the terrier, who speedily licked it dry. Sherlock Holmes's earnest demeanor had so far convinced us that we all sat in silence, watching the animal intently, and expecting some startling effect. None such appeared, however. The dog continued to lie stretched upon the cushion, breathing in a laboured way, but apparently neither the better nor the worse for its draught.
>
> Holmes had taken out his watch, and as minute followed minute without result, an expression of the utmost chagrin and disappointment appeared upon his features. He gnawed his lip, drummed his fingers upon the table, and showed every other symptom of acute impatience. So great was his emotion that I felt sincerely sorry for him, while the two detectives smiled derisively, by no means displeased at this check which he had met.
>
> "It can't be a coincidence," he cried, at last springing from his chair and pacing wildly up and down the room: "it is impossible that it should be a mere coincidence. The very pills which I suspected in the case of Drebber are actually found after the death of Stangerson. And yet they are inert. What can it mean? Surely my whole chain of reasoning cannot have been false. It is impossible! And yet this wretched dog is none the worse. Ah, I have it! I have it!" With a perfect shriek of delight he rushed to the box, cut the other pill in two, dissolved it, added milk, and presented it to the terrier. The unfortunate creature's tongue seemed hardly to have been

moistened in it before it gave a convulsive shiver in every limb, and lay as rigid and lifeless as if it had been struck by lightning.

Sherlock Holmes drew a long breath, and wiped the perspiration from his forehead.[23]

By the favorable outcome of his experiment, Holmes's hypothesis had received dramatic and convincing confirmation.

7. Application

The detective's concern, after all, is a practical one. Given a crime to solve, he has not merely to explain the facts but to apprehend and arrest the criminal. The latter involves making application of his theory, using it to predict where the criminal can be found and how he may be caught. He must deduce still further consequences from the hypothesis, not for the sake of additional confirmation but for practical use. From his general hypothesis Holmes was able to infer that the murderer was acting the role of a cabman. We have already seen that Holmes had formed a pretty clear description of the man's appearance. He sent out his army of "Baker Street Irregulars," street urchins of the neighborhood, to search out and summon the cab driven by just that man. The successful "application" of this hypothesis can be described again in Dr. Watson's words. A few minutes after the terrier's death,

> . . . there was a tap at the door, and the spokesman of the street Arabs, young Wiggins, introduced his insignificant and unsavoury person.
>
> "Please, sir," he said touching his forelock, "I have the cab downstairs."
>
> "Good boy," said Holmes, blandly. "Why don't you introduce this pattern at Scotland Yard?" he continued, taking a pair of steel handcuffs from a drawer. "See how beautifully the spring works. They fasten in an instant."
>
> "The old pattern is good enough," remarked Lestrade, "if we can only find the man to put them on."
>
> "Very good, very good," said Holmes, smiling. "The cabman may as well help me with my boxes. Just ask him to step in, Wiggins."
>
> I was surprised to find my companion speaking as though he were about to set out on a journey, since he had not said anything to me about it. There was a small portmanteau in the room, and this he pulled out and began to strap. He was busily engaged at it when the cabman entered the room.
>
> "Just give me a help with this buckle, cabman," he said, kneeling over his task, and never turning his head.
>
> The fellow came forward with a somewhat sullen, defiant air, and put down his hands to assist. At that instant there was a sharp click, the jangling of metal, and Sherlock Holmes sprang to his feet again.
>
> "Gentlemen," he cried, with flashing eyes, "let me introduce you to Mr. Jefferson Hope, the murderer of Enoch Drebber and of Joseph Stangerson."[24]

[23]Ibid.
[24]Ibid.

Here we have a picture of the detective as scientist, reasoning from observed facts to a testable hypothesis that not only explains the facts but also permits a practical application.

13.5 *Scientists in Action: The Pattern of Scientific Investigation*

As the term "scientific" is generally used today, it refers to any reasoning that attempts to proceed from observable facts of experience to reasonable (that is, relevant and testable) explanations for those facts. The scientific method is not confined to professional scientists: anyone can be said to be proceeding scientifically who follows the general pattern of reasoning from evidence to conclusions that can be tested by experience. The skilled detective is a scientist in this sense, as are most of us—in our more rational moments, at least. The pervasive pattern of all scientific inquiry is expressible in terms of the steps illustrated in the preceding section.

Those seven steps will be explained further by analyzing an important example of scientific research.[25] During the eighteenth century, the caloric theory of heat had become very widely accepted. Heat was believed to be a subtle, highly elastic fluid that could be added to or extracted from a body, thereby causing temperature changes in it. The hypothesized heat fluid was supposed to be indestructible; its particles were thought to be self-repellent but attracted by ordinary matter; and it was alleged to be all-pervading. The caloric theory of heat had considerable explanatory power. The expansion of bodies when heated was explained as the natural result of "swelling" caused by the heat fluid being forced into its pores. The production of heat by pounding on a body was explained as being due to the releasing or "jarring loose" of some of the caloric that had been condensed in the body, so that pounding increased the amount of free caloric heat in it. Even the conversion of fuel to power in the early steam engine could be explained on the caloric theory; a given quantity of caloric "falling" from a higher to a lower temperature was analogous to a given quantity of water falling from a higher to a lower level—each was capable of producing mechanical power. By the end of the eighteenth century, the caloric theory of heat as a material substance was quite generally accepted.

It was against this background of accepted theory that Count Rumford (1753–1814) encountered the problem that guided much of his subsequent research. Rumford described the beginning in these words:

> Being engaged, lately, in superintending the boring of cannon, in the workshops of the military aresenal at Munich, I was struck with the very considerable degree of heat which a brass gun acquires, in a short time, in being bored; and with the

[25]The following account is freely adapted from F. K. Richtmyer, *Introduction to Modern Physics,* copyright 1928, 1934, McGraw-Hill Book Company, New York.

still more intense heat (much greater than that of boiling water, as I found by experiment) of the metallic chips separated from it by the borer.

The more I meditated on these phaenomena, the more they appeared to me to be curious and interesting.[26]

Here we have the first step in any inquiry: a problem is felt. It should be noted that in this case the felt problem arose from an apparent conflict between the data of experience and accepted scientific theories. The relevant theories were two: first, the caloric theory, which asserted heat to be a material substance, and, second, the principle of the conservation of matter, which asserted that material substance could neither be created nor destroyed. The observed fact, on the other hand, was that considerable amounts of heat were produced—without any apparent decrease in the amounts of any other material substances. The production of as much heat as Rumford observed was inexplicable on the basis of the science of his day. The situation was problematic and demanded a solution. It should be clear that the problem would not be felt by anyone who was ignorant of the accepted theories. Nor would it be felt by an unobservant individual who took no notice of the facts before him. Finally, it would not be felt by anyone whose mind was not disturbed by gaps or inconsistencies between theory and observation. It may be remarked, then, that the requisite qualities a person must have to initiate any fruitful inquiry are three: one must be familiar with current theories, observant of new facts, and uncomfortable in the presence of any conflict or gap between fact and theory.

Judging by the various experiments he was subsequently led to perform, it seems reasonable to suppose that Count Rumford's preliminary hypothesis was something like the following. Since considerable heat was generated without appreciable diminution of other material substances present, perhaps it might be possible to obtain *unlimited* amounts of heat without exhausting the supply of matter at hand. This conjecture was certainly suggested by the original data that posed the problem. Helpful in setting up an experiment to test this hypothesis, or to collect data suggested by it, was Rumford's previous knowledge that boring with dull tools generates more heat than is obtained by using sharp ones.

On the basis of this knowledge, and being guided by the preliminary hypothesis mentioned, Rumford went about collecting some additional relevant data, which he procured by the following experimental setup. He caused a blunt steel boring tool to rotate, under great pressure, against a piece of brass while both were immersed in water. The apparatus was powered by two horses. In just two and one half hours the water actually boiled, a process that continued as long as the horses kept the machinery in motion. Rumford thus arrived at the additional fact that there was no limit to the amount of heat that could be produced without any decrease in the amount of material substance in the vicinity. This fact was clearly incompatible with the caloric

[26]From William Francis Magie, *A Source Book in Physics*, copyright 1935, McGraw-Hill Book Company, New York.

theory of heat, according to which there can be only a finite or limited amount of the heat fluid in any body.

Having gathered these additional data, Count Rumford addressed himself to the task of formulating a hypothesis to explain all the facts encountered. It was with some reluctance that he abandoned the popular caloric theory. But the facts were stubborn, and not to be got around. Rumford wrote

> . . . anything which any isolated body, or system of bodies, can continue to furnish without limitation cannot possibly be a material substance; and it appears to me to be extremely difficult, if not quite impossible, to form any distinct idea of anything capable of being excited and communicated in the manner heat was excited and communicated in these experiments, except it be motion.[27]

Rumford's hypothesis that heat is a form of motion has come to be called the "mechanical" or "kinetic" theory of heat. On the basis of the facts at his disposal he rejected the "materialistic" or "caloric" theory.

But in science, as elsewhere, progress must struggle against inertia. The caloric theory had been accepted for a very long time, and Rumford's hypothesis was so revolutionary that its acceptance was very slow in coming. (Actually, it had been anticipated by Sir Isaac Newton in Query 18 of his *Opticks* almost one hundred years earlier, but Newton's authority had not been established in this field.) Before the kinetic theory could be widely accepted, further confirmation was necessary. That confirmation was supplied by other scientists.

Here we come to another important aspect of scientific thought. Science is *social*, an activity of the group rather than an isolated individual enterprise. A scientific structure can be built or created by many investigators, and the well-developed branches of science are all joint enterprises. The cooperative nature of scientific research accounts for the "objectivity" of science. The data with which scientists deal are public data, available to any qualified investigator who makes the appropriate observations. Scientists, in reporting their experiments, include a wealth of detail, not for its own intrinsic interest but to enable other investigators to duplicate the experimental setup and thus see for themselves whether the reported result really does occur. There are many cases in which individuals are mistaken in what they think they see. In a court of law, witnesses will swear to conflicting versions of events at which both were present, with no intentional perjury on the part of either. Many times people will see what they expect, or what they want to see, rather than what actually occurs. Although the facts of experience are the ultimate court of appeal for scientists, they must be public facts that everyone can experience under appropriate conditions. When elaborate experiments are repeated by various different scientists again and again, it does not token suspicion or distrust of the other person's results, but universal agreement that to be decisive facts must be public and repeatable. Repetition and careful checking by qualified observers minimizes the intrusion of subjective factors and helps maintain the objectivity of science.

[27]Richtmyer, *Introduction to Modern Physics.*

Sir Humphry Davy (1778–1829) was the next scientist of importance to interest himself in the kinetic theory of heat. From the two theories, Davy deduced testable consequences that were strictly incompatible with each other. He argued that *if* the caloric theory were true, then two pieces of ice that were initially below the melting point and were kept in a vacuum would not be melted by any amount of friction that could be produced between them.[28] On the other hand, with the kinetic theory of heat as premiss he deduced the conclusion that two pieces of ice rubbed together would melt no matter what their initial temperatures and regardless of whether or not the operation was performed in a vacuum. These deductions pointed the way to further experimentation.

The crucial experiment made possible by these deductions was then performed by Davy, who reported his procedures in great detail, specifying that he used "two parallelopipedons of ice, of the temperature of 29°, six inches long, two wide, and two-thirds of an inch thick."[29] It was experimentally verified that under the described conditions the ice *did melt*. That result convinced Sir Humphry Davy of the correctness of the kinetic theory of heat and of the untenability of the caloric theory. In Davy's own words,

> It has . . . been experimentally demonstrated that caloric, or the matter of heat, does not exist. . . . Since bodies become expanded by friction, it is evident that their corpuscles must move or separate from each other. Now a motion or vibration of the corpuscles of bodies must be necessarily generated by friction and percussion. Therefore we may reasonably conclude that this motion or vibration is heat, or the repulsive power.
>
> Heat, then, or that power which prevents the actual contact of the corpuscles of bodies, and which is the cause of our peculiar sensation of heat and cold, may be defined as a peculiar motion, probably a vibration, of the corpuscles of bodies, tending to separate them.[30]

Davy's experimental testing of his predictions resulted in the confirmation of Rumford's hypothesis. Perhaps more decisive even than Davy's experiments were those of the British physicist James Prescott Joule (1818–1889) who made the kinetic theory *quantitative* by experimentally establishing the mechanical equivalent of heat.

Especially in its quantitative form, the kinetic theory of heat has many applications. Some of these are theoretical: especially in connection with the kinetic theory of gases, it serves to unify mechanics with the theory of heat phenomena. The almost independent science of thermodynamics has been one result of this unification. As for practical applications of the kinetic theory of heat, the most obvious is in the field of artificial refrigeration, which is only one of the technological results made possible by that theory.

---

[28]His actual deduction involved considerations having to do with the theory of "heat capacity" and the phenomenon of oxidation and is too complex to reproduce here in detail. It can be found in Magie, *A Source Book in Physics*, pp. 161–165.

[29]Ibid.

[30]Ibid. Also, see E. N. Da C. Andrade, *Nature*, Vol. 135, 1935, p. 359, or R. L. Weber, ed., *A Random Walk in Science* (New York: Crane, Russak & Co., Inc., 1974), pp. 40–41.

EXERCISES

1. Take some detective story and analyze its structure in terms of the seven steps discussed in the preceding sections.

2. Find an account of some specific line of research in a popular or semipopular book on science and analyze its structure in terms of the seven steps discussed in the preceding sections.

13.6 *Crucial Experiments and Ad Hoc Hypotheses*

From the foregoing account, a reader might form the opinion that scientific progress is ridiculously easy to make. It might appear that, given any problem, all one need do is set down all relevant hypotheses and then perform a series of crucial experiments to eliminate all but one of them. The surviving hypothesis is then "the answer," and we are ready to go on to the next problem. But no opinion could possibly be more mistaken.

It has already been remarked that formulating or discovering relevant hypotheses is not a mechanical process but a creative one: some hypotheses require genius for their discovery. It has been observed further that crucial experiments may not always be possible either because no different observable consequences are deducible from the alternative hypotheses or because we lack the power to arrange the experimental circumstances in which different consequences would manifest themselves. We wish at this time to point out a more pervasive theoretical difficulty with the program of deciding between rival hypotheses by means of crucial experiments. It may be well to illustrate our discussion by means of a fairly simple example. One that is familiar to all of us concerns the shape of the earth.

In ancient Greece, the philosophers Anaximenes and Empedocles had held that the earth is flat, and this view, close to common sense, still had adherents in the Middle Ages and the Renaissance. Christopher Columbus, however, insisted that the earth is round—or, rather, spherical. One of Columbus's arguments was that as a ship sails away from shore, the upper portions of it remain visible to a watcher on land long after its lower parts have disappeared from view. A slightly different version of the same argument was included by Nikolaus Copernicus in his epoch-making treatise *On the Revolutions of the Heavenly Spheres*. In Section II of Book I of that work, entitled "That the Earth Also Is Spherical," he presented a number of arguments intended to establish the truth of that view. Of the many found there we quote the following:

> That the seas take a spherical form is perceived by navigators. For when land is still not discernible from a vessel's deck, it is from the masthead. And if, when a ship sails from land, a torch be fastened from the masthead, it appears to watchers

on the land to go downward little by little until it entirely disappears, like a heavenly body setting.[31]

As between these two rival hypotheses about the earth's shape, we might regard the foregoing as a description of a crucial experiment. The general pattern is clear. From the hypothesis that the earth is flat, H_f, it follows that, if a ship gradually recedes from view, then neither its masthead nor its decks should remain visible after the other has vanished. On the other hand, from the hypothesis that the earth is spherical, H_s, it follows that if a ship gradually recedes from view, its masthead should remain visible after its decks have vanished from sight. The rationale involved here is nicely represented by the diagram in Figure 21.

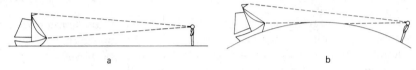

a   b

FIGURE 21

In the figure, *a* represents the situation that would obtain if H_f were true. It is clear that *if* the earth is flat there is no reason why any one portion of the ship should disappear from sight before any other portion. The figure *b* represents the situation corresponding to H_s. As the ship recedes, the curvature of the earth rises between the observer and the ship, blocking out his view of the decks while the masthead still remains visible. In each case the rays of light passing from ship to observer are represented by dashed lines. Now the experiment is performed, a receding ship is watched attentively, and the masthead *does* remain visible after the decks have disappeared. Our experiment may not have demonstrated the truth of H_s, it can be admitted, but surely it has established the falsehood of H_f. We have as clear an example of a crucial experiment as it is possible to obtain.

But the experiment described is *not* crucial. It is entirely possible to accept the observed facts and still maintain that the earth is flat. The experiment has considerable value as evidence, but it is not decisive. It is not crucial because the various testable predictions were not inferred from the stated hypotheses H_f and H_s alone, but from them plus the additional hypothesis that "light travels in straight lines." The diagrams show clearly that this additional assumption is essential to the argument. That the decks disappear before the masthead does is not deducible from H_s alone but requires the additional premiss that light rays follow a rectilinear path (H_r). And that the decks do *not* disappear before the masthead does is not deducible from H_f alone but requires the same additional premiss: that light rays follow a rectilinear path (H_r). The latter argument may be formulated as

[31]Reprinted from Nikolaus Copernicus, *On the Revolutions of the Heavenly Spheres*, as contained in John Warren Knedler, Jr., ed., *Masterworks of Science, Digests of 13 Great Classics* (Garden City, N.Y.: Doubleday & Company, Inc., 1947).

The earth is flat (H_f).

Light rays follow a rectilinear path (H_r).

Therefore the decks of a receding ship will *not* disappear from view before the masthead.

Here is a perfectly good argument whose conclusion is observed to be false. Its premisses cannot both be true; at least one of them must be false. But which one? We can maintain the truth of the first premiss, H_f, if we are willing to reject the second premiss, H_r. The second premiss, after all, is not a truth of logic. It is a contingent proposition that is easily conceived to be false. If we adopt the contrary hypothesis that light rays follow a curved path, concave upward (H_c), what follows as conclusion now? Here we can infer the denial of the conclusion of the former argument. From H_f and H_c it follows that the decks of a receding ship will disappear before its masthead does. Figure 22 explains the reasoning involved here.

a   b

FIGURE 22

In this figure, *a* represents the situation when the ship is near the shore, whereas *b* shows that, as the ship recedes, the earth (even though flat) blocks out the view of the decks while the masthead still remains visible. The light rays in this diagram too are represented by dashed lines, but in this case curved rather than rectilinear. The same experiment is performed, the decks do disappear before the masthead, and the observed fact is perfectly compatible with this group of hypotheses that includes H_f, the claim that the earth is flat. The experiment, therefore, is *not crucial* with respect to H_f, for that hypothesis can be maintained to be true regardless of the experiment's outcome.[32]

The point is that, where hypotheses of a fairly high level of abstractness or generality are involved, no observable or directly testable prediction can be deduced from just a single one of them. A whole group of hypotheses must be used as premisses, and if the observed facts are other than those predicted, *at least one* of the hypotheses in the group is shown to be false. But we have not established which one is in error. An experiment can be crucial in showing the untenability of a group of hypotheses. But such a group will usually contain a considerable number of separate hypotheses, the truth of any one of which can be maintained in the teeth of *any* experimental result, however "unfavorable," by the simple expedient of rejecting some *other* hypothesis of the group. A conclusion often drawn from these

---

[32]This illustration was first suggested by the late professor C. L. Stevenson in 1946.

considerations is that no individual hypothesis can ever be subjected to a crucial experiment.

The preceding discussion may be objected to strenuously. It may be urged that the experiment in question "really does" refute the hypothesis that the earth is flat. It may be charged that the argument to the contrary is guilty of making an *ad hoc* hypothesis to obscure and get around the plain facts of the case. It may be felt that only the invention of *ad hoc* hypotheses right and left can prevent some experiments from being crucial and decisively refuting single hypotheses. This objection deserves careful attention.

The crux of the objection would seem to lie in the phrase "ad hoc," which in this context is a highly charged term of abuse. Of its emotive significance there can be little doubt, but its literal meaning is somewhat ambiguous. There are three different senses in which the term "ad hoc" is often used. Its first and etymological meaning would seem to be that an *ad hoc* hypothesis is one that was specially made up to account for some fact *after* that fact had been established. In this sense, however, *all* hypotheses are ad hoc, since it makes no sense to speak of a hypothesis that was not devised to account for some antecedently established fact or other. Hence the first sense does not fit in very well with the derogatory emotive significance of the term. We must consider its other meanings.

The term "ad hoc" is also used to characterize a hypothesis that accounts *only* for the particular fact or facts it was invented to explain and has no other explanatory power, that is, no other testable consequences. No *scientific* hypothesis is *ad hoc* in this second sense of the term, although *every* hypothesis is *ad hoc* in the first sense explained. A hypothesis that is *ad hoc* in the second sense is unscientific; since it is not testable, it has no place in the structure of science. The second sense of "ad hoc" fits in perfectly with the derogatory emotive meaning of the term. But it should be realized that the auxiliary hypothesis about light rays traveling in curved paths, which was sufficient to save the hypothesis that the earth is flat from being definitely refuted by the experiment described, is *ad hoc* only in the first sense, not the second. For it does have a considerable number of empirically testable consequences.

There is a third sense of the term "ad hoc," in which it is used to denote a mere descriptive generalization. Such a descriptive hypothesis will assert only that all facts of a particular sort occur in just some particular kinds of circumstances and will have no explanatory power or theoretical scope. For example, limiting their diet to polished rice was found by Eijkman to cause polyneuritis in the small group of chickens with which he was working (as described in Exercise 1 on page 391 in the preceding chapter on Mill's Methods). Eijkman's hypothesis to account for this fact was *ad hoc* in the third sense: he simply drew the generalization that a diet limited to polished rice will cause polyneuritis in *any* group of chickens. His hypothesis accounts for more than just the particular facts observed; it is testable by controlling the diets of *other* groups of chickens. But it is descriptive rather than explanatory, *merely* empirical rather than theoretical. The science of nutrition has come a long way since Eijkman's contribution. Both the identification and the analysis of vitamins are required for a more adequate account of the facts observed by Eijkman. Science seeks to explain rather than merely to describe; hypotheses that consist of mere generalizations of the facts observed are said to be ad hoc.

The classical example of an *ad hoc* hypothesis in this third sense is the Fitzgerald Contraction Effect introduced to account for the results of the Michelson–Morley experiment on the velocity of light. By affirming that bodies moving at extremely high velocities contract, Fitzgerald accounted for the given data; his account was testable by repetitions of the experiment. But it was generally held to be *ad hoc* rather than explanatory, and not until Einstein's Special Theory of Relativity were the anomalous results of the Michelson-Morley experiment given an adequate, that is, a theoretical, explanation. It should be noted that the auxiliary hypothesis about the curved path of light rays is not *ad hoc* in this third sense either, since it is not a mere generalization of observed facts. (It is, in fact, an essential ingredient in the General Theory of Relativity.)

The general situation seems to be that it is not necessary to invoke *ad hoc* hypotheses—in either the second or third senses of the term, which are the derogatory ones—to prevent experiments from being crucial. Even if we confine our attention to theoretically significant hypotheses, and never invoke any *ad hoc* hypotheses at all, no experiments are ever crucial for individual hypotheses, since hypotheses are testable only in groups.[33] Our limitation here serves to illuminate again the *systematic* character of science. Scientific progress consists in building ever more adequate theories to account for the facts of experience. True enough, it is of value to collect or verify isolated particular facts, for the ultimate basis of science is factual. But the theoretical structure of science grows in a more organic fashion. In the realm of theory, piecemeal progress, one-step-at-a-time advances, can be accomplished, but only within the framework of a generally accepted body of scientific theory. The notion that scientific hypotheses, theories, or laws are wholly discrete and independent is a naive and outdated view.

The term "crucial experiment" is not a useless one, however. Within the framework of accepted scientific theory that we are not concerned to question, a hypothesis *can* be subjected to a crucial experiment. If a negative result is obtained—that is, if some phenomenon fails to occur that had been predicted on the basis of the single dubious hypothesis together with accepted parts of scientific theory—then the experiment is crucial and the hypothesis is rejected. But there is nothing absolute about such a procedure, for even well-accepted scientific theories tend to be changed in the face of new and contrary evidence. Science is not monolithic, either in its practices or in its aims.

---

[33]This view has been argued persuasively by P. Duhem, *The Aim and Structure of Physical Theory*, trans. P. P. Wiener (Princeton, N.J.: Princeton University Press, 1954). A challenging objection to it can be found in Adolf Grunbaum, "The Duhemian Argument," *Philosophy of Science*, Vol. 27, No. 1, January 1960. See also Sandra G. Harding, ed., *Can Theories Be Refuted? Essays on the Duhem–Quine Thesis* (Boston: D. Reidel Publishing Co., 1976).

Perhaps the most significant lesson to be learned from the preceding discussion is the importance to scientific progress of dragging "hidden assumptions" into the open. That light travels in straight lines was assumed in the arguments of Columbus and Copernicus, but it was a hidden assumption. Because they are hidden, there is no chance to examine such assumptions critically and to decide intelligently whether they are true or false. Progress is often achieved by formulating explicitly an assumption that had previously been hidden, and then scrutinizing and rejecting it. An important and dramatic instance of this occurred when Einstein challenged the universally accepted assumption that it always makes sense to say of two events that they occurred *at the same time*. In considering how an observer could discover whether or not two distant events occurred "at the same time," Einstein was led to the conclusion that two events could be simultaneous for some observers but not for others, depending upon their locations and velocities relative to the events in question. Rejecting the assumption led to the Special Theory of Relativity, which constituted a tremendous step forward in explaining such phenomena as those revealed by the Michelson–Morley experiment. It is clear that an assumption must be recognized before it can be challenged. Hence it is enormously important in science to formulate explicitly all relevant assumptions in any hypothesis, allowing none of them to remain hidden.

13.7 *Classification as Hypothesis*

It might be objected that hypotheses play important roles only in the more advanced sciences, not in those that are relatively less advanced. It may be urged that although explanatory hypotheses may be central to such sciences as physics and chemistry, they play no such role—at least not yet—in the biological or social sciences. The latter are still in their descriptive phases, and it may be felt that the method of hypothesis is not relevant to the so-called descriptive sciences, such as botany or history. This objection is easily answered. An examination of the nature of description will show that description itself is based on or embodies hypotheses. Hypotheses are as basic to the various systems of taxonomy or classification in biology as they are in history or any of the other social sciences.

The importance of hypothesis in the science of history is easily shown and will be discussed first. Some historians believe that the study of history will reveal the existence of a single cosmic purpose or pattern, either religious or naturalistic, which accounts for or explains the entire course of recorded history. Others deny the existence of any such cosmic design but insist that the study of history will reveal certain historical laws that explain the actual sequence of past events and can be used to predict the future. On either of these views, the historian seeks explanations that must account for and be confirmed by the recorded events of the past. On either of these views, therefore, history is a theoretical rather than a merely descriptive science, and the role of hypothesis must be admitted as central in the historian's enterprise.

There is, however, a third group of historians who set themselves what is apparently a more modest goal. According to them, the task of historians is simply to chronicle the past, to set forth a bare description of past events in their chronological order. On this view, it might seem, "scientific" historians have no need of hypotheses, since their concern is with the facts themselves, not with any theories about them.

But past events are not so easily chronicled as this view implies. The past itself is simply not available for this kind of description. What *is* available are present records and traces of the past. These range all the way from official government archives of the recent past to epic poems celebrating the exploits of half-legendary heroes, and from the writings of older historians to artifacts of bygone eras unearthed in the excavations of archeologists. These are the only facts available to historians, and from them they must infer the nature of those past events it is their purpose to describe. Not *all* hypotheses are general; some are particular. The historian's description of the past is a particular hypothesis that is intended to account for present data, and for which the present data constitute evidence.

Historians are detectives on a grand scale.[34] Their methods are the same, and their difficulties too. The evidence is scanty, and much of it has been destroyed—if not by the bungling local constabulary, then by intervening wars and natural disasters. And just as the criminal may have left false or misleading clues to throw pursuers off the scent, so many present "records" are falsifications of the past they purport to describe, either intentional, as in the case of such forged historical documents as the "Donation of Constantine," or unintentional, as in the writings of early uncritical historians. Just as the detective must use the method of science in formulating and testing hypotheses, so the historian must make hypotheses too. Even those historians who seek to limit themselves to bare descriptions of past events must work with hypotheses: they are theorists in spite of themselves.

Biologists are in a somewhat more favorable position. The facts with which they deal are present and available for inspection. To describe the flora and fauna of a given region, they need not make elaborate inferences of the sort to which historians are condemned. The data can be perceived directly. Their descriptions of these items are not casual, of course, but systematic. They are usually said to *classify* plants and animals, rather than merely to describe them. But classification and description are really the same process. To describe a given animal as carnivorous is to classify it as a carnivore; to classify it as a reptile is to describe it as reptilian. To describe any object as having a certain attribute is to classify it as a member of the class of objects having that attribute.

[34]See Robin W. Winks, ed., *The Historian as Detective: Essays on Evidence* (New York: Harper & Row, Publishers, Inc., 1969).

Classification, as generally understood, involves not merely a single division of objects into separate groups but further subdivision of each group into subgroups or subclasses, and so on. This pattern is familiar to most of us, if not from our various studies in school, then certainly from playing the old game of "Animal, Vegetable, or Mineral?" or its more recent version, "Twenty Questions." Apart from such games, there are many motives that have led people to classify objects. For primitive people to live, they were required to classify roots and berries as edible or poisonous, animals as dangerous or harmless, and other tribes as friends or enemies. People tend to draw distinctions that are of practical importance to them and to neglect those that play a less immediate role in their affairs. A farmer will classify grains and vegetables carefully and in detail but may call all flowers "posies," whereas florists will classify their merchandise with the greatest of care but may lump all the farmer's crops together as "produce." There are several motives that may lead us to classify things. One is practical, another theoretical. Having only three or four books, one could know them all well and could easily take them all in at a glance, so there would be no need to classify them. But in a public or college library containing many thousands of volumes, the situation is different. If the books there were not classified, the librarian could not find the books that might be wanted, and the collection would be practically useless. The larger the number of objects, the greater is the need for classifying them. A practical purpose of classification is to make large collections accessible. This is especially apparent in the case of libraries, museums, and public records halls of one sort or another.

In considering the theoretical purpose of classification, we must realize that the adoption of this or that alternative classification scheme is not anything that can be true or false. Objects can be described in different ways, from different points of view. The scheme of classification adopted depends upon the purpose or interest of the classifier. Books, for example, would be classified differently by a librarian, a bookbinder, and a bibliophile. The librarian would classify them according to their contents or subject matter, the bookbinder according to their bindings and a bibliophile according to their date of printing or perhaps their relative rarity. The possibilities are not thereby exhausted, of course: a book packer would divide books according to their shapes and sizes, and persons with still other interests would classify them differently in the light of those different interests.

Now what special interest or purpose do scientists have that can lead them to prefer one scheme of classification to another? The scientist's aim is knowledge, not merely of this or that particular fact for its own sake, but knowledge of the general laws to which they conform and their causal interrelations. One classification scheme is better than another, from the scientist's point of view, to the extent that it is more fruitful in suggesting scientific laws and more helpful in the formulation of explanatory hypotheses.

The theoretical or scientific motive for classifying objects is the desire to increase our knowledge of them. Increased knowledge of things is further insight into their attributes, their similarities and differences, and their interrelations. A classification scheme made for narrowly practical purposes may tend to obscure important similarities and differences. Thus a division of animals into dangerous and harmless will assign the wild boar and the rattlesnake to one class and the domestic pig and the grass snake to the other, calling attention away from what we should today regard as more profound similarities in order to emphasize superficial resemblances. A scientifically fruitful classification of objects requires considerable knowledge about them. A slight acquaintance with their more obvious characteristics would lead one to classify the bat with birds, as flying creatures, and the whale with fishes, as creatures that live in the sea. But a more extensive knowledge would lead us to classify both bats and whales as mammals, because being warm blooded, bearing their young alive, and suckling them are more important characteristics on which to base a classificatory scheme.

A characteristic is important when it serves as a clue to the presence of other characteristics. An important characteristic, from the point of view of science, is one that is causally connected with many other characteristics, and hence relevant to the framing of a maximum number of causal laws and the formulation of very general explanatory hypotheses. That classification scheme is best, then, which is based on the most important characteristics of the objects to be classified. But we do not know in advance what causal laws obtain, and causal laws themselves partake of the nature of hypotheses, as was emphasized in the preceding chapter. Therefore any decision as to which classification scheme is best is itself a hypothesis that subsequent investigations may lead us to reject. If later investigations revealed *other* characteristics to be more important, that is, involved in a greater number of causal laws and explanatory hypotheses, it would be reasonable to expect the earlier classification scheme to be rejected in favor of a newer one based upon the more important characteristics.

This view of classification schemes as hypotheses is borne out by the actual role such schemes play in the sciences. Taxonomy is a legitimate, important, and still growing branch of biology, in which some classification schemes, like that of Linnaeus, have been adopted, used, and subsequently abandoned in favor of better ones, which are themselves in turn subject to modification in the light of new data. Classification is generally most important in the early or less developed stages of a science. It need not always diminish in importance as the science develops, however. For example, the standard classification scheme for the elements, as set forth in Mendeleeff's table, is still an important tool for the chemist.

In the light of the foregoing discussion, a further remark can be made on the role of hypothesis in the science of history. It has already been remarked that the historian's descriptions of past events are themselves hypotheses based on present data. There is an additional, equally significant role that hypotheses play in the descriptive historian's enterprise. It is obvious that no historical era or event of any magnitude can be described in *complete detail*. Even if all its details could be known, historians could not possibly include them all in their narratives. Life is too short to permit an exhaustive description of anything. Historians must therefore describe the past selectively, recording only some of its aspects. Upon what basis shall they make their selection? Clearly, historians want to include what is significant or important in their descriptions, and to ignore what is insignificant or trivial. The subjective bias of this or that historian may lead to laying undue stress on the religious, the economic, the personal, or some other aspect of the historic process. But to the extent that they can make an objective or scientific appraisal, historians will regard those aspects as important which enter into the formulation of causal laws and general explanatory hypotheses. Such appraisals are, of course, subject to correction in the light of further research.

The first Western historian, Herodotus, described a great many aspects of the events he chronicled, personal and cultural as well as political and military. The so-called first scientific historian, Thucydides, restricted himself much more to the political and the military. For a long period of time, most historians followed Thucydides, but now the pendulum is swinging in another direction, and the economic and cultural aspects of the past are being given increased emphasis. Just as biologists' classification schemes embody their hypotheses as to which characteristics of living things are involved in a maximum number of causal laws, so historians' decisions to describe past events in terms of one rather than another set of characteristics embody their hypotheses as to which characteristics are causally related to a maximum number of others. Some such hypotheses are required before historians can even begin any systematic description of the past. It is this hypothetical character of classification and description, whether biological or historical, that leads us to regard hypothesis as the all-pervasive method of scientific inquiry.

EXERCISES

In each of the following passages

a. What data are to be explained?
b. What hypotheses are proposed to explain them?
c. Evaluate the hypotheses in terms of the criteria presented in Section 13.3.

★ 1. The distant universe looks quite different froom the nearby universe. To explain this, astronomers adopt an evolutionary hypothesis. Distant objects, they believe, are young objects. The signals we get from them, delivered here at the speed of light, were emitted when the objects were in an earlier stage of development than we see in the local region. If, for example, one of MacAlpine's survey objects [quasars—quasi-stellar objects whose light has traveled some billions of years to reach us] were one and one-half billion parsecs away, its light would have originated at a time when our own solar system was still forming and our sun quite young. What was our galaxy like at that time? It is hard to know except to infer that perhaps it looked then like quasars look to us today.

—BLANCHARD HIATT, *University of Michigan Research News,*
Vol. 30, Nos. 8–9, August–September 1979

2. In the United States, regardless of the way health is measured (mortality, morbidity, symptoms, or subjective evaluation), and regardless of the unit of observation (individuals, city or state averages), *years of schooling usually emerges as the most powerful correlate of good health.* Michael Grossman, an economist who has done extensive research on this question, has tended to interpret this relationship as evidence that *schooling increases the individual's efficiency in producing health,* although he recognizes that some causality may run from better health to more schooling. The way schooling contributes to efficiency in producing health has never been made explicit, but Grossman has speculated that persons with more education might choose healthier diets, be more aware of health risks, choose healthier occupations, and use medical care more wisely.

—VICTOR R. FUCHS, "The Economics of Health in a Post-Industrial Society,"
The Public Interest, Summer 1979

3. The central geographical and climatic characteristic of North Africa and the Mideast is its aridity. A current hypothesis is that there exists a feed-back relationship between the plant growth of a marginally arid area and its rainfall. If for some reason—overgrazing, for example—the area is partially denuded of growth, its albedo, or reflectivity, will increase. A greater percentage of sunlight is returned to space, the corresponding heat loss is compensated by sinking air motions; and mean cloudiness, and hence mean rainfall, decreases. Then plant growth decreases still further, and a feed-back, or vicious circle, mechanism is set in motion.

—MORTON G. WURTELE and JEHUDA NEUMANN,
"Some Areas for International Cooperation in the Geophysical Sciences,"
Middle East Review, Vol. 10, Spring 1978

4. One of the most challenging problems in all of social science has been untangling the environmental and genetic influences of the family on children's intellectual, occupational, and economic attainments. The educational level of parents correlates fairly well with both school achievement and mental ability test scores of their children. This correlation is usually assumed to indicate the strength of the influence of environment on school success, since parents with more years of schooling tend to expect their chldren to do well in school and create a richer educational environment in the home than do poorly educated parents. If the causal connection runs from the rich family environment to the academic-ability level of the child, then it makes sense to try to induce all parents to provide more educative environments, as a way of improving school performance of educationally disadvantaged children.

If mental ability is to some extent inherited, however, a different set of causal linkages may be involved: Parents possessing high levels of mental ability will tend to spend more years in school than others do, will pass on some of their ability to their children, *and* will create more educative home environments. In this view, correlation between home environment and the child's academic performance may mask a more important genetic relation between parents' abilities and children's abilities.

—HARRY L. MILLER, "Hard Realities and Soft Social Science,"
The Public Interest, Spring 1980

★ 5. The mechanism of stimulus and response in geotropism has often been studied. If very young seedlings in which the root and stem are just appearing are fixed in any position whatever, the young root will invariably grow downward and the young stem upward. The English horticulturalist Knight, more than a century ago, suggested that this behavior was due to gravity. He reasoned that if this were so, it should be possible to substitute a stronger force for gravity and thus to change the direction of growth. Knight fastened young plants in various positions to the rim of a wheel, which he revolved rapidly in a horizontal plane, thus subjecting the plants to a "centrifugal force" greater than gravity. Under these conditions the roots grew outward, in the direction of the centrifugal pull, and the stems grew inward, toward the hub, in an exactly opposite direction. Knight thus proved that plant structures orient themselves to this force in just the same way that they do to gravity.

—EDMUND W. SINNOTT and KATHERINE S. WILSON,
Botany: Principles and Problems

6. On the 7th of January 1610, at one o'clock in the morning, when he directed his telescope to Jupiter, he observed three stars near the body of the planet, two being to the east and one to the west of him. They were all in a straight line, and parallel to the ecliptic, and they appeared brighter than other stars of the same magnitude. Believing them to be fixed stars, he paid no great attention to their distances from Jupiter and from one another. On the 8th of January, however, when, from some cause or other, he had been led to observe the stars again, he found a very different arrangement of them: all the three were on the west side of Jupiter, *nearer one another than before,* and almost at equal distances. Though he had not turned his attention to the extraordinary fact of the mutual approach of the stars, yet he began to consider how Jupiter could be found to the east of the three stars, when but the day before he had been to the west of two of them. The only explanation which he could give of this fact was, that the motion of Jupiter was *directly* contrary to astronomical calculations, and that he had got before these two stars by his own motion.

In this dilemma between the testimony of his senses and the results of calculation, he waited for the following night with the utmost anxiety; but his hopes were disappointed, for the heavens were wholly veiled in clouds. On the 10th, two only of the stars appeared, and both on the east of the planet. As it was obviously impossible that Jupiter could have advanced from west to east on the 8th of January, and from east to west on the 10th, Galileo was forced to conclude that the phenomenon which he had observed arose from the motion of the stars, and he set himself to observe diligently their change of place. On the 11th, there were still only two stars, and both to the east of Jupiter; but the more eastern star was now *twice as large as the other one,* though on the preceding night they had been perfectly equal. This fact threw a new light upon Galileo's difficulties, and he immediately drew the conclusion, which he considered to be indubitable, *"that there were in the heaven three stars which revolved round Jupiter, in the same manner as Venus and Mercury revolved round the sun."* On the 12th of January, he again observed them in new positions, and of different magnitudes; and, on the 13th, he discovered a fourth star, which completed the *four* secondary planets with which Jupiter is surrounded.   —SIR DAVID BREWSTER, *The Martyrs of Science*

7. Again however solid things are thought to be, you may yet learn from this that they are of rare body: in rocks and caverns the moisture of water oozes through and all things weep with abundant drops; food distributes itself through the whole body of living things; trees grow and yield fruit in season, because

food is diffused through the whole from the very roots over the stem and all the boughs. Voices pass through walls and fly through houses shut, stiffening frost pierces to the bones. Now if there are no void parts, by what way can the bodies severally pass? You would see it to be quite impossible. Once more, why do we see one thing surpass another in weight though not larger in size? For if there is just as much body in a ball of wool as there is in a lump of lead, it is natural it should weigh the same, since the property of body is to weigh all things downwards, while on the contrary the nature of void is ever without weight. Therefore when a thing is just as large, yet is found to be lighter, it proves sure enough that it has more of void in it; while on the other hand that which is heavier shows that there is in it more of body and that it contains within it much less of void. Therefore that which we are seeking with keen reason exists sure enough, mixed up in things; and we call it void.   —LUCRETIUS, *On the Nature of Things*, Book I

8. While walking one night with Dr. Frink, we accidentally met a colleague, Dr. P., whom I had not seen for years, and of whose private life I knew nothing. We were naturally very pleased to meet again, and on my invitation, he accompanied us to a café, where we spent about two hours in pleasant conversation. To my question as to whether he was married, he gave a negative answer, and added, "Why should a man like me marry?"

On leaving the café, he suddenly turned to me and said: "I should like to know what you would do in a case like this: I know a nurse who was named as co-respondent in a divorce case. The wife sued the husband for divorce and named her as co-respondent, and *he* got the divorce." I interrupted him saying, "You mean *she* got the divorce." He immediately corrected himself saying, "Yes, she got the divorce," and continued to tell how the excitement of the trial had affected this nurse to such an extent that she became nervous and took to drink. He wanted me to advise him how to treat her.

As soon as I had corrected his mistake, I asked him to explain it, but, as is usually the case, he was surprised at my question. He wanted to know whether a person had no right to make mistakes in talking. I explained to him that there is a reason for every mistake, and that if he had not told me that he was unmarried, I should say that he was the hero of the divorce case in question, and that the mistake showed that he wished he had obtained the divorce instead of his wife, so as not to be obliged to pay alimony and to be permitted to marry again in New York State.

He stoutly denied my interpretation, but his emotional agitation, followed by loud laughter, only strengthened my suspicions. To my appeal that he should tell the truth "for science' sake" he said, "Unless you wish me to lie, you must believe that I was never married, and hence, your psychoanalytic interpretation is all wrong." He, however, added that it was dangerous to be with a person who paid attention to such little things. Then he suddenly remembered that he had another appointment and left us.

Both Dr. Frink and I were convinced that my interpretation of his *lapsus linguae* was correct, and I decided to corroborate or disprove it by further investigation. The next day, I found a neighbor and old friend of Dr. P., who confirmed my interpretation in every particular. The divorce was granted to Dr. P's wife a few weeks before, and a nurse was named as co-respondent. A few weeks later, I met Dr. P., and he told me that he was thoroughly convinced of the Freudian mechanisms.   —A. A. BRILL, *Psychoanalysis: Its Theories and Practical Applications*

9. Like multiple sclerosis, poliomyelitis in its paralytic form was a disease of the more advanced nations rather than of the less advanced ones, and of economically better-off people rather than of the poor. It occurred in northern Europe and North America much more frequently than in southern Europe or the countries of Africa, Asia or South America. Immigrants to South Africa from northern Europe ran twice the risk of contracting paralytic poliomyelitis than South-African-born whites ran, and the South-African-born whites ran a much greater risk than nonwhites. Among the Bantu of South Africa paralytic poliomyelitis was rarely an adult disease. During World War II in North Africa cases of paralytic poliomyelitis were commoner among officers in the British and American forces than among men in the other ranks. At the time various wild hypotheses for the difference were proposed; it was even suggested that it arose from the fact that the officers drank whiskey whereas men in the other ranks drank beer!

We now understand very well the reason for the strange distribution of paralytic poliomyelitis. Until this century poliomyelitis was a universal infection of infancy and infants hardly ever suffered paralysis from it. The fact that they were occasionally so affected is what gave the disease the name "infantile paralysis." With the improvement of hygiene in the advancing countries of the world more and more people missed infection in early childhood and contracted the disease for the first time at a later age, when the risk that the infection will cause paralysis is much greater.

This explains why the first epidemics of poliomyelitis did not occur until this century and then only in the economically advanced countries.

—GEOFFREY DEAN, "The Multiple Sclerosis Problem,"
Scientific American, Vol. 223, No. 1, July 1970

★ 10. Since Venus rotates so slowly, we might be tempted to conclude that Venus, like Mercury, keeps one face always toward the Sun. If this hypothesis were correct we should expect that the dark side would be exceedingly cold. Pettit and Nicholson have measured the temperature of the dark side of Venus. They find that the temperature is not low, its value being only $-9°F.$, much warmer than our stratosphere in broad daylight. It is unlikely that atmospheric currents from the bright side of Venus could perpetually heat the dark side. The planet must rotate fairly often to keep the dark side from cooling excessively.

—FRED L. WHIPPLE, *Earth, Moon and Planets*

11. A large rock balanced on a small protuberance is an object of a certain wonder. Such rocks are not rare; for example, in Goblin Valley in southern Utah there are more than 1,000 of them. But how do the rocks stay balanced?

Balanced rocks originate when a bed of sediments is dissected by erosion until a column is formed. If the strata at the top of the column are harder than the strata farther down, erosion will whittle the softer rock down to a pillar narrower than the capstone.

Nothing about the erosion process, however, guarantees that the end product will be symmetrical, and so what keeps the capstone in place? Two investigators at Kansas State University, Wilson Tripp, an engineer, and Frederic C. Appl, whose specialty is rock mechanics, suggest that a dynamic process is responsible, that it starts when the capstone first begins to tilt in any direction and that the point of contact between the capstone and its supporting pillar continuously shifts, thereby remaining exactly under the capstone's center of gravity. The principle that underlies the process is simply that rock under the stress of compression is more resistant to erosion than unstressed rock.

When the capstone first begins to tilt, Tripp and Appl note, the movement will shift the stress of compression from one section of the supporting pillar to another. Thereafter the unstressed section will erode more rapidly than before and the stressed section will erode more slowly. Successive tilts in other directions will stress successive sections of the pillar, and the differential erosion that results will make the process self-leveling. As a consequence the capstone will remain poised on the pillar until the inevitable day when the area of contact becomes too small for the self-leveling to continue, and the balancing work, ceasing its apparent defiance of the laws of statistical mechanics, crashes satisfyingly to the ground.

—"Science and the Citizen," *Scientific American*, Vol. 230, No. 3, March 1974

12. Find a sociological puzzle, and one gets, usually, a slew of esoteric explanations, couched, of course, in opaque sociological jargon. Take the question which has befuddled a number of commentators recently: Why is it that women today seem to be marrying later than before? We shall not try to list all the ingenious explanations that have been advanced, from the rise of women's liberation to the increasing proportion of open homosexuality, male and female. Suffice to say that simple statistics, once understood, provide the most likely explanations. Here is Paul C. Glick, of the U.S. Bureau of the Census, writing in *Current Population Reports:*

> One of the tangible factors that probably helps to explain the increasing postponement of marriage is the 5-to-10-percent excess of women as compared with men during recent years in those ages when most first marriages occur (18 to 24 years for women and 20 to 26 years for men). This imbalance is a consequence of past fluctuations in the birth rate. For example, women born in 1947 after the baby boom had begun were ready to marry in 20 years, but the men they were most likely to marry were born in 1944 or 1945 (about one-half in each year) when the birth rate was still low; these men were about 8 percent less numerous than the 20-year-old women. (By contrast, girls who were born during the last 15 years, while the birth rate has been declining, will be scarce as compared with eligible men when they reach the main age for marriage.)

—VICTOR R. FUCHS, "The Economics of Health in a Post-Industrial Society," *The Public Interest*, Summer 1979

13. Early in the eighteenth century Edmund Halley asked: "Why is the sky dark at night?" This apparently naive question is not easy to answer, because if the universe had the simplest imaginable structure on the largest possible scale, the background radiation of the sky would be intense. Imagine a static infinite universe, that is, a universe of infinite size in which the stars and galaxies are stationary with respect to one another. A line of sight in any direction will ultimately cross the surface of a star, and the sky should appear to be made up of overlapping stellar disks. The apparent brightness of a star's surface is independent of its distance, so that everywhere the sky should be as bright as the surface of an average star. Since the sun is an average star, the entire sky, day and night, should be about as bright as the surface of the sun. The fact that it is not was later characterized as Olbers' paradox (after the 18th-century German astronomer Heinrich Olbers). The paradox applies not only to starlight but also

to all other regions of the electromagnetic spectrum. It indicates that there is something fundamentally wrong with the model of a static infinite universe, but it does not specify what.

> —ADRIAN WEBSTER, "The Cosmic Radiation Background,"
> *Scientific American*, August 1974

14. Toxin-antitoxin reactions were the first immunological processes to which experimental precision could be applied, and the discovery of principles of great importance resulted from such studies. . . . The simplest assumption to account for the manner in which an antitoxin renders a toxin innocuous would be that the antitoxin destroys the toxin. Roux and Buchner, however, advanced the opinion that the antitoxins did not act directly upon toxin, but affected it indirectly through the mediation of tissue cells. Ehrlich, on the other hand, conceived the reaction of toxin and antitoxin as a direct union, analogous to the chemical neutralization of an acid by a base.

The conception of toxin destruction was conclusively refuted by the experiments of Calmette. This observer, working with snake poison, found that the poison itself (unlike most other toxins) possessed the property of resisting heat to 100°C., while its specific antitoxin, like other antitoxins, was destroyed at or about 70°C. Nontoxic mixtures of the two substances, when subjected to heat, regained their toxic properties. The natural inference from these observations was that the toxin in the original mixture had not been destroyed, but had been merely inactivated by the presence of the antitoxin, and again set free after destruction of the antitoxin by heat.

> —HANS ZINSSER and STANHOPE BAYNE-JONES, *A Textbook of Bacteriology*

★ 15. Dr. Konrad Buettner of the University of California at Los Angeles has recently advanced the hypothesis that, during the lifetime of the moon, the everlasting influx of cosmic rays has slowly ground the upper-surface layers of rocks into fine dust. That the moon's skin cannot consist of solid rocks has been demonstrated through temperature measurements during lunar eclipses. As soon as the shadow of the earth creeps over the measuring area the temperature drops steeply, and after half an hour it is over 200°F. lower than it was in the full sun. When the shadow has passed by, the temperature again rises at a similarly steep rate. No solid piece of rock can cool down and heat up so quickly. These drastic temperature changes can be explained only by the existence of a thick layer of heat-insulating dust as fine as face powder. The thickness of the layer must be at least several inches. The sandblasting of meteoric dust also grinds at the moon's surface, but cosmic rays can be expected to do a much better job.

> —HEINZ HABER, *Man in Space*

14

Probability

14.1 *Alternative Conceptions of Probability*

The words "probable" and "probability" have been frequently used thus far
in our discussion of inductive logic and scientific method. Even a hypothesis
that fits all the available facts is not thereby established conclusively, it was
said, but only *with probability*. And the most protracted and careful uses of
Mill's Methods of experimental inquiry do not prove the truth of the laws to
which they lead, but only tend to confirm them as being highly *probable*. Even
the best inductive arguments fall short of that certainty that attaches to valid
deductive arguments.

The words "probable" and "probability" are used in various different
ways. We say, for example, that the probability of a tossed coin showing
heads is ½; that the probability of a twenty-five-year-old woman surviving
her twenty-sixth birthday is .971; and that, on the present evidence, it is
highly probable that Einstein's Theory of Relativity is correct. There are other
contexts in which the words "probable" and "probability" are used, as in
speaking of "probable errors" of measurement, and so on. But the first three
may be taken as the most important and typical uses of the terms. The third
is the most significant for scientific hypotheses. It differs from the first two
in not assigning any numerical coefficient of probability. *Degrees* of probability
are assigned to scientific hypotheses only in terms of more and less. Thus
the Darwinian theory is regarded as more probable than the account of creation given in the Book of Genesis, and the atomic theory has a higher degree

459

of probability than any of the recent highly speculative hypotheses concerning the inner structures of nuclei.

The first two of our three examples assign numbers as measures of the probabilities they assert. The sources of these numbers seem fairly clear. Coins have two sides, heads and tails, and when they fall, one side or the other must face upward. One chance out of two will place heads up, and so the probability ½ is assigned to heads. To arrive at the probability coefficient mentioned in the second example, mortality statistics must be gathered and compared. Of 1,000 women who celebrated their twenty-fifth birthday, it was found that 971 lived at least one additional year, and on the basis of these findings the figure .971 was assigned to the probability of a twenty-five-year-old woman's surviving her twenty-sixth birthday. Such probability measurements as these are utilized by life insurance companies in fixing the size of premiums to be charged for their policies.

As the first two examples may suggest, studies of probability are bound up with gambling and mortality statistics; in fact, the modern study of probability had its beginnings in these two fields. The theory of probability is commonly regarded as having begun with the correspondence between Blaise Pascal (1623–1662) and Pierre de Fermat (1608–1665) over the proper division of the stakes in an interrupted game of chance. Another version had it begin with Pascal's advice to the Chevalier de Mere, a notorious seventeenth-century gambler, on how to wager in throwing dice. In connection with the study of mortality, in 1662 Captain John Graunt published a discussion of the mortality records that had been kept in London since 1592. Possibly as a consequence of its mixed ancestry, probability has been given two different interpretations.

The classical theory of the nature of probability, as formulated by Laplace, De Morgan, Keynes, and others, regards it as measuring degree of *rational belief*. When we are completely convinced of something, the measure of our belief may have the number 1 assigned it. And when we are utterly certain that a specified event cannot possibly happen, our belief that it *will* happen can be assigned the number 0. Thus a rational person's belief that a tossed coin will *either* show heads or not show heads is 1, and his belief that it will *both* show heads and not show heads is 0. Where he is not sure, the degree of his reasonable belief will fall somewhere between 0 and 1. Probability is predicated of an event according to the degree to which one rationally believes that it will occur. Or probability may be predicated of a statement or proposition according to the degree to which a completely rational person will believe it.

On the classical view, probability is always a result of partial knowledge and partial ignorance. If the exact motion of one's fingers in flipping a coin were known, together with the initial position, dimensions, and weight distribution of the coin, one could predict its trajectory and final resting position with complete confidence. But such complete information is not available. Only some information is known: that the coin has only two sides, that it will fall, and so on. Consequently our belief that it will show heads is measured by a consideration of the various possibilities, which are 2, of which heads is only 1. Therefore the probability ½ is assigned to the event of the coin showing heads. Similarly, when a deck of cards is about to be dealt, the cards are in just the order they are and will come off the deck, in an honest deal, in exactly the sequence of spades and hearts and diamonds and clubs, aces and kings and queens and jacks, that is determined by their arrangement in the deck. But we do not know that arrangement. We know only that there are thirteen spades, out of fifty-two cards altogether, so the probability that the first card dealt will be a spade is exactly ¹³⁄₅₂ or ¼.

This view is known as the *a priori* theory of probability. It is so called because no trials need be run before the probability is assigned, no sample deals need be examined. All that is required is a knowledge of the antecedent conditions: that there are only thirteen spades in the deck, that there are fifty-two cards altogether, and that it is an honest deal, so that one card has as much chance as any other of being dealt first. On the *a priori* view, all we need do to compute the probability of an event's occurring in given circumstances is to divide the number of ways in which it can occur by the total number of possible outcomes of those circumstances, provided there is no reason to believe that any one of those possible outcomes is more likely than any other.

An alternative to the *a priori* view is the theory that regards probability as a measure of "relative frequency." The relative frequency theory seems especially suited to take account of probability judgments arising out of statistical investigations. Thus an actuary observes a number of women in order to determine what mortality rate they exhibit. Here we have a class and an attribute, the class being that of twenty-five-year-old women, the attribute that of surviving their twenty-sixth birthdays. The probability assigned is the measure of the relative frequency with which the members of the class exhibit the attribute in question. Of 1,000 twenty-five-year-old women, if 971 exhibit the attribute of surviving at least one additional year, the number .971 is assigned as the probability coefficient for the occurrence of this attribute in any such class. On the relative frequency theory of probability, then, probability is not defined in terms of rational belief. Probability is defined as the relative frequency with which members of a class exhibit a specified attribute.

The relative frequency theory, as its name implies, regards probability as relative. Thus if the question is raised as to the probability with which blondness of hair occurs, this varies with respect to the different reference classes relative to which the attribute may occur. For example, the probability of blondness is higher relative to the class of Scandinavians than it is relative to the total population of the world.

The *a priori* theory also regards probability as relative. In the language of the classical *a priori* theory, no event has any *intrinsic* probability. It can be assigned a probability only on the basis of the evidence available to the person making the assignment. This relativity is to be expected on a view that regards probability as a measure of rational belief, for a reasonable person's beliefs change according to the state of that person's knowledge. Suppose, for example, that two people are watching a deck of cards being shuffled. When the shuffle is finished, the dealer accidentally "flashes" the top card. One observer sees that the card is black, although he is not able to observe whether it is a spade or a club. But the second observer notices nothing. If the two observers are asked to estimate the probability of the first card's being a spade, the first observer will assign the probability ½, since there are only twenty-six black cards, of which half are spades. But the second observer will assign the probability ¼, since he knows only that there are thirteen spades in the deck of fifty-two cards. The two observers thus assign different probabilities to the same event. Has one of them made a mistake? Certainly not: each has assigned the correct probability *relative to the evidence available*. Both estimates are correct—even if the card turns out to be a club. No event has any probability *by itself*, which means that any prediction will have different probabilities in different contexts, that is, relative to different sets of evidence. It is important to notice that although an event has different probabilities relative to different amounts of evidence, it would be a mistake for anyone to use less than the total evidence available in judging probabilities.

Because of their agreement upon the relative nature of probability, adherents of both theories agree on the acceptability and utility of the probability calculus, of which an elementary presentation will be made in the following section.

14.2 *The Probability Calculus*

The probability calculus is a branch of pure mathematics that can be used in computing the probabilities of complex events from the probabilities of their component events. A complex event can be regarded as a whole of which its component events are parts. For example, the complex event of drawing two spades in succession from a deck of playing cards is a whole of which the two parts are the event of drawing the first spade and the event of getting a second spade on the very next draw. Again, the complex event of a bride and groom living to celebrate their golden wedding anniversary is a whole of which the parts are the event of the bride's living an additional fifty years, the groom's living an additional fifty years, and no separation taking place. When it is known how the component events are related to each other, the probability of the complex event can be *calculated* from the probabilities of its components. Although the probability calculus has a much wider range of applications, it is most easily explained in terms of games of chance, so most of our examples and illustrations in this section will be drawn from the sphere of gambling. And the *a priori* theory will be used here, though it should be emphasized that all our results, with a minimum of reinterpretation, can be expressed and justified in terms of the relative frequency theory.

1. Joint Occurrences

Let us first turn our attention to complex events having as their component parts events that are *independent*. Two events are said to be *independent* if the occurrence or nonoccurrence of either of them has absolutely no effect on the occurrence or nonoccurrence of the other. For example, if two coins are tossed, whether one comes down heads or tails has no effect upon whether the other shows heads or tails. Let us pose as our first problem: what is the probability of getting two heads in tossing two coins? There are three possible outcomes to tossing two coins: we may get two heads, or we may get two tails, or we may get one head and one tail. *But these are not equipossible alternatives,* for there are two ways of getting one head and one tail, as contrasted with only one way of getting two heads. The first coin may be heads and the second tails, or the first coin may be tails and the second one heads; these are two distinct cases. There are four distinct possible events that may occur when two coins are tossed; they may be listed as follows:

First Coin	Second Coin
H	H
H	T
T	H
T	T

There is no reason for expecting any one of these cases to occur rather than any other, so we regard them as equipossible. The *favorable* case, that of getting two heads, is only one of four equipossible events, so the probability of getting two heads in tossing two coins is ¼. The probability for this complex event may be calculated from the probabilities of its two independent component events. The complex event of getting two heads is constituted by the joint occurrence of the event of getting a head on the first and the event of getting a head on the second. The probability of getting a head on the first is ½, and the probability of getting a head on the second is also ½. The events are presumed to be independent, so the *product theorem* of the probability calculus can be used to compute the probability of their joint occurrence. The product theorem for independent events asserts that the probability of the joint occurrence of two independent events is equal to the product of their separate probabilities. The general formula may be written

$$P(a \text{ and } b) = P(a) \times P(b)$$

where a and b are the two independent events, $P(a)$ and $P(b)$ are their separate probabilities, and $P(a \text{ and } b)$ designates the probability of their joint occurrence. In the present case, since a is the event of the first coin falling heads, and *b* is the event of the second coin falling heads, $P(a) = \frac{1}{2}$ and $P(b) = \frac{1}{2}$, so $P(a \text{ and } b) = \frac{1}{2} \times \frac{1}{2} = \frac{1}{4}$.

Let us consider a second problem of the same sort. What is the probability of getting a 12 in rolling two dice? Two dice will show twelve points only if each of them shows six points. Each die has six sides, any one of which is as likely to be face up after a roll as any other. Where *a* is the event of the first die showing a 6, $P(a) = \frac{1}{6}$. And where *b* is the event of the second die showing a 6, $P(b) = \frac{1}{6}$. *The complex event of the two dice showing a 12 is constituted by the joint occurrence of a and b.* By the product theorem, then $P(a \text{ and } b) = \frac{1}{6} \times \frac{1}{6} = \frac{1}{36}$, which is the probability of getting a 12 on one roll of two dice. We can arrive at the same result by taking the trouble to enumerate all the possible events that may occur when two dice are rolled. There are thirty-six equipossible events, which may be listed as follows, where of each pair of numbers the first stands for the number on the top face of the first die, the second for the number showing on the second one:

1–1	2–1	3–1	4–1	5–1	6–1
1–2	2–2	3–2	4–2	5–2	6–2
1–3	2–3	3–3	4–3	5–3	6–3
1–4	2–4	3–4	4–4	5–4	6–4
1–5	2–5	3–5	4–5	5–5	6–5
1–6	2–6	3–6	4–6	5–6	6–6

Of these thirty-six equipossible cases, only one is favorable (to getting a 12), so the probability is thus seen directly to be $\frac{1}{36}$.

The product theorem may be *generalized* to cover the joint occurrence of *any* number of independent events. Thus if we draw a card from a deck, replace it and draw again, and replace it and draw once more, the event of drawing three spades is the joint occurrence of the event of getting a spade on the first draw, the event of getting a spade on the second draw, and the event of getting a spade on the third draw. Where these three events are designated by *a*, *b*, and *c*, their joint probability $P(a \text{ and } b \text{ and } c)$ is equal to the product of the separate probabilities of the three events: $P(a) \times P(b) \times P(c)$. The probability is easily computed. A deck of cards contains fifty-two different cards of which thirteen are favorable to the event of drawing a spade. The probability of getting a spade is $\frac{13}{52}$ or $\frac{1}{4}$. Since the card drawn is replaced before drawing again, the initial conditions for the second drawing are the same, so each of $P(a)$, $P(b)$, and $P(c)$ is equal to $\frac{1}{4}$. *Their joint occurrence has the probability* $P(a \text{ and } b \text{ and } c) = \frac{1}{4} \times \frac{1}{4} \times \frac{1}{4} = \frac{1}{64}$. The General Product Theorem allows us to compute the probability of the joint occurrence of any number of independent events. Next we turn to events that are *not* independent.

It is frequently possible to compute the probability of the joint occurrence of several events even when they are not completely independent. In the previous example, if the card drawn is *not* replaced in the deck before the next drawing, the outcomes of the earlier drawings *do* have an effect on the outcomes of the later drawings. If the first card drawn is a spade, then for the second draw there are only twelve spades left among a total of fifty-one cards, whereas if the first card is *not* a spade, then there are thirteen spades left among fifty-one cards. Where *a* is the event of drawing a spade from the deck and not replacing it, and *b* is the event of drawing another spade from among the remaining cards, then the probability of *b*, P (*b* if *a*), is $12/51$ or $4/17$. And if both *a* and *b* occur, the third draw will be made from a deck of fifty cards containing only eleven spades. If *c* is this last event, then P (*c* if both *a* and *b*) is $11/50$. Thus the probability that all three are spades if three cards are drawn from a deck and not replaced is, according to the product theorem, $13/52 \times 12/51 \times 11/50$, or $11/850$. This is *less* than the probability of getting three spades in three draws when the cards drawn are replaced before drawing again, which was to be expected, since replacing a spade increases the probability of getting a spade on the next draw.

Let us consider another example involving the probability of the joint occurrence of dependent events. Suppose we have an urn containing two white balls and one black ball. If two balls are drawn in succession, the first one *not* being replaced before drawing the second, what is the probability that both balls drawn will be white? Let *a* be the event of drawing a white ball on the first draw. There are three equipossible draws, one for each ball. Of these, two are favorable, since two of the balls are white. The probability of getting a white ball on the first draw, $P(a)$, is therefore $2/3$. If *a* occurs, then there remain only two balls in the urn, one white and one black. The probability of getting a white ball on the second draw, which event we may call "*b*," is clearly $1/2$; that is, P (*b* if *a*) $= 1/2$. Now by the general product theorem, the probability of getting two white balls is the probability of the joint occurrences of *a* and (*b* if *a*), which is the product of the probabilities of their separate occurrence, $2/3 \times 1/2 = 1/3$. The general formula here is $P(a \text{ and } b) = P(a) \times P(b \text{ if } a)$. The probability of getting two white balls in two such successive draws can be reached, in this simple situation, by considering all possible cases. Where one white ball is designated by W_1 and the other white ball by W_2 and the black ball by B, the following equipossible pairs of draws may be listed:

First Draw	Second Draw
W_1	W_2
W_1	B
W_2	W_1
W_2	B
B	W_1
B	W_2

Of these six equipossible events, two are favorable (the first and third), which gives $1/3$ directly as the probability of getting two white balls in two successive draws with no replacement made.

EXERCISES

★ 1. What is the probability of getting tails every time in three tosses of a coin?

2. What is the probability of getting three aces in three successive draws from a deck of cards (a) if the card drawn is replaced before making the next drawing, (b) if the cards drawn are not replaced?

3. An urn contains twenty-seven white balls and forty black balls. What is the probability of getting four black balls in four successive drawings (a) if each ball drawn is replaced before making the next drawing, (b) if the balls are not replaced?

4. What is the probability of rolling three dice so the total number of points that appear on their top faces is 3, three times in a row?

★ 5. Four men whose houses are built around a square spend an evening celebrating in the center of the square. At the end of the celebration each staggers off to one of the houses, no two going to the same house. What is the probability that each one reached his own house?

6. A dentist has her office in a building with five entrances, all equally accessible. Three patients arrive at her office at the same time. What is the probability that they all entered the building by the same door?

7. Suppose that the probability that a man of twenty-five will survive his fiftieth birthday is .742 and that the probability that a woman of twenty-two will survive her forty-seventh birthday is .801. Suppose further that the probability that a marriage contract by such a couple will not end in divorce during the first twenty-five years is .902. What is the probability that such a couple will live to celebrate their silver wedding anniversay?

8. In each of two closets there are three cartons. Five of the cartons contain canned vegetables. The other carton contains canned fruits: ten cans of pears, eight cans of peaches, and six cans of fruit cocktail. Each can of fruit cocktail contains three hundred chunks of fruit of approximately equal size, of which three are cherries. If a child goes into one of the closets, unpacks one of the cartons, opens a can and eats two pieces of its contents, what is the probability that two cherries will be eaten?

9. A player at draw poker holds the seven of spades and the eight, nine, ten, and ace of diamonds. Aware that all the other players are drawing three cards, he figures that any hand he could win with a flush he could also win with a straight. For which should he draw? (A *straight* consists of five cards in numerical sequence; a *flush* consists of five cards all of the same suit.)

10. How would you distribute fifty white balls and fifty black balls in two urns to maximize the probability that a random drawing of one ball from each urn would yield two white balls?

2. Alternative Occurrences

The preceding discussion dealt with complex events constituted by the joint occurrence of two or more component events. Some events whose probability it may be desired to compute are of a different sort. These may be constituted by the occurrence of one or more of several alternative events. For example, in tossing two coins, we may be interested not in the event of getting two heads but in the event of getting *either* two heads or two tails. These component events, one of getting two heads, the other of getting two tails, are *exclusive* events, that is, they cannot both occur. The formula for computing the probability of a complex event that is said to occur when either of two *mutually exclusive* events occurs is

$$P(a \text{ or } b) = P(a) + P(b)$$

That is, the probability that at least one of two mutually exclusive events occurs is the *sum* of their separate probabilities. Because the probability of getting two heads is ¼ and the probability of getting two tails is ¼, and because these are exclusive possibilities, the probability of getting *either* two heads or two tails is ¼ + ¼ = ½. This result may also be obtained, in this simple case, by considering that the four equipossible events that could occur when two coins are tossed are H–H, H–T, T–H, T–T, of which two, the first and fourth, are favorable to the event of getting either two heads or two tails. Here direct inspection shows the probability to be 2/4 or ½.

The *addition theorem* stated in the preceding paragraph obviously generalizes to the case of any number of exclusive alternative events. The product theorem and the addition theorem may be used together to compute the probabilities of complex events. Consider the problem of computing the probability of being dealt a flush in a poker game (a *flush* consists of five cards all of the same suit). There are four exclusive alternatives here: the event of getting five spades, the event of getting five hearts, the event of getting five diamonds, the event of getting five clubs. The probability of getting five spades, according to the product theorem for dependent probabilities, is 13/52 × 12/51 × 11/50 × 10/49 × 9/48 = 33/16,660. Each of the other exclusive alternatives has the same probability, so the probability of getting a flush is 33/66,640 + 33/66,640 + 33/66,640 + 33/66,640 = 33/16,660.

One more example will be considered. In drawing one ball from each of two urns, one containing two white balls and four black balls, the other containing three white balls and nine black balls, what is the probability of getting two balls of the same color? The event in whose probability we are interested is the alternative occurrence of two mutually exclusive events, one that of getting two white balls, the other that of getting two black balls. Their probabilities are to be computed separately and then added. The probability of getting two white balls is 2/6 × 3/12 = 1/12. And the probability of getting two black balls is 4/6 × 9/12 = ½. So the probability of getting two balls of the same color is 1/12 + ½ = 7/12.

The addition theorem applies only when the alternative events are mutually exclusive. It may, however, be required to compute the probabilities of complex events that are constituted by the occurrence of at least one of two or more alternatives that are *not* mutually exclusive. For example, what is the probability of getting at least one head on two tosses of a coin? Here we know that the probability of getting a head on the first toss is ½, and the probability of getting a head on the second toss is also ½; but the sum of these separate probabilities is 1, or certainty, and it is *not* certain that at least one toss will yield a head, because both may yield tails. The point here is that the two events are *not exclusive*; both may occur. In computing the probability of the alternative occurrence of nonexclusive events, the addition theorem is *not directly applicable*. There are, however, two methods that can be used in computing probabilities of this type.

The first method of computing the probability that at least one of two nonexclusive events will occur requires that we break down or analyze the favorable cases into exclusive events. In the problem of finding the probability that at least one head will appear in two tosses of a coin, the equipossible cases are H–H, H–T, T–H, T–T. These are all mutually exclusive, and each of them has the probability ¼. The first three are favorable, that is, if any one of the first three occurs, it will be true that at least one head appears in the two tosses. Hence the probability of getting at least one head is equal to the sum of the separate probabilities of all of the mutually exclusive favorable cases, which is ¼ + ¼ + ¼ = ¾.

The other method of computing the probability that at least one of two nonexclusive events will occur depends upon the fact that *no case can be both favorable and unfavorable*. If *a* designates an event, say, the event of getting at least one head on two tosses of a coin, then we shall use the notation $\bar{a}$ to designate the event *unfavorable* to *a*, that is, the event of not getting any head at all on two tosses of the coin. Since no case can be both favorable and unfavorable, *a* and $\bar{a}$ are *mutually exclusive*; that is, *a* and $\bar{a}$ cannot possibly both occur. And since every case must be either favorable or unfavorable, it is certain that either *a* or $\bar{a}$ must occur. Since zero is the probability coefficient we assign to an event that cannot possibly occur, and 1 is the probability coefficient assigned to an event that is certain to occur, the following two equations are true:

$$P(a \text{ and } \bar{a}) = 0$$
$$P(a \text{ or } \bar{a}) = 1$$

where $P(a \text{ and } \bar{a})$ is the probability that *a* and $\bar{a}$ will both occur, and $P(a \text{ or } \bar{a})$ is the probability that either *a* or $\bar{a}$ will occur. Since *a* and $\bar{a}$ are mutually exclusive, the addition theorem is applicable, and we have

$$P(a \text{ or } \bar{a}) = P(a) + P(\bar{a})$$

The last two equations combine to give

$$P(a) + P(\bar{a}) = 1$$

which yields

$$P(a) = 1 - P(\bar{a})$$

Hence we can compute the probability of an event's occurrence by computing the probability that the event will *not* occur and subtracting that figure from 1. Applied to the event of tossing at least one head in two tosses of a coin, we can easily see that the only case in which the event does *not* occur is when both tosses result in tails. This is the unfavorable case, and by the product theorem, its probability is $\frac{1}{2} \times \frac{1}{2} = \frac{1}{4}$, whence the probability that the event of getting at least one head in two tosses *does* occur is $1 - \frac{1}{4} = \frac{3}{4}$.

Another illustration of an event composed of alternative but nonexclusive occurrences is the following. If one ball is drawn from each of two urns, the first containing two white balls and four black balls, the second containing three white balls and nine black balls, what is the probability of getting at least one white ball? This problem can be solved in either of the two ways discussed in the two previous paragraphs. We can divide the favorable cases into mutually exclusive alternatives. These are a white ball from the first urn and a black ball from the second, a black ball from the first urn and a white ball from the second, and a white ball from both urns. The respective probabilities of these three are $\frac{2}{6} \times \frac{9}{12} = \frac{1}{4}$, $\frac{4}{6} \times \frac{3}{12} = \frac{1}{6}$, and $\frac{2}{6} \times \frac{3}{12} = \frac{1}{12}$. Then the addition theorem for exclusive alternatives gives us $\frac{1}{4} + \frac{1}{6} + \frac{1}{12} = \frac{1}{2}$ as the probability of getting at least one white ball. The other method is somewhat simpler. The unfavorable case in which the draw does not result in at least one white ball is the event of getting two black balls. The probability of getting two black balls is $\frac{4}{6} \times \frac{9}{12} = \frac{1}{2}$, so the probability of getting at least one white ball is $1 - \frac{1}{2} = \frac{1}{2}$.

Let us now attempt to work out a moderately complicated problem in probability. The game of craps is played with two dice. The *shooter*, who rolls the dice, wins if a 7 or an 11 turns up on the first roll, but loses if a 2, or 3, or 12 turns up on the first roll. If one of the remaining numbers, 4, 5, 6, 8, 9, or 10, turns up on the first roll, the shooter continues to roll the dice until either that same number turns up again, in which case the shooter wins, or a 7 appears, in which case the shooter loses. The problem can be posed: What is the probability that the shooter will win? First of all, let us obtain the probabilities that the various numbers will occur. There are thirty-six different equipossible ways for two dice to fall. Only one of these ways will show a 2, so the probability here is $\frac{1}{36}$. Only one of these ways will show a 12, so here the probability is also $\frac{1}{36}$. There are two ways to throw a 3: 1–2, and 2–1, so the probability of a 3 is $\frac{2}{36}$. Similarly, the probability of getting an 11 is $\frac{2}{36}$. There are three ways to throw a 4: 1–3, 2–2, and 3–1, so the probability of a 4 is $\frac{3}{36}$. Similarly, the probability of getting a 10 is $\frac{3}{36}$. Since there are four ways to roll a 5, 1–4, 2–3, 3–2, and 4–1, its probability is $\frac{4}{36}$, and this is also the probability of getting a 9. A 6 can be obtained in any one of five ways, 1–5, 2–4, 3–3, 4–2, and 5–1, so the probability of getting a 6 is $\frac{5}{36}$, and the same probability exists for an 8. There are six different combinations that yield 7, 1–6, 2–5, 3–4, 4–3, 5–2, 6–1, so the probability of rolling a 7 is $\frac{6}{36}$.

The probability that the shooter will win on the first roll is the sum of the probability that a 7 turns up and the probability that an 11 turns up, which is $\frac{6}{36} + \frac{2}{36} = \frac{8}{36}$ or $\frac{2}{9}$. The probability of losing on the first roll is the sum of the probabilities of getting a 2, a 3, and a 12, which is $\frac{1}{36} + \frac{2}{36} + \frac{1}{36} = \frac{4}{36}$ or $\frac{1}{9}$. The shooter is twice as likely to *win on the first roll* as to *lose on the first roll*; however, the shooter is most likely not to do either on the first roll, but to get a 4, 5, 6, 8, 9, or 10. If one of these six numbers is thrown, the shooter is obliged to continue rolling the dice until he rolls that number again, in which case he wins, or until a 7 comes up, which is a losing case. Those cases in which neither the number first thrown nor a 7 occurs can be ignored, for they are not decisive. Suppose the shooter gets a 4 on the first roll. The next *decisive* roll will show either a 4 or a 7. In a decisive roll, the equipossible cases are the three combinations that make up a 4 (1–3, 2–2, 3–1) and the six combinations that make up a 7. The probability of throwing a second 4 is therefore $\frac{3}{9}$. The probability of getting a 4 on the first roll was $\frac{3}{36}$, so the probability of winning by throwing a 4 on the first roll and then getting another 4 before a 7 occurs is $\frac{3}{36} \times \frac{3}{9} = \frac{1}{36}$. Similarly, the probability of the shooter winning by throwing a 10 on the first roll and then getting another 10 before a 7 occurs is also $\frac{3}{36} \times \frac{3}{9} = \frac{1}{36}$.

By the same line of reasoning, we can find the probability of the shooter winning by throwing a 5 on the first roll and then getting another before throwing a 7. In this case, there are ten equipossible cases for the decisive roll; the four ways to make a 5 (1–4, 2–3, 3–2, 4–1) and the six ways to make a 7. The probability of winning with a 5 is therefore $\frac{4}{36} \times \frac{4}{10} = \frac{2}{45}$. The probability of winning with a 9 is also $\frac{2}{45}$. The number 6 is still more likely to occur on the first roll, its probability being $\frac{5}{36}$. And it is more likely than the others mentioned to occur a second time before a 7 appears, the probability here being $\frac{5}{11}$. So the probability of winning with a 6 is $\frac{5}{36} \times \frac{5}{11} = \frac{25}{396}$. And again, similarly, the probability of winning with an 8 is $\frac{25}{396}$.

There are eight different ways for the shooter to win: if a 7 or 11 is thrown on the first roll or if one of the six numbers 4, 5, 6, 8, 9, or 10 is thrown on the first roll *and* again before a 7. These ways are all exclusive; so the total probability of the shooter's winning is the sum of the probabilities of the alternative ways in which winning is possible, and this is $\frac{6}{36} + \frac{2}{36} + \frac{1}{36} + \frac{2}{45} + \frac{25}{396} + \frac{25}{396} + \frac{2}{45} + \frac{1}{36} = \frac{244}{495}$. Expressed as a decimal fraction, this is .493. This shows that in a crap game the shooter has *less* than an even chance of winning—only slighty less, to be sure, but still less than .500.

EXERCISES

★ 1. Calculate the shooter's chances of winning in a crap game by the second method; that is, compute the chances of his losing, and subtract it from 1.

2. In drawing three cards in succession from a standard deck, what is the probability of getting at least one spade (a) if each card is replaced before making the next drawing, (b) if the cards drawn are not replaced?

3. What is the probability of getting at least one head in three tosses of a coin?

4. If three balls are selected at random from an urn containing five red, ten white, and fifteen blue balls, what is the probability that they will all be the same color (a) if each ball is replaced before the next one is withdrawn, (b) if the balls selected are not replaced?

★ 5. If someone offers to bet you even money that you will not throw an ace on any one of three successive throws of a die, should you accept the bet?

6. From a piggy bank containing three quarters, two dimes, five nickels, and eleven pennies, two coins are shaken out. What is the probability that their total value amounts to exactly

      (a) 50¢?   (b) 35¢?   (c) 30¢?   (d) 26¢?   (e) 20¢?
      (f) 15¢?   (g) 11¢?   (h) 10¢?   (i) 6¢?   (j) only 2¢?

7. If the probability that a man of twenty-five will survive his fiftieth birthday is .742, and the probability that a woman of twenty-two will survive her forty-seventh birthday is .801, and such a man and woman marry, what is the probability (a) that at least one of them lives at least another twenty-five years, (b) that only one of them lives at least another twenty-five years?

8. One partly filled case contains two bottles of root beer, four bottles of cola, and four bottles of beer; another partly filled case contains three bottles of root beer, seven colas, and two beers. A case is opened at random and a bottle selected at random from it. What is the probability that it contains a soft drink? Had all the bottles been in one case, what is the probability that a bottle selected at random from it would contain a soft drink?

9. A player in a draw-poker game is dealt three jacks and two small odd cards. He discards the latter and draws two cards. What is the probability that he improves his hand on the draw? (One way to improve it is to draw another jack to make four-of-a-kind; the other way to improve it is to draw any pair to make a full house.)

CHALLENGE TO THE READER

Sometimes the application of the calculus of probability leads to a correct result that is not what we would have supposed on a casual consideration of the facts given. Such a result is called counter-intuitive. Exercise 5 in this set (above) will be thought counter-intuitive by many.

The following problem has been a source of some controversy among probability theorists. Is the correct solution counter-intuitive?

10. Remove all cards except aces and kings from a deck, so that only eight cards remain, of which four are aces and four are kings. From this abbreviated deck, deal two cards to a friend. If she looks at her cards and announces (truthfully) that her hand contains an ace, what is the probability that both her cards are aces? If she announces instead that one of her cards is the ace of spades, what is the probability then that both her cards are aces? Are these two probabilities the same?[1]

---

[1]For some discussion of this problem see L. E. Rose, "Countering a Counter-Intuitive Probability," *Philosophy of Science*, Vol. 39, 1972, pp. 523–524; A. I. Dale, "On a Problem in Conditional Probability," *Philosophy of Science*, Vol. 41, 1974, pp. 204–206; R. Faber, "Re-encountering a Counter-Intuitive Probability," *Philosophy of Science*, Vol. 43, 1976, pp. 283–285; and S. Goldberg, "Copi's Conditional Probability Problem," *Philosophy of Science*, Vol. 43, 1976, pp. 286–289.

14.3 *Expectation or Expected Value*

In placing bets or making investments it is important to consider not only the probability of winning or receiving a return, but also *how much* can be won on the bet or returned on the investment. These two considerations, *safety* and *productivity*, often clash; greater potential returns usually entail greater risks. The safest investment may not be the best one to make, nor may the investment that promises the greatest return *if* it succeeds. The need to reconcile safety and maximum return confronts us not only in gambling and investing, but also in choosing among alternatives in education, employment, and other spheres of life. We would like to know whether the investment—of money or of time and energy—is "worth it," that is, whether that wager on the future is wise, all things considered. The future cannot be known, but the probabilities may be estimated. To compare investments, or bets, or "chancy" decisions of any kind the concept of *expected value* is a powerful tool.

Expected value may be best explained in the context of wagers whose outcomes have known probabilities. Any bet—say an even money bet of $1 that heads will appear on the toss of a coin—should be thought of as a purchase; the money is spent when the bet has been made. The dollar wagered is the price of the purchase; it buys some *expectation,* or *expected value.* If heads appears the bettor receives a return of *$2* (one his own, the other his winnings); if tails appears, the bettor receives *$0* return. There are only two possible outcomes of this wager, a head or a tail, the probability of each is known to be ½, and there is a specified return ($2, or $0) associated with each outcome. We multiply the return yielded on each possible outcome by the probability of that outcome's being realized; the sum of all such products is the expectation or expected value of the bet or investment. The expected value of a one dollar bet that heads will appear when a fair coin is tossed is thus equal to (½ × $2) + (½ × $0), which is $1. In this case, as we know, the "odds" are even—which means that the expected value of the purchase was equal to the purchase price.

But that is not always the case. We seek investments in which the expected value purchased is greater than the cost of our investment. We want the odds in our favor. Yet we are often tempted by wagers of which the expected value is less, sometimes much less, than the price of the gamble.

The disparity between the price and the expected value of a bet can be readily seen in a raffle, in which the purchase of a ticket offers a small chance at a large return. How much the raffle ticket is really worth depends upon how small the chance *and* how large the return. Suppose that the return, if we win it, is an automobile, worth $10,000, and the price of the raffle ticket is $1. If 10,000 raffle tickets are sold, of which we buy one, the probability of our winning is $\frac{1}{10,000}$. The chances of winning are thus very small, but the return if we win is very large. In this hypothetical case the expected value of the raffle ticket is ($\frac{1}{10,000}$ × $10,000) + ($\frac{9,999}{10,000}$ × $0), or precisely $1, the purchase price of the ticket. But the usual purpose of a raffle is to raise money for some worthy cause, and that can happen only if more money is collected from ticket sales than is paid out in prizes. Therefore many more than 10,000 tickets—perhaps 20 or 50 or even 100 thousand—will be sold. Suppose that 20,000 tickets are sold. The expected value of our $1 ticket then will be ($\frac{1}{20,000}$ × $10,000) + (19,999 × $0), or 50 cents. If 100,000 tickets are sold the expected value of the $1 ticket will be reduced to 10 cents, and so on. We may be confident that the expected value of any raffle ticket we are asked to buy will be substantially less than the amount we are asked to pay for it.

Lotteries are very popular because of the very large prizes that may be won. States and countries conduct lotteries because every ticket purchased buys an expected value equal to only a fraction of the ticket's price; those who run the lottery retain the difference, reaping huge profits.

The Michigan Lottery, played by more than two-thirds of the citizens of that state, is typical. Different bets are offered. In one game, called the "Daily 3," the player may choose (in a "straight bet") any three-digit number from 000 to 999. Each evening, after all bets are placed, a number is drawn at random and announced by the State; a player who has purchased a $1 straight-bet ticket that day on that winning number wins a prize of $500. The probability that the correct three digits in correct order have been selected is 1 in 1,000; the expected value of a $1 "Daily 3" straight-bet ticket is therefore $\frac{1}{1,000}$ × $500 plus $\frac{999}{1,000}$ × $0, or *50 cents*.

Lotteries and raffles are examples of great disparity between the price and the expected value of the gambler's purchase. Sometimes the disparity is small, but the number of purchasers nevertheless insures the profitability of the sale, as in gambling casinos, where every normal bet is one in which the purchase price is greater than the expected value bought. In the preceding section we determined, using the product theorem and the addition theorem of the calculus of probability, that the dice game called craps is one in which the shooter's chance of winning is .493—just a little less than even. But that game is widely and mistakenly believed to offer the shooting player an even chance. Betting on the shooter in craps, at even money, is therefore a leading attraction in American gambling casinos. But every such bet of $1 is a purchase of expected value equal to (.493 × $2) + (.507 × $0), which is 98.6 cents. The difference of approximately a penny and a half may seem trivial; but because casinos receive that advantage (and other like advantages on other wagers) in thousands of bets made each day on the dice tables, they are very profitable enterprises. In the gambling fraternity those who regularly bet on the shooter to win at craps are called "right bettors," and among professional gamblers it is commonly said that "all right bettors die broke."

Disparities of similar kind, in which every wager costs more than the expected value it buys, are to be found in analyzing all other bets in gambling casinos. The roulette wheel, the symbol of chance all over the world, gives a further illustration of these disparities. In roulette the numbers 1–36 appear (not in numerical order) around the circumference of a large wheel, and behind each number is a small groove. The wheel, carefully balanced so as to favor no number or section of the wheel, is spun vigorously, and a small steel ball is set spinning in the opposite direction just outside it and behind the numbers. The groove in which the ball comes finally to rest marks the one number that wins that game. The payoff for a bet on one number is 35-to-1. However, in addition to the 36 numbers colored alternately red and black around the rim of the wheel, there are two other numbers (0 and 00) colored green. The probability of winning a bet on any one number on the roulette wheel, therefore, is 1 in 38. The expected value of a $1 bet on a given number in roulette is therefore ($\frac{1}{38}$ × $36) + ($\frac{37}{38}$ × $0), or just under 95 cents.

In roulette one can also bet on groups of numbers, at odds that vary with the size of the group. One may wager that the ball will come to rest on any one of a group of three numbers, at the odds of 11 to 1, but the two green numbers keep the game profitable for the house. The probability of winning such a bet will be $\frac{3}{38}$, and the return, if one wagers $1 and wins, will be $12. The expected value of the bet on a group of three numbers ($\frac{3}{38}$ × $12 = 94.7) remains just under 95 cents. Or one may bet on a group of four numbers, the bet paying 8 to 1, ($\frac{4}{38}$ × $9 = 94.7) or on two numbers at odds of 17 to 1 ($\frac{2}{38}$ × 18 = 94.7)—but the expected value of all these wagers remains a little less than 95 cents. Instead of betting on one or a few numbers, one may bet on half of them—that the winning number will be red (or black), or that it will be even (or odd), but such bets, at even money, also lose if the ball comes to rest behind either of the two greens. Of the 38 possible outcomes 18 outcomes will yield a retur.. of $2 on a $1 bet on red, (or black, or even, or odd) and 20 outcomes will yield a return of $0. The expected value of such a bet is therefore ($\frac{18}{38}$ × $2) + ($\frac{20}{38}$ × $0) = 94.7—again just under 95 cents! Gambling casinos are not places in which prudent people spend their money.

The concept of expected value is of great practical use in helping one to decide how to save (or invest) one's money most wisely. Banks pay differing rates of interest on accounts of different kinds. Let us assume that the alternative bank accounts among which we choose are all government insured, and that therefore there is no chance of a loss of the principal. At the end of a full year the expected value of each $1,000 savings investment, at 5% simple interest, is ($1,000 [the principal that we know will be returned]) + (.05 × $1,000), or $1,050 in all. To complete the calculation, this return must be multiplied by the probability of our getting it—but here we assume, because the account is insured, that our getting it is certain, so we merely multiply by 1, or $\frac{100}{100}$. If the rate of interest is 6%, the insured return will be $1,060, and so on. The expected value purchased in such savings accounts is indeed greater than the deposit, the purchase price—but to get that interest income we must give up the use of our money for some period of time. The bank pays us for its use during that time because, of course, it plans to invest that money at yet higher rates of return.

Safety and productivity are considerations always in tension. If we are prepared to sacrifice a very small degree of safety for our savings, we may achieve a modest increase in the rate of return. For example, with that $1,000 we may purchase a corporate bond, perhaps paying 9 or even 10% interest, in effect lending our money to the company issuing the bond. The yield on our loan may be nearly double that of a bank savings account—but we will be running the risk, small but real, that the corporation issuing the bond will be unable to make payment when the loan we made to them falls due. In calculating the expected value of such a bond, say at 10%, the amount to be returned to the investor of $1,000 is determined in precisely the same way in which we calculated the yield on a savings account. First we calculate the return, if we get it: ($1,000 [the principal] + 10% × $1,000 [the interest]), or $1,100 total return. But in this case the probability of our getting that return is not $100/100$; it may be very high but it is not certain. The fraction by which that $1,100 return must therefore be multiplied is the probability, as best we can estimate it, that the corporation will be financially sound when its bond is due for payment. If we think this probability is very high—say, .99—we may conclude that the purchase of the corporate bond at 10% offers an expected value ($1,089) greater than that of the insured bank account at 6% ($1,060), and is therefore a wiser investment. Here is the comparison in detail:

Insured bank account at 6% simple interest for one year:

> Return = [principal + interest] = ($1,000 + $60) = $1,060
> Probability of return (assumed) = 1
> Expected value of investment in this bank account:
> ($1,060 × 1 = $1,069 + ($0 × 0 = $0) or *$1,069 total*

Corporate bond at 10% interest, at the end of one year:

> Return if we get it = [principal + interest] = ($1,000 + $100) = $1,100
> Probability of return (estimated) = .99
> Expected value of investment in this corporate bond:
> ($1,100 × .99 = $1,089) + ($0 × .01 = $0) or *$1,089 total*

However, if we conclude that the company to which we would be lending the money is not absolutely reliable, our estimated probability of ultimate return will drop, say, to .95, and the expected value will drop also:

Corporate bond at 10% interest, at the end of one year:

> Return if we get it = [principal + interest] = ($1,000 + $100) = $1,100
> Probability of return (new estimate) = .95
> Expected value of investment in this corporate bond:
> ($1,100 × .95 = $1,045) + ($0 × .05 = $0) or *$1,045 total*

If this were our judgment of the company selling the bond, then the bank account, paying a lower rate of interest with greater safety, will be judged the wiser investment.

In trying to predict the expected value of investments, by judging the soundness of companies and the like, we are estimating, explicitly or implicitly, the fractions which, at that time, we think best represent the likelihoods of the possible outcomes foreseen. These fractions we must multiply by the returns we anticipate in the event of those outcomes, before summing the products. All such predictions are necessarily speculative, and the outcomes calculated therefore uncertain, of course. But, when we can determine the approximate value of a given return *if* we achieve it, we can—by doing calculations of the kind here described—determine what probability those outcomes *need* to have (given present evidence) in order that our investment now, our gamble on those outcomes, be worthwhile. Many decisions in financial matters, but also very many choices in ordinary life, depend on such estimates of probability and resultant expected value.

It is sometimes argued that in a game in which there are even-money stakes to be awarded on the basis of approximately equiprobable alternatives, such as tossing a coin or betting black versus red on a roulette wheel, one can be *sure to win* by making the same bet consistently—always heads, or always black, say—and doubling the amount of money wagered after each loss. Thus if I bet $1 on heads, and tails show, then I should bet heads again to the tune of $2. If tails show again, my next bet—also on heads—should be $4, and so on. One cannot fail to win by following this procedure, because extended runs are highly improbable; the longest run must *sometimes* end— and, when it does, the person who has pyramided or continued to double the bet will be money ahead!

What is wrong with this theory? Why need anyone work for a living, when we can all adopt this foolproof system of winning at the gaming table? We can ignore the fact that the usual gaming house has an upper limit on the size of the wager it will accept and focus our attention on the real fallacy contained in the prescription. Although a long run of tails, say, is almost certain to end sooner or later, it may end later rather than sooner. An adverse run *may* last long enough to exhaust any finite amount of money the bettor may have to play. To be certain of being able to continue doubling the bet each time, no matter how long the adverse run may continue, the bettor would have to begin with an infinite amount of money. But of course a player with an infinite amount of money could not possibly win—in the sense of increasing his wealth. Such a case is too fanciful, anyway; let us confine our discussion to a player who has only a fixed, finite amount of money to lose. For definiteness, we may suppose that he has decided in advance how long he will play: if he is resolved to play until all his money is gone, then he is bound to lose all his money, sooner or later (provided that the house has sufficient funds to cover all of his bets, of course); whereas if he is resolved to play until he wins some antecedently specified amount, the game might go on forever with the player never either reaching his goal or going broke.

For the sake of simplicity, suppose a player begins with just $3, so that she is prepared to sustain just one loss: two in a row would wipe her out. Let her decide to bet on heads just twice, and consider the different possible outcomes. The $3 is her purchase price; what is the expectation purchased? If two heads come up in a row, the player, winning $1 on each, will get a return of $5. If there is a head first and then a tail, the return will be just $3. If there is tail first and then a head, having lost $1 on the first toss and having bet $2 on the second, which won, the player's return will be $4. Finally, two tails will wipe her out, yielding a return of $0. Each of these events has a probability of ¼, so the expected value is (¼ × $5) + (¼ × $3) + ¼ × $4) = $3. The player's expectation is no greater when she uses the doubling technique than when she risks her entire capital on one toss of a coin.

Let us make a different supposition, that a player decides to play three times (if his money holds out) so that with luck he can double his money. The eight possible outcomes can be listed in the form of a table:

First Toss	Second Toss	Third Toss	Return	Probability
H	H	H	$6	⅛
H	H	T	$4	⅛
H	T	H	$5	⅛
H	T	T	$1	⅛
T	H	H	$5	⅛
T	H	T	$3	⅛
T	T	H	$0	⅛
T	T	T	$0	⅛

The expectation on this new strategy remains the same, still $3.

Let us consider just one more aspect of the doubling technique. Suppose some one wants to win just a single dollar, which means that she will play until she wins just once or else goes broke. With this more modest aim, what is the probable value of her investment? If heads appears on the first toss, the return is $4 (the $1 won and the original stake of $3) and having won her dollar, the woman stops playing. If tails appears on the first toss, $2 is bet on the second. If heads appears, the return is $4, and the player quits with her winnings. If tails appears, the return is $0, and the player quits because she has lost all her money. There are only these three possible outcomes, the first of which has a probability of ½, the second ¼, and the third ¼. Such a player, following such a strategy, is three times as likely to win as to lose. But of course she can lose three times as much as she can win by this method. The expected value is (¼ × $4) + (¼ × $4) + (¼ × $0) = $3. The expectation is not increased at all by following the doubling technique. The *chances* of *winning* are increased, just as by betting on more numbers at roulette, but the *amount* that can be won decreases rapidly enough to keep the *expected value constant.*

EXERCISES

★ 1. What is the expected value of a wager that consists of betting $1 each on all thirty-six numbers on one spin of a roulette wheel?

2. "Suppose we dump a complete set of chessmen into a hat—all 16 black pieces and all 16 white—shake the hat, then remove the pieces randomly by pairs. If both are black, we put them on the table to form a black pile. If both happen to be white, we put them on the table to form a white pile. If the two pieces fail to match in color, we toss them into their chess box. After all 32 pieces have been removed from the hat, what's the probability that the number of pieces in the black pile will be exactly the same as the number in the white pile?"

—MARTIN GARDNER, "Mathematical Games,"
Scientific American, Vol. 242, February 1970

3. At most crap tables in gambling houses, the house will give odds of six to one against rolling a 4 the "hard way," that is, with a pair of 2's as contrasted with a 3 and a 1, which is the "easy way." A bet made on a "hard way" 4 wins if a pair of 2's show before either a 7 is rolled or a 4 is made the "easy way"; otherwise it loses. What is the expectation purchased by a $1 bet on a "hard-way" 4?

4. If the odds are eight to one against rolling an 8 the "hard way" (that is, with two 4's), what is the expectation purchased by a $1 bet on a "hard-way" 8?

★ 5. What expectation does a person with $15 have who bets on heads, beginning with a $1 bet, and uses the doubling technique, if the bettor resolves to play just four times and quit?

6. On the basis of past performance, the probability that the favorite will win the Bellevue Handicap is .46, while there is a probability of only .1 that a certain dark horse will win. If the favorite pays even money and the odds offered are eight to one against the dark horse, which is the better bet?

7. If $100 invested in the preferred stock of a certain company will yield a return of $110 with a probability of .85, whereas the probability is only .67 that the same amount invested in common stock will yield a return of $140, which is the better investment?

8. A punchboard has a thousand holes, one containing a number that pays $5, five containing numbers that pay $2 each, and ten containing numbers which pay $1 each. What is the expected value of a punch that costs 5¢?

9. An investor satisfies herself that a certain region contains radioactive deposits, which may be either plutonium or uranium. For $500 she can obtain an option that will permit her to determine which element is present and to enjoy the proceeds from its extraction and sale. If only plutonium is present, she will lose four-fifths of her option money, whereas if uranium is present she will enjoy a return of $40,000. If there is only one chance in a hundred that uranium is present, what is the expected value of the option?

10. What was the probability of Louvrier's selecting the two cows A and D that "got better by themselves" after the anthrax inoculation described in Chapter 12 on pages 410–411?

CHALLENGE TO THE READER

We noted in this section that if the value of the return on a wager (if we achieve that return) is known, and if the decision facing us is whether to make that wager (or investment), it is possible to calculate the probability that this anticipated return must have to justify the present wager. That is the situation often facing a player in the game of poker, when she must decide whether to risk additional money to retain her chances of winning the pot by staying in the game, or to drop out. Imagine yourself such a player in the following circumstances:

11. You are playing stud poker. [In this game one card is dealt to each player on the first round, face down; on each of the following four rounds, one card is dealt to each player face up, for all to see. Betting is done after each round.] Just before the last round is dealt—each player showing three cards and having one "in the hole"—one of the other players who has the ace and king of spades and the six of diamonds showing bets the limit of $2. You must decide whether to call (that is, to match his bet and stay in the game) or to drop out. No other player remains in the game, but you are certain that he has an ace or a king in the hole. The four cards in your hand are the three and five of hearts and the four and six of clubs. If your last card gives you a straight (a numerical sequence of five cards, regardless of their suit) that would beat two pairs, and it would also beat three of a kind. Suppose you are confident that, after the last round, your opponent will do no more than check and call—that is, pass and subsequently match the $2 bet you place then. How much money must there be in the pot now for your call of his bet on this round to be worth the $2 you must now risk to stay in the game?

15

Logic and the Law

Law is order, and good law is good order.

—Aristotle

Reason is the life of the law; nay, the common law itself is nothing else but reason. . .

—Sir Edward Coke

Wherever Law ends, Tyranny begins.

—John Locke

15.1 *Laws, Courts, and Arguments*

Laws—adopted by legislatures or resulting from the decisions of courts—are the instruments of society in governing behavior. An important distinction is commonly drawn between *criminal* law and *civil* law.

In criminal law the limits of permissible behavior are laid down. Crimes are defined, and punishments may be specified. A crime is an offense against the *public* order; the dispute in criminal proceedings is therefore between the state, the accuser, and the defendant, the accused. Murder, for example, is defined in the Federal criminal code as "the unlawful killing of a human being with malice aforethought."[1] Charged with murder, a defendant on trial may deny that he was the killer, or he may admit the killing but contend that it was excusable, or he may deny that the killing was premeditated, or

---

[1] 18 U.S.C. 1111. References to statutes usually give the name of the set of laws, abbreviated, preceded by the volume number in that set, and followed by the section number in that volume. This reference is to the 18th volume of the United States Code, Section 1111. When court decisions (also called "opinions") are cited, the name of the case (e.g., *Marbury v. Madison*) usually begins the reference; the abbreviated name of the series of court reports in which it appears will then be preceded by the volume number in that series, and followed by its page number in that volume; the year the decision was made will commonly end the reference. Thus, the U.S. Supreme Court opinion in which the power of the Court to declare acts of the Federal government to be in violation of the U.S. Constitution would normally be cited as *Marbury v. Madison*, 5 U.S. 137 (1803).

480

he may contend that it was not malicious but accidental. Typically, a crime will involve both a wrongful *deed* and a wrongful *intention* or state of mind in the actor.

In *civil* law, standards for conduct are laid down for determining when one is legally obligated to fulfill an earlier agreement (the law of "contracts"), or for determining when one is liable for an injury done as a result of alleged negligence, or other fault (the law of "torts"). A civil proceeding is usually a dispute between *private* parties. The complaining party, or plaintiff, may allege that a contract has been unfairly broken, or that an injury to persons or to private property has resulted from unauthorized or negligent conduct. The responding party (here also called defendant) may dispute the factual claims, or contend that his conduct was justified by some other legal rule, or seek to show that his conduct resulted in no damage to the plaintiff. If damage is proved, and the conduct was unlawful, the defendant's good intentions will not normally be relevant.[2] It is not criminal *guilt* that is at issue in the civil law, but *liability*. Thus, a drunken driver who injures a pedestrian may be *punished* for his crime; but, in a separate proceeding, he may also be sued by the person he injured, and if found liable may be obliged to pay civil *damages* to the victim.

In both criminal and civil law it is a principal function of the judicial system to resolve disputes; a trial may be needed to insure that the resolution is definitive and fair. In this process the principles of logic are heavily relied upon. Validity and invalidity, the basic rules of deduction, principles for the evaluation of inductive inferences, and so on, remain fundamentally the same in every field, and do not change when applied in a legal context. But the absolutely central role of argument in resolving legal controversies justifies special attention here to the way logical principles apply in the world of law and the courts.

In thinking about the uses of logic in the law, three distinctions should be kept in mind, bearing respectively upon the **nature** of laws, the **sources** of laws, and the **kinds** of laws.

First: In addition to the laws of the state or the community (called, generally, the *"positive"* law) there are rules of right conduct—*"moral"* laws or principles—which may or may not be enforced by the community. Disagreement about the content and applicability of moral laws is common; the discussion in this book is restricted to the application of logic in the enforcement of the positive law, the formal rules of the community.

Second: The laws of the community have different sources. Most commonly we think of laws as being the products of a legislature of some kind—national, or state, or local. These are *statutory* laws; an example is the definition of murder, given above. Disputes over the interpretation or application of laws often require appellate courts to formulate principles having the force of law. These we call *case law*, or statutory interpretation. At a lower level,

---

[2]Punitive damages are sometimes imposed in special circumstances, under civil law. Thus the general principle that the civil law is not punitive has exceptions. Almost every general principle in law will have some exceptions, most of which cannot be noted in this book.

under the authority given by a legislature, a governmental agency often has the power to make enforceable rules, for businesses, or home-owners, or taxpayers, etc. These rules we call *administrative* law; the regulations of the Internal Revenue Service and of the Federal Food and Drug Administration are examples of administrative rules that have the force of law. At the highest level there are overriding principles that govern even what legislatures or courts may do, as for example, the principle, as formulated in the First Amendment to the U.S. Constitution, that

> Congress shall make no law respecting an establishment of religion, or prohibiting the free exercise thereof; or abridging the freedom of speech, or of the press. . . .

Such principles, sometimes but not always appearing in the founding document of a state or a nation, we call *constitutional* law. Whatever the source of a law, dispute may arise in its application; in resolving these disputes the use of logic is critical.

Third: *Criminal* law must be distinguished from *civil* law, as noted above. The Supreme Court of Minnesota, deciding a civil action against a doctor who performed needed surgery upon a patient without that patient's consent, wrote as follows:

> If it [the operation] was unauthorized, then it was . . . unlawful. It was a violent assault, not a mere pleasantry; and even though no negligence is shown, it was wrongful and unlawful. The case is unlike a criminal prosecution for assault and battery, for there an unlawful intent must be shown. But that rule does not apply to a civil action, to maintain which it is sufficient to show that the assault complained of was wrongful and unlawful or the result of negligence.[3]

In resolving disputes a legal system must apply some principle, or rule, to a set of factual circumstances—eventually reaching some judgment about guilt or liability. The facts themselves are often (but not always) in dispute, and may need to be established. That is a primary function of trials and the investigations that precede them. Then one party will claim that some specific rule of law applies to the facts, while the opposing party will claim that this rule does not apply, or that some other applicable rule takes precedence over it. Each party reaches *conclusions*—both about the facts themselves, and about the application of the law to the facts. Each party presents *arguments* in support of its position. Those arguments purport to be logically correct; that is, the premises offered are claimed to provide support, deductive or inductive, for the conclusions urged.

In the sections that follow, we examine the ways in which logical principles enter in appraising arguments in these complicated legal processes.

[3]*Mohr* v. *Williams*, 95 Minn. 261 (1905).

15.2 *Language in the Law*

1. The Functions of Legal Language

Three different uses of language were noted in Chapter 2: informative, expressive, and directive. In the law, language is rarely used only to express attitudes, sometimes used merely to inform, but most commonly used to direct conduct. Directive language may take the form of explicit commands ("You must file a tax return if . . .") or by explaining how some things are to be done if they are done at all, ("If your income was $1,900 or more, you can be claimed as a dependent on your parent's return if you were under age 19 [at the end of the tax year] or a full time student . . .")[4] or by giving notice of what is permitted ("You may make voluntary contributions to reduce the public debt")[5] or by notification that certain acts or omissions are punishable, and how they are punishable. Sentences having a declarative form will therefore often have the direction of conduct as their main function. ("If you do not file a return . . . or provide fraudulent information, the law provides that you may be charged penalties and, in certain cases, you may be subject to criminal prosecution."[6] Here as elsewhere, determining the functions of language requires an awareness of context and sensitivity to the multiplicity of possible uses.

2. Fallacies in the Law

Fallacies—of relevance or of ambiguity—are as troublesome in the law as in any other context in which we seek reliable judgments. But what may appear to be errors in reasoning in ordinary discourse may, because of the special conditions imposed by legal process, prove to be good argument here.

Several examples of these special conditions are worth noting. First, where evidence of a certain kind or degree is essential to uphold a case, emphasis upon the absence of such evidence—what might seem an appeal to ignorance (argument *ad ignorantiam*; see Section 3.2, page 93) may be logically proper. Thus, as we noted in Chapter 3, the innocence of one charged with a crime must be assumed in the absence of compelling proof to the contrary. Or again, a prosecutor may be unable to establish what criminal conviction requires: that the accused intended to do the wrongful act, or that the accused acted with negligence or recklessness, or with some other state of mind essential for criminality. This inability of the prosecutor may require the acquittal even of one whose deeds appear superficially to violate the law. Very commonly there is a positive burden upon one party in a legal dispute to prove something; then the argument by the opposing party based upon the absence of that proof is, in a sense, an argument *ad ignorantiam*. Where such

---

[4]*Instructions*, IRS Form 1040, 1987, p. 5.
[5]Ibid., p. 2.
[6]Ibid., p. 31.

a specific "burden of persuasion" applies, however, this technique is not fallacious.

Heavy reliance upon authority is a second special feature of legal reasoning. What might ordinarily seem a fallacious appeal to authority (argument *ad verecundiam;* see Section 3.2, page 95) may prove proper and even compelling in law. The reason for this is the importance of stability in the legal process. The substantive rules of law ought not be constantly in flux, and courts must be dependable in applying those rules consistently, in order that citizens may know what their legal duties are. Therefore, a rule arising from case law (i.e., from an authoritative interpretation of a statute by a higher court) governs the lower courts and may be consistently applied even when its application may appear awkward or harsh. References to the opinions of other courts therefore abound; the maxim, *stare decisis,* ("let the decision stand") plays a central, sometimes a compelling role in legal argument. Without it citizens would not know what to expect if drawn into legal dispute, and could not know how to abide by the law.

The fallacy of argument *ad verecundiam* is not merely that authority has been appealed to, but that the nature and circumstances of that appeal was *inappropriate.* The special emphasis upon stability in a just legal system alters somewhat the standards of appropriateness.

Third, an argument *ad hominem* may, in some legal circumstances, be no fallacy. Testimony and evidence presented at a trial may be in conflict. Judges (or juries when trial is by jury) often must decide what testimony is to be relied upon, which witnesses are to be most trusted. One party may therefore seek to discredit some witness who has given damaging testimony by exhibiting inconsistencies in that testimony. Or the witness may be impeached— by questioning the witness's honesty or integrity, or by exhibiting his ignorance or confusion about the matters at issue. Abraham Lincoln, when a young defense attorney, won a famous case by discrediting a witness who had sworn that he had seen the accused (Lincoln's client) at the scene of the crime, by the light of the moon. Lincoln questioned the witness about what he had seen and at what distance. Then, with almanac in hand, Lincoln declared that there was no moon at all on that date, and that the opposing witness was therefore either confused or lying. The case against his client, punctured by this argument *ad hominem,* collapsed.

Impeachment is well illustrated in the following case. Henry Lazarus, a prominent New York merchant, was accused of bribing a federal inspector. The chief witness against Lazarus was Charles Fuller, Supervising Inspector in New York City at the time. Fuller testified that Lazarus gave him money to overlook the fact that Lazarus was manufacturing defective goods for the Government. Fuller was cross-examined by defense counsel, who had investigated his history and had obtained a copy of his application for employment with the Government. The cross-examination went as follows:

> Q. "Now, Mr. Fuller, in your application you made to the government, on which I showed you your signature and affidavit, you attached your picture, did you not?"

A. Yes, sir."

Q. "You were asked, when you sought this position, these questions [about your previous employment] . . . and you wrote in 'February 1897 to August 1917, number of years 20; Where employed—Brooklyn; Name of Employer—Vulcan Proofing Company; Amount of salary—$37.50 a week; also superintendent in the rubber and compound room.'

Q. "You wrote that, didn't you?"

A. "Yes, sir."

Q. "And swore to that, didn't you?"

A. "Yes, sir."

Q. "Now, were you employed from February, 1897 to August, 1917, twenty years, with the Vulcan Proofing Company?"

A. "No, sir."

Q. "And had you been assistant superintendent of the rubber and compound room?"

A. "No, sir."

Q. "That was false, wasn't it?"

A. "Yes, sir."

Q. "You knew it was false, didn't you?"

A. "Yes, sir."

Q. "And you knew you were swearing to falsehood when you swore to it?"

A. "Yes, sir."

Q. "And you swore to it intentionally?"

A. "Yes, sir."

Q. "And you knew you were committing perjury when you swore to it?"

A. "I did not look at it in that light."

Q. "Didn't you know that you were committing perjury by swearing and pretending that you had been twenty years in this business?"

A. "Yes, sir."

Q. "And you are swearing now, aren't you?"

A. "Yes, sir."

Q. "In a matter in which a man's liberty is involved?"

A. "Yes, sir."

Q. "And you know the jury is to be called upon to consider whether you are worthy of belief or not, don't you?"

A "Yes, sir."

Q. "When you swore to this falsehood deliberately, and wrote it in your handwriting, and knew it was false, you swore to it intentionally, and you knew that you were committing perjury, didn't you?"

A. "I didn't look at it in that light."

Q. "Well, now, when you know you are possibly swearing away the liberty of a citizen of this community, do you look at it in the same light?"[7]

---

[7]Cited in R. O. Lempert and S. A. Saltzburg, *A Modern Approach to Evidence,* 2nd ed. (St. Paul, Minn.: West Publishing Co., 1982), pp. 300–301.

In a much more famous case, *ad hominem* argument was used by Socrates in his trial at Athens in the year 399 B.C. Cross-examining his accuser, Meletus, he elicited Meletus's claims both that Socrates worships new gods rather than those of the state, *and* that Socrates is an atheist. Then Socrates said:

> "Nobody will believe you, Meletus, and I am pretty sure that you do not believe yourself. . . . He [Meletus] certainly does appear to me to contradict himself in the indictment as much as if he said that Socrates is guilty of not believing in the gods, and yet of believing in them—but this is not like a person who is in earnest."[8]

Arguments *ad hominem*, whether of the abusive or of the circumstantial variety (see Section 3.2, pages 97–100) may be powerful attacks upon the case one is seeking to combat in court.

Two other non-fallacious forms of pleading common in the law resemble arguments earlier identified as fallacies. The first of these is the appeal to pity, the argument *ad misericordiam* (see Section 3.2, page 104). If such an appeal is used to support the claim of innocence for one accused of a crime it is fallacious, of course. But the appeal to pity is no fallacy when it is directed to the judge, after conviction, in an effort to win greater leniency in punishment. The poverty or misery of the accused at the time of the crime may have no relevance in determining whether he was guilty, yet may be appropriately weighed in determining the severity of punishment to be meted out.

Finally, the argument *ad baculum*, the appeal to force (Section 3.2, page 105) is in some degree the argument of law-makers themselves. Laws ought to serve good public purposes, of course, and commonly do, and the fact that laws have been enacted by a duly authorized legislature imposes a heavy obligation to obey them. But to insure general obedience, especially by those who might not obey for better reasons, punishment for disobedience is threatened by the state. Such threats of force, if effective, may be very useful to the community. Hence we commonly see public reminders of what law-breakers are threatened with: "Drunk Drivers Land in Jail!" or "No Parking—Tow-Away Zone."

Persons fearing the punishment that is threatened, or damages likely to be assessed, may refrain from criminal acts, or civilly wrongful acts to which they would otherwise be tempted. That fear and its consequences render the threat of punishment or damages *deterrent*; deterrence gives "teeth" to the law, making it an effective force in directing conduct.

3. Definitions in the Law

Legal rules directing conduct, whether adopted by legislatures or formulated by courts, need to be clear and unambiguous. Ideally, those who are subject to a law ought not be uncertain about what does and what does not constitute obedience to it. Sometimes rules of law are deliberately formulated so as to

---

[8]*Apology,* 27.

retain some vagueness, to permit flexibility in applying those rules to un-
foreseen circumstances. In general, however, the language used in stating
laws should exhibit the greatest feasible precision for the achievement of their
purpose—neither including what was to have been excluded, nor excluding
what was to have been included.

Sometimes this drive for precision results in great heaviness of language
in statutes and in formal contracts, in which lengthy qualifications are specified, or references that in ordinary discourse would be assumed clear from
context are spelled out in painful detail. Better to bear the cost of wordiness,
the lawyer may reason, than the cost of vagueness or ambiguity that might
later prove catastrophic.

This need for precision also results in careful attention being given to the
definitions of the words used in laws and in administrative rules. Persuasive
definitions and theoretical definitions, as these were explained in Chapter 4,
have little place in law. Stipulative definitions may be introduced when a
statute relies upon special terms. Thus, in a proposed statute authorizing
persons to declare in advance when certain medical procedures may later be
withdrawn or withheld from themselves, the unusual word "declarant" is
much used; its meaning in the statute is stipulated as

> a person who has executed a declaration," where 'declaration' "means a docu-
> ment executed pursuant to section 3.[9]

Precising definitions (see Section 4.2) are exceedingly common in law. A
critical word or phrase may have several different meanings in ordinary
speech, some broader and some narrower; there may be more than one ordinary, lexical definition. Legislators often will insure that a term's meaning
in a specific context is sharply delineated by presenting a precising definition
of it.

Two examples will be useful. In the statute referred to above concerning
what are known as "living wills," frequent reference is made to persons who
are "terminally ill." Within that law a precising definition of this phrase is
given:

> 'Terminally ill' means a state in which an incurable, irreversible, and uncontrol-
> lable disease or condition will, in the reasonable opinion of the attending physician,
> likely result in death within approximately one year.[10]

And since this law concerns the kinds of medical intervention that the "declarant" may direct to be withheld from himself when terminally ill, the term
"medical intervention" is also given a precising definition:

> 'Medical intervention' means any medicine, procedure, or device a physician
> prescribes, administers, performs or authorizes.[11]

---

[9]Michigan House of Representatives, Bill 4176, Section 2 (b) and (c), introduced February 24,
1987.
[10]Ibid., Section 2 (i).
[11]Ibid., Section 2 (f).

The terms "physician" and "attending physician" also receive precising definitions in this statute, and so on. Where the elimination or reduction of ambiguity is important, careful definition is of great value.

15.3 *Inductive Reasoning in Law*

Most reasoning in everyday life is a blend of induction and deduction. In this book we have dealt with the two major patterns separately (Deduction in Part Two, Induction in Part Three) because their essential principles are most easily learned in this way. But in grappling with the real problems of the world we rely upon both kinds of argument, usually combined. Often we begin with inductive reasoning, use the inductive conclusions as premisses in deductive arguments, integrate the deductive conclusions with additional inductive results, deduce more, and so on. The end product is, commonly, a fabric of which inductive and deductive elements are the warp and the woof. In legal disputes, it is the strength of this rational fabric that determines success or failure.

Examples of legal reasoning are often taken from the decisions of judges in appellate courts. There the analysis is largely deductive in character and the reasoning is set forth in the court's "opinion" on a given case. Complex arguments are devised, and arranged to have as their final conclusion the decision on the issue(s) before the court.

But this deductive process in the appellate courts, although very important indeed, is in fact secondary. The primary reasoning process in law is inductive. The facts must be determined first of all, in trial court; and in establishing them causal arguments, probability, and scientific methods of an essentially inductive kind come first. In courts—local, or state, or federal—where legal cases are "tried," a distinction is therefore drawn between those who find (i.e., determine) the *facts*, and those who direct the application of *law* to those facts.

Disputes in court are most often not about laws, but about matters of fact over which there is sharp disagreement. Was the work completed by the date contractually agreed upon? Did the negligence of X cause the injury to Y? Is the person accused of the crime the one who actually committed the deed? Questions of this kind are for the finders of fact (often, but not always, juries) to decide, after hearing evidence and argument.

Only after the facts have been determined can the legal rules (in the form of statutes, or common law principles, or administrative regulations) be applied to those facts by the court. Establishing the facts, putting them "on record," is therefore a principal objective when any case is tried in court. In doing this, the reasoning chiefly relied upon is inductive.

1. The Method of Inquiry in Law

Earlier (in Chapter 13) we examined ways in which—in science, in detection, and in all problem-solving—the method of inquiry is used. A problem is first identified, preliminary hypotheses are proposed, additional facts are collected, an explanatory hypothesis is formulated, consequences of that hypothesis are inferred and tested, and the results are then applied in practice. In such inductive investigations, of course, we never get all the evidence, or reach absolute certainty. But, with careful reasoning, we often do achieve reliable solutions to the problems confronted. In courts of law the method of inquiry is not essentially different—although the ways in which acceptable evidence is collected and applied are subject to the special restrictions of a system of justice where concern for fairness as well as concern for truth is prized.

Those who are charged with determining the facts (called the "triers of fact"—usually the jury, sometimes the judge) will commonly be confronted by several inconsistent accounts and proposed explanations of a given set of events. A mass of testimony and documents will be submitted. In opening and closing argument attorneys for the disputing parties will present conflicting hypotheses regarding the impact and coherence of this evidence. The triers of fact have the task of selecting, from the alternative hypotheses offered by the parties, that which best *explains* the mass of evidence and testimony.

But this inductive process is burdened, in a courtroom, by restrictions upon what evidence may be considered. A jury, consisting of laypersons without experience in legal process, may often be misled or confused by testimony or other evidence that is not relevant to the issue at hand, or evidence that is for some reason not fair to one of the parties. One task of the judge, therefore, is to limit the submission of evidence by the disputing parties, carefully applying a body of principles designed to insure that the competing hypotheses may be weighed fairly. These are the principles of the *law of evidence*.

Thus, for example, in American jurisprudence one who is accused of a crime cannot be required to answer questions put by the state; he may remain silent because it is a principle of fairness that no one may be forced to incriminate himself.[12] Another well-known (and very controversial) rule of evidence excludes "hearsay"—testimony by a witness about some fact, based on what some other person has said or written. One contemporary authority defines hearsay as "an out-of-court 'statement' offered for the truth of the matter asserted."[13] The difficulty hearsay creates for the trier of fact is that it rests in part on the truthfulness and competency of some third person who is not present in court, from whom the witness has received his information. But the truthfulness and competency of that other person cannot be tested by cross-examination; therefore hearsay may not be trustworthy evidence.

[12]"No person . . . shall be compelled in any criminal case to be a witness against himself. . . ." *U.S. Constitution,* Amendment V. But note that when an accused person testifies voluntarily, his testimony must be open to examination, and thus he may be required to undergo cross-examination.

[13]R. O. Lempert and S. A. Saltzburg, *A Modern Approach to Evidence,* 2nd ed. (St. Paul, Minn.: West Publishing Co., 1982), p. 357.

Rather than receiving the secondhand report from this witness—says the rule in effect—let that other person come forward and testify on the matter, allowing his direct testimony to be carefully examined.

But there are important exceptions to the "hearsay rule"—as when the person whose views are reported cannot be brought to court, or when the hearsay reported is an admission plainly opposed to the interest of the person reporting it. The underlying question raised here is: does the value of the "hearsay" evidence in proving some matter of fact (its "probative value") outweigh the danger that such evidence will mislead the jury?

Rules of evidence are intended to protect the integrity of legal process. Some exclusions are based on the need to avoid a failure by the jury to evaluate evidence wisely; others rest on the concern for human dignity; still others seek to deter police misconduct. These rules may at times hinder the pursuit of the truth. Hence there is controversy surrounding them. Establishing the facts is a principal objective in court—but the circumstances in a trial require that some of those involved in the inquiry be protected. The courtroom is not a scientific laboratory exploiting nonhuman resources, but a forum in which the fate of human beings may turn on which account of the facts is accepted by the jury. *Fairness* in this process is of the very highest importance, and that is why principles of fairness set limits within which the inductive process can proceed.

2. Causation in Legal Reasoning

Relations of cause and effect play a central role in many legal controversies. To be liable for another's injury, one must (normally) have caused it. To be convicted of a crime one must have acted in a way that caused certain unlawful outcomes. It is not causal *laws* that are sought, as in most science, but particular causal connections, as in History. Was this person or this act the cause of that particular outcome or injury?

Different possible meanings of "cause" were distinguished in Section 12.1: remote and proximate cause, cause as sufficient condition and cause as necessary condition, and cause as that which, in the presence of normal conditions, is critical in bringing the outcome to pass.

When a chain of causes leads to an event (e.g., an injury for which compensation is sought) the elements in the causal chain closest to the injury, the *proximate* causes, are most likely to be assigned legal responsibility for the outcome. Those whose actions are further back in the causal chain, and who therefore could not foresee the injurious result, are much less likely to be held responsible for it. But how far back must we trace the causal chain? One judge writes as follows:

> What we do mean by the word "proximate" [cause] is that, because of convenience, of public policy, of a rough sense of justice, the law arbitrarily declines to trace a series of events beyond a certain point. This is not logic. It is practical

politics. . . . We may regret that the line was drawn just where it was, but drawn somewhere it had to be.[14]

To make that "rough sense of justice" more consistently applicable, one rule commonly adopted is that a defendant is liable for injury to another only if the harm suffered was the natural and probable consequence of his act. In cases of alleged negligence one may be held responsible if, under the conditions that normally prevail, he should have been able to *foresee* that his act would be critical in bringing the injury to pass.

How much a reasonable person can be expected to foresee is of course controversial. The bizarre circumstances of a very famous case in American legal history, *Palsgraf* v. *The Long Island Railroad Company*,[15] nicely illustrates the problem encountered in drawing some line between proximate and remote causes to determine legal responsibility for an injury. Mrs. Palsgraf, waiting with her ticket on a railroad platform, was struck by a heavy scale that was upset by the explosion of some fireworks accidentally ignited when a train on a nearby track ran over a package of fireworks wrapped in newspaper, dropped by a passenger as train company employees were helping him to board a slowly moving train. Mrs. Palsgraf sued the train company for damages. The acts of the train company's employees were surely critical in the causal chain; if they had not pulled the passenger's arm the package would not have dropped, the fireworks would not have exploded, the scale would not have been upset—and Mrs. Palsgraf would not have been injured. Yet so distant in the causal chain were the acts of the train attendants that they could not have foreseen, and therefore could not have guarded against, the peculiar combination of events that led to the injury. The Long Island Railroad was found not to be at fault. Train companies owe a duty of very great care for the safety of their passengers; but the extent of that duty was carefully linked, in this landmark case, to the causal foreseeability of the damage done. "The risk reasonably to be perceived defines the duty to be obeyed."[16]

Legal responsibility may be traced not only to proximate acts in the causal chain, but also to proximate *omissions,* failures to act in accord with one's legal duties. Acts of omission, like acts of commission, cannot ground responsibility for injury, however, when the immediate cause of the damage, even if preventable, could not reasonably have been anticipated. Thus, the failure to foresee that an extraordinary and unprecedented rainfall might cause a flood does not give rise to legal liability for the flood damage at the end of an unforeseeable causal chain.[17] On the other hand, everyone understands the need to keep children away from attractive hazards, and thus the failure to fence a railway track, or a swimming pool, may be an important

---

[14]Justice Andrews, dissenting in *Palsgraf* v. *Long Island R.R.*, 248 N.Y. 357 (1928).
[15]248 N.Y. 339.
[16]Ibid., p. 334.
[17]*Power* v. *Village of Hibbing*, 182 Minn. 66 (1930).

and foreseeable part of the cause of a child's death when it is struck by a train, or drowns in the pool, and such omissions may therefore be the basis for legal liability. "Negligence consists" as one appellate court put it, "not alone in careless action, but also in careless omission to act."[18]

Of course, where parties in special circumstances owe special duties of care to others—because they handle very dangerous materials, or give explicit assurance of a very high degree of safety, or the like—their acts or omissions may be the basis of legal liability even when the unfortunate outcomes encountered were only very dimly foreseeable. Those engaged in some kinds of activity may be subject to a standard of "strict liability," and thus are obliged to expect the unexpected. For example, blasting companies may be held responsible even though the specific outcomes of the explosions they cause may have been unpredictable; and airlines and railroads may be responsible for some injuries to their passengers that no one could have foreseen.

Determining legal responsibility is always a matter of establishing the facts *and* fitting those facts to established rules of conduct. In cases of alleged negligence, if the defendant had no special duties of care, the rule of law will commonly fix responsibility based upon what an "ordinary, reasonable, and prudent" person may be expected to have done under the circumstances then prevailing.[19] If the interpretation of the rule is well established, and clear, the dispute in court is likely to center on the determination of the facts of a particular case, the arguments being mainly inductive; if the facts are clear, the legal dispute is likely to center upon the rule, or the interpretation of the rule, that ought to be applied to them, the arguments being (as we will see in the following section) mainly deductive.

The distinction between the sufficient and the necessary condition for an outcome (see Section 12.1) may also enter critically in determining legal responsibility. Even if a person's act or omission might have been the *sufficient* cause of injury to another, it will not result in legal responsibility if the injury clearly would have resulted from the actual prevailing conditions anyway. Thus, the failure to have a lifeboat ready will not be held the cause of death of a man who sinks without trace immediately upon falling into the ocean.[20] And the failure to give a turning signal to an automobile driver who could not have seen it if it had been given will not be held the cause of the collision that ensues.[21]

When a cause is necessary for an event it is the "*sine qua non*" of that event—a Latin expression meaning "that without which not." The causal rule often applied in law is called the "*sine qua non*" rule—that a defendant's conduct is not the cause of an event if the event would have occurred without it. Plainly it is *necessary* conditions that are of primary interest in legal arguments. Yet not all necessary conditions yield legal responsibility either. Some

[18]*Stokes* v. *City of Sac City*, 151 Iowa 10 (1911). See also: *McNally* v. *Colwell*, 91 Mich. 527.
[19]*Whitman* v. *W.T. Grant Co.*, 16 Utah 2d 81 (1964).
[20]*Ford* v. *Trident Fisheries*, 232 Mass. 400 (1919).
[21]*Rouleau* v. *Blotner*, 84 N.H. 539 (1931).

acts may be no more than part of the normally prevailing circumstances, necessary for the injurious outcome but not in themselves wrongful—as when an injury results from the presence of one who had a normal duty to be where he was. And, in some circumstances, two acts concur in bringing about an event in such a way that either one of them, operating alone, would have been sufficient to cause the harmful result; viewed as cause, neither may be necessary, and yet both may be culpable. In a notorious murder case, one man stabbed a victim with a knife, while another fractured the same victim's skull with a rock. Either wound was sufficient to cause death, and in this case neither was strictly necessary—but both men were found guilty of the crime.[22] In another case a plaintiff's property was burned by a combination of fires, one from a natural source and one negligently started; either might have had the same result; neither was strictly necessary, yet the person responsible for the negligently started fire was not absolved.[23]

Whether the defendant's conduct was the cause of an event is thus a *factual* question, which has been commonly formulated in this way: was that conduct both a "material element *and* a substantial factor" in bringing that event about?[24] The phrase "material element" seeks to incorporate part of the concept of cause as "necessary condition," while the phrase "substantial factor" seeks to incorporate part of the concept of cause as "sufficient condition," eliminating those cases in which the defendant's conduct has played an insignificant part in the result. But the ultimate determination of the cause must be argued in court, to be decided by a jury or other trier of fact.

3. Analogical Reasoning in Legal Argument

In deciding disputed factual questions heavy reliance may be placed upon *analogical arguments.* Such arguments (as we saw in Chapter 11) are built upon premises in which one or more cases are shown to be like another case that is in question, in one or more respects; the conclusion drawn is that the questionable case is like the others in some additional important respect. Analogical arguments are exceedingly common in legal controversies over who caused what.

Was an incorrect diagnosis, and subsequent injury to the patient, the result of the physician's carelessness? Other doctors may testify that the symptoms relied upon in that case almost invariably do lead, in other cases, to the diagnosis given; in this very similar case, it is concluded, the physician did precisely what is normally done, and what should have been done, in spite of the unfortunate result. Arguments having this analogical structure are presented by engineers when testifying about the normal consequences of subjecting bridges to certain stresses, or by fire-fighters when testifying about the normal effects of certain fire-fighting techniques, and so on. Most *expert*

[22]*Wilson* v. *State of Texas*, 24 S.W. 409 (1893).
[23]*Anderson* v. *Minneapolis, St. P. and S.S.M. Railroad*, 146 Minn. 430 (1920).
[24]*Connellan* v. *Coffey*, 122 Conn. 136 (1936).

testimony has precisely this form: 'In my experience, (says the expert, in effect), circumstances of such-and-such kind have usually led (or rarely lead) to results of the kind encountered here. Therefore, as an expert in these matters, it is my judgment that in this case the result was (or was not) the probable effect of just such causes.' The expert draws an analogy; an argument based upon that analogy leads to the conclusion about causal connection that aims to resolve the dispute at hand.

What is known as *"circumstantial evidence"* is similarly grounded upon analogical argument. In a recent, horrendous murder case, an Arkansas man was found guilty of the killing of 14 of his relatives by shooting and strangling. There was no evidence that he personally had fired the gun. The evidence against him, the prosecutor agreed, was entirely circumstantial: he owned the gun that had been used, and he had it in his possession when arrested, driving his dead son's car; all the bodies were found in his house, seven of them buried there, two of them hidden, others in trash bags—all of which showed (the prosecutor argued) that the crimes were "not the work of some phantom passer-by."[25] While there is little "ordinary" experience to which such gruesome killings could be likened, the jury could, and did, draw conclusions from such evidence about who (almost certainly) caused the deaths and the disposition of the bodies, based upon their knowledge of the history of people's actions in other cases.

The instances in the premises of an analogical argument may not be explicitly identified, but may be only general recollections from ordinary experience. We have all learned, for example, that unlighted stairs often lead to injurious falls. When a person has been badly hurt in a tumble down unlighted steps, it is reasonable to conclude that bad lighting played a substantial part in causing the injury, and those who failed to light the stairs may be legally responsible for it.[26] Similarly, when drawing conclusions about defective repair work, or ice-covered walks, or other kinds of circumstances with which we have had direct experience, we reason analogically. Without formulating or asserting a causal law, we understand that certain kinds of consequents often follow certain kinds of antecedents. Causal analogies are central in the inductive reasoning process; the criteria for appraising argument based upon them have been discussed in Section 11.2.

Analogical argument is occasionally used by judges in justifying the application of an established rule, or in defending a particular interpretation of some statute. Confronting the claim that a legislature had tacitly intended an exception to the general rule it had incorporated in a law, an appellate court may reason analogically thus: Exceptions to the application of a statute will normally be specified explicitly; where they have not been specified explicitly within a statute it is generally assumed that no exception was intended by the lawmakers. If in many past cases the absence of specified exception meant that none was intended, it is reasonable to conclude in the case of the statute

[25]Reported by the Associated Press, and published in *The Ann Arbor News*, February 11, 1989, p. A2.

[26]*Tullgren* v. *Amoskeag Mfg. Co.*, 82 N.H. 268 (1926).

now before us, in which no exception has been specified, that no exception was intended here either.

Analogical arguments are chiefly aimed at conclusions of fact. The fact in question may be the intention of legislators in enacting a statute, or the interpretation of a constitutional provision that is most likely to achieve the main purpose of that provision. Although abstract, such arguments are nevertheless inductive. Their premises support their conclusion (about legislative intent, and the like) not with certainty, but only with some degree of probability.

4. Probability in Legal Argument

Probability is thus a central concept in inductive legal reasoning, as in all inductive reasoning. Once the truth of certain factual premises has been presumed, conclusions may be drawn from those premises with deductive certainty. But the facts upon which such reasoning is built must first be established inductively, and therefore only with probability. The *degree* of probability with which the facts can be established often becomes, in the law as in scientific inquiry, the measure of success.

But the probability of simple factual events cannot in most circumstances be expressed as a numerical fraction, and therefore the calculus of probability, (discussed earlier in Section 14.2) cannot be readily applied in such cases. Given the testimony of several conflicting witnesses it is probable (we may say) that the accused is lying when he denies having been present at the scene of the crime. But how probable? Except as an indication of our subjective convictions in the matter, it would not be justifiable to say that the probability of his lying is .62, or .85. How then can probability be rationally used in law?

Although it may be arbitrary to assign a number to a given probability, it is often possible to characterize the general degree of probability that the evidence justifies. The rules of the legal system will usually specify what degree of probability will be needed to prove matters of different kinds. These are called "*standards of proof.*" Thus, different characterizations of the probability of some alleged fact may meet (or fail to meet) different standards or burdens. Three distinct standards are very widely relied upon.

In most cases in civil law the plaintiff and the defendant come to the court with an equal presumption of correctness. Thus, in deciding matters of fact that can be determined only with probability, the jury needs to decide which (if either) of the contesting parties' claims is more likely to be true, that is, which is supported by a *preponderance of the evidence*. Preferring one account of the facts over its competitor, as more probable, may be a "close call"—but if some call must be made, and neither party deserves preference, the question becomes that of finding the greater probability. No quantification is normally feasible or needed. Typically, the judge may instruct the jury in this way:

If you find from a preponderance of the evidence that the plaintiff has sustained injuries as alleged in her complaint, then it will be your duty to assess the damages. . ."[27]

In suits for damages under civil law the *burden* of proof (or sometimes "burden of persuasion") is generally supposed to rest upon the complaining party, the party seeking redress for injury. If the jury finds that the evidence for the two sides is evenly balanced, therefore, the plaintiff will not have sustained this burden, and the defendant will normally win. But the evidence on either side need not be overwhelming; plaintiff's burden must be sustained by more than speculation or conjecture—but it will be enough if the jury finds that the plaintiff introduced evidence from which reasonable persons may conclude that it is *more probable* that the injury complained of was caused by the defendant than that it was not.[28]

At the other extreme, in criminal law the standard of proof is very high. The mistaken conviction of the innocent is an injustice so terrible that every effort must be made to avoid it. Therefore an accused must be presumed innocent until conclusively proved guilty. Conviction of crime requires that the accused be found guilty *"beyond reasonable doubt."* This means that the probability of guilt is so great that no reasonable person, after considering all the evidence, would believe him innocent.[29] The application of this standard results in the acquittal of some persons who are probably guilty in fact. But it is far better that the guilty go free, we say, than that the innocent be convicted. Legal argument in defense of the accused need not prove his innocence, but need only show that the state has not sustained its burden of proof, has not submitted evidence of guilt that meets the required standard. Principles built into our legal system to guard against unfairness thus set limits within which inductive inquiry proceeds.

A third, intermediate standard is widely applied in circumstances of certain kinds. Legal arguments often rely upon common presumptions, which serve as accepted rules for drawing conclusions from established facts unless disproved. Most such presumptions are rebuttable, but rebutting them in a given case sometimes requires more than a preponderance of the evidence, yet less than near certainty. For example: it is a presumption of the common law that records of public agencies, including public schools and universities, are maintained accurately. A graduate of a public university may allege in a suit for damages that his records had been inaccurately maintained, and this is a matter he may prove in court—but a preponderance of the evidence will not suffice. To override what is presumed he must prove his claim with *clear and convincing evidence.*[30]

[27]*Kenwood Tire Co.* v. *Speckman,* 92 Ind. App. 419 (1931).

[28]William L. Prosser, *Handbook of the Law of Torts* (St. Paul, Minn.: West Publishing Co., 1941), p. 326.

[29]This very high standard of proof has become a constitutional requirement in the United States, as part of the "due process" guaranteed to all by the 14th Amendment. See *In re Winship,* 397 U.S. 358 (1970).

[30]Richard O. Lempert and Stephen A. Saltzburg, *A Modern Approach to Evidence,* 2nd ed. (St. Paul, Minn.: West Publishing Co., 1982), pp. 806 ff.

Probability thus plays a critical role in legal argument. Whether a matter can be proved by a preponderance of the evidence, or by clear and convincing evidence, or beyond reasonable doubt, may make all the difference in court. "These traditional devices," wrote a judge of the New Jersey Supreme Court, "provide the scales on which the persuasive impact of the sum total of the evidence must be weighed."[31]

15.4 *Deductive Reasoning in Law*

Determining the facts is fundamental in resolving a legal dispute—but after the facts have been established the appropriate rule of law must be applied to them by the court, and then some practical conclusion drawn. The legal rule, carefully formulated, is one premiss of a deductive argument; the statement of the facts exhibiting their relation to that rule is a second premiss. The outcome of applying the rule to the facts will lead to judgment. If the defendant in a civil suit is held liable, an appropriate *remedy* for the plaintiff (the person injured) must then be awarded; if the accused is found guilty in a criminal trial an appropriate *punishment* must then be imposed. The overall structure of the central argument is clear in either case: it is a deductive argument consisting of a rule together with the facts of the case as premisses, and the judgment of the court as conclusion.

This deductive process often encounters further hurdles, however. At trial, the facts are established and the law applied to them. But there are many possible grounds upon which the decision of the trial court may be appealed to higher courts. The *facts* themselves, of which an account is given in the record of trial, will not normally be the issue on appeal; appeals will usually concern the *way* in which those facts had been found, or the *rules* that ought to be applied *to* those facts. But deciding upon the rule that is correctly applied to a given set of facts can be exceedingly difficult and controversial.

1. Determining the Correct Rule of Law

The appeal to a higher court is normally based on the claim that some rule has been applied improperly, or that the wrong rule has been applied altogether. The rule in question may be *procedural* or *substantive*.

Procedural rules are fundamental in law, because confidence in the entire judicial system requires that the steps taken in reaching a decision were fair to the contesting parties. They must have been given a full opportunity to present their case, normally with the help of legal counsel. Claims must have been dealt with by the proper authorities, in the proper way, using the proper standards. The evidence heard must be relevant, and opportunity to examine it must have been provided to all parties. Even the question of "standing"—whether a complaining party has such a relation to the matter at issue that he is entitled to bring the matter to court—may be critical to the proper use

[31]*Botta v. Brunner*, 26 N.J. 82 (1958).

of the judicial system, and intensely controversial. What may appear to lay-men to be "legal technicalities" are often important procedural questions that determine whether justice has been done. Long experience has shown that to be just a legal system requires careful procedural distinctions and elaborate procedural rules.

Most often it is the *substance* of the rule applied, rather than procedure, that is the issue before an appellate court. Not every possible factual circum-stances could be anticipated when the rules were written, and depending upon which circumstances are emphasized, different rules may appear ap-plicable. Or different authorities (courts or legislatures) may have promul-gated different and conflicting rules that could be claimed to govern the matter at hand. And even if the applicable rule is agreed upon, its language may be vague, some terms within it overly broad, or ambiguous, or com-monly used in different ways.

In rejecting one interpretation of a rule in favor of another, the technique of refutation by logical analogy (discussed earlier in Sections 6.2, 8.4, and 11.3) is commonly used by judges. A disputed argument may be shown to have the *same form* as another argument that is plainly unsound. A striking example of such reasoning is found in a recent Supreme Court decision that the prohibition of cruel and unusual punishment in the U.S. Constitution[32] does not forbid imposing the death penalty for youthful murderers. Histor-ically, the Court has determined that a punishment is "cruel and unusual" when the content of the laws of the great majority of the states shows that there is a "national consensus" that it is an unacceptable form of punishment. Is there such a national consensus that would forbid the execution of 18-, 17-, and even 16-year-old offenders? Justice Scalia, writing for the Court in 1989, noted that of the 37 states that authorize capital punishment, 12 re-quire offenders to have been at least eighteen years old at the time of the crime, 3 others require offenders to have been seventeen, and 22 impose no age requirement. The national consensus that the Supreme Court normally requires to label a punishment "cruel and unusual" seems clearly lacking, he concluded. Justice Brennan, dissenting, replied that this calculation is misleading because it fails to take into account the 13 states that do not permit capital punishment under *any* circumstances. Justice Scalia rejoined: "The dissent's position is rather like discerning a national consensus that wagering on cockfights is inhumane by counting within that consensus those states that bar all wagering."[33]

In reaching decisions on substance, three steps in the processes of appellate courts may be distinguished: First, the court must decide *which* rule to apply; second the court must *state* that rule with precision; and third, the court must determine what *result* will flow from the correct application of the stated rule to the facts of the case at hand. An appellate court must **identify,** and for-**mulate,** and then correctly **apply** the rules of law. The records of this labo-

---

[32]"Excessive bail shall not be required, nor excessive fines imposed, nor cruel and unusual punishments inflicted," *U.S. Constitution,* Amendment VIII.

[33]*Stanford* v. *Kentucky,* Case No. 87-5765, U.S. Supreme Court, decided June 26, 1989.

rious process, heavily dependent upon deductive argument, fill the shelves of law libraries.

2. Identifying, Formulating, and Applying Rules of Law: The Law of Libel

The ways in which argument is used in this process can be best explained with reference to one cluster of real and continuing legal disputes. For this purpose we focus here on the law of libel.

One who is defamed in writing may be damaged in ways deserving redress. Under some circumstances the injured party may sue for damages under civil law on grounds of *libel*. But what *standard*—what rule of law—shall be applied in determining whether someone who claims to have been damaged (the plaintiff) has been libelled? There are different standards, differently stated. The steps in judicial argument—selecting the legal rule, formulating it precisely, and applying it to the established facts—can be well illustrated by examining a set of real cases in the law of libel.

The New York Times ran a paid advertisement in 1963 protesting treatment of civil rights activists in the South. The Police Commissioner of Montgomery, Alabama, although not named in the advertisement, sued the newspaper for damages; statements in the advertisement were proved to be false and defamatory. The plaintiff, Sullivan, was awarded $500,000 by the jury; this verdict was appealed by the defendant, *The New York Times,* and the case was ultimately decided by the United States Supreme Court.[34]

Two general principles, both important but in conflict with one another, were urged by the parties in this case. First, a citizen is entitled to a peaceful remedy for the widespread publication of a very damaging falsehood. This principle underlies all libel proceedings in the civil law. Mr. Sullivan was unfairly damaged, and deserved some remedy. Second, the freedom of the press deserves very special protection, and is given that protection under the First Amendment of the United States Constitution. If a newspaper must fear heavy damages for the publication, in good faith, of sharply critical judgments that turn out to be mistaken, that would strongly discourage a vigorously critical press, and would chill political debate. This was the principle urged on appeal by *The New York Times.*

Choosing among conflicting rules that *could* be applied to the facts, is the perennial problem for appellate courts. The rule chosen will generally depend upon the values given highest priority by the court. Logic by itself cannot make the choice, but logic can be used to defend the choice made. Good reasons, but different reasons, may be given for choosing one, or another, of the larger principles as controlling. If stability is the chief consideration of the court, it may believe itself bound by precedent, and will therefore choose the rule for which the strongest and most recent precedents can be found. But precedents of approximately equal strength and timeliness may be pre-

---

[34]*New York Times v. Sullivan*, 376 U.S. 254 (1964).

sented on both sides, and the task may then be that of selecting one set of precedents for reasons other than stability.

In this case of alleged libel involving a newspaper and a police commissioner, the general principle of the law of libel—that a citizen unfairly damaged is entitled to some remedy—might have prevailed, but did not. The United States Supreme Court felt bound to promote what it viewed as "good public policy" by protecting the public's interest in political debate that is "robust and uninhibited," thus favoring the defendant. In its emphasis upon the overriding importance of the special protection given to a free press by the U.S. Constitution, the Supreme Court took the first critical step in approaching judgment: it made a policy choice and in doing so **identified** the rule to be applied.

How was the general rule to be **formulated** in this case? The fact that the advertisement included statements that were false and defamatory was not in dispute; nevertheless the plaintiff was not to recover damages. The Court therefore found it necessary to refine the standard for libel (actually making new law) to require, *when the plaintiffs defamed are public officials,* that the false and defamatory statements about them were made with "actual malice"— "that is, with knowledge that it was false or with reckless disregard of whether it was false or not." False and defamatory statements made without actual malice must be protected, said the Court, because "a rule compelling the critic of official conduct to guarantee the truth of all his factual assertions—and to do so on pain of libel judgments virtually unlimited in amount—leads to . . . self-censorship."[35]

This formulation of the standard for the libel of public officials has since been widely applied. A public official, being in the public eye, is not entitled to the same level of protection from defamation as an ordinary private citizen. But some persons are in the public eye although they are not "public officials." Should the rule that is aimed at protecting vigorous public debate apply to public *figures* as well as public *officials*? Further refinement of the rule was needed.

Wally Butts, a former head football coach and director of athletics at the University of Georgia, was defamed in an article in the *Saturday Evening Post* in which he was charged with fixing a football game between The Universities of Georgia and Alabama. What was written was false and very damaging. Butts was certainly not a public official, but the Supreme Court decided that the rule in *The New York Times* case must apply to public figures as well as public officials—and Butts certainly was a public figure.[36]

Thus, in reconciling the law of libel with the First Amendment, the Supreme Court's formulation of the rule introduced a constitutional privilege for some defamatory falsehoods, varying with the *status* of the person defamed. Complications of other kinds remain unresolved. What if the person defamed is neither a public official nor a public figure, and yet the *topic* of

---

[35]Ibid.
[36]*Curtis Publishing Co.* v. *Butts,* 388 U.S. 130 (1967).

the press report is one of great public interest? A broadcasting company that defamed a distributor of nudist magazines was protected against libel damages because of the importance of the subject matter in its false broadcast. The Supreme Court wrote: "We honor the commitment to robust debate on public issues, which is embodied in the First Amendment, by extending constitutional protection to all discussion and communication involving matters of public or general concern, without regard to whether the persons are famous or anonymous."[37] The standard for press protection developed for *The New York Times* was once again adjusted, in this case formulated to offer press protection very broadly, with the distinction between public and private figures—although not erased—fading in importance.

However carefully the rule protecting a free press may be refined, it must in the end also be **applied** to the established facts of the case, in order to reach a decision. The facts are established at trial. The distinction between public and private figures (in applying the law of libel) remains consequential—but *which facts* on record will determine whether the person defamed was a public or a private figure? The final step in this judicial argument must yet be taken.

In an article entitled "Frame-Up," appearing in a periodical called *American Opinion*, published by the John Birch Society in 1969, a reputable attorney representing a family whose son had been murdered, was falsely defamed. The attorney, Gertz, was recklessly accused of being the architect of an alleged "frame-up" of the police officer who had been convicted of the killing. Gertz sued the magazine for libel.[38] Gertz had been most unjustly damaged, but the topic was one of great public interest. Does the standard as formulated in *The New York Times* case protect the magazine when it falsely defames a person in Gertz's circumstances? That depends upon how the Court chooses to describe those circumstances.

The magazine claimed that Gertz was a public figure. Whether that is true depends upon which facts are selected for emphasis. He had been active in community and professional affairs, and he was well-known in some circles. Did that make him a public figure? No, said the Supreme Court: "We would not lightly assume that a citizen's participation in community and professional affairs rendered him a public figure for all purposes."[39] But the earlier trial of the police officer, allegedly a frame-up, was a topic of much public discussion, and Gertz was marginally involved in that trial. Did that make him a public figure? That depends upon the nature of his involvement. The question of who is a public figure must be answered, the Court wrote, "by looking to the nature and extent of an individual's participation in the particular controversy giving rise to the defamation."[40] Gertz's involvement in that trial was limited to protecting the interests of the family of the victim whom he represented. The facts chosen for emphasis by the Court were not

[37]*Rosenbloom v. Metromedia*, 403 U.S. 29 (1973).
[38]*Gertz v. Welch*, 418 U.S. 323 (1974).
[39]Ibid.
[40]Ibid.

Gertz's association with a matter of some notoriety, but his professional behavior which was entirely normal, and they concluded that the false defamation of him could not be protected by the *New York Times* standard. "Absent clear evidence of general fame or notoriety in the community, and pervasive involvement in the affairs of society, an individual should not be deemed a public personality for all aspects of his life."[41]

The judicial process, appearing on the surface to be a straightforward application of rules to facts, becomes in reality one of enormous complexity. Not only must the appropriate rule be identified, and then formulated to accomplish the public purposes of the law, but there must be an ordering of the facts already established, and a selection of those facts upon which the reformulated rule bears most directly. Only then can a conclusion be reached in the case at hand.

15.5 *Logic as Right Reasoning*

Wherever intellectual problems of importance arise—in the law, in science, or in everyday life—good argument can strongly support, but can never guarantee, correct solutions, because the truth of every premiss is open to question. We reason inductively to establish the facts in a problematic situation. From what we have thus accepted as premisses, we reason deductively to establish and defend what follows from those premisses. In all the study of logic we aim to identify, master, and use the methods and principles that distinguish good reasoning from bad.

If the foundations upon which our reasoning is built are solid, and if we are consistently attentive and accurate, nothing will guide us more securely or more successfully in solving problems of every kind than the methods of logic with which this book has been concerned.

[41]Ibid.

Solutions to
Selected Exercises

Exercises on pp. 14–18

1. PREMISS: Society pays the other cost for damaged health and property, oil spills in the ocean, polluted or poisoned rivers, lakes and beaches, acid rain, killed or poisoned fish and oyster beds, and human misery.
CONCLUSION: The price of fossil and nuclear fuel is only a small fraction of their total cost.

5. PREMISS: The light that we see from distant galaxies left them millions of years ago, and in the case of the most distant object that we have seen, the light left some eight thousand million years ago.
CONCLUSION: When we look at the universe, we are seeing it as it was in the past.

10. PREMISS: Researchers don't add in such noncash benefits as food stamps or Medicaid when calculating family incomes.
CONCLUSION: Poverty statistics overstate the number of poor people.

15. PREMISSES: (1) If an opinion [whose expression is silenced] is right, all members of the human race are deprived of the opportunity of exchanging error for truth.
(2) If an opinion [whose expression is silenced] is wrong, all members of the human race lose the clearer perception and livelier impression of truth, produced by its collision with error.
CONCLUSION: The peculiar evil of silencing the expression of an opinion is, that it is robbing the human race; posterity as well as the existing generation; those who dissent from the opinion, still more than those who hold it.

20. PREMISSES: (1) A gray surface looks red if we have been looking at a blue-green one.
(2) Plain paper feels smooth if we have been feeling sandpaper or rough if we have been feeling plate glass.
(3) Tap water tastes sweet if we have been eating artichokes.
CONCLUSION: Some part of what we call red or smooth or sweet must be in the eyes or fingertips or tongue of the beholder, feeler, or taster.

25. PREMISS: I am sensible that I am deficient in judgement, in good common sense.
    CONCLUSION: I ought to be diffident and cautious.

30. PREMISS: They [the least destructive nuclear weapons] make it easier for a nuclear war to begin.
    CONCLUSION: It is probably true that the least destructive nuclear weapons are the most dangerous.

Exercises on pp. 22–25

1. ① [American farmers produce more food and fiber than they could profitably sell on a free market.] In cold economic terms (that means that) ② [we have more farmers than we need.]

5. ① [I've opposed the death penalty all my life.] ② [I don't see any evidence that it's a deterrent] and ③ [I think there are better and more effective ways to deal with violent crime.]

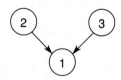

10. ① [A just society cannot possibly pay everyone the same income] (since) ② [the aptitudes and efforts of individuals diverge dramatically] and (since) ③ [the common good is far better served accordingly by systematic inequalities of reward.]

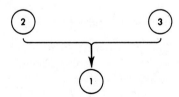

15. **Q** Dr. Koop, why does ① [the government need[s] to intervene in the treatment of handicapped infants]?
A ② [The Rehabilitation Act of 1973 states that it is illegal in any institution that receives federal aid to discriminate against anyone on the basis of race, creed, color, religion, ethnic origin or handicap.] ③ [We have good evidence that many children are deprived of their civil rights by being treated in a different way than they would be treated if they were not handicapped.]

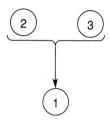

20. ① [Hunting, . . . particularly the hunting of large animals, is so complicated, difficult and hazardous that the cooperation of numerous individuals is needed.] ⟨It can be inferred, therefore, that⟩ ② [Peking man was more likely to have been living in a group than in solitude when he began to hunt deer.]

25. In 1972 Justice Thurgood Marshall wrote that "punishment for the sake of retribution is not permissible under the Eighth Amendment." ① [That is absurd.] ② [The element of retribution—vengeance, if you will—does not make punishment cruel and unusual, it makes punishment intelligible.] ③ [It distinguishes punishment from therapy.] ④ [Rehabilitation may be an ancillary result of punishment, but we punish people to serve justice, by giving people what they deserve.]

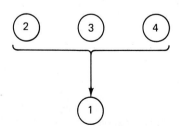

Exercises on pp. 30–33

1. ① [Now every developed capitalist nation simultaneously plays the role of colony and metropolis with respect to other such nations.] (Thus,) ② [war today between two developed nations would not be a war *for* markets but, instead, a war *against* their markets.]

5. Not an argument but an explanation of the perplexity of scientists confronted by a new phenomenon, a gamma ray source with 20,000 times more energy output than the sun.

10. Here we have an explanation for our having a man in the loop, not an argument intended to prove that we do. However, the fact that a decaying satellite can look like an incoming warhead may also serve as the premiss of an argument of which the conclusion is that a human being *ought* to be involved in the system used for detecting approaching warheads.

15. Not an argument, but an explanation of why Treason doth never prosper (although perhaps more a joke than an explanation).

20. ① [According to BLS a couple with two children needs 67 percent more income than a childless couple.] (This implies that) ② [adults spend about two thirds as much on their children as on themselves.]

25. Not an argument but an explanation of why the Tudor government in England failed to reintroduce legal slavery.

Exercises pp. 40–45

1. General Mercier, leaving for Rennes to appear as a witness, issued his Order of the Day: "① [Dreyfus will be condemned once more.] (For) ② [in this affair someone is certainly guilty] and ③ [the guilty one is either he or me.] (As) ④ [it is certainly not me,] ⑤ [it is Dreyfus.]"

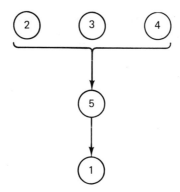

5. ① [I have a heart,] and (therefore) ② [I love;] but ③ [I am your daughter,] and (therefore) ④ [I am proud.]

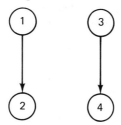

10. ① [. . . almost every advertisement you see is obviously designed, in some way or another, to fool the customer:] ② [the print that they don't want you to read is small;] ③ [the statements are written in an obscure way.] (It is obvious to anybody that) ④ [the product is not being presented in a scientific and balanced way.] (Therefore,) ⑤ [in the selling business, there's a lack of integrity.]

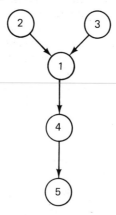

15. ① [The lower strata of the middle class—the small tradespeople, shop-keepers, and retired tradesmen generally, the handicraftsmen and peas-ants—all these sink gradually into the proletariat,] (partly because) ② [their diminutive capital does not suffice for the scale on which modern industry

is carried on, and is swamped in the competition with the large capitalists,] (partly because) ③ [their specialized skill is rendered worthless by new methods of production.] (Thus) ④ [the proletariat is recruited from all classes of the population.]

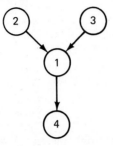

20. ① [A disease entity is defined by signs and symptoms generated by objective—that is, organic—determinants.] (Thus) ... ② [illness is organic.] (Since) ③ [mental disturbances are not organic,] ④ [mental illness is not illness.]

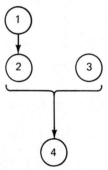

25. Why should selective cutting should be implemented? ① [The Amazonian forest contains 20 to 60 trees an acre, but only one or two can be used for industrial purposes.] ② [Only these trees can be felled economically] (because) ③ [exploration requires heavy, expensive, high-oil-consumption equipment.] ④ [This machinery can be amortized only by cutting large, high-yield trees.] ⑤ [The main advantage of selective cutting is that the younger trees get more access to light and water,] ⑥ [accelerating the natural growth cycle of the forest.] ⑦ [Selective cutting should be implemented.]

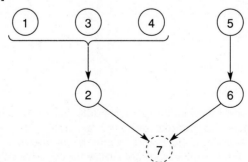

30. ". . . You appeared to be surprised when I told you, on our first meeting, that you had come from Afghanistan."

"You were told, no doubt."

"Nothing of the sort. I *knew* you came from Afghanistan. From long habit the train of thoughts ran so swiftly through my mind that I arrived at the conclusion without being conscious of intermediate steps. There were such steps, however. The train of reasoning ran, '① [Here is a gentleman of a medical type,] but ② [with the air of a military man.] (Clearly) ③ [an army doctor,] then. ④ [He has just come from the tropics,] (for) ⑤ [his face is dark,] and ⑥ [that is not the natural tint of his skin,] (for) ⑦ [his wrists are fair.] ⑧ [He has undergone hardship and sickness], (as) ⑨ [his haggard face says clearly.] ⑩ [His left arm has been injured.] ⑪ [He holds it in a stiff and unnatural manner.] ⑫ [Where in the tropics could an English army doctor have seen much hardship and got his arm wounded? Clearly in Afghanistan.]' The whole train of thought did not occupy a second. I then remarked that you came from Afghanistan, and you were astonished."

"It is simple enough as you explain it," I said, smiling.

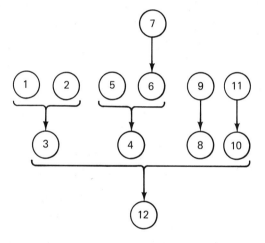

Exercises on pp. 59–64

1. If the first native is a politician, then he lies and denies being a politician. If the first native is not a politician, then he tells the truth and denies being a politician. In either case, then, the first native denies being a politician.

Since the second native reports that the first native denies being a politician, he tells the truth, and is, therefore, a nonpolitician.

The third native asserts that the first native is a politician. If the first native is a politician, then the third native speaks the truth and is, therefore, a nonpolitician. If the first native is a nonpolitician, then the third native lies and is, therefore, a politician. Hence only one of the first and third natives is a politician, and since the second is a nonpolitician, there is only one politician among the three natives.

5. Since Lefty said that Spike did it, Spike's first and third statements are equivalent in meaning and therefore either both true or both false. Since only one statement is false, they are both true.

Dopey's third statement is, therefore, false, and so his first two are true. Therefore Butch's third statement is false and so his first two are true, of which the second reveals that Red is the guilty man.

(An alternative method of solving this problem was communicated to me by Professor Peter M. Longley of the University of Alaska. All but Red both assert their innocence *and* accuse someone else. If their professions of innocence are false, so are their accusations of other persons. But no one makes two false statements, so their statements that they are innocent must be true. Hence Red is the guilty one. This solution, however, presupposes that only one of the men is guilty.)

(Still another method of solving this problem is due to James I. Campbell of Eisenhower College and Walter Charen of Rutgers College. Dopey's second statement and Butch's third statement are contradictory, so at least one must be false. But if Dopey's second statement were false, his third statement would be true and Spike would be guilty. However, if Spike were guilty, his first and third statements would both be false, so he cannot be guilty and hence Dopey's second statement cannot be false. Therefore, Butch's third statement must be false, whence his second statement is true and Red is the guilty man.)

10. Number the diamonds, 1–10, and proceed as follows:

First weighing: 1, 2, 3, 4   against   5, 6, 7, 8.

A. If they balance: the odd diamond must be 9 or 10.

Weigh 9 against 1; if 9 goes up it is the odd diamond and light; if 9 goes down it is the odd diamond and heavy; if they balance the odd diamond must be 10. Then weigh 10 against 1; if 10 goes up it is light, if it goes down it is heavy.

B. If the eight diamonds in the first trial do not balance:

Suppose that 1, 2, 3, 4 go down, while 5, 6, 7, 8 go up.

Then weigh 1, 2, 8, 9 against 3, 4, 7, 10. If 1, 2, 8, 9 go down, the odd diamond must be either 1 or 2 and heavy, or 8 and light. Then weigh 1 against 2; if either goes down it is the odd diamond and heavy. If they balance the odd diamond is 8 and light. If, on the second weighing, 3, 4, 7, 10 go down, the odd diamond must be either 3 or 4 and heavy, or 7 and light. Weigh 3 against 4; if either goes down it is the odd diamond and heavy; if they balance the odd diamond is 7 and light.

Here is another solution for Exercise 10:

Number the diamonds, 1–10; then proceed as follows:

First weighing: put the diamonds numbered 1, 2, and 3 on one side of the scale, and those numbered 4, 5, and 6 on the other side. If the two sides balance we know the odd diamond is either 7, 8, 9, or 10. In that case, as a second weighing, put numbers 7 and 8 on one side of the scale, and numbers 9 and 2 (or any other number 1–6) on the other side. If these balance the odd diamond must be 10; weigh it against any one of diamonds 1–6; if it goes down it is heavy, and if it goes up it is light. If on the second weighing, 7 and 8 go down and 9 and 2 go up, the odd diamond is heavy if it is seven or eight, and it is 9 if it is light. Then weigh 7 against 8; if either goes down, it is the odd diamond and heavy. If 7 and 8 balance, the odd diamond is 9 and light.

If, on the first weighing (1, 2, 3 against 4, 5, 6) one side (say, 1, 2, 3) goes down, then as a second trial, put 1, 2, 4, 5 on one side of the scale, and 7, 8, 9, 10 on the other. If these balance the odd diamond must be either 3 and heavy, or 6 and light. Then put 3 on one side of the scale, 7 on the other. If these two balance, the odd diamond is 6 and light. If, on this second weighing (1, 2, 4, 5 against 7, 8, 9, 10) the side with 1, 2, 4, 5 goes down, we know the odd diamond must be 1 or 2 and must be heavy. Then we weigh 1 against 2 and the one that goes down is the odd diamond and is heavy. If on the second weighing the side with 1, 2, 4, 5 goes up, we know that the odd diamond must be either 4 or 5 and must be light. Weigh 4 against 5 and the diamond that goes up is the odd diamond and is light.

There are other solutions, all of which are variations on one of the two given above.

Exercises on pp. 74–78

I. 1. Directive—stop talking about my age.
Expressive—to evoke antipathy and contempt for the "honorable gentleman" as an old fool who is "ignorant in spite of experience."
Informative—admits that the speaker is a young man.

5. Directive—rid yourselves of lawyers.
Expressive—to evoke antipathy toward lawyers.
Informative—the profession of lawyers is "to disguise matters," that is, to conceal and distort the facts.

10. Directive—Do not delay decisions until perfect clearness is achieved.
Expressive—To show disapproval of those who demand perfect understanding before deciding.
Informative—Perfect clearness is not required for wise decision making.

15. Directive—be religious; and if you study philosophy at all, study it deeply.
Expressive—to evoke piety, and also to evoke contempt for atheists as being shallow.
Informative—beginning students of philosophy tend toward atheism, but advanced students of philosophy are religious.

20. Directive—do not oppose war.
Expressive—to evoke feelings of approval and moral enthusiasm for war.
Informative—if there were no war, people would continue to have finite aims, they would become (in some obscure sense) "corrupt," and might lose their "ethical health" (a term not clearly defined in Hegel's context).

II. 1. Asserts that the speaker will not accept the nomination and would not serve even if elected president.
Intended to stop the Republican politicians from working for his (Sherman's) nomination.
Provides evidence that the speaker is forthright and unavailable.

5. Asserts that research requires continual re-examination of accepted beliefs, and asserts further (as conclusion) that research is critical of established practices.
Intended to stimulate research, to stimulate a questioning attitude and a critical spirit, and to warn people who want to enjoy the fruits of research

that they must tolerate criticism of accepted doctrines and existing practices.

Provides evidence that the speaker values and is committed to the continual re-examination of doctrines and axioms upon which current thought and action are based, and is critical of existing practices.

10. Asserts that there are three classes of citizens: rich—who are lazy and greedy; poor—who have nothing, are envious, hate the rich, and are susceptible to demagogy; and the middle class—who are law-abiding, law-enforcing, and make the state secure.

Intended to cause hostility toward the rich and (especially) toward the poor, and to produce approval of the middle class.

Provides evidence that the speaker is neither rich nor poor or at least not poor.

15. Asserts that all who speak about constitutional rights, free speech, and the free press are Communists.

Intended to cause hostility toward those who defend constitutional rights, free speech, and free press.

Provides evidence that the speaker is hostile toward constitutional rights, free speech, free press, and Communists.

20. Asserts that the painting in question is overpriced and without merit.

Intended to cause people to laugh—at Whistler, and not to buy and not to praise Whistler's paintings.

Provides evidence that the speaker is hostile toward Whistler, witty, bombastic, and not sensitive to Whistler's art.

Exercises on pp. 85–87

1. Disagreement in belief as to how a fool should be answered.
Agreement in attitude (of contempt) toward fools.

5. Disagreement in belief as to how the physical separation of two persons affects their fondness or regard for one another.
Disagreement in attitude is suggested: *a* generally approves of separation, while *b* appears to be negative (or perhaps neutral) about it.

10. Disagreement in belief is only implied or suggested here: *a* clearly believes in the truth of atheism, but that *b* disbelieves the atheist doctrine is suggested or implied by his statement that atheists are scoundrels.
Disagreement in attitude is expressed: *a* approves of atheism and atheists, whereas *b* disapproves of atheists and—by implication—of atheism.

15. Disagreement in belief as to the value of propriety of the American government: *a* believes it is disgraceful, *b* believes that though it is imperfect it is better than any other up to that time.
Disagreement in attitude: *a* disapproves, *b* approves, of the American government.

20. Disagreement in belief as to how reason can and will be used: *a* believes that reason is needed to avoid disaster, *b* believes that reason never serves spiritual things and usually serves those who oppose what comes from God.
Disagreement in attitude: *a* strongly approves of reason, while *b* strongly disapproves of reason and its consequences.

Exercises on pp. 107–113

I. 1. Begging the Question (*petitio principii*). Obviously circular: The American College Dictionary **defines** "famous" as meaning *well known.*

5. Appeal to Emotion (*argumentum ad populum*).

10. False Cause (*post hoc ergo propter hoc*).

15. Appeal to Force (*argumentum ad baculum*).

20. Appeal to Force (*argumentum ad baculum*).

II. 1. *Argumentum ad hominem* (circumstantial) can be seen to appear twice in this passage as "You cannot be against something because you do not go where it is to oppose it." Also, the *argumentum ad hominem* (abusive) appears in Phillips's more or less subtle way of telling his questioner where to go.

5. Not a fallacy.

10. *Argumentum ad hominem* (abusive).

15. *Argumentum ad hominem* (circumstantial) committed by "one evening newspaper," which divided a column into double columns to show that Q. Slide had changed his mind. The *argumentum ad hominem* (abusive) is committed by Q. Slide in his reply.

20. Begging the question (*petitio principii*). Obviously a circular argument.

Exercises on pp. 120–123

I. 1. Amphiboly.

5. Equivocation. The terms "poor" and "poorest" are relative terms, sometimes applying to financial circumstances, sometimes to skills. The poorest man who is head of government is not necessarily the poorest head of government.

10. Composition. That the parts have a specified shape does not imply that the whole itself has that shape.

II. 1. Composition. That the parts have functions does not imply that the whole has a function.

5. Amphiboly (what does the phrase "without success" really modify?)

10. Composition.

15. Composition.

Exercises on pp. 124–127

1. Equivocation.

5. Equivocation (on "other").

10. False cause. Obviously intended as a joke, this passage suggests that the daytime's light is caused by something other than the sun, whereas we know that it is the sun itself that causes the daytime to be light.

15. Begging the question (*petitio principii*).

20. Appeal to Ignorance (*argumentum ad ignorantiam*).

25. Division. Of course the author does not commit the fallacy, but he claims (facetiously, perhaps) that Whitman did commit it in thinking about himself. The argument is patently fallacious, but it is a fallacy that one might commit subconsciously.

Exercises on pp. 138–141

1. An apparently verbal dispute that is really genuine. The ambiguous phrase "greatest hitter" is used by Daye in the sense of getting the largest number of hits and by Knight in the sense of *hitting the largest number of home runs.* They really disagree in attitude toward Rose and Aaron, Daye having highest esteem for the former, as a hitter, and Knight for the latter, as a hitter.

5. A merely verbal dispute. The ambiguous phrase "business . . . good" is used by Daye in the sense of *increased sales* and by Knight in the sense of *increased profit.* There *may* be a disagreement in attitude toward the company in question. Daye approving and Knight deploring, but this is not at all clear from their words.

10. An obviously genuine dispute, with Daye affirming and Knight denying that *Dick bought himself a new car.*

15. Merely verbal; the ambiguous word "unemployed" is used by Daye in the (more usual) sense of "employable person who is ready and willing to work but not able to secure employment" and by Knight in the (somewhat odd) sense of "person who is not gainfully employed."

Exercises on p. 143

I. 1. animal, vertebrate, mammal, feline, wildcat, lynx.

Exercises on p. 146

I. 1. Gregory Peck, Paul Newman, Robert Redford.

    5. bromine, chlorine, iodine.

II. 1. movie star.

     5. halogen.

Exercises on pp. 150–151

I. 1. ridiculous.

    5. vanity.

   10. danger.

   15. portent.

II. 1. unmarried man.

     5. young offspring.

    10. very large person.

    15. very small person.

    20. very small meal.

Exercises on pp. 155–158

II. 1. Too narrow, violates Rule 3. Some teachers give instruction to adults.

5. Obscure, violates Rule 4. Also it fails to state the essence, which is to change over time, thus violating Rule 1.

10. Circular, since "produces" is synonymous with "causes." Violates Rule 2.

15. Figurative language, violates Rule 4.

20. Too narrow, violates Rule 3. But there are philosophical issues involved here, as shown by the following:

> Unless one is to abandon the physiological paradigm altogether, this definition is far too wide. Health is functional normality, and as such is desirable exactly insofar as it promotes goals one can justify on independent grounds. But there is presumably no intrinsic value in having the functional organization typical of a species if the same goals can be better achieved by other means. A sixth sense, for example, would increase our goal-efficiency without increasing our health: so might the amputation of our legs at the knee and their replacement by a nuclear-powered air-cushion vehicle.
> —CHRISTOPHER BOORSE,"On the Distinction Between Disease and Illness," *Philosophy and Public Affairs,* Vol. 5, No. 1, 1975

III. 1. Figurative language, violates Rule 4. It also fails to state the essence, violating Rule 1.

5. Too broad, since some prose records such moments; and too narrow, since some (great) poetry is tragic; violates Rule 3. It may also be criticized as being phrased in figurative language, violating Rule 4, although this is not altogether obvious.

10. Too broad, since some persons with a very low opinion of themselves tend to behave this way; and too narrow, since some supremely conceited persons do not stoop to such vainglory or social climbing; violates Rule 3. It may also be criticized for violating Rule 1 in not stating the essence, which is a trait of character rather than a tendency to overt behavior of the kinds specified.

15. Too narrow; not all political power is exercised "for the public good," certainly not "*only* for the public good"; violates Rule 3.

20. Too broad, violates Rule 3. In his *A History of Western Philosophy,* Bertrand Russell criticized this definition on the grounds that "the dealings of a drill-sergeant with a crowd of recruits, or of a bricklayer with a heap of bricks . . . exactly fulfill Dewey's definition of 'inquiry'."

25. Figurative language, violates Rule 4. Probably the definition of "liberty" is too narrow in several respects: It is not confined to people in "good social position," or to saying what "everybody believes"; violates Rule 3. And "license" is also defined in a way that is too narrow, because often people exercise license by saying what is not true; violates Rule 3. But this kind of comment runs the danger of spoiling a good joke.

30. As it stands this definition is obviously circular. It is followed in Wittgenstein's book, however, by "I.e.: if you want to understand the use of the word 'meaning', look for what are called 'explanations of meaning'." Thus

emended, the definition is made consistent with Wittgenstein's tendency to identify *meaning* with *use*. Compare: "A spade is to dig."

Exercises on pp. 164–165

1. S = historians, P = extremely gifted writers whose works read like first-rate novels. Form: particular affirmative.

5. S = members of families that are rich and famous, P = persons of either wealth or distinction. Form: particular negative.

Exercises on p. 168

1. Affirmative, particular. Subject and predicate both undistributed.

5. Negative, universal. Subject and predicate both distributed.

Exercises on p. 172

1. If a is true: b is false, c is true, d is false.
   If a is false: d is true, b and c are undetermined.

Exercises on pp. 178–181

I.   1. No reckless drivers who pay no attention to traffic regulations are people who are considerate of others. Equivalent.

II.   1. Some college athletes are not nonprofessionals.

III. 1. All nonpessimists are nonjournalists. Equivalent.

IV.   1. False   5. False.

V.   1. False   5. Undetermined.

VI.   1. Undetermined.   5. True.   10. False.
         15. False   20. True   25. Undetermined.

VII. 1. True.   5. False.   10. Undetermined.
         15. False.   20. True.   25. Undetermined.

Exercises on p. 184

I.   Step (3) to (4) is invalid (conversion by limitation).

Exercises on p. 190

1. $SP \neq 0$.

5. $SM = 0$.

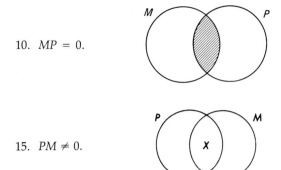

10. $MP = 0$.

15. $PM \neq 0$.

Exercises on p. 194

1. No nuclear-powered submarines are commercial vessels.
   All nuclear-powered submarines are warships.
   Therefore no warships are commercial vessels.
   EAE-3

5. All advocates of high tariff rates are Republicans.
   Some Republicans are not conservatives.
   Therefore some conservatives are not advocates of high tariff rates.
   AOO-4

Exercises on pp. 196–197

1. All bipeds are astronauts, for all astronauts are humans, and all humans are bipeds.

5. All unicorns are mammals, so some mammals are not animals, since no animals are unicorns.

Exercises on pp. 205–206

I. 1. All M is P.
       No S is M
       ∴ No S is P.

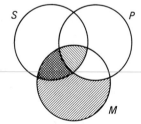

invalid.

    5. No P is M.
       Some M is S.
       ∴ Some S is not P.

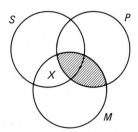

valid.

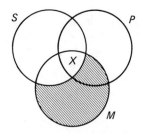

10. Some *P* is *M*.
    All *M* is *S*.
    ∴ Some *S* is *P*.

valid.

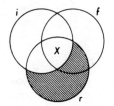

II. 1. Some reformers are fanatics.
        All reformers are idealists.
        ∴ Some idealists are fanatics.

IAI-3
valid.

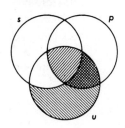

5. No pleasure vessels are underwater craft.
   All underwater craft are submarines.
   ∴ No submarines are pleasure vessels.

EAE-4
invalid.

Exercises on pp. 211–213

  I. 1. Undistributed Middle. Breaks Rule 2.
      5. Illicit Minor. Breaks Rule 3.
     10. Illicit Major. Breaks Rule 3.
 II. 1. Undistributed Middle. Breaks Rule 2.
      5. Existential Fallacy. Breaks Rule 6.
III. 1. Affirmative Conclusion from a Negative Premiss. Breaks Rule 5.
      5. Illicit Minor. Breaks Rule 3.
 IV. 1. No, for its mood would have to be *EEE* in violation of Rule 4.
      5. In Figure 2 one premiss would have to be negative to avoid violating Rule
         2. But then by Rule 5 the conclusion would have to be negative and would
         distribute its predicate, thus violating Rule 3. In all other figures (1, 3, 4) it
         is possible, as is shown by the fact that *AII*-1, *AII*-3, and *IAI*-4 are all valid.
         (*IAI*-3 is also valid, of course.)

Exercises on pp. 217–218

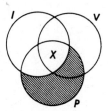

1. Some *P* is *V*.
   All *P* is *I*.
   ∴ Some *I* is *V*.

valid.

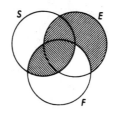

5. All *E* is *F*.
No *F* is *S*.
∴ No *S* is *E*.

valid ("Flammable" and "inflammable" are synonyms.)

Exercises on pp. 224–225

1. All roses are fragrant things.

5. All Junkos are best things that money can buy.

10. No people who face the sun are people who see their own shadows.

15. No candidates of the Old Guard are persons supported by the Young Turks. (or) No Young Turks are supporters of candidates of the Old Guard.

20. All people who love well are people who pray well.

Exercises on pp. 227–231

I. 1. All times when he is reminded of his loss are times when he groans.

5. All cases in which she gives her opinion are cases in which she is asked to give her opinion.

II. 1. No things derived from sensory impressions are items of knowledge of substance itself.
All items of knowledge are things derived from sensory impressions.
∴ No items of knowledge are items of knowledge of substance itself.

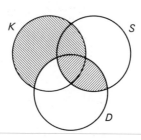

EAE-1

valid.

5. All bankrupt companies are companies unable to pay interest on their debts.
Barcelona Traction is a company unable to pay interest on its debts.
∴ Barcelona Traction is a bankrupt company.

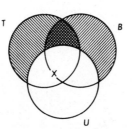

AAA-2
AII-2

invalid. (Undistributed Middle)

10. No gold is base metal.
    Some base metals are things that glitter.
    ∴ Some things that glitter are not gold.

EIO-4

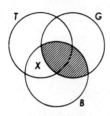

valid.

15. No persons who are truly objective are persons likely to be mistaken.
    All persons likely to be mistaken are persons who ignore the facts.
    ∴ No persons who ignore the facts are persons who are truly objective.

EAE-4

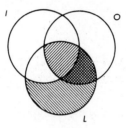

invalid. (Illicit Minor)

20. All things interesting to engineers are approximations.
    No approximations are irrationals.
    ∴ No irrationals are things interesting to engineers.

AEE-4

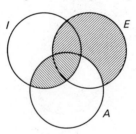

valid.

25. All excessive drinkers are debtors.
    Some executive drinkers are not unemployed persons.
    ∴ Some unemployed persons are not debtors.

AOO-3

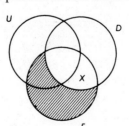

invalid. (Illicit Major)

30. All places where pickets are present are places where there is a strike.
    The factory is a place where pickets are present.
    ∴ The factory is a place where there is a strike.

AAA-1
AII-1

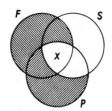

valid.

35. All valid syllogisms are syllogisms that distribute their middle terms in at
    least one premiss.
    This syllogism is a syllogism that distributes its middle term in at least one
    premiss.
    ∴ This syllogism is a valid syllogism.

AAA-2
AII-2

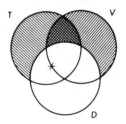

invalid. (Undistributed
Middle)

40. All persons present are employed persons.
    All members are persons present.
    ∴ All members are employed persons.

AAA-1

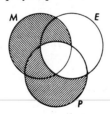

valid.

45. All times when he is sick are times when he complains.
    This time is not a time when he is sick.
    ∴ This time is not a time when he complains.

AEE-1
AOO-1

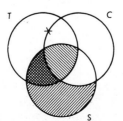

invalid. (Illicit Major)

Exercises on pp. 233–235

1. Third order.
   No well-mannered people are "alienated" people.
   The American people are well-mannered people.
   ∴ The American people are not "alienated" people.

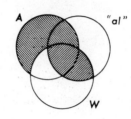

EAE-1   valid.

5. First order.
   All flesh is passive, the plaything of its hormones and of the species, the
   restless prey of its desires.
   Man is flesh.
   ∴ Man is passive, the plaything of his hormones and of the species, the
   restless prey of his desires.

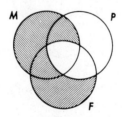

AAA-1   valid.

10. First order.
    No creatures who act not only under external compulsion, but also by inner
    necessity are possessors of freedom in the philosophical sense.
    All persons are creatures who act not only under external compulsion, but
    also by inner necessity.
    ∴ No persons are possessors of freedom in the philosophical sense.

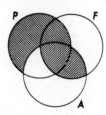

EAE-1   valid.

Valid enthymeme whose major premiss would probably be expressed as
"No one is free in the philosophical sense who acts not only under external
compulsion, but also by inner necessity."

15. Third order.
No men who serve Mammon are men who serve God.
Henry is a man who serves Mammon.
∴ Henry is not a man who serves God.

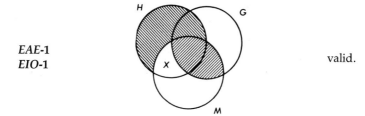

EAE-1
EIO-1

valid.

20. First order.
All fathers who know their own children are wise fathers.
He is a father who knows his own child.
∴ He is a wise father.

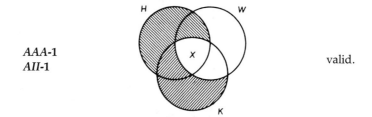

AAA-1
AII-1

valid.

Here the missing major premiss was expressed in *The Merchant of Venice* as "It is a wise father that knows his own child."

25. First order.
All those who deserve the fair are those who are brave.
Achilles is brave.
∴ Achilles is one who deserves the fair.

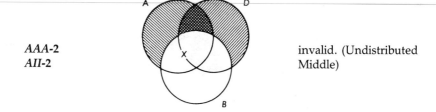

AAA-2
AII-2

invalid. (Undistributed Middle)

The missing major premiss was stated by Dryden as "None but the brave deserves the fair." To make the enthymeme into a valid syllogism, the converse of the indicated missing premiss would have to be added. If it is, the result is a valid syllogism of form **AAA-1** and **AII-1**.

30. Second order.

All times in which the theater could exist are times when it is possible to pretend to motives and abilities other than one's real ones, or to pretend to strengths of motives and levels of ability other than their real strengths and levels.

All times are times in which the theater could exist.

∴ All times are times when it is possible to pretend, etc.

AAA-1

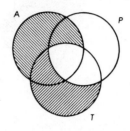

valid.

Exercises on pp. 237–238

I. 1. (1') All babies are illogical persons.
    (3') All illogical persons are despised persons.
    (2') No persons who can manage crocodiles are despised persons.
    ∴ No babies are persons who can manage crocodiles.

All *I* is *D*.
All *B* is *I*.
∴ All *B* is *D*.

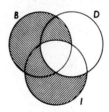

valid.

No *M* is *D*.
All *B* is *D*.
∴ No *B* is *M*.

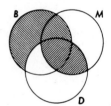

valid.

II. 1. (1') All those who take in the *Times* are those who are well educated.
     (3') No creatures who cannot read are those who are well educated.
     (2') All hedgehogs are creatures who cannot read.
     ∴No hedgehogs are those who take in the *Times*.

All *T* is *W*.
No *C* is *W*.
∴ No *C* is *T*.

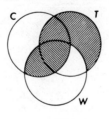

valid.

No *C* is *T*.
All *H* is *C*.
∴ No *H* is *T*.

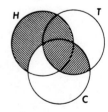

valid.

Exercises on pp. 241–244

1. Pure Hypothetical Syllogism. Valid.

5. Fallacy of Denying the Antecedent. Invalid.

10. Pure Hypothetical Syllogism. Invalid.

15. Disjunctive Syllogism. Valid.

20. Pure Hypothetical Syllogism. Valid.

25. Mixed Hypothetical Syllogism, *modus tollens*. Valid.

30. Mixed Hypothetical Syllogism, *modus tollens*. Valid.

35. Mixed Hypothetical Syllogism, *modus tollens*. Valid.

Exercises on pp. 249–252

1. Impossible to go between the horns. It would be plausible to grasp it by either horn, arguing either (a) that liberties do not properly include the right to publish false and harmful doctrines or (b) that we run no risk of losing our own liberties if we vigorously oppose false and harmful doctrines with true and helpful ones. And it could be plausibly rebutted (but not refuted) by using its ingredients to prove that "we must either be guiltless of suppressing the liberties of others or else run no risk of losing our own liberties."

5. The key to refuting this dilemma lies in exposing the ambiguity of the key phrase "going beyond," which could mean "going logically beyond to what is not implied" or "going psychologically beyond to what is not suggested." When this is done, it permits grasping it by one horn or the other depending upon which sense of "going beyond" is intended. Of course, the usual plausible but nonrefuting rebuttal can be constructed here.

10. It is very easy to go between the horns here, because people lie on a continuum of virtue stretching from saints to sinners. It can plausibly be grasped by the second horn, arguing that even very bad people may be deterred from wrongdoing by strictly enforced laws. The usual plausible but nonrefuting rebuttal can be constructed here out of the ingredients of the given dilemma.

15. Impossible to go between the horns. It is plausible to grasp it by either horn, arguing either (a) that when desiring to preserve we may be motivated simply by inertia and seek to rest in the status quo even while admitting that a change would not be worse and might even be better—but just "not worth the trouble of changing" or (b) that when desiring to change we may be motivated simply by boredom with the status quo and seek a change even while admitting that a change might not be better and might even be worse—but "let's have a little variety." These are psychological rather than political or moral considerations, but the original dilemma appears to be itself psychological. The usual rebutting counterdilemma could be used here: when desiring to preserve, we do not wish to bring about something better; when desiring to change, we do not wish to prevent a change to the worse. It is a question, however, how plausible this is.

20. Of the first dilemma one must admit that as it is formulated here that one cannot go between the horns, at least if "more than a synonym" is understood as "other than a synonym." But grasping the first horn is easy, especially along Fregean lines, which distinguish sense from reference. And grasping the second horn is also possible, with one plausible move turning on equivocations that need untangling, another turning on the legitimate

aim of improving the terms (or concepts) being analyzed. The usual non-refuting rebuttal can be constructed out of the original dilemma's ingredients. Of the second dilemma, one can go between the horns by remarking on the fact that directions for the proper use of a new term need not take the form of, or be reducible to, an explicit definition of it. This suggests a plausible way of grasping the first horn. The usual nonrefuting rebuttal can be constructed out of the original dilemma's ingredients.

Exercises on pp. 262–265

I. 1. True.   5. True.   10. True.   15. False.   20. True.

II. 1. True.   5. False.   10. True.   15. True.   20. False.

III. 1. True.   5. True.   10. False.   15. False.   20. True.

IV. 1. $I \cdot \sim L$ 5. $\sim I \cdot \sim L$ 10. $\sim(E \vee J)$.

   15. $\sim I \vee L$ 20. $(I \cdot E) \vee \sim(J \cdot S)$

Exercises on pp. 273–275

I. 1. True.   5. False.   10. True.   15. False.   20. False.

II. 1. True.   5. False.   10. False.   15. True.   20. False.

III. 1. $A \supset (B \supset C)$ 5. $(A \cdot B) \supset C$ 10. $\sim[A \supset (B \cdot C)]$

   15. $B \supset (A \vee C)$ 20. $B \vee C$

Exercises on pp. 284–285

I. a. 3 is the specific form of a.

   e. 10 is the specific form of e.

   j. 6 has j as a substitution instance, and 23 is the specific form of j.

II. 1.

p	q	$p \supset q$	$\sim q$	$\sim p$	$\sim q \supset \sim p$
T	T	T	F	F	T
T	F	F	T	F	F
F	T	T	F	T	T
F	F	T	T	T	T

valid.

5.

p	q	$p \supset q$
T	T	T
T	F	F
F	T	T
F	F	T

invalid. (Shown by second row.)

10.

p	q	$p \cdot q$
T	T	T
T	F	F
F	T	F
F	F	F

valid.

15.

p	q	r	q ⊃ r	p ⊃ (q ⊃ r)	p ⊃ r	q ⊃ (q ⊃ r)	p v q	(p v q) ⊃ r
T	T	T	T	T	T	T	T	T
T	T	F	F	F	F	F	T	F
T	F	T	T	T	T	T	T	T
T	F	F	T	T	F	T	T	F
F	T	T	T	T	T	T	T	T
F	T	F	F	T	T	T	T	F
F	F	T	T	T	T	T	F	T
F	F	F	T	T	T	T	F	T

invalid. (Shown by fourth and sixth rows.)

20.

p	q	r	s	p • q	p ⊃ q	(p • q) ⊃ r	r ⊃ s	p ⊃ (r ⊃ s)	(p ⊃ q) • [(p • q) ⊃ r]	p ⊃ s
T	T	T	T	T	T	T	T	T	T	T
T	T	T	F	T	T	T	F	F	T	F
T	T	F	T	T	T	F	T	T	F	T
T	T	F	F	T	T	F	T	T	F	F
T	F	T	T	F	F	T	T	T	F	T
T	F	T	F	F	F	T	F	F	F	F
T	F	F	T	F	F	T	T	T	F	T
T	F	F	F	F	F	T	T	T	F	F
F	T	T	T	F	T	T	T	T	T	T
F	T	T	F	F	T	T	F	T	T	T
F	T	F	T	F	T	T	T	T	T	T
F	T	F	F	F	T	T	T	T	T	T
F	F	T	T	F	T	T	T	T	T	T
F	F	T	F	F	T	T	F	T	T	T
F	F	F	T	F	T	T	T	T	T	T
F	F	F	F	F	T	T	T	T	T	T

valid.

III.

1. (A v B) ⊃ (A • B)
   A v B   has the specific
   ∴ A • B   form

   (p v q) ⊃ (p • q)
   p v q
   ∴ p • q

p	q	p v q	p • q	(p v q) ⊃ (p • q)
T	T	T	T	T
T	F	T	F	F
F	T	T	F	F
F	F	F	F	T

valid.

5. (I v J) ⊃ (I • J)
   ~(I v J)   has the specific
   ∴ ~(I • J)   form

   (p v q) ⊃ (p • q)
   ~(p v q)
   ∴ ~(p • q)

p	q	$p \lor q$	$p \cdot q$	$(p \lor q) \supset (p \cdot q)$	$\sim(p \lor q)$	$\sim(p \cdot q)$
T	T	T	T	T	F	F
T	F	T	F	F	F	T
F	T	T	F	F	F	T
F	F	F	F	T	T	T

valid.

IV. 1. $A \supset (B \cdot C)$

$\sim B$ has the specific

$\therefore \sim A$ form

$p \supset (q \cdot r)$

$\sim q$

$\therefore \sim p$

p	q	r	$q \cdot r$	$p \supset (q \cdot r)$	$\sim q$	$\sim p$
T	T	T	T	T	F	F
T	T	F	F	F	F	F
T	F	T	F	F	T	F
T	F	F	F	F	T	F
F	T	T	T	T	F	T
F	T	F	F	T	F	T
F	F	T	F	T	T	T
F	F	F	F	T	T	T

valid.

5. $M \supset (N \supset O)$

N has the specific

$\therefore O \supset M$ form

$p \supset (q \supset r)$

q

$\therefore r \supset p$

p	q	r	$q \supset r$	$p \supset (q \supset r)$	$r \supset p$
T	T	T	T	T	T
T	T	F	F	F	T
T	F	T	T	T	T
T	F	F	T	T	T
F	T	T	T	T	F
F	T	F	F	T	T
F	F	T	T	T	F
F	F	F	T	T	T

invalid. (Shown by fifth row.)

Exercises on pp. 291–292

I. 1. c is the specific form of 1.

5. c has 5 as a substitution instance, and i is the specific form of 5.

II. 1.

p	q	$p \supset q$	$p \supset (p \supset q)$	$[p \supset (p \supset q)] \supset q$
T	T	T	T	T
T	F	F	F	T
F	T	T	T	T
F	F	T	T	F

contingent.

					$p \supset$	$p \supset$
5.	p	q	$\sim q$	$q \cdot \sim q$	$(q \cdot \sim q)$	$[p \supset (q \cdot \sim q)]$
	T	T	F	F	F	F
	T	F	T	F	F	F
	F	T	F	F	T	T
	F	F	T	F	T	T

contingent.

							$(p \supset q) \equiv$
III. 1.	p	q	$p \supset q$	$\sim q$	$\sim p$	$\sim q \supset \sim p$	$(\sim q \supset \sim p)$
	T	T	T	F	F	T	T
	T	F	F	T	F	F	T
	F	T	T	F	T	T	T
	F	F	T	T	T	T	T

tautology.

5.	p	q	$p \vee q$	$p \cdot (p \vee q)$	$p \equiv [p \cdot (p \vee q)]$
	T	T	T	T	T
	T	F	T	T	T
	F	T	T	F	T
	F	F	F	F	T

tautology.

						$(p \supset q) \equiv$
10.	p	q	$p \supset q$	$p \vee q$	$(p \vee q) \equiv q$	$[(p \vee q) \equiv q]$
	T	T	T	T	T	T
	T	F	F	T	F	T
	F	T	T	T	T	T
	F	F	T	F	T	T

tautology.

					$p \cdot$			$(p \cdot q) \vee$	$[p \cdot (q \vee r)] \equiv$
15.	p	q	r	$q \vee r$	$(q \vee r)$	$p \cdot q$	$p \cdot r$	$(p \cdot r)$	$[(p \cdot q) \vee (p \cdot r)]$
	T	T	T	T	T	T	T	T	T
	T	T	F	T	T	T	F	T	T
	T	F	T	T	T	F	T	T	T
	T	F	F	F	F	F	F	F	T
	F	T	T	T	F	F	F	F	T
	F	T	F	T	F	F	F	F	T
	F	F	T	T	F	F	F	F	T
	F	F	F	F	F	F	F	F	T

tautology.

Exercises on pp. 298–303

I.   1. *Absorption (Abs.)*   5. *Constructive Dilemma (C.D.)*

     10. *Hypothetical Syllogism (H.S.)*   15. *Conjunction (Conj.)*

II.   1. 3. 1, Simp.
4. 3, Add.
5. 2,4, M.P.
6. 3,5, Conj.

5. 5. 2,4, M.P.
6. 1,5, Conj.
7. 3,4, D.S.
8. 6.7, C.D.

III.   1. 1. A
2. B /∴ $(A \lor C) \cdot B$
3. $A \lor C$ 1, Add.
4. $(A \lor C) \cdot B$ 3,2, Conj.

5. 1. $M \lor N$
2. $\sim M \cdot \sim O$ /∴ N
3. $\sim M$ 2, Simp.
4. N 1,3, D.S.

10. 1. $A \supset B$
2. $(A \cdot B) \supset C$ /∴ $A \supset C$
3. $A \supset (A \cdot B)$ 1, Abs.
4. $A \supset C$ 3,2, H.S.

15. 1. $(P \supset Q) \cdot (R \supset S)$
2. $(P \lor R) \cdot (Q \lor R)$ /∴ $Q \lor S$
3. $P \lor R$ 2, Simp.
4. $Q \lor S$ 1,3, C.D.

20. 1. $(\sim H \lor I) \lor J$
2. $\sim (\sim H \lor I)$ /∴ $J \lor \sim H$
3. J 1,2, D.S.
4. $J \lor \sim H$ 3, Add.

25. 1. $(W \cdot X) \supset (Y \cdot Z)$
2. $\sim [(W \cdot X) \cdot (Y \cdot Z)]$ /∴ $\sim (W \cdot X)$
3. $(W \cdot X) \supset [(W \cdot X) \cdot (Y \cdot Z)]$ 1, Abs.
4. $\sim (W \cdot X)$ 3,2, M.T.

IV.   1. 1. $A \lor (B \supset A)$
2. $\sim A \cdot C$ /∴ $\sim B$
3. $\sim A$ 2, Simp.
4. $B \supset A$ 1,3, D.S.
5. $\sim B$ 4,3, M.T.

5. 1. $N \supset [(N \cdot O) \supset P]$
2. $N \cdot O$ /∴ P
3. N 2, Simp.
4. $(N \cdot O) \supset P$ 1,3, M.P.
5. P 4,2, M.P.

10. 1. $E \lor \sim F$
2. $F \lor (E \lor G)$
3. $\sim E$ /∴ G
4. $\sim F$ 1,3, D.S.
5. $E \lor G$ 2,4, D.S.
6. G 5,3, D.S.

V.   1. 1. $A \supset B$
2. $A \lor (C \cdot D)$
3. $\sim B \cdot \sim E$ /∴ C
4. $\sim B$ 3, Simp.
5. $\sim A$ 1,4, M.T.
6. $C \cdot D$ 2,5, D.S.
7. C 6, Simp.

5. 1. $(Q \supset R) \cdot (S \supset T)$
2. $(U \supset V) \cdot (W \supset X)$
3. $Q \lor U$ /∴ $R \lor V$
4. $Q \supset R$ 1, Simp.
5. $U \supset V$ 2, Simp.
6. $(Q \supset R) \cdot (U \supset V)$ 4,5, Conj.
7. $R \lor V$ 6,3, C.D.

VI.   1. 1. $(G \lor H) \supset (J \cdot K)$
2. G /∴ J
3. $G \lor H$ 2, Add.
4. $J \cdot K$ 1,3, M.P.
5. J 4, Simp.

5. 1. $C \supset R$
2. $(C \cdot R) \supset B$
3. $(C \supset B) \supset \sim S$
4. $S \lor M$ /∴ M
5. $C \supset (C \cdot R)$ 1, Abs.
6. $C \supset B$ 5,2, H.S.
7. $\sim S$ 3,6, M.P.
8. M 4,7, D.S.

Exercises on pp. 308–315

I.   1. *Transposition* (Trans.)   5. *Material Equivalence* (Equiv.)

   10. *Association* (Assoc.)   15. *Distribution* (Dist.)

II.   1. 3. 2, Trans.   5. 3. 2, Dist.
   4. 3, D.N.   4. 3, Com.
   5. 1,4, H.S.   5. 4, Simp.
          6. 5, Taut.
          7. 1, Assoc.
          8. 7,6, D.S.
          9. 8, Impl.

III.   1. 1. $A \supset {\sim}A$ $/\therefore {\sim}A$ 5. 1. ${\sim}K \text{ v } (L \supset M)$ $/\therefore (K \cdot L) \supset M$
   2. ${\sim}A \text{ v } {\sim}A$ 1, Impl.   2. $K \supset (L \supset M)$ 1, Impl.
   ${\sim}A$ 2, Taut.   3. $(K \cdot L) \supset M$ 2, Exp.

   10. 1. $Z \supset A$ 15. 1. $(O \text{ v } P) \supset (Q \text{ v } R)$
   2. ${\sim}A \text{ v } B$ $/\therefore Z \supset B$ 2. $P \text{ v } O$ $/\therefore Q \text{ v } R$
   3. $A \supset B$ 2, Impl.   3. $O \text{ v } P$ 2, Com.
   4. $Z \supset B$ 1,3, H.S.   4. $Q \text{ v } R$ 1,3, M.P.

   20. 1. $I \supset [J \text{ v } (K \text{ v } L)]$
   2. ${\sim}[(J \text{ v } K) \text{ v } L]$ $/\therefore {\sim}I$
   3. ${\sim}[J \text{ v } (K \text{ v } L)]$ 2, Assoc.
   4. ${\sim}I$ 1,3, M.T.

   25. 1. $A \text{ v } B$
   2. $C \text{ v } D$ $/\therefore [(A \text{ v } B) \cdot C] \text{ v } [(A \text{ v } B) \cdot D]$
   3. $(A \text{ v } B) \cdot (C \text{ v } D)$ 1,2, Conj.
   4. $[(A \text{ v } B) \cdot C] \text{ v } [(A \text{ v } B) \cdot D]$ 3, Dist.

IV.   1. 1. ${\sim}A \supset A$ $/\therefore A$
   2. ${\sim}{\sim}A \text{ v } A$ 1, Impl.
   3. $A \text{ v } A$ 2, D.N.
   4. A 3, Taut.

   5. 1. $[(K \text{ v } L) \text{ v } M] \text{ v } N$ $/\therefore (N \text{ v } K) \text{ v } (L \text{ v } M)$
   2. $[K \text{ v } (L \text{ v } M)] \text{ v } N$ 1, Assoc.
   3. $N \text{ v } [K \text{ v } (L \text{ v } M)]$ 2, Com.
   4. $(N \text{ v } K) \text{ v } (L \text{ v } M)$ 3, Assoc.

   10. 1. $(Z \text{ v } A) \text{ v } B$
   2. ${\sim}A$ $/\therefore Z \text{ v } B$
   3. $(A \text{ v } Z) \text{ v } B$ 1, Com.
   4. $A \text{ v } (Z \text{ v } B)$ 3, Assoc.
   5. $Z \text{ v } B$ 4,2, D.S.

V.   1. 1. ${\sim}A$ $/\therefore A \supset B$ 5. 1. $K \supset L$ $/\therefore K \supset (L \text{ v } M)$
   2. ${\sim}A \text{ v } B$ 1, Add.   2. ${\sim}K \text{ v } L$ 1, Impl.
   3. $A \supset B$ 2, Impl.   3. $({\sim}K \text{ v } L) \text{ v } M$ 2, Add.
          4. ${\sim}K \text{ v } (L \text{ v } M)$ 3, Assoc.
          5. $K \supset (L \text{ v } M)$ 4, Impl.

VI.   1. 1. $A \supset {\sim}B$ 5. 1. $[(M \cdot N) \cdot O] \supset P$
   2. ${\sim}(C \cdot {\sim}A)$ $/\therefore C \supset {\sim}B$ 2. $Q \supset [(O \cdot M) \cdot N]$ $/\therefore {\sim}Q \text{ v } P$
   3. ${\sim}C \text{ v } {\sim}{\sim}A$ 2, De M.   3. $[O \cdot (M \cdot N)] \supset P$ 1, Com.

4. $C \supset \sim\sim A$ 3, Impl.

5. $C \supset A$ 4, D.N.

6. $C \supset \sim B$ 5,1, H.S.

4. $[(O \cdot M) \cdot N] \supset P$ 3, Assoc.

5. $Q \supset P$ 2,4, H.S.

6. $\sim Q \lor P$ 5, Impl.

10. 1. $[H \lor (I \lor J)] \supset (K \supset J)$
    2. $L \supset [I \lor (J \lor H)]$ $/\therefore (L \cdot K) \supset J$
    3. $[(I \lor J) \lor H] \supset (K \supset J)$ 1, Com.
    4. $(I \lor (J \lor H)) \supset (K \supset J)$ 3, Assoc.
    5. $L \supset (K \supset J)$ 2,4, H.S.
    6. $(L \cdot K) \supset J$ 5, Exp.

15. 1. $(Z \supset Z) \supset (A \supset A)$
    2. $(A \supset A) \supset (Z \supset Z)$ $/\therefore A \supset A$
    3. $[(Z \supset Z) \supset (A \supset A)] \lor \sim A$ 1, Add.
    4. $\sim A \lor [(Z \supset Z) \supset (A \supset A)]$ 3, Com.
    5. $A \supset [(Z \supset Z) \supset (A \supset A)]$ 4, Impl.
    6. $A \supset \{A \cdot [(Z \supset Z) \supset (A \supset A)]\}$ 5, Abs.
    7. $\sim A \lor \{A \cdot [(Z \supset Z) \supset (A \supset A)]\}$ 6, Impl.
    8. $(\sim A \lor A) \cdot \{\sim A \lor [(Z \supset Z) \supset (A \supset A)]\}$ 7, Dist.
    9. $\sim A \lor A$ 8, Simp.
    10. $A \supset A$ 9, Impl.

VII. 1. 1. $\sim N \lor A$
    2. N $/\therefore A$
    3. $N \supset A$ 1, Impl.
    4. A 3,2, M.P.

5. 1. $R \supset A$ $/\therefore R \supset (A \lor W)$
    2. $\sim R \lor A$ 1, Impl.
    3. $(\sim R \lor A) \lor W$ 2, Add.
    4. $\sim R \lor (A \lor W)$ 3, Assoc.
    5. $R \supset (A \lor W)$ 4, Impl.

10. 1. $(G \cdot S) \supset D$
    2. $(S \supset D) \supset P$
    3. G $/\therefore P$
    4. $G \supset (S \supset D)$ 1, Exp.
    5. $S \supset D$ 4,3, M.P.
    6. P 2,5, M.P.

15. 1. $M \supset \sim C$
    2. $\sim C \supset \sim A$
    3. $D \lor A$ $/\therefore \sim M \lor D$
    4. $M \supset \sim A$ 1,2, H.S.
    5. $A \lor D$ 3, Com.
    6. $\sim\sim A \lor D$ 5, D.N.
    7. $\sim A \supset D$ 6, Impl.
    8. $M \supset D$ 4,7, H.S.
    9. $\sim M \lor D$ 8, Impl.

20. 1. $P \supset \sim M$
    2. $D \supset M$
    3. $U \lor D$
    4. $(\sim P \supset \sim S) \cdot (\sim S \supset \sim D)$
    5. $P \lor \sim P$ $/\therefore U$
    6. $(\sim S \supset \sim D) \cdot (\sim P \supset \sim S)$ 4, Com.
    7. $\sim P \supset \sim S$ 4, Simp.
    8. $\sim S \supset \sim D$ 6, Simp.
    9. $\sim P \supset \sim D$ 7,8, H.S.
    10. $\sim M \supset \sim D$ 2, Trans.
    11. $P \supset \sim D$ 1,10, H.S.
    12. $(P \supset \sim D) \cdot (\sim P \supset \sim D)$ 11,9, Conj.
    13. $\sim D \lor \sim D$ 12,5, C.D.
    14. $\sim D$ 13, Taut.
    15. $D \lor U$ 3, Com.
    16. U 15,14, D.S.

Exercises on p. 317

 1. *A* *B* *C* *D*

   f **f** **f** **t**

 5. *S* *T* *U* *V* *W* *X*

   t **f** **f** **t** **t** **t** or any of thirteen other truth-value assignments.

Exercises on pp. 320–323

 1. 1. $(A \supset B) \cdot (C \supset D)$ $/\therefore (A \cdot C) \supset (B \lor D)$
   2. $A \supset B$ 1, Simp.
   3. $\sim A \lor B$ 2, Impl.
   4. $(\sim A \lor B) \lor D$ 3, Add.
   5. $\sim A \lor (B \lor D)$ 4, Assoc.
   6. $[\sim A \lor (B \lor D)] \lor \sim C$ 5, Add.
   7. $\sim C \lor [\sim A \lor (B \lor D)]$ 6, Comm.
   8. $(\sim C \lor \sim A) \lor (B \lor D)$ 7, Assoc.
   9. $(\sim A \lor \sim C) \lor (B \lor D)$ 8, Com.
   10. $\sim(A \cdot C) \lor (B \lor D)$ 9, De M.
   11. $(A \cdot C) \supset (B \lor D)$ 10. Impl.

 5. *X* *Y* *Z* *A* *B* *C*

   t **f** **t** **f** **t** **f**

II. 1. 1. $C \supset (M \supset D)$
   2. $D \supset V$
   3. $(D \supset A) \cdot \sim A$ $/\therefore M \supset \sim C$
   4. $D \supset A$ 3, Simp.
   5. $\sim A \cdot (D \supset A)$ 3, Com.
   6. $\sim A$ 5, Simp.
   7. $\sim D$ 4,6, M.T.
   8. $(C \cdot M) \supset D$ 1, Exp.
   9. $\sim(C \cdot M)$ 8,7, M.T.
   10. $\sim C \lor \sim M$ 9, De M.
   11. $\sim M \lor \sim C$ 10, Com.
   12. $M \supset \sim C$ 11, Impl.

 5. $(I \cdot S) \supset (G \cdot P)$
   $[(S \cdot \sim I) \supset A] \cdot (A \supset P)$
   $I \supset S$ $\therefore P$

	I	*S*	*G*	*P*	*A*	or	*I*	*S*	*G*	*P*	*A*
proved invalid by	**f**	**f**	**t**	**f**	**f**		**f**	**f**	**f**	**f**	**f**

 10. $(H \supset A) \cdot (F \supset C)$
   $A \supset (F \cdot E)$
   $(O \supset C) \cdot (O \supset M)$
   $P \supset (M \supset D)$
   $P \cdot (D \supset G)$ $\therefore H \supset G$

	H	*A*	*C*	*F*	*E*	*O*	*M*	*P*	*D*	*G*
proved invalid by	**t**	**t**	**t**	**t**	**t**	**f**	**f**	**t**	**f**	**f**

15.   1. $(J \lor A) \supset [(S \lor K) \supset (\sim I \cdot Y)]$
      2. $(\sim I \lor \sim M) \supset E$ $/\therefore J \supset (S \supset E)$
      3. $\sim(J \lor A) \lor [(S \lor K) \supset (\sim I \cdot Y)]$ 1, Impl.
      4. $[(S \lor K) \supset (\sim I \cdot Y)] \lor \sim(J \lor A)$ 3, Com.
      5. $[(S \lor K) \supset (\sim I \cdot Y)] \lor (\sim J \cdot \sim A)$ 4, De M.
      6. $\{[(S \lor K) \supset (\sim I \cdot Y)] \lor \sim J\} \cdot$
           $\{[(S \lor K) \supset (\sim I \cdot Y)] \lor \sim A\}$ 5, Dist.
      7. $[(S \lor K) \supset (\sim I \cdot Y)] \lor \sim J$ 6, Simp.
      8. $[\sim(S \lor K) \lor (\sim I \cdot Y)] \lor \sim J$ 7, Impl.
      9. $\sim(S \lor K) \lor [(\sim I \cdot Y) \lor \sim J]$ 8, Assoc.
     10. $[(\sim I \cdot Y) \lor \sim J] \lor \sim(S \lor K)$ 9, Com.
     11. $[(\sim I \cdot Y) \lor \sim J] \lor (\sim S \cdot \sim K)$ 10, De M.
     12. $\{[(\sim I \cdot Y) \lor \sim J] \lor \sim S\} \cdot$
           $\{[(\sim I \cdot Y) \lor \sim J] \lor \sim K\}$ 11, Dist.
     13. $[(\sim I \cdot Y) \lor \sim J] \lor \sim S$ 12, Simp.
     14. $(\sim I \cdot Y) \lor (\sim J \lor \sim S)$ 13, Assoc.
     15. $(\sim J \lor \sim S) \lor (\sim I \cdot Y)$ 14, Com.
     16. $[(\sim J \lor \sim S) \lor \sim I] \cdot [(\sim J \lor \sim S) \lor Y]$ 15, Dist.
     17. $(\sim J \lor \sim S) \lor \sim I$ 16, Simp.
     18. $[(\sim J \lor \sim S) \lor \sim I] \lor \sim M$ 17, Add.
     19. $(\sim J \lor \sim S) \lor (\sim I \lor \sim M)$ 18, Assoc.
     20. $\sim(J \cdot S) \lor (\sim I \lor \sim M)$ 19, De M.
     21. $(J \cdot S) \supset (\sim I \lor \sim M)$ 20, Impl.
     22. $(J \cdot S) \supset E$ 21, 2, H.S.
     23. $J \supset (S \supset E)$ 22, Exp.

Exercises on pp. 335–336

I.   1. $(x)(Bx \supset Mx)$

      5. $(\exists x)(Dx \cdot \sim Rx)$

     10. $(x)(Cx \supset \sim Fx)$

     15. $(x)(Vx \supset Cx)$

II.   1. $(\exists x)(Ax \cdot \sim Bx)$

      5. $(\exists x)(Ix \cdot \sim Jx)$

Exercises on pp. 341–342

I.   1.   1. $(x)(Ax \supset \sim Bx)$
          2. $(\exists x)(Cx \cdot Ax)$ $/\therefore (\exists x)(Cx \cdot \sim Bx)$
          3. $Ca \cdot Aa$ 2, **EI**
          4. $Aa \supset \sim Ba$ 1, **UI**
          5. $Aa \cdot Ca$ 3, Com.
          6. Aa 5, Simp.
          7. $\sim Ba$ 4,6, M.P.
          8. Ca 3, Simp.
          9. $Ca \cdot \sim Ba$ 8,7, Conj.
         10. $(\exists x)(Cx \cdot \sim Bx)$ 9, **EG**

5. 1. $(x)(Mx \supset Nx)$
    2. $(\exists x)(Mx \cdot Ox)$ $/\therefore (\exists x)(Ox \cdot Nx)$
    3. $Ma \cdot Oa$ 2, **EI**
    4. $Ma \supset Na$ 1, **UI**
    5. Ma 3, Simp.
    6. Na 4,5, M.P.
    7. $Oa \cdot Ma$ 3, Com.
    8. Oa 7, Simp.
    9. $Oa \cdot Na$ 8,6, Conj.
    10. $(\exists x)(Ox \cdot Nx)$ 9, **EG**

II. 1. 1. $(x)(Ax \supset \sim Bx)$
    2. Bc $/\therefore \sim Ac$
    3. $Ac \supset \sim Bc$ 1, **UI**
    4. $\sim\sim Bc$ 2, D.N.
    5. $\sim Ac$ 3,4, M.T.

5. 1. $(x)(Mx \supset Nx)$
    2. $(\exists x)(Ox \cdot Mx)$ $/\therefore (\exists x)(Ox \cdot Nx)$
    3. $Oa \cdot Ma$ 2, **EI**
    4. $Ma \supset Na$ 1, **UI**
    5. Oa 3, Simp.
    6. $Ma \cdot Oa$ 3, Com.
    7. Ma 6, Simp.
    8. Na 4,7, M.P.
    9. $Oa \cdot Na$ 5,8, Conj.
    10. $(\exists x)(Ox \cdot Nx)$ 9, **EG**

Exercises on p. 346

I. 1. $(\exists x)(Ax \cdot Bx)$ logically $Aa \cdot Ba$
    $(\exists x)(Cx \cdot Bx)$ equivalent $Ca \cdot Ba$
    $\therefore (x)(Cx \supset \sim Ax)$ in $\boxed{a}$ to $\therefore Ca \supset \sim Aa$

    proved invalid by Aa Ba Ca

                           t   **t**   **t**

5. $(\exists x)(Mx \cdot Nx)$ logically $(Ma \cdot Na) \vee (Mb \cdot Nb)$
    $(\exists x)(Mx \cdot Ox)$ equivalent $(Ma \cdot Oa) \vee (Mb \cdot Ob)$
    $\therefore (x)(Ox \supset Nx)$ in $\boxed{a, b}$ to $\therefore (Oa \supset Na) \cdot (Ob \supset Nb)$

    proved invalid by Ma Mb Na Nb Oa Ob

                           t   **t**   **t**   **f**   **t**   **t**

or any of several other truth value assignments.

II. 1. $(x)(Ax \supset Bx)$ logically $Aa \supset Ba$
    $(x)(Cx \supset Bx)$ equivalent $Ca \supset Ba$
    $\therefore (x)(Ax \supset Cx)$ in $\boxed{a}$ to $\therefore Aa \supset Ca$

    proved invalid by Aa Ba Ca

                           t   **t**   **f**

5. $(\exists x)(Mx \cdot Nx)$ } logically $\begin{cases} (Ma \cdot Na) \text{ v } (Mb \cdot Nb) \\ (Oa \cdot \sim Na) \text{ v } (Ob \cdot \sim Nb) \\ \therefore (Oa \supset \sim Ma) \cdot (Ob \supset \sim Mb) \end{cases}$
   $(\exists x)(Ox \cdot \sim Nx)$ } equivalent
   $\therefore (x)(Ox \supset \sim Mx)$ } in $\boxed{a, b}$ to

proved invalid by

Ma	Mb	Na	Nb	Oa	Ob
t	t	t	f	t	t

or any of several other truth-value assignments.

Exercises on pp. 350–353

I. 1. $(x)[(Ax \text{ v } Ox) \supset (Dx \cdot Nx)]$ 5. $(x)(Gx \supset (Wx \equiv Lx))$

II. 1. 1. $(x)[(Ax \text{ v } Bx) \supset (Cx \cdot Dx)]$ /∴ $(x)(Bx \supset Cx)$
         2. $(Ay \text{ v } By) \supset (Cy \cdot Dy)$ 1, **UI**
         3. $\sim(Ay \text{ v } By) \text{ v } (Cy \cdot Dy)$ 2, Impl.
         4. $[\sim(Ay \text{ v } By) \text{ v } Cy] \cdot \sim(Ay \text{ v } By) \text{ v } Dy]$ 3, Dist.
         5. $\sim(Ay \text{ v } By) \text{ v } Cy$ 4, Simp.
         6. $Cy \text{ v } \sim(Ay \text{ v } By)$ 5, Com.
         7. $Cy \text{ v } (\sim Ay \cdot \sim By)$ 6, De M.
         8. $(Cy \text{ v } \sim Ay) \cdot (Cy \text{ v } \sim By)$ 7, Dist.
         9. $(Cy \text{ v } \sim By) \cdot (Cy \text{ v } \sim Ay)$ 8, Com.
        10. $Cy \text{ v } \sim By$ 9, Simp.
        11. $\sim By \text{ v } Cy$ 10, Com.
        12. $By \supset Cy$ 11, Impl.
        13. $(x)(Bx \supset Cx)$ 12, **UG**

5. $(\exists x)(Sx \cdot Tx)$ } logically $\begin{cases} (Sa \cdot Ta) \text{ v } (Sb \cdot Tb) \text{ v } (Sc \cdot Tc) \\ (Ua \cdot \sim Sa) \text{ v } (Ub \cdot \sim Sb) \text{ v } (Uc \cdot \sim Sc) \\ (Va \cdot \sim Ta) \text{ v } (Vb \cdot \sim Tb) \text{ v } (Vc \cdot \sim Tc) \\ \therefore (Ua \cdot Va) \text{ v } (Ub \cdot Vb) \text{ v } (Uc \cdot Vc) \end{cases}$
   $(\exists x)(Ux \cdot \sim Sx)$ } equivalent
   $(\exists x)(Vx \cdot \sim Tx)$ } in   a, b, c
   $\therefore (\exists x)(Ux \cdot Vx)$ } to

proved invalid by

Sa	Sb	Sc	Ta	Tb	Tc	Ua	Ub	Uc	Va	Vb	Vc
t	f	t	t	t	f	f	t	f	t	f	t

or any of several other truth value assignments.

III. 1. 1. $(x)[(Ax \text{ v } Bx) \supset Cx]$
           2. $(x)(Vx \supset Ax)$ /∴ $(x)(Vx \supset Cx)$
           3. $(Ay \text{ v } By) \supset Cy$ 1, **UI**
           4. $Vy \supset Ay$ 2, **UI**
           5. $\sim Vy \text{ v } Ay$ 4, Impl.
           6. $(\sim Vy \text{ v } Ay) \text{ v } By$ 5, Add.
           7. $\sim Vy \text{ v } (Ay \text{ v } By)$ 6, Assoc.
           8. $Vy \supset (Ay \text{ v } By)$ 7, Impl.
           9. $Vy \supset Cy$ 8,3, H.S.
          10. $(x)(Vx \supset Cx)$ 9, **UG**

5. $(x)\{[Ex \cdot (Ix \text{ v } Tx)] \supset \sim Sx\}$
    $(\exists x)(Ex \cdot Ix)$
    $(\exists x)(Ex \cdot Tx)$
    $\therefore (x)(Ex \supset \sim Sx)$

This argument is logically equivalent in ⎡ *a, b* ⎤ to

$\{[Ea \cdot (Ia \text{ v } Ta)] \supset \sim Sa\} \cdot \{[Eb \cdot (Ib \text{ v } Tb)] \supset \sim Sb\}$
$(Ea \cdot Ia) \text{ v } (Eb \cdot Ib)$
$(Ea \cdot Ta) \text{ v } (Eb \cdot Tb)$
$\therefore (Ea \supset \sim Sa) \cdot (Eb \supset \sim Sb)$
which is proved invalid by

	Ea	Eb	Ia	Ib	Ta	Tb	Sa	Sb
	t	t	t	f	t	f	f	t
or	t	t	f	t	f	t	t	f

IV. 1. 1. $(x)[(Cx \cdot \sim Tx) \supset Px]$
    2. $(x)(Ox \supset Cx)$
    3. $(\exists x)(Ox \cdot \sim Px)$ $/\therefore (\exists x)(Tx)$
    4. $Oa \cdot \sim Pa$ 3, **EI**
    5. $Oa \supset Ca$ 2, **UI**
    6. $(Ca \cdot \sim Ta) \supset Pa$ 1,**UI**
    7. Oa 4, Simp.
    8. Ca 5,7, M.P.
    9. $\sim Pa \cdot Oa$ 4, Com.
    10. $\sim Pa$ 9, Simp.
    11. $Ca \supset (\sim Ta \supset Pa)$ 6, Exp.
    12. $\sim Ta \supset Pa$ 11,8, M.P.
    13. $\sim\sim Ta$ 12,10, M.T.
    14. Ta 13, D.N.
    15. $(\exists x)(Tx)$ 14, **EG**

5. $(\exists x)(Dx \cdot Ax)$
    $(x)[Ax \supset (Jx \text{ v } Cx)]$
    $(x)(Dx \supset \sim Cx)$
    $(x)[(Jx \cdot Ix) \supset \sim Px]$
    $(\exists x)(Dx \cdot Ix)$
    $\therefore (\exists x)(Dx \cdot \sim Px)$

This argument is logically equivalent in ⎡ *a, b* ⎤ to

$(Da \cdot Aa) \text{ v } (Db \cdot Ab)$
$[Aa \supset (Ja \text{ v } Ca)] \cdot [Ab \supset (Jb \text{ v } Cb)]$
$(Da \supset \sim Ca) \cdot (Db \supset \sim Cb)$
$[(Ja \cdot Ia) \supset \sim Pa] \cdot [(Jb \cdot Ib) \supset \sim Pb]$
$(Da \cdot Ia) \text{ v } (Db \cdot Ib)$
$\therefore (Da \cdot \sim Pa) \text{ v } (Db \cdot \sim Pb)$
is proved invalid by

	Da	Db	Aa	Ab	Ja	Jb	Ca	Cb	Ia	Ib	Pa	Pb
	t	t	t	f	t	f	f	f	f	t	t	t
or	t	t	f	t	f	t	f	f	t	f	t	t

Exercises on pp. 360–363

1. Analogical Argument.   5. Analogical Argument.
10. Analogical Argument.   15. Nonargumentative use of analogy.
20. Nonargumentative use of analogy.

Exercises on pp. 366–371

I. 1. (a) more, (b) more, (c) more, (d) more, (e) less, (f) neither.

II. 1. Large diamonds, armies, great intellects all have the attributes of greatness [of value for diamonds, of military strength for armies, of mental superiority for intellects], and of divisibility [through cutting for diamonds; dispersion for armies; interruption, disturbance, and distraction for intellects].
Large diamonds and armies all have the attribute of having their greatness diminish when they are divided.
Therefore great intellects also have the attribute of having their greatness diminish when they are divided.

(1) There are only three kinds of instances among which the analogies are said to hold, which is not very many. On the other hand, there are many, many instances of these kinds. By our first criterion the argument is fairly cogent.

(2) There are only three respects in which the things involved are said to be analogous. This is not many and the argument is accordingly rather weak.

(3) The conclusion states only that, when "divided," a great intellect will sink to the level of an ordinary one. This is not terribly strong a conclusion relative to the premises, and so by our third criterion the argument is fairly cogent.

(4) The instances with which the conclusion deals are enormously, fantastically different from the instances mentioned in the premises. There are so many disanalogies between intellects, on the one hand, and large diamonds and armies, on the other, that by our fourth criterion Schopenhauer's argument is almost totally lacking in probative force.

(5) There are but two kinds of instances in the premises with which the conclusion's instances are compared. Armies and large diamonds are, however, quite dissimilar to each other, so from the point of view of our fifth criterion, the argument is moderately cogent.

(6) Schopenhauer recognizes that the question of relevance is important, for he introduces a separate little discussion on this point. He urges that the superiority (the "greatness") of a great intellect "depends upon" its concentration or undividedness. Here he invokes the illustrative or explanatory (nonargumentative) analogy of the concave mirror which focuses all its available light on one point. There is indeed some merit in this claim, and by our sixth criterion the argument has a fairly high degree of cogency.

Finally, however, it must be admitted that the whole passage might plausibly be analyzed as invoking large diamonds and armies for illustrative and explanatory rather than argumentative purposes. The plausibility of this alternative analysis, however, derives more from the weakness of the analogical argument than from what is explicitly stated in the passage in question.

5. This passage can be analyzed in two different ways. In both ways the analogical argument is presented primarily as an illustration of the biologist's reasoning.

(I) Porpoises and men all have lungs, warm blood, and hair.

Men are mammals.

Therefore porpoises are also mammals.

(1) There are many instances examined, which makes the conclusion probable.

(2) There are only three respects noted in the premisses in which porpoises and men resemble each other. In terms of their sheer number, this is not many: not enough to make the argument plausible.

(3) The conclusion is enormously strong relative to the premisses, because so many attributes are summarized in the term "mammal" (shown by the variety of other, specific attributes confidently predicted by the zoologist). This tends, of course, to weaken the argument.

(4) There are many disanalogies between men and porpoises: porpoises are aquatic, men are terrestrial, porpoises have tails, men do not, porpoises do not have the well-developed, highly differentiated limbs characteristic of men, and so on. These tend to weaken the argument.

(5) There are very few dissimilarities among men—biologically speaking—and by our fifth criterion this tends to weaken the argument too.

(6) But in terms of relevance the argument is superlatively good, because biologists have found the three attributes remarked in the premisses to be such remarkably dependable indicators of other mammalian characteristics.

(II) Porpoises and men all have lungs, warm blood, and hair.

Men also nurse their young with milk, have a four-chambered heart, bones of a particular type, a certain general pattern of nerves and blood vessels, and red blood cells that lack nuclei.

Therefore porpoises also nurse their young with milk, have a four-chambered heart, bones of the same particular type, the same general pattern of nerves and blood vessels, and red blood cells that lack nuclei.

This version of the analogical argument contained in the given passage is evaluated in much the same way as the first one discussed. It is somewhat stronger an argument than the first one according to the third criterion, because in spite of the apparently greater detail in the second version's conclusion, it is weaker than that of the first version because being a mammal entails all these details plus many more.

Nature has a way of reminding us that such arguments are only probable, however, and never demonstrative. For the platypus resembles all other mammals in having lungs, warm blood, hair, nursing their young with milk, and so on. Other mammals are viviparous (bearing their young alive). Therefore the platypus. . . ? No, the platypus lays eggs.

10. Gram-positive bacteria in culture mediums and gram-positive bacteria in the living body all have much the same properties: ways of growing, of

reproducing, etc. Gram-positive bacteria in culture mediums have the property of being destroyed by the presence of penicillium. Therefore gram-positive bacteria in the living body also will be destroyed by the presence of penicillium.

(1) There are very many kinds and instances that have been examined, which makes the conclusion very probable.

(2) There are very many respects hidden in the "etc." in which gram-positive bacteria resemble each other whether in culture mediums or in the living body. These make the conclusion highly probable.

(3) The conclusion is strong relative to the premises, though it could have been stronger. A weaker conclusion would have been that the presence of penicillium in the living body would have inhibited the growth of gram-positive bacteria there. A stronger conclusion would have stated that exactly that same amount of penicillium in the living body would destroy the gram-positive bacteria there in exactly the same time that it did in a culture medium. In the light of subsequent knowledge (!) the conclusion could have been regarded at the time as highly probable.

(4) There are relatively few disanalogies between the living body and culture mediums *relative to the growth in them of bacteria.* (Of course, this is a consequence of bacteriologists designing culture mediums to simulate the living body in the respects in which it is an acceptable habitat for bacteria.) So from this point of view also the conclusion is probable.

(5) There were many dissimilarities among the instances mentioned in the premises: Dr. Fleming "found that quite a number of species" were destroyed by penicillium. So here too the conclusion is highly probable.

(6) The analogy is very relevant because it was well known long before Dr. Fleming's discovery that a fungus subsists on organic matter. By this criterion also the conclusion is very probable.

Exercises on pages 373–376

1. The argument being refuted is alleged to be the following:
   Psychoanalysis is very difficult and time consuming.
   Therefore psychoanalysis is the most valuable method of psychotherapy.
   The refuting analogy is
   The Model T (a Ford car last produced during the 1920s) is very difficult and time consuming (which it was: because of its stiff springs it was uncomfortable to ride in, and it was hazardous in traffic because of its low horsepower, and it was prone to breakdown because of its ancient vintage).
   Therefore the Model T is the most valuable method of wheeled transportation.
   These two arguments have the same form, and since the refuting analogy has a true premiss and a false conclusion, it is invalid and therefore a very effective refutation of the given argument.

5. The argument being refuted is alleged to be the following:
   There are many things wrong with society—some of which are increasingly conspicuous.
   We have also had decades of uninterrupted growth.

Therefore the growth must be the cause of the various social and economic ills that we see around us.

The refuting analogy is

There are many ills of society.

People spend more time these days in cleaning their teeth.

Therefore the fact that people spend more time these days in cleaning their teeth must be the cause of all the ills of society.

The two arguments have the same form, and since the refuting analogy has true premises and a false conclusion, it is obviously invalid and therefore a very effective refutation of the given argument.

In fact, both arguments commit the Fallacy of False Cause, of the *post hoc ergo propter hoc* variety discussed in Chapter 3, pages 101–102.

10. The argument being refuted is the following: Mr. Clark is qualified to manage America's conservation lands, because his father and grandfather were forest rangers.

    The refuting analogy is: Someone should be Secretary of Transportation because he comes from a long line of cab drivers.

    These two arguments have very similar form, and since the refuting analogy could have a true premiss and a false conclusion, it is invalid and therefore looks like an effective refutation of the original argument.

    The original argument, however, could be elaborated by claiming that forest rangers are motivated by love of conservation, learned from one's parents, rather than simply by the money they earn. The parallel claim about cab drivers would be highly implausible.

15. There is here a tangle of analogical argument, nonargumentative use of analogy, and refutation by logical analogy.

    The analogical argument is: Although the use of force is wrong, at times force can justly be used to counter force. Therefore although lying is wrong, at times lies can rightly be used to counter lies.

    And the inference is drawn that just as someone forfeits his rights to noninterference by others when he threatens them forcibly, so a liar has forfeited the ordinary right to be dealt with honestly.

    The proposition inferred is offered as an *explanation* why "Many find it easier to lie to those they take to be untruthful themselves. It is as though a barrier had been let down." (The second sentence here is a nonargumentative use of analogy.)

    Augustine's argument against the conclusion is that: Countering a lie with a lie is like countering sacrilege with sacrilege. And since sacrilege is *absolutely* wrong, so is lying.

Exercises on pp. 385–386

1. *A B C D* occur together with *a b c d.*

   A E F G occur together with *a e f g.*

   Therefore *A* is the cause ("the major factor") in *a.*

   Where *A* is the introduction of nicotine into the body; *B* is the introduction of hot carbon particles into the body; *C* is the introduction of assorted carcinogens into the body; *D* is the oral stimulation of the lips by cigarettes; *E* is the activity of preparing a hypodermic injection; *F* is the piercing of the skin with the hypodermic needle; *G* is the activity of cleaning the hy-

podermic equipment afterward; *a* is a pleasant sensation; *b* is rawness of
tongue, palate, and throat; *c* is gradual debilitation and increased susceptibility to emphysema, and so on; *d* is oral gratification; *e* is the satisfaction
of preparing the injection; *f* is the slight pain at the site of the injection;
and *g* is the bother of cleaning the hypodermic equipment afterward.
WARNING: Serious reflection on this example may be dangerous to your
smoking habit.

Exercises on pp. 389–390

1. Two arguments are present, both proceeding by the Method of Difference.
   (1) *A B* occur together with *a b*.
       B occurs together with *b*.
       Therefore *A* is the cause of *a*.
           Where *A* is air (containing microorganisms), *B* is boiled meat broth,
       a is the presence of living microorganisms in and putrefaction of the
       meat broth, *b* is the usual (other) phenomena connected with meat broth
       in a flask.
   (2) *A B* occur together with *a b*.
       B occurs together with *b*.
       Therefore *A* is the cause of *a*.
           Where *A* is ordinary, unfiltered air, *B* is a previously sterile filter, *a*
       is the presence of microorganisms in the filter after *A* has been passed
       through *B* (proved by showing that it can set up putrefaction), *b* is the
       other physical phenomena common to filters whether or not they have
       been contaminated with microorganisms. That *A* is absent in the second
       instance is the result of the second instance's *B* being the second filter
       through which air was passed. That *a* is absent in the second instance
       is proved by the fact that Pasteur could not set up putrefaction with it.

Exercises on pp. 391–393

1. (1) *A B C* occur together with *a b c*.
       A D E occur together with *a d e*.
       A F G occur together with *a f g*.

       . . . .
       . . . .
       . . . .

       Therefore *A* is the cause of *a*.
           Where the instances are the first group of chickens described, and *A*
       is the circumstance of feeding exclusively on white rice, *B, C, D, E, F,*
       G, . . . are other circumstances in which the chickens probably differed
       among themselves; *a* is the phenomenon of developing polyneuritis and
       dying; and *b, c, d, e, f, g,* . . . are other phenomena attending the various
       chickens in this experiment. This is of course the Method of Agreement.
   (2) *U B C* occur together with *u b c*.
       U D E occur together with *u d e*.
       U F G occur together with *u f g*.

       . . . .
       . . . .
       . . . .

       Therefore *U* is the cause of *u*.

Where the instances are the second group of chickens described, and *U* is the circumstance of being fed unpolished rice, *B, C, D, E, F, G,* . . . are other circumstances in which these chickens probably differed among themselves but resembled the various chickens in the first group; *u* is the phenomenon of remaining healthy (or *not* contracting polyneuritis); and *b, c, d, e, f, g,* . . . are other phenomena attending the various chickens in this (second) experiment. This too is the Method of Agreement.

(3) *A B C* occur together with *a b c.*

     B C occur together with   *b c.*

Therefore *A* is the cause of *a.*

Where the instances are the first chicken of the first group and the first chicken of the second group, and *A, B, C, a, b, c* are as described above (the *absence* of *A* and *a* correspond to the presence of *U* and *u,* respectively, so here the latter need not be symbolized explicitly). This is the Method of Difference, and there are as many uses of the Method of Difference here as there are "matching" pairs of chickens in the two groups.

(4) *A B C* occur together with *a b c.*

     B C occur together with   *b c.*

Therefore *A* is the cause of *a.*

Here is each instance of the polyneuritic chickens that recovered when fed polishings from rice. Here *A* is feeding the polishings from rice; *B, C* are other circumstances of the chicken in question; *a* is recovery from polyneuritis; and *b* and *c* are other phenomena attending the chicken in question. Here is the Method of Difference again.

Exercises on pp. 395–397

1. *A B* occur together with *a b.*

   B is known to be the cause of *b.*

   Therefore *A* is the cause of *a.*

   Where *A* is "sensory and perceptual factors" in rats, *B* is "alimentary factors" in rats (appetite, hunger, general need for and concern with food), *a* is rats hoarding "worthless inedible pellets" covered with aluminum foil, *b* is rats hoarding plain food pellets.

Exercises on pp. 399–401

1. *A*   *B* *C* ——— *a*   *b* *c.*

   A⁻ *B* *C* ——— *a*⁻ *b* *c.*

   A⁺ *B* *C* ——— *a*⁺ *b* *c.*

   Therefore *A* is a cause of or causally connected with *a.*

   Where *A* is gasoline consumption (or automobile pollution of air), *B* and *C* are other circumstances roughly constant over the years, *a* is lung cancer incidence in U.S. white males, and *b* and *c* are other phenomena roughly constant over the years. *A*⁻ is the 35 percent drop in gasoline consumption between 1940 and 1945; *a*⁻ is the drop in incidence of lung cancer in U.S. white males "by approximately the same percentage" between 1940 and 1945; *A*⁺ is the nineteenfold increase in the rate of gasoline consumption between 1914 and 1950; and a^+ is the nineteenfold increase in lung cancer mortality between 1914 and 1950.

Exercises on pp. 411–417

1. (1) *A B C* occur together with *a b c.*
    A D E occur together with *a d e.*
    Therefore *A* is the cause of *a.*
       Here *A* is the circumstance of being sprayed with aqueous solutions of 2,4,5-T at 100- or 200-ppm concentrations; *B, C, D,* and *E* are other circumstances attending Rome Beauty apples; *a* is the phenomenon of ripening early; and *b, c, d,* and *e* are other phenomena attending ripening Rome Beauty apples. This is the Method of Agreement.
  (2) *A B C* occur together with *a b c.*
      B C occur together with   *b c.*
    Therefore *A* is the cause of *a.*
       Here *A, B, C, a, b, c* are as above, where the first instance is a sprayed apple, the second is an unsprayed one that did not ripen early. This is the Method of Difference.
  (3) *A*   *B   C* ——— *a*   *b   c.*
      A$^+$ *B   C* ——— *a*$^+$ *b   c.*
      A^{++} *B   C* ——— *a*$^{++}$ *b   c.*
      A^{+++} *B   C* ——— *a*$^{+++}$ *b   c.*
    Therefore *A* is the cause of *a.*
       Here *A* is application of 0-, *A*$^+$ application of 10-, *A*$^{++}$ application of 100-, *A*$^{+++}$ application of 200-ppm concentrations of 2,4,5-T in aqueous solution, *a* is softness of fruit measured at 25.9 lb, *a*$^+$ is softness of 24.8 lb, *a*$^{++}$ softness of 19.8 lb, and *a*$^{+++}$ softness of 18.9 lb. This is the Method of Concomitant Variation.

5.   *B C* occur together with   *b c.*
    A B C occur together with *a b c.*
    Therefore *A* is the cause of *a.*
       The instance in the first line is the particular rabbit used by Ehrlich and Hata, already infected with syphilis. The instance in the second line is the same rabbit after being injected with 606 solution. Here *A* is the circumstance of injecting 606 solution; *B, C* are other circumstances attending the rabbit in question; *a* is the absence of spirochetes and the remission of ulcers; *b, c* are other phenomena attending the rabbit in question. This is the Method of Difference.

10. *A B C* occur together with *a b c.*
    A B D occur together with *a b d.*
    Therefore *A B* is the cause of *a.*
       The instances here are different monkeys undergoing stress, *A,* and suffering electric shock, *B,* with *C* and *D* being other circumstances attending each of the monkeys, respectively. Here *a* is the phenomenon of ulcers, *b* is the pain induced by the electric shock, and *c* and *d* other phenomena attending the two monkeys, respectively.
       This use of the Method of Agreement establishes only that *A B* is the cause of ulcers, but not that *A* alone is the cause. The second experiment does that.

A B C occur together with *a b c*.
  B C occur together with   *b c*.
Therefore *A* is the cause of *a*.

The instance in the first line is the "executive" monkey who undergoes the stress *A* of having to prevent the electric shocks *B*. The other circumstances attending him are combined as *C*. The instance in the second line is the control monkey who undergoes the shock *B* but not the stress *A*, and also the other circumstances *C* of the rigid schedule arranged by the experimenters. They found ulcers *a* in the "executive" but not in the control, though they shared the other phenomena of pain *b* and miscellaneous *c*. This is the Method of Difference. The entire experiment proceeds by way of the Joint Method of Agreement and Difference.

Exercises on pp. 452–458

1. The data to be explained are the striking differences in appearance between objects that are very far away and objects that are (relatively) nearby. The hypothesis adopted by astronomers to explain these differences is that the distant objects are much younger than nearby objects.

   The hypothesis is surely relevant, because it is well known that the passage of time, or aging, makes a difference to things both in their character and in their appearance.

   Because of the immense distances involved (and the limiting character of the velocity of light), there is little chance of any *direct* testing of the hypothesis. But if astronomers could manage to acquire good data on the appearances of galaxies at various intermediate distances between our own and the most distant ones, and found that their appearances differed in ways that could be correlated with the differences in their distances from us, that would constitute a test (and a verification) of the hypothesis, since aging produces relatively continuous or gradual change.

   The hypothesis is compatible with previously well-established hypotheses and physical laws, which assign no influence to spatial location *as such*, and which therefore require some explanation of *why* things at different distances present different appearances. That light travels at finite velocity, and thus *takes time* to move from one place to another, entails that what we see at any time is the way things looked at an earlier time. The further the light has to travel to reach us, the longer ago it must have left the surface of the object seen. Where the distances are vast, that would entail that the time elapsed was sufficient for the distant galaxies to age perceptibly, and thus not only to be but to look different from galaxies closer by.

   The hypothesis has some predictive power, as suggested in what was said about testing it. And it has explanatory power not only in accounting for the data to be explained, but also, by implication, in explaining what *our* galaxy was like in its earlier, formative period.

   Finally, the hypothesis is reasonably simple, being based on well-established views such as that light travels at a finite velocity, and that aging changes the appearances of things.

5. The data to be explained are that a plant's roots grow *down* and its stem grows *up* regardless of the orientation in which a young seedling is fixed.

Knight's hypothesis to explain this data was that "this behavior was due to gravity," meaning by this that the plant's roots are positively gravity sensitive and its stem negatively gravity sensitive.

The hypothesis is relevant because the gravitational attraction of the earth is well established and would exercise a constant "pull" on the gravity-sensitive roots regardless of how the seedling is placed.

The hypothesis is testable in a variety of ways, some only recently available. If the astronauts who reached the moon had been able to stay there longer, they could have arranged seedlings in various positions and then observed the direction in which their roots and stems grew. If the roots grew in the direction of the moon and their stems in the opposite direction, that would show that its gravity rather than anything else about the earth (e.g., its magnetic field or its iron core) was the cause of the phenomenon observed on earth. Or if in an artificial satellite far removed from all external massive bodies, the roots and stems of seedlings arranged in different positions continued to grow in quite different directions, that too would provide an affirmative test of Knight's hypothesis. Knight's own test using centrifugal force stronger than gravity was extremely ingenious.

The hypothesis seems to be perfectly compatible with previously well-established hypotheses. Its predictive power is also considerable, because it enables us to predict how plants would grow on the moon or in artificial satellites.

The hypothesis is simple in the sense that it explains the data in terms of an already well-established theory concerning the earth's gravity. It is incomplete, of course, in that it leaves unanswered the question of what makes the roots positively gravity sensitive, and what there is in the stem to make it negatively gravity sensitive.

10. The first datum to be explained is the apparent slowness of rotation of the planet Venus. The first hypothesis considered is that Venus, like Mercury, rotates at the same rate that it revolves about the sun, thus keeping the same side always toward the sun and the other side always dark.

This hypothesis is surely relevant: if Venus does rotate slowly, that would explain why it appears to rotate slowly. It is testable by various means, not all of which are as yet technically feasible. It is especially compatible with the previously established hypothesis that Mercury behaves the same way. It has predictive power not only to explain the original datum, but also other phenomena that can be used in testing it. It is an admirably simple hypothesis.

The first hypothesis leads to the prediction that the dark side of Venus must be exceedingly cold. But Pettit and Nicholson measured the temperature of the dark side of Venus and found it to be comparatively mild, $-9°F$. This disconfirms the first hypothesis, unless it can be salvaged by some other hypothesis that could explain the apparent discrepancy.

The second hypothesis considered as a possible way to save the first one is that atmospheric currents from the warm and bright side of Venus could perpetually heat the cold and dark side. This second hypothesis could save the first one.

The second hypothesis is clearly relevant. It is testable by various means, not all technically feasible at present. It has predictive power and is fairly simple. But it is not compatible with previously well-established hypotheses about the size of Venus and—especially—the behavior of atmospheric currents. So the second hypothesis is rejected, and with it the first.

The third hypothesis intended to replace the first two is that Venus rotates "fairly often."

This third hypothesis is relevant, for if Venus rotates only *fairly* often, that would explain the original datum that Venus appears to rotate slowly, and if it rotates fairly *often,* that would explain why the dark side does not cool excessively. This is of course very loose: the actual hypothesis in this case must ultimately be made quantitative to take account of the actual measurements that are made. The third hypothesis also satisfies the several other criteria discussed in the text.

15. The data to be explained here are the steep rates at which the surface of the moon cools down and heats up during and after lunar eclipses.

The hypothesis that the surface of the moon is solid rock, or composed of rocks of macroscopic size, is rejected because it is incompatible with the previously well-established hypothesis that "no solid piece of rock can cool down and heat up so quickly."

The alternative hypothesis is that the upper surface of the moon is "a thick layer of heat-insulating dust as fine as face powder." This hypothesis is relevant, for it would certainly explain the extremely rapid changes of surface temperature: only the few inches of dust change temperature, the insulated substratum remains relatively constant in temperature. It is testable, though at the time it was proposed the techniques were not technically feasible. It is compatible with the previously established hypothesis. It has predictive power: it could be used to predict what would happen if a meteorite should land on the surface of the moon. And it is fairly simple.

But there is the question: How did the surface of the moon become so minutely pulverized? Here Dr. Buettner proposed his hypothesis that the moon's rocks have been ground to dust not merely by "the sandblasting of meteoric dust" but by "the everlasting influx of cosmic rays."

This hypothesis is relevant, testable, compatible with previously well-established hypotheses, has predictive and explanatory power, and is simple.

And yet moon rocks brought back to earth by our Apollo flights show that the moon is not covered by "dust as fine as face powder." This should help emphasize the fact that scientific theories and hypotheses are continually subject to revision as new data are accumulated.

Exercises on p. 466

1. $1/2 \times 1/2 \times 1/2 = 1/8$

5. $1/4 \times 1/3 \times 1/2 \times 1/1 = 1/24$

Exercises on pp. 470–471

1. Probability of losing with a 2, a 3, or a 12 is 4/36 or 1/9.
Probability of throwing a 4, and then a 7 before another 4, is $3/36 \times 6/9 = 1/18$.
Probability of throwing a 10, and then a 7 before another 10, is likewise 1/18.

Probability of throwing a 5, and then a 7 before another 5, is 4/36 × 6/10 = 1/15.

Probability of throwing a 9, and then a 7 before another 9, is likewise 1/15.

Probability of throwing a 6, and then a 7 before another 6, is 5/36 × 6/11 = 5/66.

Probability of throwing an 8, and then a 7 before another 8, is likewise 5/66.

The sum of the probabilities of the exclusive ways of the shooter's losing is 251/495.

So the shooter's chance of winning is 1 − 251/495 = 244/495 or .493.

5. No, for the probability of throwing an ace is 1 − 125/216 = 91/216 or .421 +.

Exercises on pp. 478–479

1. $34.11

5. $15.00

Special Symbols

INDEX